Contemporary Mental Health Issues Among African Americans

Edited by

Debra A. Harley
John Milton Dillard

AMERICAN COUNSELING ASSOCIATION
5999 Stevenson Avenue
Alexandria, VA 22304
www.counseling.org

Contemporary
Mental Health Issues
Among
African Americans

10   9   8   7   6   5   4   3   2   1

American Counseling Association
5999 Stevenson Avenue
Alexandria, VA 22304

Director of Publications
Carolyn C. Baker

Production Manager
Bonny E. Gaston

Copy Editor
Elaine Dunn

Type and cover design by Bonny E. Gaston.
Note on the cover graphic: Diamond patterns are very prominent in
African textile tradition and are symbolic of the cycles of birth, life, death, and rebirth.

Library of Congress Cataloging-in-Publication Data
Contemporary mental health issues among African Americans/edited by Debra A. Harley, John Milton Dillard
  p. cm.
  ISBN 1-55620-236-9 (alk. paper)
  1. African Americans—Mental health. 2. African Americans—Social conditions—1975– 3. African American families. 4. Cultural psychiatry—United States. 5. Mental health services—United States. 6. United States—race relations—Psychological aspects. I. Harley, Debra A. II. Dillard, John M.

RC451.5.N4C66 2005
616.89´0089´96073—dc22   2004015611

Dedication

To my parents, Morise and Thelma J. Harley
—Debra A. Harley

To my lovely wife, Frances,
and grandson, Harrison Milton
—John Milton Dillard

Table of Contents

Section I
Current Issues

Section II
Special Issues

Section III
◉
Community

Section IV
◉
Application

Foreword

The art of healing and the energy associated with the practice is a gift that is bestowed on all whose mind, body, and spirit are inclined to extend and receive it reciprocally. It is not reserved for professionally trained clinicians, nor is it restricted to members of the medical community. In fact, experience has taught me that healing is not relegated only to those with titles. Rather, healing is associated with the cognitive, affective, behavioral, and spiritual attributes each person possesses, and then uses, to bring comfort to those in need of assistance, clarity, support, encouragement, and intervention.

So simple, and yet so complex, is this notion of healing. Those who are committed to treating people of African descent are searching for that balance between conceptual depth and practical application, between rigor and relevance, between genuine cultural congruence and traditional counseling standards of practice. Well, Debra A. Harley and John Milton Dillard may have achieved that balance in this latest book, *Contemporary Mental Health Issues Among African Americans*. Those of us who engage this work on a daily basis welcome the arrival of this latest resource.

This text by Harley and Dillard is a marvelous compendium for those who are committed to working competently with clients of African descent. Far beyond being just another intellectual tool, this text meets several needs of professionals and students alike, simultaneously. First, professionals and students are in need of affirmation and validation about definitions of mental health and mental illness, factors that affect mental health status, and specific techniques that can help clinicians develop greater levels of competence and proficiency. This book does that.

Second, professionals and students are in need of perspectives that recognize social pathologies such as racism, sexism, oppression, and discrimination as contributors to mental illness, and not just the traditional views that see only intrapsychic phenomena as the etiology of client distress and dysfunction. This book does that!

Third, practitioners are in need of an infusion of hope and promise that the professional training and skill they have acquired thus far can be somehow transformed into practices that are culturally congruent, that can ultimately contribute to successful outcomes. This book does that!

Drs. Harley and Dillard have assembled a strong list of contributors and topics in this edited volume, which is organized into four primary sections—Current Issues, Special Issues, Community, Application—and a conclusion. While these sections appear to be distinct, readers will find a much more integrated approach as they read from chapter to chapter. Nowhere is this more evident than in the topics covered under Section I: Current Issues. Dr. Dillard begins with a discussion on the scope of mental health and African Americans, in which he defines mental health and illness in a historical and contemporary context. From there, chapters on the African American family, African American women,

African American males, and male–female relationships provide the context for analyzing mental health challenges faced by each group.

Sections II, III, and IV covering Special Issues, Community, and Application, respectively, provide coverage on populations such as the elderly; lesbian, gay, and bisexual populations; people with HIV/AIDS; people dealing with substance abuse issues; and those struggling with issues of biracial and multiracial identity. Also included are discussions around people with disabilities, as well as children and adolescents. Unlike other texts whose coverage is more limited, this text also addresses issues of community mental health, strength-based approaches using the Black church, spirituality and religion in counseling and psychotherapy, indigenous counseling practices, and ethics. Indeed, this is a very comprehensive volume that will be a must-read for professionals and students alike.

In publication and professional convention/conference circles, I have consistently argued that the biggest problem confronting people of African descent is not poverty, drugs, gangs, violence, racism, or White supremacy. Rather, I believe that the need for *mental liberation* is our biggest challenge. Similarly, professionals and students alike who are committed to addressing the mental health needs of people of African descent must confront the ways they (we) have conceptually been incarcerated by the mental health/illness paradigms to which we are exposed in our training. This work by Harley and Dillard is an important key that can be utilized to unlock our minds, insight our behaviors, and inspire our spirits to do the great work the African-descent community so desperately needs.

—Thomas A. Parham, PhD
Assistant Vice Chancellor
Counseling and Health Services
Director, Counseling Center
Adjunct Faculty Member
Distinguished Psychologist
Association of Black Psychologists
Fellow
American Psychological Association

Preface

Mental health among African Americans is a topic that has received attention in the literature primarily from a pathological perspective. Over time, African Americans have been described as violent in behavior, as inferior in intellect, and as a special interest group in sociopolitical contexts. Too infrequently are African Americans presented and discussed with regard to their resiliency and strengths. In conceptualizing this book, we sought to move mental health issues of African Americans from the periphery to the center, and to organize and present information about them from a positive and empowering perspective rather than a perfunctory one.

We recognize African Americans as a heterogeneous group. Thus, our use of such terms as the *African American community* and the *Black church* is not intended to present African Americans as one-in-the-same. Rather, our intent is to present the collective, communal, and cultural/kinship ties that characterize them. The goal of this book is to provide a comprehensive and concise summary of contemporary mental health issues among African Americans. The chapters include varied and comprehensive topics pertaining to African Americans, which address the community; family; women; men; male–female relationships; children and adolescents; spirituality and religion; the elderly; lesbian, gay, and bisexual persons; HIV/AIDS; biracial and multiracial identity; disabilities; indigenous counseling; and ethics. These chapters describe African Americans across various domains, within different contexts, and from historical and contemporary perspectives. Because of the increasing diversity of the population in the United States and the presence of African Americans as one of the historical racial minority groups, it is imperative that counselors and human service practitioners who have contact with African Americans better understand and apply Afrocentric perspectives into their practices and increase multicultural competence.

The contributing authors to this book represent a broad spectrum of the counseling profession and education in terms of discipline (e.g., rehabilitation, counseling psychology, school psychology, behavioral sciences, sociology, mental health, and curriculum design), race and ethnicity, gender, sexual orientation, religion, geographic locale, and nationality. Each of these professionals has a commitment to promoting the knowledge, skills, and competence of others in the area of diversity and multicultural training.

Book Contents

This book is organized into four major sections. Each section begins with a brief introduction prepared by the editors that provides the reader with an "operational map" of sorts to help maximize the utility of each chapter.

Section I: Current Issues presents five chapters, which include theories and definitions of mental health, the application of traditional theories to African Americans, and the influence of multicultural theories. In addition, chapters in this section address coping strategies of African American families in contending with overt and covert criticism of their patterns of family interaction and kinship, psychological impediments faced by African American women and men, and male–female marital status. These chapters provide evidence that issues of racism, sexism, privilege, power, and oppression need to be addressed in mental health counseling with African Americans.

Section II: Special Issues contains five chapters. In this section, the authors identify certain issues related to specific subpopulations among African Americans. Various chapters address the elderly; lesbian, gay, and bisexual persons; HIV/AIDS; substance abuse; and biracial and multiracial identity. Collectively, these chapters examine some of the most pressing psychosocial issues that impact African Americans.

Section III: Community explores African Americans' collective attitudes toward mental health counseling as well as cultural/community characteristics. Some attention is also given to the impact of violence, crime, and gangs in the African American community. The role of the Black church is explored from a strength-based approach as a way of promoting mental health wellness in the community.

Section IV: Application emerges as the integrating part of the book. Themes from previous chapters are used to discuss how to work with African Americans with mental health issues. The community is recognized as a crucial component in this section. Assessment is discussed from the relevance of the importance of starting intervention with an unbiased, accurate, and culturally appropriate evaluation of the presenting problems. Two traditionally recognized assets of the African American community, spirituality and religion and indigenous counseling, are discussed as having particular value to the counselor or practitioner. Finally, ethical implications are presented.

The final chapter is a reflection of emerging themes and key concepts throughout the book. Moreover, this chapter serves as a thought-provoking summary to encourage the reader to be continuously curious about mental health issues among African Americans and to ask questions and seek additional information.

This book offers the perspectives of 28 scholars in the fields of counseling, education, and behavioral science. It provides insight into specific issues of an underserved population in mental health services. It is our desire that upon completion of this book, the reader will either become or continue to be an advocate for equity of African American clients in the mental health and other human service arenas. In the words of Thomas A. Parham (2001),

> An opportunity is a threat to those who predict failure but a challenge to those who think they might win. If you think you might win, if you think we might have the power to promote a greater level of respect for diversity and a greater level of multicultural competence in our profession . . . then make a commitment to do something different. (p. 881)

It has been an excellent experience to work with the contributors to the book.

—Debra A. Harley and John Milton Dillard

Reference

Parham, T. A. (2001). Bridging the gap between imposition and acceptance. In J. G. Ponterotto, J. M. Casas, L. A. Suzuki, & C. M. Alexander (Eds.), *Handbook of multicultural counseling* (2nd ed., pp. 871–881). Thousand Oaks, CA: Sage.

Acknowledgments

We would like to thank all of the individuals who have contributed to this project. The contributing authors have written insightful and informative chapters. These authors contributed their knowledge, expertise, and valuable time without financial remuneration; they contributed because of their commitment to equity and to the development of a mental health care system that will appropriately serve African Americans. With gratitude, we acknowledge the role of Carolyn Baker, American Counseling Association's director of publications, in the process to completing this book. Finally, we acknowledge our families, communities, and heritage for emotional support and cultural richness.

About the Editors

Debra A. Harley, PhD, CRC, CPC, CCFC, is a professor in the Department of Special Education and Rehabilitation Counseling and the Women's Studies program at the University of Kentucky. She received her BS and MA from South Carolina State University in psychology and rehabilitation counseling, respectively, and her PhD in special education from Southern Illinois University at Carbondale. She has taught graduate courses in rehabilitation counseling and special education and has developed courses on cultural diversity; group and family counseling; substance abuse; gender, disability, and *positionalities*; and the science and politics of disability.

Dr. Harley has a special interest in cultural diversity, substance abuse, gender issues, and ethics. She is past editor of the *Journal of Rehabilitation Administration* and the *Journal of Applied Rehabilitation Counseling*. In addition, Dr. Harley edited and co-edited special issues of the *Rehabilitation Counseling Bulletin* (cultural diversity), the *Journal of Rehabilitation Administration* (an anthology and retrospective), the *Journal of Applied Rehabilitation Counseling* (cultural diversity), *Rehabilitation Education* (pedagogy in rehabilitation education at historically Black colleges and universities), and the *1989 Proceedings on the President's Committee on Employment of People With Disabilities*.

Dr. Harley has also published more than 50 articles in refereed journals, 13 book chapters, 23 book reviews, and several conference proceedings. She has a book on *Adult Career Counseling and Development* in press. Dr. Harley has made more than 50 national, state, and local presentations. Her presentations have focused on a wide variety of subjects broadly classified under counseling, multicultural counseling, and ethics.

Dr. Harley also has received numerous honors and awards for her professional accomplishments. Such accolades include the following: 2001 Mary E. Switzer Scholar in Rehabilitation, 2001 Sylvia Walker Educator of the Year Award of the National Association of Multicultural Concerns, and 2002 Provost's Award for Outstanding Teaching for Tenured Faculty at the University of Kentucky.

John Milton Dillard, PhD, is a professor and former department chair in the Department of Educational and Counseling Psychology at the University of Louisville. Dr. Dillard is director of the Counselors for the New Millennium program, designed to prepare African American certified teachers to become elementary and secondary school counselors.

He received his master's and doctorate degree from the State University of New York at Buffalo. Dr. Dillard is also a graduate of Harvard University's Management Development Program. He was professor at Texas A&M University, Oklahoma State University, and University of Carabobo, Valencia, Venezuela, South America.

Most of Dr. Dillard's manuscripts and state and national conference presentations focused on African Americans and other ethnic minority groups. He has written and coauthored several books, book chapters, and more than 60 journal articles on topics dealing with cross-cultural counseling, career development, and career planning across ethnic and cultural groups. His most recent coauthored book chapter is "Eastern–Western Healing Systems: Considerations for Mental Health Through Counseling and Psychotherapy."

Dr. Dillard is author of such books as *Multicultural Counseling: Toward Ethnic and Cultural Relevance in Human Encounters*, *Lifelong Career Planning*, and *Systematic Interviewing*. He was a member of the American Psychological Association's Division 17 and the American Counseling Association. He has served on several journal editorial boards and reviewed numerous counseling books, such as Donald Atkinson and Gail Hackett's two 2004 publications: *Counseling American Minorities: A Cross-Cultural Perspective* (6th ed.) and *Counseling Diverse Populations* (3rd ed.).

About the Contributors

Reginald J. Alston, PhD, CRC, NCC, is an associate professor and associate head and coordinator of the Rehabilitation Counseling Master's Program in the Department of Community Health at the University of Illinois at Urbana–Champaign. He has taught numerous courses such as medical aspects of disability, psychosocial aspects of disability, theories of counseling, counseling techniques, testing and measurement, and research methods in health sciences. His primary research interest is the influences of ethnicity on rehabilitation success and psychosocial adjustment for people with physical and mental disabilities, particularly African Americans. Dr. Alston is a former principal investigator of a National Science Foundation research project on science, engineering, and math for people with disabilities. He has numerous publications in leading journals and has conducted workshops and conference presentations on diversity issues in human services. Dr. Alston is a former board member for the American Rehabilitation Counseling Association and the Council on Rehabilitation Education.

Patricia Bethea-Whitfield, EdD, NCC, is an associate professor in the Department of Human Development and Services at North Carolina Agricultural and Technical State University in Greensboro, North Carolina. Dr. Bethea-Whitfield writes in the areas of African American males in counseling, African American male–female relationships, and the career and travel issues of African American women. Her most recent work is titled *African American Males in Counseling: Who's Pulling the Trigger Now?* She is a past chair of the Public Awareness and Support Committee of the American Counseling Association.

Madonna G. Constantine, PhD, is professor of psychology and education and chair of the Department of Counseling and Clinical Psychology at Teachers College, Columbia University. She received her PhD in counseling psychology from the University of Memphis. Dr. Constantine has over 80 publications related to her research and professional interests. She currently serves as associate editor of both the *Journal of Black Psychology* and *Cultural Diversity and Ethnic Minority Psychology*. She also has served as senior editor of the *Journal of Multicultural Counseling and Development*. Her research and professional interests include mental health of people of African descent; multicultural competence issues in counseling, training, and supervision; and career development of people of color and psychologists in training.

Charlotte G. Dixon, RhD, is an associate professor and chair of the Department of Rehabilitation and Mental Health Counseling at the University of South Florida in Tampa. She maintains a private counseling and vocational consulting practice.

Yolanda V. Edwards, PhD, CRC, is an assistant professor in the Counseling and Personnel Services Department at the University of Maryland, College Park. She received her PhD from the University of Iowa in rehabilitation counseling. Dr. Edwards has published in the areas of counseling in technology, rehabilitation education, and racial disparities in mental health.

Ellen S. Fabian, PhD, CRC, is an associate professor and the director of the Rehabilitation Counseling program in the Department of Counseling and Personnel Services at the University of Maryland, College Park. She has numerous publications within her research area of rehabilitation and significant mental disorders.

Anita Fernander, PhD, is an assistant professor in the Department of Behavioral Science at the University of Kentucky. She received her doctorate in clinical health psychology from the University of Miami. Dr. Fernander's research focuses on health disparities, particularly among African Americans. She examines the influence of ethnoculturally specific constructs, acculturation, and racism on risk factors for cardiovascular disease and cancer. Most recently, Dr. Fernander has been funded by the National Institute on Drug Abuse to examine psychosocial factors related to tobacco use and nicotine metabolism among African American women.

Travis A. Gayles, is an MD/PhD student in the Medical Scholars program at the University of Illinois at Urbana–Champaign. He graduated from Duke University with a BA in public policy studies and a BA in African American studies. Mr. Gayles served as a research assistant for the Institute of Medicine's Committee on Palliative and End of Life Care for Children and Their Families. He also worked with the Advisory Board Company of Washington, DC, as an analyst in the syndicated clinical research division, specializing in cardiovascular imaging, clinical trials, and physician leadership. He has served as an executive board member for the Council on African American Affairs, Inc. His primary research interests are pediatric health policy, geographical and cultural health disparities, and small business employer-based health insurance.

Rosalind P. Harris, PhD, is an associate professor in the Department of Community and Leadership Development in the College of Agriculture at the University of Kentucky. Her research has focused on spatial inequality and rural poverty, with a particular focus on gender inequality and the impacts of poverty on children and youths.

Deneese L. Jones, PhD, is an associate professor in the Department of Curriculum and Instruction at the University of Kentucky. She received a BS in elementary education from Texas Women's University and MEd and PhD from Texas A&M University. Dr. Jones's research focus is equity pedagogy. She has expertise in the areas of multicultural education, teacher education, and complex instruction for diverse populations. She presently serves as a co-researcher in the Collaborative Center for Literacy Development and director of the Center for the Study of Academic Achievement in Learning Environments. She has served as an associate dean of the Graduate School for Recruitment and Diversity. Dr. Jones was selected as an American Council on Education Fellow 2002–2003 at the University of Kansas studying institutional change for higher education.

Ye Jung Kim, MA, is a graduate student in the Department of Sociology at the University of North Texas. She earned her master's degree in political science from Ewha Woman's University, Seoul, South Korea. Her research interests include gender, social inequality, and religion.

Mai M. Kindaichi, MA, MEd, is a doctoral student in the Department of Counseling and Clinical Psychology at Teachers College, Columbia University. She earned her BA in psychology from Georgetown University. Her interests include family dynamics and gender identity development in multicultural families, the influence of diverse values in counseling processes, and multicultural counseling training issues.

Erma Jean Lawson, RN, PhD, is an associate professor in the Department of Sociology at the University of North Texas. She received her doctorate from the University of Kentucky. Dr. Lawson has investigated health issues in Zimbabwe, Cuba, New Zealand, and Australia. She received a prestigious postdoctoral fellowship to investigate African American health issues at Harvard University. Her research areas include family and medical sociology.

Renée A. Middleton, PhD, is an associate professor in the Department of Counseling and Counseling Psychology at Auburn University. Dr. Middleton also serves as director of human resources and outreach for the College of Education. She received her doctorate from Andrews University in Berrien Springs, Michigan. Dr. Middleton has presented workshops and has published in the areas of multicultural counseling, racial identity development, rehabilitation cultural diversity, and multiculturalism. Dr. Middleton is past president of the National Association of Multicultural Rehabilitation Concerns of the National Rehabilitation Association.

Marie L. Miville, PhD, is an associate professor of psychology and education at Teachers College, Columbia University. Dr. Miville also is the program coordinator and director of training of the Counseling Psychology program at Teachers College. She received her PhD from the University of Maryland, College Park. Her research explores the interrelations of collective identity and personal identity among Latinos and Latinas. Dr. Miville also developed the Miville–Guzman Universality–Diversity Scale, which measures social attitudes of awareness and acceptance of how people are both similar to and different from each other.

Elias Mpofu, PhD, CRC, is an associate professor in the Department of Counselor Education, Counseling Psychology, and Rehabilitation Services at The Pennsylvania State University. He is a former professor at the University of Zimbabwe, Africa. Dr. Mpofu was a Fulbright Fellow. He received his PhD in rehabilitation psychology from the University of Wisconsin—Madison. Dr. Mpofu has numerous articles, book chapters, and books to his credit.

Marva Nelson, MFA, is an assistant professor of English at Parkland College in Champaign, Illinois. She teaches poetry and literature, with special emphases on race, gender, and health care. Her past work experiences include serving as writer-in-residence at Marion Federal Penitentiary, Marion, Illinois, and executive assistant at the National Black Women's Health Project, Atlanta, Georgia.

Theresa M. Nowak is a doctoral candidate in educational psychology at the University of Kentucky. She has an MA in counseling psychology and is a certified school psychologist. Ms. Nowak is project coordinator of the National Early Childhood Transition Center through the Interdisciplinary Human Development Center at the University of Kentucky. Her areas of expertise include temperament, school adjustment, disabilities, and assessment of infants and young children. Ms. Nowak's publications are in the area of disabilities.

Jo Anne Rainey, PhD, is an associate professor with the Division of Education and Human Services at Kentucky State University. She received her PhD in educational psychology from the University of Texas at Austin, and she is a licensed psychologist and certified school psychologist. Dr. Rainey's areas of expertise include youth mental health, youth aggression, youth sexuality, and valid assessment strategies for minority populations. She has published in the area of collaboration and mental health.

Carolyn W. Rollins, RhD, is an assistant professor at Albany State University. Dr. Rollins's area of expertise is ethics counseling practice and behavior. She is a past board member of several rehabilitation counseling associations. Dr. Rollins has published in the areas of ethics, multicultural counseling, and rehabilitation education.

Todd A. Savage, PhD, is an assistant professor in the Department of Counseling and Educational Psychology at New Mexico State University. He has served as a consultant for the Bethune Institute for Culturally Responsive Education in Lexington, Kentucky. He earned his doctorate in school psychology from the University of Kentucky and received his BA in psychology from the University of Minnesota. He is active in research focusing on lesbian, gay, bisexual, and transgender issues in education and counseling.

Betty Brown Smith, PhD, is an assistant professor in the School of Psychology at Spalding University, Louisville, Kentucky. She is a licensed clinical psychologist. Dr. Brown-Smith worked as a clinical psychologist for Seven Counties Family Services for Kentucky in Louisville. Her research and writing interests were Africentric perspectives in providing mental assistance to African Americans. Her local and national presentations mostly focused on the African American family. Dr. Brown-Smith has written numerous articles and book chapters, most of which dealt with African Americans.

David Staten, PhD, is an assistant professor and the interim department chair for the Department of Human Services and program director for the master's-level Rehabilitation Counseling program at South Carolina State University (SCSU). He received his doctorate in rehabilitation with a specialization in counseling psychology from the University of Iowa. Dr. Staten is a member of the SCSU interdisciplinary research committee, judiciary committee, and the School of Graduate Studies Admissions committee. He teaches courses in psychological aspects of disabilities, vocational placement, and numerous other areas.

Kim Vaz, PhD, LMHC, is an associate professor of women's studies at the University of South Florida, Tampa. She is a psychoanalytic training fellow at the Carter Jenkins Center and maintains a private practice.

Keith B. Wilson, PhD, CRC, NCC, LPC, ABDA, is an associate professor and director of rehabilitation programs in the Department of Counselor Education, Counseling Psychology, and Rehabilitation Services at The Pennsylvania State University. Dr. Wilson received his doctorate from Ohio State University. His research interests are primarily focused on two areas: cross-cultural and multicultural issues among people with disabilities, and privilege-based hue/color skin in the vocational rehabilitation system and in the general population in the United States. Dr. Wilson has numerous publications and national and international presentations to his credit, including an invited presentation at Oxford University in England. He has also received several national and university awards for research, teaching, and service.

Lynda Brown Wright, PhD, is an associate professor and chair in the Department of Educational and Counseling Psychology at the University of Kentucky. She received her doctorate in counseling psychology from Texas A&M University. Her current areas of research include psychosocial and familial influences on African American child and youth development and academic achievement, psychosocial and environmental correlates of the development of cardiovascular disease risk factors in children and youths, and the development of cultural sensitivity and competency among helping professionals. Dr. Brown Wright is a National Institutes of Health award recipient.

Section I

Current Issues

The chapters presented in the first section illustrate some of the major issues involving African Americans. The central concept woven through the five chapters is mental health risk factors associated with African Americans. In chapter 1, Dillard lays the foundation for this volume as well as the issues in this section. The universal definitions of mental health and mental illness or disorders are supported by universal or traditional theories. However, some emerging African American proponents challenge these definitions, arguing that the two concepts are not two dichotomous variables. Further, the African American authors in this section advocate that these concepts fall short of presenting African Americans in a positive light. There are several factors affecting the lives of African Americans, including African American families, women, men, and the male–female relationship through marriage.

Brown Wright and Fernander, in chapter 2, discuss the multiple family structures among African Americans. In their historical review, they provide a very convincing argument regarding African Americans' connection with their African roots, emphasizing a balanced view of African American families. To this end, Brown Wright and Fernander underscore early research findings of positive factors representing strengths of African families. Despite these strengths, however, many African American families are still faced with several environmental challenges. Family members, including children, may be required to use their coping skills, family support, or professional assistance.

Although African American women have made great strides in various professional fields, they simultaneously experience oppression and mental fatigue. In chapter 3, Bethea-Whitfield argues that some African American women encounter psychological impediments. The male–female relationship can have both a positive and a negative impact on women. Individual perceptions of another's economic, educational, or career achievement often affect the psychological well-being and the stability of the male–female relationship. Physical violence most often occurs in marriages and single male–female relations. Despite these impediments, Bethea-Whitfield explores the resiliency of African American women and creative environments that support positive mental health.

African American men, too, encounter many environmental factors, such as discrimination, ethnocentrism, and unemployment, that frequently affect their psychological well-being. In chapter 4, Gayles, Alston, and Staten present several issues pertaining to African American men, such as violence and crime, health care, imprisonment, and discrimination and racial profiling. These authors discuss the psychological constraints of racism and masculinity. They also emphasize the need for change toward constructed behavior among African American men.

While African American men and women have their own separate concerns, they are faced with some similar barriers. In chapter 5, Jones discusses the union of the two, African American women and men, through marriage, which has received considerable examination and criticism as more problematic, conflictual, destructive, and a disappearing institution. She also presents the marital issues for counseling and techniques for empowering the emotional well-being of African American female–male relationships and marriage.

1

Scope of Mental Health Issues Among African Americans

John Milton Dillard

Mental health literature on African Americans in the United States is often sparse or limited in scope regarding their frequently encountered situations. For example, African Americans encounter numerous conditions that often affect their everyday lives. Many African American individuals and families have the necessary coping skills or defense mechanisms for dealing with their many daily concerns, whereas other African Americans are often strapped with burdens of managing their lives in the midst of negative factors, such as stereotypes, discrimination, gender bias, homophobia, unemployment, poor housing, poor education, and the like. How well they manage these and other factors often determines their quality of life.

The purpose of this chapter is to provide an overview and a description of the organization of this book. Two major concepts central to the discussions presented in this book are mental health and mental disorder among African Americans. The meaning of these terms can be elusive when ethnicity/race and culture are considered. What is the significance of these concepts for the African American population in the United States? I begin the discussion with historical factors occurring in the lives of African Americans followed by an examination of demographic factors influencing the psychological well-being of African Americans.

Brief Historical Overview

Pre-Civil Rights Era

Fifty years ago most Blacks were indeed trapped in poverty, although they did not mainly reside in inner cities (West, 1993). Conditions and opportunities were less than desirable for most Blacks, mainly because of racial prejudices and discrimination. Marable (1981) cited DuBois (1961) as saying that as great as the problem of the color line and race was, a much greater problem was that so many Black people were still willing to embrace comfort even if they had to endure poverty, ignorance, and disease of the majority of their fellowmen. The burden of racial prejudice or racism was more fundamentally the problem of class exploitation. Kenneth Clark, a Black psychologist and author of the book *Dark Ghetto* (1965), described the Black socioeconomic inequality as a function of ethnocentrism or racial discrimination.

The struggles in life for many Blacks are more complex than for those who are capable of withstanding the constant uncertainties and turbulence. These experiences often took their toll on the well-being of Black individuals and their families. Most Blacks had to contend with limited job opportunities, economically distressed conditions, and unfair racial treatment. Cornel West (1993) argued in his book, *Race Matters*, that

> the proper starting point for the crucial debate about the prospects for [B]lack America is an examination of the nihilism that increasingly pervades [B]lack communities. Nihilism is to be understood here not as a philosophic doctrine that there are no rational grounds for legitimate standards or authority; it is, far more, the lived experience of coping with a life of horrifying meaninglessness, hopelessness, and (most important) lovelessness. The frightening result is a numbing detachment from others and a self-destructive disposition toward the world. Life without meaning, hope, and love breeds a coldhearted, mean-spirited outlook that destroys both the individual and others. (p. 15)

West (1993) concluded that the lack of hope for Blacks can be the defeating element of destruction. We must come to grips with this notion and recognize that the negative potential of no hope is as though we have succumbed to this threat. West suggested that

> the major enemy of [B]lack survival in America has been and is neither oppression nor exploitation but rather the nihilistic threat—that is, loss of hope and absence of meaning. For as long as hope remains and meaning is preserved, the possibility of overcoming oppression stays alive. The self-fulfilling prophecy of the nihilistic threat is that without hope there can be no future, that without meaning there can be no struggle. (p. 15)

However, it was apparent that Blacks were still clinging to their hopes and will for removal of their deplorable conditions and paucity of opportunities. Although most Blacks were living in the South, they realized that it was necessary for them to relocate where employment opportunities might help them realize their dreams for a better life.

The Great Migration From the South

According to Marable (1981), many broad economic changes occurred following the post-World War II period and civil rights era affecting most socioeconomic levels in the Black community. Blacks made a significant move from the rural south to the urban north central and northeastern states. As a consequence, for example, with the scarcity of workers in northern manufacturing plants following the post-World War II period, southern Blacks in search of jobs boarded trains and buses in a great migration that lasted through the mid-1960s. They secured what they had long desired: wages so strikingly high in the North that in 1953 the average income for a Black family was almost twice that of those who remained in the South. Through much of the 1950s wages rose steadily and unemployment was low (Thernstrom & Thernstrom, 1999).

The Moynihan Report

A decade later, Daniel Patrick Moynihan's 1965 report, *The Negro Family: The Case for National Action*, delineated Black families as "a tangle of pathology in the social fabric of the ghetto underclass" (see Marable, 1981, p. 70). His report was viewed by many Black activists and intellectuals as negative and received considerable criticism for his portrayal of Black families. Moynihan's report, however, brought national attention of American society to see and comprehend urban Black families' living conditions and the need for intervention. Despite the criticism, Moynihan's report inspired considerable positive economic change in many Black families and the Black community (seldom mentioned) through the federal government as a result of federal dollars for improving these conditions.

Black Power Movement

The Black power movement was in place at the time and was considered by some as an elitist movement that created the gulf between the new Black professional and managerial privileged power brokers and the permanent underclass (Marable, 1981). Marable stated that there was a crisis in the Black power movement suggesting a lack of understanding the real significance of the economic problems within the Black ghetto. Yet the Black movement demanded that the Black community control the schools, which was an atypical approach to earlier activists such as Booker T. Washington. The efforts of the Black power movement appeared by some not to have improved the economy or the educational status in the ghetto for the Black underclass. Clark and Gershman (1980) perceived racism as a pattern of biased social attitudes and intolerant behavior by White people rather than as a systemic or structural part of modern capitalist political economy. Clark and Gershman also perceived racism as "a dangerous social disease" and not the logical outcome of consistent and coherent social structure, worldview, and economic order (Marable, 1981).

In general, the benefits of race-conscious policies appear much more limited than their advocates suggest. The greatest economic gains for African Americans since the early 1960s were in the years 1965 to 1975 and occurred mainly in the South. Hence, by the 1970s, Black employment was reduced in nonagricultural work with an increase in white-collar jobs. However, during this period, the unemployment rate remained higher for Blacks than it did for Whites. The majority of Blacks were employed in service, industrial, or clerical jobs.

Black Pride

In the 1970s, the progress of the civil rights movement led to the rise of the sentiment "Black is beautiful." This was an extraordinary feat because Black people chose to call themselves Black as a sign of pride. (In contrast, in American culture the connotations of the word *black* are usually negative.)

> The racial pride inherent in the use of the term Black led to greater feeling of kinship with other people of African descent, and so the next popular term of self-identity was Afro-American. Most recently, the term African American is the preferred term for many Black individuals in the United States. . . . Blacks have chosen to use the name African American because it gives recognition to the continent of their ancestors and to their cultural and citizenship ties to the United States. (Sanchez-Hucles, 2000, p. 9)

However, some Black Americans did not care to make the switch to calling themselves African or African American. Some older Black Americans have spent their lifetimes hearing negative and inaccurate information and stereotyping of Blacks and Africans and still feel uncomfortable or ambivalent about these newer terms.

A decade later the gains were even more striking. Between 1940 and 1970, African American men cut the income gap by about a third, and by 1970 they were earning (on average) more than half of what White men earned. The advancement of African American women was even more striking. Furthermore, African American life expectancy increased significantly, as did African American home ownership rates. African American college enrollment also increased. During this period, African Americans made significant educational achievements under adverse conditions. Marable (1981) reported, for example, that African Americans attained college education and postgraduate degrees. These graduates were closely approaching Whites in the corporate and professional ranks.

Post-Civil Rights Era

Although African Americans saw improvements during the 1980s, they continued to perceive racism and discrimination to be a part of their life. Wage discrimination was viewed as a more common problem. The economists John J. Donahue III and James Heckman discovered "virtually no improvement" in the wages of Black men compared with those of White men outside the South over the entire period from 1963 to 1987 and attributed most southern gains to the powerful antidiscrimination provisions of the 1964 Civil Rights Act. Sigelman and Welch (1991) stated that a 1986 survey revealed that Black Americans experienced discrimination in securing a quality education, obtaining decent housing, and getting a job and were victims of wage discrimination. They faced greater discrimination in employment than in education. At the time, African Americans were making progress in educational gains, but their unemployment situation had worsened compared with their White counterparts. Sigelman and Welch also reported significant effects on African Americans' perceived discrimination against oneself as related to their socioeconomic status. For instance, the African American working class perceived themselves as experiencing greater discrimination against themselves than did the middle-class African Americans. That is, the more affluent African Americans were, the fewer discrimination incidents occurred. Sigelman and Welch concluded that the perceptions of discrimination against African Americans and the trend in anti-Black emotions were similar among young and older African Americans.

New data for this same period suggested a change in the picture of African Americans' circumstances. For example, the 1990 U.S. Census suggested that African Americans were still about as segregated within major metropolitan areas as they were a decade earlier (O'Hare & Usdansky, 1992). Yet Black flight to the suburbs that began in the 1970s has steadily and significantly increased during the 1980s and 1990s (O'Hare, Pollard, Mann, & Kent, 1991). Also, between 1987 and 1990, the earned income increased by 1% for African American families, whereas White family income declined at a similar rate. However, African Americans' family income continued to trail their White counterparts. Not all of the social and economic changes occurring since 1987 narrowed the Black–White socioeconomic disparity (Sigelman & Welch, 1991). For instance, 42% of African American women were heads of households in 1987, whereas the percentage increased to 46% by 1991. Because the income for families of female-headed households was only a third of the income of African American married-couple families, it is likely that the economic well-being for these families was affected (O'Hare et al., 1991; Sigelman & Welch, 1991).

There were some signs indicating that African American–White relations had improved. For example, a 1997 Gallup poll revealed that 83% of Whites ages 18 to 34 approved of interracial marriage, and only 12% of Whites objected to sending their children to a school that included more than half the students who were African American. Further, only a small number of Whites have no African American friends, and one has to look hard to find a White person who objects to an African American family living next door (Thernstrom & Thernstrom, 1999).

Both the racial climate and the status of African Americans have changed. More than 40% of African Americans now consider themselves as middle class. Forty-two percent own their own homes, which rises to 75% if we look just at African American married couples. African American two-parent families earned only 13% less than two-parent White families. Almost a third of the African American population lives in the suburbs. In a 1991 Gallup poll, about one fifth of all White but almost half of African American respondents said that at least three of four African Americans were impoverished urban residents, "by implication living in ghettos, in high-rise public housing projects, with crime and the welfare check as their main source of income" (Thernstrom & Thernstrom, 1999, p. 32). Yet, in fact, African Americans who consider themselves to be middle class outnumber, by a wide margin, those with incomes below the poverty line (Thernstrom & Thernstrom, 1999).

In subsequent years, these patterns continued, although at a rather slow rate. For instance,

> by 1999, more than 30 percent of African American men and nearly 60 percent of African American women hold white-collar jobs. Whereas in 1970 only 2.2 percent of American physicians were African American, the figure is now 4.5 percent. While the faction of African American families with middle-class incomes rose almost forty points between 1940 and 1970, it has inched up only another ten points since then. (Thernstrom & Thernstrom, 1999, p. 32)

This brief discussion of African Americans' historical past over the last 50 years demonstrated roles that racial discrimination and prejudice played in their struggles to gain economic social success in a less than sympatric society. Cornel West (as cited in Cowan, 2003) argued that although racial oppression has been a persistent theme throughout American history, there is a well-known perception that the civil rights movement abolished the legacies of segregation and subordination and made ethnocentrism nonexistent. Cowan (2003) wrote:

> While the meaning of racial discrimination was once clear for all to see in the presence of [W]hite and colored signs, we now live in a racially murky era where racial antipathy is harder to prove. But America remains a racialized society where race is engraved on individual identities and sewn into the seams of the social fabric, no matter how seductive the illusion that racial equality has been achieved. Although Jim Crow segregation is now an anachronism and vitriolic expressions of racism have been forced underground, [Cornel] West contends that racism persists and echoes Malcolm X by asserting that one cannot stab a person six inches in the back and then pull the knife out two inches and conclude that progress has been made. [Cornel] West suggests that the legacy of explicit racism as condoned by state and federal laws has been replaced by the subtler but no less insidious racism of stereotyping, problematization, and exclusion of the [B]lack community. Such expressions of racism, entwined with a general feeling of paranoia, continue to undermine African-American humanity and demonstrate that race still matters. He also suggests that the consequences of racism are apparent in the state of crisis found in the [B]lack ghettos. (p. 20)

Summary

African Americans endured many economic, social, and employment changes over the last 50 years, which were plagued with prejudice and discrimination. In spite of them, they did not give up hope for an improved and more promising future. African Americans made progress, however slowly, despite such prevailing conditions. Much of their gains were made in educational advancements followed by improved working conditions and better job opportunities. African Americans experienced less discrimination in education than in employment. The Black–White disparity in employment and earned income continued, particularly for African American men and women. Other gains over the course of this period for some African Americans were social and economic gains, including African Americans perceiving themselves as middle class and some experiencing a suburban lifestyle. Blacks now saw themselves in a new light: African Americans with a strong sense of self-pride. Although racism and discrimination were the common threads that ran through these past decades, they also persist in various degrees in the lives of most African Americans, as evident in the following discussion on their demographics affecting their well-being.

Demographics Affecting African Americans' Well-Being

There are many social, geographic, and economic changes that occurred among African Americans over the past decade. These changes have had a significant impact on their lives and well-being. Because of within-group differences, African Americans constitute a diverse rather than a homogeneous group. Thus, we can expect these demographic changes not to have an equal impact across individual African Americans.

Geographical Locations

According to a recent U.S. Census report, African Americans or Blacks constituted 36 million people in the United States, or 13% of the civilian noninstitutionalized population (U.S. Census Bureau, 2002). Most of them (55.3%) maintained regional residence in the South, 18.1% in the Northeast, 18.1% in the Midwest, and 8.6% in the West. More than half (52%) of all African Americans resided in a central city within a metropolitan area as compared with 21% of non-Hispanic Whites. Only 13% of African Americans and 22% of non-Hispanic Whites resided in nonmetropolitan areas.

Marital Status

Among the 26.2 million African Americans and the 158.3 million non-Hispanic Whites ages 15 and older, 10% of each were divorced and about 6% of each were widowed, but 43% of African Americans had never married, compared with 25% of non-Hispanic Whites. African Americans were less likely than non-Hispanic Whites to be currently married (35% and 57%, respectively). Note that married included those with a spouse present or a spouse absent (U.S. Census Bureau, 2002).

In 2002, there were 8.8 million African American families and 53.6 million non-Hispanic White families in the United States. Approximately one half (48%) of all African American families were married-couple families, 43% of African American families were maintained by women with no spouse present, and 9% were maintained by African American men with no spouse present. The 2002 U.S. Census Bureau report indicated that among married-couple families, 33% of African American families had two members, compared with 47% of non-Hispanic White families. African American married-couple families were more likely than their non-Hispanic White counterparts to have five or more members (20% and 12%, respectively). Among families maintained by women with no spouse present, 40% of African American families had two members, compared with 55% of non-Hispanic White families.

Age and Gender

In 2002, 33% of all African Americans were younger than 18 years of age, compared with 23% of non-Hispanic Whites. Only 8% of African Americans were 65 and older, compared with 14% of non-Hispanic Whites. A larger percentage of African American men than non-

Hispanic White men were younger than age 18 (36% compared with 24%). In contrast, 7% of African American men and 12% of non-Hispanic White men were 65 and older. A higher percentage of African American women (30%) than non-Hispanic White women (22%) were under age 18, whereas 9% of African American women and 16% of non-Hispanic White women were 65 and older.

Educational Achievement and Workforce Participation

Of the 20.4 million African Americans 25 years and older, 79% had earned at least a high school diploma. Seventeen percent of African Americans had attained at least a bachelor's degree. More African American women (18%) than African American men (16%) had earned at least a bachelor's degree.

Of the 216.8 million members of the civilian population age 16 and older in 2002, 25.4 million (12%) were African Americans. The unemployment rate for African Americans was twice that for non-Hispanic Whites (11% and 5%, respectively). African American men had a higher rate of work participation compared with African American women. There was a higher rate for African American women (62%) in the workforce than for White women (60%).

According to the 2002 U.S Census report, African American men were more than twice as likely as non-Hispanic White men to work in service occupations (19% and 8%, respectively). Also, African American women (26%) were less likely to work in managerial and professional specialty positions compared with non-Hispanic White women (37%), as well as performing in technical, sales, and administrative support positions (36% for African American women compared with 40% for non-Hispanic White women). Furthermore, fewer non-Hispanic White women worked in service positions (15%) compared with African American women (27%). Only 5% of African American women worked in operator, fabricator, and laborer positions compared with non-Hispanic White women (9%).

Economic Conditions

The 2002 Census report also indicated that 27% of African American married-couple families had earned incomes of $75,000 or more, compared with 40% of comparable non-Hispanic White families. African American families maintained by women with no spouse present had incomes that concentrated in the lower range; that is, 58% of African American families' earned incomes were less than $25,000. In 2001, the poverty rate, which was 12% for the total population, was 23% for African Americans and 8% for non-Hispanic Whites. During the same period in 2001, 6.8 million families in the United States received incomes below the poverty level. Of these families, 1.8 million were African American and 3.1 million were non-Hispanic White families. However, a higher percentage of African American families than of non-Hispanic White families were poor, 21% for African Americans and 6% for non-Hispanic Whites. Poverty was highest among African American families (35%) headed by women with no spouse present compared with non-Hispanic White families. African American families headed by men with no spouse present were more likely to live in poverty (19%) compared with 10% of non-Hispanic White families.

Homelessness

Individual and family homelessness have increased steadily during the last two decades (Lindsey, 1998). Lindsey stated that the vast majority of families of this group is headed by women. They become victims of homelessness for a variety of reasons, among them "employment issues, declining support from public assistance, scarcity of available low-income housing, lack of health insurance, domestic violence and other family disruptions, mental illness, . . . substance abuse" (Waxman & Trupin, 1997, pp. 45–46), physical illness, and lack of or insufficient income. According to the U.S. Department of Housing and Urban Development (1994), families are the fastest growing segment of the homeless population. "The ethnic make-up of the homeless population varies widely, reflecting the overall U.S. population. Furthermore, as with poverty, the population is disproportionately African American (58%), while less than 3% are from among the Hispanic and Native American populations" (Waxman & Trupin, 1997, p. 41). Rocha, Johnson, McChesney, and Butterfield (1996) conducted a study to determine the demographic predictors of families' ability to access permanent housing upon departing shelters after a 10-year period. Their findings indicated that large families and African American families were less likely to move into permanent housing than were smaller families and White families. Research results suggest that, in urban areas, 25% of the homeless are children younger than 18 years old (Waxman & Trupin, 1997).

Dail (2000) contended that there is no commonly accepted figure of the actual number of homeless in the United States presently available. However, approximately 12 million of the adult population in the United States experienced homelessness at some stage in their lives (Burt et al., 1999).

Levy (2000) cited research funded by the National Institute of Mental Health that suggested that the prevalence of major mental illness among homeless individuals ranged from 28% to 37% and that nearly half of this population were addicted to drugs and/or alcohol. Despite the efforts of outreach workers, many homeless individuals with major mental illness are unable to access mental health care services such as psychotherapy, day treatment, and residential programs. Levy argued that there are substantial numbers of people with major illness who reside on the street and in shelters without adequate access to housing or health care.

Summary

African Americans are indeed a diverse group of people. They are the second largest ethnic minority group in the United States. Most of them reside in urban cities within metropolitan areas; however, this historical review indicated that most African Americans reside in the South. It appears there has been a geographical shift back to the South, with slightly more than half of African Americans now residing in the South. This shift back to the South may be because of greater opportunities for many African Americans than in other regions. Approximately half of all African Americans are married couples. They are a younger group than their White counterparts. The unemployment rate for African Americans significantly outpaced the unemployment rate for Whites. More than twice the number of African American men worked in service jobs than White men. As discrimination and prejudice negatively affected earlier employment practices, they continue to affect current employment patterns of African American men and women. Further, discrepancies in earning power for African American married couples and White couples are relatively consistent with past decades. Many African Americans are and still live below the poverty line.

African American homelessness has increased steadily since the last decade. Most families, including children, of this group were headed by women. Several issues suggest why they are without adequate housing, such as employment issues, mental health, and alcohol and drug use. The stress and strain in which African Americans find themselves indeed warrant the need for improved psychological health. Accessibility and awareness of these sources are critical.

Mental Health and Mental Illness

Any attempt to define mental and emotional health is a complex and ambiguous task, particularly considering the fact that the scope of individual differences is so vast. According to the Surgeon General's report (U.S. Department of Health and Human Services, 1999),

> mental health is a state of successful performance of mental function, resulting in productive activities, fulfilling relationships with other people, and the ability to adapt to change and to cope with adversity. Mental health is indispensable to personal well-being, family and interpersonal relationships, and contribution to community or society. (p. 4)

Klag (1999) stated that "each individual is born with a distinct disposition—a characteristic that adds to individual variations in emotions—that colors our attitudes about and responses to our surroundings" (p. 1207). The symptoms involving behavior and the extent of what is normal are so sweeping that labeling a behavior as a disorder is seldom unequivocal. An emotion, response, or attitude that seems consistent (completely in keeping) with one person's temperament may be an indication that something is wrong for another. For example, Klag (1999) proffered:

> Add to individual variations in emotions and a behavior the variations that arise in regard to context and culture. Certain subjective experiences, emotions, and behavior that may be defined as disordered in one context or one culture may be perfectly acceptable and within normal boundaries in another. For example, it is considered normal to giggle at a party but not at a funeral. At the same time, it may be normal to enjoy yourself at a wake. (p. 1207)

Klag (1999) further delineated mental health and mental illness and what and how some factors can cause or trigger these conditions. He stated:

> Given the wide range of normal emotional states and responses, as well as the capriciousness of life circumstances, it is seldom easy to define with great precision just what constitutes mental and emotional health. Almost always, mental health or mental illness is determined on an individual basis. As with physical illness, some mental disorders are diseases, arising from biologic imbalance and disruption. Often, however, mental health and emotional well-being are the products of the struggle between a person's vulnerabilities and strengths as they surface in [the person's] interactions with his [her] world. (p. 1207)

Does this suggest that everyone's psychological health is gauged by these concepts? It appears that these two concepts, mental health and mental illness/disorders, are universal and fit all Whites, African Americans, and other ethnic/racial groups as well as age and gender groups. Ramseur (2002), however, examined several mental health models and studies and argued that there is no polarity between mental or psychological health and mental illness. For example, Ramseur (2002) stated:

> Freedom from symptoms or illness is the most medical model of psychological health. Health is the absence of illness, and implicitly the ability to function adequately. This model has been characterized as inadequate by theorists like Maslow (1968) who stresses the importance of "positive" characteristics like creativity, "growth," and self-actualization in psychological functioning. Psychological health defined as being essentially like the average "modal" member of society [or] of being "adjusted" to one's social/cultural surroundings was once common models in the literature. However, both concepts are rarely used now. "Adjustment" seems to evoke conformity and blandness to many theorists, and culture-bound notion that they want to transcend. (p. 430)

Ramseur (2002) further stated that there is no general support for a defined meaning for mental health that includes African Americans and their experiences. Ramseur argued:

> How should psychological health be defined? . . . No theory or model of adult psychological health has achieved a consensus or accumulated a convincing body of empirical evidence to address [this question]. In addition, while existing models of psychological health claim to be "universal," that is applicable and explanatory for all persons, in fact, they usually have little or nothing to say about the unique social/cultural circumstances of African Americans and the impact of such circumstances on African American adult psychological health. (p. 428)

Afrocentric models of African American personality, such as Kambon's (1998), Baldwin's (1991), and Nobles's (1991), have implications for psychological health and healthy functioning for African Americans, which are becoming ever more apparent in the literature on psychological health. Kambon's model, for example, emphasizes the value of congruent and self-affirming cultural values and worldviews for African American psychological health. He believes that African Americans need to be rooted in a positive sense of culture and social history. Ramseur (2002), however, concluded that Kambon's model lacks supporting evidence for his belief "that the average African American is 'mentally disordered' because of Cultural Misorientation" (p. 436).

Based on Marie Jahoda's (1958) pioneering model that emphasizes positive mental health, an increasing number of models, such as by Anderson, Eaddy, and Williams (1990), Franklin and Jackson (1990), and Shade (1990), have adopted Jahoda's approach in presenting African Americans' mental health. Jahoda's model was presented in her book, *Current Conceptions of Positive Mental Health* (1958). Jahoda (1958) suggested two methods for defining mental health:

> as a relatively constant and enduring function of personality, leading to predictable differences in behavior and feelings depending on the stresses and strains of the situations in which a person finds himself; or as a momentary function of personality and situation. (p. 8)

She also identified six dimensions that contribute to positive mental health, suggesting that a person's mental health is more than the absence of symptoms but involves the presence of that person's positive, for example, healthy, characteristics. Jahoda's (1958) six dimensions are

1. the attitudes of a person toward one's own self
2. the extent to which an individual is cognizant of one's potentialities as a result of action
3. the integration of function in the person's personality
4. the extent of a person's autonomy of social influences
5. the way a person's views his or her environment
6. the ability of a person to accept life as it occurs and control it.

However, Ramseur (2002) stated that none of the emerging or existing theories of positive mental health satisfactorily explain and delineate African American psychological health. He proposed a synthesis of certain aspects from these existing theories that will be significant for African Americans across the life span. Based on these theories, Ramseur (2002, pp. 437–438) suggested six issues:

1. maintaining an overall positive conception of the self
2. maintaining a positive conception of African Americans as a group and a positive sense of connection and involvement with the African American community and its culture

3. maintaining an accurate perception of the social environment (including its racism)
4. adapting to both African American and White community/cultures and using effective, nondestructive ways to cope with both
5. developing and maintaining emotional intimacy with others
6. maintaining a sense of competence and ability to work productively.

He contended that how well a person manages these issues and the balance between successful and dysfunctional adaptation might be the measure of psychological health for African Americans.

Franklin and Jackson (1990) contended that "in both [African American] and the general populations, the vast majority of people are not reported as having a definable mental disorder" (p. 292). Thus, it is unclear what the nature of mental health is throughout the life span. Mental health and mental illness are not two independent or contrasting conditions, but each individually has simultaneously healthy and illness aspects (Jahoda, 1958). Hence, mental health is not simply the absence of mental illness, anymore than mental illness is the absence of mental health (Franklin & Jackson, 1990; Jahoda, 1958; Ramseur, 2002).

For the purpose of this book, our emphasis is on positive mental health among African Americans. We are concerned with the psychological strengths as the foundation for their positive mental health. Positive mental health is more than the absence of illness or disorder, and it includes the presence of positive healthy characteristics that promote wholesome and healthy development. Positive mental health aims for nonpathological outcomes and characteristics affecting positive psychological development. The importance of positive mental health for African Americans is being proficient and functioning effectively in a pluralistic society. The individual has the ability to function effectively despite social demands and expectations. Factors contributing to positive mental health include healthy self-esteem, adequate shelter, a good education, a successful career, a full-time job, intelligence, access to good health care, and well-defined role responsibilities. These constitute the basic psychological and physical needs of every human being. Yet thousands of people in the United States go to bed hungry, and thousands more sleep on city streets throughout urban America. Thus all Americans do not share quality health care and quality education.

In summary, several emerging theoretical frameworks have been proposed suggesting positive mental health of African Americans. These positions are contrary to traditional theories on mental health that is supposedly universal for all ethnic/racial groups. Mental health is not necessarily the absence of symptoms of mental disorder. Thus, mental health and mental illness are not viewed as two polarized concepts. Our aim in this book is to promote positive mental health among African Americans. As part of this promotion, we must examine some of the problems that prevent effective mental health treatment involving African Americans.

Barriers to Mental Health Treatment

Counseling and psychotherapy have been applied by mental health practitioners with clients well before the 1950s (Ridley, 1995). Kendall (1996) contended that "the majority of research and professional literature dealt with processes and outcomes of psychotherapy. It was used as an intervention for mental health difficulties that included primarily White populations with little emphasis on ethnicity, culture, or class" (p. 13).

According to Cain and Kington (2003), discrimination based on race/ethnicity is detrimental to the individuals who experience discrimination as well as to society at large. They further suggested that there are serious mental health and physical health consequences for people who routinely live with discrimination (Cain & Kington, 2003; Williams & Williams-Morris, 2000). Perceptions and experiences of racial/ethnic bias leading to unfair treatment can result in personal negative emotional and stress responses, which in turn have been shown to be related to hypertension, cardiovascular disease, mental health, and other negative states of health (Cain & Kington, 2003; Karlsen & Nazroo, 2002; Williams & Williams-Morris, 2000). Cain and Kington (2003) argued that

> ways in which racial bias can affect mental health range from limits on access to quality [mental and] medical care and economic deprivation to the physiological responses to experience of chronic discrimination and to inequitable exposures to occupational and environmental hazards. (p. 191)

African Americans have a strong sense of ethnic identity and self-worth that may have been protective against perceptions of ethnocentrism and ethnic prejudice and the stress resulting from bias situations (Cain & Kington, 2003; Williams, Spencer, & Jackson, 1999). To the extent that racism is a major source of stress, individuals can be taught stress-reduction techniques and to draw on the strength of their community (Bowen-Reid & Harrell, 2002).

There are numerous studies (Cain & Kington, 2003; Feagin & Sikes, 1994; Ridley, 1995; Sigelman & Welch, 1991; Williams, Neighbors, & Jackson, 2003) regarding the mental health status of African Americans and other ethnic minorities. In Cain and Kington's (2003) research regarding bias or discrimination and unfair treatment, for example, about 70% to 80% of most African American and White men and women indicated that they usually attempted to do something about being treated unfairly and talked to others about it, whereas some accepted this treatment as a fact of life but told others about it. Yet others kept the treatment to themselves and either did something about it or accepted it as a routine event. Both African American and White men were more likely to report the incident at work and most likely to do something about the situation.

Cain and Kington's (2003) study indicated that blood pressure was elevated most among working-class African American women who accepted unfair ethnocentric/discriminatory treatment as a fact of life and kept it to themselves and among working-class African American men who accepted this type of treatment but told others. Blood pressure was also elevated among working-class African American men but not women, who reported having experienced racial discrimination in three or more situations. Cain and Kington concluded that these results suggest that women may feel less restrained to share their emotions in a manner that provides validation, whereas men may talk about what happened in a more resigned manner and consider it not prudent to express their actual emotions of the hurt and anger. On the other hand, patterns among professional African American women and men may speak to their greater social and economic resources and, thus, perhaps greater willingness to identify and challenge discriminatory treatment (Feagin & Sikes, 1994; hooks, 1995; Sigelman & Welch, 1991). Another challenge is identifying effective methods used for assessing African Americans' mental health and mental disorders.

Traditional Method of Assessing Mental Health and Mental Illness

Assessing mental health and mental illness across diverse ethnic and cultural groups is a complex and arduous task. Ivey, Ivey, and Bradford (1998) stated that the *Diagnostic and Statistical Manual of Mental Disorders* (4th ed.; *DSM–IV*; American Psychiatric Association,

1994) "is a classification system focused on labeling or naming specific groupings of attitudes and behaviors, primarily for classification purposes" (p. 336) and is commonly used with African Americans and other ethnic minorities. However, some reports (Ivey et al., 1998; Kurasaki & Okazaki, 2002; Ridley, 1995; Thomas & Sillen, 1972) have questioned the accuracy and misuse of diagnostic systems and techniques particularly when applied to African Americans and other ethnic minorities. For example, Kurasaki and Okazaki (2002) argued:

> There is a danger in not responding to individuals within our diverse society with assessment techniques that are sensitive to cultural variations in symptom presentation. Assessments that are not culturally informed can result in missed diagnoses of real and treatable psychological problems, as well as over-pathologizing culturally normal thoughts and behaviors. How then do we distinguish between psychopathology and culturally appropriate thoughts and behaviors? (p. 1)

Moreover, to what extent does the *DSM–IV* system have universal appropriateness for determining psychological problems of African Americans? Parham (2002) spoke specifically to this single system or type of an assessment tool that is often applied to classify mental disorders among African Americans:

> Classification of African descent people using terms and constructs developed for and used by a European American oriented profession assumes a universality that may not be accurate. Most, if not all, of the conditions or diagnostic labels used to classify mental disorders come from diagnostic nosologies (e.g., *DSM–IV* or theoretical orientations) that have not been normed or influenced by cultural standards that differ from those of White populations. Even the latest attempt to infuse some cultural information into the *DSM–IV* diagnostic system is, at best, substandard. Obviously, this raises the question of whether African descent people can be appropriately and accurately classified and diagnosed using these systems. (p. 5)

It appears that the assessment tools, such as the *DSM–IV*, must include ethnic and cultural differences in their diagnostic classifications. Cross-cultural assessment training must be given to mental health professionals to ensure sensitivity to and awareness of the cultural and within-group differences and similarities among African Americans. Effective mental health professionals must be required to be knowledgeable of and culturally responsive to mental health needs of African Americans.

Mental Health Professionals and Cultural Responsiveness

Therapy outcomes have raised some concern regarding the ability of mental health professionals who are primarily White to provide psychotherapeutic services to African American clients. Kendall (1996) found in her study that White clients tended to stay in therapy, whereas African American clients prematurely dropped out before completing treatments. Further, she concluded that ethnicity is an important variable that must be considered in terms of how clients engage in psychotherapy. African Americans often view therapy as an indication of a person's weakness, and individual verbal therapy often places the African American client in a paradoxical situation (Boyd-Franklin, 1989).

The issues of ethnicity and race play a significant role in how the client participates in therapy. To be successful in obtaining meaningful outcomes working with African Americans, it is imperative that helping professionals become culturally responsive to the mental health needs of African Americans in a therapeutic encounter. This approach is likely to lead to positive outcomes that are consistent with the goals of positive mental health for African Americans.

Need for Positive Mental Health Perspective for African Americans

Much of the traditional literature focuses on the pathology of the African American as a type of debilitation and a failure to society. A disproportionate number of African American inmates are in correction facilities, yet there are few discussions of positive mental health approaches. Ruiz (1990) advocated for greater focus on preventive mental health perspectives rather than the dysfunctional or the mentally impaired African American. Although there are limited numbers of existing models emphasizing positive mental health, most of the following chapters in this book illustrate a more positive/preventative perspective regarding African Americans.

Summary

African Americans represent a very diverse group of people with many values and worldviews. There are many demographic factors that have shaped or influenced their values, worldviews, thoughts, behaviors, and lifestyles. The mental health and mental disorders among African Americans are examples of how the two variables can affect each person's life. Mental health facilities are available, but not all African Americans have equal access to these facilities because of such barriers as social stigma, ability to pay for services, or lack of transportation. In the Surgeon General's report urging attention to African Americans' mental health and mental illness, his message included taking preventative measures to ensure the most appropriate mental health care for all African Americans regardless of their economic and social status.

Methods for assessing mental health and mental illness must incorporate African American culture to begin approaching some degree of accuracy in diagnoses and treatment for this group. Professionals who use mental assessment tools must be made aware of the flaws inherent in many of the current tools. Obviously, there is a need for professionals to ascertain effective usage, such as experience, with African American populations.

Plan of the Book

This book is organized into four primary sections that include a broad range of chapters about many important aspects of the lives of African Americans. The final chapter provides a summary for the reader. These chapters were written by an outstanding and distinguished group of practitioners and educators. Section I deals with current issues affecting the lives of African Americans: general scope of mental health, family, women, men, and marital status and female–male relations. Section II provides pertinent data on special issues concerning African Americans: elderly; lesbians, gays, and bisexuals; HIV/AIDS; substance abuse; and biracial and multiracial identity. Section III deals with the African American community: cultural characteristics; perceptions of mental health counseling; impact of violence, crime, and gangs; the Black church; and public and mental health. Section IV discusses how the concepts presented in earlier discussions can be implemented into practice for African Americans. Chapters in this section focus on practical application of concepts and strategies for African Americans: community mental health, selective counseling interventions for the disabled, mental health assessment for children and adolescents, spirituality and religion in counseling and psychotherapy, and professional ethics. The final chapter of the book concludes with a summary and future implications.

References

American Psychiatric Association. (1994). *Diagnostic and statistical manual of mental disorders* (4th ed.). Washington, DC: Author.

Anderson, L. P., Eaddy, C. L., & Williams, E. A. (1990). Psychosocial competence: Towards a theory of understanding positive mental health among Black Americans. In D. S. Ruiz (Ed.), *Handbook of mental health and mental disorder among Black Americans* (pp. 255–271). New York: Greenwood Press.

Baldwin, J. A. (1991). African (Black) psychology: Issues and synthesis. In R. L. Jones (Ed.), *Black psychology* (3rd ed., pp. 125–135). Hampton, VA: Cobb & Henry.

Bowen-Reid, T. L., & Harrell, J. P. (2002). Racist experiences and health outcomes: A dreaminization of spirituality as a buffer. *Journal of Black Psychology, 28,* 18–36.

Boyd-Franklin, N. (1989). *Black families in therapy: A multisystems approach.* New York: Guilford Press.

Burt, M. R., Aron, L. Y., Douglas, T., Valente, J., Lee, E., & Iwen, B. (1999, August). *Homelessness: Programs and the people they serve—Findings of a national survey of homeless assistance: 1996 summary report.* Washington, DC: The Urban Institute.

Cain, V. S., & Kington, R. S. (2003). Investigating the role of racial/ethnic bias in health outcomes. *American Journal of Public Health, 93,* 191–192.

Clark, K. (1965). *Dark ghetto: Dilemmas of social power.* New York: Harper & Row.

Clark, K., & Gershman, C. (1980, October 5). The Black plight: Race and class? *New York Times Magazine,* Section 6.

Cowan, R. (2003). *Cornel West: The politics of redemption.* Malden, MA: Polity Press.

Dail, P. W. (2000). Introduction to the symposium on homelessness. *Policy Studies Journal, 28,* 331–337.

Feagin, J., & Sikes, M. P. (1994). *Living with racism: The Black middle-class experience.* Boston: Beacon Press.

Franklin, A. J., & Jackson, J. S. (1990). Factors contributing to positive mental health among Black Americans. In D. S. Ruiz (Ed.), *Handbook of mental health and mental disorder among Black Americans* (pp. 291–308). New York: Greenwood Press.

hooks, B. (1995). *Killing rage: Ending racism.* New York: Henry Holt.

Ivey, A. E., Ivey, M. B., & Bradford, M. (1998). Reframing *DSM–IV*: Positive strategies from developmental counseling and therapy. *Journal of Counseling & Development, 76,* 334–351.

Jahoda, M. (1958). *Current conceptions of positive mental health.* New York: Basic Books.

Kambon, K. K. K. (1998). An African-centered paradigm for understanding the mental health of Africans in American. In R. Jones (Ed.), *African American mental health* (pp. 33–50). Hampton, VA: Cobb & Henry.

Karlsen, S., & Nazroo, J. Y. (2002). Relation between racial discrimination, social class, and health among ethnic minority groups. *American Journal of Public Health, 92,* 624–631.

Kendall, J. (1996). Creating a culturally responsive psychotherapeutic environment for African American youths: A critical analysis. *Environment and Health Advances in Nursing Science, 18*(4), 11–28.

Klag, M. J. (1999). Mental health. In M. J. Klag (Ed.), *Johns Hopkins family health book* (pp. 1206–1267). New York: Harper Collins.

Kurasaki, K. S., & Okazaki, S. (2002). Introduction. In K. S. Kurasaki, S. Okazaki, & S. Sue (Eds.), *Asian American mental health: Assessment theories and methods* (pp. 1–27). New York: Kluwer Academic/Plenum.

Levy, J. S. (2000). Homeless outreach: On the road to pretreatment alternatives. *Families in Society, 81,* 360–368.

Lindsey, E. W. (1998). Service providers' perception of factors that help or hinder homeless families. *Families in Society, 79,* 160–172.

Marable, M. (1981). *Blackwater: Historical studies in race, class consciousness, and revolution.* Dayton, OH: Black Praxis Press.

Nobles, W. W. (1991). Extended self: Rethinking the so-called Negro self-concept. In R. Jones (Ed.), *Black psychology* (3rd ed., pp. 295–304). Hampton, VA: Cobb & Henry.

O'Hare, W. P., Pollard, K. M., Mann, T. L., & Kent, M. M. (1991). *African Americans in the 1990s* (Vol. 46, No. 1). Washington, DC: Population Reference Bureau.

O'Hare, W. P., & Usdansky, M. L. (1992, September). What the 1990 census tells us about segregation in 25 large metros. *Population Today,* 6–7.

Parham, T. A. (2002). *Counseling persons of African descent: Raising the bar of practitioner competence.* Thousand Oaks, CA: Sage.

Ramseur, H. (2002). Psychologically healthy African American adults. In R. L. Jones (Ed.), *Black psychology* (4th ed., pp. 427–455). Hampton, VA: Cobb & Henry.

Ridley, C. R. (1995). *Overcoming unintentional racism in counseling and therapy: A practitioner's guide to intentional intervention.* Thousand Oaks, CA: Sage.

Rocha, C., Johnson, A. K., McChesney, K. Y., & Butterfield, W. H. (1996). Predictors of permanent housing for sheltered homeless families. *Families in Society, 77,* 50–57.

Ruiz, D. S. (1990). Introduction. In D. S. Ruiz (Ed.), *Handbook of mental health and mental disorder among Black Americans* (pp. xv–xxii). New York: Greenwood Press.

Sanchez-Hucles, J. (2000). *The first session with African Americans: A step-by-step guide.* San Francisco: Jossey-Bass.

Shade, B. J. (1990). Coping with color: The anatomy of positive mental health. In D. S. Ruiz (Ed.), *Handbook of mental health and mental disorder among Black Americans* (pp. 273–289). New York: Greenwood Press.

Sigelman, L., & Welch, S. (1991). *Black Americans' views of racial inequality: The dream deferred.* Cambridge, England: Cambridge University Press.

Thernstrom, A., & Thernstrom, S. (1999). Black progress. In C. H. Foreman Jr. (Ed.), *The African American predicament* (pp. 29–44). Washington, DC: Brookings Institute Press.

Thomas, A., & Sillen, S. (1972). *Racism and psychiatry.* Secaucus, NJ: Citadel Press.

U.S. Census Bureau. (2002). *The Black population in the United States: March 2002—Current Population Reports, Series P20-541.* Washington, DC: Author.

U.S. Department of Health and Human Services. (1999). *Mental health: A report of the Surgeon General.* Rockville, MD: Author.

U.S. Department of Housing and Urban Development. (1994). *Priority: Home! The federal plan to break the cycle of homelessness.* Washington, DC: Author.

Waxman, L., & Trupin, R. (1997). *A status report on hunger and homelessness in America's cities.* Washington, DC: U.S. Conference of Mayors.

West, C. (1993). *Race matters.* Boston: Beacon Press.

Williams, D. R., Neighbors, H. W., & Jackson, J. S. (2003). Racial/ethnic discrimination and health: Findings from community studies. *American Journal of Public Health, 93,* 200–208.

Williams, D. R., Spencer, M. S., & Jackson, J. S. (1999). Race, stress, and physical health: The role of group-identity. In R. J. Contrada & R. D. Ashmore (Eds.), *Self, social identity and physical health: Interdisciplinary explorations* (pp. 71–100). New York: Oxford University Press.

Williams, D. R., & Williams-Morris, R. (2000). Racism and mental health: The African American experience. *Ethnicity & Disease, 5,* 243–268.

2

The African American Family

Lynda Brown Wright and Anita Fernander

Numerous scholars agree that there is no such thing as *the* African American family. To the contrary, a diverse array of African American family configurations, structures, customs, and ideologies is evident within the African American community. Yet, there are "traditional" characteristics that help to describe the African American family experience (Boyd-Franklin, 1989a; R. B. Hill, 1972; Nobles, 1972). While African American families share many features with families from other racial/ethnic groups, they also hold their own distinctive features that set them apart, and as such, it is important that these unique patterns are considered when working with African American families (Boyd-Franklin, 1989a; Brinson, 1992; Littlejohn-Blake & Darling, 1993; Spaights, 1990). The purpose of this chapter is to provide a greater understanding of African American families, by reviewing the sociocultural factors that have influenced their diverse family types, their strengths, and the challenges they face, as well as provide mental health professionals with suggestions for their consideration when working with families from within the African American community.

Historical and Cultural Influences

The African American family experience cannot be adequately understood without acknowledging its historical and cultural influences. There is strong support for the notion that many African American family traditions have their roots in Africa and that they have been adapted over time in an effort to cope with the ramifications of the institution of slavery (Herskovits, 1941; Nobles, 1972; Sudarkasa, 1980). The traditional African American family structure, for example, has been greatly influenced by characteristics of West African families who held strong extended family ties and tended to have a matrilineal family organization (Barbarin, 1983; Surdarkasa, 1980). During slavery, however, a major part of the goal of controlling African Americans was to take away their connection with the homeland of Africa by stripping them of their African language, identity, and culture. Any emotional ties the enslaved Africans sought to create were consistently undermined by dominant beliefs and social conditions (Pinderhughes, 2002). Thus, the focus was to replace traditional African family values and customs with those that could be conducive to slave identity functioning. Despite these attempts to destroy their African identity, however, many slaves organized themselves into family structures and thus made their own adaptations to family life in America (Staples & Johnson, 1993).

Until the 1950s, few scholars wrote about or researched African American family structures. However, since their arrival as slaves in America, negative perceptions of inferiority have been formed, many of which have continued to shape ideologies today. These early notions of African American family life were developed primarily by non-African American scholars and political leaders who based their conclusions on Eurocentric standards (e.g., Frazier, 1957; Moynihan, 1965). African American families were viewed as "distinctive" and even "pathological" rather than different when compared with White families (Heiss, 1975).

E. Franklin Frazier's (1957) work no doubt helped to set the stage for many of the negative views of African American family structures and the impact of those structures on the survival of the African American community. His book, *The Negro Family in the United States*, offers one of the first extensive writings that specifically characterized African American families as distinctively inferior. Frazier referred to the African American family structure as "disorganized" and suggested this disorganization affected the functioning of the entire African American community and had thus impeded the African American family's ability to function in the larger White society. He contended that limited stability in the African American family has resulted in a lack of tradition and thus a large number of fragmented families (Frazier, 1957). Consequently, scholarly credibility was given to the view that African American family structures were inferior compared with White family structures.

Daniel Patrick Moynihan's (1965) work is another pivotal point in which the African American family structure was assaulted. As a politician, his work was arguably more influential; it set the stage for many public policies that would later affect African American family life across many domains. In his 1965 report, *The Negro Family: The Case for National Action*, Moynihan alleged a unique "pathology" of the overall African American community, which he traced to the African American family structure, a structure he described as "matriarchal," "disorganized," and "dysfunctional." His report described the African American family as the "principal source of the most aberrant, inadequate, or antisocial behavior that did not establish but now serves to perpetuate the cycle of poverty and deprivation" (Moynihan, 1965, p. 30).

It was not until African American scholars began to write about the African American family that deficit views were challenged and clearer, more balanced pictures of African American family structures and systems of functioning began to emerge in the literature (e.g., Allen, 1978; Billingsley, 1968a, 1968b; Boyd-Franklin, 1989a, 1989b; Hatchett & Jackson, 1993; R. B. Hill, 1972; Logan, 1996; Scott & Black, 1989; Staples, 1971; Sudarkasa, 1980; Taylor, Chatters, & Jackson, 1993). These scholars began to challenge the previously held ideology that African American family structures should be viewed only from a Eurocentric perspective, which tended to assess them in terms of male–female unions and parental status in which legal and biological relationships were emphasized (Billingsley, 1968a, 1968b, 1992; Gaines, 1997; R. B. Hill, 1972; J. L. McAdoo, 1993; Mosley-Howard & Evans, 2000; Staples & Johnson, 1993).

Billingsley (1968b), in his seminal research *Black Families in White America*, was one of the first scholars to challenge the ways in which African American families had been viewed historically. He concluded that the strengths of African American families, many of which were adaptive mechanisms of survival during tremendously oppressive conditions in America, far outweighed their weaknesses. In a close examination of the various configuration patterns of African American families, Billingsley (1968b) also challenged the belief that female-headed families automatically provide less conducive family environments than male-headed families. Additionally, he declared that there were more than two types of family structures among families within the United States. Billingsley (1968b) proposed three categories of families: *primary families* (e.g., two-parent families), *extended families* (other relatives and in-laws), and *augmented families* (e.g., no blood relation). His work, along with the work of the many other contemporary scholars that followed, helped to bring recognition to the fact that African American family structures, while not always consistent with the trends of European American family structures, are viable and functioning units within the African American community (Boyd-Franklin, 1989a; Chatters, Taylor, & Jayakody, 1994; Hatchett & Jackson, 1993; R. B. Hill, 1972; Logan, 1996; Scott & Black, 1989; Sudarkasa, 1993; Taylor et al., 1993; Zinn & Eitzen, 1996).

Contemporary African American Family Structures

As is the case with most family structures in the United States, African American family structures have developed in numerous ways over the past decades while still maintaining certain historical patterns. Some of the contemporary configurations of African American family structures that are addressed in this chapter are those of marriage and the extended family network.

While marriage has always been and remains a very important aspect of African American life, overall, the rates of marriage among African Americans have declined steadily since the 1960s (U.S. Census Bureau, 2000a). Specifically, the percentage of African American women and men who marry has declined by 20% over the past 50 years when compared with other ethnic groups (Tucker & Mitchell-Kernan, 1995). Pinderhughes (2002) noted that marriage among African Americans was at its height during the 1880s, when 80% of all African American families consisted of a husband and wife. In 1998, single women headed 54% of African American households (U.S. Census Bureau, 2000a). While overall, African American families headed by a woman have increased steadily, it should be noted that among families above the poverty level, married couples constitute the majority of African American family structures (R. B. Hill, 1972; S. A. Hill, 1999).

Extended families, which Boyd-Franklin (1989a) described as "families in which relatives with a variety of blood ties have been absorbed into a coherent network of mutual emotional and economic support" (p. 43), continue to exist in many diverse forms among African American families. Billingsley (1968b) further delineated the diversity of African American extended family units by suggesting four major types: (a) subfamilies, those that consist of at least two or more relatives; (b) families with secondary members, which R. B. Hill (1977) referred to as minor relatives (e.g., grandchildren, nieces, nephews, cousins, siblings under 18), "peers of the primary parents," such as cousins, "elders of the primary parents," such as aunts and uncles, and "parents of the primary parents"; (c) augmented families, in which children are being raised by families in which there is no blood relation; and (d) "nonblood" relatives, "fictive kin" individuals who are a part of the family in terms of their involvement but who are not related by blood ties (Boyd-Franklin, 1989a; Stack, 1974).

Extended family living within the African American community has continued for a number of reasons and may vary depending on the household. Boyd-Franklin (1989a) noted that there can be endless combinations of extended family units within the African American community. In a review, Kane (2000) outlined three ways in which extended family households function. In the first, some extended families combine their financial incomes and manpower for the care of the old and the young members of the family. Some are more holistic in that they combine all of their efforts together for the family, including emotional and financial support. A second extended family structure is one in which members of the family live close to one another but in separate households. A third family configuration is one in which familial relationships are established with others who are not biologically related (close friends and neighbors) and who may or may not live with the nuclear family.

The many social ills that have plagued some African American youths and young adults have also affected the African American family, which has resulted in a growing number of multigenerational extended family units. The growing numbers of teenage mothers have resulted in more unique multigenerational configurations. A relatively new type of extended family has emerged, one in which many households are composed of grandmothers, young mothers, and their young children (Gordon, Chase-Landsdale, Matjasko, & Brooks-Gunn, 1997). Increasingly, grandparents are becoming parents again, as they take responsibility for the rearing of often very young grandchildren. Additionally, social problems (drugs, HIV/AIDS, institutionalization of young African American men and women, etc.) have resulted in growing numbers of children becoming a part of the foster care system. This new phenomenon has resulted in what Scannapieco and Jackson (1996) referred to as *formal kinship* care, whereby a relative will care for a child who has been placed in the legal system. Historically, informal adoptions have been common. However, legal adoptions of relatives are becoming more common.

Recognition of the diverse family structures among African Americans provides a more realistic view of the majority of settings in which African Americans live. This information can be particularly significant and important for helping professionals in their quest to understand some of the dynamics of African American family life (Boyd-Franklin, 1989a).

Traditional African American Family Strengths

R. B. Hill (1972), in his early examination of African American families, pointed out many strengths within the African American family that can be very useful for mental health professionals when working with African American families. Twenty-five years later, he reexamined these strengths and found that although life for African American families was even more challenging, most of the strengths could still be noted (R. B. Hill, 1997). A few of these strengths are listed here and are discussed later in terms of how they can be used by mental health professionals in their work with African American families.

Strong Kinship Bonds

African Americans have a long history of attempting to keep strong family connections (R. B. Hill, 1972). Ever since African American families struggled to survive and stay together as their family members were being sold off during slavery, they have fought against societal forces that have tried to tear them apart. These strong bonds continue to persist today in many families through the aforementioned extended family networks, care of elderly family members, and informal adoptions of children. In a national Black survey, Hatchett and Jackson (1993) found that African Americans support the notion of family cohesiveness (Kane, 2000).

Strong Religious Orientation

The often strong religious orientation among African Americans has been a characteristic of many African American families. Historically, the Black church has been a central part of the African American experience in America and appears to be one of the few institutions that was not destroyed by slavery or other forms or disenfranchisement (Barbarin, 1983; Boyd-Franklin, 1989b; Richardson, 1991). The church has served numerous functions within the African American community, including as support systems in time of trouble. Research shows that African Americans are more likely to use prayer and support of the church in times of crises (Dressler, 1985, 1991). For many, church members function as part of extended family networks. From slavery through the civil rights movement, the Black church has been viewed as a survival mechanism and, for many, continues to serve that function today.

Strong Orientation Toward Work

Contrary to the perceptions and myths that African Americans are "lazy" and "shiftless," most members of African American families exhibit a strong work ethic. Studies have found that African Americans and Whites exhibit similar attitudes toward work (S. A. Hill, 1999). In fact, African American parents tend to support the notion that hard work is the way to open doors to other opportunities (Boyd-Franklin, 1989b; R. B. Hill, 1972). Additionally, social scientists contend that acts of racism and discrimination have led to tremendous economic inequality that has affected the African American family life in the United States (Feagin & Spikes, 1994; W. Wilson, 1987), which suggests that because of racism and discrimination, many African Americans have to work even harder to get to the same end as their White counterparts.

Adaptability of Family Roles

African American families have been found to exhibit role flexibility within the family unit. The myth of the African American matriarchal family system has been a common stereotype that has likely grown out of this phenomenon. African American families have been found to be more egalitarian compared with White families, which have traditionally tended to be more patriarchal. This "difference" in family roles has primarily allowed the persistent perception of the predominant matriarchal African American family system, even when there is a man in the home (S. A. Hill, 1999). Additionally, many African American family members tend to more readily take on parenting roles for relatives or fictive kin should it become necessary (Barbarin, 1983; Boyd-Franklin, 1989b). While this could cause other issues to develop, it is considered a strength in that young children who need care are informally adopted by someone within the family.

Strong Achievement Orientation

Traditionally, education has been greatly valued and stressed within the African American family and community, regardless of the income status or educational level of the parents. It has been seen as a vehicle to help open doors of opportunity that have previously been closed to African Americans. Research has also shown that when compared with low-income Whites, low-income African Americans aspire to higher occupations (R. B. Hill, 1997). However, the socioeconomic status of the African American family continues to lag far behind that of White families (U.S. Census Bureau, 2000b). Traditionally, African American parents have maintained high expectations for their children, despite their income or educational levels.

In recent years, the academic achievement gap has become a well-documented phenomenon among African American students (Donlevy, 2002; English, 2002; Haycock, 2001; Hunter & Bartee, 2003; Jencks & Phillips, 1998; Lee, 2002; Rothman, 2002). There is evidence to suggest that compared with European Americans, African American students score lower on standardized tests of academic ability (Jencks & Phillips, 1998; Levine & Eubanks, 1990; Rothman, 2002; Steele, 1992), receive lower grades in school (National Center for Education Statistics, 2000), are disproportionately tracked into low-ability and vocational programs (Dauber, Alexander, & Entwisle, 1996; White & Parham, 1990), and have higher rates of grade retention (Owings & Magliaro, 1998).

The ongoing debate to determine the causes of the achievement gap has yielded multiple hypotheses and rationales toward its origin. Although one specific theory has not been able to account for all of the variance, it is postulated that several factors may contribute to the overall achievement gap. (A full discussion, however, is beyond the scope of this chapter. For further reviews, see Cook & Ludwig, 1998; Ferguson, 1998, 2001; Hale, 2001; Hale-Benson, 1982; Jencks & Phillips, 1998; Ogbu, 1991, 2003; M. Phillips, Brooks-Gunn, Duncan, Klebanov, & Crane, 1998; Steele & Aronson, 1998; W. Wilson, 1998.) It is clear that the achievement gap among African American children and youths is a complex phenomenon, and more research is needed to fully gain insight regarding why the gap exists.

African American Family Challenges

Historically, African American families have faced many challenges with great amounts of fortitude and adaptability (Billingsley, 1991; Feagin & Spikes, 1994). Strong family units have empowered African American families to endure despite the many challenges they have faced. In this section we discuss some of the challenges faced by African American families.

Poverty

Despite numerous gains in levels of education, higher status occupations, and increasing numbers of African American families that are now members of the middle and upper classes, there continue to be disproportionate numbers of African Americans who remain in poverty (U.S. Census Bureau, 2000b). Hopes for the "American dream" or even equal opportunity do not appear to be attainable for all, because the legacy of poverty can become intergenerational (Billingsley, 1991; Wilkinson, 1995).

Upward Mobility

As African Americans are advancing in careers, they are becoming increasingly more mobile; thus it has become necessary for many to redefine their "normal" relationships within their extended family units. For example, more families now do not live as close to family members and, as a result, may be unable to travel to visit parents and grandparents as much as they would like. Additionally, many are required to move often to pursue their career goals. Such moves can have an impact on the nuclear family as well as the extended family. Depending on the makeup of the family unit, such moves may require small children to adjust to new environments and schools on a regular basis, which can be stressful. Also, it could make it more challenging to maintain close ties with grandparents, aunts, and other extended family members.

Stereotypes

Many stereotypes persist about African American families and family members. Data on stereotypes reveal African Americans continue to be viewed negatively by many Whites. For example, in the well-cited General Social Survey (National Opinion Research Center, 1990), 29% of Whites viewed most African Americans as unintelligent, 56% believed most prefer to live off welfare, 21% believed most are prone to violence, and 44% believed most African Americans are lazy. These perceptions are not without consequences. For example, African American students face negative stereotypes that portray them as less intelligent than their White peers (Steele, 1997). This theory, labeled *stereotype threat*, was developed by

Claude Steele. He defined stereotype threat as the threat of being viewed through the lens of a negative stereotype or the fear of doing something that would inadvertently conform to that stereotype (Steele, 1999). In a chapter in the book *The Black–White Test Score Gap*, Steele and Aronson (1998) discussed five research experiments that attempted to uncover the existence of a stereotype threat. The combined results indicate that by making African American students aware of negative stereotypes about their group's intellectual ability, their test performance scores tend to decrease in comparison with European American students' scores. Steele and Aronson indicated that the level of stereotype threat may vary depending on the type of test being presented, such as whether or not the test is a measure of intellectual ability. In the case of intellectual ability labeled measures, stereotype threat reduced academic efficacy. According to Steel and Aronson, if an African American was about to take the SAT and was made aware of the negative stereotypes concerning his or her group, it is hypothesized that the student's test performance would decrease. While some of the educational gaps are closing, these stereotypes are reinforced by statistics that have historically found that African American children, on the average, obtain lower scores on achievement tests and have lower grade point averages compared with their White peers (Steele, 1997).

Racial and Ethnic Identity Development

Although often used interchangeably, the concepts of racial and ethnic identity are two separate constructs. Racial identity is a social construction that "refers to a sense of group or collective identity based on one's perception that he or she shares a common heritage with a particular racial group" (Helms, 1993). In comparison, according to Yinger (1976, as cited in Chavez & Guido-DiBrito, 1999, p. 40), ethnic identity is also a social construct that is viewed as an individual's identification with

> a segment of a larger society whose members are thought, by themselves or others, to have a common origin and share segments of a common culture and who, in addition, participate in shared activities in which the common origin and culture are significant ingredients.

The degree of racial/ethnic identity development of family members can affect the African American family. In today's society, African Americans are faced with numerous challenges, including how to negotiate between the different worlds in which they must live. For many, the degree to which they are able to maneuver within the majority culture and interact within their own culture will greatly affect them as individuals and as a member of a family unit. Boykin (1986) referred to this phenomenon as a triple quandary. Others have referred to it as biculturalism or bicultural competence. Bicultural competence refers to the degree to which one can both feel comfortable and function effectively in two distinct cultural contexts (Dubois, 1903/1961; Sue & Sue, 2003). The extent to which family members are prepared to do this will affect their functioning in society and thus will affect the particular family unit.

Tatum (2004) queried upper-middle-class African American college students who were enrolled in two exclusive New England area colleges concerning their experiences regarding their upbringing in predominantly White communities. She found that positive same-race peer relationships, information about African American achievements, the availability of role models, and the encouragement of significant adults were important for academic success and the resolution of identity conflicts. Specifically, Tatum used Cross's model of racial identity development (see Cross, 1978; Parham, 1989, for further elaboration) to analyze the students' racial identity development. In all of the cases presented, the perception that teachers did not expect excellence from their Black students (in fact, were surprised by it), the invisibility of African Americans in the curricula of their high schools, and the stereotypical expectations of both Black and White peers hindered the development of a positive Black identity. According to Tatum, the extent to which the individuals had strong and supportive families mediated the negative impact of school and helped to further their identity development.

Institutional Barriers

Compared with other ethnic groups, contemporary African Americans are plagued by inordinate amounts of stress (Billingsley, 1992; Locke, 1992). Family stress theories maintain that when individual family members are overwhelmed by social and environmental stress in their life, their psychological functioning is compromised, which, in turn, negatively affects their interactions with other family members and the family unit as a whole (i.e., Conger et al., 1990; McCubbin et al., 1980). A common and unique stressor that African Americans confront (compared with White Americans) is race-related stress. *Race-related stress* is defined as transactions involving invidious forms of racism between individuals or groups that are perceived as taxing to individual and collective resources (Harrell, 2000; Utsey, 1999). Although many types and forms of racism have been proposed, Clark, Anderson, Clark, and Williamson (1999) pointed out that racism can be conceptualized into two categories: attitudinal racism and ethnic discrimination (behavioral racism). *Attitudinal racism* refers to attitudes and beliefs that denigrate others because of phenotypic characteristics or ethnic group affiliation (Yetman, 1985), whereas *ethnic discrimination* refers to actions that individuals or institutions take to deny equitable treatment to others because of phenotypic characteristics or ethnic group affiliation. Ethnic discrimination not only influences an individual's psychological well-being but also directly and indirectly influences African American family processes and well-being. The primary mode through which ethnic discrimination manifests itself in today's society is through institutional racism in the areas of health, welfare, politics, economics, and other structured organizations. This form of racism has a direct influence on the socioeconomic status of the African American family. Dill (1998) and Horton and Allen (1998) pointed out that the socioeconomic status of the African American family is more the result of institutional racism than lack of values, aspirations, or desire. Institutional racism inhibits African Americans from catching up to White Americans in terms of housing, career advancement, and other social and professional arenas (Gardere, 1999). Despite controlling for other social and demographic factors, African American families continue to experience levels of poverty that exceed that of White American families. For example, according to the 2000 U.S. Census report, 26% of White Americans age 25 or older had a 4-year college degree compared with 16% of African Americans, and the median household income for White Americans in 1998 was $41,000 compared with just $25,000 for African Americans (U.S. Census Bureau, 2000b). Gardere (1999) asserted that as long as society maintains this form of behavioral racism, no matter what level of socioeconomic status African American families achieve, they will still have a difficult time gaining equitable status.

Coping Strategies and Strength-Based Approaches

The psychological consequences of racism contribute to traumatic feelings of inferiority among African Americans (Stevenson, Davis, & Abdul-Kabir, 2001). However, it is clear that although the negative consequences of racism exist in the lives of African American families, many African American families have developed positive coping strategies and strength-based approaches that have allowed them to counteract racism and overcome social barriers to achieve what might be ascribed as a paradox of middle- to upper-middle-class social and economic status when contrasted against high levels of poverty among many other African American families. The social and economic success of many African American families are attributed to strength-based racial socialization strategies that promote positive coping styles among family members, including adopting a healthy cultural paranoia, having an open discussion of racial struggles, performing egalitarian and flexible family roles, having a commitment to a strong education and work ethic, utilizing extended family kinship networks, and maintaining a strong religious/spiritual orientation (Barbarin, 1983; Boyd-Franklin, 1989a; Boykin & Toms, 1985; R. B. Hill, 1972; Kane, 2000; Nobles, 1972). Each of these is discussed briefly in turn.

Grier and Cobbs (1968) promoted the use of healthy cultural paranoia among African Americans to function effectively in a society where ethnic discrimination appears to be all encompassing. Healthy cultural paranoia refers to the normal (nonpathological) response of African Americans to racism. Manifestations of healthy cultural paranoia include distrust and suspicion of Whites and a feeling that, if one is not cautious, one is at risk with the majority culture.

Many authors have reported that parental initiation of discussions with their children of the long history of slavery and racial struggles of African Americans is an important coping strategy for African American families (Bowman & Howard, 1985; Boykin & Toms, 1985; Feagin & Spikes, 1994; Harrison, 1985; Jackson, McCullough, & Gurin, 1988; Jackson, McCullough, Gurin, & Broman, 1991; H. P. McAdoo, 1985; Peters, 1985; Spencer, 1983, 1987; Thornton, Chatters, Taylor, & Allen, 1990). Parental instruction helps prepare children to expect such social stress, initiates the development of skills for children to handle this social conflict when it arises, and protects against trauma that could lower their self-perceptions and contribute to feelings of inferiority (Gardere, 1999; Greene, 1992; Stevenson & Renard, 1993).

As previously mentioned, research documents that African American families incorporate egalitarian and flexible family roles (i.e., Barbarin, 1983; J. L. McAdoo, 1993; Willie, 1993). Decisions regarding finances, the household, and child care are made based on the family member's ability and opportunity rather than gender. Parenting roles may be undertaken not only by mothers and fathers but also by other adult relatives, grandparents, fictive kin, and other siblings (Barbarin, 1983; Scott & Black, 1989).

African American parents generally promote education and hard work as necessary tools for their children to surpass them socioeconomically (Boyd-Franklin, 1989a; Coleman, 1986; R. B. Hill, 1972; Hines & Boyd-Franklin, 1982). To promote these values, African American parents teach their children to share family responsibilities including child rearing and household chores and encourage high academic performance and career ambitiousness.

It is also within their own communities that African American families find the social support needed to cope and survive. Extended family kinship networks are common among African American families and provide valuable sources of social support, such as the pooling of resources such as money, emotional support, and information (Barbarin, 1983; Barnes, 1985; Billingsley, 1968b; Dressler, 1985; H. P. McAdoo, 1992; Sudarkasa, 1993; M. Wilson, 1984).

Spirituality and religiosity have been identified as a fundamental aspect of the daily lives and worldview of individuals of African descent (Akbar, 1991; L. J. Myers, 1988; F. B. Phillips, 1990; Taylor, Chatters, Jayakody, & Levin, 1996). In fact, African Americans have been reported to cite spiritual and religious coping as their most frequent coping mechanism (i.e., Pargament, Poloma, & Tarakeshwar, 2001). In addition, African American churches provide a place for self-expression and release of emotional tension, leadership development, solidarity, and support (R. B. Hill, 1972; H. Myers, 1982).

Issues in Therapeutic Treatment

As a mental health professional, one must realize and own any stereotypes that might be present and then work to gain a better understanding about the specific African American family unit with which one is working. While many African American families may share common customs, traditions, and strengths, the mental health professional must realize that levels of education, occupations, and resources will vary and should be assessed. Knowledge about a family's religious orientation and church attendance may be useful in learning more about the family's support system(s). Additionally, because the use of religion and spirituality in therapy has become more acceptable (Boyd-Franklin, 1989b), such information could be useful in the therapeutic process. Similarly, because of extended family and fictive kin networks, the therapist must be careful to assess the important persons and role functions in the particular family system.

Knowledge of diverse African American family structures should be used to put into context the family system that may be operating within the particular family unit. For example, White (1991) suggested that information about extended family networks within African American families can provide helping professionals with more realistic views of how roles are assumed within the family and who may be the significant caregiver(s) of young children within African American family units (Boyd-Franklin, 1989b). The mental health professional must be able to understand that racism, classism, and other sources of discrimination are very real issues for many African American families. This awareness will prevent the notion of Black paranoia when such issues are mentioned.

An understanding of African American cultural expressions, values, customs, holidays, and so on can provide a therapist with tools to establish rapport. To gain a better understanding of worldviews of the family members, one should explore ethnic identity issues within the family unit.

Summary

In this chapter we have described some of the historical influences that have shaped the lives of African American families. Whereas early research on the African American family often presented unsupported, stereotypical, and pathological views of African American families, recent research has described the African American family as socially and culturally distinct from other ethnic/racial family systems. Many of these sociocultural distinctions have contributed to the phenomenal strengths within the African American family that have enabled the family unit to not only survive but also thrive. It is clear that the long-standing, far-reaching, and ever-present impact of racism has contributed to and shaped the structural and functional aspects of the African American family. However, contemporary African American families have developed unique ways of coping to maintain the "spirit of the family." Helping professionals must make every effort to understand the unique sociocultural dynamics, strengths, and coping styles that contribute to the successful functioning of the African American family unit.

References

Akbar, N. (1991). The evolution of human psychology for African Americans. In R. L. Jones (Ed.), *Black psychology* (3rd ed., pp. 99–123). Berkeley, CA: Cobb & Henry.

Allen, W. R. (1978). The search for applicable theories of Black family life. *Journal of Marriage and the Family, 40,* 117–129.

Barbarin, O. A. (1983). Coping with ecological transitions by Black families: A psychosocial model. *Journal of Community Psychology, 11,* 308–322.

Barnes, A. S. (1985). *The Black middle class family.* Bristol, IN: Wyndham Hall.

Billingsley, A. (1968a). *Black families in Black America.* Englewood Cliffs, NJ: Prentice Hall.

Billingsley, A. (1968b). *Black families in White America.* Englewood Cliffs, NJ: Prentice Hall.

Billingsley, A. (1991). The church, the family and the school in the African American community. *Journal of Negro Education, 60,* 427–440.

Billingsley, A. (1992). *Climbing Jacob's ladder: The enduring legacy of African-American families.* New York: Simon & Schuster.

Bowman, P. J., & Howard, C. (1985). Race-related socialization, motivation, and academic achievement: A study of Black youths in three-generation families. *Journal of the American Academy of Child Psychiatry, 24,* 134–141.

Boyd-Franklin, N. (1989a). *Black families in therapy: A multi-systemic approach.* New York: Guilford Press.

Boyd-Franklin, N. (1989b). Five key factors in the treatment of Black families. In S. W. Saba, B. M. Karrer, & K. V. Hardy (Eds.), *Minorities in family therapy* (pp. 53–69). New York: Haworth.

Boykin, A. W. (1986). The triple quandary and the schooling of Afro American children. In U. Neisser (Ed.), *The school achievement of minority children: New perspectives* (pp. 57–92). Hillsdale, NJ: Erlbaum.

Boykin, A. W., & Toms, F. D. (1985). Black child socialization: A conceptual framework. In H. P. McAdoo & J. L. McAdoo (Eds.), *Black children: Social, educational, and parental environments* (pp. 35–51). Newbury Park, CA: Sage.

Brinson, J. A. (1992). A comparison of the family environments of Black male and female adolescent alcohol users. *Family Therapy, 19,* 179–186.

Chatters, L. M., Taylor, R. J., & Jayakody, R. (1994). Fictive kinship relations in Black families. *Journal of Comparative Family Studies, 25,* 297–312.

Chavez, A., & Guido-DiBrito, F. (1999). Racial and ethnic identity development. *New Directions for Adult and Continuing Education, 84,* 39–47.

Clark, R., Anderson, N. B., Clark, V. R., & Williamson, D. R. (1999). Racism as a stressor for African Americans: A biopsychosocial model. *American Psychologist, 54,* 805–816.

Coleman, P. P. (1986). Separation and autonomy: Issues of adolescent identity development among the families of Black male status offenders. *American Journal of Social Psychiatry, 6,* 43–49.

Conger, R. D., Elder, G. H., Lorenz, R. O., Conger, K., Simons, R. L., Whitbeck, L. B., et al. (1990). Linking economic hardship to marital quality and instability. *Journal of Marriage and the Family, 52,* 643–656.

Cook, P., & Ludwig, J. (1998). The burden of acting White: Do adolescents disparage academic achievement? In C. Jencks & M. Phillips (Eds.), *The Black–White test score gap* (pp. 375–400). Washington, DC: Brookings Institution Press.

Cross, W. E. (1978). The Cross and Thomas models of psychological nigrescence: A review. *Journal of Black Psychology, 5,* 13–31.

Dauber, S. L., Alexander, K. L., & Entwisle, D. R. (1996). Tracking and transitions through the middle grades: Channeling educational trajectories. *Sociology of Education, 69,* 290–307.

Dill, B. T. (1998). A better life for me and my children: Low-income single mothers' struggle for self-sufficiency in the rural South. *Journal of Comparative Family Studies, 29,* 419–428.

Donlevy, J. (2002). Closing the achievement gap: Plausible solutions, multiple dimensions. *Instructional Journal of Instructional Media, 29,* 143–148.

Dressler, W. W. (1985). Extended family relationships, social support, and mental health in a southern Black community. *Journal of Health and Social Behavior, 26,* 39–48.

Dressler, W. W. (1991). Social support, lifestyle incongruity, and arterial blood pressure in a southern Black community. *Psychosomatic Medicine, 53,* 608–620.

Dubois, W. E. B. (1961). *The souls of Black folk.* Greenwich, CT: Fawcett. (Original work published 1903)

English, F. (2002). On the intractability of the achievement gap in urban schools and the discursive practice of continuing racial discrimination. *Education and Urban Society, 34,* 298–311.

Feagin, J. R., & Spikes, M. P. (1994). *Living with racism: The Black middle-class experience.* Boston: Beacon Press.

Ferguson, R. (1998). Teachers' perceptions and expectations and the Black–White test score gap. In C. Jencks & M. Phillips (Eds.), *The Black–White test score gap* (pp. 273–317). Washington, DC: Brookings Institution Press.

Ferguson, R. (2001). A diagnostic analysis of Black–White GPA disparities in Shaker Heights, Ohio. In D. Ravitch (Ed.), *Brookings papers on education policy 2001* (pp. 347–396). Washington, DC: Brookings Institution Press.

Frazier, E. F. (1957). *The Negro family in the United States.* New York: Macmillan.

Gaines, K. (1997). Rethinking race and class in African American struggles for equality, 1885–1941. *American Historical Review, 102,* 378–388.

Gardere, J. (1999). *Smart parenting for African Americans.* New York: Kensington.

Gordon, R., Chase-Landsdale, P., Matjasko, J., & Brooks-Gunn, J. (1997). Young mothers living with grandmothers and living apart: How neighborhood and household contexts relate to multigenerational coresidence in African American families. *Applied Developmental Science, 1,* 89–106.

Greene, B. (1992). Racial socialization as a tool in psychotherapy with African American children. In L. A. Vargas & J. J. Koss-Chioino (Eds.), *Working with culture: Psychotherapeutic interventions with ethnic minority children and adolescents* (pp. 63–84). San Francisco: Jossey-Bass.

Grier, W. H., & Cobbs, P. M. (1968). *Black rage.* New York: Basic Books.

Hale, J. E. (2001). *Learning while Black: Creating educational excellence for African American children.* Baltimore: Johns Hopkins University Press.

Hale-Benson, J. (1982). *Black children: Their roots, culture, and learning styles.* Provo, UT: Brigham Young University Press.

Harrell, S. P. (2000). A multidimensional conceptualization of racism-related stress: Implications for the well-being of people of color. *American Journal of Orthopsychiatry, 79,* 42–57.

Harrison, A. O. (1985). The Black family's socializing environment: Self-esteem and ethnic attitude among Black children. In H. P. McAdoo & J. L. McAdoo (Eds.), *Black children* (pp. 174–193). Beverly Hills, CA: Sage.

Hatchett, S. J., & Jackson, J. S. (1993). African American extended kin systems: An assessment. In H. P. McAdoo (Ed.), *Family ethnicity: Strength in diversity* (pp. 90–108). Newbury Park, CA: Sage.

Haycock, K. (2001, March). Closing the achievement gap. *Educational Leadership,* 6–11.

Heiss, J. (1975). *The case of the Black family: A sociological inquiry.* New York: Columbia University Press.

Helms, J. E. (1993). Introduction: Review of racial identity terminology. In J. E. Helms (Ed.), *Black and White racial identity: Theory, research and practice* (pp. 3–8). Westport, CT: Praeger.

Herskovits, M. J. (1941). *The myth of the Negro past.* New York: Harper.

Hill, R. B. (1972). *The strengths of Black families.* New York: Emerson-Hull.

Hill, R. B. (1977). *Informal adoption among Black families.* New York: National Urban League.

Hill, R. B. (1997). Demographic differences in selected work ethic attributes. *Journal of Career Development, 24,* 3–23.

Hill, S. A. (1999). *African American children: Socialization and development in families.* Thousand Oaks, CA: Sage.

Hines, P. M., & Boyd-Franklin, N. (1982). Black families. In M. McGoldrick, J. K. Pearce, & J. Giordano (Eds.), *Ethnicity and family therapy* (pp. 84–107). New York: Guilford Press.

Horton, H. D., & Allen, B. L. (1998). Race, family structure and rural poverty: An assessment of population and structural change. *Journal of Comparative Family Studies, 29,* 397–407.

Hunter, R. C., & Bartee, R. (2003). The achievement gap: Issues of competition, class, and race. *Education and Urban Society, 35,* 151–160.

Jackson, J. S., McCullough, W. R., & Gurin, G. (1988). Family, socialization environment, and identity development in Black Americans. In H. P. McAdoo (Ed.), *Black families* (pp. 242–256). Newbury Park, CA: Sage.

Jackson, J. S., McCullough, W. R., Gurin, G., & Broman, C. L. (1991). Race identity. In J. S. Jackson (Ed.), *Life in Black America* (pp. 238–253). Thousand Oaks, CA: Sage.

Jencks, C., & Phillips, M. (Eds.). (1998). *The Black–White test score gap.* Washington, DC: Brookings Institution Press.

Kane, C. M. (2000). African American family dynamics as perceived by family members. *Journal of Black Studies, 30,* 691–702.

Lee, J. (2002). Racial and ethnic achievement gap trends: Reversing the progress toward equity. *Educational Researcher, 31,* 3–12.

Levine, D. U., & Eubanks, E. E. (1990). Achievement disparities between minority and nonminority students in suburban schools. *Journal of Negro Education, 59,* 186–194.

Littlejohn-Blake, S., & Darling, C. (1993). Understanding the strengths of African American families. *Journal of Black Studies, 23,* 460–472.

Locke, D. C. (1992). *Increasing multicultural understanding.* Newbury Park, CA: Sage.

Logan, S. L. (1996). A strength perspective on Black families. In S. L. Logan (Ed.), *The Black family: Strengths, self-help, and positive change* (pp. 8–21). Boulder, CO: Westview Press.

McAdoo, H. P. (1985). Racial attitude and self-concept of young Black children over time. In H. P. McAdoo & J. L. McAdoo (Eds.), *Black children: Social, educational, and parental environments* (pp. 213–242). Newbury Park, CA: Sage.

McAdoo, H. P. (1992). Upward mobility and parenting in middle-income Black families. In A. Burlew, W. C. Banks, H. P. McAdoo, & D. A. Azibo (Eds.), *African American psychology: Theory, research, and practice* (pp. 63–86). Newbury Park, CA: Sage.

McAdoo, J. L. (1993). Decision making and marital satisfaction in African American families. In H. P. McAdoo (Ed.), *Family ethnicity: Strength in diversity* (pp. 109–119). Newbury Park, CA: Sage.

McCubbin, H. I., Joy, C. B., Cauble, A. E., Comcau, J. K., Patterson, J. M., & Needle, R. H. (1980). Family stress and coping: A decade review. *Journal of Marriage and the Family, 41,* 237–244.

Mosley-Howard, S., & Evans, C. (2000). Relationships and contemporary experiences of the African American family: Ethnographic case study. *Journal of Black Studies, 30,* 428–452.

Moynihan, D. P. (1965). *The Negro family: The case for national action.* Washington, DC: U.S. Government Printing Office.

Myers, H. (1982). Research on the Afro-American family: A critical review. In B. A. Bass, G. E. Wyatt, & G. J. Powell (Eds.), *The Afro-American family* (pp. 35–68). New York: Grune & Stratton.

Myers, L. J. (1988). *An Afrocentric worldview: Introduction to an optimal psychology.* Dubuque, IA: Quintal-Hunt.

National Center for Education Statistics. (2000). *National Assessment Educational Process (NAEP): 1999 long term trend assessment.* Washington, DC: Office of Educational Research and Improvement, U.S. Department of Education.

National Opinion Research Center. (1990). *General social survey.* Retrieved October 1, 2003, from http://www.norc.uchicago.edu/projects.gensoc.asp

Nobles, W. (1972). African philosophy: Foundations for a Black psychology. In R. L. Jones (Ed.), *Black psychology* (pp. 22–36). New York: Harper & Row.

Ogbu, J. (1991). Minority responses and school experiences. *Journal of Psychohistory, 18,* 433–456.

Ogbu, J. (2003). *Black American students in an affluent suburb: A study of academic disengagement.* Mahwah, NJ: Erlbaum.

Owings, W., & Magliaro, S. (1998). Grade retention: A history of failure. *Educational Leadership, 56,* 86–88.

Pargament, K. I., Poloma, M. M., & Tarakeshwar, N. (2001). Methods of coping from the religions of the world: The bar mitzvah, karma, and spiritual healing. In C. R. Snyder (Ed.), *Coping with stress: Effective people and processes* (pp. 259–284). London: Oxford University Press.

Parham, T. (1989). Nigrescence: The transformation of Black consciousness across the life cycle. In R. Jones (Ed.), *Black adult development and aging* (pp. 151–166). Berkeley, CA: Cobb & Henry.

Peters, M. F. (1985). Racial socialization of young Black children. In H. P. McAdoo & J. L. McAdoo (Eds.), *Black children: Social, educational, and parental environments* (pp. 159–173). Newbury Park, CA: Sage.

Phillips, F. B. (1990). NTU psychotherapy: An Afrocentric approach. *Journal of Black Psychology, 17,* 55–74.

Phillips, M., Brooks-Gunn, J. Duncan, G., Klebanov, P., & Crane, J. (1998). Black–White test score convergence since 1965. In C. Jencks & M. Phillips (Eds.), *The Black–White test score gap* (pp. 103–148). Washington, DC: Brookings Institution Press.

Pinderhughes, E. (2002). African American marriage in the 20th century. *Family Processes, 41,* 269–282.

Richardson, B. L. (1991). Utilizing the resources of the African American church: Strategies for counseling professionals. In C. C. Lee & B. L. Richardson (Eds.), *Multicultural issues in counseling: New approaches to diversity* (pp. 65–75). Alexandria, VA: American Association for Counseling and Development.

Rothman, R. (2002). Closing the achievement gap: How schools are making it happen. *Journal of the Annenberg Challenge, 5,* 2–12.

Scannapieco, M., & Jackson, S. (1996). Kinshipcare: The African American response to family preservation. *Social Work, 41,* 190–197.

Scott, J. W., & Black, A. (1989). Deep structures of African American family life: Female and male kin networks. *Western Journal of Black Studies, 13*(1), 17–24.

Spaights, E. (1990). The therapeutic implications of working with the Black family. *Journal of Instructional Psychology, 17,* 183–190.

Spencer, M. B. (1983). Children's cultural values and parental rearing strategies. *Developmental Review, 3,* 351–370.

Spencer, M. B. (1987). Black children's ethnic identity formation: Risk and resilience in castelike minorities. In J. S. Phinney & M. E. Rotheram (Eds.), *Children's ethnic socialization* (pp. 103–116). Newbury Park, CA: Sage.

Stack, C. (1974). *All our kin: Strategies for survival in a Black community.* New York: Harper & Row.

Staples, R. (1971). Towards a sociology of the Black family: A theoretical and methodological assessment. *Journal of Marriage and the Family, 33,* 119–135.

Staples, R., & Johnson, L. (1993). *Black families at the crossroads: Challenges and prospects.* San Francisco: Jossey-Bass.

Steele, C. M. (1992, April). Race and the schooling of Black Americans. *Atlantic Monthly,* 68–78.

Steele, C. M. (1997). A threat in the air: How stereotypes shape intellectual identity and performance. *American Psychologist, 52,* 613–629.

Steele, C. (1999, August). Stereotype threat and Black college students. *Atlantic Monthly,* 54–62.

Steele, C., & Aronson, J. (1998). Stereotype threat and the test performance of academically successful African Americans. In C. Jencks & M. Phillips (Eds.), *The Black–White test score gap* (pp. 401–430). Washington, DC: Brookings Institution Press.

Stevenson, H. C., Davis, G., & Abdul-Kabir, S. (2001). *Stickin' to, watchin' over, and gettin' with.* San Francisco: Jossey-Bass.

Stevenson, H. C., & Renard, G. (1993). Trusting ole' wise owls: Therapeutic use of cultural strengths in African-American families. *Professional Psychology: Research and Practice, 24,* 433–442.

Sudarkasa, N. (1980). African and Afro-American: Family structure—A comparison. *Black Scholar, 11*(8), 37–60.

Sudarkasa, N. (1993). Female-headed African American households: Some neglected dimensions. In H. P. McAdoo (Ed.), *Family ethnicity: Strength in diversity* (pp. 81–89). Newbury Park, CA: Sage.

Sue, D. W., & Sue, D. S. (2003). *Counseling the culturally different: Theory and practice.* New York: Wiley.

Tatum, B. (2004). Family life and school experience: Factors in the racial identity development of Black youth in White communities. *Journal of Social Issues, 60,* 117–135.

Taylor, R. J., Chatters, L. M., & Jackson, J. S. (1993). A profile of familial relations among three generation Black families. *Family Relations, 42,* 332–341.

Taylor, R. J., Chatters, L. M., Jayakody, R., & Levin, J. S. (1996). Black and White differences in religious participation: A multi-sample comparison. *Journal for the Scientific Study of Religion, 35,* 403–410.

Thornton, M. C., Chatters, L. M., Taylor, R. J., & Allen, W. R. (1990). Sociodemographic and environmental correlates of racial socialization by Black parents. *Child Development, 61,* 401–409.

Tucker, M. B., & Mitchell-Kernan, C. (1995). Trends in African American family formation: A theoretical and statistical overview. In M. B. Tucker & C. Mitchell-Kernan (Eds.), *The decline in marriage among African Americans: Causes, consequences, and policy implications* (pp. 3–26). New York: Russell Sage Foundation.

U.S. Census Bureau. (2000a). *Current population reports, household and family characteristics.* Washington, DC: U.S. Government Printing Office.

U.S. Census Bureau. (2000b). Poverty rate comparison: Census 2000, Current Population Survey (CPS), and Census 2000 Supplementary Survey (C2SS) (2000 annual demographic supplement). Washington, DC: U.S. Government Printing Office.

Utsey, S. (1999). Development and validation of a short form of the Index of Race-Related Stress (IRRS)–Brief Version. *Measurement and Evaluation in Counseling and Development, 32,* 149–167.

White, J. (1991). Toward a Black psychology. In R. L. Jones (Ed.), *Black psychology* (3rd ed., pp. 5–13). Berkeley, CA: Cobb & Henry.

White, J. L., & Parham, T. H. (1990). *The psychology of Blacks: An African-American perspective* (2nd ed.). Englewood Cliffs, NJ: Prentice Hall.

Wilkinson, D. (1995). Gender and social inequality: The prevailing significance of race. *Daedalus, 124,* 167–178.

Willie, C. (1993). Social theory and social policy derived from the Black family experience. *Journal of Black Studies, 23,* 451–459.

Wilson, M. (1984). Mothers' and grandmothers' perceptions of parental behavior in three-generational Black families. *Child Development, 55,* 1333–1339.

Wilson, W. (1987). *The truly disadvantaged: The inner city, the underclass, and public policy.* Chicago: University of Chicago Press.

Wilson, W. (1998). The role of the environment in the Black–White test score gap. In C. Jencks & M. Phillips (Eds.), *The Black–White test score gap* (pp. 501–510). Washington, DC: Brookings Institution Press.

Yetman, N. (1985). Introduction: Definitions and perspectives. In N. Yetman (Ed.), *Majority and minority: The dynamics of race and ethnicity in American life* (4th ed., pp. 1–20). Boston: Allyn & Bacon.

Zinn, M., & Eitzen, S. (1996). Using textbooks for the multicultural transformation: The case of sociology. *Transformations, 7,* 1–10.

3

African American Women and Mental Health

Patricia Bethea-Whitfield

Contemporary African American women have emerged from a tapestry of historical and political issues in a paradox of oppression and empowerment. Oppressed because of their race and their gender (King, 2003; Staples, 1973), these women often find that this double jeopardy (Staples, 1973) is further compounded by the detriments of class or poverty (hooks, 1993, as cited in Holcomb-McCoy & Moore-Thomas, 2001). Including both psychological and physical injury (Robinson & Howard-Hamilton, 1994), this oppression is rooted in the historical images of the African American woman as nurturer, temptress, and matriarch. In many ways, these stereotypes have become the essential fabric of the way African American women view themselves and define their place in society (Cole & Guy-Sheftall, 2003). As the negative images of African American women proliferate more rapidly than the positive ones, Cole and Guy-Sheftall maintained that many African American women are as "endangered" as African American men, often being valued by no one. This chapter explores the images of African American women, the violence that follows their devaluation, the barriers to their therapy-seeking behaviors, and their perennial resilience.

Images of African American Women

African American women were brought to the United States to "work, produce, and to re-produce" (Almquist, 1995, as quoted in Holcomb-McCoy & Moore-Thomas, 2001), giving them a unique role among American women. This role, of necessity, had to be supported by images that cast the African American woman in a different light than her White counterpart and cleared the way for her to bear the burden of capitalist ambition.

Lerner (1972) reported that one such distortion was the myth of the "bad" Black woman:

> By assuming a different level of sexuality for all Blacks than that of Whites and mystifying their greater sexual potency, the black woman could be made to personify sexual freedom and abandon. A myth was created that all black women were eager for sexual exploits, voluntarily "loose" in their morals and therefore, deserved none of the consideration and respect granted to White women. (p. 163)

While White women were promoted to a position of moral rectitude (Giddings, 1984), "every black woman was, by definition, a slut according to this racist mythology" (Lerner, 1972, p. 163), and eventually, slave traders openly marketed African American women for their supposed lascivious nature (Jordan, 1969). These women could be exploited at will without regard to the usual sanctions against such behavior and so Black women were "impaled on the cutting edges of this race/sex dialectic" (Giddings, 1984, p. 35).

Having codified slavery in 1661, Virginia passed legislation in 1662 stipulating that the child of a Black woman would take the status of the mother, thus clearing the way for masters to create their own labor force through the exploitation of these vulnerable women. Finally, by 1705, it was decided that although White women would not be put "to ground" to work at the risk of heavier taxes, it was acceptable for slave women to work in the home or in the ground without penalty (Giddings, 1984). This meant that Black women worked the fields alongside men and animals in what has been called a "negative equality" (Davenport & Yurich, 1991) without the pretense of femininity afforded women of other ethnic groups. In conclusion, Giddings (1984) stated:

> By the early eighteenth century an incredible social, legal, and racial structure was put in place. Women were firmly stratified in the roles that Plato envisioned. Blacks were chattel, White men could impregnate a Black woman with impunity, and she alone could give birth to a slave. Blacks constituted a permanent labor force and metaphor that were perpetuated through the Black woman's womb. And all this was done within the context of the Church, the operating laws of capitalism, and the psychological needs of White males. Subsequent history would be a variation on the same theme. (p. 39)

Frame, Williams, and Green (1999) agreed that these historical realities have been the foundation of the dilemmas African American women face. Collins (1990, as cited in Sklar, 1995) stated that the breeder woman image of the slave era has been updated into the myth of the welfare mother today. Also from these roots, society now connotes the African American woman as "the asexual, caretaking 'mammy'; the seductive and licentious siren; as well as the long-suffering or emasculating matriarch" (Cole & Guy-Sheftall, 2003, p. 200).

Perhaps nothing has been more instructive in the perpetuation of these images than the media (Wilson & Russell, 1996). First portrayed in print as devoted asexual mammies, tragic mulatto figures, and domestics, by mid-century, African American women were delivered by television as "the loud-mouthed, strong-willed, emasculating Sapphire" (Wilson & Russell, 1996, p. 250). In 1973, Staples interpreted this image as that of "a masculinized female who must be subordinated in order that the Black male may take his rightful place in society" (p. 10), and today, the Sapphire image still connotes a woman who is controlling and bent on degrading her mate (Hughes, 2003).

Like "gangsta" films in which women are portrayed as superficial girlfriends and targets of rape and abuse, the music video has become a visual accompaniment to gangsta rap, demeaning lyrics directed to African American women as objects of male manipulation (Wilson & Russell, 1996). Cole and Guy-Sheftall (2003) hastened to point out that while the devaluation of African American women has been around a lot longer than gangsta rap, this music has "transformed it into an enticing mantra of Black women as 'bitches' and 'hos' and released it for mass consumption" (p. 202). According to Cole and Guy-Sheftall, these terms, once considered derogatory, have been internalized by younger African American women who now refer to themselves as *bitches* and *hos*, a gesture considered by some a mere "transgressive" (p. 204) venture into male territory to capture language and by others as a sign that women can be as uninhibited about their sexual desires as men. Far from benign, Cole and Guy-Sheftall maintained that the media has instructed an entire generation in "problematic gender messages" (p. 203) that once internalized become damaging to self and relationships. In other words, this is not just entertainment (Sanders, 1997). These images have been very influential in terms of identity development and violence in the lives of African American women.

African American Women and Violence

Taken together, the conclusion must be made that African American women are often not valued as individuals (Cole & Guy-Sheftall, 2003; Wilson & Russell, 1996). Gillum (2002), in a study of stereotypic images and intimate partner violence, found a positive relationship between the endorsement of stereotypic images of women and the justification of violence against women. In that study, many African American men endorsed both views largely because men have been socialized to see domination as an "entitlement" (Stets & Pirog-Good, 1987, p. 237) that infiltrates personal relationships. This socialization is fully consistent with a general social acceptance of violence as a way to reinforce social hierarchies such as those based on race, gender, and class, which are discussed in this chapter, as well as ethnicity, age, and others (Collins, 1998). Specifically, Collins identified rape, battering, sexual harassment, and pornographic images in the media as violence used to support a social system of gender-based privilege for men. This devaluation, combined with the idea that African American women must be kept in their place, sets up dangerously high stakes for maintaining order and makes African American women easy targets for violence.

Several studies (e.g., Hampton, Oliver, & Magarian, 2003; Lee, Sanders, & Mechanic, 2002) have shown that intimate partner violence is more common and more violent in the African American community than in the Caucasian community. This violence can be as extreme as homicide but ranges to emotional, verbal, or psychological abuse that is wrongly perceived as more innocuous, with physical injury, rape, or stalking in between (Lee et al., 2002). African American women also experience more devastating abuse and more abuse in which weapons are involved. Further, Lee et al. stated that intimate partner violence has been shown to contribute to a variety of health-related issues as well as losses in psychological functioning, deficits in interpersonal relating, and deterioration in the performance of roles in parenting and at work. Finally, Lee et al. stated that African American women have greater mental health consequences than some other groups. Notwithstanding, they added, African American women report violent intimate partner abuse (with the exception of rape) at twice the rate of Caucasian women who are less likely to report.

Stets and Pirog-Good (1987) saw control as the central variable in the use of violence and asserted that individuals will first try other strategies such as "talking, pouting or crying" (p. 238) before resorting to striking. Some men, they concluded, who are more emotional or dependent may be more likely to use violence as a control mechanism, as will men who view acts of violence as nonviolent. The perception of control and violence among African American men and women could be related to the desensitizing effect of media influences as discussed by Cole and Guy-Sheftall (2003).

Further, it may be that "anger, hatred and frustration" (Hampton et al., 2003, p. 533) as by-products of institutional racism affect the romantic relationships between African American men and women and ignite the violence. The complexities of African American male–female relationships are well documented (Bethea, 1995; Cazenave, 1983; Davenport & Yurich, 1991; Staples, 1988). Cazenave asserted that oppression, particularly in the racial and economic arenas, results in hostilities that African American men ventilate in their relationships with African American women. Here, the earning disparity between African American men and women could be a root cause.

Hughes (2003) pointed out that "brothers don't mind their woman being an aggressive lioness when they're out in the world taking care of business, but they want that same woman—their woman—to be a soft and cuddly kitten when she comes home to him"

(p. 100). Such a view, reinforced through a publication popular in the African American community, replays the old dilemma of the African American woman expected to work outside the home and at the same time fulfill the traditional feminine role. Conversely, Hughes added, African American women may be less likely to lament their lack of softness and more likely to feel the problem is the lack of an equally strong partner. Staples (1988) stated that "the greater a woman's educational level and income, the less desirable she is to many Black males. While a man's success adds to his desirability as a mate, it detracts from a woman's" (p. 189).

Although these images hold a certain level of legitimacy, the generalizations should be accepted critically. For example, the use of some of these images and language is generation specific, depicting more contemporary individuals. There also exist, though not so well documented, images of African American women as strong nurturers and fierce defenders of their families. These heroines represent a very valid image as well.

"The good news," according to Hughes (2003), "is that Black women are strong, resourceful and tenacious" (p. 98). As a result of slavery and its aftermath, these women "came to know their own strength in a way that women in other cultures rarely have" (Davenport & Yurich, 1991, p. 68). Davenport and Yurich added that this role of "strength and resourcefulness" (p. 69) was defined for African American women unlike the treatment of women of other ethnic groups. So the domination of the Sapphire role is morphed into a kind of strength that is glorified in the Black community. According to Dansby (1975, as cited in Davenport & Yurich, 1991), of 200 African American women surveyed, 76% identified "being a good provider" as a part of successful mothering although this role is usually a male domain. This image, while heroic, has emerged out of a need for Black survival.

Identity

Gilligan (1993) concluded that identity develops differently for women than for men and that while individuation is the cornerstone of male development, women become more relational, speaking "in a different voice." During adolescence, girls prepare to embrace the reality of womanhood, which often requires dissociation from self or a kind of "privatization" (p. xxii) of experience. So at a time when developmental challenges abound, adolescence brings a decrease in much needed "psychological resilience and self esteem" (L. M. Brown, 1993, p. 10). Ultimately, this plays out in the mental health arena because girls, culturally forbidden to externalize or act out (Sachs-Ericsson & Ciarlo, 2000), turn their distress on themselves.

Using Gilligan's (1993) notion of voice, Morgan (1993) described young Black girls as "loud," using loudness as a metaphor for their "contrariness" and "resistance to nothingness" or invisibility. Davenport and Yurich (1991) stated that "their unique gender role socialization but also their somewhat higher status leads African American women *away* from the traditional, deferent behavior that so often has been culturally expected of women" (p. 69). Going a step further, Turner (1987, as cited in Gibbs & Fuery, 1994) found that African American women, like the women described in Gilligan's work, develop identity in the context of relationships with others ("self-in-relation" theory) but are still able to create a sense of self. Powell (1985) found that African American girls had greater self-esteem than Caucasian girls.

In a study conducted by Petersen (2000), women stated that they felt special as children and at an early age decided to reject the traditional female role. These women, in addition to recalling positive images of themselves, also identified family and coping strategies as important themes in the development of identity. Additionally, they identified career achievement as an important force in defining a sense of self. Petersen concluded that African American women who are, for the most part, outside the mainstream have a vantage point from which they can evaluate messages of the dominant culture and circumvent negative stereotypes without internalizing them. This conclusion evokes the image of the strong African American woman and a precarious balancing act that by itself could be at the root of some mental health issues. Contrary to what the circumstances indicate, African American women have emerged with self-definition that has enabled them to overcome "externally-driven images designed to exert control" (Collins, 1991, as quoted in Petersen, 2000).

Prevalent Psychiatric Disorders

Still, institutional racism takes a toll on mental health among African American women. The U.S. Surgeon General's report (1999) referenced historical influences such as slavery and exclusion from services and resources on the basis of race as the foundation of socioeconomic deficits among African Americans. The report further concluded that the resulting poverty relegates people who are poor to an at-risk status that includes the homeless, incarcerated, and substance abuse populations. Finally, the report found that socioeconomic status is directly linked to mental health, with people who are poor reporting more problems of mental health. Because of oppression and economic deficits, African Americans are overrepresented in vulnerable populations.

Further, Williams and Morris-Williams (2000) concluded that racism has led to deficits in socioeconomic mobility and resources among African Americans. Specifically, residential segregation has helped to ensure that many African Americans live in areas fraught with environmental risk and economic blight isolated with others equally bereft of resources. Poverty, unemployment, relegation to lower paying jobs, and differential purchasing power are also ways that race affects African Americans in the general society, according to Williams and Morris-Williams. For example, Landrine, Klonoff, Alcaraz, Scott, and Wilkins (1995), in a study of salary data in Florida, found that when education and job category were controlled for, African American women earned significantly less than White men and women. In a more recent report, Fleck (2004) stated that African American and Hispanic consumers who chose to finance a car loan through the dealership were "targeted more often than other consumers" (p. 22) for hidden fees that amounted to $1,000 or more. This kind of racial bias in marketing is reflected repeatedly in neighborhood markets where higher prices disproportionately affect racially segregated consumers. Basically, this means that African Americans, when they can find employment, may well take home less pay and more often see their economic resources siphoned by racial prejudice.

Williams and Morris-Williams (2000) asserted that discriminatory experiences can lead to adverse effects on mental health. Specifically, A. C. Brown, Brody, and Stoneman (2000) identified the daily grind of life under adverse economic circumstances as integral to stress among African American women. Additionally, they found a significant interaction between high socioeconomic stress and the ability to manage important tasks such as checking the behavior of an errant child. This finding indicates that economic strain mediates the woman's ability to cope with other stressors and contributes to other problems such as depression.

In 1991, Robins and Regier (as cited in Williams & Morris-Williams, 2000) reported in the Epidemiological Catchment Area Study of psychiatric disorders that adults with lower socioeconomic status were likely to have a psychiatric disorder at three times the rate of their counterparts with higher socioeconomic status. The study, which included 4,638 African American respondents, indicated that phobic disorder was the most often reported mental disorder among that group. Similarly, the National Comorbidity Survey, reported in 1994 by Kessler et al., included 666 African American respondents. This study found the largest number of mental disorders in the area of depression, anxiety, and phobic disorders (U.S. Surgeon General, 1999). Further, the report identified higher rates of these disorders among African American women. An interesting example comes from research by Kasl and Harburg (1975, as cited in Gibbs & Fuery, 1994) regarding the relationship between emotional distress and quality of life in Detroit communities. They found that women who lived in certain areas of the city reported feeling more tense, vulnerable, and unhappy. In fact, Gibbs and Fuery reviewed a number of studies with similar findings regarding demographic factors and the increased risk of mental disorders in African American women, highlighting economic constraints, being a single parent, and living in unsafe neighborhoods.

Stressful life events predict depression in women (Kendler et al., 1993, as cited in Gregory, 1999). According to Yonkers and Chantilis (1995, as cited in Gregory, 1999), stressors may include not having a confidant, having less than a high school education, having young children at home, having feelings of helplessness, having an unstable marital history, and not working outside the home. All of these, except the last, read like a laundry list of the realities of life for many African American women.

Further, Gibbs and Fuery (1994), in a comprehensive review of the literature, identified factors that they called *protective* in that they seemed to delimit psychological distress. These factors included connectedness with family, church and social networks, marriage, more income, and higher education. From these findings, they concluded that African American women with substantial earning power who are married and employed will experience more psychological well-being than single, unemployed, lower income women. Ironically, the current marriage rate among African American women may forestall the achievement of this mental health advantage.

Barriers to Efficacy in Mental Health Counseling

The literature evidences a number of barriers to efficacy in mental health counseling among African American women, beginning with a sense of empowerment or self-efficacy. Efforts to achieve self-definition, a complex task for women, are confounded by definitions of attractiveness found in the dominant culture and the negative images promoted in the media (hooks, 1993, as cited in Holcomb-McCoy & Moore-Thomas, 2001). P. B. Jackson and Mustillo (2001) concluded from their review of the literature that the physical self is the "most important predictor of self-image among African-American youth" (p. 36). People who are considered physically attractive often receive preferential treatment, and people with lighter complexions are treated better in certain situations than African Americans with darker complexions. Notwithstanding, P. B. Jackson and Mustillo found in their research that women who have dark skin have higher levels of self-efficacy and that physically attractive women and women who are satisfied with their role in the family are all happier.

On the down side, the characterization of the strong African American woman, which has been a much needed source of self-efficacy for many, also leaves some women feeling no alternative but to shoulder the burden at home and at work to the detriment of their own well-being. Many of these women concentrate in service occupations and low-paying jobs because of historical oppressions. Consequently, they experience less sense of competence and more discrimination (P. B. Jackson & Mustillo, 2001). Frame et al. (1999) stated that racism fosters internalized oppression, which causes women to doubt their own credibility in comparison with Whites and experience a poorer quality of mental health (P. B. Jackson & Mustillo, 2001). Further, the economic strain of being a single head of household also puts African American women at greater risk for poverty and mental health problems (Williams, Takeuchi, & Adair, 1992). These women, it seems, not only fail their own career aspirations but also are unable to fulfill their sense of responsibility to provide for their families.

Finally, women with more education and higher incomes experience more self-efficacy, leading P. B. Jackson and Mustillo (2001) to conclude that self-esteem and self-efficacy are significant predictors of mental health among African American women. However, these factors alone are not enough to stave off poor mental health. Ultimately, the strong African American woman image as well as the very real strength that it evokes is a big gun that fires both ways. Used to create doors and opportunities, it works well. However, women driven by the idea that they are supposed to be able to master any situation may too often choose to go it alone for too long trapped by their isolation. According to Roan (2003), a part of the solution may be giving up the notion that one can do it all.

Other issues of efficacy lie in the society itself. The U.S. Surgeon General's report (1999) pointed out that racism continues to affect the quality of services for African Americans because of a historical mistrust of agencies that are not viewed as supportive of African Americans. For example, the image of welfare mothers as lazy collectors of welfare checks not only labels welfare recipients as irresponsible but also identifies their children as a drain on taxpayers and encourages a social response designed to control their reproductive freedom (Davis, 1983, as cited in Barbee & Little, 2003). Further, the Surgeon General's report pointed out that certain high-need populations such as the incarcerated, people in psychiatric hospitals, people in the inner city, and the rural poor are less accessible to research and their mental health needs are less well known. Access to services may also be dictated by urban or rural location (Lee et al., 2002).

In the area of abuse, Collins (1998) stated that institutionalized racism has impeded the recognition of violence in the lives of African American women. Specifically, there has been little support for their claims of rape and little emotional support in communities that are accepting of abuse for maintaining social order and punishment. One reason for this lack of support is the image of African American women as morally loose (Anderson & Cummings, 1993; Collins, 1998). Further, some of the very factors that create the climate for abuse may act to deter reporting. These include fear of retaliation and limited availability of financial or social support (Lee et al., 2002).

Even when women leave home to escape abuse, they encounter some of the same challenges in the homeless lifestyle. Hatty (1996) stated that women who live outside the home and traditional family structures are considered "out of place" (p. 417) and are often the victims of physical and sexual assaults. Further, some homeless women fall into the sex trade to support themselves and become even more at risk for health problems related to unsafe sex, poor nutrition, poor hygiene, and drug abuse. Finally, homeless women often create a new identity for themselves with a new street name. As these women sink deeper into the street culture, they experience "institutional distancing" (Hatty, 1996, p. 416), which makes it more difficult for them to reach out to agencies that could offer support. So women who are homeless also experience barriers to mental health. It is estimated that one out of four homeless persons has a severe psychiatric illness, with schizophrenia and mood disorders being the most common (U.S. Surgeon General, 1999).

Help-Seeking Behaviors and Resiliency

In the area of treatment, Thompson and Isaac (2004) stated that there are conflicting findings regarding utilization rates among African Americans. Their survey of the literature suggests that African Americans state a need for or seek mental health services but are less likely to follow up with using the services. Also, they found that African Americans have been misdiagnosed more frequently than Whites, particularly in the area of depression, in which they are underdiagnosed, and in the area of schizophrenia, in which they are over-diagnosed. In 2001, the U.S. Surgeon General's report also stated that African Americans were less likely to receive appropriate mental health care. Thompson and Isaac concluded that race and culture may contribute to some of these deficits.

Gibbs and Fuery (1994) stated that African American women turn to both formal and informal resources for support. Although they will seek help, they are more likely to go to ministers or medical facilities. O'Malley, Forrest, and Miranda (2003) found that primary care physicians play a vital role in a woman's health when they care about their patients, providing comprehensive services such as depression screening. Barbee and Little (2003) pointed out that some health care providers may fail to recognize the need for help presented by some women because the strong African American woman image is so pervasive. These findings indicate the need for women to be vigilant about developing quality primary care relationships and advocating for quality care for all women, including the indigent and homeless.

In addressing why women do not pursue formal services, Gibbs and Fuery (1994) cited inaccessible health care facilities, lack of health insurance, negative or ambivalent attitudes about mental health services, and differential treatment, which means that sometimes African American women are not only inaccurately diagnosed but also relegated to services that require the least from them such as drug treatments. Thompson and Isaac (2004) elaborated that African Americans may choose such groups to reduce their contact with mental health personnel. Realistically, this distancing may be the result of the lack of diversity or cultural awareness among the mental health staff as well.

Indications are that most African American women choose formal mental health services largely when the issue is very serious and when less formal interventions have not prevailed. According to Gibbs and Fuery (1994), African American women will first seek alternative stress-relieving strategies such as prayer, which has been a powerful source of support (A. P. Jackson & Sears, 1992). Olphen et al. (2003) found that individuals who reported praying less often also reported a greater number of depressive symptoms.

Extended family support, social networks, and the church also serve as alternative interventions, according to Gibbs and Fuery (1994). The church has long been a source of support in the African American community, fulfilling many needs for worship, justice, social support, and leadership (Frame et al., 1999). From this institution, many African American women have found strength.

Robinson and Howard-Hamilton (1994) stated that empowerment is a process in which people become aware of the dynamic of power and the impact of internalized racism on their lives. Petersen (2000) offered an example of empowerment in a study on identity in which African American women with a strong sense of self had a ready descriptor of themselves that demonstrated a preparation for survival. They began speaking with "I was always a . . . ." Here, the word *fighter* or *hard worker* might be used to reinforce the notion that the women had strategies for success and images of themselves as survivors. Robinson and Howard-Hamilton maintained that an Afrocentric worldview that embraces the historical and cultural realities of African Americans has a greater potential for strength and identity development than more traditional approaches. Finally, Gibbs and Fuery (1994) recommended community-based interventions that foster independence and empower African American women to be partners in their own change. Whether women pursue formal or informal intervention, the goal is more positive self-images and behaviors.

Implications for Practice

Counselors who serve African American women need to be sensitive to the impact of historical and cultural influences on their mental health. While viewing the woman as very much the strong individual she was socialized to be, they must consider her dilemmas in the social context that framed them and the stressors that drain her resources. In many cases, historical and social circumstances are the etiology of a range of issues, including identity development, economic opportunity and work or career success, relationships, the achievement of marriage and family, as well as the need for security, belonging, support, and role fulfillment. Understanding that socioeconomic status can define the opportunity structure, confound relationships, and serve to deter or reinforce mental well-being must become central to the realistic assessment of challenges faced by African American women.

Consequently, career development and counseling must become an important aspect of service to this population. Women need to assess their skills and interests and make short- and long-term goals that can realistically lead to a fulfilling lifestyle. Many welfare-to-work programs rely on the woman herself to choose a job instead of a career direction, and this is based on her often limited knowledge of what she can do and what options are available. Career choice begins with self-awareness and awareness of the workplace (Herr, Cramer, & Niles, 2004). Further, these programs and others need to accept racism as a given and empower women in the workforce with strategies and support that can assure their survival.

Additionally, the attitudes of the counselor and his or her ability to build relationships are essential. The counselor must avoid stereotypes that blatantly categorize African American women based on their perceived racial or cultural heritage and strive instead to understand each woman and the world that she presents. For example, there will be generational issues. Some of the contemporary music and film influences will be more important to understanding younger African American women as these media further mystify their already complex developmental struggles and relationships. Older women may face issues related to career development, truncated salary opportunities, health, marriage, or aging dilemmas.

Finally, to be effective, mental health services have to be perceived as "okay," and therapists must be viewed as resonant with their clients. When African American women present for counseling, they need to find mental health professionals with whom they can identify. Consequently, there is a critical need for counselors from all ethnic backgrounds, and the challenge for counselor education programs is to begin training ethnic counselors at a rate that will make a real difference in their accessibility in practice settings.

Further, consideration should be given to the fact that African American women need access to both formal and informal treatment interventions. Mental health professionals must become advocates for African American women to assure proper diagnosis and treatment in the mental health facility as well as adequate resources in the community. Community here is meant to describe a wider geographic and social sphere than the traditional African American community where increasing numbers of African Americans no longer live. The use of creative strategies to foster social networks can reduce isolation and provide support and healing without robbing women of more discretionary leisure and creating more work. Most African American women have enough to do. Consequently, these networks or *sister circles* should not be as much about groups baking cookies and carpooling children as about a time for women to reflect and meet their own needs. Support groups at work or local community centers and weekend retreats are examples of alternative delivery strategies that can be readily accessible. Again, support services made available through the church will continue to be vital.

Implications for Future Research

An intensified research effort is needed with regard to many facets of mental health among African American women. Some studies are dated but still cited throughout the literature because they provide a rare piece of the puzzle. In addition to the need to constantly update the literature, there is a need to rethink how research with women is done. Many studies fail to identify participants by race, whereas other studies that include African American women do not achieve a representative sample when compared with the numbers of Caucasians. Further, there is a need to acknowledge that African American women are not a homogeneous group, and there is still considerable work to be done to better understand the mental health needs of homeless women, incarcerated women, HIV-positive women, women with somatic illnesses, and women in predominantly White work environments. More clinical research is needed on depression and anxiety and how continual socioeconomic oppression and institutional racism amount to physical and mental abuse for so many women, including the working poor—women who are working but not able to earn a living wage despite the one, two, or three jobs they maintain.

Additionally, more research is needed on the wellness issues of African American women. The mental health community needs to understand how so many African American women overcome and how counselors can share that special combination of chutzpah with other women who are seeking their own strength and empowerment. Not enough is known about issues that are not clinical but equally important. For example, how are African American women faring in the caregiver role with aging parents as they balance career and child-rearing responsibilities? More research is needed on how African American women who did not have children or marry are faring as they move toward midlife with careers in place. Does it feel like no more worlds to conquer, or are they successfully moving toward generativity? Erikson (1963, as cited in Berger, 1998) defined generativity as the stage in psychosocial development in which aging individuals find affirmation in reaching out to support younger generations through child rearing or other creative work. African American baby boomers have experienced enormous educational and career success and benefited their communities in numerous ways. Is this enough?

At the other end of the age spectrum, research on the identity development of African American girls will provide an important underpinning to the understanding of mental health needs of women. As African American girls venture into new career directions and experiment with new sex role definitions, we need to better understand who they are and what influences their well-being. Particularly, more research is needed regarding the impact of music such as gangsta rap on the images of African American women. Further, this research can explore the relationship between the media devaluation of women and violence at the hands of intimate partners as proposed by Cole and Guy-Sheftall (2003).

Also, as more African American women attempt to negotiate the career ladder, the stress of racial discrimination continues as a very real challenge. Further research is needed to help mental health professionals understand the impact of discrimination on physical and mental health. For example, women who seek treatment because of racial or sexual discrimination on the job receive little support in the workplace. Far from receiving affirmation of the painful experience, they often find their motives challenged along with their credentials. Williams and Morris-Williams (2000) found in their study that approximately 50% of White Americans viewed African Americans as lazy and wanting to live off welfare. Such negative views, if held by an employer or a counselor to whom a woman turns for help, would confound efforts to find relief in counseling and regain mental health. Certainly, further research is needed to illuminate the values of the counselor regarding discrimination and the depth of empathy for African American women among counselors from different ethnic backgrounds. Now over 10 years into the full force of the multicultural counseling movement, it is still not clear that all individuals can receive adequate counseling despite their diversity.

Finally, the research community needs to reach out to African American women to develop their trust in research and what it can do for them. Only then will these women come to the telephone, return the survey, or volunteer to join a cohort when a researcher calls. Without their willing participation, many questions will remain unanswered.

Summary

Building on the footprint of slavery, African American women have developed in remarkable ways. Not only have they managed to transcend the limitations of one of the most oppressive social systems ever to exist, but they have also developed a sense of self with a trademark strength that has empowered them to nurture their children and their grandchildren, the elderly, and the community. Having identity forced on them, African American women have evolved among the vanguard of empowered women.

At the same time, it is important to realize that the challenges of institutional racism and socioeconomic limitation strain the physical and emotional resources of many African American women. Increasingly, negative images threaten to inundate self-perception and warp relationships with those who would rightly provide a pivotal support network. This is especially true in the area of intimate partner domestic violence. Mental health practice needs to be attuned to historical and social realities and accepting of women in the context of their individual lives. Acknowledging individuals, their achievements, and strengths provides critical affirmations of identity and empowerment in the therapeutic environment.

Further, mental health services need to be made available to these women in both formal and informal settings. In the mental health facility, services need to be inviting. Too many African American women are disenchanted with services that remain unresponsive to their needs. Alternative support systems need to be encouraged. Through the local church or community center, services need to be made accessible to women to network and explore identity development. Further, these innovative programs are needed to reach out to women regardless of their socioeconomic resources as well as women who are incarcerated or homeless.

Finally, more research is needed. African American women need to be included in large numbers in studies investigating any facet of mental health. The research community needs to foster a bond with African American women to encourage their research participation, and the research, when it is conducted, must focus on both clinical disorders and wellness issues among African American women, recognizing the heterogeneous breadth of their remarkable reality.

References

Anderson, W. P., & Cummings, K. (1993). Women's acceptance of rape myths and their sexual experiences. *Journal of College Student Development, 34,* 53–57.

Barbee, E. L., & Little, M. (2003). Health, social class and African American women. In E. Disch (Ed.), *Reconstructing gender* (pp. 553–568). New York: McGraw Hill.

Berger, K. S. (1998). *The developing person: Through the life span.* New York: Worth.

Bethea, P. D. (1995). African American women and the male–female relationship dilemma: A counseling perspective. *Journal of Multicultural Counseling and Development, 23,* 87–95.

Brown, A. C., Brody, G. H., & Stoneman, Z. (2000). Rural Black women and depression: A contextual analysis. *Journal of Marriage and Family, 62,* 187–199.

Brown, L. M. (1993). Hidden girls. *Instructor: Middle Years, 102,* 10–13.

Cazenave, N. A. (1983). Black male–Black female relationships: The perceptions of 155 middle-class Black men. *Family Relations, 32,* 341–350.

Cole, J. B., & Guy-Sheftall, B. (2003). *Gender talk: The struggle for women's equality in African American communities.* New York: Random House.

Collins, P. H. (1998). The ties that bind: Race, gender and US violence. *Ethnic & Racial Studies, 21,* 917–939.

Davenport, D. S., & Yurich, J. M. (1991). Multicultural gender issues. *Journal of Counseling & Development, 70,* 64–71.

Fleck, C. (2004). Driving off hidden fees. *AARP Bulletin, 45*(4), 22.

Frame, M. W., Williams, C. B., & Green, E. L. (1999). Balm in Gilead: Spiritual dimensions in counseling African American women. *Journal of Multicultural Counseling and Development, 27,* 182.

Gibbs, J. T., & Fuery, D. (1994). Mental health and well-being of Black women: Toward strategies of empowerment. *American Journal of Community Psychology, 22,* 559–583.

Giddings, P. (1984). *When and where I enter.* New York: William Morrow.

Gilligan, C. (1993). *In a different voice.* Cambridge, MA: Harvard University Press.

Gillum, T. L. (2002). Exploring the link between stereotypic images and intimate partner violence in the African American community. *Violence Against Women, 8*(1), 64–87.

Gregory, T. (1999). Understanding depression in women. *Patient Care, 33,* 19, Article A58310554. Retrieved October 6, 2003, from http://web2.infotrac.galegroup.com

Hampton, R., Oliver, W., & Magarian, L. (2003). Domestic violence in the African American community. *Violence Against Women, 9,* 533–579.

Hatty, S. E. (1996). The violence of displacement: The problematics of survival for homeless young women. *Violence Against Women, 2,* 412–428.

Herr, E. L., Cramer, S. H., & Niles, S. G. (2004). *Career guidance and counseling: Through the lifespan.* Boston: Allyn & Bacon.

Holcomb-McCoy, C. C., & Moore-Thomas, C. (2001). Empowering African-American adolescent females. *Professional School Counseling, 5*(1), 19–27.

Hughes, Z. (2003, March). Who says sisters can't be nice? Softness for tough girls. *Ebony, 58,* 98–102.

Jackson, A. P., & Sears, S. J. (1992). Implications of an Africentric worldview in reducing stress for African American women. *Journal of Counseling & Development, 71,* 184–191.

Jackson, P. B., & Mustillo, S. (2001). I am woman: The impact of social identities on African American women's mental health. *Women & Health, 32*(4), 33–59.

Jordan, W. D. (1969). *White over Black: American attitudes toward the Negro 1550.* New York: Norton.

King, K. S. (2003). Do you see what I see? Effects of group consciousness on African American women's attributions to prejudice. *Psychology of Women Quarterly, 27,* 17–31.

Landrine, H., Klonoff, E. A., Alcaraz, R., Scott, J., & Wilkins, P. (1995). In B. Lott & D. Maluso (Eds.), *The social psychology of interpersonal discrimination* (pp. 183–224). New York: Guilford Press.

Lee, R. K., Sanders, T. V., & Mechanic, M. B. (2002). Intimate partner violence and women of color: A call for innovations. *American Journal of Public Health, 92,* 530–535.

Lerner, G. (1972). *Black women in White America: A documentary history.* New York: Vintage Books.

Morgan, J. (1993). Professor studies "those loud Black girls": Acceptance of gender diversity key to understanding young Black females. *Black Issues in Higher Education, 10,* 20–21.

Olphen, J., Schulz, A., Isreal, B., Chatters, L., Klem, L., Parker, E., & Williams, D. (2003). Religious involvement, social support, and health among African-American women on the East Side of Detroit. *Journal of General Internal Medicine, 1,* 549–568.

O'Malley, A. S., Forrest, C. B., & Miranda, J. (2003). Primary care attributes and care for depression among low-income African American women. *American Journal of Mental Health, 93,* 1328–1345.

Petersen, S. (2000). Multicultural perspective on middle-class women's identity development. *Journal of Counseling & Development, 78,* 63–72.

Powell, G. J. (1985). Self-concept among Afro-American students in racially isolated minority schools: Some regional differences. *Journal of the American Academy of Child Psychiatry, 24,* 142–149.

Roan, S. (2003, August). Flippin' out. *Heart & Soul, 10,* 94–97.

Robinson, T. L., & Howard-Hamilton, M. (1994). An Afrocentric paradigm: Foundation for healthy self-image and healthy interpersonal relationships. *Journal of Mental Health Counseling, 16,* 327–340.

Sachs-Ericsson, N., & Ciarlo, J. A. (2000). Gender, social roles, and mental health: An epidemiological perspective. *Sex Roles: A Journal of Research, 34,* 605, Article A75959827. Retrieved October 6, 2003, from http://web2.infortrac.galegroup.com

Sanders, A. J. (1997, February). From video hos to deathbed divas. *Essence, 2,* 160.

Sklar, H. (1995). The upperclass and mothers in the hood. In M. L. Andersen & P. H. Collins (Eds.), *Race, class and gender: An anthology* (pp. 123–134). Belmont, CA: Wadsworth.

Staples, R. (1973). *The Black woman in America.* Chicago: Nelson Hall.

Staples, R. (1988). An overview of race and marital status. In H. P. McAdoo (Ed.), *Black families* (pp. 187–189). Newbury Park, CA: Sage.

Stets, J. E., & Pirog-Good, M. A. (1987). Violence in dating relationships. *Social Psychology Quarterly, 50,* 237–246.

Thompson, C. E., & Isaac, K. (2004). African-Americans: Treatment issues and recommendations. In D. R. Atkinson (Ed.), *Counseling American minorities* (pp. 125–143). New York: McGraw Hill.

U.S. Surgeon General. (1999). *Mental health: A report of the Surgeon General.* Washington, DC: U.S. Department of Health and Human Services, Office of the Surgeon General, SAMHSA. Retrieved October 6, 2003, from http://www.mentalhealth.org/cre/ch3.asp

U.S. Surgeon General. (2001). *Mental health: Culture, race, ethnicity—A supplement to "Mental health: A report of the Surgeon General."* Washington, DC: U.S. Department of Health and Human Services, Office of the Surgeon General, SAMHSA. Retrieved October 6, 2003, from http://www.mentalhealth.org/cre/fact1.asp

Williams, D. R., & Morris-Williams, R. (2000). Racism and mental health: The African American experience. *Ethnicity and Health, 5,* 243–269.

Williams, D. R., Takeuchi, D. T., & Adair, R. K. (1992). Marital status and psychiatric disorders among Blacks and Whites. *Journal of Health and Social Behavior, 33,* 140–157.

Wilson, M., & Russell, K. (1996). *Divided sisters.* New York: Doubleday.

4

Understanding Mental Illness
Among African American Males:
Risk Factors and Treatment Parameters

Travis A. Gayles, Reginald J. Alston, and David Staten

No matter the source on African American men and mental health, the article or chapter is sure to begin with a depiction of their struggle to express manhood and achieve full status in society. No other demographic group faces such dire impediments as lowered life expectancy, higher incarceration rates, and lowered economic wealth (American Sociological Association, 2001; Centers for Disease Control and Prevention, 2000, 2001). In other words, race remains a predominant factor in influencing the daily lives of African American males. African American males and White males have similar expectations at birth. Society's gender constructs expect men to be in charge and assume powerful roles in their families and communities (American Counseling Association, 1998). The difference is the number of impediments to achieving these goals for African American males. This is especially important, with a growing Black youth population that is facing increased suicide rates, exposure to violence, and criminal imprisonment (Centers for Disease Control and Prevention, 2001).

African American males struggle to cope with the heightened effects of racism, yet they underutilize mental health services (Centers for Disease Control and Prevention, 2001). Mental illness carries a stigma in the African American community; in particular, African American males view acknowledging mental illness as a weakness (Diala et al., 2002). There is a strong presence of nontraditional sources of support—peer networks and churches—to compensate for the lack of more formal treatment. However, African American males continue to cope through maladaptive behaviors, leading to myriad problems.

Improvements to the counseling process have been gradual as it pertains to African Americans overall. Now the improvements must continue as research must be done to account for differences between males and females and also heterogeneity in the male population. As class divisions become larger, it will be imperative to not assume that all African American males have the same experience. This chapter examines the plight that African American males face, highlighting general disparities that heavily influence one's mental health status and expanding on how these influences translate to access and utilization of mental health services. Also, the chapter examines the need for counselors to acknowledge the effects of race on African American males and to incorporate race in the counseling process through environmental changes such as open disclosure, active engagement, and promotion of an improved racial and self-identity.

The Plight

Whether it is Chris Rock using humor to lighten the onerous burden that it carries or the soulful sounds of singer Angie Stone to highlight the accomplishments of her "strong Black brothers," we are all well acquainted with the plight of the African American male. According to Mincy (1994), "historically, manhood has not been a birthright for black males, who have not generally been granted traditional masculine privilege or power in the United States" (p. 35). Racism in the form of social, economic, and cultural vices has worked to prevent Black men from achieving this privilege. It has arguably led to the development of poor self-esteem, depression, and heightened stress. Existence has become survival.

The history of slavery in the United States provides a backdrop for this struggle. The male role is usually the protector of the family and the economic breadwinner. Black men were not allowed to assume these roles during these times (American Counseling Association, 1998). Instead, a tenuous balance was sought between shielding the family and not being so aggressive that it led to death. Black men were often unable to protect their wives from sexual advances from slave masters and were not allowed to obtain jobs that paid wages to support their families. As a result, many women and children had to assume some of these roles to keep the communities standing.

The enduring struggles of the past 150 years have been chronicled through history: the fight to vote, separate but equal, and the civil rights movement of the 1950s and 1960s. At every turn, African American men have been at the forefront actively advocating for change and receipt of basic human rights. They have sought to protect their families and be leaders of their communities while simultaneously trying to shape their own self-image against society's many stereotypes (American Counseling Association, 1998). Many would argue that the battles have not ended. The questions of injustice are precarious ones, as progress has been made on different levels, and as African American men do climb corporate, governmental, athletic, and societal ladders. But images of Rodney King, James Byrd, and Amadou Diallo are still too fresh in our minds to concede that the path to manhood is a free pass without daunting, unparalleled obstacles that others in society do not face.

For instance, for African American males the outlook is not bright economically, health-wise, or legally. He makes less money for similar jobs, has a much lower life expectancy than any other demographic group in U.S. society, and is disproportionately an inhabitant of the U.S. penal system (American Sociological Association, 2001).

On average, Black men earned 9% less than otherwise similar White men in the private sector. The percentage difference in earnings between Blacks and Whites was smallest in the lowest paid occupations and greatest in the highest paid occupations (American Sociological Association, 2001). For men working in the public sector, on the other hand, the average difference in earnings between Blacks and Whites in the same occupation was only 5% (American Sociological Association, 2001). These differences were magnified in the highest paid private sector jobs, in which Black men earned as much as 20% less than White men in similar positions. In addition, Black men with a bachelor's degree made $19,000 less than their White counterparts (American Sociological Association, 2001; Armas, 2003).

Health Status

According to the Centers for Disease Control and Prevention (2000), Black men have a lower life expectancy than any other demographic group in U.S. society at 68.2 years, trailing White women (80.0 years), Black women (74.9 years), and White men (74.8 years). Black men also have a lower life expectancy when accounting for men of all races (74.1

years). African American male infants had higher infant mortality rates also, at 14.8 deaths per 1,000 in comparison with the overall average of 6.8 per 1,000 (Centers for Disease Control and Prevention, 2000).

Homicide is the leading cause of death for Black men ages 15–34. In contrast, homicide is the fourth leading cause of death for White males during these same ages (Centers for Disease Control and Prevention, 2000). African American men die from complications from HIV/AIDS at a rate of 62.7 per 100,000, compared with 19.1 for African American women, 12.5 for White men, 1.8 for White women, 25.5 for Latino men, and 5.9 for Latino women (Center for the Advancement of Health, 2003).

Amount of suicides remains lower for Black males in comparison with White males; however, the rate for Black men, in particular using handguns, has doubled over the past 20 years (Associated Press, 2002). African American men die from cerebrovascular disease at a rate of 50.5 per 100,000, twice as likely as White men or women. And 221.1 per 100,000 African American men die of cancer, more than twice the rate for White women (Center for the Advancement of Health, 2003).

Jail Levels

Nationally, Black men ages 18–64 had a significantly higher rate of incarceration at 7.9% versus 1.1% for White men and 2.7% for Hispanics (Human Rights Watch, 2000a). And African American male juveniles are 3.3 times more likely to be in juvenile detention centers than their White counterparts (Human Rights Watch, 2000b). The latter statistic is evidence of an alarming trend. Black male youths present an emerging population that will require attention. Youths are being exposed to more violence than ever before, not only on television but in real-life situations (Centers for Disease Control and Prevention, 2001). Many of them develop harmful behavioral patterns long before adulthood, yet they rarely receive the type of nurturing treatment needed to produce mentally and physically positive outcomes.

Socialization of African American Males

Black men do not reach the age of 21 feeling alienated; it is a cycle that begins early in adolescent growth. Identity construction focuses more on fitting into one's environment, which is often in contradiction to the mainstream notions we see daily (Mincy, 1994). All of the things that youths see as Black are portrayed as "counter culture" to the mainstream. Whether it is the rap music that they listen to or the baggy clothing that they wear, youths are reminded daily that their culture is not the right way and that in order to be successful they must abandon their natural tendencies to adopting a mainstream attitude (Mincy, 1994).

There is evidence that African American males handle stress and mental angst differently. Each individual develops a racial component to his personality that is shaped by outside social influences (Carter, 1995). This component is compounded by how they interpret the images society portrays to them about their race. For African American men there are few positive images, which can lead to low self-esteem and depression.

Historical Progression of Counseling African American Men

Most of the empirical data on treatment have centered around studies that looked at severely mentally ill patients. These patients are most often in state mental hospitals; state hospitals are the primary inpatient source of treatment for African Americans (Williams, 1995).

This research has offered some suggestions of how race may influence mental health status. But the bulk of older research is limited to this population and ignores the heterogeneity of the African American male population. Differences in African American males' experiences may influence the attitudes a client brings into counseling and the types of counseling methods that may be effective. Despite these differences, many mental health officials struggle to handle the effect of race on the client's mental status. Discounting the patient sometimes translates to relationship barriers. Race is essential because it relates to client referral, patient–therapist dynamics, descriptions, conceptualizations, and treatment planning (Carter, 1995).

The process of counseling African American men has focused more on resocialization. *Resocialization* is defined as the process wherein an individual, defined as inadequate according to societal norms, is subjected to a dynamic program of behavior intervention aimed at installing those values that would allow the individual to function according to the norms of society (Savage & Kelley, 1980). Guys "on the street" would potentially term this as "selling out." Building skill sets that will lead to success in the real world should be a goal of all therapies; counseling cannot devalue an individual's culture as a means of measuring success. The client must be counseled to develop not only a sense of individual esteem but racial pride as well. Cross and Vandiver (2001) proposed a model of nigrescence that examines Black consciousness development. Unlike previous theories, their model presupposes the existence of multiple Black identities and identifies eight different identity types.

Black men usually do not seek treatment until they experience severe symptoms of mental illness. This is significant because these severe emotions manifest themselves in potentially harmful actions not only to themselves but also to those around them (American Counseling Association, 1998). If these actions are criminal, then offenders may be arrested, and the psychological assistance that they need will only be further delayed.

Casework models of the past have been based on solely looking at the victim, ignoring the effects of his surroundings. Such a limited scope places the entirety of the illness on the individual, citing his inability to perform at a mentally healthy state. This is one potential reason why counseling is viewed with mistrust, for fear of being blamed for one's plight (Green, 1982). For African American men, this is significant because to them it affirms their beliefs that society is against them.

Defining the Need

Overall, African Americans have experienced similar rates of mental illness with non-Hispanic Whites, as evidenced by the data from the Epidemiologic Catchment Area Study (1980–1985); however, differences arise for specific diagnoses. According to Williams (1995):

- African Americans are more likely to suffer from phobias, somatization (sleep paralysis), and cultural-bound syndromes than Whites.
- Non-Hispanic Whites are nearly twice as likely as African Americans to commit suicide. One startling statistic though is that the suicide rate for young Black men is similar to White males, and steadily climbing. For African American males ages 10 to 14, the suicide rate climbed from 1980 to 1995 by 233%, compared with 120% for Whites.
- African Americans are six times more likely to receive a diagnosis of alcohol and substance abuse, whereas Whites are four times more likely to receive a diagnosis of personality disorder. African Americans with higher socioeconomic status than Whites were still three times more likely to be tested for alcohol and substance abuse.

- African Americans are diagnosed with schizophrenia more frequently than Whites but less for affective disorders.

Whites received antidepressants 17% more than did African Americans. However, new classes of drugs, including selective serotonin reuptake inhibitor medicines with fewer side effects, are less often prescribed to African American patients (Centers for Disease Control and Prevention, 2001). One of the potential drawbacks from this is that African Americans may stop taking medicines more often because of the heightened side effects.

Data from the Centers for Disease Control and Prevention (2001) show that African Americans, especially men, are overrepresented in special needs populations:

- 40% of homeless populations
- 50% of all prisoners in state and federal penal systems
- 40% of juveniles in custody
- 25% of African American youths, based on exposure to violence, qualify for post-traumatic stress disorder (PTSD)
- 21% of Black Vietnam veterans suffer from PTSD compared with 14% of non-Hispanic Whites.

Utilization Patterns

Nearly one third of mentally ill Americans receive care. African Americans, however, seek treatment half as much as their White counterparts (Centers for Disease Control and Prevention, 2001). Oddly, African Americans are more likely to have a positive attitude toward use of mental health services than are Whites in both behavioral and emotional responses to these services (Diala et al., 2002). They are also more likely to seek professional care if they have serious emotional problems. The negative association does not arise until after the initial visit (Diala et al., 2002).

Mental illness, however, still carries a tremendous stigma in the African American population. Many are not aware that mental illness is indeed a medical illness (Diala et al., 2002). Mental illness is often ridiculed in Black communities, with phrases like "He just ain't right in the head" or "He rode the short bus." Such characterizations establish a negative connotation to weakened mental status. Men who are in touch with their emotions are effectively known as "punks." Regardless of the community, *punk* is a derogatory term that runs counter to one's level of masculinity. Dealing with mental illness is exposing one's vulnerable side. By doing so, it gives others an opportunity to exploit one's weaknesses, using them against him for greater gain.

Treatment

African American males are more likely to receive treatment from primary care facilities and emergency services (Centers for Disease Control and Prevention, 2001). This is important to note because African Americans may be receiving prescriptions from practitioners who may not be specifically trained in the nuances of mental diagnoses. These physicians may also not be aware of alternative treatments, instead relying solely on the pharmacological properties of medicines. African American men are also more likely to receive assistance from community centers (Centers for Disease Control and Prevention, 2001).

Overall, non-Whites are admitted to mental institutions at a rate of 328 to 136 for Whites per 100,000 (Diala et al., 2002). In all age groups, African American males are disproportionately represented in inpatient treatment services yet underrepresented in outpatient treatment models.

Sources of Referrals

A majority of African American men are referred to counseling by judges, social workers, and parole officers; the purpose of counseling becomes a rehabilitative or reform process, and it may also be seen as a source of punishment (American Counseling Association, 1998). Such views invoke negative associations with the counseling process and governmental agencies, and clients may be resistant to counseling. Many African American males bypass traditional medical services to receive support from their friend groups and community entities, such as churches (Carter, 1995).

Friend groups provide support for many African American males, especially younger males. These peers effectively have "their back." This peer group formation has come under fire for heavily influencing the development of masculinity in young Black males, in particular in inner-city urban areas. While this may be true, these peer groups are the only source for many young Black males to gain male support or interaction. When they experience problems, they are likely to confide in their "boys" because they trust them and have shared experiences.

This concept continues through ages and education levels. Black fraternities are prevalent on college campuses, and other groups such as Masonic lodges and Black Men United clubs are growing. These organizations provide a venue for Black men to interact with others who look like them and are facing similar issues. These similarities translate to trust (Majors & Gordon, 1994).

Throughout history, the church has been the bedrock of support for the African American community, whether through the civil rights movement or a haven for those befallen on hard times. It has somehow trumped more official agencies in understanding the emotional crises men face; its techniques have been highly effective in providing counseling-like services through spirituality (Owens, 1980).

African American churches provide another interesting feature. It is a place where Black men can participate freely in leadership roles in respected, powerful positions. Such leadership positions can be affirming to these men, who otherwise may never experience any type of power in their daily lives (Carter, 1995). Churches also provide a place of comfort because the question of authenticity and qualifying experiences is a minute, if not nonexistent, issue. Many men feel that they can speak with their pastors or other church officials because of a shared experience, if nothing more than also being a Black man (American Counseling Association, 1998).

For many African American males, religion provides a spiritual cleansing of their problems; their faith in God is used as the treatment. An interesting case study is the influence of the Muslim religion in prisons. The foundation of the Black Muslim prison program is based on the belief that the individual was not aware of his external surroundings before incarceration (Owens, 1980). The goal is to educate the individual to raise his self-concept level. It is hoped the inmate would develop a positive racial component of his personality, and thereby positive racial coping skills (Owens, 1980).

Barriers to Counseling

One of the biggest obstacles to counseling is the lack of trust related to differences in race between the client and the mental health professional. Instead of seeking assistance, many African American males internalize their depression because of this mistrust (American

Counseling Association, 1998). This is dangerous because it can lead to stress-related illnesses, such as hypertension, or maladaptive behavior including substance abuse. A potential solution would be to send the client to an African American counselor. Carter (1995) noted that there are positive effects from clients seeing a counselor of the same race, such as not having to educate the counselor on what being Black in society means. The only problem is that African Americans make up only 2% of psychiatrists, 2% of psychologists, and 4% of social workers (Centers for Disease Control and Prevention, 2001). Sharing the same race still may not buffer a counselor from preconceived notions about clients, and it is imperative that all counselors be aware of the aforementioned obstacles and implement therapy techniques tailored to their clients. With such a small population of African American professionals, all counselors must be trained and understand potential barriers to providing treatment to African American males.

Other barriers to effective counseling that arise, as noted in Exhibit 4.1 by the American Counseling Association, include heightened aggression, alienation, and disconnect from friends and family.

Counseling Framework Models

There are several key steps that counselors can follow regardless of the counseling model that they choose to use. Exhibit 4.2 lists the American Counseling Association's key guidelines that form an effective intervention in African American men that works to lessen some of the aforementioned obstacles to treatment. Each of these pieces reflects the need for building an environment of trust and open disclosure. It is imperative for African American men to feel a connection with their counselor, especially if the counselor is of another race (American Counseling Association, 1998). As stated earlier, African American men are conditioned to internalize issues. And when a lot of their problems are caused by

Exhibit 4.1
Barriers to Counseling

Problems of aggression and control
Aggression and control present themselves in one of three ways. First, African American men demonstrate too little control over aggression and control; they often exhibit immature or limited coping skills. Second, they exhibit too much control over their emotions, manifesting in suppression or repression. And last, African American men internalize their emotions through inappropriate channeling.

Cultural alienation/disconnection
When African American men feel marginalized, they often disconnect from personal relationships, jobs, and community to cope with their anger. Such disconnection leads to cultural alienation.

Self-esteem
The inability to fulfill masculine roles leads to diminished self-esteem and an internalized negative self-image. In order to compensate for this lack of self-esteem, men often partake in maladaptive behavior.

Dependency issues
African American men may relieve their stress by developing unhealthy dependencies, such as drug abuse. This behavior may become engrained as a problem-solving mechanism that is repeated consistently in the face of adversity.

Reluctance to ask for help
For African American men, seeking mental health treatment is admitting weakness and deconstructs masculine identity. The view of threatening one's manhood is compounded by the aforementioned lowered self-esteem. In addition, African American men are generally not raised to disclose to strangers.

Note. Adapted from *Counseling African Americans: Counseling African American Men,* by the American Counseling Association (1998). Retrieved September 20, 2003, from http://aca.convio.net/site/News2?page=NewsArticle&id=7164&news_iv_ctrl=1023

Exhibit 4.2

Framework for Effective Intervention With African American Males

---

Developing rapport
One of the most substantial barriers to treatment is antitrust. Counselors must work to establish an initial personal connection. This can be accomplished by shifting the initial focus of interactions on verbal and nonverbal communication as opposed to setting up counseling goals. A good rapport lays the foundation for open communication between counselor and client.

Pace engagement of counseling process
Counseling is most effective when therapeutic work evolves naturally from the open relationship with established rapport, trust, and openness.

Possible self-disclosure
A potential tool in establishing rapport is a level of self-disclosure. Often African American male clients gain trust through asking direct, often intimate questions to their counselors. A counselor's willingness to answer directly on a personal level may increase credibility with the client. It is important to note, however, that a counselor should disclose to their client only to their level of comfort.

Encouraging introspection
Many of the issues African American men face, such as cultural alienation and disconnection, influence the level of sharing intimate feelings in counseling sessions. The counselor needs to foster an open environment that facilitates client introspection.

Explore spirituality
Helping clients to explore their personal meaning of life and sense of spirituality can provide a focus for processing issues of alienation, anger, or frustration. An open, trust-filled rapport is essential for success.

Sensitive to racism
There is a great deal of variability in how racism affects psychosocial development of African American men, yet the influence cannot be overstated. It is integral in problem etiology and resolution and important to not discount the effects in the client's life.

Psychoeducational counseling
It is important that counseling be viewed as an educative process for clients. The primary focus of counseling may need to be developing new behaviors or skills to deal more effectively with challenges that African American men face daily, such as social and economic obstacles.

Note. Adapted from *Counseling African Americans: Counseling African American Men*, by the American Counseling Association (1998). Retrieved September 20, 2003, from http://aca.convio.net/site/News2?page=NewsArticle&id=7164&news_iv_ctrl=1023

racism, they will inherently view the counselor as a part of that oppressive system (American Counseling Association, 1998). Trust is built and concerns of racism reduced when the counselor opens up to the African American male client.

Five Stages of Counseling Process

The American Counseling Association (1998) has also proposed a framework in five stages (see Exhibit 4.3) similar to a model proposed by Gibbs and Huang (1989). The framework addresses some of the initial concerns and responses of African American males about mistrust and discomfort in a counseling environment. The stages emphasize building on the counselor's ability to obtain positive responses to one's actions from the client (American Counseling Association, 1998).

Counseling Models

Counseling models have made great progress over the past decade to include race and the effects of racism on African American males. Numerous counseling models have emerged in an effort to include race in the counseling process, including racially inclusive and culturally specific models.

Exhibit 4.3
Five Stages to Address Initial Client Concerns

Stage 1: Initial Contact/Appraisal

Many African American men enter counseling reserved, untrusting, passive–aggressive, or potentially hostile; on the other hand, they could appear superficially pleasant. Hidden by all of these different emotions is potential mistrust of the counselor or hostility toward the counselor. It is essential for the counselor to convey personal authenticity.

Stage 2: Investigative

The client will often attempt to minimize any educational, economic, or social distinctions he may perceive between himself and the counselor. He seeks to relate to the counselor on some level, sometimes through inquiring about potential commonalities. These commonalities are important in establishing an open environment. It requires the counselor to be comfortable with stepping outside of the professional role to interact on a more personal level of commonality.

Stage 3: Involvement

It is at this stage that the client decides whether he can identify with the counselor as a person. This is based upon the honest self-disclosure of the counselor. The client begins to engage in an identification process, characterized by asking the counselor personal questions. The degree to which a counselor is able to engage in self-disclosure and get personal with an African American male client can promote trust and transition into a working counseling relationship.

Self-disclosure to promote trust #

Stage 4 : Commitment

The client usually makes a decision on whether or not he can trust the counselor. This decision is based on his evaluation of the counselor as an honest individual that he can relate to on a personal level.

Stage 5: Engagement

The final decision on the counselor's authenticity and trustworthiness is made during this time. This marks the working stage where the counseling process begins.

Note. From *Counseling African Americans: Counseling African American Men*, by the American Counseling Association (1998). Retrieved September 20, 2003, from http://aca.convio.net/site/News2?page=NewsArticle&id=7164&news_iv_ctrl=1023

The racially inclusive model is based on the idea that race is a psychological factor, not just a social or cultural factor; it integrates practices from traditional therapeutic models, such as psychodynamic, behavioral, and humanistic models (Carter, 1995). From this perspective the racially inclusive model weaves together racial identity theory and the therapeutic interaction model (Carter, 1995). It allows counselors to determine the level of importance that race-related issues mean to the client (Carter, 1995).

The culturally specific therapy model uses the values of the client's culture to determine abnormal behavior and potential treatment approaches (Carter, 1995). According to Carter (1995, p. 28), culturally specific models are likely to be used when culturally diverse groups grow in size, economic conditions are stable, and political and racial issues are less evident in social interactions.

Each model can be applied to a different portion of the African American male population. The important lesson to take home is that all models must acknowledge race. However, it is essential not to assume that all Black men have identical experiences. Counselors must be aware of the client's background, economically, educationally, and socially. Counselors must be cautious not to abandon previous practices but work to incorporate guidelines such as those proposed by the American Counseling Association for African American males.

Summary

Addressing mental illness in the African American male population is a huge undertaking, but one that is desperately needed. African American males present a unique segment of society. No other group faces the number of institutional obstacles yet is conditioned so heavily to reject the idea of receiving outside help to cope with these burdens. Counselors must admit the devastating and negative effects of racism. Racism must be acknowledged in therapy by both the counselor and the client.

Counselors must respect the powerful impact that community resources, such as social networks and churches, have on African American males. Instead of discouraging these support systems, counselors can pick up helpful insights that can be applied in counseling.

There is a continuing shortage of African American mental health professionals. An increase in the number of African American counselors, especially male counselors, would have a potentially profound effect on improving the mental health of African American males.

Regardless of the race of the counselor, however, there is an overall need for expanding training for all mental health professionals. Counselors should continue to be trained in how to encounter race in the counseling process. They must also learn that diversity also exists within different cultures; not all individuals will have the same experience. This is crucial as the population of African American males becomes more diverse economically and socially.

Academe must continue to refine counseling models for African Americans overall and in particular for African American men. It will become increasingly important as a new generation of young boys become men and encounter the dire obstacles that Black men face each day.

References

American Counseling Association. (1998). *Counseling African Americans: Counseling African American men*. Retrieved September 20, 2003, from http://aca.convio.net/site/News2?page=NewsArticle&id=7164&news_iv_ctrl=1023

American Sociological Association. (2001). *Earnings inequality between Black and White men in the private sector greatest at the top*. Retrieved September 20, 2003, from http://www.asanet.org/media/grodsky.html

Armas, G. C. (2003). *Educational gaps narrow between men, women, races*. Retrieved September 20, 2003, from http://www.nwaonline.net/pdfarchive/2003/march/21/3-21-03%20B9.pdf

Associated Press. (2002, March 20). Black male suicide rates increase. Retrieved March 25, 2004, from http://www.psycport.com/showArticle.cfm?xmlFile=associatedpress_2002_03_20_5177-3551-Black-Suicides..xml&provider=Associated+Press

Carter, R. T. (1995). *The influence of race and racial identity in psychotherapy: Toward a racially inclusive model*. New York: Wiley.

Center for the Advancement of Health. (2003, May). *Facts of life: Issue briefings for health reporters*. Retrieved September 20, 2003, from http://www.cfah.org/factsoflife/vol8no5.cfm

Centers for Disease Control and Prevention. (2000). *Infant mortality statistics from the 2001 period linked birth/infant death data set*. Retrieved September 20, 2003, from http://www.cdc.gov/nchs/data/nvsr/nvsr52/nvsr52_02.pdf

Centers for Disease Control and Prevention. (2001). *African American mental health fact sheet*. Retrieved September 20, 2003, from http://www.surgeongeneral.gov/library/mentalhealth/cre/fact1.asp

Cross, W. E., & Vandiver, B. J. (2001). Nigrescence theory and measurement: Introducing the Cross Racial Identity Scale (CRIS). In J. G. Ponterotto, J. M. Casas, L. A. Suzuki, & C. M. Alexander (Eds.), *Handbook of multicultural counseling* (2nd ed., pp. 371–394). Thousand Oaks, CA: Sage.

Diala, C., Muntaner, C., Walrath, C., Nickerson, K. J., LaVeist, T. A., & Leaf, P. J. (2002). Racial differences in attitudes towards professional mental health care and the use of services. In T. A. LaVeist (Ed.), *Race, ethnicity, and health* (pp. 591–606). New York: Wiley.

Gibbs, J. T., & Huang, L. N. (1989). *Children of color: Psychological interventions with culturally diverse youth.* San Francisco: Jossey-Bass.

Green, J. W. (1982). *Cultural awareness in the human services.* Englewood Cliffs, NJ: Prentice-Hall.

Human Rights Watch. (2000a). *Race and incarceration in the United States.* Retrieved September 20, 2003, from http://hrw.org/backgrounder/usa/race/pdf/table3.pdf

Human Rights Watch. (2000b). *Rates of confinement in juvenile detention facilities, by race.* Retrieved September 20, 2003, from http://hrw.org/backgrounder/usa/race/pdf/table6.pdf

Majors, R. G., & Gordon, J. U. (Eds.). (1994). *The American Black male: His present status and his future.* Chicago: Nelson-Hall.

Mincy, R. B. (1994). *Nurturing young Black males: Challenges to agencies, programs, and social policy.* Washington, DC: Urban Institute.

Owens, C. E. (1980). *Mental health and Black offenders.* Lexington, MA: Lexington Books.

Savage, J. E., & Kelley, Y. (1980). Counseling–psychotherapy and Black men. In T. M. Skovholt, P. G. Schauble, & R. Davis (Eds.), *Counseling men* (pp. 130–136). Monterey, CA: Brooks/Cole.

Williams, D. R. (1995). *African American mental health: Persisting questions and paradoxical findings.* Retrieved September 20, 2003, from http://www.rcgd.isr.umich.edu/prba/perspectives/spring1995/dwilliams.pdf

5

Marital Status: Female–Male Relationships of African Americans

Deneese L. Jones

The genius of our Black foremothers and forefathers was . . . to equip Black folk with cultural armor to beat back the demons of hopelessness, meaningless, and lovelessness.

—*Cornel West*

Historically, marriage within the African American community has been described as having uniqueness and cultural relevance. Ceremonial beliefs and methodological approaches to marriage are, indeed, culturally defined. African American women and men recognize marriage as a preservation of race, identity, and heritage. However, in recent years, the role and value of marriage in the African American community has received considerable examination and criticism as being more problematic, conflictual, destructive, and a disappearing institution without a cultural connection (Gladding, 2002; Willis, 1990).

Rodney and Marilyn, two African American professionals, had been married for 29 years. Up to this point, theirs had been a beautiful marriage but not without some years of ups and downs that could be contributed to spousal misunderstandings, drug usage, financial burdens, child-rearing hazards, and career challenges. Rodney, in a government, upper-management position, and Marilyn, as a college professor, often commented on how they had learned over the years to overcome difficult situations and their adverse effects through open and sometimes "tough" communication with each other and learning to pray about everything. Both had managed to ascend to successful careers despite physical separation sometimes because of his military service as well as the challenges of racism that they had experienced many times in their separate careers and lifestyles. Following their arrival to middle-class-level living and after rearing two children to adulthood, Marilyn and Rodney surmised that in spite of everything, life had been good to them.

But, this year brought a new challenge for them. Marilyn had been offered an opportunity to receive apprenticeship-type training for a future job promotion. As she would be an African American female in a nontraditional job role, they took great pride in this opportunity. The catch was that it would mean her living several thousand miles away from Rodney for 10 months. But, they reasoned that because this experience would ultimately lead to helping her achieve a long-term goal, they both were happy and made plans for the move by setting her up in a luxury apartment in the city where she would live. They purchased furniture together and planned to visit each other periodically during the year. When she finally left, they talked on the phone nightly and expressed their loneliness but endured it knowing that there was a time limit on this arrangement.

An avid cook, Rodney kept busy with household chores and yard work when he came home from work. He read nightly and played pool once a week with his friends. Marilyn worked long hours and enjoyed all the new skills that she was acquiring. She spent the weekends reading, shopping, and going to see movies whenever she was not traveling or attending seminars. On one occasion, Marilyn became physically ill and Rodney traveled to her new living quarters to spend time taking care of her because he knew that she had no one else there to care for her. She felt affirmed in her relationship and expressed her delirious appreciation for his sacrifice.

At the end of the apprenticeship experience and the physical separation, Rodney helped Marilyn make the move back home. He said that he had learned that if he had to live this life, it is best to have someone to share life with and he was glad that she was home to share his life. This warmed her heart, but after Marilyn returned home, she and Rodney faced the issue of learning how to live together again. Having learned to make do without the other, they had to relearn how to make time for each other and renew the communication patterns that they had established. Nothing could be taken for granted; adjustment was inevitable for almost every area of their lives. Marilyn found herself, once again, "studying" her spouse to pay attention to his unspoken needs. Rodney rediscovered the importance of spending quality time with Marilyn and really listening to her during their times together.

The unintended consequences of sacrifice for a career promotion had created an area of conflict for this couple but, luckily, they realized early the need to address their issues. They talked about their needs and prayed for a renewal of their relationship. Next they were purposeful and diligent in being watchful during this time of reentry. The lesson they learned is that while it is great to have career goals, it is most important to prepare for the adjustments and understanding needed on both parts for making such a transition. Truly female–male marital relationships are hard work!

This case study illuminates the understanding of many that African American families are known for being "strong" in the areas of religious orientation and spirituality; they often utilize the resources of their clergy and churches (Cherlin, 1992). But, as further exhibited in this case study, African American male–female relationships are faced with many stressors associated with money, work, success, and even leisure (Turner, 1993). Suffice it to say that there have always been tension and conflict between the sexes of all races, but for African Americans, the discord seems to have reached crisis proportions. An examination of the census shows that 35% of Americans between 24 and 34 years of age have never married. For African Americans that figure is 54% (Peterson, 2000). Whether conscious or unconscious, the legacies of slavery and a changing society have resulted in fewer African Americans marrying today than at any time in history despite their belief in the institution of marriage and an increase in affluence (Cherlin, 1992).

Without question the African American female–male marital relationship struggle has been the focus of countless magazine articles, church and convention symposiums, rap music lyrics, and many books and films written or produced by African American artists. According to African American sociologist Larry Davis, author of the best-selling book *Black and Single*, two of every three African American marriages end in divorce (Washington, 1996). In addition, according to sociologist William Julius Wilson, 22% of all married African American women are currently separated from their husbands. What's more, African Americans are the only major ethnic group in America in which more adults are single than married (Washington, 1996).

Nevertheless, the soaring divorce rate among African Americans is just the tip of the iceberg when one considers the historical legacy for which such results are rooted. Most African American men and women genuinely desire to establish and maintain a meaningful, loving relationship. To love and be loved is among the most basic of human needs. And the inability to achieve this desire certainly could contribute to the incidence of domestic violence, psychological instability, increased imprisonment of African American males, child abuse, alcoholism, substance abuse, poor physical health, HIV/AIDS, depression, and suicide presently afflicting the African American community. Given the enormity of mental affronts levied against African American women and men individually (as well as other major ethnically diverse groups) and collectively as a spousal unit, the fact is that fewer African Americans marry today than at any time in history (Cherlin, 1992). This chapter examines African American female–male marital status as a primary focus in mental health counseling. It includes a discussion of the traditional evolution of marriage for African American women and men from the African roots to its American counterpart. Additionally, this chapter highlights some stereotypes and controlling images found in African American female–male relationships and the issues that signal the need for counseling. Finally, it addresses those techniques that empower the well-being of African American female–male relationships and marriage.

The Evolution of Marriage Among African Americans

I was born in the Congo
I walked to the fertile crescent and built the sphinx
I designed a pyramid so tough that a star
That only glows every one hundred years falls
Into the center giving divine perfect light—I am bad
—*Nikki Giovanni*

A good reason to write of contemporary mental health issues for African Americans in female–male marital relationships is because, like other special groups with their own history and culture (e.g., Hispanics, Jews, Native Americans), African Americans have special issues and concerns that no one else has. And, frankly, African Americans really seem to have more than their share of issues because no other group has had to deal with the legacy of slavery in the United States—which ended 150 years ago—and the amazingly persistent cloud of relentless racism that has continued ever since. Many African Americans know these issues even if they are not always talked about, and these issues and concerns are brought along into the marriage scene whether anyone wants to bring them along or not. This difference does not necessarily make African Americans *relationship deficit* but rather *relationship different*. It is totally understandable; nevertheless, the African American struggle to be Americans has made them have to be strong and resilient even in their relationships. Blessed with resilient ancestors, who found ways to stay alive, to keep tradition intact, and, despite extraordinary adversity, to preserve some semblance of family ties, their legacy of survival is a source of inspiration. Indeed, this history should have a direct influence on how African Americans view themselves and how they relate to others. And it is this recognition of the past on present-day situations that will allow them to gain control over their destiny.

When one examines the chronological history of African Americans and the male–female relationship, it is a history of tragedy and endurance. Starting before the rape of a continent by slave traders, Africans shared a heritage of collectivism, spirituality, openness, and loyalty (Peterson, 2000). And, although European slave traffickers advanced the myth that Africans were a savage, primitive group of people, the reality is that Africans shared an advanced society many centuries before Europe began to emerge from its medieval period. For the Africans, their dominant allegiance was to the tribe—an organism with many faces but a single set of shared goals (Hopson & Hopson, 1994). The concerns of the community were the focus of every decision. All members of the tribe were part of a chain linking them both to their ancestors and to their unborn children. Generally speaking, African societies viewed marriage not only as the joining of one man with one woman but as a means of linking two extended families to expand their influence as an economic, religious, and political unit (Hopson & Hopson, 1994). Marriages could be arranged by the prospective partners or by their kin; in either case, all parties had to consent before the ceremony took place. After marriage, a couple usually lived together in an existing family compound typically comprised of a series of adjoining dwellings (Hopson & Hopson, 1994). And although monogamy was the norm, in some regions, it was accepted practice for a man to have two or more wives. When children were born in Africa, they were tended both by parents and by other kin. Aunts and uncles were expected to assume certain responsibilities, and grandparents, who were viewed as the vital links between the past and the present, held positions of special influence and honor (Willis, 1988). Within a family compound, all children were considered brothers and sisters; the distinction between cousins and siblings was largely irrelevant. Men were intimately involved with their children, especially their sons, to whom they passed down the crucial survival skills of warrior, hunter, and carpenter. Children were the center of family life within the female–male relationship to improve conditions for the next generation and to pass down an enduring heritage (Hopson & Hopson, 1994).

If the African experience is demonstrative of strength seeped in tradition, the American experience for Africans is one of a tradition of sorrow seeped in inevitable frustration. The physical and mental bondage of the heart and soul of African Americans surrounded by the brutality of slavery in the United States has cast a long shadow of struggle. There are three distinct facts concerning this history of African Americans in the United States:

1. They were not immigrants but were involuntarily taken from their African homes, violently severed from families, and brought to the United States in chains.
2. They were transported to a world of different values and traditions that were radically different from what they had known or experienced; it was a nation not of collective decision making but individualism and entrepreneurship.
3. They were, by law and by custom, denied the rights and privileges awarded to White people in the U.S. society, resulting in economic and social pressures that fostered further family fragmentation. (Akbar, 1994, p. 10)

As enslaved persons, African Americans had very little control over their own lives. William Goodell (1853) described the institution of marriage as it was viewed by the slaveholders for African Americans:

The slave has no rights, of course, he or she cannot have the rights of a husband a wife. The slave is a chattel and chattels do not marry. The slave is not ranked among sentient beings, but among things, and things are not married. (p. 9)

Goodell continued in his graphic description of slave marriage relationships:

The obligations of marriage are evidently inconsistent with the conditions of slavery, and cannot be performed by a slave. The husband promises to protect his wife and provide for her. The wife promises to be the helpmeet of her husband. They mutually promise to live with and cherish each other, 'til parted by death. But what can such promises by slaves mean? The legal relation of master and slave renders them void! It forbids the slave to protect even himself. It clothes his master with authority to bid him inflict deadly blows on the woman he has sworn to protect. It prohibits his possession of any property wherewith to sustain her . . . it gives master unlimited control and full possession of her own person, and forbids her, on pains of death, to resist him, if he drags her to his bed! It severs the plighted pair at the will of their masters, occasionally or forever. (p. 10)

Ultimately, the African American man was evaluated by his ability to endure strenuous work and to produce children. He was viewed by the slave master as a stud—or having the ability to impregnate a woman—and a workhorse to the degree of his physical strength (Akbar, 1994). The African American woman was valued primarily as a breeder or sexual receptacle to show the capacity to have healthy children. Her worth as a human being was reduced to the particular financial value or personal pleasure she could hold for the master (Akbar, 1994). These historical images, which African Americans have inherited, appear to continue to sabotage many efforts for true manhood (fatherhood) and womanhood (motherhood). Though the current attitudes and conditions (e.g., unemployment) may feed these patterns and keep them growing, the origins of the African American female–male relationship issues seem to rest in the plague of slavery.

Stereotypes and Controlling Images of African American Female–Male Relationships

Take a day to heal from the lies you've told yourself and that have been told to you.
—*Maya Angelou*

I believe it is important in a discussion of marriage within the African American community to highlight the stereotypical views of African American women and men because, too often, these images penetrate how individuals may see their mates and influence how they interpret what they do and mean to do. More importantly, one of the strongest challenges in creating and sustaining a positive marriage is to be able to see your mate for who she or he is—not for what the latest situation comedy, rap video, or book by a racist may depict.

Racism

Racism is a judicious and often underestimated factor in the stress that can occur in female–male marital relationships for African Americans. The forms of racism range from ignorance, to unjust treatment, to blatant acts of hatred and violence. The results are that those on the receiving end can become angry, hostile, bitter, or frustrated (Gollnick & Chinn, 1998). Or it could subtly wear away at one's personhood, leaving one distrustful of others or even of one's self. The insidious nature of racism is the fact that when it is subtle, it can be disguised and difficult to realize at times; this creates many levels of stress that is difficult to understand and endure. For example, a couple who is house-hunting can be "directed" by some real estate agents to certain communities or presented with apparently insurmountable problems with getting a home loan. Or racial profiling while driving a vehicle because one fits the supposed description of people who traffic in drugs or commit crimes creates a daily dose of stress that can tear at a relationship. Or the gender-based racism of employers offering more opportunities to African American women than African American men can be difficult for African American men as they seek employment.

Realizing these subtle and not-so-subtle situations can serve as a psychological chain that the African American couple, and particularly the African American male, can take home with them as a measure to be overcome (Akbar, 1994). Major for African American men is the preconceived notion by Whites that African American men do not work hard and are always late or that, regardless of qualifications, if a man is to get the job he should be

White. Another form of stress for African American men is the common fear of Whites, especially White women, that they should feel fear of physical harm toward all African American men (Hopson & Hopson, 1994). Knowledge of such racist beliefs can be a hurtful challenge for African American men. Understanding the doubts and trying to be objective to eliminate all other explanations can be tough. But, the result is that all of these subtle or obvious situations build to produce frustration and uncertainty about the world in which African Americans must walk. In relationships, African Americans need to have the presence of mind and strength to put the racist acts of the world into perspective.

Racism can also enter into the female–male relationship when individuals have a Eurocentric perception of beauty. Many African American males and females define beauty as long hair, blue eyes, and light skin. A regular display of a media image of White women has subtly sent the message in such a way that African American men may expect African American women to act like White women (Akbar, 1994). In the same regard, some African American women want their men to act like White men—buy them a house in the suburbs, own two cars, and vacation in the Bahamas once a year. All of these instances serve to highlight that it is important not to underestimate the impact that racism has had on the stability of African American female–male relationships.

Sexism

Beyond the impact of racism, sexism has an equally severe impact on relationships for African American women and men. One of every two husbands physically abuses his wife (Kunjufu, 1993). But, the issue of date and marital rape has until recently rarely been discussed primarily because of male privilege. Sexism is expressed in multiple ways—from some rappers who cannot produce a complete song without denigrating African American women to the words used by many African American men to describe their sexual exploits. Sexism is beliefs in the inherent superiority of one sex over all others and thereby the right to dominance (Lorde, 1995). Often this type of gender discrimination is practiced by individuals in personal situations of marriage and family life. As a result, there are statistics that say a female with a college degree has a 10% greater chance of divorce if she is engaged in a female–male marital relationship. If she has 2 years of graduate school or pursues a PhD, the rate increases to 19% (Kunjufu, 1993).

Bill Cosby illustrates the role of sexism and power and their dynamics in a relationship when he wrote:

> If any man truly believes that he is the boss of the house, then let him do this: pick up the phone, call a wallpaper store, order new wallpaper for one of the rooms in his house, and then put it on. He would have a longer life expectancy sprinkling arsenic on his eggs. Any husband who buys wallpaper, drapes, or even a prayer rug on his own is auditioning for the Bureau of Missing Persons. (Cosby, 1989, pp. 158–159)

Financial Burdens

Economic pressures in relationships are by no means a new concept. In 1920, 90% of African American children lived with their fathers. In 1960, about 80% of African American children lived at home with both parents. In the 1990s, the number of African American children living with both parents has dropped to a low 38% (Kunjufu, 1993). It would be naive not to understand the direct parallels in the economic changes from agriculture, to manufacturing, to high technology and the role these play in female–male marital relationships for African Americans. It is difficult to stay together or maintain relationships when economic resources become scarce. In a capitalistic society in which money is a means of exchange as well as an indicator of power and self-esteem for so many, money further serves as a vehicle to express values and control. Thus, one of the major issues in female–male relationships is money and who controls it (Hopson & Hopson, 1994).

There is a real need for most African Americans to work—not only one but two jobs in an effort to stay ahead of the bills and live at a desirable level. The difficulty in this behavior in relation to the female–male marital status is that it leaves less time for families and relationships. In helping the family or spouse situation, a vacuum of time is created. To complicate the issues, African Americans are bombarded with media images of "the great life." But the path to obtaining that life is not accessible for many. Transitioning from a low socioeconomic level to a middle-class status can create a cycle of working to have more but not saving or having money at the end of the month (Peterson, 2000).

Additional pressures can be brought into the relationship by the varying perspectives of the individuals. For example, some will think that playing the lottery is how they can strike it rich. Others may think about using insurance money from an accident or suing someone as the avenue to financial gain. Still others may think that as African Americans, they will never be rich. But, historically, because men have been perceived as the major breadwinners, they oftentimes feel that they should be able to control all of the movements, lifestyle, and expenditures of their spouse (Hopson & Hopson, 1994). However, as more and more women enter the workplace because of the aforementioned issues of gender-based racism, this creates a greater tension between African American men and women when they allow themselves to be defined by money (D. W. Sue & Sue, 1999).

In this way, issues of money and the ideas of financial success are in part tied to the historical racism in the United States. African Americans realize not only that it is hard for them to get and keep a job but also how difficult it is to obtain a job at the same wages or with the same opportunities of advancement as Whites. The reality is that African Americans still endure unemployment at greater rates than other ethnically diverse groups (Gollnick & Chinn, 1998). Also, labor statistics show that they make less than Whites in every white-collar occupational category (e.g., clerical, technical, administrative, professional) with the difference sometimes ranging from a few hundred to several thousand dollars per year (Whitfield, Markman, Stanley, & Blumberg, 2001).

Other issues of finances can be found in how a couple chooses to handle their money. Whether one person is delegated as the manager of the money or whether the couple chooses to establish separate accounts with a "joint pot" to which each contributes to pay bills, spouses may feel that they do not have enough connections in how the money is to be spent. Such financial struggles can easily and eventually escalate into major relationship battles.

Myths and Lies

The media-induced, consistently negative portrayals and images of African Americans are shaping the images not only of the opposite sex but of themselves as well—and not for the better. "The things that keep [African American] women and men apart," said Rutgers University professor of psychology Nancy Boyd-Franklin (1998, p. 235), "are partly external but are also partly our own internalization of negative, victimizing messages about each other that have been laid upon us by a Eurocentric society." America has historically demeaned African American intelligence, morals, and physical attributes through literature and the printed and now electronic media. In place of reality, White America, or what some have referred to as "White supremacist ideology," has presented negative, stereotypical images of African Americans and their culture (Washington, 1996). African American men are often portrayed as big, dumb, and abusive, with incorrigible criminal minds. By the same token, African American women are projected as devious, promiscuous Jezebels, prostitutes, or welfare mothers with a house full of dependent children (Washington, 1996).

This systematic negative portrait is older than America itself and helped to justify slavery, colonization, and discrimination. Even today, virtually every major newspaper and magazine in the country have presented stories about claims that African Americans are genetically less intelligent than Whites. *Newsweek* magazine even used the book *The Bell Curve*, by Richard Herrnstein and Charles Murray (1994), for a cover story. But, the fact that many eminent scientists had found Murray's analysis seriously flawed did not prevent the media from publicizing this recurring stereotype.

Additionally, the negative depictions of the African American physical body have flourished. The eyes and skin are too dark, noses are too flat, lips and hips are too large, and even the hair is too kinky. At the same time, though, the blond-haired, blue-eyed White woman became the subtle standard of beauty and was rendered goddess status in advertisements, magazines, movies, and television programs. Even more challenging are the glaring omissions that can be found regularly in major newspapers and television programs that are far more preoccupied with African American failure than their achievement (D. Sue, 1994).

This consistent lack of positive imagery is psychologically devastating to African Americans and their own female–male relationships. If African American men or women have contempt for themselves because of their racial identity, how can they love and cherish another African American? In fact, negative myths and lies abound. For example, many African American men espouse the following opinions about African American women: "[Black] women keep scorecards and measure your assets and job titles," "They don't allow us to be ourselves, they want to remake us," "Today, a lot of [Black] women are going for White men," "[Black] women don't respect brothers unless they live up to the materialistic image of a man put out by White society," and "It's sad that some of our sisters . . . will do anything for money and fame." Likewise, African American women have strongly held beliefs about African American men. For example, "There are no good [Black] men available," "So many brothers are unemployed because they are lazy," "The shortage of [Black] men has made them think of themselves as a prize," "[Black] men, in general, are extremely sexist," and "A brother will drop a sister for a White woman in a second."

The irony of these stereotypical images held by so many African Americans about their own folk is that African Americans have been fighting against such negativism and self-hatred ideas since day one in America. Today, these most cruel of myths are still being perpetuated, albeit modernized, updated, and improved. Unfortunately, far too many African American females and males find it exceedingly difficult to love or respect their brothers and sisters—or themselves for that matter. "Can genuine human relationships flourish for [African American] people in a society that assaults [African American] intelligence, moral character and possibility?" (Washington, 1996).

Counseling Issues

For every one of us that succeeds, it's because there's somebody there to show you the way out.
—*Oprah Winfrey*

Have you ever seen a couple who seems happy all the time? They look so in love and do not ever appear to have a difference of opinion or problems relating to each other. One might wonder if they even have the same life situation and problems as the rest of the world. The reality is that they do have problems and issues. But, they have either learned to hide them well or found productive ways to address them. As with Rodney and Marilyn, discussed earlier, you may also know couples who do well for many years and then have major problems. This is because the nature of problems that occur in a marriage can change over time.

In the past, relationship norms in the African American community reflected the realities of African American family life (D. W. Sue & Sue, 1999). For example, often professional African American women married blue-collar men without regard for who earned the most money or had the best education. And many African American women—unlike their White counterparts—have always worked outside the home. As discussed previously, African American female–male marital relationships face unique challenges. Today, African Americans desperately need to define their own relationship norms as they did in the past. Issues of money, power, racism, and sex may simmer at the core of every relationship, influencing the way one responds to crisis and manipulating the behaviors that are exhibited. Too many African Americans are using Eurocentric values as the yardstick to evaluate each other. These values, however, do not take into account the tremendous odds that the average African American woman or man has to overcome to achieve even a modest amount of success in America. And though there are common problems, a particular one may sometimes be smaller or larger than at other times. Because African American male–female relationships are dynamic and influenced by others as well as the changes in roles in the success of a couple, they may experience a need to problem solve. In this case, assertive communication is an effective tool for diffusing the tension often associated with jobs, money, racism, and sexism (Willis, 1990).

When one sees and understands how the outside world affects the marital relationship for African American women and men, it is easy to see how counseling can become an issue. Feeling trapped in a complex web of conflict, confusion, mistrust, misdirected anger, and doubt, they may not understand how the web got spun and are at a loss at how to extricate themselves. All too often, people approach problems as if their partner were an enemy to be conquered (Wilson & Stith, 1991). They may approach problems as if there must be a winner and a loser, and no one wants to be a loser. Looking for love, they may not realize that they must first begin the search within themselves. In fact, the first stage of healing the divisions between African American women and men involves doing some hard work on each other (D. W. Sue & Sue, 1999). By confronting the past, one can begin to understand the damage inflicted by negative images, painful experiences, and racism.

Counseling and therapy as a tool for attaining self-knowledge and confronting conflict may be unfamiliar and threatening to many African American couples. Usually African Americans will go to their minister, a close friend, or relatives (Cherlin, 1992). Many will even confide in their family physician rather than think of going to a mental health specialist. They may have been raised to believe that admitting troubles is a betrayal. Like other historically oppressed groups, many believe counseling to be like "airing dirty laundry" with the fear that others will use it against them. The thought of talking about personal things to a stranger may cause others to hesitate to seek professional counseling or think of it as only a last-resort measure in a time of crisis (Hopson & Hopson, 1994).

Nevertheless, some of this is changing. The whole country is becoming more sophisticated about using therapists, and as mental health services become more demystified and have fewer stigmas, the use should grow. But, a needed advantage would be to have culturally sensitive counselors work to persuade African Americans to feel best about who they are as individuals (D. W. Sue & Sue, 1999). They will need to assist African American couples to nurture ancestral traditions while respecting their connections with America and learning to relate comfortably with people of different heritages (Hopson & Hopson, 1994). The key to maintaining successful personal and work relationships is to be genuinely respectful of one another's traditions and the perspectives they provide while acknowledging and accepting the differences and viewing them as a source of strength, not a reason for divisiveness.

> Selena was a successful businesswoman who had developed her own small-scale real estate business from scratch. She had been raised to believe that equal opportunities were available if the individual was willing to work hard. Selena dislikes being referred to as the "African American real estate woman" in her town of about 12% African American population. When she decided to seek counseling, she said her husband's strong sense of ethnicity made her feel uncomfortable. A lawyer, he constantly wanted to decorate their home with African statues, he only listened to jazz, and he insisted on calling himself an African American. She perceived that this obsession of his jeopardized their marital relationship.
>
> Selena claimed that she was at ease with her own racial identity but felt it was something to accept rather than emphasize. When she discussed her upbringing, it was obvious that some conflicts remained unresolved. Her mother, in an effort to steer her daughter toward success and away from the gangs in the streets of her neighborhood, taught Selena that assimilation was the best way to achieve material success. Yet, Selena admitted a stronger attraction to Black-identified men. In time, she began to understand that it was not necessary to minimize the importance of her African heritage or to immerse herself exclusively in things associated with African Americans, as if she had to prove something. Having previously assumed that she had to come down firmly in the camp of either the African American or White world, Selena found duality to be a real awakening that strengthened her relationship with her spouse.

As illustrated in this case study, there is widespread agreement among licensed African American therapists and counselors that the first step toward building emotional well-being and healthy relationships is self-knowledge (D. W. Sue & Sue, 1999). This is an age-old concept and is repeated in many world religions, philosophies, and literature.

Techniques That Empower the Emotional Well-Being of African American Female–Male Relationships and Marriage

In the previous case description of Selena, her ability to seek counseling was empowering for Selena and contributed to her well-being as an individual and in her relationship with her husband. It was an indicator of strength and courage—not an admission of weakness. Her willingness to explore the issues, learn more about herself, confront awkward or unpleasant truths, and work toward change was symbolic of the fight for healthy African American female–male relationships.

In the area of female–male relationships for African Americans, the topic of communication is probably the most needy area for the well-being of any relationship (D. W. Sue & Sue, 1999). Although many African American couples may be great communicators in every other instance, they seem to have never learned to communicate well when it comes to conflict. But clear communication is critical to the future of any relationship. We have all experienced the frustration of being misunderstood. One may think one is being clear, but the partner just does not seem to get it. Or one is just sure that one knows what was said yesterday, but today what is being said is something different.

Filters change what goes through them. For example, a furnace filter takes dust and dirt out of the air. A filter on a camera lens alters the properties of the light filtering through. A coffee filter lets the flavor through and leaves the grinds behind. As with any other filter, what goes into our communication filters is different from what comes out. Everyone has a style of communicating, and differing styles can lead to filtering. As in my own marriage, one of us is expressive and the other is more reserved. Because of this, we have challenges understanding each other because we use and understand such different styles. Styles are determined by many influences, including gender and upbringing (Gollnick & Chinn, 1998). Sometimes, differences in style, rooted in family backgrounds, can cause great misunderstanding, becoming a powerful filter that distorts communication. Effective counseling techniques emphasize that filters can affect couples as they struggle for clear communication.

One way to do this is to use agreed-upon strategies and techniques to help during the important conversations. This added structure to the interaction is exactly what is done all the time in work and political settings. Recently I had the opportunity to speak on a panel session for the Congressional Black Caucus. While there, I thought about the things I had considered in writing this chapter. Consider for a moment what a typical session of the Congressional Black Caucus would look like if the members did not agree on the rules of how and when things can be shared. With the appropriate structure, there is less opportunity to damage relationships and more chances to manage conflict.

The goal of most relationships should be to establish intimacy. But in African American relationships, the goal is not to get hurt, not to be used. There has been so much hurt in previous experiences, African Americans begin to take a self-protective stance that gets in the way of their getting close and healing as a couple. So the partners are suspicious of others and afraid of being manipulated. Somebody is always trying to place blame for problems that come up. But, there is no right and wrong—there are good choices and bad choices, and good things happen when one makes good choices and bad things happen when one makes bad choices. The empowering technique advises that one is not wrong if one makes a bad choice, one just needs to make another choice (Willis, 1990). This releases the "blame game" and allows the couple to negotiate and come together.

As African Americans, what may be needed is to look at healthy ways to be together. The beginning of that is dialogue or communication. Sitting down regularly—on a weekly or monthly basis—and talking to each other about our pain, about our joy, about our anger, about our fears, and about our frustration is healthy. And this will need to occur on a large scale and soon in order to stay the destructive forces that exist.

Summary

The history of African American relationships from slavery until today profiles relationship "role models" and "villains." It represents the best and the worse in the relationship struggle. This chapter has attempted to highlight some of the key issues and the factors that make maintaining a healthy relationship so difficult. These issues range from economic pressures, racial discrimination, sexism, financial burdens, and the myths and lies that continue to persevere in the growing dilemmas faced by African American female–male marital relationships. As an educator and not a counselor, I have sought to offer encouragement that empowers the emotional well-being for these relationships. And if, in fact, African American marriages are in trouble just as they are for the rest of the people in the United States, it is my belief that it does not have to stay that way. With the know-how of prepared culturally sensitive counselors and the will of determined couples, there stands a good chance of making good things happen. It is my further belief that one cannot prevent marriage from being hard work at times, but if the individuals can work hard together, they can make their relationship the kind that deepens and grows over the years, whatever comes their way.

References

Akbar, N. (1994). *Chains and images of psychological slavery.* Jersey City, NJ: New Mind Productions.

Boyd-Franklin, N. (1998). *Black families in therapy: A multisystems approach.* New York: Guilford Press.

Cherlin, W. W. (1992). *Marriage, divorce, remarriage.* Cambridge, MA: Harvard University Press.

Cosby, B. (1989). *Love and marriage.* New York: Doubleday.

Gladding, S. T. (2002). *Family therapy: History, theory, and practice* (3rd ed.). Columbus, OH: Merrill Prentice Hall.

Gollnick, D. M., & Chinn, P. C. (1998). *Multicultural education in a pluralistic society* (5th ed.). Columbus, OH: Merrill.

Goodell, W. (1853). *The American slave code.* New York: American and Foreign Anti-Slavery Society.

Herrnstein, R. J., & Murray, C. (1994). *The bell curve: Intelligence and class structure in American life.* New York: Free Press.

Hopson, D. S., & Hopson, D. P. (1994). *Friends, lovers, and soul mates: A guide to better relationships between Black men and women.* New York: Simon & Schuster.

Kunjufu, J. (1993). *The power, passion and pain of Black love.* Chicago: African American Images.

Lorde, A. (1995). Age, race, class, and sex: Women redefining difference. In J. Arthur & A. Shapiro (Eds.), *Campus wars: Multiculturalism and the politics of difference* (pp. 191–198). Boulder, CO: Westview Press.

Peterson, K. S. (2000, March 8). Black couples stay the course. *USA Today*, p. 8D.

Sue, D. (1994, Spring). Incorporating cultural diversity in family therapy. *The Family Psychologist, 10,* 19–21.

Sue, D. W., & Sue, D. (1999). *Counseling the culturally different* (3rd ed.). New York: Wiley.

Turner, W. L. (1993, April). Identifying African-American family strengths. *Family Therapy News, 24,* 9, 14.

Washington, E. (1996). *Uncivil war: The struggle between Black men and women.* Chicago: Noble Press.

Whitfield, K. E., Markman, H. J., Stanley, S. M., & Blumberg, S. L. (2001). *Fighting for your African American marriage.* San Francisco: Jossey-Bass.

Willis, J. T. (1988). An effective counseling model for treating the Black family. *Family Therapy, 15,* 185–194.

Willis, J. T. (1990). Some destructive elements in African-American male–female relationships. *Family Therapy, 17,* 139–147.

Wilson, L. L., & Stith, S. M. (1991). Cultural sensitive therapy with Black clients. *Journal of Multicultural Counseling and Development, 19,* 32–34.

Section II

Special Issues

To open this section on special issues, in chapter 6 Middleton presents an intriguing chapter on the psychological well-being of African American elders. African American elders witnessed many historical changes, both negative and positive. These events included wars, movement from agricultural and automation to technology, and personal tragedies including ethnocentrism, segregation, lynching and other unprecedented acts of violence, racial hate crimes, death, and bereavement. In spite of these events, this group exhibited resiliency that might include some degree of denial. The major concern is, how do African American elders manage to deal with their traumatic events without mental health counseling? The suggested therapy implications must include cultural and economic factors significant to the lives of the elderly African American.

In chapter 7, Savage and Harley address lesbian, gay, and bisexual African Americans. They take on a topic that is very much neglected in the professional literature. Much can be gained from this chapter as the authors present an in-depth discussion of identity development and sexual identity development. They also explore intriguing concerns of many individuals in this group. Unlike other groups discussed in this volume, African American lesbian, gay, and bisexual individuals are faced with both racism and discrimination because of their sexual orientations. The chapter contains well-developed implications and recommendations for providing counseling to members of this group.

The impact of HIV and AIDS on different subgroups of African Americans has been striking. Many African American men and women are affected with this disease. In chapter 8, Nelson presents an excellent discussion of HIV and AIDS among African Americans and their involvement in the Black church. The Black church is a highly respected institution in the Black community that is often viewed as a change agent for social justice. Nelson describes the effects of homophobia within the Black church and the psychosocial behaviors among its members. There are community counseling and health care services for those facing HIV/AIDS. Well-developed sections presenting practical implications for therapy with HIV/AIDS clients and future research are also included.

Another issue among African Americans is alcohol use and abuse. Alcohol use can develop into a personal problem for some individuals who drink excessively without self-control, whereas others are able to handle their drinking habits relatively well. In chapter 9 Harley notes that fewer African Americans use alcohol as part of their lifestyles compared with their White counterparts. Alcohol abuse is one of the potential cognitive and behavioral coping responses to a stressful circumstance.

There are several barriers to mental health treatment that attribute to African Americans' underutilization of mental health services. Harley calls for prevention and intervention strategies for reducing African Americans' dependency on alcohol use. And because alcohol abuse continues, suggested research implications are presented.

The final chapter in this section includes identity among biracial and multiracial individuals who identify as African Americans. Recent research on this topic suggests that the number of mixed marriages and interracial dating are steadily increasing. In chapter 10, Constantine and her colleagues present an extensive examination of the many concerns involved in the sometimes complex biracial or multiracial identity process. Biracial and multiracial African Americans attain the advantage of psychological preparedness against ethnocentrism through exposure to racial identity socializing agents. An excellent discussion is presented on the biracial and multiracial identity development models. Several suggestions are made for mental health professionals who work with biracial and multiracial clients with identity concerns.

6

Mental Health Challenges of African American Elders: Issues, Interventions, and Cultural Considerations

Renée A. Middleton

What is the state of the art of counseling and psychotherapy for elder African Americans in today's society? What are the pressing personal problems encountered by African American elders, and how might they be solved through counseling and psychotherapy? How do African American elders work through psychological trauma? What is the role of the counselor in advocating for the rights, mental health, or otherwise of older/elder adults? These questions seem worth asking and answering for older Americans in general; however, because older African Americans often experience multiple binds of ageism, racism, poverty, disabilityism, and in the case of females, sexism (Middleton, Rollins, Flowers, & Crow, 1997), these questions seem particularly relevant for this population. Many African American elders who are on the receiving end of these multiple binds may show evidence of vulnerability; however, more often than not, in spite of these vulnerabilities they are highly resilient people who have survived devastating life experiences. Perhaps this is a sign that mental health organizations should consider using a strengths/resiliency model.

There is a growing literature arguing for the value of the strengths perspective/resilience enhancement paradigm in clinical practice. This chapter focuses on addressing these questions from a multicultural and social action perspective. I examine resiliency as a strength-based multicultural counseling approach. Additionally, the resolve of elder African Americans is examined for characteristics that provide insight into their mental health resiliency. The chapter concludes with recommendations for the counseling profession on how it might play a more vital role as a catalyst for change, working both with and on behalf of older persons in general, and African Americans in particular.

Within the older adult population itself, there are important differences between the various age segments and ethnic/racial groups in terms of their health and socioeconomic characteristics. Therefore, the reader will first be provided with general population demographics for older adults in an effort to highlight and contrast the enormity of the challenges specific to African Americans. Further, I take a comparative futuristic look at what might be expected in relation to the needs of the elderly of today and tomorrow. However, prior to engaging in these discussions, it is important to understand how I use the terms *older adults, elder, elderly,* and *ageism.*

Population Descriptors and Demographics

A first step in establishing services for older adults is that of defining the population. Many agencies and programs use 65 as their definition of the aged or older adults (Blake, 1981). For example, the Social Security Act of 1935 established age 65 as the age of retirement, thus establishing this stage in life as old age (Ganikos, 1979). According to Wray (1992), current health and social policies often identify people chronologically as follows: younger-old (ages 65 to 74), old (ages 75 to 84), and older-old or elderly (age 85 and above). While one's chronological age is useful in determining eligibility for certain services, our greatest concern should be with capabilities or potential rather than with limitations set arbitrarily because of age (Blake, 1981). Additionally, different cultures mark entrance into older age through social changes such as becoming grandparents, retirement, or functional status rather than chronological age. Therefore, people may be recognized as elders at widely divergent ages—as early as 40 for some Southeast Asian and Native American groups (Wray, 1992). Consequently, beyond chronological age, an individual who is "old" may be defined as one who accepts the stereotypes of aging or ageism, or eventually experiences physical, emotional, or a psychological breakdown because of that acceptance (Middleton & McDaniel, 1990). Although chronological age may be a necessary component, it is not an automatic prerequisite for classification, nor is it the most important criterion. Rather, the emphasis is on the individual's attitude and overall adjustment toward his or her own aging.

In this chapter I use the terms *older* and *elder* synonymously, generally to describe the population of individuals who are 65 years of age or older. However, use of the term *elder* is not synonymous with the term *elderly*. The term *elder* is used to refer to any individual who is held in high respect who is older than the person using the term in reference to another. Use of the term *elderly* is restricted to referencing individuals who are 85 years of age or older. Finally, one cannot make reference to the aging population in America without defining ageism in America. *Ageism* is the general prejudice in both attitude and treatment toward individuals based on chronological age (Myers, 1990). Ageism is similar in nature to racism, sexism, disabilityism, and other -isms. To the extent that mental health practitioners observe that their clients are victims of ageism, either intentionally or unintentionally, practitioners have a responsibility to intervene in some capacity. More importantly, we must ensure that as mental health practitioners, we are not responsible for perpetrating ageist acts or attitudes.

The Nation's Aging: General Population Demographics

The number of people 65 years and over increased by a factor of 11, from 3.1 million in 1900 to 33.2 million in 1994 (U.S. Census Bureau, 1995). To be sure, the surge that has been seen up to now will pale in comparison with what the future is expected to bring. The number of people 65 years and over could more than double by 2050 to 80 million. About one in eight Americans were elderly in 1994, but about one in five could be elderly by the year 2030 (U.S. Census Bureau, 1993). For older adults in general, better health care, diets, and lifestyles have been prolonging life expectancies for decades, resulting in a remarkable increase in the number of people living past age 70, 80, and even 90. The age group 85 and over is projected to be the fastest growing part of the elder population throughout the rest of this century. According to Census Bureau middle series projections, the population age 85 and over will more than double, from 3 million in 1990 to 7 million in 2020. This group will again double in size to 14 million by 2040, as the survivors of the baby-boom cohort reach the oldest ages (U.S. Census Bureau, 1993).

The elderly population is predominantly European American. European Americans represent a higher proportion of elderly than any other racial group largely because they have a better rate of survival to age 65 as well as a lower recent fertility. Further, immigration may be a contributing factor. The proportion of European American immigrants over the past 30 years has declined. However, one can expect to see more racial diversity within America's elderly population in the coming years. With this in mind with respect to the general population of older adults, it provides a reference point for discussing African American elders in particular.

The Nation's Aging: African American Elders

African Americans have primarily entered the United States from the Caribbean and Africa through the slave trade. Consequently, African Americans are likely to be of mixed ethnic heritage, including American Indian and Northern European elements (Baker, 1994). According to the U.S. Census Bureau (1993), of the 80.1 million people age 65 and older projected for the year 2050, 8.4 million will be African Americans. Comparatively, 6.7 million will be races other than White or Black, and 12.5 million will be Latino/Latina Americans (Mexican Americans, Central and South Americans, Puerto Ricans, Cubans, and other Hispanic groups). The African American population 85 years and over is projected to increase from 223,000 in 1990 to 1.4 million by 2050. African Americans have accounted for a smaller share of the 85-and-over population in recent census than in earlier census.

To better understand this population, I discuss issues of longevity and general health characteristics of the African American elder. Additionally, specific mental health challenges among this population are addressed. While frequent demographic comparisons among other racial groups are made, I recognize that some subgroups among African American elders are potentially more at risk than others. Three of those groups—rural African Americans, African American women, and older-aged African Americans—are discussed later in this chapter.

Longevity and General Health Characteristics

We face numerous questions raised by the growth and increasing longevity of the older population. According to Perry (1993), some of the most urgent are the following: Will tomorrow's generation of older people be healthy? Will they be independent? Will societies provide productive and purposeful roles for them? Many assume health among older adults has improved because more are living longer. Others hold a contradictory image of older adults, particularly the elderly, as dependent and frail. Neither view is completely accurate.

In 1991, life expectancy at birth reached a record high of 75.5 years. Life expectancy at birth is defined as the average number of years a person would live given the age-specific mortality rates of a specified year or period (Taeuber & Taeuber, 1971). In 1991, the life expectancy at birth for European American men compared with African American men was 72.9 and 64.6 years of age, respectively, and 79.6 and 73.8 years of age for European American women and African American women, respectively. This racial/ethnic gap in life expectancy persists at 65 years and 75 years of age. Under the mortality conditions of 1991, at age 85, African American women would live an additional 6.3 years and African American men 5.1 years. Just as for life expectancy at birth, African American women can still expect to live longer than African American men (U.S. Census Bureau, 1993).

The three major causes of death among older adults in 1991 were heart disease, cancer, and stroke. These three major causes of death were responsible for 7 of every

10 deaths in older adults in 1991. Smoking has been associated with all three major causes of death. Men are more likely to smoke and to smoke more heavily than women. Men, however, are relatively more likely to have quit smoking than women. Elderly African American men are about twice as likely as elderly European American men to be a current smoker (National Center for Health Statistics, 1994). Smoking is known to be a high risk factor for certain types of cancer. Additionally, the rates of hypertension are especially high among elderly African Americans.

The U.S. Census Bureau (2001b) reported that African Americans and Hispanic Americans suffer from hypertension at a rate of 59% and 11%, respectively, greater than their White counterparts. However, African American women appear to have a higher incidence of hypertension, heart disease, and stroke than African American men (Dancy & Ralston, 2002).

In general, aging African Americans are more likely to suffer from complications of diabetes (e.g., vision problems, renal problems, and amputations). It has been noted that diabetes is the fourth leading cause of death among African American women (Rajaram & Vinson, 1998), and they have higher mortality rates for breast cancer than European American women (Adderley-Kelly & Green, 1997).

AIDS is another issue on the health care front. In recent years, increased attention has been given to children dying of AIDS. Yet, in 1992, nearly three times as many people age 60 years and over died of AIDS as did people under 20 years of age (National Center for Health Statistics, 1994). The number of people age 60 years and over who died from AIDS nearly doubled during the 5-year period from 1987 to 1992. As the AIDS rate continues to grow among African Americans, these rates are likely to increase significantly among older African Americans.

Many of these health care challenges can become very debilitating. For older adults, performing ordinary activities of daily living may be problematic. Difficulty in performing personal care tasks and home management tasks are referred to as *functional limitations*. These are measures of ability to live independently and are used as indicators of the need for health services.

The scale used to measure the ability to perform physical tasks related to personal care is called the Activities of Daily Living (ADLs; Wiener, Hanley, Clark, & Van Nostrand, 1990). Most lists include activities such as eating, bathing, dressing, toileting, and getting in or out of a bed or chair. An additional commonly used measure, the Instrumental Activities of Daily Living (IADLs), measures more complex tasks, including handling personal finances, preparing meals, shopping, doing housework, traveling, using the telephone, and taking medications.

The need for personal assistance with everyday activities increases with age. The extent of need for personal assistance with everyday activities is an indicator of need for health and social services. At older ages, the percentage requiring assistance ranged from 9% of those age 65 to 69 up to 50% for those age 85 or older. Elderly African Americans (25.2%) and Latino/Latina Americans (25.3%) are more likely than European Americans (17.1%) to need assistance. Hing and Bloom (1990) defined *functional dependency* as people dependent on at least one of seven ADLs or seven IADLs. From this definition, the rate of functional dependency was higher among elderly African Americans than European Americans. Among the population 65 years and over, 59% of African Americans had one or more functional limitations compared with 49% of European Americans. The limitations were more likely to be severe among elderly African Americans as 40% had limitations that were severe compared with 27% of elderly European Americans.

Given these particulars, perhaps the single most significant development in the counseling profession is the issue of serving aging Americans with various chronic health conditions, in particular aging racial/ethnic groups. Legislation such as the 1990 Americans With Disabilities Act (ADA) and current counseling practices must extend service provisions to increase general health services and opportunities for this growing population. What about mental health issues and services?

Mental Health Issues and Challenges

Older adults are as vulnerable as younger people to the most prevalent mental health disorders in our population: depression, anxiety, and alcohol abuse. Unfortunately, less is known about these disorders than about acquired cognitive disorders such as dementia and delirium in the elder population (Kelley, 2003). Inconclusive evidence exists regarding the influence of race or ethnicity on psychological well-being and mental health.

There has been an increase in research on ethnicity and mental health; however, scholars are not in agreement on exactly how culture, ethnic, and racial status influence psychopathology. However, culture and ethnicity remain relevant and important in mental health (Kales et al., 2000). Much of the literature approaches the subject from a social stress or social causation perspective commonly evoked to account for greater psychopathology among the lower social classes, a finding documented in a variety of community surveys and other studies of psychiatric epidemiology (Blazer, Hays, & Salive, 1996; Cutrona, Russell, Hessling, Brown, & Murry, 2000; Dancy & Ralston, 2002; Kessler & Cleary, 1980).

For some African American elders who have limited economical resources, there is a greater possibility that they will be exposed to a larger number of stressors and also are likely to have fewer psychological and social resources for coping with stress. Likewise one might expect that, for some African American elders, race can be expected to affect levels of mental disorder because they experience more stressful events and also because segments of this population may have fewer resources for dealing with stress (Glasgow & Brown, 1998).

In a study by Cook, Pearson, Thompson, Black, and Rabins (2002), the frequency of suicidality and associated characteristics in a sample of 835 African American older adult residents of six urban public housing developments was assessed. The frequency of passive and active suicidal ideation was 2.5% and 1.4%, respectively. Characteristics of individuals with both active and passive suicidality included elevated anxiety, social dysfunction, somatic symptoms, low social support, lack of a confidant, and low religiosity. Characteristics of those with passive, but not active, ideation also included older age, lower levels of education, elevated depressive symptoms, poorer cognitive functioning, and having recently discussed emotional problems with a health care provider.

Kales et al. (2000) evaluated the impact of race on mental health care utilization among older patients within given clinical psychiatric diagnoses. Kales et al. identified that significant racial differences in mental health care utilization found over a subsequent 2-year period were related to outpatient (but not inpatient) care. For example, African American patients with psychotic disorders had significantly fewer outpatient psychiatric visits, and African American patients with substance abuse disorders had significantly more psychiatric visits than European American patients in their respective groups. Kales et al. believed the differences were likely due to such factors as compliance, treatment efficacy, access to health care, or possible clinician bias.

Although discrimination and exclusion are important mechanisms potentially capable of exacerbating or leading to greater psychological disorders among African American elders, an additional concept that has special relevance to immigrant groups is migration and the resulting acculturative stress (Markides, 1986). These acculturative stresses may be due to clinician bias or a lack of understanding of behaviors and cultural practices among descendants of Africa (Caribbean, Haiti, Africa, etc.) who migrate into the United States. Behaviors and health practices consistent with their culture may be viewed as deviant and assessed as a mental disorder or illness.

Misdiagnosis as a specific cause of differential rates of clinical psychiatric diagnosis in elderly patients has been supported by several studies (Baker, 1995; Coleman & Baker, 1994; Kales et al., 2000). Coleman and Baker (1994), in a Veterans Affairs setting, found that seven of eight middle-aged and elderly African American patients with affective disorders had been misdiagnosed with schizophrenia. Yet, whether the emphasis is on migration and acculturative stress or on ethnic/racial status, clinical bias, misdiagnosis, or discrimination, the theoretical perspective resorted to for understanding the mental health and psychological well-being of elder African Americans is a social stress perspective that emphasizes the negative effects of being ethnic.

While these stressors are very real, the majority of African American elders possess a core of personality characteristics and dispositions that enable highly stressed elders to maintain a sense of competence and control in their lives. Two factors contribute to a successful individual's greater resiliency: the family interaction system and the work and community milieu (Hakim & Wegmann, 2002; Klohnen, Vandewater, & Young, 1996). So what is resilience, and where does this strengths perspective come from?

Resiliency and African American Elders

Many counselors and educators who endorse multicultural counseling competency have grown tired and disillusioned with the traditional disease model that has dominated their professional practice for decades (Larkin, Alston, Middleton, & Wilson, 2003; Middleton & McDaniel, 1990; Middleton et al., 1997; Myers, 1990, 1994). The traditional disease model, borrowed from medicine, highlights injury, pathology, victimization, and learned helplessness. A new model is needed. In social work this change in model and emphasis has been dubbed the *strengths perspective* (Saleebey, 1996).

A strengths outlook is not new to the counseling profession; it has been identified as resiliency. However, resiliency is an attribute that has remained in the background and has not been thoroughly understood or researched with respect to its influence or impact on the health and well-being of African American elders. Consistent with the multicultural counseling competency research (Arredondo et al., 1996), the counseling professional is encouraged to look at African American elder clients in light of their capacities, talents, competencies, possibilities, visions, values, and hopes. Resiliency is the attribute, the concept, and the process that epitomizes and operationalizes the strengths perspective.

Resiliency is usually defined as successful adaptation under adverse conditions (Klohnen, 1996) or as the factors and processes enabling sustained competent functioning even in the presence of major life stressors (Klohnen et al., 1996). A person's ability to recover, to adapt, or to bounce back to a normal condition varies over the person's lifetime. According to Norman (2000), there are several important considerations to keep in mind when thinking about resiliency:

1. It is not a fixed attribute. It is a process of interaction between environmental and personal factors. If circumstances change, outcomes may be different.
2. A person may become dependent or addicted to adversity over time. The larger the number of factors stressing an individual, the more likely maladaptive, rather than resilient, outcomes will result.
3. Resilient behavior does not necessarily mean good emotional health. Behaviorally resilient individuals can be emotionally troubled.

Perkins and Tice (1995) have applied the paradigm of resiliency to the elderly, and there is a strong case for the usefulness of this approach; however, its actual utilization in practice remains limited (Saleebey, 1996). Clinical practice continues to focus on pathology and dysfunction. There is a limited use of the strengths/resiliency model on the part of counselors and other mental health practitioners and the systems in which they practice.

C. P. Kaplan, Turner, Norman, and Stillson (1996) offered a modified consultation resilience model for social workers that may be useful for counselors and other mental health practitioners to consider. The model utilizes psychodynamic, cognitive, cognitive–behavioral, humanistic, supportive, and psychoeducational methods in their treatment. The client's strengths as they relate to *cognition* (e.g., has an understanding of right and wrong from their cultural and ethical perspective, considers and weighs alternatives in problem solving, sees the world as most other people see it in their culture), *emotion* (e.g., has emotions congruent with situation, has a range of emotions, expresses love and concern for intimate others), *motivation* (e.g., does not want to be dependent on others, willing to seek help and share problem situation with others they can trust, wants to improve current and future situations), *coping* (is persistent in handling family crises, is well organized, is resourceful and creative with limited resources), and *interpersonal skills* (has a sense of humor, performs social roles appropriately, is patient, makes sacrifices for friends, family members, and others) are assessed. C. P. Kaplan et al. stressed that training in the use of this model must be tailored to the skills and training of the staff called upon to implement the model. Certainly, counselors are highly skilled to implement such a model. The model by C. P. Kaplan et al. requires the counselor to seek to understand the worldview of the African American elder (Arredondo et al., 1996; Middleton et al., 2000). No group would benefit more by this model of intervention than African Americans in rural settings, female elders, and those who are older-aged.

Implications of Population Demographics and Characteristics

Dancy and Ralston (2002) profiled the subgroups of greatest need among African American elders whom they believed to be at risk in terms of health. The three groups they identified are older African Americans (a) who are in rural settings, (b) who are female, and (c) who are older-aged. Observations by Dancy and Ralston are consistent with the population demographics and health information previously discussed. These groups are not mutually exclusive. In fact, overlapping demographic characteristics of place of residence, gender, and age are three key factors identified by Dancy and Ralston in determining whether or not elder African Americans are at risk in terms of health.

In general, there is a paucity of literature on rural elders, and even less is known about African American rural elders. Data on self-reported health demonstrate that nearly one in three (30.3%) African American rural elders report that their health is poor compared with 16.6% of urban African Americans and 12.2% of rural European Americans (Coward, Bull, Kukulka, & Galliher, 1994). According to Parks (1988), the typical rural African American elder is 72 years of age, widowed, and retired and has received some high school education. The individual lives alone, probably in a house that he or she owns, but prefers to be close to relatives. Social contacts occur on a regular basis, and morale is high even though things do seem a bit worse with age. The person is affiliated with a church and religion, and the church plays a large role in the individual's life.

Factors related to the health status of older African American women are numerous. Economic risk is a key factor for older African American women 70 years of age and older. These women have the lowest median income in comparison with Black men and European Americans of both sexes (Watson, 1990). Very often illness is endured in order to fulfill roles and responsibilities. Thus, when a major illness occurs, older African American women may delay formal health care or seek intermittent treatment, not only because of a lack of resources but also because any accumulated income must be spent to a minimal level to receive Medicaid benefits (Lewis, 1992). Older African American women underuse the health care system, often overestimate their health status, and are often unwilling to discuss health problems (Dancy & Ralston, 2002).

Older-aged (75 years of age or older) African American elders need and seek social support. Use of health care services, including in-home care and nursing homes, continues to be less likely for African Americans than for European Americans. For older-aged African Americans, the major barriers are lack of confidence in the formal health care system, dependence on informal supports for health care, underutilization of formal supports, and lower socioeconomic levels due to this cohort's education and occupational status (Dancy & Ralston, 2002).

During the last century, life expectancy has improved dramatically, although unevenly, across historically underrepresented racial/ethnic groups (African Americans, Asian Americans, Native Americans, and Latino/Latina Americans) and European Americans. A concentrated effort to eliminate the barriers due to segregation and discrimination in education, politics, economics, and health care is needed. The fact that the older population is predominantly White or European American is not solely related to the fact that there are more Caucasians in the population. While we can only speculate on the precise number, direction, pace, and synergistic effects of the social and demographic changes referenced above, we know that the rates estimated are likely to be influenced by actual levels of international migration and survivorship. If the chance of survival improves more rapidly for each group, the numbers predicted could be even higher. Likewise, if the chance of survival decreases for specific groups or populations, the numbers predicted could be lower. Therefore, the question must be asked. Prior to and since the September 11 terrorist attacks, who are more likely to be allowed to immigrate into the United States: Europeans, Latinos, or people of African descent? Also, who is more likely to survive into their advanced years?

Already, African Americans have accounted for a smaller share of the 85-and-over population in recent census than in earlier census. This may be due to improvements in age reporting because of improved knowledge of actual age through the wider availability of birth certificates and increased literacy, resulting in a diminished tendency to exaggerate age among the oldest old (U.S. Census Bureau, 2001a). However, it may also be due to decreased survivorship. A population's age composition can change only through three fundamental demographic processes: birth, death, and migration. Birth rates for African Americans and Latino Americans proportionally exceed that of European Americans (Ventura, Peters, Martin, & Maurer, 1997). Therefore, actual shifts in demographics for African Americans and other ethnically diverse populations will largely be due to longevity and migration. We have taken a focused look at longevity and health characteristics of African Americans in comparison with other racial groups. Clearly, there are challenges that will decrease longevity and migration. Therefore, it is important to understand the implications of how factors relating to resiliency, population growth, and health affect the work of the mental health practitioner.

Implications for Mental Health Practice

Cultural Influences

African American culture is highly influenced by traditional African values that emphasize collectivism, sharing, obedience to authority, belief in spirituality, and respect for elders (Baker, 1994). For many African American elders, family, religion, and spirituality play significant roles in their lives. Regarding family, there is great strength in the African American family structure. In that strength, there is the possibility of an extended or nontraditional family arrangement. The extended family network of relatives, older children, and close friends provides emotional and economic support. Among families headed by females, the rearing of children is often undertaken or supported by African American elders. Within the African American family are an adaptability of family roles, strong kinship bonds, a strong work and achievement ethic, and strong religious and spiritual orientations (Hildebrand, Phenice, Gray, & Hines, 1996; McCollum, 1997).

Second in importance only to family, the church is perceived as the primary institution in the African American community. Spirituality and religion play an important role in providing comfort in the face of numerous stressors encountered over the years by African American elders. The majority of African Americans are evangelical Christians with religious experiences originating in the regions of ancient Africa (Cush, Punt, and, to a great extent, Egypt), as well as African American adaptation of Hebraic, Jewish, Christian, and Islamic beliefs and rituals (Carter, 2002). Slavery and segregation denied African American older adults access to the full rights and privileges granted to other Americans. Fortunately, the church historically was the only institution that African American elders had to meet their emotional and spiritual needs. Even today, the church remains at the center of community life, attending to the social, spiritual, and psychological needs of numerous African American elders and their families (Richardson & June, 1996).

These realities have specific implications for counseling practitioners. First, differences in family function should not automatically be seen as deficits. The counselor should seek to identify the family structure of the elderly client. For example, the elder African American grandparent may be faced with having to play a key role in the raising of grandchildren or great grandchildren. Rather than utilizing a monolithic approach to counseling, the counselor would be well advised to develop nontraditional approaches to deal with late-life transitions that older adults may be facing. One must realize that mental health counselors are subjected to negative stereotypes of African American elders that are common to all in our society. Mental health counselors have largely been socialized and trained, and therefore have a preference for working with the YAVIS client—youthful, attractive, verbal, intelligent, and successful (Schofield, 1964). Certainly, African American elders may totally contradict the YAVIS syndrome. Indeed, forming the backbone of the African American family, African American elders defy the myths often attributed to the elderly—senile, dependent, hard of hearing, physically impaired, lacking in common sense, helpless, and always in need of their family to care for them. On the contrary, frequently, significant help and support come from African American elders. Often, an African American elder such as the grandmother is faced with assuming a key role in helping to raise grandchildren. Her influence and help should not be eliminated; rather, the goal might be to make the working alliance with the other caregivers more efficient.

Very often, among African American elder women, seeds of self-neglect may be seen. Taking care of self becomes secondary. It is as if their own individual needs are not as important as the needs of others in their lives. As caregivers, there is the perception that if they stop to take care of themselves (rest, exercise, outpatient exams, inpatient care, etc.), there will be no time or no one left to take care of the children and grandchildren. Culturally competent counselors will seek to understand and strengthen the family structure as it exists. Culturally competent counselors should not seek to impose their own middle-class Eurocentric perspective of who constitutes a family or who must head or care for the family. For many African American elders, to be of service to others and family, in particular, is paramount where a high value is placed on caretaking.

Second, asking about religion/spirituality during the health assessment or intake can help the counselor determine whether religious/spiritual factors will influence the client's medical decisions and compliance. If the family is heavily involved in church activities or has strong spiritual beliefs, the counselor might enlist resources (e.g., the pastor, minister, bishop) to deal with problems involving conflicts within the family or community. The counselor should consider churches as much a potential source of information as clinics, schools, hospitals, or other mental health professionals (Carter, 2002). The history of slavery for African American elders has contributed to the disruption of the African American family. Despite this, African American elders have held their families together by sheer strength of character, using extended kinship and church ties, and by their strength of spirit and spirituality. It would be highly beneficial if counselors recognized these strengths in the African American elder rather than falling prey to myths and damaging misconceptions.

Third, a culturally competent counselor acknowledges the possibility that race or culture might play a role in the presenting problem of the African American elder and is viewed as more competent than is a culture-blind counselor. If the problem is due to discriminatory practices by an institution, the counselor must enter into an expansive problem-solving mode and assist the client in addressing the problem and anticipate possible mistrust from African American elders (Atkins, 1988).

Socioeconomic Influences

The U.S. Department of Commerce reported in a June 2001 news release that people age 65 years and older represent 14% of the civilian workforce, and 9.7% had incomes below the poverty level (U.S. Department of Commerce, 2001). The poverty rate among all people 65 and over was 10% in 2001. Among men 65 and over, the rate for African Americans was three times as high (16%) as the rate for European Americans (5%). The poverty rate for African American women 65 and older was nearly three times as high (26%) as the rate for European American women (10%; McKinnon, 2003).

Poverty needs to be considered in any explanation of mental health problems among African American elders. While there is a relationship between psychological disorders and socioeconomic status, the relationship is a complex one that has only begun to be examined through the research of the last 30 or 40 years. Many African American elders were educated during a time when equal access to quality education was severely limited. Only 19% have completed high school, and 3.5% have no formal education at all, resulting in lower wages, fewer skilled jobs, and longer period of unemployment (U.S. Census Bureau, 2001b). The median income for African American older adults is approximately $7,328 for men and $5,239 for women (U.S. Department of Commerce, 2001). Further, rural older adults in general are poorer than urban older adults, and their rate of exit from poverty is lower than urban elders (Glasgow & Brown, 1998; Jensen & McLaughlin, 1997). The majority of African American elders reside in urban areas; however, 16.2% reside in rural areas and are concentrated in the southeastern region of the United States (Coward et al., 1994). In urbanized areas, 34% live in poverty, and in rural areas that number increases to 50% (American Association of Retired Persons, 1996).

Diversity and growth are two terms that best describe America's older population. They are a heterogeneous group, inasmuch as they differ in age, gender, race, and ethnic backgrounds. Some have significant financial and health problems, whereas others lead more secure and healthier lives. Some stay in the workforce until death, whereas others are able to select a more leisurely lifestyle. Many older Americans are living longer into retirement. These changing trends will continue to affect the nation's workforce and economic base well into the 21st century (U.S. Department of Commerce, 1993). Subsequently, appropriate avocational (volunteer or hobby activities), counseling services, and financial resources will be required to support older adults who live longer into retirement. From the perspective of economic security, the adaptation made by many older African Americans today is a fairly comfortable one. However, there are pockets of people, particularly African American women, rural elderly, and the older elders (85+), whose sparse work history has placed them in economic jeopardy. Additionally, the restructuring of the American work-force has affected older and younger workers alike, and the psychological effects of forsaking one's work role can be profound.

African American Elders of Tomorrow

With the increasing numbers of African Americans in the middle class, the aging cohort of African American elders will most likely not be disadvantaged in the same way as their low-income counterparts (Dancy & Ralston, 2002). With one in seven African American families having an income of $50,000, there will be an increasing portion of the older African American population that will be affluent. Therefore, there is differential jeopardy within the African American community; it is not a monolithic population.

While there are uncertainties about how the younger generations of African Americans today will age, most would agree that older people of tomorrow will be enormously diverse and surviving in even greater numbers into advanced old age. Older African Americans of tomorrow promise to be very different on a number of parameters, not the least of which is the pattern of adult attitudes and behaviors that are already seen in younger people of today. I believe that older African American elders will be far more confident about being old—a confidence derived from being part of the largest cohort group in the history of hu-mankind that has enjoyed huge strides in education and technological advances. Functional rather than chronological markers will designate age (Larkin et al., 2003; Middleton & McDaniel, 1990). Ageism will not be easily tolerated by tomorrow's older population, and the impact of this attitudinal difference from today's older African American popula-tion cannot be underestimated.

Passivity to disability will be the exception, not the norm, and disability will be far less likely to translate into dependency as it does for older African Americans today (Larkin et al., 2003). Older African American elders will seek more control over their health care, par-ticularly older African American women. Even for the more frail elderly, global diagnoses and labels of dementia or conditions dismissed as normal aging will not be readily ac-cepted, and the number of mutual support groups will proliferate. On the whole, older African American elders of tomorrow will be far less reluctant to use mental health services to aid in solving problems of family and individual crises and in dealing with the lifelong depressive episodes as well as those that accompany disability.

Recommendations for Counselors and Counselor Educators

The counseling profession advances a facilitative service-oriented process enabling people with mental health challenges and disabilities to attain usefulness and satisfaction in life. There is a need for preventive and innovative strategies in the provision of counseling ser-vices for African American elders (Larkin et al., 2003). Some African American elders may just be exiting the workforce or making personal and social adjustment transitions from work roles to avocational roles (Middleton & McDaniel, 1990). For many of these indi-viduals, counseling may be needed to make these transitional adjustments effectively. Therefore, the following are some recommendations for working with this population.

First, the counselor should seek to build on or maintain the positive and healthy aspects of the client's resiliency. Those African American elders who are the most vulnerable (rural elderly, women, and older elders) who are "struggling" or "suffering" have the potential for resiliency, and the counselor should seek to be effective in finding ways to enhance the client's resiliency and view the client's resiliency from a strengths-based perspective. In many ways, it becomes important to bring to the surface the strengths of the African American elder for his or her own self-awareness. Often, these elders are not aware of their own strengths and characteristics of resiliency. These may need to be uncovered and brought to the awareness of the African American elder to be used as tools for health maintenance.

Second, attitudinal barriers and social integration remain obstacles to overcome (Hershenson, 1992; S. P. Kaplan, 1990). The goal, as a counselor for African American elders, should be to assist African American elders in dealing effectively with present and future difficulties. Assistance may also be needed to deal with those difficulties that occur because one is perceived or treated as if one is unhealthy, a victim, or a person with disability.

Third, mental health counseling of older persons continues to be an emerging specialty. Consequently, counseling training programs rarely provide opportunities for interdisciplinary collaborations, thus doing a disservice to the real fact that no single discipline—counseling, psychology, rehabilitation, medicine, nursing, biology, sociology, or psychiatry—can meet the needs of this multifaceted population. The preparation of counselors who have specialized training and skills to meet the multifaceted needs of African American elders must be expanded to reflect the demographic changes of our society if they are to effect positive changes. We must continue to expand our interdisciplinary collaborations.

Fourth, practitioners are encouraged to know the cultures of the multicultural client population they are serving in the United States (Arredondo et al., 1996). Therefore, it becomes the responsibility of the counselor to involve himself or herself in the experiences that are a part of aging, dying, and death (J. T. Kemp, 1984) if these experiences and opportunities are not already a part of one's counselor preparation program (Middleton, Fowers, & Zawaiza, 1996). The older person becomes the teacher, and it is the practitioner's responsibility to become the student (J. T. Kemp, 1984). This may mean engaging in workshops, seminars, and other self-directed experiential activities and learning opportunities.

Finally, if collaboration among the professions is to be a reality, what is needed is our advocacy for a national social policy that supports a vital and productive old age to pair with the needed policy on older persons with disabilities. The professions have been asking for years for a coordinated federal policy in each of these areas (Bass, Kutza, & Torres-Gil, 1990; Hansen & Perlman, 1991; Myers, 1994).

Summary

Older African American elders with disabilities and other health care issues are an underserved population within the counseling and rehabilitation professions (Hansen & Perlman, 1991; Larkin et al., 2003; Middleton & McDaniel, 1990; Myers, 1986). Older persons, none more so than African American elders, experience negative stereotypes and are often regarded as having a physical or mental impairment (Butler, 1994; McCracken, Hayes, & Dell, 1997; Middleton & McDaniel, 1990). Consequently, by either regard or actuality, they are covered under the ADA.

Some examples of disabling conditions covered by the ADA that some older people may be currently dealing with include anxiety disorders, bipolar disorder, AIDS, narcolepsy, alcohol or drug addiction (so long as the individual is not a current user or an unlawful drug user), and cardiac disease. The courts have held that these impairments and other conditions may render a person disabled (Lindsay, 1989/1990). However, some of these same conditions might not result in making an individual disabled if it is unclear whether the impairment limits a *major life activity*. Major life activity denotes functions such as caring for oneself, performing manual tasks, walking, seeing, hearing, speaking, breathing, learning, and, most important, walking (see ADLs and IADLs discussed earlier).

What is clear, however, is that this population, like any other, can benefit from counseling and other health care and human services. Research seems to suggest that resilient individuals have the ability to differentiate between the possible and impossible and are able to appraise the consequences of their actions realistically. If we are to plan and provide effective services for older people, assessing and evaluating the combined impact of both disabling and mental conditions are important (Myers, 1994). Therefore, finding ways to enhance resiliency may be a very useful counseling approach.

Physical illness and disability do not occur in isolation. Rather, biological processes interact with psychological and social factors. Therefore, avocational activities and meaningful socialization in an individual's personal and social adjustment to aging are also important (Middleton et al., 1997). It is also known that physical problems can lead to mental and emotional disturbance, emotional distress can exacerbate physical symptoms, and other combinations of both can lead to significant clinical impairments (Cohen, 1990; B. Kemp, 1986). However, where this population is concerned, there exists an extraordinary potential for real reform in mental health policy and practice in both the counseling and rehabilitation professions.

If real reform is to be achieved, I believe that practitioners seeking to serve this population must become proactive in seeking collaborative involvement with other health care and human service professions—vocational rehabilitation, medicine, nursing, biology, sociology, and psychiatry. Counselor education training programs must begin thinking about training their students to recognize the importance of interdisciplinary assessment and treatment for older people (Myers, 1994). This truly becomes an important consideration when working with older ethnic African American populations given the demographic information previously cited regarding the growth of members in this group.

References

Adderley-Kelly, B., & Green, P. (1997). Breast cancer education, self-efficacy, and screening in older African American women. *Journal of the Black Nurses Association, 9,* 45–57.

American Association of Retired Persons. (1996). *A profile of older Americans.* Washington, DC: Author.

Americans With Disabilities Act of 1990, 42 U.S.C.A. § 12101 *et seq.* (West 1993).

Arredondo, P., Toporek, R., Brown, S., Jones, J., Locke, D., Sanchez, J., & Stadler, H. (1996). Operationalization of the multicultural counseling competencies. *Journal of Multicultural Counseling and Development, 24,* 42–78.

Atkins, B. J. (1988). An asset-oriented approach to cross-cultural issues: Blacks in rehabilitation. *Journal of Applied Rehabilitation Counseling, 19*(4), 45–49.

Baker, F. M. (1994). Issues in psychiatric care of African American elders. In *The American Psychiatric Association Task Force on Ethnic Minority Elderly: A task force of the American Psychiatric Association* (pp. 21–62). Washington, DC: American Psychiatric Association.

Baker, F. M. (1995). Misdiagnosis among older psychiatric patients. *Journal of the National Medical Association, 87,* 872–876.

Bass, S. A., Kutza, E. A., & Torres-Gil, F. M. (Eds.). (1990). *Diversity in aging.* Glenview, IL: Scott, Foresman.

Blake, R. (1981). A demographic analysis. *Journal of Rehabilitation, 47,* 19–27.

Blazer, D. G., Hays, J. C., & Salive, M. E. (1996). Factors associated with paranoid symptoms in a community sample of older adults. *The Gerontologist, 36,* 70–75.

Butler, R. N. (1994). Dispelling ageism: The cross-cutting intervention. In D. Shenk & W. A. Achenbaum (Eds.), *Changing perceptions of aging and the aged* (pp. 137–143). New York: Springer.

Carter, J. H. (2002). Religion/spirituality in African American culture: An essential aspect of psychiatric care. *Journal of the National Medical Association, 94,* 371–375.

Cohen, G. D. (1990). Psychopathology and mental health in the mature and elderly adult. In J. E. Birren & K. W. Schaie (Eds.), *Handbook of the psychology of ageing* (pp. 221–291). San Diego, CA: Academic Press.

Coleman, D., & Baker, F. M. (1994). Misdiagnosis of schizophrenia among older, Black veterans. *Journal of Nervous Mental Disorders, 182,* 527–528.

Cook, J. M., Pearson, J. L., Thompson, R., Black, B. S., & Rabins, P. V. (2002). Suicidality in older African Americans: Findings from the EPOCH study. *American Journal of Geriatric Psychiatry, 10,* 437–446.

Coward, R. T., Bull, C. N., Kukulka, G., & Galliher, M. (1994). *Health services for rural elders.* New York: Springer.

Cutrona, C. E., Russell, D. W., Hessling, R. M., Brown, P. A., & Murry, V. (2000). Direct and moderating effects of community context on the psychological well-being of African American women. *Journal of Personality and Social Psychology, 79,* 1088–1101.

Dancy, J., & Ralston, P. A. (2002). Health promotion and Black elders. *Research on Aging, 24,* 218–242.

Ganikos, M. L. (Ed.). (1979). *Counseling the aged.* Falls Church, VA: American Personnel and Guidance Association.

Glasgow, N., & Brown, D. (1998). Older, rural and poor. In R. T. Coward & J. A. Krout (Eds.), *Aging in rural settings* (pp. 187–207). New York: Springer.

Hakim, H., & Wegmann, D. J. (2002). A comparative evaluation of perceptions of health of elders of different multicultural backgrounds. *Journal of Community Health Nursing, 19,* 161–171.

Hansen, C. E., & Perlman, L. G. (1991). Aging and the rehabilitation process: An overview of the 15th Mary E. Switzer memorial seminar. *Journal of Rehabilitation, 3,* 7–10.

Hershenson, D. B. (1992). Conceptions of disability: Implications for rehabilitation. *Rehabilitation Counseling Bulletin, 35,* 154–160.

Hildebrand, V., Phenice, L. A., Gray, M. M., & Hines, R. P. (1996). *Knowing and serving diverse families.* Englewood Cliffs, NJ: Prentice-Hall.

Hing, E., & Bloom, B. (1990). *National Center for Health Statistics: Long-term care for the functionally dependent elderly, vital and health statistics* (Series 13, No. 104, DHHS Pub. No. PHS 90-1765). Hyattsville, MD: Public Health Service.

Jensen, L., & McLaughlin, D. K. (1997). The escape from poverty among rural and urban elders. *The Gerontologist, 37,* 462–468.

Kales, H., Blow, F., Bingham, C., Roberts, J., Copeland, L., & Mellow, A. (2000). Race, psychiatric diagnosis, and mental health care utilization in older patients. *American Journal of Geriatric Psychiatry, 8,* 301–309.

Kaplan, C. P., Turner, S., Norman, E., & Stillson, K. (1996). Promoting resilience strategies: A modified consultation model. *Social Work in Education, 18,* 158–168.

Kaplan, S. P. (1990). Social support, emotional distress, and vocational outcomes among persons with brain injuries. *Rehabilitation Counseling Bulletin, 34,* 16–23.

Kelley, S. (2003). Prevalent mental health disorders in the aging population: Issues of co-mordity and functional disability. *Journal of Rehabilitation, 69*(2), 19–25.

Kemp, B. (1986). Psychosocial and mental health issues in rehabilitation of older persons. In S. J. Brody & G. E. Ruff (Eds.), *Ageing and rehabilitation: Advances in the state of the art* (pp. 122–158). New York: Springer.

Kemp, J. T. (1984). Learning from clients: Counseling the frail and dying elderly. *Personnel and Guidance Journal, 62,* 270–272.

Kessler, R. C., & Cleary, P. D. (1980). Social class and psychological distress. *American Sociological Review, 45,* 463–478.

Klohnen, E. C. (1996). Conceptual analysis and measurement of the construct of ego-resiliency. *Journal of Personality and Social Psychology, 70,* 1067–1079.

Klohnen, E. C., Vandewater, E. A., & Young, A. (1996). Negotiating the middle years: Ego-resiliency and successful midlife adjustment to women. *Psychology and Aging, 11,* 431–442.

Larkin, V., Alston, R., Middleton, R., & Wilson, K. (2003). Underrepresented ethnically and racially diverse aging populations with disabilities: Trends and recommendations. *Journal of Rehabilitation, 69*(2), 26–31.

Lewis, I. (1992, November). *Health issues of older Black women.* Discussant remarks at symposium presented at the annual meeting of the Gerontological Society of America, Washington, DC.

Lindsay, R. A. (1989/1990). Discrimination against the disabled: The impact of the new federal legislation. *Employee Relations Law Journal, 15,* 333–345.

Markides, K. S. (1986). Minority status, aging, and mental health. *International Journal of Aging and Human Development, 23,* 285–300.

McCollum, V. J. C. (1997). Evolution of the African American family personality: Considerations for family therapy. *Journal of Multicultural Counseling and Development, 25,* 219–229.

McCracken, J. E., Hayes, J. A., & Dell, D. (1997). Attributes of responsibility for memory problems in older and younger adults. *Journal of Counseling & Development, 75,* 385–391.

McKinnon, J. (2003). *The Black population in the United States: March 2002* (U.S. Census Bureau, Current Population Reports, Series P20-541). Washington, DC: U.S. Census Bureau.

Middleton, R. A., Fowers, C., & Zawaiza, T. (1996). Multiculturalism, affirmative action, and Section 21 of the 1992 Rehabilitation Act Amendments: Fact or fiction? *Rehabilitation Counseling Bulletin, 40,* 11–30.

Middleton, R. A., & McDaniel, R. S. (1990). The (re)habilitation needs of the older non-disabled handicapped person: Expanding the role of the rehabilitation professional. *Journal of Rehabilitation, 54*(4), 23–27.

Middleton, R. A., Rollins, C., Flowers, C., & Crow, G. (1997, April). *Counseling and older adults with disabilities: A multicultural perspective.* Paper presented at the American Counseling Association 1997 World Conference, Orlando, FL.

Middleton, R. A., Rollins, C., Sanderson, P. L., Leung, P., Harley, D., Ebener, D., & Leal-Idrogo, A. (2000). Endorsement of professional multicultural rehabilitation competencies and standards: A call to action. *Rehabilitation Counseling Bulletin, 43,* 219–240.

Myers, J. E. (1986). Preparing counselors for work with older persons. *Counselor Education and Supervision, 26,* 137–145.

Myers, J. E. (1990). Aging: An overview for mental health counselors. *Journal of Mental Health Counseling, 12,* 245–259.

Myers, J. E. (1994). Education and training of aged-care providers. *Disability and Rehabilitation, 16,* 171–180.

National Center for Health Statistics. (1994). *Health United States: 1993* (Table 48). Hyattsville, MD: Public Health Service.

Norman, E. (2000). *Resiliency enhancement: Putting the strengths perspective into social work practice.* New York: Columbia University Press.

Parks, A. G. (1988). *Black elderly in rural America: A comprehensive study.* Bristol, IN: Wyndham Hall.

Perkins, K., & Tice, C. (1995). A strengths perspective in practice: Older people and mental health challenges. *Journal of Gerontological Social Work, 23*(3/4), 83–97.

Perry, D. (1993, May). *Aging research and public policy in the United States.* Paper presented at the European Federation of Pharmaceutical Industries' Association, Salzburg, Austria.

Rajaram, S. S., & Vinson, V. (1998). African American women and diabetes: A sociocultural context. *Journal of Health Care for the Poor and Underserved, 9,* 236–247.

Richardson, B. L., & June, L. N. (1996). Utilizing and maximizing the resources of the African American church: Strategies and tools for counseling professionals. In C. C. Lee (Ed.), *Multicultural issues in counseling: New approaches to diversity* (pp. 155–170). Alexandria, VA: American Counseling Association.

Saleebey, D. (1996). The strengths perspective in social work practice: Extensions and cautions. *Social Work, 41,* 296–305.

Schofield, W. (1964). *Psychotherapy: The purchase of friendship.* Englewood Cliffs, NJ: Prentice Hall.

Taeuber, I. B., & Taeuber, C. (1971). *U.S. Bureau of the Census: People of the United States in the 20th century.* Washington, DC: U.S. Government Printing Office.

U.S. Census Bureau. (1993). *Population projections of the United States, by age, sex, race, and Hispanic origin: 1993 to 2050* (Current Population Reports, P25-1104). Washington, DC: U.S. Government Printing Office.

U.S. Census Bureau. (1995). *Population profile of the United States.* Washington, DC: U.S. Government Printing Office.

U.S. Census Bureau. (2001a). *Demographic profile.* Washington, DC: Author.

U.S. Census Bureau. (2001b). *Projections of resident population by age, sex, race, and Hispanic origin, 1999 to 2100.* Washington, DC: Author.

U.S. Department of Commerce. (1993). *We the American elderly* (Age and Sex Statistics Branch Population Division, Bureau of the Census). Washington, DC: Author.

U.S. Department of Commerce. (2001). *Country's older population profiled by the U.S. Census Bureau* (U.S. Census Bureau Public Information Office, Publication No. CB01). Washington, DC: Author.

Ventura, S. J., Peters, K. D., Martin, J. A., & Maurer, J. D. (1997). Births and deaths: United States, 1996. In *Monthly vital statistics report: Vol. 46* (No. 1, Suppl. 2). Hyattsville, MD: National Center for Health Statistics.

Watson, W. H. (1990). Family care, economics and health. In W. H. Watson (Ed.), *Black aged: Understanding diversity and service needs* (pp. 50–68). New Brunswick, NJ: Transaction Books.

Wiener, J. M., Hanley, R. J., Clark, J. F., & Van Nostrand, J. F. (1990). Measuring the activities of daily living: Comparisons across national surveys. *Journal of Gerontology: Social Sciences, 45,* S229–S237.

Wray, L. A. (1992). Health policy and ethnic diversity in older Americans—Dissonance or harmony? [Special issue: Cross-cultural medicine—A decade later]. *Western Journal of Medicine, 157,* 357–361.

7

African American Lesbian, Gay, and Bisexual Persons

Todd A. Savage and Debra A. Harley

African American lesbian, gay, and bisexual (LGB) individuals face multiple forms of oppression, including racism, sexism, and heterosexism. These individuals contend with discrimination not only in the society at large but within their racial/ethnic and the homosexual communities as well. That there are homophobia and heterosexism among African Americans is largely reflective of the homophobic and heterosexist culture in which we live (Clarke, 1999). Social norms, stereotypes, and life experiences influence the identity development of African Americans who identify as LGB. LGB individuals belong to a group whose membership is defined by their sexual orientation (McIntyre, 1992). For African Americans who identify as LGB, sexual orientation is but one criterion that defines their identity. They are also defined by their skin color (i.e., race) and gender (Greene & Boyd-Franklin, 1996). The added pressures of racism and sexism no doubt affect the overall identity development of African American LGB persons, challenging them constantly to navigate several oppressed identities. According to Lorde (1984, p. 120), "constantly being encouraged to pluck out some one aspect of self and present this as the meaningful whole, eclipsing or denying the other parts of self" is characteristic of the multiplicity of oppression experienced by African American LGB individuals. Furthermore, they risk estrangement from the African American community and alienation from the LGB community, which historically has had primarily a White face associated with it (Jones & Hill, 1996). The feeling of having to choose between the two communities adds to the inner conflict experienced by many African American LGB individuals.

The purpose of this chapter is to explore the multiple forms of oppression encountered by African Americans who identify as homosexual or bisexual (i.e., racism, sexism, and heterosexism) and the resulting psychosocial implications of such phenomena. In the sections that follow, information is presented as to how African American LGB individuals are marginalized in the broader LGB community and how their devalued position in the broader social hierarchy subjects them to multilayered levels of discrimination. We seek to accomplish these goals by addressing (a) racial identity development; (b) gender identity development; (c) sexual identity development; (d) the intersection of race, gender, and sexual orientation in the African American community; and (e) adjustment issues and acceptance in the coming-out process. Finally, implications and recommendations for counseling African American LGB individuals are outlined.

Racial Identity Development

Identity development has been theorized as occurring through a series of stages. Helms (1995) indicated that all people go through a stepwise process of developing racial and ethnic consciousness. The process is a part of personal growth and comes about as a result of one's effort to understand and integrate life experiences (Parker, Archer, & Scott, 1992) and is ongoing throughout the life span (Baruth & Manning, 1999). According to Poston (1990), racial identity development involves different levels of development and specific attitudes associated with these various levels. Although there are numerous theories and models of racial identity development applicable to people of color other than White (e.g., Downing & Roush, 1985; Helms, 1990, 1995; Morten & Atkinson, 1983; Parham & Helms, 1985; Wooden, Kawasaki, & Mayeda, 1983), models specific to African Americans are the focus here.

African American Identity Development

The essence of racial identity for African Americans has been explained through *nigrescence* models (Cross, 1971). *Nigrescence* is defined as the process by which a person "becomes Black" (D. L. Plummer, 1996, p. 169). Cross's 1971 model was one of the first nigrescence models to appear in the literature and is characterized as a five-stage process. The initial stage, the *preencounter* stage, involves prediscovery of one's racial identity. "Individuals view the world from a White frame of reference such that they [African Americans] think and behave in ways that negate their Blackness" (Ford, Harris, & Schuerger, 1993, p. 410). As a result of a crucial incident in which race becomes salient, it is during the second stage, *encounter*, that African Americans explore their Blackness. According to Ford et al. (1993), "in the face of conflicting and startling information from an encounter, they reevaluate their self-image, thereby becoming vulnerable and otherwise uncertain about their identity" (p. 410). The conscious awareness of one's Blackness rises to the top. *Immersion–emersion,* the third stage, represents the transition between one's historic view of her- or himself as an African American and an emerging Black identity. Individuals in this stage adopt a new frame of reference and struggle to rid themselves of an invisible identity, clinging to all elements of Blackness (Ford et al., 1993). Through the transition into the fourth stage, *internalization*, the individual becomes more bicultural, pluralistic, and better able to see commonalities across racial groups, making her or him better able to relate effectively with individuals from racial backgrounds different from her or his own (Cross, 1978). The final stage, *internalization–commitment*, is characterized by the individual becoming more active politically to bring about change for other Blacks (Ford et al., 1993). That is, the individual has formed a positive self-identity and takes action to promote self-pride and works to ensure that the rights of others from her or his group are protected. Although Cross's model as outlined here appears to have rigid boundaries, it seems to encompass many of the psychological and social dilemmas confronted by African Americans (Ford et al., 1993). However, identity development is a complex construct. A fuller understanding of African American racial identity requires breaking down the notion of African American culture as being monolithic (D. L. Plummer, 1996). It is clear that within-group differences exist among African Americans. Nevertheless, identity development is, in part, predicated on the individual's ability to adopt the mores of her or his identified community and to exhibit specific culturally related behaviors (D. L. Plummer, 1996; Poston, 1990). Furthermore, racial identity development for African Americans is influenced by cultural and ecological variables present in the society at large, such as negative stereotypes about people with black skin (Spencer & Markstrom-Adams, 1990). For example, Erikson (1968) reported people of color being at risk of internalizing and accepting negative self-images imposed on them by Whites as well as some members of their own racial group. Thus, African Americans "must achieve congruence between the real self and the ideal-perceived self if they are to function fully with well-integrated identities" (Ford et al., 1993, p. 412).

Gender Identity Development

Gender identity development is grounded in traditional models of human development that, in turn, have their roots in the Freudian theory of psychosexual development (Nelson, 1996). Because the traditional theories reflect a Western view of male development, "many feminist psychologists question whether the individuation process is the same for girls and women as it is for boys and men" (Nelson, 1996, p. 339). Gender-related issues for identity development are conceptualized on the basis of *relational competence* that involves separation (e.g., individuation), connection (e.g., movement toward relationships; Nelson, 1996), and mutuality (e.g., empathic responsiveness of participants in a dyad to attend and respond to the affective state of the other; Jordan, 1991). Because it is not within the scope of this chapter to outline every theory of human development, differences in gender role expectations are highlighted. And, given the fact that much attention has been given to male identity development and little attention to female identity development (Hays, 1996), gender-related identity development for women is the primary focus here.

An examination of gender development and sexism reveals that men, as well as women, are controlled by associated phenomena (Schur, 1984). For example, men have been historically limited and restricted by narrow definitions of masculinity. Conversely, women have been punished for violating or threatening to violate gender-related norms (Schur, 1984). According to Chodorow (1989), the formulation of core identity is conflicted for boys but not for girls. On the one hand, girls get their start in life connected to and identified with their mothers, who recognize their daughters as similar to themselves. On the other hand, boys see the need to identify apart from the mother, with the mother reinforcing this need (Nelson, 1996). Clearly, these are traditional views of identity development. Likewise, several feminist theorists (e.g., Benjamin, 1988; Chodorow, 1978) developed psychological theories that "assume a heterosexual reproductive imperative" (Bloom, 1994, p. 305) in which the role of females is linked directly with the role of motherhood. Bloom also stated that the emphasis on mothering remains the cornerstone of psychological development and is strongly present in feminist psychological theories, reinforcing "a naturalized story of identity formation" (p. 305). As a result, women without children (including some lesbians) are often not represented in most traditional or feminist theories of gender identity development. Therefore, deconstructing women's identity with biological motherhood is critical (Bloom, 1994).

Another aspect of gender identity is race. "Despite the good intentions of the formulator, feminist formulations of psychotherapy have been assailed for their failure to reflect the full spectrum of diversity among women" (Greene, 1994, p. 335). Furthermore, Greene stated that the assumption of feminist therapy that "gender is the primary focus of oppression for all women" (p. 336) fails

> to recognize, or minimizes, the importance of race, sexual orientation, culture, socioeconomic level and other forms of oppression, the intersection of these factors with one another, and the impact of these intersections on the experiences, perceptions, and values held by women of color. (p. 336)

The presumption of gender oppression as the primary focus in feminist theory often leads to the misperception that women of color and White women have greater similarities than between women of color and their male counterparts (Greene, 1994). As a result, African American women have expressed a sense of estrangement from feminist ideologies because racial oppression is not being addressed within these discussions.

Although African American women and White women share some experiences, they also are from fundamentally different places. That is, White women are in a position of power and privilege in terms of race, and African American women are seen as "other" in terms of race and gender in the American social order (Parks, Carter, & Gushue, 1996). "Whereas racial identity development must occur from a position of social power, gender identity is formed from a culturally subordinate position" (Parks et al., 1996, p. 626). Given the focus here on African Americans (women), Helms's (1990) *womanist identity development* (WID) model is presented below.

The WID model consists of four stages: *preencounter* (Womanist I), *encounter* (Womanist II), *immersion–emersion* (Womanist III), and *internalization* (Womanist IV; Parks et al., 1996). The WID model focuses on an internally defined identity. During the first stage, the African American woman accepts traditional gender roles and denies social bias. In the second stage, the woman may question and experience confusion about gender roles in society. Women move to this stage when they experience an external event that challenges their prior worldview. In addition, the woman "cautiously explores alternative solutions to role conflict" (Parks et al., 1996, p. 625). Stage 3 is characterized by the resolution of the discomfort experienced in Stage 2. The woman chooses a different externally determined perspective. She rejects traditional gender roles, expresses hostility toward men, idealizes women, seeks positive female role models, and develops intense interpersonal connections with other females (Parks et al., 1996). In the final stage, "the woman achieves an internally defined and more fully integrated identity" (Parks et al., 1996, p. 625). In this stage the woman develops a view of womanhood independent of either the traditional or the feminist perspective of gender identity development. In essence, as the realities of the effects of race and gender oppression converge, the WID model provides African American women with a "space" through which the core self-(identity) can emerge (King & Ferguson, 1996). Succinctly, identity development for African American women represents self-actualization.

Sexual Identity Development

The development of an LGB identity and the coming-out process can be lengthy, difficult, and exasperated by age, race, gender, religion, socioeconomic status, culture, and geographic location (Fassinger, 1991). Negative attitudes, expressed verbally and nonverbally, have an impact on LGB identity development (Walters, 1997). Specifically, "lesbians and gay men of color and those from ethnic or religious backgrounds with especially negative attitudes about homosexuality would find it difficult to come-out and develop a positive gay male or lesbian identity" (Garnets & Kimmel, 1991, p. 160). Therefore, LGB individuals are coerced to deny important aspects of themselves and their lives to gain community support (Walters, 1997). Moreover, LGB individuals "must deal with enormous amounts of stress as a result of living in a heterosexual and homophobic society" (Diplacido, 1998, p. 138).

The challenges for African American bisexuals are more complex because they live in a culture that sees sexual orientation as either a gay/lesbian or straight proposition (Conerly, 2000). According to Conerly, bisexuals generally lack institutional and other forms of communal supports specific to them and are forced to emphasize a preference for one gender over the other. Moreover, bisexuals must either socialize in cultural spaces that support their gender preference or go back and forth between straight and lesbian or gay communities. "African American gays and lesbians usually have the option of socializing in a community where their sexual identity is centered. Bisexuals usually do not" (Conerly, 2000, p. 7).

Yet, African American gay and bisexual men must contend with racism and heterosexism as part of their identity development. Likewise, African American lesbian and bisexual women face challenges of racism, sexism, and heterosexism as they struggle for identity. Thus, African American LGB persons must simultaneously develop a racial identity, a gender identity, and a sexual identity. Furthermore, these individuals have to establish both an individual and a group identity. This phenomenon is what Walters and Simoni (1993) called "a common experience of oppression" (p. 94) and what Loiacano (1989) referred to as "having several oppressed identities" (p. 21). It is clear that African American LGB individuals must simultaneously maneuver multiple identities.

Numerous models explaining sexual identity development exist in the literature (e.g., Cass, 1979; Coleman, 1982; K. Plummer, 1975; Ponse, 1978; Sophie, 1985–1986; Troiden, 1988), and regardless of the model examined (e.g., Morles's [1989] five-stage ethnic gay and lesbian identity model), none are specific to an African American context. According to Loiacano (1989), "choices about coming-out to others, becoming involved in primary relationships, and becoming politically active in the sexual minority community may be complicated by status as a Black American" (p. 22). Loiacano elaborated with the explanation that "because these tasks are all related to gay identity development, it follows that this process may be different for Black Americans and other people of color than it is for White Americans" (p. 22). In other words, for gay people of color, coming out in a multicultural context limits participation in social activities within their ethnic community to protect their families from stigmatization and humiliation (Merighi & Grimes, 2000). Merighi and Grimes asserted that these restrictions on gay people of color underscore the complexities and marginalization that LGB "people of color confront while simultaneously defining their cultural and sexual identities in a predominantly heterosexual society" (p. 32). For example, Merighi and Grimes cited a study of how young gay men disclosed their sexual identities to family members and how their family members responded to such disclosures; the majority of African Americans acknowledged how their cultural norms and ideas worked against disclosure. Several participants in the study viewed the importance of family loyalty and preservation as a foundation on which to feel less fearful of being rejected (see Merighi & Grimes, 2000).

The primary socialization of African Americans into Black cultural norms, combined with their simultaneous socialization into White American culture, "largely structures how they negotiate sexual identity questions and confer meaning to homosexual behavior" (Almaguer, 1991, as quoted in Nardi & Schneider, 1998, p. 537). Moreover, diversity is the touchstone of African American LGB identity (Boykin, 1996). For example, increasing numbers of African American LGB persons comfortably negotiate their way through the African American community, the White homosexual and bisexual community, and the African American homosexual and bisexual community in ways they feel are genuine to their full identities (Boykin, 1996).

Perhaps because of their multiplicity of identities, African American LGB individuals seem less likely than their White counterparts to be open about their sexual orientation or to consider themselves out of the closet (Boykin, 1996). Furthermore, for African Americans, sexual orientation can be just another example of their "otherness," making them less likely to view this aspect of their identity as central to who they are (Boykin, 1996). Partly because of isolation, conflicting identities, and exclusion from the homosexual and bisexual community, many African American LGB individuals avoid the use of certain terms when self-identifying as homosexual or bisexual (Boykin, 1996; Icard, 1986). For example, many African American lesbians and gay men do not use the term *queer* and question if they should use the term *gay* because these are White cultural terms that White people created (Boykin, 1996). The impact of labeling for African American lesbians has specific implications in their identity development. According to Eisenstein (1979) and Greene and Boyd-Franklin (1996), the derogatory stereotype of African American lesbians as *bulldaggers* or *funny women* is another assault on the multilayered texture of these individuals. Hence, the fact that African American LGB persons express such disconnection with a gay identity reveals the chasm between them and the homosexual and bisexual community at large (Boykin, 1996).

While visible and tangible characteristics and differences exist for African American LGB individuals, their multiple identities must be understood and addressed from the dual dimensionality of the two group identities in conjunction with self-identity development (Walters, 1997). In other words, the African American identity and the sexual identity in combination with the stage of coming out are integral to development of a full identity. It should be noted that acculturation (e.g., the infusion of White Western values among African Americans) plays a part in sexual identity development of African American LGB persons. Wherever African American LGB individuals fit on the identity continuum, these individuals have experiences with several oppressed identities (Boykin, 1996; Loiacano, 1989).

The Intersection of Race, Gender, and Heterosexism in the African American Community

For African American LGB persons, unlike heterosexual African Americans, their sexual orientation does not insulate them from the oppression of heterosexism, and unlike White LGB individuals, their skin color does not insulate them from the oppression of racism (Boykin, 1996). Similarly, African American lesbians and African American heterosexual women experience sexism within their community and from society at large (Loiacano, 1989). However, "lesbianism is largely considered incompatible with the role expectations of women in the Black community" (Loiacano, 1989, p. 21). Thus, any deviation from the expected role (e.g., propagation of the race and parenting) by lesbians is "construed as a betrayal of one's appropriate roles and identity" (Walters, 1997, p. 51).

The intersection of race, gender, and heterosexism in the African American community is organized around the subordination and devaluation of LGB individuals. According to Ellis and Murphy (1994), our society is organized "around misogynist, sexist, heterosexist, and homophobic beliefs and practices" (p. 48). Olkin (1999) and Walters (1997) stated that differences (e.g., Black and White, women and men, homosexual and heterosexual, presence and absence of disability) are used to create and maintain power. Moreover, Ellis and Murphy (1994) asserted that "differences are used to justify discrimination against, and oppression of, one group of people (e.g., women, homosexuals) by another (e.g., men and heterosexuals)" (p. 48). Given the multiplicity of oppression experienced by African Americans who identify as LGB, integration of their ethnicity and sexual orientation is challenging to achieve.

The marginalization of African American LGB individuals within the African American community is influenced by the community's view that homosexuality is a White phenomenon largely irrelevant to the interests of the African American community (Boykin, 1996; Loiacano, 1989; Walters, 1997). According to Greene and Boyd-Franklin (1996), "the African American community is perceived by many of its lesbian members as extremely homophobic" (p. 51). However, it should be noted that while the discussion in this chapter addresses heterosexism in the African American community, the whole African

American community is not heterosexist. Cheryl Clarke stressed this point in an interview with Boykin (1996) when she stated that the "accusation of homophobia" (p. 185) directed toward the whole African American community is inaccurate because no one has studied the African American community's attitudes on homosexuality. Therefore, inferences are being reported on the basis of perceptions.

In addition, as members of a historically oppressed group, African Americans have placed great importance on reproductive sexuality to ensure continued existence of the group in the face of racist, genocidal practices by the dominant (i.e., White) group (Greene & Boyd-Franklin, 1996). However, this does not mean that African American LGB persons are not parents. For example, Greene and Boyd-Franklin (1996) reported that it is not uncommon for African American lesbians to have children from prior relationships. Furthermore, because of the cultural tradition of "multiple mothering," African American lesbians are more likely to have been involved in child rearing than White lesbians.

Among African Americans, several cultural values are in direct conflict with values held by the larger LGB community. First, African Americans value privacy. In contrast, the dominant LGB community stresses the value of coming out. Being openly homosexual or bisexual is valued as part of healthy psychosocial development among the LGB community (Cass, 1984). In addition, African Americans promote privacy (e.g., secrecy, denial) through pretense. For example, rather than dealing with the issue of a lesbian relationship and lifestyle, the African American family pretends that the relationship does not exist and accepts the lover in the culturally accepted role of "girlfriend" or "sister" (Greene & Boyd-Franklin, 1996). Thus, discussion of lesbianism, gayness, or bisexuality is considered taboo. It is clear that the African American community perpetuates oppression within itself against LGB individuals. A second cultural value of African Americans is a strong religious and spiritual orientation. African Americans who have a Western Christian religiosity may use biblical scripture to support and reinforce heterosexist beliefs (Greene, 1994). Similarly, non-Christian African Americans such as Muslims view homosexuality and bisexuality as decadent European practices (Greene & Boyd-Franklin, 1996).

Third, African Americans value family and kinship ties. Any deviation from this value is viewed as a betrayal of the family (Walters, 1997). For example, African American gay men receive pressure to be secretive about their sexual orientation, and the message given is that marriage and family always come first (Loiacano, 1989). More than likely, the family will present a united front against an LGB member. The family may disown the individual with the result being no contact or communication between the individual and the family and community. Once this happens, the sense of unity that helps to form identity is lost. According to Butler (1992), "kinship controls all relationships in the community and binds together the interdependent relationships of all members of the group" (p. 46).

Finally, African Americans have a "worldview that is made manifest through the language, symbols, customs, values, and ideas of the people" (Butler, 1992, p. 29). Butler went on to say that more recently, the African American worldview has been given more concrete expression and been made functional for contemporary purposes. "The Principles of Nguzo Saba (i.e., African American Value System) have become widely acknowledged and accepted as the guiding standards for functioning in an Afrocentric frame of reference" (Butler, 1992, p. 29). The seven principles—*umoja* (unity), *kujichagulia* (self-determination), *ujima* (collective work and responsibility), *ujamaa* (cooperative economics), *nia* (purpose), *kuumba* (creativity), and *imani* (faith)—form the foundation from which the group identity of African Americans is established and differentiated from other groups of people in the United States (Butler, 1992). Although there is no discussion in the literature of Nguzo Saba in relation to the LGB community, given the value system and heterosexism in the African American community, some latitude can be made for inference. That is, because homosexuality and bisexuality are perceived as threats to the sur- vival of the African American family and community, they are in conflict with these principles.

Unfortunately, in the African American community, heterosexism is frequently not seen as prejudice but as a survival skill for the African American race or the particular individ- ual (Boykin, 1996). Heterosexism plays a role in the activities of everyday people, with het- erosexism frequently occurring in ways too subtle to be detected (Boykin, 1996). Likewise, gender distinction between lesbians and gay men is also prevalent in the perception of in- dividuals in the African American community. On the one hand, for example, African American lesbians are talked about solely in negative terms because they are seen as a threat to the social structure of the family, whereas African American gay men are often known and seen in a positive light as long as they remain closeted (e.g., the organ player in church known or perceived to be gay, which is okay as long as it is never discussed or made ex- plicit). On the other hand, African American men believe that they are to be strong and that their gay counterpart is inherently weak: "The African American male is often forced to denounce homosexuality in order to avoid suspicion" (Boykin, 1996, p. 172). Clearly, heterosexism is interwoven into the African American culture wherein a contradiction ex- ists between supporting sexual discrimination on the one hand and fighting racism on the other. Often, African American LGB individuals experience conflicts in allegiances because of the discrimination that exists within both the African American community (i.e., het- erosexism) and the gay and lesbian community (i.e., racism; Walters, 1997).

Psychosocial Adjustment and Acceptance in the Coming-Out Process

Although African Americans who identify as LGB prefer to have their multiple identities acknowledged by both their ethnic community and the LGB community (Walters, 1997), when given the choice between the two communities, many African American LGB indi- viduals tend to gravitate toward the African American community as a primary reference group and source of support (Boykin, 1996; Loiacano, 1989). Partly because African Americans tend to be more economically and socially disadvantaged than Whites and sub- jected to racism, the LGB members of this community find racial identification more im- portant. Conversely, White LGB individuals consider sexual orientation identification as more important (Boykin, 1996). Therefore, LGB African Americans need to find cultur- ally relevant ways to come out that do not deny or separate the LGB aspect of self from the African American identity. In response to a racist and heterosexist mainstream society, as well as heterosexist ethnic communities and racist gay communities, African American LGB persons have engaged in a number of efforts to redefine themselves and to create com- munities and cultures that embrace them (Kumashiro, 2001). In addition, African American LGB youths recognize the racialization that exists in school support groups for sexual mi- nority students. In a study examining why Black gay high school males stay away from a school-sponsored project for sexual minority students, McCready (2001) found the fol- lowing results. First, the microdynamics of racial separation have many layers, including his- torically produced microdynamics that are both personal (stemming from childhood experiences) and institutional (such as racially separating school structures that have been created over time). Second, everyday microdynamics maintain and challenge the histori- cally laid groundwork through face-to-face interactions. Third, issues of gender, class, and sexuality further complicate the microdynamics of racial formation and racial separation.

As African American LGB individuals explore the possibility of coming out, consider- ation needs to be given to what allies may be present in the family who can assist or be sup- portive in the process. Given the African American community's emphasis on privacy, the decision to come out must be weighed with great discretion. In essence, the mental health functioning of the individual and the beliefs of the community are in conflict with each other. Furthermore, if the challenges experienced by African American LGB individuals are less internal (e.g., the person is coping fairly well) and are more external (e.g., due to heterosexism and racism), more attention should be given to social injustice and societal inconsistency (Walters, 1997). Merighi and Grimes (2000) found that coming out for racial minority gay males "served as an important means of affirming a core aspect of their overall identity and creating new, and potentially difficult, dialogues with their family members" (p. 38). However, the importance of preserving and upholding strong family relations was a salient factor in their decision to come out. In other words, concerns for family well-being and how others perceive the family were identified as key factors for initially avoiding disclosure of their sexual orientation to family members. Another interesting finding of Merighi and Grimes is that the majority of the participants in their study who disclosed their sexual identity to a family member did so directly, indicating high levels of comfort with their sexuality.

In a study to evaluate the relationship between lesbian and gay identity and subsequent psychological adjustment, Miranda and Storms (1989) found that positive lesbian and gay identity was related to psychological adjustment as measured by lower neurotic anxiety and greater ego strength in both an older and a younger sample of lesbians and gay men. Furthermore, two coping strategies, self-labeling as a sexual minority and self-disclosure of sexual orientation to others, were related to development of a positive lesbian or gay identity. It is clear that the development of a positive lesbian or gay identity is an important task in promoting the psychological adjustment of lesbians and gay men. Although the study by Miranda and Storms did not specify race of the participants, the findings are consistent with those of other studies indicating that self-identity and self-disclosure as LGB are essential to healthy psychological adjustment. However, within the cultural context for African American LGB persons, their racial/ethnic cultural community is highly important (Croom, 2000). Disclosure among African American LGB persons may not be forthcoming and not an indication of pathology or unhealthy adjustment, but rather a coping strategy to balance the relationship with the family of origin and to counteract the negative effects of disclosure (Greene & Boyd-Franklin, 1996; Mobley & Levey, 1998). In some ways, nondisclosure may be a sign of resilience. While African American lesbians perceive the African American community to be conservative in their views on homosexuality, most lesbians' interest in participation in their ethnic community overshadows their concerns about negative reactions to their homosexuality (Mays, Cochran, & Rhue, 1993).

Implications and Recommendations for Counseling

Providing counseling or intervention to African Americans who identify as LGB takes place in the midst of many different systems (e.g., racism, sexism, heterosexism, and multiple identities) that are antagonistic and provide little support for them as individuals or in their relationships (Greene & Boyd-Franklin, 1996). Given their multiple identities, African American LGB individuals do not have the luxury of focusing their attention solely on one form of oppression in their lives (Boykin, 1996). To facilitate an integration of the multiple identities of African American LGB persons, counselors first need to educate themselves about racial identity development, gender identity development, sexual identity development, acculturation, cultural values, conflicting allegiances, racism, sexism, and heterosexism.

In addition, practitioners need to prepare themselves with accurate knowledge and learn how coming out can affect the family ecology. Either coming out or keeping one's sexual orientation a secret can be stressful and provoke intense anxiety for LGB persons

(Merighi & Grimes, 2000). Merighi and Grimes suggested that practitioners working with LGB clients and their families need to (a) not minimize the ramifications of coming out and help them prepare for the potential hostile responses from family members, (b) carefully assess if the client is emotionally prepared to come out to the family, and (c) equip the client with resources and information about homosexuality or bisexuality to offer the family members. The last suggestion is based on the premise that in view of initial ambivalence or negative reactions that often occur after initial disclosure of sexual orientation, with the passage of time family members may eventually become supportive of their LGB family member. It is important for the counselor or therapist to work with the clients to remember that just as they did not accept their sexual orientation and identity overnight, an affirmative understanding or acceptance need not take place immediately for family members either (Greene & Boyd-Franklin, 1996). Therefore, the counselor or therapist should work with the client to develop strategies to identify the stages of acceptance of family members that may occur over time.

Equally as important in the counseling process regarding disclosure issues is for the counselor or therapist "to know the range in which formally forbidden practices are tolerated within a culture as they are not discussed and not labeled" (Greene & Boyd-Franklin, 1996, p. 58). In addition, the counselor/therapist should not equate tolerance (predicated on an LGB person's silence) with approval. For example, when an African American lesbian takes her partner home, the relationship is considered a friendship by the family until the lesbian nature of the relationship is openly acknowledged (Greene & Boyd-Franklin, 1996). The focus of disclosure for the client should include the "safest" way to come out to individuals within the family and to the collective family (Greene & Boyd-Franklin, 1996; Mobley & Levey, 1998).

Hays (1996) proposed that counselors use the ADRESSING model for organizing and systematically considering complex cultural influences in the counseling field. The ADRESSING model focuses on nine main cultural influences that counselors need to consider in their work with African American gay and lesbian individuals: "Age and generational influences, Disability, Religion, Ethnicity (which may include race), Social status, Sexual orientation, Individual heritage, National origin, and Gender" (Hays, 1996, p. 332). The ADRESSING model is intended to incorporate groups of people who have traditionally been marginalized by the counseling profession in a more integrated way (Hays, 1996). This is an essential initial step because the more education and awareness counselors have, the greater the possibility that oppression will not thrive in the counseling profession.

Another counseling implication is for counselors to gain an awareness of the survival strategies African American LGB individuals have already developed to deal with racism, sexism, or heterosexism. In fact, LGB African Americans may deal with sexual oppression more easily than do their White counterparts because they have struggled with racial discrimination years before many of them recognized their sexual orientation (Boykin, 1996). Thus, the counselor should put emphasis on the counseling relationship as a partnership between the client and her- or himself. This can prove to be empowering for African American LGB persons because they are experts about themselves and have experience functioning in at least two worlds (e.g., White society and LGB communities). Mays et al. (1993) found that one strategy used by African American lesbians to deal with race and sex discrimination included avoidance of certain people and situations.

In terms of coping and resilience, development of supportive networks for African American LGB individuals is an additional implication for counseling. These networks need to be established in both the broader LGB community and the African American community. Community-based support groups for African American LGB individuals may provide a forum for debunking stereotypes and nurturing the development of positive group identity attitudes (Walters & Simoni, 1993). Given the multiple oppressed statuses of African American LGB persons and the potential rejection they face by their family of origin and ethnic communities, support for these individuals may be found in the families they have created for themselves (Greene & Boyd-Franklin, 1996). In addition, spirituality (not necessarily religion) serves as a source of coping and resiliency for LGB individuals (Ritter & O'Neill, 1989). Ritter and O'Neill also suggested that counselors can assist LGB persons to "create a spirituality unique to their experience" as they move through the stages of coming out and through the accompanying losses and grief (p. 14).

A frequently overlooked aspect of counseling LGB persons involves issues of safety. "Perhaps the most egregious obstacle to successful adjustment for gay/lesbian [persons] is the anticipation and presence of violence in their lives" (Lipkin, 1999, p. 145). Helping clients to recognize the potential dangers posed by others who respond violently to their sexual identity is one area of counseling that must be addressed for LGB persons, particularly for African Americans because of the intersection of identities. Sexual and racial identities are more than constructs across context and time. However, the integrative models of identity continue to focus on psychological factors of individuals and fail to fully accommodate the fluid nature of identities (Lowe & Mascher, 2001). Safety issues for African American LGB persons must be considered independently across race, ethnicity, gender, and sexual orientation and across interaction of categories.

Another example of a counseling issue that may be encountered when working with LGB African Americans is that of interracial coupling, particularly when the non-Black partner is White (Boykin, 1996). According to Greene (1994), lesbian interracial relationships face even greater challenges than heterosexual interracial relationships because of the lack of family and community support. Several other challenges associated with LGB interracial relationships include increased visibility, heterosexist and racist reactions from family and community members, and issues of guilt and associated feelings about racism by a White partner (Greene & Boyd-Franklin, 1996). Greene and Boyd-Franklin stated that both partners in an interracial relationship must guard against two behaviors: the White partner claiming she or he understands what the experience of racism is like for the African American partner, and the African American partner being jealous or resenting the White partner's privileged status in the dominant culture and in the LGB community. Having awareness of some of these issues can assist counselors in being responsive in their work with interracial LGB couples.

A discussion of counseling implications for African American LGB persons is not complete without mention of mental health and risk assessment. Ignoring this population in the development and usage of assessment protocols is a flagrant dereliction by practitioners, educators, and researchers. Similarly, the medical profession is cited as another area in which specific health care needs of LGB persons are neglected (O'Hanlan, Robertson, Cabaj, Schatz, & Nemrow, 1996). Given the levels of stress, substance abuse, domestic violence, public violence, and economic effects of homophobia and heterosexism experienced by African American LGB persons, racism, heterosexism, and homophobia are deemed as a "health hazard" (O'Hanlan et al., 1996). In essence, homophobia can lead to misrepresentation of facts by clients and misinterpretation of facts by counselors, therapists, and physicians (Lowe & Mascher, 2001; O'Hanlan et al., 1996).

A final implication for counseling is connecting education, research, and practice. Locating African American LGB persons can pose many realistic obstacles to research scientists. Educators and practitioners can collaborate with researchers to establish and maintain outreach to African American LGB persons. According to Croom (2000), the exclusion of more representative LGB ethnic minority subjects "limits the information we gather on the development of self-esteem, disclosure, the impact of diversity on and within ethnic minority group members, parenting, and so forth" (p. 272). Croom stressed that some of the misinformation about LGB persons in general and LGB African Americans in particular may be fueled by the lack of diversity in research samples and the tendency to view the LGB communities as if they were a monolithic entity. If African American LGB persons are not represented in mainstream research, gaining an understanding of their specific needs and developing culturally appropriate strategies for intervention will continue to fall short. Thus, the issue of research also includes modification of curricula in psychology and social science programs to be inclusive of training experiences with LGB issues specific to African Americans.

Summary

African Americans who identify as LGB are confronted daily by racism, sexism, and heterosexism, resulting in a multiplicity of oppression. Notably, all three forms of oppression are supported and reinforced by a hierarchy of White social power and privilege, a culturally subordinate position for African Americans, a male sexist superiority, and an automatic assumption of heterosexuality as a right to dominance in society. Moreover, racial identity development of African American LGB persons is influenced by negative stereotypes. Likewise, such individuals must deal with exclusion or subordination in the larger LGB community and rejection or estrangement from the African American community.

The intersection of gender and sexuality in the African American community is organized around devaluation of LGB individuals and the view that homosexuality and bisexuality are a White phenomenon. In the African American community, heterosexism is seen as necessary for the survival of the African American race. Nevertheless, African American LGB persons identify more with their racial group than with the White LGB community because of the racism that exists in this community.

A call has been issued to the mental health profession in debunking dangerous myths and removing the stigma attached to homosexuality and bisexuality in society (e.g., American Psychological Association, 2000; Carver, 1995), as well as in eradicating the exclusionary pose of African Americans as participants in research and the development of culturally appropriate intervention. The field of mental health counseling has both an opportunity and an initiative to include and propel equitable counseling for African American LGB persons.

References

American Psychological Association. (2000). Guidelines for psychotherapy with lesbian, gay, and bisexual clients. *American Psychologist, 55,* 1440–1451.

Baruth, L. G., & Manning, M. L. (1999). *Multicultural counseling and psychotherapy: A lifespan perspective.* Upper Saddle River, NJ: Merrill.

Benjamin, J. (1988). *Bonds of love: Psychoanalysis, feminism and the problem of domination.* New York: Pantheon.

Bloom, J. B. (1994). The counterrevolution: Sex, politics, and the new reproductive technologies. In M. P. Mirkin (Ed.), *Women in context: Toward a feminist reconstruction of psychotherapy* (pp. 284–309). New York: Guilford Press.

Boykin, K. (1996). *One more river to cross: Black and gay in America.* New York: Anchor Books.

Butler, J. B. (1992). Of kindred minds: The ties that bind. In *Cultural competence for evaluators: A guide for alcohol and other drug abuse prevention practitioners working with ethnic/racial communities* (DHHS Publication No. ADM 92-1884). Rockville, MD: Office for Substance Abuse Prevention.

Carver, C. A. (1995). Where professional reality meets political distortion: What mental health professionals can do about the anti-gay movement. *Journal of Humanistic Education and Development, 33,* 113–122.

Cass, V. C. (1979). Homosexual identity formation: A theoretical model. *Journal of Homosexuality, 4,* 219–235.

Cass, V. C. (1984). Homosexuality identity formation: Testing a theoretical model. *Journal of Sex Research, 20,* 143–167.

Chodorow, N. (1978). *The reproduction of mothering.* Berkeley: University of California Press.

Chodorow, N. (1989). *Feminism and psychoanalytic theory.* New Haven, CT: Yale University Press.

Clarke, C. (1999). The failure to transform: Homophobia in the Black community. In E. Brandt (Ed.), *Blacks, gays, and the struggle for equality: Dangerous liaisons* (pp. 31–44). New York: New Press.

Coleman, E. (1982). Developmental stages of the coming out process. *Journal of Homosexuality, 7,* 31–43.

Conerly, G. (2000). Are you Black first or are you queer? In D. Constantine-Simms (Ed.), *The greatest taboo: Homosexuality in Black communities* (pp. 7–23). Los Angeles: Alyson Books.

Croom, G. L. (2000). Lesbian, gay, and bisexual people of color. In B. Greene & G. L. Croom (Eds.), *Education, research, and practice in lesbian, gay, bisexual, and transgendered psychology: A resource manual* (pp. 263–281). Thousand Oaks, CA: Sage.

Cross, W. E. (1971). Negro-to-Black conversion experience: Toward a new psychology of Black liberation. *Black World, 20*(9), 13–27.

Cross, W. E. (1978). The Cross and Thomas models of psychological nigrescence. *Journal of Black Psychology, 5,* 13–19.

Diplacido, J. (1998). Minority stress among lesbians, gay men, and bisexuals: A consequence of heterosexism, homophobia, and stigmatization. In G. M. Herek (Ed.), *Stigma and sexual orientation: Understanding prejudice against lesbians, gay men, and bisexuals* (pp. 138–159). Thousand Oaks, CA: Sage.

Downing, N. E., & Roush, K. L. (1985). From passive acceptance to active commitment: A model of feminist identity development for women. *The Counseling Psychologist, 13,* 695–709.

Eisenstein, Z. R. (1979). A Black feminist statement. In Z. R. Eisenstein (Ed.), *Capitalist patriarchy and the case for socialist feminism* (pp. 362–372). New York: Monthly Review Press.

Ellis, P., & Murphy, B. C. (1994). The impact of misogyny and homophobia on therapy with women. In M. P. Mirkin (Ed.), *Women in context: Toward a feminist reconstruction of psychotherapy* (pp. 48–73). New York: Guilford Press.

Erikson, E. H. (1968). *Identity: Youth and crisis.* New York: Norton.

Fassinger, R. E. (1991). The hidden minority: Issues and challenges in working with lesbian women and gay men. *The Counseling Psychologist, 19,* 157–176.

Ford, D. Y., Harris, J., & Schuerger, J. M. (1993). Racial identity development among gifted Black students: Counseling issues and concerns. *Journal of Counseling & Development, 71,* 409–416.

Garnets, L., & Kimmel, D. (1991). Lesbian and gay male dimensions in the psychological study of human diversity. In J. D. Goodchild (Ed.), *Psychological perspectives on human diversity: Masters lecturers* (pp. 143–189). Washington, DC: American Psychological Association.

Greene, B. (1994). Diversity and difference: The issue of race in feminist therapy. In M. P. Mirkin (Ed.), *Women in context: Toward a feminist reconstruction of psychotherapy* (pp. 333–351). New York: Guilford Press.

Greene, B., & Boyd-Franklin, N. (1996). African American lesbian couples: Ethnocultural considerations in psychotherapy. *Women & Therapy: A Feminist Quarterly, 19*(3), 49–60.

Hays, P. A. (1996). Addressing the complexities of culture and gender in counseling. *Journal of Counseling & Development, 74,* 332–338.

Helms, J. E. (1990). An overview of Black racial identity theory. In J. E. Helms (Ed.), *Black and White racial identity: Theory, research and practice* (pp. 9–32). Westport, CT: Greenwood Press.

Helms, J. E. (1995). An update of Helms's White and people of color racial identity models. In J. G. Ponterotto, J. M. Casa, L. A. Suzuki, & C. M. Alexander (Eds.), *Handbook of multicultural counseling* (pp. 181–191). Thousand Oaks, CA: Sage.

Icard, I. (1986). Black gay men and conflicting social identities: Sexual orientation versus racial identity. In J. Gripton & M. Valentich (Eds.), *Social work practice in sexual problems* (pp. 83–93). New York: Haworth.

Jones, B. E., & Hill, M. J. (1996). African American lesbians, gays, and bisexuals. In R. P. Cabaj & T. S. Stein (Eds.), *Textbook of homosexuality and mental health* (pp. 549–561). Washington, DC: American Psychiatric Press.

Jordan, J. V. (1991). The meaning of mutuality. In J. V. Jordan, A. G. Kaplan, J. B. Miller, I. P. Stiver, & J. L. Surey (Eds.), *Women's growth in connection* (pp. 81–96). New York: Guilford Press.

King, T. C., & Ferguson, S. A. (1996). "I am because we are": Clinical interpretations of communal experience among African American women. *Women and Therapy, 18*(1), 33–45.

Kumashiro, K. K. (2001). Queer students of color and antiracist, antiheterosexist education: Paradoxes of identity and activism. In K. K. Kumashiro (Ed.), *Troubling intersections of race and sexuality: Queer students of color and anti-oppressive education* (pp. 1–25). New York: Rowman & Littlefield.

Lipkin, A. (1999). *Understanding homosexuality, changing schools: A text for teachers, counselors, and administrators.* Boulder, CO: Westview Press.

Loiacano, D. K. (1989). Gay identity issues among Black Americans: Racism, homophobia, and the need for validation. *Journal of Counseling & Development, 68,* 21–25.

Lorde, A. (1984). *Sister outsider.* Freedom, CA: Crossing Press.

Lowe, S. M., & Mascher, J. (2001). The role of sexual orientation in multicultural counseling. In J. G. Ponterotto, J. M. Casas, L. A. Suzuki, & C. M. Alexander (Eds.), *Handbook of multicultural counseling* (2nd ed., pp. 755–778). Thousand Oaks, CA: Sage.

Mays, V. M., Cochran, S. D., & Rhue, S. (1993). The impact of perceived discrimination on the intimate relationships of Black lesbians. *Journal of Homosexuality, 25,* 1–14.

McCready, L. (2001). When fitting in isn't an option, or, why Black queer males at a California high school stay away from Project 10. In K. K. Kumashiro (Ed.), *Troubling intersections of race and sexuality: Queer students of color and anti-oppressive education* (pp. 37–53). New York: Rowman & Littlefield.

McIntyre, T. (1992). Invisible culture in our schools: Gay and lesbian youth. *Beyond Behavior, 3*(3), 6–12.

Merighi, J. R., & Grimes, M. D. (2000). Coming out to families in a multicultural context. *Families in Society: The Journal of Contemporary Human Services, 81,* 32–41.

Miranda, J., & Storms, M. (1989). Psychological adjustment of lesbians and gay men. *Journal of Counseling & Development, 68,* 41–45.

Mobley, M., & Levey, M. (1998). Lesbian, gay, and bisexual students of color. In M. Levey, M. Blanco, & W. T. Jones (Eds.), *How to succeed on a majority campus: A guide for minority students* (pp. 171–197). Belmont, CA: Wadsworth.

Morles, E. S. (1989). Ethnic minority families and minority gays and lesbians. *Journal of Homosexuality, 17,* 217–239.

Morten, G., & Atkinson, D. R. (1983). Minority identity development and preference for counselor race. *Journal of Negro Education, 52,* 156–161.

Nardi, P. M., & Schneider, B. E. (Eds.). (1998). *Social perspectives in lesbian and gay studies: A reader.* New York: Routledge.

Nelson, M. L. (1996). Separation versus connection. The gender controversy: Implications for counseling women. *Journal of Counseling & Development, 74,* 339–344.

O'Hanlan, K. A., Robertson, P., Cabaj, R. P., Schatz, B., & Nemrow, P. (1996, November 1). Homophobia is a health hazard. *USA Today Magazine, 125,* 26–29.

Olkin, R. (1999). The personal, professional, and political when clients have disabilities. *Women and Therapy: A Feminist Quarterly, 22*(2), 87–103.

Parham, T. A., & Helms, J. E. (1985). The relationship of racial identity attitudes to self-actualization and affective states of Black students. *Journal of Counseling Psychology, 32,* 431–440.

Parker, W. M., Archer, J., & Scott, J. (1992). *Multicultural relations on campus: A personal growth approach.* Muncie, IN: Accelerated Development.

Parks, E. E., Carter, R. T., & Gushue, G. V. (1996). At the crossroads: Racial and womanist identity development in Black and White women. *Journal of Counseling & Development, 74,* 624–631.

Plummer, D. L. (1996). Black racial identity attitudes and stages of the lifespan: An exploratory investigation. *Journal of Black Psychology, 22,* 169–181.

Plummer, K. (1975). *Identities in the lesbian world: The social construction of self.* Westport, CT: Greenwood Press.

Ponse, B. (1978). *Identities in the lesbian world: The social construction of self.* Westport, CT: Greenwood Press.

Poston, W. S. C. (1990). The biracial identity model: A needed addition. *Journal of Counseling & Development, 69,* 152–155.

Ritter, K. Y., & O'Neill, C. W. (1989). Moving through loss: The spiritual journey of gay men and lesbian women. *Journal of Counseling & Development, 68,* 9–15.

Schur, E. M. (1984). *Labeling women deviant: Gender, stigma, and social control.* New York: McGraw-Hill.

Sophie, J. (1985–1986). A critical examination of stage theories of lesbian identity development. *Journal of Homosexuality, 12,* 39–51.

Spencer, M. B., & Markstrom-Adams, C. (1990). Identity process among racial and ethnic children in America. *Child Development, 61,* 290–310.

Troiden, R. R. (1988). *Gay and lesbian identity: A sociological analysis.* New York: General Hall.

Walters, K. L. (1997). Urban lesbian and gay American Indian identity: Implications for mental health service delivery. In L. B. Brown (Ed.), *Two spirit people: American Indian lesbian women and gay men* (pp. 43–65). Binghamton, NY: Harrington Park Press.

Walters, K. L., & Simoni, J. M. (1993). Lesbian and gay men identity attitudes and self-esteem: Implications for counseling. *Journal of Counseling Psychology, 40,* 94–99.

Wooden, W. S., Kawasaki, H., & Mayeda, R. (1983). Lifestyles and identity maintenance among gay Japanese-American males. *Alternative Lifestyles, 5,* 236–243.

8

Let the Choir Say "Amen":
The Impact of Intragroup Perceptions on
African Americans With HIV/AIDS

Marva Nelson

Intracultural perceptions in African American communities nourish a climate whereby HIV/AIDS continues to flourish, particularly among African American women. Because of the early identification of AIDS with the gay White community, many African Americans associate stigma and shame with this disease. As a result, African Americans tend to shun formal counseling venues. Instead, many seek out sites of nonprofessional counseling such as churches, which have traditionally served as places where African Americans may "lay their burdens down." However, African American churches, despite being traditionally vocal advocates for the health and welfare of the community, have responded lethargically to the AIDS crisis in the African American community. More specifically, many have ignored the psychosocial needs of congregants with HIV/AIDS, unfortunately reinforcing the stigma and shame associated with this disease. Consequently, many African Americans with HIV/AIDS and their caregivers, in effect, have become psychological refugees pushed out into the fringes of a community already historically marginalized.

Moreover, more formalized support structures (i.e., public and private counseling outlets) have also been frustratingly slow to acknowledge the specific psychosocial needs of African Americans with HIV/AIDS. This has served to further heighten the wariness of African Americans with HIV/AIDS because of intracultural, as well as intraracial, perceptions of not only HIV/AIDS but also mental illness. Therefore, it is essential that counselors more fully understand and engage the hydra-headed psychological traumas experienced by African Americans with HIV/AIDS in the form of intracultural and intraracial perceptions. By doing so, counselors may develop more effective strategies that specifically attend to this population's psychosocial needs.

Demographics

HIV/AIDS, initially thought to affect primarily gay White men, is rapidly approaching pandemic status within the African American community. African Americans accounted for half of the new reported HIV cases in the United States in 2001. African American men constituted 43% of reported HIV cases, and African American women constituted 64% of reported HIV1 cases (Centers for Disease Control and Prevention, 2003). This represents a statistically significant threat in that African Americans currently account for approximately 13% of the U.S. population (U.S. Census Bureau, 2002). In stark contrast, the HIV/AIDS mortality rate is steadily declining among the gay White population.

African Americans bore witness to the devastating arrival of the HIV/AIDS epidemic of the 1980s along with the rest of America. However, the epidemic disparately affected the African American community. As Maya Rockeymoore (as quoted in Daniels, Brown, & Mayeri, 2002) noted in *State of Black America*:

> Early surveillance data issued by the Centers for Disease Control and Prevention (CDC) revealed that African Americans were among the first cases of AIDS in America and that their rate of infection was disproportionate to their representation in the general population. (p. 124)

However, the initial images that inundated the entire nation's newspapers, magazines, and televisions were those of gay White men. Already injected with a healthy dose of mistrust rooted in sociocultural biases and experiences with health care and counseling systems, African Americans chose to silently ride out the subsequent campaign of misinformation of who was and was not at risk for the disease. As gay White men such as actor Rock Hudson became the icon of HIV/AIDS, African Americans, specifically gay men, watched HIV/AIDS ravage their social networks. Unfortunately, there was very little organized hue and cry from within the greater African American community owing to the aforementioned mistrust, which was additionally complicated by communal perceptions of homosexuality.

African Americans' Views Toward Sexuality

African Americans have traditionally retreated behind a thickly veiled silence when confronting issues of sexuality. Thanks to slavery's legacy of sexual exploitation of Black bodies, an inordinate amount of shame and stigma has been attached to African American sexualities. The African American community has usually sought refuge from racist mythologies that have prevailed since the 1600s well into this century by ratcheting up the emphasis on heterosexuality. Consequently, the discourse of homosexuality has been articulated as abnormal and deviant behavior, historically viewed as extant only within the White community—even though scholarly research has provided evidence that homosexual cultures were existent in precolonial Africa and, therefore, logically have extended out among the peoples of the African Diaspora. "A . . . pattern of male–male marriages is found among the Berber culture of Siwa (Egypt) where 'men and boys entered into alliances . . . with family approval and these alliances had many of the traits of formal marriage'" (Adam, 1968, as quoted in Constantine-Simms, 2001, p. 136). However, despite historical documentation, African American gay men are, quite often, viewed as having embraced so-called White values or told that they have succumbed to the "White man's disease."

Additionally, research regarding intragroup perceptions of homosexuality suggests that African Americans may demonstrate a higher degree of homophobia than the predominantly White population. "African Americans are believed to have less tolerance of homosexuality than Whites. This degree of difference is thought to result in greater stigmatization of homosexuality in African American communities, causing more 'closeted' behaviors and subsequently producing more stress" (Rose, 1998, as quoted in Battle & Lemmelle, 2002, p. 134). Consequently, conjectures regarding sexuality may very well result in having one's "race card" called into question within the community. That is to say that those who are deemed to be homosexual within the African American community tend to be vilified as "acting White" and, consequently, become marginalized within their communities—even though they share the communal experience of racial oppression.

> Individuals who are militantly opposed to racism in all its forms still find lesbianism and male homosexuality something to snicker about or, worse, to despise. Homophobic people of color are oppressive not just to white people, but to members of their own groups—at least 10 percent of their own groups. (Smith, 1998, p. 114)

These attitudes may be directly attributable to intragroup perceptions related not only to sexual taboos within the African American community but also to gender role expectations and the unequivocal support expressed by the leadership of many formal organizational structures within the community that are viewed as "authentic" transmitters of African Americans' perspectives, for example, churches, political organizations, and social clubs.

Granted, the sexually repressive attitudes expressed by African Americans mirror those of the general population; however, slavery's aftermath of sexual exploitation of both male and female African Americans indelibly inscribed an unwholesome sense of sexual repression rooted in bestialized and submissive imagery of African American men and women that persists even now. Correspondingly, the African American community has continually exerted extraordinary efforts toward negating these images, primarily by fervently embracing hegemonic gender roles as idealized by the general (read: White) population. In addition, African Americans have sought to deracinate these historical blemishes by exalting heterosexuality and, more specifically, heterosexual masculinity.

Even though this amplification of Black manhood has been existent within the community for decades, recurrent issues have intensified the relatively recent discussions focused on Black masculinity that gained impetus in the 1960s—most likely due to a convergence of ideologies. The birth of the Black nationalist movement in conjunction with the (re)birth of the feminist movement created heated debates on intragroup perceptions about the ostensible emasculation of Black men. The flames of these debates were further stoked by the findings contained within the famous Moynihan Report of 1965 titled *The Negro Family: The Case for National Action* (written by Senator Daniel P. Moynihan) that garnered national and international attention for its scrutiny of the changing demographics of the African American (then Negro) family. Accordingly, its findings reported a significant increase in female-headed households, which, consequently, affirmed one of the key agenda points of the predominantly male, Black nationalist movement: that Black men, disempowered and disenfranchised, were in danger of becoming even more psychologically emasculated because of the increase of female-headed households. Furthering their cause were the ever-disproportionate educational attainment, employment, and incarceration rates for African American men in contrast to African American women and the general population at large. All of these factors helped to shape a communal ideal of extolling Black masculinity. As a consequence, the resultant effect further marginalized African American women and, as noted earlier, Black gay men, thereby relegating them to the periphery of a community itself already historically marginalized.

Homophobia Within the African American Community

Many of the militant architects of the Black nationalist movement were enthusiastically sexist and homophobic. While, in theory, race trumped gender, the exact opposite appears to be true. The valorization of patriarchy, while espousing a breaking away from "traditional" White and bourgeoisie Black values, along with a call for "unity," actually mirrored the very

values many sought to reject; to wit: promotion of intragroup inequality as well as de-
nunciation of those African Americans, usually women and gays, who believed that true
transformation could take place only by presenting a united front.

Much of the hypermasculinized discourse of the Black power movement is reflected in
the poetics of the Black arts movement that was tremendously influential within the African
American community. Poets such as Haki Madhubuti (formerly known as Don L. Lee) and
Imamu Amira Baraka (formerly known as LeRoi Jones) charged the atmosphere with their
writings:

> . . . Swung on a faggot who politely
> Scratched his ass in my presence.
> He smiled broken teeth stained from
> His over-used tongue, fisted-face.
> Teeth dropped in tune with Ray
> Charles singing "yesterday."
> (*Madhubuti, "Don't Cry, Scream"; in* Call and Response, *Liggins Hill et al., 1997, pp. 1539–1540*)

No doubt, many African American gay men ran "screaming" into their psychological
closets, choosing to adopt the militant Black male pose to physically survive an environment that was racially and sexually oppressive.

Similarly, Baraka, viewed by many as one of the fathers of the Black arts movement, subtly articulates the misogyny and homophobia that were the order of the day with regard
to Black nationalism:

> . . . For all of him, and all of yourself, look up,
> Black man, quit stuttering and shuffling, look up,
> Black man, quit whining and stooping, for all of him,
> For Great Malcolm[1] a prince of the earth, let nothing in us rest
> Until we avenge ourselves for his death, stupid animals
> That killed him, let us never breathe a pure breath if
> We fail, and white men call us faggots till the end of
> The earth.
> (*Baraka, "Poem for Black Hearts"; in* Call and Response, *Liggins Hill et al., 1997, pp. 1503–1504*)

This polemic of masculinity, exhorting Black men to assume a pose of exaggerated
manhood, grounded itself in gender roles being biologically deterministic in nature.
Therefore, African American women were expected to support "The Movement" and their
Black men from behind the scenes (or "the margins") by provisioning the ranks, so to
speak, with soldiers for this New Black Order through reproduction. "The racial discourse
. . . of influential cultural nationalists involved in Black liberation struggles during the
'machismo' sixties include[d] an embrace of a biologically-based natural order with respect to gender roles" (Cole & Guy-Sheftall, 2003, p. 80). Therefore, procreation served
as a form of racial uplift, thereby legitimating Black womanhood.

In short, Black group identity became and continues to remain subject to licensure by
certain group leaders who, through the construction of a formulaic equation of Blackness,
affirm or deny group membership based on a set of predetermined, highly subjective set

---

[1]Malcolm refers to Nation of Islam minister and Black nationalist, Malcolm X, who was assassinated in
February 1965.

of criteria. Those found lacking in measuring up to standards of "true Blackness" are shunted toward the outer boundaries of the African American community.

Cohen (1999) addressed this in her scholarly study of AIDS in the African American community, *The Boundaries of Blackness: AIDS and the Breakdown of Black Politics*:

> Group members employ a "calculus" of indigenous membership, which can include an assessment of personal or moral worth, such as an individual's contribution to the community, adherence to community norms and values, or faithfulness to perceived, rewritten, or in some cases newly created African traditions. Thus indigenously constructed definitions of black group identity seek to redefine and empower blackness to the outside world by policing the boundaries of what can be represented to the dominant public as "true" blackness. (p. 74)

Over the past 40 years, subsequent to the aforementioned sociopolitical movements, communal and national perspectives, as articulated through various media (e.g., books, news, comedy, and musical venues), myopically address problems prevalent in the African American community such as incarceration and educational attainment rates for males, while ignoring the equally important problem of HIV/AIDS. Music tends to serve as a predominant form of articulating and affirming the "cool pose" of strident heterosexuality expected of African American men. Musical lyrics by many rap, hip-hop, and reggae artists bear witness to this. For example,

> The world is in trouble/Anytime Buju Banton come/Batty boy[2] get up and run/ah gunshot in ah head man/Tell dem crew . . . it's like/Boom bye bye, in a batty boy head, rude boy nah promote no nasty man, them hafi dead. (Banton, 2001)

The importance of this cultural venue cannot be overstated. This prevalent attitude of censure by "any means necessary" fuels intracultural discrimination and stigmatization of "The Other," specifically African Americans who are significantly affected by HIV/AIDS. In short, a hierarchy of oppression exists whereby heterosexism trumps race and race trumps homophobia.

Perceptions of Heterosexual Behavior

Another major contributory factor to the stigmatization of African Americans with HIV/AIDS is the perception of sexual behavior. While the existence of HIV/AIDS among the homosexual African American community should not be given short shrift, the continued focus on this community, in turn, marginalizes those engaging in risky heterosexual behavior. Consequently, the community, until recently, has turned a blind eye to the fastest growing demographic of people with HIV/AIDS—especially African American women. As stated earlier, African Americans accounted for half of the new reported HIV cases in the United States in 2001. African American men constituted 43% of reported HIV cases, and African American women constituted 64% of reported HIV cases (Centers for Disease Control and Prevention, 2003). Although a significant increase in reported cases has occurred over the past decade, we must recognize several barriers to garnering a more holistic picture of HIV/AIDS within the African American community. Negative perceptions toward homosexuality and assumption of a "cool pose" by many Black men serve to hide the true depth of this epidemic within the larger heterosexual community.

---

[2]"Batty boy" is the pejorative term commonly used for gay men in Jamaica.

Given African American communal disdain for homosexuality, which is oftentimes rooted in religious reasoning, men who have sex with men tend to be less forthcoming about their sexual behavior and are unwilling to see themselves as other than heterosexual. Consequently, due to the perceptions surrounding Black sexualities, many are less likely to seek out health care services that will inform them of their HIV status. Additionally, many of these men will retain female sex partners who may, unknowingly, become infected with HIV/AIDS. A prime example of this can be seen among African American men who have been incarcerated either in jail or in prison. Currently, African American men are disproportionately represented among incarcerated populations in the United States. According to a U.S. Bureau of Justice Statistics report (see Harrison & Karberg, 2003), 12.9% of African American men between the ages of 25 and 29 were incarcerated compared with 4.3% of Hispanic and 1.6% of White men (p. 11). Even though the rate of incarceration drops for Black men as their age increases, they are still incarcerated at twice the rate of Whites. Many of these African American men have been incarcerated for drug-related crimes, oftentimes receiving disproportionate sentencing because of relatively recent changes in sentencing laws. In addition, there has been a significant increase in the incarceration rate of women, especially African American women, again due in no small part to significant changes in drug sentencing laws. Incarceration conjures negative stereotypes, particularly for African American men, of becoming submissive to other men within the more dominant, hypermasculinized prison culture. Prison sexual assaults among men tend to be underreported for, if no other reason, self-preservation. Consequently, upon release into a community that exalts male heterosexuality, many men remain silent about sexual relations formed on the basis of necessity or coercion within the penal system. This same mindset holds true among African American women who have been incarcerated. Oftentimes, their incarceration is connected to African American men who possess a history of illicit drug use or incarceration. In addition, the lack of quality access to health care further adds to the stigma tenaciously attached to convict populations. However, this underreporting is not the sole realm of the incarcerated.

The phenomenon of engaging in what has been coined as *down-low* sexual behavior is becoming more and more a part of the social discourse involving HIV/AIDS. Because of the resistance to labeling oneself, many men who have sex with men within the general African American community tend to not disclose their sexual orientation, not even to their female partners, thereby leaving the women to presume that they are heterosexual. Consequently, owing to continued misperceptions about who can and cannot get HIV/AIDS, these men and the women who become their sexual partners are less likely to know their HIV status. Those courageous enough to disclose their sexual orientation or seek out counseling services run the risk of further stigmatization given the African American community's participation in "the oppression olympics" whereby race takes precedence over gender and any deviance from prescribed gender roles (i.e., acting like a man) is viewed as socially unacceptable behavior.

The Black Church

This volatile admixture of homophobia and heterosexism has also been consistently fueled by highly influential social forces within the African American community that have, for the most part, assimilated; in other words, they have, by and large, adopted middle-class (read: White) values. One of the most revered and highly influential institutions in the African American community is the Black church. Although there is no monolithic "Black church" per se, many African Americans view these institutions as an amalgamation. These churches arose during a critical juncture in African American history. Churches often served as proponents for abolition, and similarly, slaves seeking civil justice found some vestiges of equality inside the walls of these institutions. As freedom was gained, many Black churches co-opted the predominantly White Protestant ethic that valued work, family, and education under the aegis of religious worship. Therefore, the "Black church" is used in this context to speak of those churches predominantly rooted in Protestantism because they tend to function as "authentic" transmitters of the collective African American experience.

African Americans have historically looked to the Black church as a change agent of social justice, thereby focusing their collective gaze on the liberating aspects of the Bible, specifically the messages inherently contained within the New Testament: Jesus as champion for the oppressed and the possibility of freedom being gained through resurrection.

> Unlike many white Americans, blacks have often seen religion and spirituality not so much as a mere set of rules but as a mechanism for liberation in the struggles of their lives and times, which have taken them from slavery to segregation to economic dislocation. (Boykin, 1996, pp. 125–126)

Today, however, significant numbers of African Americans adhere to a more fundamentalist reading of biblical scripture rooted in Old Testament admonishments that mirror the collective mindset of sexual conservatism that exists throughout the United States. That is to say, sex should be an experience derived solely from within the bounds of heterosexual marriage with the endpoint being procreation. Once again, as was the case in the 1960s, procreation has become the vehicle for racial uplift within the African American community. Similarly, African Americans once more face repression of any erotic/sexual desires that fall outside marital parameters.

African American churches, seeking assimilation into mainstream Christian society, have staunchly reinforced these traditional sexual mores. In fact, many exemplars of Black church leadership, while proclaiming the liberating aspects of the biblical scripture, have, nonetheless, failed to critically engage the Black church in a much-needed dialogue of how the scriptures have been continually used to negate the multidimensionality of African ancestral faith traditions that held long-established gender role expectations, addressed the consequences of immoral behavior, and correspondingly, revered marriage and family. Instead, many church leaders discriminately use scriptural injunctions to denounce gender rebels—those who face stigma and shame because of intragroup differences. Boykin (1996) affirmed this as a replication of the psychology slave owners once used:

> The use of religion to justify discrimination is, of course, not new. In 1845, Frederick Douglass described how his master converted to Christianity and then found religious sanction and support for his slave holding cruelty. "I have seen him tie up a lame young woman," wrote Douglass, "and whip her with a heavy cowskin upon her naked shoulders, causing the warm red blood to drop; and in justification of the bloody deed he would quote the passage of Scripture—'He that knoweth the master's will, and doeth it not, shall be eaten with many stripes.'" (p. 147)

Within the African American community, gender rebels have become the designated boogeyman that is to blame for many communal ailments, even though many of these rebels serve silently as functionaries within the Black church. Once again, Boykin (1996) provided anecdotal evidence:

> Despite the widespread awareness of homosexuality in the black church, we still find black ministers, deacons, ushers, choir members, music directors, organists, congregations, and homosexuals themselves participating in an elaborate conspiracy of silence and denial. Several of the black ministers I interviewed—even those with reputations for homophobia—acknowledged the pres-

ence of large homosexual contingents in their churches, but this fact has not stopped their homophobic preaching, particularly because the lesbian and gay parishioners accept and even participate in the rhetorical gay bashing. (p. 127)

Consequently, intragroup perceptions regarding legitimacy of needs help to reinforce the ever-present hierarchy of oppression. Therefore, many church members with HIV/AIDS still abide by church dogma even though they must endure blatant intragroup discrimination because the church may be the only point of social support for them even as it tacitly endorses intragroup segregation. This, no doubt, adds to the psychosocial burden many African Americans with HIV/AIDS already shoulder.

The significance of the church as an institution of power within the Black community is so prevalent that many Blacks dare not stray from it. In addition to serving as a change agent for social justice, the Black church has met more individualized needs, specifically functioning as a surrogate source of psychosocial counseling, in opposition to more formalized public and private organizations. This is true, too, of other spaces within the African American community, such as sociopolitical organizations, fraternities, sororities, community centers, and others. This surrogacy may be directly attributable to African Americans' reticence toward seeking assistance from so-called White venues (i.e., psychologists, psychotherapists, psychiatrists, etc.).

Given the constancy of the Black church not only as a means of worship but also as a social support network, accessibility to the church, usually located within the heart of any given African American community, has seemed to provide a more logical means of psychosocial support. Many other more formal institutions tend not to be situated immediately within the community. Given this, we can see why many African American communities utilize church clergy as counselors, despite the imminent possibility of being further stigmatized. Those who stray away from the fold and seek social support outside of the community run the risk of facing communal humiliation for seeking services from institutions that have traditionally not been encouraging to the African American community. Many an African American child has been punished for telling family business or "airing dirty laundry." Therefore, anyone breaking the conspiracy of silence that is prevalent within the community may be branded as a race traitor, subject to communal ridicule and intragroup discrimination.

Community Counseling and Health Care Services

African Americans with HIV/AIDS possess a collective reticence toward seeking more formalized counseling because the majority of counseling services that may be attentive to their needs tend to be physically located outside community boundaries, be they urban or rural. In addition, the faces of HIV/AIDS counselors mirror a predominantly White face extant within the field as a whole. In addition, many such counseling services are provided in sites more amenable to visitation by gay White men and are placed in neighborhoods relatively distant from African American communities. This further serves to validate intragroup perceptions that the face of HIV/AIDS is represented by primarily White gay men. Therefore, it stands to reason that those African Americans who seek out counseling resources may be viewed as "telling White folks" information that not only reflects personal experiences but may speak to and be perceived as a collective indictment of the failure of the African American community to address the individual needs of African Americans with HIV/AIDS.

An additional complication has been the historical shutting out of African Americans to accessible, quality health care. This has been further compounded by differential diagnoses based on intercultural and intragroup distinctions on the basis of class and race.

Access to quality health care is premised on socioeconomic worth in American society as a whole. Conversely, the history of the African American community has been threaded through and through with economic disenfranchisement. This history is rife with examples of how health care agencies have only served to heighten intragroup differences. Good health belongs to the haves rather than the have-nots. In other words, those who are White or appear to subscribe to White values and possess the economic means to do so will be afforded accessible, quality health care. All others need not apply—unless they are willing to submit to mediocre treatment.

One of the most strikingly nefarious incidences of this is the infamous Tuskegee Syphilis Experiment conducted for 40 years by the U.S. Public Health Service on the poorest of the poor, illiterate Black sharecroppers suffering from tertiary syphilis. Informed by federal public health officials that they were being treated for "bad blood," these men served, in fact, as laboratory guinea pigs being observed by researchers as they suffered the ravages of syphilis. The participants were being told that they were benefiting the "public good." (See also this volume, chap. 15, for more discussion on the Tuskegee Experiment.)

Keeping this in mind, communal paranoia is often stoked when clinical protocols seeking African American participation are broadcast throughout the collective community. The Tuskegee Experiment has become the bellwether for African Americans' cultural mistrust. In addition, this communal paranoia has been further exacerbated by clinicians' continued failure to incorporate holistic and culturally sensitive approaches. The resultant effect is that many African Americans with HIV/AIDS already stigmatized within their communities steer clear of potential psychosocial trauma and stigmatization by failing to respond to calls for participants in studies that have oftentimes cast a negative light on the African American community, reinforced discriminatory attitudes among health care providers, and historically benefited the dominant population.

For example, current drug protocols for people with HIV/AIDS have been highly effective in predominantly White populations but revealed much poorer outcomes in the African American population. Maya Rockeymoore (as quoted in Daniels et al., 2002) provided probable evidence of intercultural discrimination related to inequities in health care.

> A study published in the *Archives of Internal Medicine*[3] found that Medicaid patients treated for AIDS-related Pneumocystis Carinii Pneumonia (PCP) were 75 percent more likely to die than those with private insurance. Medicaid patients who are more likely to be African American . . . were dramatically less likely to receive the proper treatment for PCP or even have their complication diagnosed. Those Medicaid patients, who did receive proper treatment, received it later in their hospital stay than those . . . who were privately insured. Findings from this study have been corroborated by a more recent study conducted by the Institute of Medicine, which found that African Americans had a higher death rate due to pervasive discrimination that made them less likely to receive appropriate AIDS treatment. (p. 137)

Cultural Awareness and Sensitivity

The lethargic response of the mental health community toward addressing issues of cultural sensitivity has exacerbated the already prevalent intragroup mistrust and suggests in-

---

[3]Bennett, C. L., Horner, R. D., Weinstein, R. A., Dickinson, G. M., DeHovitz, J. A., Cohn, S.E., et al. (1995). Racial differences in care among hospitalized patients with pneumocystis carinii pneumonia in Chicago, New York, Los Angeles, Miami, and Raleigh–Durham. *Archives of Internal Medicine, 155*, 1586–1592.

tercultural discrimination. This has profoundly contributed to the decreasing likelihood that African Americans with HIV/AIDS may seek out more formalized, professional resources (e.g., counseling or psychotherapy). In addition, a lack of ethnic mirroring as well as a dearth of outreach services further serves to socially isolate African Americans with HIV/AIDS.

Mental health practitioners and other health service providers usually reflect the faces of the predominantly White population. African Americans with HIV/AIDS, when they do take the initiative to seek out appropriate counseling services, are often confronted with self-disclosing their sexual health status to someone who may not appear to be either physically or verbally empathetic to them. As a consequence, this discomfiture may create a sense of having to choose allegiances. If clients' perception that their needs will not be heard or adequately addressed is confirmed by a counselor, then they face castigation and isolation within their community upon their return for having stepped "out of their place" by "airing their dirty laundry."

Oftentimes, potential counseling resources are located in more affluent neighborhoods, which facilitate access for gay White men and others of the dominant population who have HIV/AIDS. Consequently, African Americans with HIV/AIDS may have to travel outside of their neighborhoods. Again, the significance of situational and economic disenfranchisement and how they may affect intracultural perceptions should not be overlooked. Many African Americans are criticized for seeking to "act White" if they choose to step outside the prescribed boundaries of Blackness.

Implications for Practice and Future Research

The counseling professions, although somewhat more cognizant of issues of cultural mistrust, must push for greater awareness of intragroup differences (such as those discussed here) that speak to the multidimensional issues faced by African Americans with HIV/AIDS. Disseminating culturally sensitive literature, for example, pamphlets, booklets, and videos that reflect the diversity of people afflicted with HIV/AIDS, is a laudable, albeit one-dimensionally simplistic approach that plays into treating these diseases by means of a template. This methodology calls into question ownership of life-saving information and further utilizes cultural tools historically used to oppress African people of the Diaspora. This, in turn, only serves to intensify the already prevailing cultural mistrust and corroborates communal suspicions toward the dominant group. Viable alternatives must include more holistic approaches that account for a more in-depth reading of intragroup differences among African Americans.

Additionally, given the prominent role that the Black church continues to play in many African Americans' lives, especially those with HIV/AIDS, outreach by initiating sustained contact and developing collaborative strategies that provide opportunities for cross-cultural education may help to draw African Americans with HIV/AIDS back in from the borderlands, thereby re-creating truly safe spaces for worship as well as sites for much-needed intragroup dialogues.

However, even before these initial contacts are made, mental health practitioners must expand their knowledge base in respect to the multidimensional aspects of African Americans' spiritual beliefs, for example, the critical role religiosity plays in those who attend church as well as those who do not. To that end, training should be provided to not only established professionals but also students going into counseling in order not to replicate the same barriers African Americans with HIV/AIDS currently face. Constantine, Lewis, Conner, and Sanchez (2000) provided insights into how counseling training programs may breach existing barriers:

Hence, counselor training programs may wish to identify strategies that encourage students to explore their own spiritual and religious orientations and the impact these ideologies have on their work with African American clients. In particular, counselors' religious and spiritual orientations may greatly influence therapeutic issues, such as their conceptualizations of clients' presenting concerns, the counseling relationships, and choice of clinical interventions. It is also conceivable that supervision, as an integral part of counselor training, focuses on the awareness and exploration of spiritual and religious issues regarding how they may affect various therapeutic phenomena. (p. 35)

In addition, given the demographic shifts occurring within the United Stated and the related increase in culturally diverse populations, more concerted recruitment efforts targeting racial/ethnic minority teaching faculty and staff outside of the usual venues (e.g., urban vs. rural, university vs. community) must be undertaken. Robinson and Morris (2000) noted the potential significance of this:

Training directors at university counseling centers reported significantly greater emphasis on multicultural issues than did training directors at community mental health centers, state hospitals, medical schools, and private psychiatric hospitals. . . . If these types of sites are actually offering the most training in multicultural issues, what can be said about the training offered at other types of sites? (p. 246)

Education of outreach teams that provide mobility of services may not only help close the gap between service needs and delivery but also cultivate healthy dialogues regarding intragroup and intercultural perceptions of HIV/AIDS. The argument can be made regarding potential costs of implementing these programs under ever-present budgetary constraints that counseling services operate under. However, such an approach may well focus attention on this national dilemma. More importantly, implementation of such a strategy will, hopefully, provide positive mental and physical outcomes, thereby lightening the load in the long run on our increasingly overburdened health systems.

Summary

African Americans' historical underutilization of services based on (a) service sites located outside of clients' neighborhood, which may further marginalize clients; (b) cultural mistrust rooted in historical encounters and perceived lack of empathy by counselors; (c) limited resources such as income and transportation; and (d) the potential for debilitation from the disease itself all serve as potential areas of critical examination whereby African Americans with HIV/AIDS may be better served by utilization of more culturally appropriate and holistic approaches. Given the near-pandemic impact on African Americans with HIV/AIDS, their caregivers, and the community as a whole, it is imperative that mental health professionals take the lead in developing effective delivery models such as collaborative ventures with community churches, halfway houses, and other community organizations that cultivate productive dialogues and models that, in turn, will offer significantly better mental and physical outcomes for African Americans with HIV/AIDS.

References

Banton, B. (2001). *Buju Banton: Ultimate collection* [CD]. Santa Monica, CA: Hip-O Records.
Battle, J., & Lemmelle, A. J., Jr. (2002). Gender differences in African American attitudes toward gay males. *Western Journal of Black Studies, 26,* 134–139.

Boykin, K. (1996). *One more river to cross: Black and gay in America*. New York: Doubleday.

Centers for Disease Control and Prevention, National Center for HIV, STD, and TB Prevention, Divisions of HIV/AIDS Prevention. (2003). *HIV/AIDS among African Americans fact sheet*. Retrieved March 1, 2004, from http://www.cdc.gov/hiv/pubs/Facts/afam.htm

Cohen, C. (1999). *The boundaries of Blackness: AIDS and the breakdown of Black politics*. Chicago: University of Chicago Press.

Cole, J. B., & Guy-Sheftall, B. (2003). *Gender talk: The struggle for women's equality in African American communities*. New York: Ballantine.

Constantine, M. G., Lewis, E. L., Conner, L. C., & Sanchez, D. (2000). Addressing spiritual and religious issues in counseling African Americans: Implications for counselor training and practice. *Counseling & Values, 45*, 28–38.

Constantine-Simms, D. (Ed.). (2001). *The greatest taboo: Homosexuality in Black communities*. Los Angeles: Alyson Books.

Daniels, L. A., Brown, D., & Mayeri, S. K. (Eds.). (2002). *The state of Black America*. New York: National Urban League.

Harrison, P. M., & Karberg, J. C. (2003, April). *Bureau of Justice Statistics Bulletin: Prison and jail inmates at midyear 2002* (No. NCJ 198877). Washington, DC: U.S. Department of Justice, Office of Justice Programs. Retrieved March 1, 2004, from http://www.ojp.usdoj.gov/bjs/pub/pdf/pjim02.pdf

Liggins Hill, P., Bell, B. W., Harris, T., Harris, W. J., Miller, R. B., O'Neale, S. J., & Porter, H. (Eds.). (1997). *Call and response: The Riverside anthology of the African American literary tradition*. New York: Houghton Mifflin.

Moynihan, D. P. (1965). *The Negro family: The case for national action*. Washington, DC: U.S. Department of Labor.

Robinson, D. T., & Morris, J. R. (2000). Multicultural counseling: Historical context and current training considerations. *Western Journal of Black Studies, 24*, 239–253.

Smith, B. (1998). *The truth that never hurts: Writings on race, gender, and freedom*. New Brunswick, NJ: Rutgers University Press.

U.S. Census Bureau. (2002). *American community survey profile: Tabular profile*. Retrieved September 5, 2003, from http://www.census.gov/acs/www/Products/Profiles/Single/2002/ACS/Tabular/010/01000/US1.htm

9

African Americans and Substance Abuse

Debra A. Harley

Substance abuse is recognized as a major health issue with various causes and implications, affecting women and men, all age groups, and diverse racial and ethnic groups in the United States, with African Americans being affected disproportionately (Fisher & Harrison, 2000). Although African Americans have higher rates of abstinence from alcohol than White Americans, African Americans who drink have higher rates of medical problems associated with drinking (Craig, 2004). In fact, some researchers have characterized alcohol abuse as the number one mental and social problem of African Americans (Bouie, 1993; Watts & Wright, 1983). "African Americans have been particularly vulnerable to the negative social and health consequences of substance abuse" (Stevens & Smith, 2001, p. 263). These consequences include earlier onset of substance abuse problems, greater likelihood of incarceration rather than treatment, higher rates of illness such as liver cirrhosis and esophageal cancer, poverty, unemployment, low educational level, residential segregation, and greater risk for HIV/AIDS (Dawkins & Williams, 1997; Fisher & Harrison, 2000; U.S. Census Bureau, 2000; Wallace & Brown, 1995). For African Americans, substance abuse is a mental health issue that has its origins in historical patterns (e.g., how alcohol was introduced to and used for slaves) and contemporary circumstances (e.g., poverty, racism, oppression, and war; Beatty, 2003; James & Johnson, 1996). African Americans must also contend with classism, which is composed of the oppressed and the oppressive, involving exploitation and economic issues based on class structures (Dittmar, 1995). In addition, African American women must deal with issues of sexism, which manifests as lower socioeconomic status and poverty, stress, violence, and trauma, placing them at greater risk for substance abuse (Beatty, 2003). In the United States, race is closely linked with class, and, thus, the individual influences of each cannot be easily distinguished (Blauner, 1992).

Although mental disorders account for four of the leading causes of disability in the United States, the Substance Abuse and Mental Health Services Administration's (SAMHSA) survey on drug use and health found that less than half of adults (age 18 and older) with a serious mental illness received treatment or counseling for a mental health problem during the past year (SAMHSA, 2003). More than 2 million adults with serious mental illness reported that they did not receive treatment. Cost of treatment was the primary reason for not getting mental health treatment. Other reasons included concerns about stigma, not knowing where to go for treatment, fear of being committed or having to take medicine, and lack of time or transportation (SAMHSA, 2003). Unfortunately, no differentiation was made between these figures and reasons pertaining to African Americans.

African American addiction is often evaluated without close examination of the traditional uses of alcohol and other drugs (AOD), without an understanding of psychological trauma people of African descent suffered when separated from their culture, and without consideration of risk factors and predisposition. This chapter examines issues about African American alcohol and drug consumption in response to psychological events and social stressors. Information is presented on the following: (a) background and early stereotyping of African Americans, (b) the marketing of substances to African Americans, (c) living in high-stress environments (e.g., low income, high rates of crime, high unemployment) and other risk factors, (d) the psychology of victimization versus resiliency, (e) barriers to treatment, and (f) prevention and intervention. Implications for practice and future research are also presented.

Although African Americans are discussed in this chapter in relation to substance abuse as a negative response to stressors, many African Americans do not drink excessively in response to stress. In fact, most African Americans drink socially and moderately and experience no problems from alcohol (Grace, 1992; Mosley, Atkins, & Klein, 1988). In addition, the reader is cautioned to keep in mind the diversity within the African American community and not to presume that all African Americans are alike. Some information discussed here may be more relevant for some subgroups than for others.

Background and Stereotyping

The presence of AOD in specific areas of Africa and the role of these drugs have a long history of trading relations between the West African coast and Europe. Anthropologically, well-established drinking patterns in which alcohol has become a focus of group interest have a minimal amount of disruptive behavior related to alcohol use in Africans. When Africans were brought to the New World, they brought their indigenous social patterns and drinking styles with them. Slaves were relatively sober when compared as a group with European settlers and American Indians because they drank largely when the "master" allowed it to happen (e.g., weekends, holidays, celebrations). Many slave masters permitted and encouraged alcohol use during harvest and agricultural layover times. In addition, liquor was used as an incentive and reward for prodigious feats of labor (James & Johnson, 1996). Ironically, legislation prohibited slaves from using alcoholic beverages except that the stimulant be given in relief of real physical distress (Fisher & Harrison, 2000).

Alcohol consumption and use of other drugs by African Americans evolved into more disruptive patterns of use after the civil war. The end of slavery stimulated the beginning of a rapid increase in migration north and in southern cities. "This increasing urbanization was to change African American patterns of occasional alcohol use into patterns of addiction" (James & Johnson, 1996, p. 12). The expansion of the urban ghetto has encouraged the growth of substance abuse as an industry. Alcohol began to be used more widely as a medication to treat the emotional suffering brought on by racism, economic deprivation or poverty, stress, and hopelessness (B. D. Johnson & Muffler, 1997). Other events such as the Vietnam war and racial integration led to increased AOD use and addiction (James & Johnson, 1996). African Americans must also contend with gender-based stereotypes. For example, African American men are perceived as physically powerful, emotionally immature, and demanding of respect at all costs as the ultimate expression of strength (Poussaint & Alexander, 2000). For African American women, the expectations are that they are strong, savvy, "not taking anything off any body," and stoic (hooks, 1993).

Many African Americans drink exclusively on weekends, traditionally a time of relaxation, visitation, and celebration (Fisher & Harrison, 2000). African American drinkers are further characterized by the following: (a) begin drinking at an earlier age, (b) tend to be younger alcoholics, (c) experience more severe substance abuse, (d) are involved in manual labor and more often go to bars after work, (e) are at higher risk for alcohol-related morbidity and mortality, (f) have more severe psychiatric consequences associated with substance abuse, (g) often lack factual information about substance abuse, and (h) are less likely to seek treatment (Craig, 2004; Lex, 1985).

According to James and Johnson (1996), perhaps the most significant event to affect patterns of African American addiction happened outside the United States in the Latin American country of Chile during the early 1970s, with the consolidation of the drug trade. Large amounts of cocaine were coming into the United States, and much of it was heading directly into African American communities. Subsequently, usage of variations of cocaine (e.g., crack, crank) expanded in African American communities because they were more affordable.

The use of illicit drugs is a major problem in the African American community (Grace, 1992). African Americans, especially those in the inner city, are identified as having addiction to cocaine, and there is an alarming increase in the number and younger age of individuals with addictions to illicit drugs. In fact, narcotics dependency among African Americans increased with their migration to northern urban areas (James & Johnson, 1996). According to L. S. Brown and Alterman (1992), African Americans are more likely to have used crack cocaine than any other racial/ethnic group. The use of and addiction to opiates among African Americans are accompanied by violence and criminal activity in their communities. Illicit drugs not only have brought more addiction, crime, and violence to African American communities but have also contributed substantially to the HIV/AIDS crisis (James & Johnson, 1996).

Marketing of Substances to African Americans

The specific demographic characteristics (e.g., age, education, income, sex) of African Americans who purchase and consume alcoholic beverages are not well known. However, we do know that the alcohol industry spends over a billion dollars annually to market its products and that African Americans are targeted disproportionately as consumers (Hacker, Collins, & Jacobson, 1987; Scott, Denniston, & Magruder, 1992; Wallace & Brown, 1995). The industry hires African American advertising agencies to conduct research and to develop sophisticated Black-oriented advertising programs that use African American language, culture, music, and role models to sell alcoholic beverages. Many African American popular magazines carry advertisements that glamorize alcohol and cigarette use. Coupled with the higher concentration of billboards in the African American community is the equally high concentration of alcohol outlets. That is, liquor stores are highly visible parts of residential areas heavily populated by African American people (Hacker et al., 1987; Wallace & Brown, 1995).

Many businesspersons have found a lucrative market locating their establishments in African American communities. It is suggested that African Americans drink more because alcohol is readily accessible (Mosley et al., 1988). In general, there are 10 times more liquor stores in African American communities than in predominantly White communities (Gordon, 1994). Availability of alcohol in relation to geographical factors among culturally and ethnically diverse populations reveals that the risk for substance abuse appears to have increased among individuals residing in impoverished areas (L. S. Brown & Alterman, 1992). Brown and Alterman further echoed that

> to the extent that many African Americans are and continue to be impoverished and deprived of many of the resources and benefits of our society, we should expect to find greater rates of substance abuse and more severe consequences of drug use. (p. 861)

Wallace and Brown (1995) stressed that it is not possible to draw a direct causal link from the alcohol industry's race-specific advertisement targeting to the negative health outcomes that alcohol use and abuse have on many African American people each year. They continued,

> Nevertheless, it seems very plausible that the money the alcohol industry pumps into Black employment, advertising, community service, and other organizations helps to silence efforts by African American churches, leadership, and celebrities to make African Americans aware that the legal drug, alcohol, devastates more families and takes more lives than all the illicit drugs combined. (p. 357)

Inevitably, the economic dependence of many African American corporations and individuals on the alcohol industry may limit both their ability and desire to advocate against the industry. In many ways, the African American community is in a catch-22 situation with neither the economic clout nor the social support to resist the pressure to purchase and consume alcoholic beverages (Wallace & Brown, 1995). Cigarettes and smoking among African Americans have produced similar results. According to James and Johnson (1996), "the tobacco industry casts a wide net of economic and political influence in the African American community that has devastating effects" (p. 58). In many African American communities, alcohol- and tobacco-related illness are the leading cause of death, with heart disease and cancer rates running above the national average (Breo, 1993).

Packaging and pricing of alcoholic beverages in conjunction with high levels of availability are other marketing strategies aimed specifically at African Americans. "The '40 ounce' malt liquor, ubiquitous in African American communities, is a particularly poignant example of availability" (Wallace & Brown, 1995, p. 359). The 40-ounce malt liquor is oversized, relatively inexpensive, extremely high in alcohol content, and heavily sold and marketed within African American communities (Scott et al., 1992).

The region of the country and the size of the city in which one lives are positively correlated to the prevalence and level of alcohol use (U.S. Department of Health and Human Services [U.S. DHHS], 1990). Despite evidence that African Americans are more likely to abstain from alcohol use and drink less than Whites, ethnographic data suggest that alcohol use and abuse are widespread problems among African Americans in urban, high-density, low-socioeconomic areas (Wallace & Brown, 1995). Chemical substances are frequently used as an escape mechanism from negative aspects of life (e.g., denial of equal opportunities for employment, education, and health care). Numerous African Americans are crowded into ghettos and inner cities, which breeds frustration that could lead to abuse of AOD.

High-Stress Environments and Other Risk Factors

African Americans currently experience psychosocial problems because of alcohol use. These problems include crime, homicide, suicide, impaired job performance, automobile accidents, environmental factors, and difficulty in intrapersonal and interpersonal relationships (Fisher & Harrison, 2000; U.S. DHHS, 1990). Intrapersonal risks refer to individual or personal behavior that puts an individual at risk for AOD abuse. Examples of these risk factors include sensation seeking, poor grades, low self-esteem, depression, expectation to drink in the future, and lack of bonding to societal institutions (e.g., family, school, community, work, and church; Wallace & Brown, 1995). Interpersonal risks are those that result from interaction with others. The most frequently cited interpersonal risk factors include those related to family and peers (e.g., modeling of alcohol abuse by parents and siblings, high levels of family conflict and stress, and pressure to drink; Hawkins, Catalano, & Miller, 1992). Environmental factors include those that relate to the broader social environment (e.g., racism) and those that relate specifically to AOD (Wallace & Brown, 1995).

Research indicates that alcohol consumption and alcohol-related social and physical problems are highest where there are high levels of poverty, unemployment, and crime; where there are high concentrations of alcohol outlets and low alcohol prices; where Sunday sales and advertising are not restricted; and where the minimum drinking age is low (O'Malley & Wagenaar, 1991). African Americans are disproportionately exposed to and affected by these factors (Wallace & Brown, 1995). The tragedy for African Americans is that most of them are subjected to all of the conditions of social injustice, social inconsistency, and personal impotence as the norm, which creates fertile ground for developing dependence on AOD (Bouie, 1993). Bouie indicated that "these conditions are not mutually exclusive, but interrelated and interdependent, and within them are elements of racism and manifestations of poverty, unemployment, and so forth" (p. 191).

K. A. Johnson and Jennison (1994) conducted a study of stressful loss and the buffering effect of social support on drinking behavior among African Americans and found that those who experienced stressful losses, or whose extended family members had experienced such losses, were significantly more likely to drink excessively. Thus, utilitarian drinking among African Americans may, in part, be a reaction to life circumstances in which alcohol represents an attempt to cope with traumatic social and psychological stress.

African Americans drink primarily to reduce tension and distress (James & Johnson, 1996). The abuse of alcohol is only one of an array of potential cognitive and behavioral coping responses to a stressful event (K. A. Johnson & Jennison, 1994). K. A. Johnson and Jennison indicated that according to the *additional burden model,* African Americans are more likely to experience unremitting or unmitigated stress in terms of their perceptions of a hostile and exclusionary social environment. This notion is supported by others reflecting that the frequency of exposure to various stressors is much greater for African Americans than for other groups (Jackson, 1991). In fact, there is the suggestion that African Americans are suffering from "posttraumatic slavery syndrome," the connection of racial oppression, hopelessness, self-hatred, economics, stress, and the patterns of self-destructive behavior (Poussaint & Alexander, 2000). Poussaint and Alexander provided an example of posttraumatic slavery syndrome with the cases of Carl Burton and Kenneth Poussaint (two African American males who were caught in a cycle of drug abuse, criminal activity, and self-loathing that fit the profile of young Blacks who self-destruct) in the following way:

> Both Burton and Poussaint began experimenting with drugs at an early age. . . . Both young men had contact with the criminal justice system and had served time for crimes related to their addictions. . . . Both were diagnosed with mental illnesses, yet declined to stay on a medication schedule; indeed, their drug abuse might possibly be seen as an attempt at self-medication. . . . . Both young men became increasingly isolated from their families while family members struggled to find effective means of helping them. . . . Both expressed, within their respective forms of mental illness, a preoccupation with the influence that they believed whites, and a white-dominated "system," held over their lives. . . . And both young men grew to devalue themselves to such a degree that an early death was not discounted as an alternative to the struggle that living had become. (p. 13)

Although these two young men "cannot possibly stand as exact mirrors of every black person who has self-destructed during the past twenty years," they possess "several important threads in their experiences that are relevant to the suicides of thousands of African Americans in recent years—and to the state of our society as a whole" (Poussaint &

Alexander, 2000, p. 13). Poussaint and Alexander stressed that diagnostic models have not always been effective in addressing the unique mental health concerns of African Americans. The high rate of homicide among African Americans might be viewed as evidence of a peculiar kind of communal self-hatred that leads to a devaluation of the lives of fellow African Americans. In addition, that same self-hatred may also lead to a devaluation of self, which can result in life-threatening, self-destructive, or suicidal behavior. Similar dynamics of self-devaluation and hopelessness may account, in part, for the high rates of AOD use among African Americans in U.S. society.

Victimization Versus Resiliency

Victimization is a term frequently used in the literature when referring to African Americans, whereas the term *resiliency* is used less frequently. Victimization refers to a process in which an individual or a group of people is coerced to conform or acquiesce to external forces. Conversely, resiliency is the ability to respond to and overcome adversity or socially constructed obstacles. Although no consensus about how to operationally define resiliency exists, most definitions include two basic elements: the presence of serious stress or adversity and the manifestation of competence or effective functioning (Beardslee, 1989). Through music, literature, and poetry, African Americans have echoed a legacy in which they must be capable of coping with any stress that comes along. According to Poussaint and Alexander (2000), "the idea [that] strength is required to endure the difficulties of life on earth has been central to black culture, and psychological, spiritual, and physical endurance enabled African Americans to withstand more than three hundred years of oppression" (p. 109). However, the question has been raised to determine if African Americans are engaging in self-destructive behavior through AOD addiction in response to an unfair burden and expectation to be strong at all costs. In other words, AOD abuse may be a sign of the degree to which African Americans have internalized the one-dimensional perception of themselves as "preternaturally strong" (Poussaint & Alexander, 2000). The expectation is that African Americans are to remain strong in spite of what hooks (1993) referred to as "psychological abuse in black life" (p. 70).

Several factors are inherent in the concept of resilience: social support, downward comparison (e.g., "things could have been worse"; Wills, 1991), and self-efficacy. According to Wills, when people are feeling discouraged, they try to feel better about themselves or their situation by comparing themselves with someone less fortunate. For African Americans who abuse alcohol, the comparison may be one of saying, "At least I don't use drugs." Making downward comparisons can improve one's sense of well-being and enhance one's self-esteem.

Barriers to Treatment

African Americans have historically been underserved by traditional mental health counseling services because of poverty, lack of accessible facilities, lack of awareness of service facilities or their purpose, and the absence of culturally acceptable treatment models (Exum, Moore, & Watt, 1999). Underutilization of mental health services by African Americans is also attributed to the fact that some may have a historically hostile response because of their prolonged inferior treatment in American society (Vontress & Epp, 1997). Cultural mistrust among African Americans of mental health services reveals that African Americans underutilize these services because (a) of fear of treatment and of being hospitalized, (b) they are often misdiagnosed and overrepresented among involuntary hospital admissions, and (c) mental health services are viewed by the African American community as a microcosm of the larger White society (Whaley, 2001). It is clear that cultural beliefs of African Americans play a significant role in mental health utilization or underutilization.

African Americans' perception of counselors as insensitive to their needs, the belief that counselors do not invest equal energy and time working with racial minority groups, and the feeling that counselors do not accept, understand, or respect cultural differences account for other reasons why African Americans overwhelmingly do not use mental health counseling services (S. P. Brown, Lipford-Sanders, & Shaw, 1995). Heavy reliance of African Americans on their church for help is yet another factor that explains underutilization of mental health services (Baruth & Manning, 1999). In fact, "a major 'protective factor' against alcohol abuse to which many Black people are exposed is religion" (Wallace & Brown, 1995, p. 345). Other barriers that contribute to underutilization of mental health services for African Americans include (a) a lack of awareness and understanding of the unique characteristics of the value systems of African American families, (b) communication barriers that hinder the development of trust between the African American client and the non-African American therapist, and (c) lack of a historical perspective on the development of the family and support systems within the African American community (Baruth & Manning, 1999; James & Johnson, 1996; Sue & Sue, 1999).

A final barrier to treatment for African Americans with AOD addiction is that they are frequently admitted to prison hospitals. In such cases, the distribution throughout the United States is not even. Over 90% of these admissions were concentrated in the District of Columbia and nine states, with New York (New York City), Illinois (Chicago), the District of Columbia, Ohio, and Michigan accounting for 75% of the admissions (James & Johnson, 1996). Speculation and research are now directed toward the lack of equity in the criminal justice system with regard to the sentencing of African Americans for drug arrests being disproportionately higher than for Caucasian and other racial minority groups.

Philosophically, the issue of African Americans' distrust of health care in general has been examined. Distrust of African Americans toward the health care system does not mean that the system is unfair to them. A part of what we mean by a good health care system is that it is perceived so by those who use it. Therefore, "even if the system is just, and the distrust is not well founded, the long and troubled relationship between African Americans and various components of the health care system may explain the distrust if not justify it" (McGary, 2002, p. 216). Nevertheless, African Americans' experiences with regard to type of treatment received in the health care system are documented in the medical (e.g., *Journal of the American Medical Association*; Rhodes, Battin, & Silvers, 2002), social work (e.g., *Journal of Social Work* and *Journal of Social Work Education*), rehabilitation (Wilson, Turner, Liu, Harley, & Alston, 2002), and counseling (e.g., *Journal of Counseling & Development*) literature. Moreover, African Americans' skepticism toward the medical and mental health care communities has deep roots in our nation's history (e.g., White-defined normal behavior for African Americans; Poussaint & Alexander, 2000).

Prevention and Intervention

It is important to know that no single treatment approach is appropriate for all individuals. Finding the right treatment program involves careful consideration of such things as setting, length of care, philosophical approach, and the needs of the individual and the family (SAMHSA, 2003). Access to treatment has sometimes been a problem for African Americans; however, the rate of treatment success is comparable with that of Caucasian Americans (National Institute on Alcohol Abuse and Alcoholism, 1994). Prevention and intervention of substance abuse with African Americans is a complex process and yet practical if strategies are developed to meet culturally specific individual, family, and community needs (Stevens & Smith, 2001). Traditionally, African Americans have relied on the family, church, and community for assistance and support with psychosocial and emotional problems (SAMHSA, 1997). According to Carter and Rogers (1996), mental health counselors must be capable of analyzing adaptive behavior patterns, coping strategies, cultural dynamics of substance use, and specific sociopolitical influences of substance abuse with African Americans. It is clear that any type of intervention and prevention programming should fit the worldview of the African American client (Grace, 1992; Stevens & Smith, 2001). A practical starting point of intervention is the use of a cultural assessment in which counselors should ask about patients' background to understand their AOD use and the role culture may play in recovery (Craig, 2004).

Bouie (1993) indicated that "the real culprits of AOD abuse in local African American communities throughout the U.S. are racism, poverty, unemployment, low or no self-esteem, and many other psychosocial manifestations" (p. 190). Therefore, the focus of intervention should be on the social and economic ills that lead to an individual's psychological and physical need to use AOD. Bouie highly endorsed the notion that intervention and prevention approaches should be anchored in the Afrocentric perspective, which is grounded in the psychosocial cultural struggles and experiences of African American people. This perspective has two primary functions. The first is that it provides an initial step in the development of a paradigm that begins to capture the exemplars of the African American culture and experiences. Second, it serves as an insider's perception of the world (Morris, 2000), or a "cultural construction of reality" (Dana, 1998, p. 62). According to Morris, the insider's perception is "a perception that is based on the juxtaposition of a horrid historical past and the realities of the here and now" (p. 32).

In working with African Americans, Glide Memorial United Methodist Church (GMUMC) developed an Afrocentric drug prevention and intervention program based on Eleven Steps (Williams, 1992). GMUMC is a community-based program that does not focus on running out the users and pushers; rather, it is designed to bring them into the fellowship of love, hope, acceptance, and recovery from substance abuse. GMUMC program labeled these steps the "Terms of Faith and Resistance," and they are as follows:

1. Gain control over my life.
2. Tell my story to the world.
3. Stop lying.
4. Be honest with myself.
5. Accept who I am.
6. Feel my real feelings.
7. Feel my pain.
8. Forgive myself and forgive others.
9. Practice rebirth: a new life.
10. Live my spirituality.
11. Support and love my brothers and sisters. (Williams, 1992, p. 17)

Unlike the Twelve Steps of Alcoholics Anonymous (AA), with these Eleven Steps an individual does not have to identify him- or herself as "powerless." Such an admission by African Americans can prove to be more disempowering than empowering, and more victimizing than liberating. In other words, with the Twelve Steps of AA, African Americans as a people who are already emotionally, psychologically, politically, educationally, and financially disadvantaged are being asked or told to submit to and declare themselves even more disadvantaged, if not more inferior. The GMUMC's "Terms of Faith and Resistance" is a strength-based approach, not a deficit-based approach as are so many mental health and substance abuse treatment interventions. While the intent here is not to make a comparison of the AA's Twelve Steps and these Eleven Steps, it is noteworthy to mention that the vast majority of AA members in the United States are White, and only a few studies have investigated the program's effectiveness for ethnic minorities (Tonigan, Connors, & Miller, 1998).

In addition to the factors identified previously, other factors to consider in working with African Americans who abuse substances include (a) drinking patterns (group drinking vs. utilitarian drinking), (b) acculturation, and (c) generational definition and perception of substance abuse. Convivial drinking among African Americans is believed to facilitate sociability, good feelings, and group recreation. On the other hand, utilitarian drinking is used to cope with the struggles and challenges of living, with traumatic events, and with the numerous hardships and issues of personal adjustments (K. A. Johnson & Jennison, 1994). The way African Americans define "a drink" is another consideration in prevention and intervention. Different generations define a drink differently. For example, while older African Americans tend to define a drink by a pint bottle or the 40-ounce malt liquor, their younger counterparts define a drink by the ounce (e.g., a 12-ounce bottle of beer, an 8-ounce glass of wine). Therefore, prevention and intervention programs must involve educational issues regarding the social, cultural, and scientific definition of what constitutes a drink. Poussaint and Alexander (2000) suggested that mental health providers develop necessary skills to maintain therapeutic alliances with African Americans clients. Two key skills include the ability to recognize and appropriately respond to verbal and nonverbal communications with African American clients.

The Academy of Family Physicians identified and recommended specific skills for doctors working with racial minority clients. Poussaint and Alexander (2000) endorsed these recommendations as appropriate for mental health practitioners working with African American and other racial minority clients. The relevant recommendations as they pertain to mental health counseling of African Americans are modified and described below:

1. Constructing a medical and psychosocial profile in a culturally sensitive fashion.
2. Prescribing treatment in a culturally sensitive manner.
3. Using family members, community gatekeepers, and other community resources and advocacy groups.
4. Working collaboratively with other human service professionals.
5. Working with alternative and complementary counseling practitioners and/or indigenous, lay, or folk healers when professionally, ethically, and legally appropriate.
6. Identifying how one's cultural values, assumptions, and beliefs affect patient care and clinical decision making. ("Learning Cultural Competence," 1997, p. 9)

The delivery of mental health counseling services to African Americans with AOD problems and dependence requires a multifocal approach.

Implications for the Future

The future direction of society's role in prevention and intervention is applying a participatory research model to AOD prevention in the African American community. Unlike traditional research, which is to advance academic knowledge and evaluation of services, the goal of participatory research is to advance practical knowledge and intervention. Other characteristics of this research model that are advantageous to the study of and intervention with African Americans are that its methods are interpretive and inductive and its measures are generated in response to local situations. In addition, the researcher and the client are a part of the community and have co-control of the research. Finally, the client is an active participant and has ownership of the data in participatory research (Langton & Taylor, 1995).

While the literature acknowledges oppression as a stressor for African Americans, it frequently separates oppression from racism. For African Americans, stress is both intracultural and intercultural. That is, African Americans go back and forth between the African American community and the dominant culture and experience different types of stresses in each of these environments. Thus, research needs to examine the stressors related to African American substance abuse in relation to their place within their culture and across cultural boundaries.

African Americans are underrepresented in clinical trials. Research needs to identify and define cultural significance in clinical trails. Finally, research needs to understand and explore that in African American communities there is still the fear factor of genocide and of being used as guinea pigs. According to Mitchell (1995), mental health practitioners have an opportunity to learn from clients and to forge alliances with African American communities as never before.

Summary

In general, African Americans' use of alcohol is less than that of White Americans. African Americans tend to abuse AOD in response to stressors. In addition, African Americans' use of AOD rests in historical patterns and influences. AOD use among African Americans frequently results in more adverse outcomes with regard to severity and devastation in their lives, families, and communities. Treatment must focus on a strength-based perspective. Given African Americans' negative experiences with both medical and mental health care, some attention should be directed toward reducing the stigma many of them experience when they or their family acknowledges addiction to substances and mental health problems. In addition, accessibility of mental health services for African Americans involves not only community-based programs but also culturally appropriate ones. African Americans share many common values and beliefs; however, they represent a homogeneous group with just as many different views and behaviors. Mental health and intervention services for substance abuse for African Americans must be individualized to meet their unique needs. Moreover, substance abuse and its collateral issues (e.g., racism, discrimination, poverty) must be addressed concurrently and sequentially. In the final analysis, African Americans' responsiveness to mental health treatment rests with having *all* of their basic needs met that affect their psychosocial adjustment.

References

Baruth, L. G., & Manning, M. L. (1999). *Multicultural counseling and psychotherapy: A lifespan perspective* (2nd ed.). Upper Saddle River, NJ: Merrill/Prentice Hall.

Beardslee, W. R. (1989). The role of self-understanding in resilient individuals: The developmental perspective. *American Journal of Orthopsychiatry, 145,* 63–69.

Beatty, L. A. (2003). Substance abuse, disabilities, and Black women: An issue worth exploring. *Women & Therapy, 26,* 223–236.

Blauner, R. (1992). The ambiguities of racial change. In M. L. Andersen & P. H. Collins (Eds.), *Race, class, and gender: An anthology* (pp. 54–65). Belmont, CA: Wadsworth.

Bouie, J. (1993). A community-organization model for the prevention of alcohol and other drug abuse, HIV transmission, and AIDS among African Americans. In *The second national conference on preventing and treating alcohol and other drug abuse, HIV infection, and AIDS in Black communities: From advocacy to action* (CSAP Monograph, DHHS Publication No. ADM-93-1969). Rockville, MD: U.S. Department of Health and Human Services.

Breo, D. L. (1993). Kicking butts—AMA, Joe Camel, and the "Black Flag" war on tobacco. *Journal of the American Medical Association, 270,* 1978–1984.

Brown, L. S., & Alterman, A. I. (1992). African Americans. In J. H. Lowinson, P. Ruiz, R. B. Millman, & J. G. Langrod (Eds.), *Substance abuse: A comprehensive textbook* (2nd ed., pp. 861–867). Baltimore: Williams & Wilkins.

Brown, S. P., Lipford-Sanders, J., & Shaw, M. (1995). Kujichagulia—Uncovering the secrets of the heart: Group work with African American women on predominately White campuses. *Journal for Specialists in Group Work, 20,* 151–158.

Carter, J. H., & Rogers, C. (1996). Alcoholism and African American women: A medical sociocultural perspective. *Journal of the National Medical Association, 88,* 81–86.

Craig, R. J. (2004). *Counseling the alcohol and drug dependent client: A practical approach.* Boston: Pearson.

Dana, R. H. (1998). Multicultural assessment of personality and psychopathology in the United States: Still art, not science, and controversial. *European Journal of Psychological Assessment, 14,* 62–70.

Dawkins, M. P., & Williams, M. M. (1997). Substance abuse in rural African American populations: Rural substance abuse. In E. B. Robertson, Z. Sloboda, G. M. Boyd, L. Beatty, & N. J. Kozel (Eds.), *Rural substance abuse: State of knowledge and issues* (NIDA Research Monograph). Washington, DC: U.S. Department of Health and Human Services.

Dittmar, L. (1995). All that Hollywood allows: Films and the working class. *Radical Teacher, 46,* 38–45.

Exum, H. A., Moore, Q. L., & Watt, S. K. (1999). Transcultural counseling for African Americans revisited. In J. McFadden (Ed.), *Transcultural counseling* (2nd ed., pp. 171–219). Alexandria, VA: American Counseling Association.

Fisher, G. L., & Harrison, T. C. (2000). *Substance abuse: Information for school counselors, social workers, therapists, and counselors.* Boston: Allyn & Bacon.

Gordon, J. U. (1994). *Managing multiculturalism in substance abuse services.* Thousand Oaks, CA: Sage.

Grace, C. A. (1992). Practical considerations for program professionals and evaluators working with African American communities. In M. A. Orlandi, R. Weston, & L. G. Epstein (Eds.), *Cultural competence for evaluators: A guide for alcohol and other drug abuse prevention practitioners working with ethnic/racial communities* (OSAP Cultural Competence Series I, DHHS Publication No. ADM 92-1884). Rockville, MD: U.S. Department of Health and Human Services.

Hacker, G., Collins, R., & Jacobson, M. (1987). *Marketing booze to Blacks.* Washington, DC: Center for Science in the Public Interest.

Hawkins, J. D., Catalano, R. F., & Miller, J. Y. (1992). Risk and protective factors for alcohol and other drug problems in adolescence and early adulthood: Implications for substance abuse prevention. *Psychological Bulletin, 112,* 64–105.

hooks, B. (1993). *Sisters of the yam: Black women and self-recovery.* Boston: South End Press.

Jackson, J. S. (1991). Black American life course. In J. S. Jackson (Ed.), *Life in Black America* (pp. 264–273). Newbury Park, CA: Sage.

James, W. H., & Johnson, S. J. (1996). *Doin' drugs: Patterns of African American addiction.* Austin: University of Texas Press.

Johnson, B. D., & Muffler, J. (1997). Sociocultural. In J. H. Lowinson, P. Ruiz, R. B. Millman, & J. G. Langrod (Eds.), *Substance abuse: A comprehensive textbook* (3rd ed., pp. 107–117). Baltimore: Williams & Wilkins.

Johnson, K. A., & Jennison, K. M. (1994). Stressful loss and the buffering effect of social support on drinking behavior among African Americans: Results of a national survey. *Journal of Alcohol and Drug Education, 39,* 1–24.

Langton, P. A., & Taylor, E. G. (1995). Applying a participatory research model to alcohol research in ethnic communities. In *The challenges of participatory research: Preventing alcohol-related problems in ethnic communities* (CSAP Cultural Competence Series, DHHS Publication No. SMA 95-3042). Rockville, MD: U.S. Department of Health and Human Services.

Learning cultural competence. (1997). *Journal of Minority Medical Students, 10,* 9.

Lex, B. W. (1985). Alcohol problems in special populations. In J. Mendelson & N. Mello (Eds.), *The diagnosis and treatment of alcoholism* (2nd ed., pp. 96–97). New York: McGraw-Hill.

McGary, H. (2002). Racial groups, distrust, and the distribution of health care. In R. Rhodes, M. P. Battin, & A. Silvers (Eds.), *Medicine and social justice: Essays on the distribution of health care* (pp. 212–223). New York: Oxford University Press.

Mitchell, J. L. (1995). Comments on alcohol prevention research in Black American communities. In *The challenges of participatory research: Preventing alcohol-related problems in ethnic communities* (CSAP Cultural Competence Series, DHHS Publication No. SMA 95-3042). Rockville, MD: U.S. Department of Health and Human Services.

Morris, E. F. (2000). An Africentric perspective for clinical research and practice. In I. B. Weiner (Ed.), *Handbook of cross-cultural and multicultural personality assessment* (pp. 17–41). Mahwah, NJ: Erlbaum.

Mosley, B., Atkins, B. J., & Klein, M. (1988). Alcoholism and Blacks. *Journal of Alcohol & Drug Education, 33,* 51–58.

National Institute on Alcohol Abuse and Alcoholism. (1994, January). *Alcohol alert* (No. 23, PH347). Washington, DC: U.S. Department of Health and Human Services.

O'Malley, P. M., & Wagenaar, A. C. (1991). Effects of minimum drinking age laws on alcohol use, related behaviors and traffic crash involvement among American youth: 1976–1987. *Journal of Studies on Alcohol, 52,* 478–491.

Poussaint, A. F., & Alexander, A. (2000). *Lay my burden down: Unraveling suicide and the mental health crisis among African Americans.* Boston: Beacon Press.

Rhodes, R., Battin, M. P., & Silvers, A. (Eds.). (2002). *Medicine and social justice: Essays on the distribution of health care.* New York: Oxford University Press.

Scott, B. M., Denniston, R. W., & Magruder, K. M. (1992). Alcohol advertising in the African-American community. *Journal of Drug Issues, 22,* 455–469.

Stevens, P., & Smith, R. L. (2001). *Substance abuse counseling: Theory and practice.* Upper Saddle River, NJ: Merrill.

Substance Abuse and Mental Health Services Administration. (1997). *Promoting addiction treatment to diverse populations: African Americans.* Washington, DC: National Clearinghouse for Alcohol and Drug Information.

Substance Abuse and Mental Health Services Administration. (2003). *Reasons for not receiving treatment among adults with serious mental illness.* Retrieved October 27, 2003, from htpp://www.samhsa.gov/oas2k3/MhnoTX.cfm

Sue, D. W., & Sue, D. (1999). *Counseling the culturally different: Theory and practice.* New York: Wiley.

Tonigan, J. S., Connors, G. J., & Miller, W. R. (1998). Special populations in Alcoholics Anonymous. *Alcohol Health & Research World, 22,* 281–293.

U.S. Census Bureau. (2000). *Population profile of the United States.* Washington, DC: U.S. Government Printing Office.

U.S. Department of Health and Human Services. (1990). *The seventh special report to the U.S. Congress on alcohol and health.* Rockville, MD: Author.

Vontress, C. E., & Epp, L. R. (1997). Historical hostility in the African American client: Implications for counseling. *Journal of Multicultural Counseling and Development, 25,* 170–184.

Wallace, J. M., & Brown, L. S. (1995). Alcohol abuse prevention research in African American communities. In *The challenges of participatory research: Preventing alcohol-related problems in ethnic communities* (CSAP Cultural Competence Series, DHHS Publication No. SMA 95-3042). Washington, DC: U.S. Department of Health and Human Services.

Watts, T., & Wright, R. (1983). *Black alcoholism: Toward a comprehensive understanding.* Springfield, IL: Charles C Thomas.

Whaley, A. L. (2001). Cultural mistrust and mental health services for African Americans: A review and meta-analysis. *The Counseling Psychologist, 29,* 513–531.

Williams, C. (1992). *No hiding place: Empowerment and recovery for our troubled communities.* San Francisco: Harper.

Wills, T. A. (1991). Similarity and self-esteem in downward comparison. In J. Suls & T. Wills (Eds.), *Social comparison: Contemporary theory and research* (pp. 51–78). Hillsdale, NJ: Erlbaum.

Wilson, K. B., Turner, T., Liu, J., Harley, D. A., & Alston, R. J. (2002). Perceived vocational rehabilitation service efficacy by race: Results of a national customer survey. *Journal of Applied Rehabilitation Counseling, 33,* 26–34.

10

Biracial and Multiracial Identity: Influence on Self-Identity as African American

Madonna G. Constantine, Marie L. Miville, and Mai M. Kindaichi

Demographic and social climate shifts have brought greater attention to people of mixed racial and ethnic heritage in the United States, although not without challenges. The 2000 U.S. Census marked a historical change in the national discussion about race by permitting respondents to indicate more than one racial classification. The Association of MultiEthnic Americans, Project RACE, and other national organizations led various lobbying efforts to include a mixed-race classification in the census, which had not occurred previously. Arguments against the mixed-race initiative were heard from leaders in the African American community, including Jesse Jackson and Kweisi Mfume, who asserted that a biracial or multiracial category would dilute documentation of racial inequities and increase the difficulty of collecting data on the effects of racial discrimination (Rockquemore & Brunsma, 2002). Rather than including a separate biracial or multiracial category, respondents were given the option to indicate more than one racial group affiliation (Jones & Smith, 2001).

According to the 2000 U.S. Census, 6.8 million people, or 2.4% of the national population, identified themselves by two or more races (i.e., biracial or multiracial; Jones & Smith, 2001). Nearly 1.8 million of these individuals reported being Black or African American in combination with another racial or ethnic group. Reported population figures regarding biracial African Americans, however, may be underestimations of the actual size of this population (Brown, 1995; Root, 1996). In particular, the degree to which parents of interracial children address their children's racial group orientation and how people of mixed-race heritage identify with either or both racial groups may influence population estimates (Winn & Priest, 1993).

The term *biracial* generally describes individuals with two parents of different racial categories, irrespective of their personal racial self-identity (Rockquemore & Brunsma, 2002). The term may also refer to someone who has parents of the same socially designated race, even if one or both of the parents are biracial, or if there is an acknowledgment of cross-racial mixing in the family history (Root, 1996). Some researchers (e.g., Poston, 1990; Rockquemore, 2002) have used the term biracial as a synonym for individuals whose parentage is both Black and White, to the exclusion of individuals who consider racial mixing from prior generations to be salient to their present identity. *Multiracial* is a broader term that includes people who claim two or more racial backgrounds, as in individuals who have at least one parent who self-identifies as biracial and another parent of a different racial background (Root, 1996). We use both terms multiracial and biracial as befits the topic at hand.

In this chapter, we provide some background information pertaining to the historical and current experiences of biracial and multiracial African Americans. We also discuss considerations in the self-identification process for biracial and multiracial African Americans, and we present several prominent identity development models for biracial and multiracial people. In addition, we present issues that mental health counselors might wish to consider when working with biracial and multiracial African Americans.

Relevant Background

Despite the persistent social divide between Blacks and Whites in the United States (Rockquemore & Brunsma, 2002), the number of Black–White unions has increased steadily since the *Loving v. Virginia* case in 1967 led to the legal recognition of interracial unions (Root, 1996). Increased interactions between members of Black and White racial groups have contributed to a rise in interracial unions and biracial births. Race-based shifts in the social climate and evolving social movements necessitate reevaluation of existing models of racial and ethnic identity development and expansion of psychological frameworks related to the experiences of biracial and multiracial African Americans (Celious & Oyserman, 2001).

In light of the increase in the number of biracial and multiracial African American individuals in the United States, there is a need for counselors and other mental health professionals to develop a working knowledge of dynamics specific to the experiences of this population (Harris, 2002; Winn & Priest, 1993). For example, some biracial or multiracial African Americans may be perceived as exclusively of one race (e.g., White or African American), Latino/Latina, of mixed-race descent, or racially "other" (Cunningham, 1997). The experiences of ambiguity or fluidity regarding self-definition (Bradshaw, 1992), "passing" as a member of a particular race (Daniel, 1992; Rockquemore & Brunsma, 2002), and guilt associated with cultural disloyalty (Winn & Priest, 1993) may be particularly salient issues to consider for mental health professionals working with biracial and multiracial African Americans. As such, conceptualizations of racial identity development and ethnic identity development relevant to biracial and multiracial African Americans need to be expanded to include the unique identity development experiences of this group, especially with regard to issues that may influence the development of a positive racial identity (e.g., Allen, 2001). Further, explorations into the adaptive components of various resolutions of biracial and multiracial identity development, including the adoption of a monoracial identity, may inform research, training, and practice with biracial and multiracial African Americans (Cunningham, 1997; Deters, 1997; Rockquemore, 2002; Rockquemore & Laszloffy, 2003; Sebring, 1985).

A brief examination of some of the historical influences on potential psychological experiences of biracial and multiracial African Americans may be of special importance, particularly concerning the meanings of skin color gradation among African Americans (Cunningham, 1997). As a social construction, race has been a means of social stratification and hierarchy that ensures privilege to White people. The rule of *hypodescent*, or the *one-drop rule*, was used to delineate the racial category of individuals who straddle racial boundaries, particularly between Blacks and Whites (Rockquemore & Brunsma, 2002), and served to maintain White privilege. That is, "one drop" of non-White blood was believed to "contaminate" people, barring them from full inclusion in White society and relegating them to classification to a lower status race (Daniel, 1992). Social norms defining Whiteness and Blackness were companions to antimiscegenation laws enacted to maintain social stratifications; antimiscegenation laws addressed the social value of presumed White racial purity only and did not address interracial unions among people of color who occupied similar levels of status (i.e., Native Americans, Latinos, and African Americans). The one-drop rule also led to social constructions of race in binary terms (Black and White), seeming to disallow both interracial unions and identities of multiple heritages (e.g., Black and American Indian, or Black and Latina/Latino; Root, 1996).

From a historical perspective, the rule of hypodescent influenced attitudes toward gradations of skin color from Whites as well as African Americans (Rockquemore & Brunsma, 2002). In the pre-Civil War southern slave economy, exploitative unions between slave owners and Black female slaves resulted in biracial offspring, who were often included in the slave population. Within the population, individuals with lighter skin were elevated to the status of "house slave" versus "field slave," a social division that reflected preferences for lighter skin as a potential means of higher status and greater acceptance (Cunningham, 1997). Prior to the Civil War, communities of offspring of interracial unions had access to education and skilled trades and often acted as buffers between White and Black societies. The ideological social divisions that characterized the slave economy were reinforced during the Civil War, after which biracial Blacks aligned with freed slaves as a result of alienation from White society. In fact, because of their education, many biracial and multiracial people emerged as social leaders through teaching, involvement in churches, and legislation. However, their unique "racial" definitions as mulatto, Creole, or "blue-vein" (Daniel, 1992) were often unavailable after the Civil War, as racial definitions shifted and emphasis on discriminating White from non-White intensified in the social climate.

Already a heterogeneous population by skin color, African American society then became more visibly diverse as biracial and multiracial African Americans parented children and as interracial unions, forceful and consensual, persisted. Through the period of the Harlem Renaissance, mixed-race African Americans emerged as artistic and creative voices of the Black experience. With the surfacing of Black power movements in the 1960s (Cunningham, 1997; Rockquemore & Brunsma, 2002), within-group variance of skin color was brought to the political foreground; previously unspoken suspicions between fair-complexioned and dark-complexioned African Americans drew greater attention in this social climate. Within these movements, the one-drop rule had become an avenue through which biracial and multiracial African Americans came to view themselves with reference to the larger Black community, as well as a barometer of the degree to which individuals may have differential access to social privileges.

Self-Identification Issues Among Biracial and Multiracial African Americans

Black identity is not characterized by phenotype alone, as attested by the myriad shades among Black people, as well as the complex definitions of racial and ethnic identity development (Newsome, 2001). Instead, Black identity develops through the collective experience of being regarded as Black in America, which includes, but is not limited to, experiences of racial discrimination and oppression. When societal definitions of Black and White racial group membership are determined by issues associated with hypodescent, it can be argued that biracial and multiracial African Americans are likely to be regarded as Black. Thus, the complexities of the interfaces of social and personal meanings attached to racial classification (Brown, 1995) may be influenced by peer, familial, social, and political forces (Kerwin & Ponterotto, 1995; Kerwin, Ponterotto, Jackson, & Harris, 1993; Renn, 2003; Root, 1998). In particular, biracial and multiracial children and adolescents shape their identity development with reference to a variety of sources, including siblings' appearance, identification with parents of different racial groups, and society's reactions to them (Root, 1998).

Biracial and multiracial African Americans often self-identify as Black to respond adaptively to social forces that validate a monoracial identity (Winn & Priest, 1993). Recent studies among biracial and multiracial African American children and young adults (Brown, 1995; Winn & Priest, 1993) have indicated that a majority of participants experienced pressure to assume a monoracial Black identity. Indeed, even biracial or multiracial African Americans who adopt a racially neutral identity, usually in primarily White environments, may shift this self-definition upon adolescence and entering dating relationships (Twine, 1996). Twine found this shift occurring for biracial and multiracial African American women upon encountering "patterns of exclusion and anti-Black racism" beginning to operate during puberty (p. 217).

The assumption of a monoracial Black identity for biracial and multiracial African Americans has both advantages and disadvantages (Brunsma & Rockquemore, 2002). Biracial and multiracial African Americans, who have been exposed to Black racial identity socializing agents, such as family, community, and peer groups, likely have the advantage of psychological preparedness against discrimination (Rockquemore & Laszloffy, 2003). Biracial and multiracial African Americans may have experienced societal and interrelational "push" factors that reinforced self-designation as Black (Brunsma & Rockquemore, 2002; Twine, 1996). In addition, the historical variations of skin color and phenotype among African Americans can foster an implicit sense of validation. At the same time, biracial and multiracial African Americans who identify solely as Black may encounter challenges concerning their authenticity as Black people (Bradshaw, 1992).

Adding to the complexity of identity development and social acceptance for biracial and multiracial African Americans is the notion of "passing," that is, phenotypically appearing as White to maximize social power and privileges and presumably to escape the oppression experienced by other darker-hued African Americans (Root, 1998). Biracial or multiracial African Americans also may attempt to "pass" as a member of either the White or the Black/minority racial group, depending on the social context, to escape marginality by members of a particular racial group (Daniel, 1992, 1996; Deters, 1997). Membership into predominantly Black social groups may be fraught with tests of credibility for biracial and multiracial African Americans, particularly for those with visible European features (Cunningham, 1997). Feelings of resentment about biracial and multiracial African Americans' perceived fluidity between racial worlds and the associated privileges, deriving from members of the Black community, may intensify feelings of alienation and marginalization for biracial and multiracial African Americans. At the same time, public designation as Black may mask internal conflicts about racial identity and cloud the cultivation of personal meanings of African American identity. Unfortunately, much of the information regarding passing among biracial and multiracial African Americans is anecdotal; little research has been conducted on the experiences of passing and its psychological sequelae (i.e., *passing* is not the same as *being* and may result in feelings of dissonance, alienation, anxiety, and so on).

Models of Black and Afrocentric identity development may illuminate understandings of experiences of biracial and multiracial African Americans who self-identify as Black. Early models of Black racial identity development (i.e., Cross, 1971; Helms, 1984) influenced early conceptualizations of biracial identity development (e.g., Kerwin & Ponterotto, 1995; Kich, 1992; Poston, 1990). In general, these models asserted that an integrated sense of self as African American, characterized by a positive internal and collective commitment to one's racial group (Cross, 1971; Helms, 1984; Helms & Cook, 1999), is considered to be the most sophisticated level of Black racial identity development. According to Cross's (1971) nigrescence model, African Americans progress through five stages of increasing awareness and internalization of Black identity with respect to oppressive forces of the majority culture. Alternative models of Black racial identity development have focused less on having an original negative view of the self based on external oppressive forces and emphasized the development of a healthy and fully integrated self-concept based on African consciousness and spirituality (Constantine, Richardson, Benjamin, & Wilson, 1998). For example, optimal theory, developed by Linda James Myers and her colleagues (e.g., Myers, 1993; Myers & Speight, 1994; Myers et al., 1991), provides a framework of identity development founded on African-centered belief systems and a definition of self-worth absent of material and external influences.

Developmental models of Black racial identity development have been formidable catalysts of research and conceptualizations of cross-racial counseling processes. However, the application of these models to biracial and multiracial African Americans has been challenged (Myers et al., 1991; Root, 2002). Although most Black racial identity models originate from a position of unawareness of the self as African American and naive adoption of beliefs about Black people as defined by an oppressive White structure, it is important to consider that biracial or multiracial African Americans may have strong feelings attached to negotiating identification with both the oppressed (Blacks) and the oppressors (Whites). That is, Whiteness and White culture may not be perceived by biracial or multiracial African Americans as monolithically oppressive agents or entities (particularly given White parentage). Black racial identity development is guided by individuals' identification and internalization of collective experiences relative to a single racial group; however, the racial identity development for biracial or multiracial people is likely a function of integrating and internalizing two or more racial group identities (Kerwin & Ponterotto, 1995; Poston, 1990).

Most existing conceptualizations of Black racial identity development assume a universal process that affects identity development across people (Root, 2002), although the experiences of biracial or multiracial African Americans may be inherently different. For example, it is possible that some biracial African Americans are socialized to label themselves as "both Black and White" rather than "either Black or White" (Root, 1998). Still others may nominally identify as Black or attempt to pass as White or Black. Biracial or multiracial African Americans who self-identify as Black may immerse themselves in Black culture but adopt an exaggerated Black persona that is incongruent with the realities of their life experiences (Gibbs, 1989). Depending on family structures and community environments, positive Black role models or Black communities may not be accessible to some multiracial African Americans, thereby limiting their exposure to a wider range of African Americans. Additionally, immersion experiences with other biracial or multiracial African Americans may be rare outside of familial interactions for multiracial African Americans who were socialized to self-identify as "both/and"; immersion in academic knowledge of biracial and multiracial African Americans may be unavailable or may speak to multiracial experiences in purely cognitive or overgeneralizing ways (Rockquemore & Brunsma, 2002).

Conceptual and empirical literature concerning components of racial identity development among biracial and multiracial people have focused primarily on childhood and adolescence (e.g., Deters, 1997; Fatimilehin, 1999; Gibbs, 1989; Gibbs & Hines, 1992; Newsome, 2001; Sebring, 1985; Winn & Priest, 1993). Research has highlighted the potential influences of familial, peer, and academic socialization agents as salient components of identity development (e.g., Root, 1996, 1998). For example, interracial family values regarding race may be affected by interrelated factors such as family background, structural factors, and family dynamics (Johnson, 1992). Family background variables may include income, education, and parental occupations, which can have an effect on attitudes about power and status, as well as influence access to diverse communities and people of color. Structural factors, such as living arrangements, family composition, and contact with extended family, also may affect how biracial and multiracial African Americans self-identify.

For example, biracial African Americans who were raised by single White mothers may have limited access to the racial or cultural experiences of their fathers, and they may have limited contact with extended paternal family members. Such experiences would almost certainly influence the degree to which they internalize or identify with Black culture. Identification with an oppressed minority group can generate feelings of inferiority for biracial African Americans, particularly if both the children and the parent of color are treated as unwanted members of the extended family (Root, 1998). In the next section, theoretical models of racial identity development among biracial and multiracial individuals discuss the potential influences of peer, family, and other socialization agents on identity development.

Biracial and Multiracial Identity Development Models

In response to the criticisms of applying Black racial identity development conceptualizations to biracial and multiracial people, models of biracial and multiracial identity development have been developed. Linear models of biracial identity development (e.g., Kerwin & Ponterotto, 1995; Kich, 1992; Poston, 1990) consider the most sophisticated level of racial identity awareness to be a function of adulthood, when the integration of multiple racial or ethnic identities exists and individuals display flexibility in adapting to various racial, ethnic, and cultural environments. Many of these models center on biracial identity (majority/minority descent) rather than multiracial identity or identity emanating from minority/minority descent.

Poston (1990) presented a biracial identity development model based on the experiences of individuals with Black and White parents. In the early childhood stage of his model, racial group orientation attitudes are not developed, and *personal identity* is primarily based on self-esteem factors that are fostered within the family. Preadolescent biracial individuals may experience alienation and crises as they feel pushed to choose a monoracial self-designation (i.e., *choice of group categorization*) in order to facilitate participation in peer, family, and social groups. In adolescence, biracial individuals struggle with dissonance between an externally defined monoracial identity and internal loyalty to both cultures, as reflected in their relationships to parents of differing racial groups (i.e., *enmeshment/denial*). Feeling unable to identify with both parents, a biracial adolescent also struggles with feelings of disloyalty over potentially rejecting one parent. An *appreciation* and exploration of one's multiple racial identities begins in early adulthood and is exhibited in active learning about racial and ethnic heritages; however, there is a remaining tendency to identify with one racial group. In adulthood, biracial individuals are believed to experience *integration*, in which a racial identity that recognizes various racial group influences is secured.

Kich (1992) offered a conceptualization of biracial identity development that paralleled Poston's (1990) emphasis on movement from dissonance between choosing a monoracial self-identity toward an integrated biracial self-identity as a function of age progression. In Kich's three-stage model of biracial identity development, individuals move from feelings of incongruence between self-perceptions and external perceptions (i.e., Stage 1—3 to 10 years old), through struggles for social and self-acceptance (i.e., Stage 2—8 years old through young adulthood), until they fully internalize a bicultural and biracial identity (i.e., Stage 3—late adolescence or young adulthood).

Similar to Poston's (1990) and Kich's (1992) models, Kerwin and Ponterotto's (1995) model of biracial identity development used age-based developmental markers to illustrate progression in racial awareness. However, unlike the above models, the Kerwin–Ponterotto model acknowledged variance among resolution styles (e.g., establishing a public racial identity that differs from a private one) as influenced by personal, societal, and environmental factors. The Kerwin–Ponterotto model also diverged from the other models in their acknowledgment that biracial individuals may experience exclusion from groups of color as well as Whites. In the *preschool* stage, which occurs up to 5 years of age, biracial children recognize similarities and differences in physical appearance; this awareness may be a function of the degree of parental sensitivity to and addressing of race-related issues. In the *entry to school* stage, biracial children are in greater contact with social groups and may be asked to classify themselves according to a monoracial label. In the *preadolescence* stage, there is an increased awareness of social meanings ascribed to social groups as characterized by skin tone, physical appearance, ethnicity, and religion; environmental factors, such as entry into a more diverse or more monocultural context, and direct or vicarious exposure to racism also may heighten these young adolescents' sensitivity to race. As biracial children enter *adolescence*, pressures to identify with one social group may be intensified by expectations of identification with the racial group of a parent of color. In the *college/young adulthood* stage, there may be a continued immersion in a monoracial group, accompanied with an acute awareness of the contexts in which race-related comments are made. The *adulthood* stage is characterized by a continued exploration and interest in race and culture, including self-definitions of racial and cultural identities, and increased flexibility in adapting to various cultural settings.

One limitation of some models of biracial identity development has been their assumption that the desired end-state is that of a fully integrated biracial identity (Root, 1998). Recent conceptual literature (e.g., Rockquemore, 1999; Root, 1998) has suggested alternative resolutions of the biracial and multiracial identity development process. Root (1998) proposed an ecological meta-model for understanding the potential effects of inherited influences (e.g., parents' identities, nativity, phenotype, and extended family), traits (e.g., temperament, coping skills, and social skills), and socialization agents (e.g., family, peer, and community) on resolution of racial identity for multiracial people. These components are nested in class, historical, and gender contexts particular to the individual. Different sources of experiential conflict lead to feelings of alienation and marginality, discrimination, and ambiguity that challenge the development of a healthy sense of self. Root (1996) also noted that multiracial individuals can negotiate identity development concerns through four possible "border crossings" or comfort in, across, and between racial categories: ability to carry multiple cultural perspectives simultaneously; situational identity, or shifting racial identity with respect to the social environment; claiming an independent multiracial reference point; and maintaining a monoracial identity when entering different cultural environments. A fifth pattern also was identified (Renn, 2003) in which biracial individuals do not claim a specific racial identity category.

Typologies of racial identity resolution options for multiracial individuals (Root, 1998) and Black–White biracial individuals (Brunsma & Rockquemore, 2002; Rockquemore, 1999) offer frameworks for expanding conceptualizations of adaptive racial identity development for multiracial African Americans. Individuals may adopt a singular (e.g., Black or White) identity (Rockquemore, 1999) by accepting categories imposed on them passively (i.e., acceptance of the identity society assigns) or choosing to identify with a particular racial group (Root, 1998). Passive acceptance of societal categorization may be adaptive to the extent that individuals feel a sense of belongingness to the given group; however, racial groups are not monoliths, and individuals' experiences of one group of Black or White people will not be the same throughout life. Additionally, biracial or multiracial African Americans who passively identify as Black may not have developed self-awareness about race or a multidimensional appreciation for cultural meanings and values characteristic of African Americans. On the other hand, choosing to identify as Black may be advantageous psychologically, provided that individuals do not feel marginal to the reference group and do not deny other parts of their racial composition (Root, 1998).

Border identity (Rockquemore, 1999), or identification with both or many racial groups (Root, 1998), may be considered positive when personality and sense of self remain constant across racial contexts, although social validation of racial identity may be specific to regions of high concentrations of biracial and multiracial people, such as the West Coast (Jones & Smith, 2001). Brunsma and Rockquemore (2002) noted that border identities may not be "validated" or acknowledged by some individuals, in which case biracial and multiracial African Americans are categorized as Black, as per the hypodescent rule. Biracial and multiracial African Americans may adopt a protean identity (Rockquemore, 1999), in which people present a variety of identities, depending on the social context. Protean individuals reference themselves in several group orientations (e.g., Black, White, multiracial), as a function of their genuine identities or the utility of bicultural or multicultural adaptation despite internal comfort that favors one or the other race (Daniel, 1996). Adopting a transcendent identity (Rockquemore, 1999) allows individuals to detach themselves from racial categorization, whereas identification with a new racial group (Root, 1998) affords the opportunity to assume a novel identity with others who feel positively about generating a new reference group. Both of these options share a sense of empowerment in the self-designation as "other"; rather than being categorized as "other," biracial and multiracial individuals may take control of "otherness" through semantic separation from existing racial designations. Empirical evidence supporting variations of adaptive identity development resolutions for biracial and multiracial people is in its infancy (Root, 2002).

Another limitation of current biracial and multiracial identity development models is the lack of thorough integration of the intersections of racial and gender identity development for biracial people (Rockquemore, 2002). This issue may be evident through limited discussion of the differential socialization messages from mothers and fathers of different racial groups. Johnson (1992) stated that the mother's race may be particularly important in shaping identity development for biracial African Americans. That is, mothers generally may have greater contact with biracial children during their development and may represent racial socialization agents both implicitly and explicitly. However, it is often the case that the parent and extended family members of color in interracial unions will provide primary racial socialization messages to biracial children (Root, 1996).

The possible intersections of gender and racial identity development for biracial and multiracial African Americans who self-identify as Black shape conflicts through life stages, particularly regarding dating and partnership (Rockquemore, 2002). For example, biracial (specifically Black and White) African American males and females may receive different messages about their attractiveness from both genders of both Black and White reference groups. In addition to status markers, privileges awarded based on lighter skin tone and European features have traditionally included perceptions of greater physical attractiveness, particularly for women. Although standards of aesthetics or beauty change with social shifts, White culture widely considers European features to be normative and beautiful and tends to label African and other non-European (Asian, Latino/Latina) features as "ethnic" or "exotic."

Another limitation of many current biracial and multiracial identity development models is the presumption of White/person of color mixture on which these models are based. Although this statistically is the most likely combination of individuals of mixed-raced descent in the United States, particularly for African Americans, there has been an increase of biracial and multiracial African Americans from a variety of racial backgrounds. Hall (1992) conducted a watershed study examining identity development for biracial Black and

Japanese adults, assessing a number of factors affecting their identity development, such as ethnicity of neighbors and friends, languages spoken, racial resemblance, and perceived acceptance by others. She concluded by describing her biracial Black and Japanese participants as "at-risk" survivors who "in spite of (or because of) all the detours and adjustments, . . . were well adjusted in their heterogeneous heritage" (Hall, 1992, p. 264). Few biracial and multiracial identity models address the unique challenges faced by multiracial African Americans who claim a multiplicity of racial heritages, including Asian, Latino/Latina, American Indian, or a blend of racial heritages that includes White as well.

Although some researchers have reported that many biracial and multiracial individuals compartmentalize their racial identity into public and private dimensions, biracial and multiracial identity development frameworks do not speak to this resolution of racial identity development (e.g., Brown, 1995; Winn & Priest, 1993). It may be adaptive for biracial and multiracial African Americans to assert a Black identity publicly as a defense against social marginalization. Private identity as biracial or multiracial, however, may be more congruent with their familial values and internal self-concepts. Thus, the compartmentalization of racial identities into public and private dimensions may allow some biracial and multiracial African Americans to maintain a positive self-identity in the face of societal pressures (Brown, 1995).

Many biracial identity development models (e.g., Kerwin & Ponterotto, 1995; Kich, 1992; Poston, 1990) and research on the identity development experiences of multiracial African Americans (e.g., Brown, 1985; Gibbs, 1989; Gibbs & Hines, 1992) tend to emphasize phases of life that precede adulthood. Although this may be a function of the influence of Eriksonian conceptualizations of developmental tasks specific to adolescence (i.e., identity vs. role confusion), the assumption that identity development ends at early adulthood denies contextual influences that continue to affect identity development over the life span. It is important to note that some biracial or multiracial African Americans who self-identify exclusively as Black as young adults may not have cultivated a deeply personal meaning of Black identity. Neither Black racial identity nor biracial and multiracial identity development models in isolation may articulate fully the racial identity development process for biracial and multiracial African Americans across the life span. However, considerations of the intersection of components from various models and typologies, in light of various developmental life span issues, may enrich psychological understandings of biracial and multiracial African Americans' experiences.

Implications for Counselors and Other Mental Health Professionals

Biracial and multiracial African Americans may resolve racial identity development issues in various ways, depending on their histories of resolving other identity development issues. For example, biracial or multiracial African Americans may present a unitary Black identity through adolescence and adulthood, but upon encountering new environmental contexts, they reevaluate their individual experiences of race and racial identity. In other words, it may be possible for biracial and multiracial African Americans to recycle through racial identity development processes that conclude with a variety of identity resolutions. More specifically, individuals may identify publicly or privately with certain racial groups (i.e., protean identity) throughout the life course, depending on contextual circumstances such as perceived social climate, chronology, and gender. Counselors and mental health providers who work with biracial and multiracial African Americans have unique opportunities to explore processes of recycling through racial identity development processes by being mindful of individuals' experiences of race throughout the life span and contextual influences.

Mental health professionals working with biracial and multiracial African Americans should be aware of the impact of multiple racial identifications among their clients (Deters, 1997; Root, 1998). For example, themes of cultural mistrust typically evident in cross-racial dyads between African American clients and White service providers also may be exhibited with biracial and multiracial African American clients. Moreover, therapists and counselors who have been trained in existing models of racial and ethnic identity development and multicultural counseling may conceptualize biracial and multiracial African American clients' situations from these Black racial identity frameworks without a more holistic understanding of clients' experiences. In other words, although mental health professionals may attempt to use racially or culturally sensitive frameworks in counseling, their interventions and conceptualizations may not be congruent with clients' public and private understandings of their own racial or cultural identity.

Through individual and group counseling interventions, counselors and other mental health professionals could offer safe environments for biracial and multiracial African American clients to explore their understandings of their racial identity with respect to micro-, meso-, exo-, and macrosystems, for example, personality factors, peer relationships, school/work environments, and historical attitudes toward biracial and multiracial African Americans, respectively (Renn, 2003). Further, acknowledging racial ambiguity and fluidity as healthy components of racial identity development for biracial and multiracial African Americans allows safe discussions about racial identity that may foster psychological well-being (Deters, 1997). In particular, group counseling with other biracial and multiracial African Americans could facilitate a sense of normalization, offer opportunities for biracial and multiracial African Americans to learn through their peers, and foster personal understandings of collective experiences of biracial and multiracial African Americans.

Despite the increasing numbers of biracial and multiracial people of all backgrounds (Jones & Smith, 2001), multicultural training experiences likely do not provide sufficient knowledge or awareness of biracial and multiracial issues to inform effective counseling interventions. Recent reports have noted therapists' (e.g., Deters, 1997) and school counselors' (e.g., Harris, 2002) self-reported lack of training in the unique developmental and psychological concerns of biracial and multiracial people. Furthermore, lack of training and experience in working with multiracial students has been associated with greater endorsement of myths related to biracial and multiracial people (e.g., beliefs that biracial people "have the best of both worlds" and that the behavioral problems of biracial and multiracial children are associated with their racial identity conflicts; Harris, 2002). It may be valuable for mental health professionals to seek opportunities to supplement academic multicultural counseling training regarding the potential needs of biracial and multiracial African Americans.

National conferences devoted to understanding the experiences of biracial and multiracial individuals may offer opportunities for mental health professionals to interact with researchers and practitioners who focus on biracial and multiracial African Americans. Additionally, attendance at informal colloquia or presentations concerning biracial and multiracial African Americans could provide counselors and other mental health professionals with insights into shared and unique experiences of these populations. Further, it may be valuable for mental health professionals to explore and incorporate nonfiction literature written by biracial or multiracial African Americans into counseling interventions, such as autobiographies and collections of poetry. Fairly recent examples of such works include *Black, White, and Jewish: An Autobiography of a Shifting Self* (Walker, 2002); *The Color of Water: A Black Man's Tribute to His White Mother* (McBride, 1997); and *What Are You: Voices of Mixed-Race Young People* (Gaskins, 1999).

Summary

Much shifting has occurred in the last decade regarding the societal recognition of the rights and realities of biracial and multiracial people. This evolution has been paralleled in the social sciences by an increasing emphasis on better understanding the lived experiences of biracial and multiracial people. Theory, research, and practice have begun to focus on the struggles and strengths of biracial and multiracial people, by listening to the spoken stories of these individuals rather than imposing myths and stereotypes. Recent models regarding identity development of biracial and multiracial people (Rockquemore, 2002; Root, 1998) are more closely linked to these experiences, reflecting authenticity rather than rigid theorizing that only serves to continue and promote harmful myths.

Some of the most common and detrimental myths about biracial and multiracial African Americans are a lack of community and potential confusion of identity. This chapter has described a more complex picture regarding the history and current context of biracial and multiracial American Americans that places these groups within a larger societal and historical domain. That is, the experiences of biracial and multiracial Americans reflect the collective history of African Americans in the United States and the sociopolitical construction of race therein. The challenges of evolving a positive racial identity as a person of color in the United States (whether as a monoracial individual or a biracial or multiracial individual) occur in a social context historically embedded in struggle, oppression, survival, and resilience. The challenge of developing a healthy sense of self and positive relations with others may not be any more or less challenging to biracial and multiracial African Americans than to African Americans claiming a singular heritage. The specific constellation of these identity challenges for each person no doubt changes with the individual and his or her unique blending of race and culture, family system, and so on. However, it is critical that researchers and practitioners recognize the unique challenges faced by monoracial, biracial, and multiracial African Americans as well as the common struggles shared with others considered to be people of color in the United States (e.g., overt racism and discrimination, invisibility or negative visibility in the larger media, etc.).

References

Allen, R. L. (2001). A culturally based conception of the Black self-concept. In V. H. Milhouse, M. K. Asante, & P. O. Nwosu (Eds.), *Transcultural realities: Interdisciplinary perspectives on cross-cultural relations* (pp. 161–185). Thousand Oaks, CA: Sage.

Bradshaw, C. K. (1992). Beauty and the beast: On racial ambiguity. In M. P. P. Root (Ed.), *Racially mixed people in America* (pp. 77–88). Newbury Park, CA: Sage.

Brown, U. M. (1995). Black–White interracial young adults: Quest for a racial identity. *American Journal of Orthopsychiatry, 65,* 125–130.

Brunsma, D. L., & Rockquemore, K. A. (2002). Socially embedded identities: Theories, typologies, and process of racial identity among Black/White biracials. *The Sociological Quarterly, 43,* 335–356.

Celious, A., & Oyserman, D. (2001). Race from the inside: An emerging heterogeneous race model. *Journal of Social Issues, 57,* 149–165.

Constantine, M. G., Richardson, T. Q., Benjamin, E. M., & Wilson, J. W. (1998). An overview of Black racial identity theories: Limitations and considerations for future theoretical conceptualizations. *Applied & Preventive Psychology, 7,* 95–99.

Cross, W. E. (1971). The Negro-to-Black conversion experience: Toward a psychology of Black liberation. *Black World, 20,* 13–27.

Cunningham, J. L. (1997). Colored existence: Racial identity formation in light-skin Blacks. *Smith College Studies in Social Work, 67,* 375–400.

Daniel, G. R. (1992). Passers and pluralists: Subverting the racial divide. In M. P. P. Root (Ed.), *Racially mixed people in America* (pp. 91–107). Newbury Park, CA: Sage.

Daniel, G. R. (1996). Black and White identity in the new millennium. In M. P. P. Root (Ed.), *The multiracial experience: Racial borders as the new frontier* (pp. 121–139). Thousand Oaks, CA: Sage.

Deters, K. A. (1997). Belonging nowhere and everywhere: Multiracial identity development. *Bulletin of the Menninger Clinic, 61,* 368–385.

Fatimilehin, I. A. (1999). Of jewel heritage: Racial socialization and racial identity attitudes amongst adolescents of mixed African-Caribbean/White parentage. *Journal of Adolescence, 22,* 303–318.

Gaskins, P. F. (Ed.). (1999). *What are you: Voices of mixed-race young people.* New York: Henry Holt.

Gibbs, J. T. (1989). Biracial adolescents. In J. T. Gibbs & L. N. Huang (Eds.), *Children of color: Psychological interventions in minority youth* (pp. 322–350). San Francisco: Jossey-Bass.

Gibbs, J. T., & Hines, A. M. (1992). Negotiating ethnic identity: Issues for Black–White biracial adolescents. In M. P. P. Root (Ed.), *Racially mixed people in America* (pp. 223–238). Newbury Park, CA: Sage.

Hall, C. C. I. (1992). Please choose one: Ethnic identity choices for biracial individuals. In M. P. P. Root (Ed.), *Racially mixed people in America* (pp. 250–264). Newbury Park, CA: Sage.

Harris, H. L. (2002). School counselors' perceptions of biracial children: A pilot study. *Professional School Counseling, 6,* 120–129.

Helms, J. E. (1984). Toward a theoretical explanation of the effect of race on counseling: A Black and White model. *The Counseling Psychologist, 12,* 153–165.

Helms, J. E., & Cook, D. A. (1999). *Using race and culture in counseling and psychotherapy: Theory and process.* Boston: Allyn & Bacon.

Johnson, D. J. (1992). Developmental pathways: Toward an ecological theoretical formulation of race identity in Black–White biracial children. In M. P. P. Root (Ed.), *Racially mixed people in America* (pp. 37–49). Newbury Park, CA: Sage.

Jones, N. A., & Smith, A. S. (2001). *Census 2000 brief: Two or more races.* Washington, DC: U.S. Census Bureau. Retrieved May 30, 2003, from http://www.census.gov/prod/2001pubs/c2kbr01-6.pdf

Kerwin, C., & Ponterotto, J. G. (1995). Biracial identity development: Theory and research. In J. G. Ponterotto, J. M. Casas, L. A. Suzuki, & C. M. Alexander (Eds.), *Handbook of multicultural counseling* (pp. 199–217). Thousand Oaks, CA: Sage.

Kerwin, C., Ponterotto, J. G., Jackson, B. L., & Harris, A. (1993). Racial identity in biracial children: A qualitative investigation. *Journal of Counseling Psychology, 40,* 221–231.

Kich, G. K. (1992). The developmental process of asserting a biracial, bicultural identity. In M. P. P. Root (Ed.), *Racially mixed people in America* (pp. 250–264). Newbury Park, CA: Sage.

Loving v. Virginia, 388 U.S. 1 (1967).

McBride, J. (1997). *The color of water: A Black man's tribute to his White mother.* New York: Riverhead Books.

Myers, L. J. (1993). *Understanding an Afrocentric worldview: Introduction to an optimal psychology* (2nd ed.). Dubuque, IA: Kendall/Hunt.

Myers, L. J., & Speight, S. L. (1994). Optimal theory and the psychology of human diversity. In E. J. Trickett, R. J. Watts, & D. Birman (Eds.), *Human diversity: Perspectives on people in context* (pp. 101–114). San Francisco: Jossey-Bass.

Myers, L. J., Speight, S. L., Highlen, P. S., Cox, C. I., Reynolds, A. L., Adams, E. M., & Hanley, C. P. (1991). Identity development and worldview: Toward an optimal conceptualization. *Journal of Counseling & Development, 70,* 54–63.

Newsome, C. (2001). Multiple identities: The case of biracial children. In V. H. Milhouse, M. K. Asante, & P. O. Nwosu (Eds.), *Transcultural realities: Interdisciplinary perspectives on cross-cultural relations* (pp. 145–159). Thousand Oaks, CA: Sage.

Poston, W. S. C. (1990). The biracial identity development model: A needed addition. *Journal of Counseling & Development, 69,* 152–155.

Renn, K. A. (2003). Understanding the identities of mixed-race college students through a developmental ecology lens. *Journal of College Student Development, 44,* 383–403.

Rockquemore, K. A. (1999). Between Black and White: Exploring the biracial experience. *Race and Society, 1,* 197–212.

Rockquemore, K. A. (2002). Negotiating the color line: The gendered process of racial identity construction among Black/White biracial women. *Gender and Society, 16,* 485–503.

Rockquemore, K. A., & Brunsma, D. L. (2002). *Beyond Black: Biracial identity in America.* Thousand Oaks, CA: Sage.

Rockquemore, K. A., & Laszloffy, T. A. (2003). Multiple realities: A relational narrative approach in therapy with Black–White mixed race clients. *Family Relations, 52,* 119–128.

Root, M. P. P. (1996). *The multiracial experience: Racial borders as the new frontier.* Thousand Oaks, CA: Sage.

Root, M. P. P. (1998). Resolving "other" status: Identity development of biracial individuals. In P. B. Organista, K. M. Chun, & G. Marin (Eds.), *Readings in ethnic psychology* (pp. 100–122). New York: Routledge.

Root, M. P. P. (2002). Methodological issues in multiracial research. In G. C. N. Hall & S. Okazaki (Eds.), *Asian American psychology: The science of lives in context* (pp. 171–193). Washington, DC: American Psychological Association.

Sebring, D. L. (1985). Considerations in counseling interracial children. *Journal of Non-White Concerns, 13,* 3–9.

Twine, F. W. (1996). Brown skinned White girls: Class, culture and the construction of White identity in suburban communities. *Gender, Place, and Culture, 3,* 205–224.

Walker, R. (2002). *Black, White, and Jewish: An autobiography of a shifting self.* New York: Riverhead Books.

Winn, N. N., & Priest, R. (1993). Counseling biracial children: A forgotten component of multicultural counseling. *Family Therapy, 20,* 29–36.

Section III

Community

This section focuses on community issues related to mental health practice in the African American community. The five chapters form a conceptualization of how the term *community* is used to describe various aspects of African Americans, including specific cultural characteristics, relationships, cooperation and collaboration, perceptions and beliefs, and strength-based attributes.

In chapter 11, Wilson focuses on cultural characteristics of the African American community. The chapter proposes that African Americans constitute a diverse group of people and there is no one description that can accommodate their various identities, behaviors, and perceptions. The author stresses the importance of understanding general population trends related to the African American community in the United States. Wilson provides key characteristics of the African American population that contribute to a process of mutual understanding between mental health and human service providers and some of the clients they serve. In addition, recommendations of culturally defined response factors to counseling approaches when working with African Americans are presented.

In chapter 12, Dixon and Vaz examine the perceptions of African Americans regarding mental health counseling. They provide a historical context of how mental illness has been treated as a closet phenomenon within the African American community. In addition, the authors discuss the basis of African Americans' pejorative negative perceptions of mental illness and their negative attitudes toward the mental health system. Dixon and Vaz include information on what the research has found regarding barriers to mental health treatment of African Americans.

Chapter 13 addresses the impact of violence, crime, and gangs in the African American community. Harris explores the upsurge of violence within African American communities from historical changes and the mental health challenges that African Americans face that are specifically linked to the traumas associated with violence. The author theorizes about violence in relation to the experiences in African American communities and provides a descriptive overview of the forms of violence encountered within African American communities and the resulting mental health challenges and therapeutic approaches.

In chapter 14, Harley considers the Black church in mental health counseling as a strength-based approach. She asserts that the Black church has been and continues to be a dominant force and a symbol of hope and spiritual presence for African Americans that offers a sense of community and personal and psychological support. In this chapter, Harley examines the interplay of religion, spirituality, the Black church, and psychosocial adjustment in addressing the mental health of African

Americans. Information is presented on the historical Black church, the Black church today, and religious beliefs that support or conflict with mental health counseling. Harley recommends using a strength-based approach in Black churches to provide a multidimensional perspective of mental health counseling.

This section finishes with a chapter by Lawson and Kim in which they examine the separation between public health and mental health services and its consequences for African Americans. The authors discuss the dualism of mental and public health communities to explain the current schism between the two disciplines. Lawson and Kim also discuss barriers that prohibit public health and mental health research, services, and teaching collaboration. The chapter concludes with a model of public health and mental health collaboration.

In reading this section of the book, it becomes apparent that many different attributes characterize the African American community and the practice of mental health counseling. Furthermore, the practice of service delivery of mental health intervention to African Americans is influenced by both clients' perceptions of the mental health system and service providers' conceptualizations of African Americans. These chapters raise a number of important issues and help to set the scene for the next section of the book.

11

Cultural Characteristics of the African American Community

Keith B. Wilson

African Americans comprise a diverse group of people, and there is no one description that can accommodate their various identities, behaviors, and perceptions. However, there are certain themes appropriate for discussion with the African American population that are highlighted in this chapter. With the changing demographic shift that is currently under way with more racial minorities populating the United States, it is inevitable that more racial minorities will be seeking human services in greater numbers than before. Thus, it is vital to understand general population trends related to the African American community in the United States. This chapter provides key characteristics of the African American population that contribute to a process of mutual understanding between mental health and human service providers and some of the clients they serve. The chapter concludes with some recommendations of culturally defined response factors to counseling approaches when working with people who identify as African American.

Operationally Defining Race and Ethnicity

Because a lot of confusion surrounds the word *race* (Banks, 1997; Wilson & Senices, in press), it is important to first discuss the contextual differences between race and ethnicity. More importantly, the distinction between these two social–political terms is important because many human and medical service professionals tend to use the two words interchangeably and out of context. In many situations, the word *ethnicity* tends to diffuse deep-seated feelings dealing with certain kinds of discrimination (e.g., discrimination based on the color or pigmentation of the skin). However, the distinctions discussed below relating to race and ethnicity will serve to lay the foundation for what is communicated in this chapter in relation to the characteristics of the African American community in the United States. Finally, deconstructing race and ethnicity will highlight the complexities of how one judges people in the United States who may look different (phenotypically) from the mainstream norm (i.e., White Americans).

As recently adduced by Wilson and Senices (in press), in 1990, Zuckerman reported that in the field of psychology, the word *race* is avoided because of the various ways researchers in many disciplines define and use the word. Contextually defining both race and ethnicity also serves as a way to communicate an essential element in the way many people in U.S. society discriminate based on phenotype (skin hue/color; Carter, 1995; Hacker, 1995;

Schulman et al., 1999; Wilson, 2002; Wilson & Senices, in press), which is rarely discussed in most professional journals in the human service disciplines (e.g., many areas of psychology, social work, rehabilitation counseling). Sue et al. (1998) reported that the two dominant definitions of race are based on either physical or biological traits, which is consistent with the common thread communicated in most definitions of race in the social science literature. Tajfel (1981) indicated that the notion of race was more salient for ethnic minorities, particularly African Americans, because of the physical/biological evidence of skin pigment and other physical features possessed by most. To further support the assertion made by Tajfel, Carter (1995) and Wilson and Senices (in press) prefer to use the word *race*, as opposed to *ethnicity*, because they also believe that many experiences that African Americans encounter are made more intense by a person's phenotype. The many negative connotations attached to a particular phenotype, such as the darker hue that most African Americans are likely to share, when compared with White Americans, will engender perceptions of negativity from White Americans (Wilson & Senices, in press). In contrast, White Americans are viewed most positively because of their light phenotype (i.e., hue or color). In addition, because of the images associated with both African and White Americans, White Americans are likely to be viewed as less intimidating than African Americans in the United States. While it is recognized that most races may appear on the rainbow continuum from darker to lighter hues, empirical evidence (Hacker, 1995; Rosenbaum, 1996; Schulman et al., 1999) suggests that people with darker hues tend to be discriminated against more often that those with lighter hues, even within groups like Black and White Hispanics in the United States. Most of the discrimination practices are found even when variables like education and socioeconomic status are held constant. To further reinforce the skin hue assertion, Thomas and Sillen (1972) informed us that various mental disorders were as much to do with the hue of one's skin as any other demographic variable during the time of slavery in the Americas. Thus, many present conditions of African Americans can be traced historically back to the emphasis put on skin color (darker skin hue) over 400 year ago. Thus, the term *racial minorities* is used to refer to those who may be considered visible minorities (darker hue) in the United States (e.g., African Americans, Native Americans). And in this case, the operative word *visible* is primarily translated to represent people of color.

As acknowledged in the opening paragraph of this section, there is much confusion about the terms race and ethnicity. "Hispanics constitute an ethnic group rather than a racial category, and their members may classify themselves as White, Black, or some other race" (Rawlings & Saluter, 1994, p. xii; also see Rehabilitation Services Administration, 1995; U.S. Census Bureau, 2001). I believe that a general consensus of what is meant by ethnicity was recently captured eloquently by Dana (1998) when he adduced that ethnicity is one's shared culture, values, beliefs, loci of control, language, and the spirituality of a particular group of individuals (also see Banks, 1991, 1997). As Phinney (1990) indicated, ethnicity is wide ranging and includes both race and culture of origin. Because many groups in the United States (e.g., people of Italian, German, or French ancestry) are categorized under the term ethnicity, the kind of present intense discrimination (e.g., salary, housing) encountered by most White ethnic groups tends to be far less than discrimination encountered by ethnic groups that are considered Black "people of color" (e.g., African Americans) in the United States (see Bennett, 1995; Hacker, 1995; Herbert & Martinez, 1992; Wilson, Harley, McCormick, Jolivette, & Jackson, 2001). For example, Rosenbaum (1996) compared both White and Black Hispanics and controlled for a host of independent variables (e.g., socioeconomic status). His findings indicated that White Hispanics have privileges similar to those enjoyed by White Americans in the United States. More recently, Wilson (2004) reported that people with disabilities who are White Hispanic tended to have similar success as White Americans who are able-bodied in the United States. A tangential inference from both the Rosenbaum and Wilson investigations is that some individuals who classified as ethnic minorities (e.g., Hispanics) may not have similar discrimination experiences when compared with racial groups like African Americans and Black Hispanics, as available evidence suggests.

African Americans and Acculturation

While it is recognized that people get discriminated against for a plethora of reasons on a continuum of variables that could extend indefinitely, and that many variables that people get discriminated on may be correlated with one another (e.g., gender and race), being a racial minority tends to negatively intensify perceptions about African Americans and other people of color on the North American continent. And of course, these unconstructive emotional reactions lead to a lack of social and judicial justice evidenced by recent incidents of unwarranted racial profiling. Banks (1997) reported that acculturation involves two groups: the racial minority (e.g., African Americans) and the dominant culture and race (i.e., White Americans). More specifically, acculturation is a process by which racial minorities give up many of their values, beliefs, and traditions to be accepted into the White American culture or mainstream society. Contextually speaking, it is the process by which racial minorities are expected to give up many of their traditions and values, especially if these values and traditions of the racial minority group are in direct conflict with those held by the White American culture (Bennett, 1995, Wilson, 2004). Inherent in the aforementioned practice of acculturation is the concept of inequality and the lack of mutual respect the dominant culture tends to project, consciously or unconsciously, on racial minorities, such as African Americans in the United States. As far back as 1967, Ayers reported that

> Black people suffer from discrimination and prejudice, which is perhaps the most relentless and detrimental disadvantage and intensifies the other disadvantages. Handicapped white groups have greater economic mobility and more chance of being assimilated into the larger society. The obstacles against such assimilation are more formidable for the black man, largely because everyone can see his [her] ethnic identity. (p. 55)

Although race, and in the context of this chapter, one's phenotype in relation to hue, is a highly charged topic that people usually whisper or shout to one another, it is apparent that racial minorities tend to have a more difficult time acculturating and assimilating than individuals who are not considered part of the racial minority category in the United States (Bennett, 1995).

Researchers have asked for some time what factors contribute to the quality of life (e.g., socioeconomic and educational) of the nation's citizenry. As indicated by Wilson, Harley, et al. (2001), racial minority status appears to be a significant variable in determining the quality of life (e.g., vocations, bank loans) for people of color in the United States. According to accepted norms of the larger society, if the hue of one's skin is light, the assimilation opportunities will be enhanced in American society (Bennett, 1995). The "blending-in" process of people of color in the United States is quite interesting when compared with other groups who migrated or were forced to come to the United States for political or economical reasons. By some accounts, assimilation appeared to be associated with the shade of one's skin, with people having a lighter skin color being more easily assimilated into the mainstream society (Bennett, 1995).

The generations of White ethnic groups who visually did not appear much different from White European Americans in the United States could assimilate by giving up their original names, language, and traditions. However, this was not possible for people of color who were of the darker hue (Bennett, 1995). Consequently, "white ethnic groups (e.g., people of German or Irish descent) were able to attain full inclusion into the mainstream society once they were culturally identical to Anglo-Saxon Protestants" (Banks, 1991, p. 254). White ethnic groups did not have an assimilation problem if they were culturally identical to the prevailing norms of the majority culture; not so with African Americans and people of color (Bennett, 1995). What is also inherent in the observations by Banks is that African Americans would have a problem assimilating even though they might have been culturally similar to White Americans. Realizing that we live in an imperfect society, the rights and rudimentary amenities and social justice of African Americans may be jeopardized because of certain physical characteristics and, in particular, what values are attached to the phenotype of many people of color in the United States.

To corroborate the assertion that racial minorities have a more difficult time assimilating than groups who do not classify themselves under the racial minority category, Smith (2000) carried out an ambitious national study surveying intergroup relations. He confirmed that out of all the groups in the investigation (i.e., Blacks, Jews, Hispanics, fundamentalist Christians, Asians, Muslims, atheists, people with disabilities, Native Americans, gays and lesbians, Whites, immigrants, the poor, the elderly, the illiterate, and people on welfare), White Americans and African Americans have the most variant opinions on issues relating to levels of racism, group tension, and educational parity. The results of Smith's investigation are viewed as a thematic trend in several studies that have examined multiple variables dealing with race and issues of sociopolitical outcomes in the United States (e.g., vocational and educational consequences); an earlier study, by Chideya (1995), had concluded similar findings to those adduced by Smith. In one of the most recent studies that investigated and controlled several demographic variables and race, Smith's study reveals that not only do African Americans and White Americans differ in their perceptions about racial discrimination and educational equality, but these differences are inherent with many of the barriers African Americans encounter when attempting to assimilate (both psychically and perceptually) into mainstream America.

Because the attitudes and behaviors of any organization or system (e.g., educational, mental health, business) form a fairly accurate microcosm of the general society in which we live (Sue, 1994; Thomas & Sillen, 1972; Wilson, Alston, Harley, & Mitchell, 2002; Wilson, Edwards, et al., 2001; Wilson, Jackson, & Doughty, 1999), Smith's (2000) and Chideya's (1995) findings are particularly relevant to any discussion of intergroup tension occurring within social service organizations in which African Americans may be seeking psychological services, for example. Generally, White American middle-class values could be perceived as covertly biased toward racial minorities, an observation that supports the possibility of tension between the counselor and the client. The inevitable strain between White American human service providers and racial minorities tends to enhance the overall complexities of African Americans not only assimilating into the American mainstream but being accepted and validated during daily interactions with White Americans inside and outside of the counseling environment.

Demographics

As the demographic shift is well under way in the United States, people in human service professions (e.g., counseling, social work, and health care) are likely to find more racial minorities seeking to access social and medical services. As consistent with prior census reports, African Americans represent approximately 13% of the total noninstitutionalized population in the United States. When we observe the metropolitan and nonmetropolitan areas where most African Americans are likely to live, we see that the vast majority of African

Americans reside in metropolitan areas (urban) inside a city (55%), compared with only 21% of White Americans (non-Hispanic Whites). As would be expected, given the racial geographical patterns in prior years, there is also a higher number of White Americans (22%) residing in nonmetropolitan areas (rural) compared with their African American (12%) counterparts. As consistent with the aforementioned trend of African Americans living in urban areas, White Americans (57%) are more likely to reside in metropolitan areas outside central cities than their African American (36%) counterparts. Finally, there is an overwhelming number of African Americans (55.3%) living in the southern part of the United States. Although not in large percentages when compared with African Americans, White Americans tend to live in the southern and midwestern (33.3% and 27%, respectively) parts of the nation (U.S. Census Bureau, 2002). While there are several explanations for the residential patterns of African Americans and White Americans in the United States, one explanation why African Americans tend to live in urban areas would be the relatively higher number of jobs located in urban centers compared with rural areas in the United States. However, based on housing demographics and residential segregation patterns among African Americans and White Americans in the United States, a primary reason why White Americans tend to live in metropolitan areas outside central cities would be their attempt to not live where African Americans live. While there are several possible reasons why White Americans would prefer to live outside of metropolitan areas (e.g., lower crime rates, more affordable housing, better schools, etc.), one common theme attached to the meaning of "Blackness" in the United States is frequently adduced. For example, Hacker (1995) reported that White Americans tend to live in mixed racial areas until the percentage of African Americans reach 10% or higher in the residential community. In addition, another important empirical finding from Hacker's study revealed that this particular "White flight" pattern is observed even when African Americans move into neighborhoods with White Americans and hold analogous educational and socioeconomic markers as their White American counterparts. While more controversial, another reason why White Americans might not consider residing in communities with African Americans could be the devaluing of property value that accompanies the stereotypes of people of color. It is common that separate neighborhoods primarily composed of African Americans and White Americans with similar educational, social, and socioeconomic backgrounds will have different property values. Consequently, many White Americans are moving from neighborhoods that are becoming populated by African Americans (Hacker, 1995) because of the meanings that they attach to being African American (Blackness) in the United States, which tends to be negative and unrelenting in all facets of living and social conditions (e.g., educational, social, political, economical). Wilson (2002) called this kind of generalization of attitudes a microcosm of the attitudes of the society in which we live.

Family Type and Size of the African American Family

When we examine the family structure of African Americans, we see that African Americans are less likely to be married than White Americans. However, when marriage is examined across race and gender, we see that African American and White American women are more likely to be separated, widowed, or divorced than men (U.S. Census Bureau, 2002). When comparing the sizes of African American and White American families, we see that "Black (African American) married-couple families were more likely than their non-Hispanic White counterparts to have five or more members (20% and 12%, respectively)" (U.S. Census Bureau, 2002, p. 3). Only 40% of African American families were maintained by women with no partner present compared with 55% of White American families. Eleven percent of African American families were maintained by women compared with 5% of White American families (U.S. Census Bureau, 2002).

While there are varying degrees of consensus why both African Americans and White Americans differ relative to the size and type of family structure, it is important to acknowledge and respect cultural considerations that may influence the size of a particular family, for example.

African Americans and Educational Attainment

Although formal education has been a tremendous contextual sense of pride for many African Americans, African Americans (79%) still lag behind White Americans (89%) in the completion of high school and earning at least a bachelor's degree in the United States. However, when bachelor's degree completion is compared across gender with African Americans, there is evidence that African American women are more likely to earn a bachelor's degree than African American men. In addition, when educational attainment data are examined among African American and White American women, available evidence suggests that there is not a significant difference in the proportions of high school graduates and individuals who have had some college or completed an associated degree (U.S. Census Bureau, 2002). Sociopolitical realities (e.g., racism, colorism, sexism) for African Americans do account for many of the discrepancies in educational attainment between the two groups. While general data on educational attainment are somewhat mixed when one compares African Americans with White Americans in the United States, the theme that White Americans are more likely to have more education across the variables of race and gender continues to be consistent. Because African Americans get discriminated against in so many areas, the phrase "if everything were equal" should be used only when it is clear that "apple-to-apple" comparisons are made. In the case of many African Americans, this particular phrase is usually taken out of context.

African Americans and Worldview and Identity

When one looks at worldview and culture, one will inevitably find a clash between the majority culture (White Americans) and other cultures that may not be considered mainstream in the United States (e.g., African Americans). Kearney (1975) reported that worldview is a cultural construction of reality that is formed under certain sociopolitical conditions that assist groups in adapting and even surviving in certain conditions. Generally, worldview is a way that people view the world based on the unique experiences of an individual or a group. In many instances, one's worldview is determined by the experiences (e.g., historical and present-day), values, and traditions of a particular group. The fact that people tend to have different worldviews based on numerous dimensions (e.g., race and socioeconomic status) is something that should be celebrated in a society that values such diversity. From a historical perspective, however, when values expressed by, say, African Americans are projected within many contexts of the United States, those values tend to be labeled as wrong and deviant by many White American people. Dana (1998) reported that the perception that one's worldview is reality and that particular worldview has pervaded human history is called *ethnocentrism*. Thus, the problem is not that people tend to have different worldviews; it is the negative meanings that we tend to attach to worldviews that are different from our own worldview that are the problem. The worldviews of each group tend to be a "reality check" within the group to make sense out of the internal and external milieu. Fairly often, the worldview of African Americans is discounted as paranoid and highly pathologized by many White Americans in the United States, as suggested by Sue (1994) and others (Litwack, 1961; Thomas & Sillen, 1972; Wilson, Harley, et al., 2001). Because we cannot separate the attitudes of the general society (i.e., mainstream) from those of health care providers, it is not surprising that empirical evidence suggests that

African Americans are likely to be overpathologized when compared with their White American counterparts (Geller, 1988; Lawson, Hepler, Holladay, & Cuffel, 1994). In talking about the experiences of African Americans, Vontress and Epp (1997) described a primary historical event that continues to reflect the worldview of most African Americans in the United States:

> The psychology experience of African Americans has no exact parallel in human history. Exposed to three centuries of slavery, discrimination, and constant, if unconscious, fear of unequal treatment by the majority culture, African Americans may have developed a unique psychology that requires a special sensitivity and approach from the counselor. (p. 170)

There are several observations that would strongly suggest that African Americans and White Americans tend to have divergent worldviews. The first example would be the verdict in the Rodney King incident that occurred in the mid-1990s. Although both African Americans and White Americans observed police officers beating Mr. King on national television, when police officers were acquitted in the Rodney King incident, people in both communities reacted in different ways to the verdict. In contrast to most White Americans, most African Americans thought the police officers should have been found guilty. Another similar reaction based on race is found in the criminal and civil trials of O. J. Simpson. Again, one's experiences (e.g., historical and contemporary) tend to influence how events and behaviors are interpreted, and whether one's interpretation is valid will depend on whose worldview is serving as the dominant worldview in any given society. It goes without saying that tension between the African American client and the White American counselor may have detrimental outcomes when carried over into the social and mental health arenas. It is very difficult, if not impossible, for most of us to separate our racial biases. And because most counselors and mental health and medical personnel tend to be White Americans, different worldviews might be a barrier during the treatment process, thus leaving many African Americans with a less than adequate feeling about revisiting a counseling center, for example.

While there are many distinctions in worldview between African Americans and the majority culture, linear/nonrelational and nonlinear/relational communication styles are of primary concern when reasons why African Americans terminate early during the treatment process are highlighted. A major difficulty with African Americans terminating counseling sessions prematurely is the *nonrelational* way in which information is gathered in many human service settings. This perceived detachment on the part of the White American counselor is viewed as noncaring for many African American clients. In fact, it is hypothesized that this perception of being detached by White American counselors results in many premature terminations and also a lack of rapport with the White American counselor. Because this detached appearance seems to be consistent with many White American human service workers, it is inevitable that ethnocentric beliefs and training in our educational institutions, consciously or unconsciously, are perpetuating many unhealthy behaviors and thoughts among the human service professions. To reinforce the ethnocentric premise, Wright (1983) submitted that the subjugation of people of color stems from an ethnocentric attitude by White Americans toward non-White Americans:

> Ethnocentricism is the tendency to view one's own cultural group as the center of everything, the standard against which all others are judged. It assumes that one's own cultural patterns are the correct and best way to act. Historically, many whites have judged culturally different persons in terms of the values and behaviors of their white culture. This lack of understanding and respect for ethnic and cultural differences may lead to discrimination, which can be conveyed both subtly and overtly. (Vitaliti, 1998, p. 19)

Group identity usually progresses from the historical and cultural heritage of a group of people (Glazer & Moynihan, 1976). However, after 1933, the word *ethnicity* began appearing in print and was used to describe group membership and identity. Additionally, other residuals in using the term ethnicity were beginning to surface with pride in one's ethnicity and can be used to describe group membership and cultural background (Betancourt & López, 1993). Because the African American community is somewhat heterogeneous, there is a perception, going back to slavery in the United States, that African Americans who are of a lighter hue had more advantages than those with darker hues. To reinforce the hue distinction even further, Carter (1995) reported that race (e.g., hue) supercedes all of the experiences of people of color, in this case African Americans in the United States. Nonetheless, regardless of an African American's hue, many African Americans tend to identify with one another because of the similar experiences of discrimination based on phenotype. This seems to make hue a very salient variable for discrimination, partly because hue tends to be a marker that one cannot change or alter. It is not only a marker that announces to others at a distance that someone is African American, but it also has unspoken negative connotations that will signal to those in the majority culture that African Americans are not to be trusted or believed. The converse (African Americans being told that White Americans are not to be trusted) may also be true in some cases. Sexual orientation, religion, and nationality, for example, might not be as identifiable as hue and therefore less likely, when compared with African Americans, to be targeted for discrimination based on the overt marker of hue. Thus, the identity for most African Americans surrounds the "hue factor" not only for saliency of identity but also for the sociopolitical term of what most people think of when they hear the word *race* in the United States.

African Americans and Employment

In many of the human services agencies (e.g., vocational rehabilitation), African Americans tend to come into the system with less education than their White American counterparts. It is not surprising that because of the negative images embedded in the psyche of many White American health care providers and White American people in the general population (see Sue, 1994), discrimination in employment occurs. Hacker (1995) reported that for as long as records have been kept, the unemployment rate for African Americans has always been twice that of White Americans, regardless of the vibrancy or lack of vibrancy in the economy. Consequently, in economic prosperity and the lack thereof, African Americans tend not to gain any distance on White Americans in terms of the proportions of individuals employed in the United States.

To reinforce the employment assertions by Hacker (1995), the U.S. Census Bureau (2002) reported that African Americans were unemployed at twice the rate of White Americans, which is somewhat consistent across gender as well. There are many reasons for this discrepant unemployment rate between African Americans and White Americans. The sociopolitical realities of hue discrimination seem to be a very salient variable in determining the rate of employment of African Americans and White Americans in the United States, as the television documentary *True Colors* (Houser, 1996) supported several years ago.

Mental Health Services and African Americans

While present conditions of mental health services are far from adequate for African Americans, I believe that the present form of inadequate services for people of color, and, in particular, African Americans, started over 400 years ago with the institution of slavery in the United States. The sociopolitical realities regarding people of color are lined with past postulations in the counseling, psychiatry, and psychology areas indicating African Americans were less intelligent and were inferior to White Americans. Additionally, the current sociopolitical indicators (e.g., earnings and educational policies) imply that numerous presumptions about African Americans can be traced back to the early transportation of African people to the United States over 400 years ago (Wilson, Edwards, et al., 2001). While associating mental health and slavery, Thomas and Sillen (1972) adduced that various mental and psychological disorders were as much to do with the hue of one's skin than any other demographic variable during the time of slavery in the Americas. Thus, mental health and intellectual comparisons serve to underscore the present condition of many people of color with disabilities in rural centers (Wilson, Edwards, et al., 2001).

As would be expected, slavery produced several myths that presently persist in the United States. Although slavery subsisted in many parts of the globe, the kind of slavery encountered in the Western hemisphere was different and more demoralizing than in other parts of the world (Browder, 1992). In the United States, Thomas and Sillen (1972) reported that rationalizations of certain mental disorders (e.g., dysaethesia) served to sanctify a hierarchical social order of race. Even though psychology was not recognized as a specific profession until after the emancipation of Africans and African Americans, to validate slavery, White Americans claimed that African Americans were uniquely fitted for bondage by their elementary way of thinking and behaving. People of color were considered inferior to the White race based on the subjective rates of "insanity and idiocy" (Litwack, 1961). African Americans were thought to have good mental health if they were subservient (being controlled and docile), whereas protesters were categorized as deranged and mentally ill. Likewise, many Africans were labeled with dysaethesia aethiopica, or rascality (mischievous, disreputable, or dishonest character, behavior, or action) if they did not abide by the expectations of the White American slaveholders. As far back as 1928, psychiatrists believed that being associated with people of color (African Americans) would destroy the White American race (Freud, 1938). In many instances, not only was the area of psychology a system used to justify negative mental and emotional conditions and enslavement of Africans and African Americans, but it also started a process that is continued today within the field of psychology/psychiatry and the human service professions (see Dana, 1998, 2002). As a historical footnote, several acknowledged explanations for certain mental illnesses for African Americans have been since proven bogus by the psychological community (Thomas & Sillen, 1972). While the fields of psychology and human service have recently produced some top-notch scholars of people of color (e.g., Thomas Parham and Robert T. Carter), it is important to recognize that many of the psychological, sociological, and political ills that African Americans endure today started over 400 years ago with the importing of Africans to the North American continent.

Currently, mental health services for people of color and for African Americans in particular have been reactive to sociopolitical events. Services have emphasized the similarities between African Americans and White Americans. However, this ethnocentric way of thinking has contributed to the bias, lack of availability, clinical diagnoses, and underutilization of services for African Americans in the United States. Because of events like slavery in the United States, many African Americans are suffering from personal hurt that has resulted in transgenerational pain (Dana, 2002). Because training paradigms have been predicated on the White American philosophy and tend to represent that particular group (Dana, 1998), it is obvious that more diversity training to health care providers, such as psychologists, mental health counselors, and rehabilitation counselors, must take a giant leap to improve services for a growing population of clients seeking human services. It is also important to evaluate the training. Regarding mental health services, Sue (1994) reported several contemporary and unjustified findings of pathology found in the literature regarding people of color:

Racial ethnic minorities are often seen as deficient in certain desirable attributes (intelligence, motivation, good hygiene, etc.). Many in our society continue to believe, for example, that African Americans lack innate intelligence due to "genes." For now, instead of blaming the genes, they blame culture! The terms cultural deprivation and cultural impoverishment do not make conceptual sense. Because, isn't everyone born with a culture? What the early advocates of cultural impoverishment were saying was that minorities did not inherit the "right culture." (p. 24)

The history of psychological and human services for African Americans in the United States has been below adequate at best, and destructive to the emotional, psychological, social, and physical conditions of African Americans at worst. As would be anticipated, it may be common for many African Americans to express some form of hostility when they encounter White Americans not only when seeking mental health and social services but also in their workplaces (Vontress & Epp, 1997). The strategies below are recommendations for White American human service providers (e.g., counselors, therapists, social workers, etc.) to use when working with African Americans.

Culturally Defined Response Factors to Counseling African Americans

It is apparent that there is a litany of interventions that can be specified to facilitate African Americans through the human service system. Although every attempt is made to be inclusive of literature themes in this section of possible solutions, it is expected that the list below will not be an exhaustive list of intervention strategies to facilitate people of color through the maze of human services in the United States. However, I attempted to cover themes that will facilitate the counseling and social process for African Americans.

Recognizing and Addressing Historical Hostility

Vontress and Epp (1997) reported that it would be difficult for counselors to assist African American clients in therapy without recognizing that some African Americans may have problems associated with historical hostility relating to past dealings with White Americans and the White American system. All too often White American counselors will not validate the experiences of African Americans because most White American counselors do not have analogous experiences. Though expressions of historical hostility tend to be directed outward, historical hostility may be manifested inward as depression and alcohol or other substance abuses. Because of the complexities and broad range of symptoms of historical hostility, it is prudent to use a holistic approach to consider such effects as the relationship of mind and body. Finally, it is vital to consider the effects of resentment, anger, and other feelings on the client's overall health, including interpersonal relationships (Vontress & Epp, 1997).

Acknowledging and Validating Experiences of Racism

In any counseling relationship, mutual respect and understanding are vital to increase trust and positive outcomes. In this light, it is important for White American counselors to validate the experiences of African American clients. The word *validate* in this context does not mean to agree with and even to comprehend the experiences of African American clients. Validation here means to accept that the client beliefs are true to the client without invalidating his or her experiences based on the experiences, or lack of, of the counselor. This is actually the crux of the interpersonal relationship dilemma in which many African

American clients and White American counselors increasingly find themselves. In fact, for many White American therapists, it would be truly difficult, although not impossible, to validate and also allow themselves to step into the daily world of destructive interactions of the African American client and believe that the racism experiences expressed by the client are indeed true, as far as the client is concerned. Because research indicates that many White American counselors do not feel competent to provide services to African American clients (Allison, Echemendia, Crawford, & Robinson, 1996), yielding to another's worldview may be not only helpful to the client but also liberating and ultimately insightful to the White American counselor. If White American counselors do not validate the experiences of racial minorities, the tendency to overpathologize will continue within the psychology and counseling communities.

Integrating Spirituality in Therapy

A major problem human service workers (e.g., counselors) encounter is that many of them believe that spirituality and religion are pathological to the nature of psychotherapy (Frame, Williams, & Braun, 1996). From a historical perspective, for example, Freud (1913) viewed religion as a form of irrational illusion. And Freud's view continues to contribute to the disconnect between religion and psychotherapy (Frame et al., 1996). With many racial minorities' beliefs in the supernatural and a power greater than themselves, it is not surprising why African Americans, in particular, could be disfranchised even more in psychotherapy by the mainstream counseling techniques and approaches to psychological and emotional healing.

"African American culture is rich with religious and spiritual traditions and practices have been ignored in traditional approaches to counseling with this population" (Frame et al., 1996, p. 13). African rhythms to blues, soul, and jazz are all considered aspects of the aforementioned spirituality that have continued to be disregarded by mainstream counseling practices (Lee, 1990) in the North American continent. Mental health professions recognize that, to be effective with people who are African Americans, nontraditional methods of service delivery not only are necessary (Lee, 1990) but should be a required means in every counselor's toolbox of intervention strategies. Spirituality (see Frame et al., 1996, for definitions of religion and spirituality) has been with people of African descent since antiquity. Being communal and seeing the connection of body, mind, spirit, and the universe are typical perspectives that African Americans share in common. Thus, relating or associating oneself with a higher being might be a way to connect with African Americans. When necessary, referring out to a community church or reading scripture to reinforce treatment options might also be a way to increase cooperation and rapport with African Americans during therapy and interventions. While this option of nontraditional involvement might appear uncomfortable for many health care providers, being able and willing to validate the spirituality component of African Americans will go a long way to providing appropriate treatment options for a population who has historically been denied access and underserved in the human services and psychological arena. Integrating religion intervention approaches to treatment is a way for White American human service workers to connect and communicate a sense of connectedness that could enhance rapport and positive outcomes for many African Americans seeking human services.

Below are sociopolitical realities that tend to be different for African Americans and White Americans in the United States. Understanding how African Americans view these discrepancies might enhance communication and rapport between African Americans and White Americans, not only in the human service area but in the day-to-day interactions as well.

- African American women more active in church than African American men
- historical and contemporary racism and discrimination
- lack of education
- differing cultural characteristics and customs
- unequal employment and housing opportunities
- communication problems caused by misunderstood communication patterns and dialects
- depression and depressive symptoms resulting from living in high-stressed environments (e.g., high unemployment and low income). (Adapted from Baruth & Manning, 2003)

Summary

African Americans comprise a diverse group of people who have been discriminated against, marginalized, and dehumanized for over 400 years in the United States. While there are many variables that people are likely to get discriminated on (e.g., sexual orientation, gender), people of color are many times discriminated against because of the hue of their skin, as evidenced by several studies that were able to control or hold variables constant. Unfortunate accessories to the bondage of African Americans were and are the fields of psychiatry and psychology (e.g., social work, rehabilitation counseling). Because it is very difficult to separate certain philosophical beliefs in the fields of psychiatry and psychology and the general population of the United States, the fields of psychiatry and psychology are considered by many to represent a microcosm of the general attitudes of mainstream society. With the changing demographic shift that is currently under way with more racial minorities populating the United States, it is inevitable that more racial minorities will be seeking human services in greater numbers than in the past. Thus, it is important for White American counselors to adopt modern ways of providing services to African Americans and other people of color in the United States.

References

Allison, K. W., Echemendia, R., Crawford, I., & Robinson, L. (1996). Predicting cultural competence: Implications for practice and training. *Professional Psychology: Research and Practice, 27,* 386–393.

Ayers, G. E. (1967). *Rehabilitating the culturally disadvantaged.* Mankato, MN: Mankato State College.

Banks, J. (1991). *Teaching strategies for ethnic studies.* Needham Heights, MA: Allyn & Bacon.

Banks, J. (1997). *Teaching strategies for ethnic studies* (2nd ed.). Needham Heights, MA: Allyn & Bacon.

Baruth, L. G., & Manning, M. K. (2003). *Multicultural counseling and psychotherapy: A lifespan perspective* (3rd ed.). Columbus, OH: Merrill/Prentice Hall.

Bennett, C. (1995). *Comprehensive multicultural education: Theory and practice* (3rd ed.). Needham Heights, MA: Allyn & Bacon.

Betancourt, H., & López, S. R. (1993). The study of culture, ethnicity, and race in American psychology. *American Psychologist, 48,* 629–637.

Browder, A. T. (1992). *Exploding the myths: Vol. 1. Nile Valley contributions to civilization.* Washington, DC: Institute of Karmic Guidance.

Carter, R. T. (1995). *The influence of race and racial identity in psychotherapy: Toward a racially inclusive model.* New York: Wiley.

Chideya, F. (1995). *Don't believe the hype: Fighting cultural misinformation about African Americans.* New York: Penguin Group.

Dana, R. H. (1998). *Understanding cultural identity in intervention and assessment: Multicultural aspects of counseling, Series 9.* Thousand Oaks, CA: Sage.

Dana, R. H. (2002). Mental health services for African Americans: A cultural/racial perspective. *Cultural Diversity and Ethnic Minority Psychology, 8,* 3–18.

Frame, M. W., Williams, C. B., & Braun, C. (1996). Counseling African Americans: Integrating spiritually in therapy. *Counseling and Values, 41,* 13–16.

Freud, S. (1913). *The interpretation of dreams.* New York: Macmillan.

Freud, S. (1938). *The basic writings of Sigmund Freud* (A. Brill, Trans.). New York: Modern Library.

Geller, J. D. (1988). Racial bias in the evaluation of patients of psychotherapy. In L. D. Comas-Dias & E. E. H. Griffith (Eds.), *Clinical guidelines in cross-cultural mental health* (pp. 112–134). New York: Wiley.

Glazer, N., & Moynihan, D. P. (1976). Introduction. In N. Glazer & D. P. Moynihan (Eds.), *Ethnicity: Theory and experience* (pp. 1–26). Cambridge, MA: Harvard University Press.

Hacker, A. (1995). *Two nations: Black and White, separate, hostile, unequal.* New York: Macmillan.

Herbert, J. T., & Martinez, M. Y. (1992). Client ethnicity and vocational rehabilitation case service outcome. *Journal of Job Placement, 8,* 10–16.

Houser, E. (1996). *True colors* [Film]. Retrieved August 28, 2004, from http://www.viewingrace.org/browse_title.php?film_id=385&curr_letter=t

Kearney, M. (1975). Worldview theory and study. *Annual Review of Psychology, 4,* 247–270.

Lawson, W. B., Hepler, N., Holladay, J., & Cuffel, B. (1994). Race as a factor in inpatient and outpatient admissions and diagnosis. *Hospital and Community Psychiatry, 45,* 72–74.

Lee, C. C. (1990). Black male development: Counseling the "native son." In D. Moore & F. Leafgren (Eds.), *Problem solving strategies for men in conflict* (pp. 125–137). Alexandria, VA: American Association for Counseling and Development.

Litwack, L. F. (1961). *North of slavery: The Negro in the free states: 1790–1860.* Chicago: University of Chicago Press.

Phinney, J. S. (1990). Ethnic identity in adolescents and adults: Review of research. *Psychological Bulletin, 108,* 499–514.

Rawlings, S. W., & Saluter, A. F. (1994). *Household and family characteristics: Current population reports* (P20-483). Washington, DC: U.S. Census Bureau.

Rehabilitation Services Administration. (1995). *Reporting manual for the case service report* (RSA-911; RSA-PD-95-04). Washington, DC: Author.

Rosenbaum, E. (1996). The influence of race on Hispanic housing choices: New York City, 1978–1987. *Urban Affairs Review, 32,* 217–243.

Schulman, K. A., Berlin, J. A., Harless, W., Kerner, J. F., Sistrunk, S., Gersh, B., et al. (1999). The effect of race and sex on physicians' recommendations for cardiac catheterization. *New England Journal of Medicine, 340,* 618–628.

Smith, T. W. (2000). *Taking America's pulse: II. A survey of intergroup relations—The National Conference for Community and Justice.* Chicago: University of Chicago, National Opinion Research Center.

Sue, D. W. (1994). The challenge of cultural diversity: Overcoming barriers. In P. Leung & R. A. Middleton (Eds.), *Proceedings of the National Association of Multicultural Concerns* (pp. 20–27). New Orleans, LA: National Association of Multicultural Rehabilitation Concerns.

Sue, D. W., Carter, R. T., Casas, J. M., Fouad, N. A., Ivey, A. I., Jensen, M., et al. (1998). *Multicultural counseling competencies: Vol. 11. Individual and organizational development.* Thousand Oaks, CA: Sage.

Tajfel, H. (1981). *Human groups and social categories.* Cambridge, England: Cambridge University Press.

Thomas, A., & Sillen, S. (1972). *Racism and psychiatry.* New York: Carol Publishing.

U.S. Census Bureau. (2001, March). *Overview of race and Hispanic origin: Census 2000 brief.* Retrieved October 15, 2003, from http://www.census.gov/prod/2001pubs/cenbr01-1.pdf

U.S. Census Bureau. (2002, March). *The Black population in the United States: Population characteristics.* Retrieved October 21, 2003, from http://www.census.gov/prod/2003pubs/p20-541.pdf

Vitaliti, L. U. T. (1998). Rural Americans and persons with disabilities. In T. S. Smith (Ed.), *Rural rehabilitation: A modern perspective* (pp. 14–39). Arnaudville, LA: Bow River Publishing.

Vontress, C. E., & Epp, L. R. (1997). Historical hostility in the African American client: Implications for counseling. *Journal of Multicultural Counseling and Development, 45,* 170–184.

Wilson, K. B. (2002). The exploration of vocational rehabilitation acceptance and ethnicity: A national investigation. *Rehabilitation Counseling Bulletin, 45,* 168–176.

Wilson, K. B. (2004). *Reason for closure between Hispanics and non-Hispanics in the United States vocational rehabilitation system.* Manuscript in preparation.

Wilson, K. B., Alston, R. J., Harley, D. A., & Mitchell, N. (2002). Predicting vocational rehabilitation acceptance based on race, gender, education, work status at application, and primary source of support at application in the United States. *Rehabilitation Counseling Bulletin, 45,* 132–142.

Wilson, K. B., Edwards, D. W., Alston, R. J., Harley, D. A., & Doughty, J. D. (2001). Vocational rehabilitation and the dilemma of race in rural communities: The debate continues. *Journal of Rural Community Psychology, 2,* 55–81. Retrieved April 14, 2002, from http://www.events.im.com.au/reviewers/search.asp

Wilson, K. B., Harley, D. A., McCormick, K., Jolivette, K., & Jackson, R. L. (2001). A literature review of vocational rehabilitation acceptance and rationales for bias in the rehabilitation process. *Journal of Applied Rehabilitation Counseling, 32*(1), 24–35.

Wilson, K. B., Jackson, R., & Doughty, J. (1999). What a difference a race makes: Reasons for unsuccessful closures within the vocational rehabilitation system. *American Rehabilitation, 25,* 16–24.

Wilson, K. B., & Senices, J. (in press). Exploring the vocational rehabilitation acceptance rates of Hispanics and non-Hispanics in the United States. *Journal of Counseling & Development.*

Wright, B. A. (1983). *Physical disability: A psychological approach* (2nd ed.). New York: Harper & Row.

Zuckerman, M. (1990). Some dubious premises in research and theory on racial differences. *American Psychologist, 45,* 1297–1303.

12

Perceptions of African Americans Regarding Mental Health Counseling

Charlotte G. Dixon and Kim Vaz

The 1999 Surgeon General's report on mental health brought the status of mental health care to the forefront of mainstream America. According to that report, one in five Americans suffers from some kind of mental disorder that can be successfully treated. The report goes on to say that only one fourth of those who suffer receive help. With regard to African Americans, the report indicated that the prevalence of mental disorders is estimated to be higher among African Americans than among Whites, a factor that has been attributed more to socioeconomic differences than to intrinsic differences between the races (U.S. Department of Health and Human Services, 2000). Lower socioeconomic status, in terms of income, education, and occupation, has been strongly linked to mental illness, and research has long held that people in the lowest socioeconomic strata are about two and a half times more likely than those in the highest strata to have a mental disorder (Holzer et al., 1986; Regier et al., 1993). However, according to the Surgeon General's report, the U.S. mental health system is not well equipped to meet the needs of racial and ethnic minority populations, an assertion that dates back to the 1960s and 1970s with the rise of the civil rights and community mental health movements and with successive waves of immigration from Central American, the Caribbean, and Asia (U.S. Department of Health and Human Services, 2000). Consequently, those who may have the greatest need for mental health counseling services are also the ones most likely to receive inadequate or inappropriate services. This may in part explain why studies have consistently found that ethnic minorities in the United States underuse formal systems of mental health services (Cheung & Snowden, 1990; Snowden, 1999; Sue, Fujino, Hu, Takeuchi, & Zane, 1991). According to Matthews and Hughes (2001), African Americans seek professional mental health services at rates lower than those of Whites (Mindel & Wright, 1982), and 50% of ethnic minority clients drop out of treatment following their initial session, compared with 30% for White Americans (Atkinson, Morten, & Sue, 1998; Sue & Zane, 1987). A variety of factors affect help-seeking behaviors among African Americans. This chapter examines the perceptions of African Americans toward mental health counseling and identifies factors influencing the rate at which African Americans utilize mental health services.

Perceptions of Mental Illness

Mental illness has historically been treated as a closet phenomenon within the African American community in the sense that mental illness is not a subject openly and candidly discussed among Africans Americans, their families, or communities (Whitaker, 2000). Several historical and cultural factors within the Black community have thwarted efforts to bring mental illness out of the closet and into the open; primary among them is African Americans' perceptions of mental illness. For example, the literature reports that some African Americans view mental illness as a problem that can be resolved within the family or community and, consequently, may avoid outside help (Boyd-Franklin, 1989). Others assert that African Americans hold misconceptions about the nature and cause of mental illness and believe that mental illness results from character flaws that can be overcome by an "avoidance of morbid thoughts" (Hall & Tucker, 1985, p. 911). Milstein, Guarnaccia, and Midlarsky (1995) included African Americans among the general lay population that view mental illness in strongly religious terms and consider psychiatric disorders to reflect the will of God. Few Blacks view mental illness as a biological disorder that can be treated, and consequently, the admission of a mental illness is often equated with weakness. It is acceptable to experience physical problems or illness, but the same is not true of mental illness or emotional disturbances. Seeking mental health counseling is considered taboo and can cause one to be looked upon as "crazy" for going to a "shrink" ("Why Blacks Must Educate Themselves," 2001). Consequently, pejorative perceptions associated with mental illness have lingered within the Black community for generations and have led to extreme stigmatization and shame, and they continue to keep millions from getting desperately needed help. Many Blacks are so concerned about what others will think of them that they would rather suffer in silence than risk being labeled crazy by members of their community ("Why Blacks Must Educate Themselves," 2001).

African Americans have historically relied on themselves, family, friends, and religious leaders for aid in dealing with difficult situations and circumstances. This strong sense of reliance on self, according to Dr. Steve Hyman, director of the National Institute of Mental Health, which can be and is positive in many aspects, has proved detrimental with regard to seeking mental health counseling services and is another factor contributing to the closet phenomenon of mental illness within the African American community (Whitaker, 2000). Blacks tend to see themselves as invincible and strong and to believe that they can get through a mental illness without professional assistance. Consequently, African Americans tend to seek professional counseling services as a last resort—after prayer, punishment, pleading, and others in the community have failed to arrest increasingly bizarre and occasionally violent behaviors (Whitaker, 2000).

Skepticism toward the medical system in general and the mental health care system in particular is another relevant factor affecting African Americans' perceptions regarding mental health counseling. Research documents that African Americans hold negative attitudes toward the mental health system (Nickerson, Helms, & Terrell, 1994), tend to be suspicious toward psychiatry (Whitaker, 2000), have a fear of hospitalization (Sussman, Robins, & Earls, 1987), and in general report high levels of mistrust (Bailey, 1987; Biafora et al., 1993) compared with Whites. Again, historical realities have contributed significantly to this mistrust.

Closely aligned with the skepticism and mistrust are a number of external factors that combine to negatively affect African Americans' perceptions of mental health counseling services. For example, researchers have documented decades of misdiagnosis of African Americans (Poussaint, 1983; A. Solomon, 1992; P. Solomon, 1988) as well as severe and stigmatizing diagnoses of those African Americans seeking mental health services (Cole &

Pilisuk, 1976; Sue, 1977). Snowden (2003) indicated that African Americans have higher than expected rates of diagnosed schizophrenia—56% compared with 32% for Whites (National Institute of Mental Health, 1987)—and lower rates of diagnosed affective disorders than Whites. Moreover, Snowden (2003) reported differences between African Americans and Whites in how they present symptoms of mental illness to clinicians that play a central role in making diagnostic decisions. Presentation of symptomatology also affects the way in which clinicians interpret the signs and symptoms observed.

A corollary factor identified in the literature addresses the training of mental health counseling providers. Presently, most providers of mental health services are trained in traditional psychotherapeutic approaches, that is, psychoanalytic, Adlerian, Jungian, cognitive–behavioral, humanistic, behavioral, and the like. None of these approaches were founded by African Americans or ethnic researchers, nor were the theories on which these approaches are based inclusive of African American or other ethnic minority clients. Consequently, their appropriateness for treatment with clients from ethnic backgrounds, though routinely used, are questionable at best. Clinicians who have not made sufficient efforts to understand minority identity development nor tried to integrate other cross-cultural training approaches into their practice have been questioned with regard to their level of competency in meeting the mental health counseling needs of African Americans and other ethnic clients. This assertion can be supported in part by the work of Allison, Crawford, Echemendia, Robinson, and Knepp (1994), who surveyed members of the American Psychological Association regarding their feelings of competence in working with various clients. It is also interesting to note that a 1992 survey of 126 U.S. medical schools found only 13 of the schools offered cultural sensitivity courses to their students; of that number, only 1 school required cultural sensitivity training (Lum & Korenman, 1994). This finding is significant when one considers that mental disorders among African Americans are frequently presented as physical complaints to primary care physicians. In fact, according to the Johns Hopkins Medical Institutions (1999), Office of Communications and Public Affairs (www.hopkinsmedicine.org/press/1999), the greatest increase in the use of mental health services during the past decade has been among African Americans in general primary care settings. The Johns Hopkins study reported that a higher percentage of African Americans (14.9%) than Whites (10.8%) received mental health services in general medical settings, without seeing a mental health specialist.

The lack of African American mental health counseling providers is notable and may further affect perceptions of mental health treatment. According to the 1999 Surgeon General's report, African Americans account for only 2% of psychiatrists, 2% of psychologists, and 4% of social workers in the United States (U.S. Department of Health and Human Services, 2000). However, the availability of an African American mental health care provider may be insufficient to affect utilization rates. In a 1977 study by Sattler (as cited in Brice-Baker, 1999), the race of the therapist ranked fifth in importance after therapist's level of education, similarity of attitude between therapist and client, older age, and similarity in personality between therapist and client.

The literature indicates that when African Americans do receive mental health services, most do so on an inpatient basis. According to Snowden (2003), epidemiological research has revealed that African Americans are greatly overrepresented in inpatient settings and in psychiatric emergency rooms, partly because they delay seeking treatment until their symptoms are severe. Moreover, some researchers found that African Americans are more likely to be mandated into treatment (Acosta, 1979), have higher rates of involuntary civil commitment than Whites, and are more likely to be brought to the emergency room by police.

Sue et al. (1991) examined ethnic utilization and client characteristics, premature termination rates, number of sessions, and treatment outcome in one of the nation's largest mental health systems over a 5-year period. With regard to African Americans, they found the following: (a) Ethnic match with counselor was not as important a consideration in predicting premature termination (failure to return after one visit) as was having a psychotic diagnosis; (b) there was no evidence that ethnic minority clients attended fewer sessions than Whites did; and (c) African Americans were the least likely to improve after treatment, but those African Americans who were married showed the most improvement. Overall, Sue et al. found that African Americans use the mental health care system but tend to exhibit relatively few positive changes, terminate quickly, and average fewer sessions than other ethnic minority groups.

Not only do most African Americans hold pejorative negative perceptions of mental illness, but they also tend to hold negative perceptions of the mental health counseling system. These pejorative perceptions combine to significantly influence the rate at which African Americans seek help and ultimately the rate at which they utilize mental health counseling services. Several other factors bear mentioning because of their relevance to help seeking and utilization of mental health counseling. These include the cost of therapy, the lack of insurance, and the lack of perceived need for the service (Matthews & Hughes, 2001). According to Snowden (1998), the use of privately financed care, especially individual outpatient practice, paid for by either fee-for-service arrangements or managed care, constitutes the most underutilized segment of the mental health care system.

Barriers: What the Research Has Found

Lay Beliefs About Accessing Mental Health Treatment

Racial differences in ideas about the causes of mental illness can have an impact on help-seeking behaviors. African Americans' attributions to the causes of mental illness are complex and contradictory. Schnittker, Freese, and Powell (2000) found that while African Americans may accept that mental illness is related to chemical imbalances, they will not accept theories that implicate family upbringing but will accept theories that accuse life's stresses. The rejection of genetic or family explanations may be due to the way these factors have been used against the Black community. Social science explanations, which also have been popularized on television and sometimes enshrined in public policy, cite family dysfunction (e.g., single-parent families) and intellectual deficits (e.g., lagging standardized test scores are due to inherent racial learning disabilities) in comparison with Whites. These authors also noted that irrespective of level of education, African Americans tended to attribute certain etiology to specific types of mental illness. In cases of schizophrenia or depression, the respondents saw the affliction as due to biological factors or divine purpose, whereas bad character was invoked for substance abuse. Such beliefs about the legitimacy of certain types of distress as illness will affect consumer behavior. These findings are supported by the results of African American focus groups. V. Thompson, Bazile, and Akbar (2004) found that in most cases only "severe" mental health issues were seen as requiring psychotherapy: cases of depression, schizophrenia, suicide, substance abuse, grief, rape, and victims of violent acts.

The Church of Scientology Antipsychiatry Movement

Psychiatrist Carl Bell is a strident opponent of the publications and outreach to the African American community by the Church of Scientology because it exploits the suspicions of the community about the adverse effects of psychiatric treatment that have historical legitimacy. The Church of Scientology bombards the African American community with publications bearing provocative titles such as "Psychiatry's Betrayal: Creating Racism" and features Black celebrities on their Web site who liken regulated psychiatric medications to street drugs and allege that the school counseling interventions create criminals rather than scholars. Bell (2002) asserted that the overriding message is that there exists a geno-cidal plot to put African Americans on antidepressant medications and to place Black children on Ritalin (see also Marano, 2003). Anna Ferguson, an African American psychiatrist and former president of the California Psychiatric Association, is similarly alarmed at the targeting of school administrators with the Church of Scientology's Citizens Commission on Human Rights' publication, "Psychiatry: Education's Ruin," charging that the psychological programs of the 1960s have led the educational system down a destructive path. Women are alerted to refrain from seeking therapy because of the danger of becoming sexual prey for therapists; these allegations are described in the publication "Betraying Women: Psychiatric Rape." The American Psychiatric Association has conducted outreach to these communities when alerted and has formed a statement that it regards the Church of Scientology as an extremist organization whose statements are inflammatory, underinformed, and out of context (Psychiatric News, 1996). Ferguson believes the response of trained professionals is critical because the commission's propaganda will discourage some African Americans from seeking treatment.

Lasser, Himmelstein, Woolhandler, McCormick, and Bor (2002) analyzed rates of outpatient mental health treatment seeking behavior (per 1,000 population), using data from the 1997 National Ambulatory Medical Care Survey and National Hospital Ambulatory Medical Care Survey. In comparison with Whites, Blacks and Hispanics visited their primary care doctor fewer times, had less visits to psychiatric settings to obtain talk or drug therapy, and visited psychotherapists less often than their White counterparts. The Church of Scientology's commission's literature may be seductive to African Americans because it appeals to certain beliefs and values that White society has used Blacks ruthlessly in its quest to advance its scientific agendas. In a community that severely underutilizes the efficacious treatments available, Bell (2001) recommended concerted and sustained culturally sensitive social marketing as an important corrective.

Cultural Mistrust

Terrell and Terrell (1981) developed the construct of cultural mistrust to evaluate social phenomena they found to permeate the Black community: suspiciousness of White institutions such as businesses, educational and legal systems, the police, and interracial interactions. They created the Cultural Mistrust Inventory (Terrell & Terrell, 1981) to assess Black people's perceptions of Whites in these four dimensions. Over the decade, their research suggested the examiner's race was inversely correlated with the level of cultural mistrust of Black test takers (Terrell, Terrell, & Taylor, 1981), educational and occupational expectations (Terrell, Terrell, & Miller, 1993), the relationship between counselor race and premature termination of psychotherapy (Terrell & Terrell, 1984), and expectations of the counseling experience in interracial therapy dyads, with Blacks high in cultural mistrust expecting less from their White counselors (Watkins & Terrell, 1988). In a follow-up study, Watkins, Terrell, Miller, and Terrell (1989) found that Blacks high in cultural mistrust perceived that Black counselors could help them more with four common presenting problems: shyness, anxiety, dating, and feelings of inferiority. Poston, Craine, and Atkinson (1991) reported that Blacks high in cultural mistrust were more reluctant to self-disclose to White counselors and they found these counselors to be less credible sources of help. Similarly, among 100 Black women respondents, C. E. Thompson, Worthington, and Atkinson (1994) found that high cultural mistrust was associated with less client disclosure, but when counselors used a cultural orientation instead of a universal orientation (e.g., this problem happens to everyone), Black clients saw White counselors as more credible. Nickerson et al. (1994) discovered that among Black men, cultural mistrust was a significant and consistent predictor of willingness to seek mental health treatment from White counselors. And even more recently, among Black men, results continue to indicate that older, lower socioeconomic, Black male students with lower cultural mistrust tended to have more positive attitudes toward seeking professional psychological help (Duncan, 2003).

Whaley (2001a, 2001b, 2001c, 2001d) has incorporated the construct of cultural mistrust extensively in his studies of seriously mentally ill African Americans. Vontress and Epp (1997) offered a sociopsychological explanation for the continuing reasons that Blacks may tend to feel suspicious of mainstream mental health facilities and treatment modalities. They contended that there is a collective psychology called "historical hostility" that "carries the emotional charge and historical consciousness" (p. 171) found in the psyches of many African Americans. Schnittker et al. (2000) also contended that for those in their study on Black ideas of the etiology of mental illness, even if a particular racist event had not happened to them personally, their strong group identification encouraged them to view social problems that continue to happen to other African Americans as continuing significant events. Alston and Bell (1996), in an outstanding application of these ideas to rehabilitation clients, posited that while cultural mistrust may interfere in the important dimensions related to counseling by provoking anxiety-related irrational self-talk and low expectations about the counseling effort, cultural mistrust may represent a healthy adaptation and may constitute an important psychological defense to living in a racially stratified society.

Influence of the American Ethos of Rugged Individualism

African Americans, like all Americans, are bombarded with advertisements of a variety of medications to treat mental illnesses. African Americans' receptivity to drug therapy and their compliance rates must be considered in the context of the general hesitancy of Americans to use psychotropic remedies when faced with a mental problem. Americans possess a clear understanding of the efficacy of these medications, indicating that such medications help people cope with stress, get along with people, and increase self-esteem. However, they are disinclined to use psychiatric medications if they are experiencing difficult personal problems. The gap between the perceived effectiveness of psychotropic medications and the reluctance to rely on them is due in part to some concern about their potential adverse effect on the body. It is not due alone to race, gender, or having health insurance. Instead, there is a strong current of self-efficacy that runs through the culture (Ahmed, 2001). The emphasis on exercising one's autonomy and marshaling one's self-control may contribute to the preference for the use of nonmedical healing or self-determined prescriptions (Croghan et al., 2003).

Moral Masochism in Women

Lebe (1997) described moral masochistic suffering in women as originating from their reactions to excessively critical early attachment figures. The resultant personality is one in which they are compassionate, organized individuals who experience low self-worth, dysthymia, and an incapacity to celebrate their achievements. They are generously felicitous to others but cannot be to themselves. African American culture encourages and rewards women who exhibit fortitude when confronted with inadequate living conditions and resources and are able to shield their family members from encountering the full force of those social realities. Poet June Jordan (1992) likened this effort to "making a way out of no way," something "too much to ask, too much of a task for any one woman." Equally applicable is the colloquialism of Gilkes's (1980) community mothers "holding back the ocean with a broom." Moral masochism is seen as ego syntonic within the Black community. C. Thompson (2000) identified the challenge for African American women as getting their own needs met while taking care of others. The poem "The Strong Black Woman Is Dead," a highly circulated piece decrying this behavior as symptomatic, vividly captures the price paid for moral masochism:

> On August 15, 1999, at 11:55 p.m., while struggling with the reality of being a human instead of a myth, the strong black woman passed away. Medical sources say she died of natural causes, but those who knew her know she died from being silent when she should have been screaming, smiling when she should have been raging, from being sick and not wanting anyone to know because her pain might inconvenience them. She died of an overdose of other people clinging to her when she didn't even have energy for herself.
>
> —*Laini Mataka*

Black women's power and selflessness have been adaptive in the survival of the community. C. Thompson (2000) noted that "the strong Black woman" stands as a symbol of ethnic identity. The women see themselves as resilient rather than as suffering.

> They are strong, autonomous beings who can survive anything without help, despite any and all difficulties they confront. In fact, many perceive the need to ask for and accept help from anyone as an intolerable expression of weakness. Seeking psychotherapy is often seen as a sign of weakness for many African American women, a problem that can delay their obtaining much-needed help. (C. Thompson, 2000, p. 239)

Social Role Strain in African American Men

In a recent study of middle-class African Americans, Haynes (2000) discovered that both husbands and wives endorsed the husband as provider for the family even though they expected wives to work. While the men did not anticipate their wives submitting to them, both men and women had staunch allegiance to the ideals that women should be nurturers and men fulfill the duties of securing the family materially. The respondents endorsed the notion that a man's identity is derived from his ability to provide. These ideals were so strongly held that the respondents intended to encourage their children to adopt them. If problematizing these inherited gender prescriptions is not an option for the respondents and if these sentiments hold for many middle-class African Americans, men may continue to face the problem of role strain at home in addition to struggling with the problem of racism in the public arena.

In comparison with men of other nationalities, American men see success, power, and competition as more intimately tied to their self-esteem. Mahalik, Locke, Theodore, Cournoyer, and Lloyd (2001) attributed this to the value placed on men's achievement such that failures to accomplish are felt more severely by a group of American men than an Australian comparison group. With American success defined for men as "winning" and "getting ahead," Mahalik et al. conjectured that American men may enact the behaviors of success, power, and competition in an effort to improve their self-esteem. Pleck (1995) interpreted the problems of failing to live up to traditional standards of masculinity as stemming from gender role discrepancies, dysfunction, or trauma. Discrepancies emerge from an inability to accomplish the tasks of the male role, dysfunction is exhibited when performing the masculine role is unsuitable to the context (e.g., being competitive rather than compassionate with a partner), and trauma strain results from the negative consequences of many aspects of the male socialization process.

Franklin and Boyd-Franklin (2000) added racism to the contentious forces confronting African American men as they attempt to live consistently with masculine norms. Repeated racial slights create an "invisibility syndrome," affecting a man's ability to live up to his provider role because it involves the conscious processing of one's treatment by others. Feeling acknowledged, ignored, or invalidated derives from an internal evaluation of daily experience. Maintaining a dignified sense of self when faced with "microaggression" (i.e., subtle hostilities) requires "repair" (i.e., stirring up curative thoughts, healing interactions, and overt behaviors intended to comfort hurt feelings). Some lower socioeconomic men are at increased risk for hypertension in attempting to provide an economically sound existence for their families. John Henryism is a high-effort coping pattern that is permeated by a conviction that environmental events can be positively handled through hard work and determination (Clark, Adams, & Clark, 2001). Behaving in the same manner as John Henry (a mythic steeldriver who overcame insurmountable odds) is one method of meeting social expectations for lower socioeconomic men. But this coping style leads to higher blood pressure and risks of developing hypertension in the long run (Dressler, Bindon, & Neggers, 1998).

Summary

This chapter examined the perceptions of African Americans toward mental health counseling and identified factors influencing the rate at which African Americans utilize mental health services. We identified the barriers to help seeking, examined the types and patterns of care that African Americans receive, and noted the high usage of inpatient services. African Americans tend to wait until a crisis arises before accessing the mental health system. We explored the role of pejorative attitudes held by African Americans that prevent them from benefiting from the available psychopharmacological and therapy treatments and emphasized the important need for greater psychoeducational outreach to African American communities. Attention must be paid to African American lay beliefs about the causes of mental illness because these influence help-seeking behaviors and community and family support for treatment recommendations. Political movements that seek to win African American converts to their cause deploy inaccurate messages about racism in the mental health system and circulate their propaganda in the Black community, helping to further erode the confidence of Blacks in the efficacy of mental health care. Finally, the American ethos of rugged individualism is a major obstacle to health-seeking behavior as many Americans believe that medications may be effective but are very wary and conflicted about using them. Black men and women have social role strains that perpetuate the belief that they must be strong and never ask for help or admit needs. The African American community must educate itself to realize that demands it places on its members are unrealistic and may in themselves lead to negative health outcomes.

References

Acosta, F. (1979). Pre-therapy expectations and definitions of mental illness among minority and low-income patients. *Hispanic Journal of Behavioral Sciences, 1,* 403–410.

Ahmed, I. (2001). Psychological aspects of giving and receiving medication. In W. Tseng & J. Streltzer (Eds.), *Culture and psychotherapy: A guide to clinical practice* (pp. 123–134). Washington, DC: American Psychiatric Publishing.

Allison, K., Crawford, I., Echemendia, R., Robinson, I., & Knepp, D. (1994). Human diversity and professional competence. *American Psychologist, 49,* 792–796.

Alston, R., & Bell, T. (1996). Cultural mistrust and the rehabilitation enigma for African Americans. *Journal of Rehabilitation, 62,* 16–20.

Atkinson, D. R., Morten, G., & Sue, D. W. (1998). Addressing the mental health needs of racial/ethnic minorities. In D. R. Atkinson, G. Morten, & D. Sue (Eds.), *Counseling American minorities* (pp. 51–80). Boston: McGraw-Hill.

Bailey, E. J. (1987). Sociocultural factors and health care seeking behaviors among Black Americans. *Journal of the National Medical Association, 79,* 389–392.

Bell, C. (2001, September). *Education is Whitey's thing* [Abstract of paper presented at an international conference on "Stigma and Global Health: Developing a Research Agenda," Bethesda, MD]. Retrieved from http://www.stigmaconference.nih.gov/abstracts/BellAbstract.html

Bell, C. (2002, February 23). African-Americans, psychotherapy and spirituality [Radio broadcast]. *Weekend Edition.* Washington, DC: National Public Radio.

Biafora, F. A., Warheit, G. J., Zimmerman, R. S., Gil, A. G., Apaspori, E., & Taylor, D. (1993). Racial mistrust and deviant behaviors among ethnically diverse Black adolescent boys. *Journal of Applied Social Psychology, 23,* 891–910.

Boyd-Franklin, N. (1989). *Black families in therapy: A multisystems approach.* New York: Guilford Press.

Brice-Baker, J. (1999). Reflections on the symbolic and real meaning of money in the relationship between the female African American client and her therapist. *Women & Therapy, 22,* 69–80.

Cheung, F. K., & Snowden, K. R. (1990). Community mental health and ethnic minority populations. *Community Mental Health Journal, 26,* 277–291.

Clark, R., Adams, J., & Clark, V. (2001). Effects of John Henryism and anger-coping on mean arterial pressure changes in African American women. *International Journal of Behavioral Medicine, 8,* 270–281.

Cole, J., & Pilisuk, M. (1976). Differences in the provision of mental health services by race. *American Journal of Orthopsychiatry, 46,* 510–525.

Croghan, T., Tomlin, M., Pescosolido, B., Schnittker, J., Martin, J., Lubell, K., et al. (2003). American attitudes toward and willingness to use psychiatric medications. *Journal of Nervous and Mental Disease, 191,* 166–174.

Dressler, W., Bindon, J., & Neggers, Y. (1998). John Henryism, gender, and arterial blood pressure in an African American community. *Psychosomatic Medicine, 60,* 620–624.

Duncan, L. (2003). Black male college students' attitudes toward seeking psychological help. *Journal of Black Psychology, 29,* 68–86.

Franklin, A., & Boyd-Franklin, N. (2000). Invisibility syndrome: A clinical model of the effects of racism on African-American males. *American Journal of Orthopsychiatry, 70,* 33–41.

Gilkes, C. T. (1980). "Holding back the ocean with a broom": Black women and community work. In L. Rose (Ed.), *The Black woman* (pp. 217–232). Beverly Hills, CA: Sage.

Hall, L., & Tucker, C. (1985). Relationships between ethnicity, conceptions of mental illness, and attitudes associated with seeking psychological help. *Psychological Reports, 57,* 907–916.

Haynes, F. E. (2000). Gender and family ideals: An exploratory study of Black middle-class Americans. *Journal of Family Issues, 21,* 811–837.

Holzer, C., Shea, B., Swanson, J., Leaf, P., Myers, J., George, L., et al. (1986). The increased risk for specific psychiatric disorders among persons of low socioeconomic status. *American Journal of Social Psychiatry, 6,* 259–271.

Johns Hopkins Medical Institutions. (1999). *African Americans more likely to get counseling from general health provider.* Retrieved from http://www.hopkinsmedicine.org/press/1999/DEC99

Jordan, J. (1992). *Oughta be a woman.* Performed by Sweet Honey in Rock [Breathe Audio CD]. Chicago: Flying Fish Records.

Lasser, K., Himmelstein, D., Woolhandler, S., McCormick, D., & Bor, D. (2002). Do minorities in the United States receive fewer mental health services than Whites? *International Journal of Health Services, 32,* 567–578.

Lebe, D. (1997). Masochism and the inner mother. *Psychoanalytic Review, 84,* 523–540.

Lum, C. K., & Korenman, S. G. (1994). Cultural-sensitivity training in U.S. medical schools. *Academic Medicine, 69,* 239–241.

Mahalik, J., Locke, B., Theodore, H., Cournoyer, R., & Lloyd, B. F. (2001). A cross-national and cross-sectional comparison of men's gender role conflict and its relationship to social intimacy and self-esteem. *Sex Roles: A Journal of Research, 45,* 1–14.

Marano, H. (2003, October 8). Race and mental health disparity. *Psychology Today.* Retrieved from http://www.psychologytoday.com/htdocs/prod/PTOArticle/pto-20031008-000002.asp

Matthews, A. K., & Hughes, T. L. (2001). Mental health service use by African American women: Exploration of subpopulation differences. *Cultural Diversity and Ethic Minority Psychology, 7,* 75–87.

Milstein, G., Guarnaccia, P., & Midlarsky, E. (1995). Ethnic differences in the interpretation of mental illness: Perspectives of caregivers. *Research in Community and Mental Health, 8,* 155–178.

Mindel, C. H., & Wright, R. J. (1982). The use of social services by Black and White elderly: The role of social support systems. *Journal of Gerontological Social Work, 43,* 107–125.

National Institute of Mental Health. (1987). *Mental health, United States, 1987.* Washington, DC: U.S. Department of Health and Human Services.

Nickerson, K. J., Helms, J. E., & Terrell, F. (1994). Cultural mistrust, opinions about mental illness, and Black students' attitudes toward seeking psychological help from White counselors. *Journal of Counseling Psychology, 41,* 378–386.

Pleck, J. (1995). The gender role strain paradigm: An update. In R. F. Levant & W. S. Pollack (Eds.), *A new psychology of men* (pp. 11–32). New York: Basic Books.

Poston, W. C., Craine, M., & Atkinson, D. R. (1991). Counselor dissimilarity confrontation, client cultural mistrust, and willingness to self-disclose. *Journal of Multicultural Counseling and Development, 19,* 65–73.

Poussaint, A. (1983). The mental health status of Blacks—1983. In J. D. Williams (Ed.), *The state of Black America—1983* (pp. 187–239). New York: National Urban League.

Psychiatric News. (1996, October 10). *APA helps members respond to Scientology's attacks.* Retrieved from http://www.psych.org/pnews/96-10-18/cchr.html

Regier, D. A., Narrow, W., Rae, D., Manderscheid, R., Locke, B., & Goodwin, F. (1993). The de facto U.S. mental and addictive disorders service system: Epidemiologic Catchment Area prospective 1-year prevalence rates of disorders and services. *Archives of General Psychiatry, 50,* 85–94.

Schnittker, J., Freese, J., & Powell, B. (2000). Nature, nurture, neither, nor: Black–White differences in beliefs about the causes and appropriate treatment of mental illness. *Social Forces, 78,* 1101–1132.

Snowden, L. R. (1998). Racial differences in informal help seeking for mental health problems. *Journal of Community Psychology, 26,* 429–438.

Snowden, L. R. (1999). African American folk idiom and mental health service use. *Cultural Diversity and Ethnic Minority Psychology, 5,* 364–369.

Snowden, L. R. (2003). Bias in mental health assessment and intervention: Theory and evidence. *American Journal of Public Health, 93,* 239–243.

Solomon, A. (1992). Clinical diagnosis among diverse populations: A multicultural perspective. *Families in Society: The Journal of Contemporary Human Services, 73,* 371–377.

Solomon, P. (1988). Racial factors in mental health service utilization. *Psychosocial Rehabilitation Journal, 11,* 4–12.

Sue, S. (1977). Community mental health services to minority groups. *American Psychologist, 32,* 616–624.

Sue, S., Fujino, D. C., Hu, I., Takeuchi, D. T., & Zane, N. W. (1991). Community mental health services for ethnic minority groups: A test of the cultural responsiveness hypothesis. *Journal of Consulting and Clinical Psychology, 42,* 794–801.

Sue, S., & Zane, N. (1987). The role of culture and cultural techniques in psychotherapy: A critique and reformulation. *American Psychologist, 42,* 37–45.

Sussman, L., Robins, L., & Earls, F. (1987). Treatment-seeking for depression by Black and White Americans. *Social Science and Medicine, 24,* 187–196.

Terrell, F., & Terrell, S. (1981). An inventory to measure cultural mistrust among Blacks. *The Western Journal of Black Studies, 5,* 180–185.

Terrell, F., & Terrell, S. (1984). Race of counselor, client sex, cultural mistrust level, and premature termination from counseling among Black clients. *Journal of Counseling Psychology, 31,* 371–375.

Terrell, F., Terrell, S., & Miller, F. (1993). Level of cultural mistrust as a function of educational and occupational expectations among Black students. *Adolescence, 28,* 573–578.

Terrell, F., Terrell, S., & Taylor, J. (1981). Effects of race of examiner and cultural mistrust on the WAIS performance of Black students. *Journal of Consulting and Clinical Psychology, 49,* 750–751.

Thompson, C. (2000). African American women and moral masochism: When there is too much of a good thing. In L. C. Jackson & B. Greene (Eds.), *Psychotherapy with African American women: Innovations in psychodynamic perspective and practice* (pp. 239–250). New York: Guilford Press.

Thompson, C. E., Worthington, R., & Atkinson, D. R. (1994). Counselor content orientation, counselor race, and Black women's cultural mistrust and self-disclosures. *Journal of Counseling Psychology, 41,* 155–161.

Thompson, V., Bazile, A., & Akbar, M. (2004). African Americans' perceptions of psychotherapy and psychotherapists. *Professional Psychology: Research and Practice, 35,* 19–26.

U.S. Department of Health and Human Services. (2000). *Mental health care for African Americans: A report of the Surgeon General.* Rockville, MD: U.S. Department of Health and Human Services, Substance Abuse and Mental Health Services Administration, Center for Mental Health Services.

Vontress, C., & Epp, L. (1997). Historical hostility in the African American client: Implications for counseling. *Journal of Multicultural Counseling and Development, 25,* 170–184.

Watkins, C. E., Jr., & Terrell, F. (1988). Mistrust level and its effects on counseling expectations in Black client–White counselor relationships: An analogue study. *Journal of Counseling Psychology, 35,* 194–197.

Watkins, C. E., Jr., Terrell, F., Miller, F. S., & Terrell, S. L. (1989). Cultural mistrust and its effects on expectational variables in Black client–White counselor relationships. *Journal of Counseling Psychology, 36,* 447–450.

Whaley, A. L. (2001a). Cultural mistrust: An important psychological construct for diagnosis and treatment of African Americans. *Professional Psychology: Research and Practice, 32,* 555–562.

Whaley, A. L. (2001b). Cultural mistrust and mental health services for African Americans: A review and meta-analysis. *Counseling Psychologist, 29,* 513–531.

Whaley, A. L. (2001c). Cultural mistrust and the clinical diagnosis of paranoid schizophrenia in African American patients. *Journal of Psychopathology and Behavioral Assessment, 23,* 93–100.

Whaley, A. L. (2001d). Cultural mistrust of White mental health clinicians among African Americans with severe mental illness. *American Journal of Orthopsychiatry, 71,* 252–256.

Whitaker, C. (2000). The mental health crisis in Black America. *Ebony, 55,* 74–78.

Why Blacks must educate themselves about mental health care. (2001, May 14). *Jet, 99,* 12–17.

13

The Impact of Violence, Crime, and Gangs in the African American Community

Rosalind P. Harris

The 1991 book, *There Are No Children Here: The Story of Two Boys Growing Up in the Other America,* by Alex Kotlowitz contributed significantly to making visible the stunning poverty, racism, and resulting psychological and physical violence African Americans confront daily within economically and politically disempowered inner-city communities. Through the vividly painful stories of Lafayette and Pharoah Rivers growing up in Chicago's Henry Horner Homes, a public housing development, a broader sampling of American readers were able to bear witness to the complex psychological and material forces that have made survival a tenuous proposition for the majority of African American inner-city residents.

Lafayette and Pharoah were born in the wake of the economic and social devastation that resulted from the deindustrialization within Chicago. With industries moving south and then overseas in search of cheaper labor, labor unions and jobs paying a living wage and decent benefits went into decline. Even though African Americans had been concentrated within the lowest paying sectors of these industries, strong labor unions had ensured adequate livelihoods and benefits. Together with a preintegration era complement of community-based African American businesses and professional services, economic security for the community's families based on access to adequate income had provided a foundation for solvent and at times thriving community economies and civic engagements.

The convergence of deindustrialization and racial desegregation forces resulted in African American communities losing vital human, social, and economic capital in the form of businesses, professional services, and middle- and upper-middle-class residents as they moved to White neighborhoods. Simultaneously, a significant number of working-class families were becoming pauperized as a result of job losses and dependence on the welfare state as the only economic alternative. As a result, communities lost wealth and concentrated poverty; more importantly, vital social buffers and institutions that could have protected communities from the most severe impacts of these changes were eroded (Wilson, 1987).

This chapter explores the upsurge of violence within African American communities resulting from these historical changes and the mental health challenges that African Americans face that are specifically linked to the traumas associated with violence. The following discussions attempt to theorize violence in relation to the experiences in African American communities and provide a descriptive overview of the forms of violence encountered within African American communities and the resulting mental health challenges and therapeutic approaches.

Violence Theorizing

African Americans: The Historical Web of Violence

Competing theories about the nature and causes of human violence abound and are characterized by definitions and conceptual frames delimited by disciplinary boundaries. This delimiting of disciplinary boundaries has particular implications for attempting to make use of the conceptual tools that might be helpful in understanding violence within the African American community. The following brief review of some of these theoretical frameworks provides a sense of how these disciplinary boundaries have been delimited.

Biological and physiological theories propose that there is either some innate tendency within humans or some physiological or genetic abnormality that causes them to behave violently (Moyer, 1976). These are the frameworks that are often invoked by policymakers summarily dismissing social explanations for violence and that lead to policies, for example, that would rather punish than rehabilitate someone implicated in a crime.

Psychological theories tend to focus on the individualistic sources of violence, especially those resulting from abnormal psychological development (Berkowitz, 1986; Patterson, 1989). While psychology has helped to illuminate much about inner dynamics leading to aggressive behavior that might result in violence, it has done little to make sense of patterns of violence on a broader scale.

Political science examines how states are formed and theorizes regarding state-generated violence and security against violence. It offers conceptual guidance on macrolevel scale conflicts between states.

While these descriptions are overgeneralizations about violence—theorizing within the respective disciplines—it is fair to say that there has been very little interdisciplinary work that would help to illuminate the links among interpersonal, collective, national, and global levels of violence. Theorizing about these macro–micro linkages is very important for understanding the history of violence and upsurge of violence within the last 30 years within the African American community. Moreover, understanding the micro–macro linkages has the potential to give a much more robust assessment of the cumulative traumas resulting from sustained violence directed at African Americans over a long historical period and the distinctive implications for mental health and treatment.

Framing Violence in the Lives of African Americans

The horrific violence of forced removal from Africa and Middle Passage to the Americas, enslavement, and the cultural and psychological subjugation that accompanied plantation work and life once in America are rarely acknowledged in contemporary theorizing about violent crime, gangs, and drugs within the African American community. Yet violence provided the very scaffolding for the integration of African labor into the American economy. Violence within the South in the form of beatings, rape, lynching, and so forth continued after the emancipation of slaves and became even more pronounced when the U.S. government abandoned African Americans to the Southern plantocracy during the postwar Reconstruction period (Du Bois, 1967). The very abandonment by the government served to lay the foundation for the disenfranchisement of newly liberated African Americans and for the resulting growth in structural inequalities that continue to condition the life circumstances of African Americans to this day.

Structural violence conceptualized by Galtung (1975) to acknowledge violence that results from inequitable social arrangements in contrast to overt physical violence can be recognized in the enduring forms of institutional racism, which largely came into existence during Reconstruction and have prevented African Americans from being educated, owning land, and accessing employment, medical care, and so forth on par with White Americans. Some of the consequences of structural violence include the high rates of poverty for African Americans, lower rates of education and employment, higher rates of illness for preventable and chronic diseases, higher rates of maternal and infant mortality, and lower rates of life expectancy. By virtue of these disadvantages, an image of the African American as the inferior "other" has generally been deployed through policy and practice, giving shape to a very specific and deformed representation of African Americans and their life worlds.

This practice of the construction of "otherness" has been interrogated incisively by cultural studies scholars as representational practices. Essentially, representational practices provide for forms of symbolic violence, which according to Hall (1997) allow dominant groups within society (i.e., those in control of cultural production) to allocate, naturalize, and fix differences in ways that devalue, demean, and deprave certain groups of people. The representational practice of stereotyping, in particular, has had a long history of signifying and naturalizing ideas about Blackness that have allowed for such stereotypes as Toms, good Negroes, Coons, the eye-popping piccanninnies, Mammies, usually big and fat bossy house-servants, Bad Bucks, oversexed and violent Black men, and so forth to persist in print, films, and other forms of media.

These images and stereotypes mobilize power and knowledge in ways that shape consciousness subconsciously and have dramatic consequences for the impact of symbolic violence. The stereotype of Bad Bucks, for instance, has carried over into the common vivid images accompanying texts and crime statistics that have successfully constructed Black youths as the violent criminal other. These carefully constructed representations have helped to produce a reality that holds African American youths to be desperate, violent, and criminal from the inside out—to be feared, avoided, and dealt with in the most punitive ways, through surveillance, intimidation, labeling by schools and law enforcement agencies, and ultimately through imprisonment and death, thus giving state authority an ultimate license to carry out acts of violence.

State violence, through the police, courts, and the prison system, has escalated in tandem with the passage of laws that have disproportionately criminalized African American men and women (Chambliss, 1999). Police surveillance, especially in the forms of target surveillance in African American communities and racial profiling, has resulted in dramatic increases in arrests and convictions. Police brutalities at arrest and questioning are often concomitants of community surveillance and racial profiling, often resulting in crippling injuries and at times death.

This discussion has attempted to make explicit the broader historical, political, and discursive contexts in which violence is conditioned and played out within African American communities. It is clear that such complex, interlinked patterns of violence require the reframing and broadening of conceptual and theoretical frameworks to assist in understanding the dynamics of violence and the approaches that might be taken to lessen it and heal the wounds caused by it. The following section uses this discussion as background and context for providing a descriptive overview of the nature and kinds of violence experienced within the African American community.

American Apartheid

By 1990 more than half a million African Americans had left their homes in the North to move South. This reverse migration as it has been called continues into the 21st century, defying the assumptions and predictions of many scholars who believe that "the great migrations that formed the modern states were, one way, permanent movements" (Stack,

1996, p. xiv). Many are fleeing disintegrating communities and economic options within inner cities of the North. As they move into new communities, the skills, ideas, and perspectives they bring from the North contrast with local skills and modes of accommodating the political status quo. As a result, many have come up against long-entrenched patterns of race/class discrimination that have consistently prevented African American families from escaping poverty or at best moving into better economic circumstances.

Returnees have faced difficulties getting hired, though clearly possessing the human capital required for available jobs. They also have faced difficulty finding safe and adequate day cares and schools for their children (Stack, 1996). Perhaps more painful is the ongoing witness they bear to institutionalized patterns of racial discrimination. They observe the consequences of these patterns in the loss of entitlements to land, adequate livelihoods, quality educations, health care, child care, environmental health and protection, and so forth for the majority of African Americans in their new home communities. The development of a political base and social fabric for nurturing a civically engaged African American population strong enough to challenge these oppressions has been discouraged by the very nature of the rural southern political economy. It is clear from the anecdotal as well as the statistical evidence that the communities to which many are returning, by virtue of high levels of joblessness, poverty, and dislocated families, reflect the worst consequences of American apartheid. These communities have existed as enclaves of desperation and poverty, physically distinct and isolated from the resources the dominant society takes for granted, for decades without relief. This is a poignant case of the structural violence Galtung (1975) theorized.

The enclaves of desperation and poverty these returnees were escaping from in the North were in fact created by the earlier migrations of African Americans out of the South fleeing from poverty, racism, and violence. Jobs created by the growth of industries in these urban centers also attracted African Americans, who had been increasingly losing farm land and employment in agriculture in the South as a result of the Great Depression and the discriminatory practices of New Deal programs (Mandle, 1992).

Although these newly formed urban northern communities were not without their problems, until the historic developments noted in the introduction (i.e., desegregation and deindustrialization), they were characterized by intact families and close-knit neighborhoods, replete with Black-owned professional services (e.g., physicians, attorneys) and businesses (e.g., barbers, hairdressers, grocers). Mutual aid societies and churches joined in with neighborhood associations and other civic groups to provide for families and individuals living on the margins.

As noted earlier, all of this began to change when deindustrialization eroded the income and tax bases of these communities and desegregation attracted middle- and upper-middle-class residents to areas once restricted to Whites. Key institutions such as schools and businesses were also increasingly lost, as were key human and social capital resources in the form of professionals such as physicians and teachers (Wilson, 1987).

Over time, the neighborhoods left behind saw an increasing number of people out of work. Joblessness led to increased poverty, and the intense stresses on a family's emotional resources when financial resources are strained led to increased levels of intrafamily violence and the fracturing of family units (Wilson, 1987).

Joblessness and the erosion of the community's economic base often led to desperate efforts to find alternative ways to make a living. Unfortunately, the same global forces that resulted in the deindustrialization of the Northeast and Midwest (i.e., the search for cheaper labor to bolster sagging corporate profits) also led to drug and weapons production, control, and sales becoming an increasingly significant part of the corporate wealth accumulation process aided by state institutions. As a result, drugs and guns began entering African American communities at increasing rates, tying an increasing number of young men and women desperate to earn money to the vicious violence that is inherent to the gun and drug trades (Paolucci, 2001).

This discussion provides the historical and structural framework for the following descriptive overview of the nature and kinds of violence experienced within the African American community today.

Violence in the African American Community

Violence is experienced on a number of levels within the African American community, and these experiences are clearly gendered with the majority of violent incidents involving men occurring in public and the majority of incidents involving women occurring within the household. African American children are exposed to the violence of the streets, the violence of schools, and the violence of the household, and increasingly they are claimed as its victims through injury and death. The following discussion is organized along these lines to provide an in-depth description of how men, women, and children experience violence and how their experiences overlap and link with each other, creating a web of community violence.

African American Men and Violence

African American men are disproportionately represented among perpetrators and victims of violent crimes as reported in arrest statistics, criminal victimization surveys, and mortality reports (Maguire & Pastore, 1998). Homicide is the most serious violent crime in which African American men are disproportionately represented among known offenders and victims. Young African American men ages 15 to 24 have a homicide death rate nearly nine times greater than similar-ages White men (123 per 100,000 compared with 14 per 100,000, respectively). Moreover, from 1 to 85 years of age African American males have higher homicide death rates than White males of similar ages (National Center for Health Statistics, 1998).

Putting these statistics into a meaningful context, as the previous discussion on the historical and structural factors shaping conditions of violence in the African American community indicated, the lack of viable, legal, economic options has made drug and weapons trafficking the economic alternatives of choice for an increasing number of African American youths. In addition to short-term economic gains, involvements in trafficking provide young men with a sense of power, success, respect, and admiration from peers (Weinfurt & Bush, 1995; Whitehead, Peterson, & Kaljee, 1994).

Trafficking is more times than not organized and commandeered through youth gangs, which in the absence of other forms of initiatory experiences into the adult worlds of work and responsibility attract significant numbers of youths. Gang membership often provides the only sense of family and belonging for youths whose families have been fractured and obliterated by the same forces threatening their young lives (i.e., poverty, drugs, gun violence, and so forth). Initiatory rites into gang membership and ongoing activities to prove allegiance and loyalty are themselves fraught with violence. Prospective gang members can be expected to endure life-threatening beatings to prove they are "real" men. Often they are expected to inflict violence on rival gang members or randomly in the community. Conceptions of masculinity, roles in the life of the community, and relationships with women and children are solidified through years of gang affiliation and prove to be enduring intergenerational frames of reference.

One of the most serious consequences of drug trafficking is the tendency for youths to begin to use drugs themselves and to become addicted. Research indicates that upwards of two thirds of those who become involved in drug trafficking become drug users (Li, Stanton, Feigelman, Black, & Romer, 1994). Drug use and addiction are marked by their own peculiar aggressions and risks. They require increasing amounts of money obtained through robberies and burglaries often with accompanying violence. If drug use and addiction are fed by ripping off others who are dealers and suppliers in the trafficking ring, then the individual involved risks injury or death.

Young adolescents have become the preferred target group for drug trafficking because they work for lower wages, they are less likely to worry about getting hurt, and when they are arrested they are rapidly returned to the community (Kaufman, 1998; Leviton, Schindler, & Orleans, 1994). However, repeated arrests and time in juvenile detention shape a trajectory that results in an increasing number of youths serving prison terms once they become adults.

Nationwide there is a one in four chance of an African American man being locked up during his lifetime. The total number of African American men in state and federal prisons exceeds 50% and continues to grow. The majority of convictions are the result of violent offenses and other crimes tied directly to the drug trade (see Paolucci, 2001).

The War on Drugs has provided the legal pretext for intensified surveillance and arrests in the African American community. It has also provided for the imbalances in the criminalization of drugs funneled to the African American community (e.g., crack cocaine) compared with drugs used mostly by Whites that have resulted in the disproportionate convictions of African American men on drug charges.

Young Black men comprise about 6% of the population but make up 50% of those convicted of violating drug laws (Johnston, O'Malley, & Bachman, 1998). The young White male population is five times greater than that of Black males but accounts for only 37% of drug offense convictions, despite the results of national household surveys indicating that Whites are more likely to use illegal drugs than African Americans and Latinos (Maguire & Pastore, 1998).

In prison, African American men confront interracial and intraracial violence in the forms of physical assaults and sexual assaults, murder, and suicide. Violence issues from other inmates as well as from prison guards and the prison experience can be particularly dehumanizing when the prison is designed to enhance tactile and sleep deprivation. Prison programs within the United States are expressly designed to be punitive and debilitating. Very few offer opportunities for improving on education, social skills, and political and emotional literacy, all experiences that could help an individual return to the community prepared to change and to contribute in constructive ways.

The circuit of violence takes young Black men from their communities to detention centers, prisons, and back to their communities and homes where women and children are often victims of their violence. The following discussions look at the unfolding of violence in the domestic sphere within the African American community.

African American Women and Violence

Witnesses

Violence in the forms of whippings, lynchings, murder, rape, and other forms of sexual violence by African American and White men are all a part of the historical experience of African American women. In addition, African American women have borne witness to the violence experienced by their children throughout history. Today they are witnesses and victims of a substantial amount of violence within their communities and within their homes. They are also the perpetrators of violence within these respective spheres.

Exposure to violence as witnesses has taken the forms of witnessing beatings, muggings, and murders resulting from stabbing and shooting. Research indicates that this exposure to violence is both frequent and severe, with 100% of African American women in one study reporting that they both witnessed and experienced violence (Wolfer, 2000). Two thirds of the women in this study reported that the incidents they witnessed resulted in either serious injury or death (Wolfer, 2000), and loss of a loved one due to violence is also a common experience for African American women. Two studies reported rates of 23% and 55%, respectively (Jenkins & Bell, 1997; Sanders-Phillips, 1996). These rates compare with the rate of 13% in a national sample of adult women who have lost a loved one to violence (Resnick, Kilpatrick, Dansky, Saunders, & Best, 1993).

An increasing number of African American women, especially young women, have become involved in gangs and drug-trafficking activities either directly as runners and suppliers or indirectly through the involvements of their intimate partners. It is in this way that women have increasingly become witnesses and victims of the violence of drug trafficking and of the War on Drugs. The dramatic increase in the imprisonment of African American women is directly connected to convictions for violent and nonviolent crimes resulting from drug-related charges. In prison, women are often confronted with the violence of physical abuse, rape, and other sexual assaults from prison guards that continues the battering and sexual abuse experienced with intimate partners in their communities.

Victims: Intimate Partner Violence

Battering, most often by men who are their intimate partners, is the leading cause of premature death of African American women between the ages of 15 and 44 (Office of Justice Programs, 1998). Near-fatal battering also results in long-term disabling injuries and conditions. It is therefore no surprise that battering has been identified as the number one health issue for African American women by the National Black Women's Health Project (Joseph, 1997).

Given the broader community context in which the lives of many African American women unfold, it is also not surprising that research shows that the factors consistently placing these women at risk for intimate partner violence include poverty, low incomes, problem drinking, and illicit drug use especially by the intimate partner (Campbell, 1995). The most important demographic risk factor associated with the perpetrator for intimate partner violence, however, is that of being unemployed and not seeking work (Centerwall, 1995; Hawkins, 1993).

As the earlier discussion about African American men and violence suggests, the circuit of poverty and violence they negotiate does not provide for the development of the human or social capital needed to sustain a livelihood or to nurture intimacy in relationships. Nor does the circuit of poverty and violence negotiated by African American women permit for these. The emotional strains and multiple stresses in the face of repeated failures for each nurtures hopelessness and rage in relationships. In addition to battering, this hopelessness and rage often take the form of sexual abuse in its many forms.

Victims: Sexual Abuse

Stereotypes objectifying the sexuality of African American women have had a long history and enduring impact. The stigmatizing of African American women as loose and immoral Jezebels served to justify the rape and forced breeding of African women slaves. Today this stereotype is reflected in such images as welfare queens and *hoochies* and serves to naturalize and fix the idea that African American women are sexually available and sexually deviant (Collins, 2000). This is an example of the symbolic violence Hall (1997) talked about. This symbolic violence has served over time to inscript and deploy forms of sexual violence that have traumatized African American women's psyches for decades.

The sexual abuse of African American women often begins in childhood as fondling or anal, oral, or digital penetration usually by a male family member, although women have been offenders as well (West, 2002). Upwards of one third of women sampled in a range of surveys have indicated being sexually abused as children (West, 2002). The majority of women reporting abuse indicated experiencing the most severe forms of violence, including vaginal, anal, and oral penetration (Huston, Prihoda, Parra, & Foulds, 1997). Many of these girls are revictimized as women, and this victimization can take a number of forms.

Sexual harassment can take the form of unwanted talk about sex, jokes, sexual pranks, touching, and pressure for sex or sexual favors in exchange for certain benefits such as a raise at work. The workplace has been the site of struggle for African American women historically in contending with harassment because they have usually been relegated to the lowest paying, most isolated positions, which makes them particularly vulnerable. In a survey conducted in Los Angeles, one third of the African American women indicated that they had been sexually harassed at work (Wyatt & Riederle, 1995).

Sexual harassment can also take the form of sexual assault, which can include rape and sex without consent. Although women are raped by strangers, most are actually raped by acquaintances, husbands, or boyfriends. In a national study 7% of African American women indicated that they had been raped; however, self-reports indicated that close to 20% of African American adolescent girls had been raped (Tjaden & Thoennes, 2000).

Low-income African American women are especially at risk for sexual assault, and women who are battered have an increased risk of being raped by their partners. This combination of abuse is particularly dangerous with victims more likely to be psychologically abused and to be more severely abused physically (Campbell & Soeken, 1999).

Long constrained by a conspiracy of silence that discouraged African American women from speaking out about their sexual victimization by African American men, an increasing number are telling their stories in the hope that others will tell their stories too. This mobilization challenges the privileging of outrage of violence against African American men over the outrage of violence against African American women (Tillet, 2002).

African American Children and Violence

A review of selected research indicated that between 26% and 70% of inner-city children have been exposed to severe violence (Jenkins, 2001). For a majority of these children, this included witnessing the victimization of a friend or relative. Even more had sustained the loss of a loved one as a result of murder.

Increasingly, children have also become the victims of violence themselves within the community, a result of drive-by shootings and other gang activities usually related to the trafficking of drugs. Children are also the victims of violence at neighborhood schools. Jenkins and Bell (1997) reported that over 25% of the youths in a sample from an inner-city neighborhood school had experienced one or more types of victimization. These included being shot, killed, beaten, robbed with a weapon, stabbed, and raped. Over half had also been shot at, and even more had been in a position to hear gun shots and believed their lives were in danger.

African American children are also witnesses to and victims of violence within the household. This includes being witnesses to intimate partner battery and sexual assaults and being the victims of battery and sexual assaults themselves.

Psychological Impacts of Violence

The previous discussions indicate that violence is pervasive throughout inner-city African American communities, touching the lives of men, women, and children in painful and profound ways. Daily living under such conditions produces similar challenges to those confronting people living in war zones such as the Middle East, Bosnia, northern Uganda, and other violent-prone places (Garbarino, Kostelny, & Dubrow, 1998). The following discussion provides a beginning framework for understanding the accumulated psychological risks associated with living under such conditions.

Traumatic Stress and Posttraumatic Stress Disorder

The types and patterns of violence previously described for African American men, women, and children living in the inner cities of the United States take place, as described earlier, within a much broader context of risk (e.g., poverty, joblessness, fractured families), with children and adults often incapacitated as a result by depression and substance abuse. Both the chronic and explosive violence touching the lives of many within the community therefore deepens and intensifies the stress that is a part of everyday life. The violence itself, however, can tip the fragile psychological balance, producing a state of trauma known as traumatic stress resulting in a range of symptoms associated with compensatory psychic processes, collectively known as posttraumatic stress disorder (PTSD).

PTSD was the first stress-related disorder to be referenced in the third edition of the *Diagnostic and Statistical Manual of Mental Disorders* of the American Psychiatric Association (1980) primarily as a result of the experiences of shell-shocked soldiers returning from the war in Vietnam. In essence, PTSD was named to describe the response that one has to an extremely stressful life event, such as "actual or threatened death or serious injury, or a threat to the physical integrity of self or others" (American Psychiatric Association, 1994, p. 427). Individuals with PTSD are known to manifest symptoms that fall into three general categories: episodes in which the traumatic event is reexperienced, behaviors to avoid reminders or stimuli associated with the trauma, and psychic numbing and increased arousal (American Psychiatric Association, 1994). The traumatic event can be reexperienced during everyday activities and in sleep during dreaming as intrusive images and sounds associated with the trauma. Individuals may also show signs of withdrawing into themselves, pulling back from activities they previously enjoyed while their behavior may be subdued, which are signs of avoidance and psychic numbing. Signs of increased sensitivity and arousal may also be evident as startle reactions and sleep disturbances. Reactions to the trauma in the form of symptoms associated with PTSD may occur either immediately or months or years later.

Posttraumatic Stress Disorder and Its Complications

PTSD often presents in the guise of other problems and is rarely diagnosed initially. Presenting problems such as substance abuse, suicidal behavior, eating disorders, depression, and difficulties at work or school are often the outcomes or coping strategies used by those suffering from PTSD. If PTSD goes undiagnosed as the underlying or accompanying (comorbid) disorder, the individual's chances for proper treatment and hope of recovery are lessened considerably. Moreover, failure to make an initial diagnosis for appropriate referral and treatment of traumatized adults and children may condition circumstances that place an individual at risk for exposure to more stress and trauma.

Consider the case of a child who has coped with the challenges of chronic community violence all of her life and has recently witnessed the murder or severe beating of a family member. At home, the adults in her life have been exposed to the same levels of chronic community violence and the more recent violence involving a family member and are themselves traumatized. As a result, they are unable to provide the care, emotional support, and the referral the child needs to community resources that will help her to cope with the trauma that she is experiencing. At school, PTSD symptoms such as withdrawal from classroom activities, failure to complete work, and resulting failing grades as well as sporadic and uncharacteristic aggressive behavior are misread by her teachers and school counselor as behavioral problems stemming from an attitude problem or tendency toward delinquency. As a result, the student is eventually removed from the regular classroom and placed within a special education program for behaviorally and emotionally disturbed (BED) students. In the BED program her stress is intensified as she faces unfamiliar circumstances and a learning milieu clearly inappropriate for her quality and level of intelligence. To cope with this change in circumstances, she may turn to more aggressive behaviors or indulge in sex or drugs or other activities that put her at risk for exposure to violence or involvement with the juvenile court system.

The adults in this young girl's life face similar patterns of complication if their traumas are left undiagnosed and untreated. Working adults may lose time at work because of depression and anxiety or as the result of physical/medical problems related to the stress of the trauma. This may result in the loss of jobs and income, leading to further stress and alienation and perhaps the exploration of illegal income-generating strategies or dependence on drugs and/or alcohol as a way to cope. All of these trajectories heighten the possibility of involvement with the criminal justice system and the institutionalized violence that it proffers.

The scenarios described above are played out daily in communities in which chronic violence prevails. Within such contexts, people attempt to go about their daily lives with some semblance of normalcy, but the trauma of violent acts, injuries, and losses of life and the sheer number of losses through injury and death throughout the community result in immobilizing trauma on a mass scale, such as in a war zone.

Mental Health Interventions

To date, federal, state, and local policies have not been shaped to respond to conditions within the inner cities as if they were indeed war zones. Violence by and large continues to be conceptualized as an individual-level phenomenon preventable and treatable through law enforcement, the courts, and medical establishments. The underlying causes of chronic community violence (i.e., eroded economies and social networks with resulting poverty and social alienation) are left unacknowledged and unaddressed.

Because the problem has largely been defined as an individual-level phenomenon, the major efforts in addressing the traumas associated with community violence in the African American community have manifested as an array of programmed interventions designed for early identification, referral, and treatment of those in the community suffering from PTSD. The programs can be as simple as training teachers how to identify, interact with, and refer students to the appropriate mental health professionals, to more comprehensive programs that attempt to involve parents, teachers, children, law enforcement officials, and medical professionals in planning and carrying out interventions. Still these programs are few and far between in most communities, especially in the communities where they are needed the most (Jenkins & Bell, 1997).

The following discussion describes general approaches to treating PTSD and related disorders followed by a discussion of some notable program interventions for treating PTSD.

Subsequent discussions will move into considerations of alternative programs and modalities that seek to recognize opportunities for addressing structural change and deeper cultural issues within communities experiencing chronic violence.

Treating Posttraumatic Stress Disorder

Men, women, and children suffering from PTSD need a safe place and therapists skilled in treating PTSD specifically to help in processing the trauma. This is one of the greatest challenges within the African American community (i.e., lack of availability of mental health services and skilled therapists). Once a referral is made, however, and an individual has made a successful connection with a skilled therapist, the ideal is the development of a negotiated treatment plan molded to the needs of the individual.

Therapists working with PTSD consider a range of psychological schools of thought such as humanistic, psychoanalytic, cognitive–behavioral, and so forth that shape their perspectives on treating PTSD. The usual route is an eclectic approach comprising several key stages within the treatment plan.

The initial assessment interview is very important for establishing rapport as the foundation for the therapeutic relationship. Ideally, during this interview the counselor combines a finely honed knowledge of PTSD with an equally well-honed ability to listen deeply to the experience of her or his client. Essentially the counselor needs to know about trauma—the symptoms and how they manifest, something of the stages of integration and change—and yet be open to meeting the client as an individual whose experience and way of being the counselor knows nothing about (Scott & Stradling, 2001).

As part of the assessment process the counselor will use one or more psychometric self-report or interview tests, such as the Impact of Event Scale (Weiss & Marmar, 1997), to measure the frequency and types of experiences (i.e., numbing, intrusive thoughts, dissociation, and so forth) individuals are having following a traumatic event. Key in the correct diagnosis of PTSD is the careful linking of traumatic events with the manifestation of symptoms characteristic of PTSD. On the basis of the information compiled during the assessment, a treatment plan is developed.

Based on the school of thought the therapist works out of and the experiences and prerogatives of the client, treatment modalities could include body-centered work, gestalt therapy, art therapy, and so forth. The central objective of any PTSD treatment plan, however, is to create a relationship of safety between the therapist and the client that serves as a relational model to help the client begin renegotiating broken connections resulting from the trauma. The treatment plan should also provide for deepening the client's understanding of his or her trauma experience and reactions to it as deeply emotional. This involves therapeutic strategies that help the client to understand the emotional–imaginal nature of flashbacks and intrusive thoughts, but nevertheless the necessity to engage them albeit in brief encounters and small doses to weaken their imaginal impact. In this way the trauma can be processed by the client at a safe time and in a safe place. This can be done during the actual meeting with the therapist through narrative recounting and analysis or through the work of the client through journaling, art therapy, conversations with significant others, and so forth. Ultimately, the treatment plan should accomplish the return of the client to an engagement with life and relationships and a sense that life is worth living (Dunn, 2002).

The question confronting African Americans living in the war zones of the inner cities, however, is how can one realistically restore a sense of engagement with life, relationships, and the sense that life is worth living when the therapy ends and immersion in the chronic violence within the community is again unmitigated? Intervention programs, most of them shaped to work with children suffering from PTSD, have attempted to sustain support for reducing violence and treating PTSD within a communitywide context. Two of these programs are discussed below.

Program Interventions for Treating Posttraumatic Stress Disorder

The Child Witness to Violence Project was established at Boston City Hospital in 1992. It was designed to provide therapeutic intervention to young children witnessing violence. The project approached treatment holistically by working with the children, families, and teachers to provide a scaffolding of education and support to strengthen the therapeutic impact and to provide sustaining support once the therapy was concluded. Key components of the project included counseling for the parents to help them help their children and in-service education for teachers to help them identify children traumatized by violence, develop an understanding of the impacts of violence, and make referrals for appropriate therapeutic intervention.

Because the adults in a child's life can hypothetically provide the best support for healing and referral for appropriate mental health intervention once a child has been traumatized by violence, it was reasoned that educating parents about violence and PTSD would be very helpful. Moreover, by providing parents with actual counseling for themselves, they would be able to work through their own sense of powerlessness and helplessness as a result of their own traumas in strengthening the inner resources for helping their children.

Because teachers are often confronted in the classroom with the behaviors characteristic of PTSD, the project sought to provide high-quality training that would allow them to heighten awareness of situations in which a child might be suffering from PTSD and of their own responses. The training for teachers consisted of three components offered within the context of an intensive summer institute. The first component provided information on general child development and effects of violence on children at respective developmental levels. The second component focused on resilience and coping in children. The final component focused on helping teachers to become familiar with their own reactions to and experiences with violence.

Central to this project was the recognition that children experience and process exposure to traumatic events and evidence different types of symptoms characteristic of PTSD at different developmental levels. Counseling approaches and training modules were thus developed to take these issues into consideration.

The Inglewood Safe School Program in Los Angeles, California, also focused on developing treatment modalities and training modules that accounted for the differential impacts of trauma at different developmental levels for children in elementary school. The program's intervention model comprises three phases: individual psychotherapy, group psychotherapy, and mentorship. The program also interfaces with a community-based policing program.

Individual psychotherapy focuses on the trauma itself and the meaning that it has to the child. While parents do not participate in a fully developed counseling component designed for parents per se, counselors do work with the parents during this phase to provide them with a clear understanding of the child's experiences and the ongoing concerns that they will need to respond to in relation to the trauma and the child's ongoing exposure to violence. Group therapy is designed to create a relatively safe social context that will serve to enhance the emotional responsiveness of the children and to develop the social skills that will allow children to more fully and comfortably give expression to their experiences.

Mentors provide opportunities outside of the formal counseling contexts for children to discuss and elaborate upon their experiences through play, drawing, narratives, and so forth. They also assist children in making positive connections with potential social support agents in the community who also may model future career choices (e.g., police, fire-fighters, medical personnel, librarians, and so forth).

In conjunction with this, the community-based policing interface with this program provides for the training of police officers on the psychological effects of violence on children. This serves as a way to lower barriers and create relationships between local police and neighborhood children and in this way integrates law enforcement into community life in a positive way.

This discussion offers samples of intervention programs introduced into communities to address community violence, primarily through the venue of therapeutic programs buttressed by links to family, school, and law enforcement institutions. But questions arise as to the sustainability of such programs and their effectiveness in the face of the depth and breadth of the structural violence that spawns the community violence that these programs attempt to combat. Questions also arise about the level of cultural sensitivity reflected in assessment instruments, treatment modalities, and pedagogies that these programs use. The following discussion attempts to address these questions through an exploration of political/cultural approaches to healing community violence.

Political/Cultural Approaches to Trauma Resulting From Violence

Revisiting the PTSD case discussed earlier of the young girl exposed to chronic violence all of her life and recently experiencing the trauma of witnessing violence directed at a loved one, it is instructive to note that guilt and shame can play a significant role in intensifying and sustaining the trauma for her. Without a broader historical or political context for understanding why such violence is occurring within her community, within her home this young girl is left to interpret and internalize events in a way in which she feels burdened by responsibility for these events. Such interpretations affect her very sense of self and sense of worth and ability to heal. It is in this way, the internalizing of a sense of shame about who we are because we don't know or we forget how such circumstances came to be shaped by colonizing racism, that the impact on us as a colonized people is most insidious (Fanon, 1961; Memmi, 1965).

Any approach that is to make a significant impact on violence and the traumas of violence experienced within the African American community will need to help individuals and communities make sense of their experiences politically and culturally. In addition to the consciousness-raising models for politicizing communities used, for example, by Freire (1993), African Americans have a wealth of tradition to draw upon from Africa and from the various Native American tribes in creating models and approaches.

For example, indigenous models of conflict resolution accessed through African oral traditions in Ghana, Nigeria, and South Africa set forth practices that emphasize the involvement of community elders in conflicts and disputes and ritual as a way of giving presence to ancestor guides in bringing problems to resolution (Zartman, 2000). The Truth and Reconciliation Commission convened in South Africa to begin the process of healing the wounds of apartheid was conceived and carried out in such a spirit to stem the tide of violence.

Increasingly, Native American communities are creating healing circles made up of elders from the communities who offer historical and political perspectives for understanding the current circumstances and conditions under which Native Americans live. Within this context they offer guidance to the young people in making decisions about their life journeys. These have been particularly powerful forums for reclaiming their youths from official/legal court systems when implicated in crime. Through such forums elders provide guidance to these youths within the context of their own cultures to help them to make positive changes in their lives. In this way youths are accountable to their families and their communities for the harm that they have done, not just an abstract legal system meting out punitive sentences that fail to deepen the youths' appreciation for the real impact of their

actions and entangle them within a system that often short-circuits life chances and opportunities (Ross, 1996).

Liberation psychology is a nontraditional mode of mental health practice that can easily incorporate the approaches discussed above because it takes a holistic approach to treating and attempting to heal the traumas of colonized people. Its practices reflect an explicit
acknowledgment of the subjugating impacts of colonialism and the needs of a subjugated
people to reclaim their power and identity often by reclaiming treatment modalities embedded within their own traditions. Such modalities might take the form of shamanic soul
retrievals, sweat lodge ceremonies, dreamwork, and so forth that would speak to the deeply
spiritual wounding wrought by the violence of colonizing racism and its traumatizing manifestations within African American communities currently. But liberation psychology also
provides for the integration of Western modalities such as the more traditional therapist–
client dialogue with its emphasis on narrative recounting and processing with non-Western
treatment modalities in attempting to develop the most effective practices for healing and
mobilization.

Essentially, liberation psychology emphasizes the importance of providing the most
effective psychological and political tools for helping colonized people to make sense of their
structural location in the social/power order and for understanding how they became thus
situated. This emphasis reflects the belief that there is a genuine sense of power that comes
from awakening to this understanding and recognizing that there are possibilities for reimagining and working toward building a society supportive of genuine human development.

Summary

There is no disputing that violence is endemic within most inner-city African American communities, debilitating the very souls and spirits of many. It is also clear that current patterns
of violence within these communities have deep roots in the legacy of colonizing racism
that continues forms of structural violence largely denied or ignored when it comes to addressing such violence. Although current programs, policies, and treatment modalities
might be helpful to some members of the community and might give the appearance of
moving things in an overall positive direction, it is hard to ignore the overriding trends and
statistics that suggest that not much is changing and that in fact for many communities
things are getting worse.

On this basis, it is clear that there needs to be a reimagining of possibilities for addressing the traumas wrought by violence in these communities and that this reimagining
might possibly draw on the strengths of traditions thought long obliterated by colonizing
racism. Addressed through the agency and strengths of cultural traditions that acknowledge the deep soul wounding of such widespread, long-standing violence and that offer
approaches that speak to and offer healing to the soul, there is an almost unimaginable potential for the freeing of energy to make the political, social, economic, and cultural transformations necessary to deeply heal and empower African American communities.

References

American Psychiatric Association. (1980). *Diagnostic and statistical manual of mental disorders* (3rd ed.). Washington, DC: Author.

American Psychiatric Association. (1994). *Diagnostic and statistical manual of mental disorders* (4th ed.). Washington, DC: Author.

Berkowitz, B. D. (1986). *American security: Dilemmas for a modern democracy.* New
Haven, CT: Yale University Press.

Campbell, J. C. (1995). *Assessing dangerousness: Violence by sexual offenders, batterers, and child abusers*. Thousand Oaks, CA: Sage.

Campbell, J. C., & Soeken, K. L. (1999). Women's responses to battering: A test of the model. *Research in Nursing and Health, 22*, 49–58.

Centerwall, B. S. (1995). Race, socioeconomic status, and domestic homicide. *Journal of the American Medical Association, 273*, 1755–1758.

Chambliss, W. J. (1999). *Power, politics and crime*. Boulder, CO: Westview Press.

Collins, P. H. (2000). *Black feminist thought: Knowledge, consciousness, and the politics of empowerment*. New York: Routledge.

Du Bois, W. E. B. (1967). *Black reconstruction in America: An essay toward a history of the part which Black folk played in the attempt to reconstruct democracy in America, 1860–1880*. New York: Meridian Books.

Dunn, A. (2002). Trauma aftercare: A four-stage model. In T. Spiers (Ed.), *Trauma: A practitioner's guide to counselling* (pp. 97–130). New York: Brunner–Routledge.

Fanon, F. (1961). *Wretched of the earth*. New York: Grove Press.

Freire, P. (1993). *Pedagogy of the oppressed*. New York: Continuum.

Galtung, J. (1975). *Peace: Research, education, and action. Vol. 1: Essay in peace research*. Copenhagen, Denmark: Christian Ejlers.

Garbarino, J., Kostelny, K., & Dubrow, N. (1998). *No place to be a child: Growing up in a war zone*. San Francisco: Jossey-Bass.

Hall, S. (1997). Spectacle of the "other." In S. Hall (Ed.), *Representation: Cultural representations and signifying practices* (pp. 225–280). Thousand Oaks, CA: Sage.

Hawkins, D. F. (1993). Inequality, culture and interpersonal violence. *Health Affairs, 12*(4), 80–95.

Huston, R. L., Prihoda, T. J., Parra, J. M., & Foulds, D. M. (1997). Factors associated with the report of penetration in child sexual abuse cases. *Journal of Child Sexual Abuse, 6*, 63–74.

Jenkins, E. J. (2001). Violence and trauma in the lives of African American children. In A. M. Neal-Barnett, J. M. Contreras, & K. A. Kerns (Eds.), *Forging links: African American children clinical developmental perspectives* (pp. 107–128). Westport, CT: Praeger.

Jenkins, E. J., & Bell, C. C. (1997). Exposure and response to community violence among children and adolescents. In J. Osofsky (Ed.), *Children in a violent society* (pp. 9–31). New York: Guilford Press.

Johnston, L. D., O'Malley, P. M., & Bachman, J. G. (1998). *National survey results on drug use from monitoring the future, 1995–1997*. Washington, DC: U.S. Department of Health and Human Services, National Institute on Drug Abuse.

Joseph, J. (1997). Woman battering: A comparative analysis of Black and White women. In G. Kantor & J. L. Jasinski (Eds.), *Out of darkness: Contemporary perspectives on family violence* (pp. 161–169). Thousand Oaks, CA: Sage.

Kaufman, J. (1998, October 27). Locked in: Prison is all around for a girl growing up in inner-city Baltimore. *The Wall Street Journal*, p. A1.

Kotlowitz, A. (1991). *There are no children here: The story of two boys growing up in the other America*. New York: Doubleday.

Leviton, S., Schindler, M. A., & Orleans, R. S. (1994). African American youth: Drug trafficking and the justice system. *Pediatrics, 93*, 1078–1084.

Li, X., Stanton, B., Feigelman, S., Black, M., & Romer, D. (1994). Drug trafficking, substance abuse, and illicit drug use among urban African American youths. *Pediatrics, 93*(Suppl.), 1044–1049.

Maguire, K., & Pastore, A. L. (Eds.). (1998). *Sourcebook of criminal justice statistics, 1997*. Washington, DC: U.S. Department of Justice, Bureau of Justice Statistics.

Mandle, J. R. (1992). *Not slave, not free: The African American economic experience since the Civil War*. Durham, NC: Duke University Press.

Memmi, A. (1965). *Colonizer and the colonized*. New York: Orion Press.

Moyer, K. E. (1976). *The psychobiology of aggression*. New York: Harper & Row.

National Center for Health Statistics. (1998). *Health, United States—1998*. Washington, DC: U.S. Department of Health and Human Services.

Office of Justice Programs. (1998). *Bureau of Justice Statistics factbook: Violence by intimates—Analysis of data on crimes by current or former spouses, boyfriends and girlfriends* (NCJ No. 167237). Washington, DC: U.S. Department of Justice.

Paolucci, P. (2001). *Dialectical methodology, power, and capital: Dialectical methods, Foucaults's encounter with Marxism, and techniques of class domination in the global era*. Unpublished doctoral dissertation, University of Kentucky.

Patterson, G. R. (1989). *Depression and aggression in family interaction*. Hillsdale, NJ: Erlbaum.

Resnick, H. S., Kilpatrick, D. G., Dansky, B. S., Saunders, B. E., & Best, C. L. (1993). Prevalence of civilian trauma and posttraumatic stress disorder in a representative national sample of women. *Journal of Counseling and Clinical Psychology, 61*, 984–991.

Ross, R. (1996). *Returning to the teachings: Exploring Aboriginal justice*. Toronto, Ontario, Canada: Penguin.

Sanders-Phillips, K. (1996). The ecology of urban violence: Its relationship to health promotion behaviors in low income Black and Latino communities. *American Journal of Health Promotion, 10*, 308–317.

Scott, M. J., & Stradling, S. G. (2001). *Counselling for post-traumatic stress disorder* (2nd ed.). London: Sage.

Stack, C. (1996). *Call to home: African Americans reclaim the rural South*. New York: Harper Collins.

Tillet, S. (2002). Fragmented silhouettes. In C. M. West (Ed.), *Violence in the lives of Black women: Battered, black, and blue* (pp. 161–177). New York: Haworth Press.

Tjaden, P., & Thoennes, N. (2000). *Extent, nature and consequences of intimate partner violence: Findings from the National Violence Against Women Survey* (NCJ 181867). Washington, DC: U.S. Government Printing Office.

Weinfurt, K. P., & Bush, P. J. (1995). Peer assessment of early adolescents solicited to participate in drug trafficking: A longitudinal analysis. *Journal of Applied Social Psychology, 25*, 2141–2157.

Weiss, D. S., & Marmar, C. R. (1997). The Impact of Event Scale—Revised. In J. P. Wilson & T. M. Keane (Eds.), *Assessing psychological trauma and PTSD* (pp. 399–411). New York: Guilford Press.

West, C. M. (2002). Types of violence In C. M. West (Ed.), *Violence in the lives of Black women: Battered, black, and blue* (pp. 7–8). New York: Haworth Press.

Whitehead, T. L., Peterson, J., & Kaljee L. (1994). The "hustle": Socioeconomic deprivation, urban drug trafficking and low income African American male gender identity. *Pediatrics, 93*, 1050–1054.

Wilson, W. J. (1987). *The truly disadvantaged: The inner city, the underclass, and public policy*. Chicago: University of Chicago Press.

Wolfer, T. A. (2000). Coping with chronic community violence: The variety and implications of women's efforts. *Violence and Victims, 15*, 283–302.

Wyatt, G. E., & Riederle, M. (1995). The prevalence and context of sexual harassment among African American and White American women. *Journal of Interpersonal Violence, 10*, 309–321.

Zartman, I. W. (2000). *Traditional cures for modern conflicts: African conflict "medicine."* Boulder, CO: Lynne Rienner.

14

The Black Church: A Strength-Based Approach in Mental Health

Debra A. Harley

The phrase "the Black church" is used to refer collectively to the many denominations of faith observed by African Americans. Lincoln and Mamiya (1990) defined the African American church as an institution that is independently controlled by African Americans, who make up the core of African American Christians. Throughout this chapter, the terms *African American* and *Black* are used interchangeably to reflect inclusiveness of those who are of African descent. The Black church is the first fellowship organization to help African Americans deal with the oppression of slavery and a racist society and is recognized as a significant force in the movement of African Americans toward freedom of mind, body, and spirit (James & Johnson, 1996; Lincoln & Mamiya, 1990). The church has been a dominant force and a symbol of hope and spiritual presence for African Americans.

The church has thrived because of the strong belief African Americans hold that the burdens of life would eventually transcend to the promised land (Stuckey, 1987). A commonly acknowledged adage and belief among many African Americans is that "God gave us the strength to suffer." According to Poussaint and Alexander (2000), "the Christian faith claimed by most African Americans has historically upheld the philosophy of 'bearing up' at any cost under the pain of slavery and the long-lasting effects of discrimination" (p. 101). Poussaint and Alexander further explained that the public's collective understanding of the word *strength* as it is commonly used in relation to Blacks has come to mean almost superhuman endurance. I propose that a more accurate translation is that African Americans have developed the strength to suffer, struggle, survive, and succeed. In essence, it is not acquiescence to victimization but an acknowledgment of perseverance. However, the Christian faith's interpretation and the public's perceptions of the word *strength* among African Americans, along with the stigma attached to appearing weak, are one explanation of African Americans' reluctance to seek mental health treatment.

The Black church has always offered a sense of community, personal and psychological support, coping strategies, role models, and a sense of collective achievement (James & Johnson, 1996). Today, the Black church continues to function as an institution that affects the psychological health of African Americans. Both religiosity and spirituality are vital components of African American racial and cultural activities. Religion supplies perhaps the best vantage point from which to describe the development of African Americans in relationship to themselves, others, and the larger universe (Laderman & Leon, 2003). In fact, "the history and content of African American religious culture provide glimpses into what it means to be African American in the United States and what it means to be culturally American" (Laderman & Leon, 2003, p. 3). Because of this existence and the fact that religion and spirituality are different but not mutually exclusive concepts, both concepts are addressed throughout this chapter. Religion involves an organized body of beliefs with a specific creed and membership boundaries (Peck, 1997). Spirituality is much broader and best described as the attempt to be in harmony with an unseen order of things that are usually functioning on a higher plane affirming a transcendent connectedness with the universe (Kelly, 1995).

Over the past several years, the counseling profession has given increased attention to spirituality and religiosity issues. Articles have appeared in the literature that address religion, guilt, and mental health (Faiver, O'Brien, & Ingersoll, 2000) as well as approaches to religious and spiritual issues in counseling (Zinnbauer & Pargament, 2000), and a special issue of the journal *Rehabilitation Education* (1995, Vol. 9, Nos. 2 & 3) was published with increased attention given to spirituality and religiosity in counseling. Lukoff, Lu, and Turner (1992) argued that religion and spirituality are the core dimensions that edify human experiences, beliefs, behaviors, and patterns of illness. In addition, Richards and Bergin (1997) recommended that counselors assess the spiritual systems of their clients on a regular basis to obtain a more accurate and full diagnostic picture. In fact, Dr. William Hathaway, a Christian psychologist, stressed that just being sensitive to a possible role of religion in a client's life can broaden mental health practitioners' evaluation and provide different solutions to mental health issues (as cited in Kersting, 2003).

Various techniques related to religion have been used in counseling, including the use of prayer during a session, ways to direct clients to pray, spiritual journaling, forgiveness protocols, use of biblical texts to reinforce healthy mental and emotional habits, and working to change punitive God images (Kersting, 2003). According to Dr. William Hathaway, "being able to help a person connect with the variable of spirituality in their lives can be a beneficial and important therapeutic accommodation" (as quoted in Kersting, 2003, p. 40). While this attention has led to increased understanding of some of the unique psychological strengths and needs of racial minorities, mental health practitioners continue to do a poor job in effectively meeting the psychosocial and personal needs of African American clients (Cartwright & D'Andrea, 2004; U.S. Surgeon General, 2001).

Religion, spirituality, the Black church, and psychosocial adjustment need to be examined further to better understand the role of the church in addressing mental health. The purpose of this chapter is to offer a historical look at the role of the Black church in the mental health of African Americans and a discussion of the church as a strength-based strategy for counseling. This chapter addresses the following topics: (a) the historical Black church, (b) the Black church today as an institution that affects the psychological and social health of African Americans for the good of the community, (c) religious beliefs that support and conflict with mental health counseling, and (d) use of a strength-based approach in Black churches to provide a multidimensional perspective of mental health counseling. Recommendations for the future are also presented.

The Historical Black Church

An extensive presentation of the historical development of the Black church is beyond the scope of this chapter. However, it is noteworthy to present an overview of the evolution of the Black church to illustrate its significance in the psychosocial and ecological contexts in the lives of African Americans. Exact dates of the establishment of the first formal African American church are questionable. For example, Lincoln and Mamiya (1990) indicated that the first known formal African American church was established in 1750, and other historians place this date between 1773 and 1775 (T. Moore, 1991). Without providing a history lesson, I acknowledge that many enslaved Africans were introduced or exposed to Christianity during colonial times because some colonists saw slavery as an opportunity to bring Africans into a proper understanding of God's word. In fact, European missionaries and evangelists maintained the system of slavery while preaching the gospel and providing religious instruction without exposing slaves to literacy. Recognizing this contradiction, Africans who embraced the Christian tradition moved beyond these falsehoods with the development of what is commonly referred to as the "Invisible Institution" (T. Moore, 1991; Raboteau, 1978). The Invisible Institution refers to the secret religious gatherings, sometimes called the *hush harbor* meetings, held by enslaved Africans away from the observation of the slaveholders during which they forged unique religious symbols, myths, and doctrine. These hush harbor churches permitted the development of a sense of community, spiritual companionship, and religious expression among slaves that could not be practiced and nurtured in churches run by slaveholders.

The hush harbor churches addressed the particular needs of Africans in America and marked the lingering presence of African structures through the importance of water baptism and possession, complete with "dancing in the spirit" (Raboteau, 1978; Stuckey, 1987). Enslaved Africans were able to blend African and European worldviews and religious sensibilities into a unique expression of the Christian faith. Although the Christian God replaced other representations of the African High God, some Africans maintained religious/theological connections to African belief systems through a continuing devotion to deities (Pinn, 1998). According to Laderman and Leon (2003), "what these churches represented was not just Christianity in African communities; rather, they pointed to the Africanization of the Christian faith" (p. 5). Today, much of what African Americans recognize as the Black Church tradition took shape in these hush harbor churches (Lincoln & Mamiya, 1990).

Pentecostalism is the only African American Christian communion without White origins. Black churches hold membership in seven national communions (three Methodist, three Baptist, and one Pentecostal—The Church of God in Christ). Overwhelmingly, African Americans are affiliated with the Baptist (e.g., Missionary, not Southern) denomination followed by the Methodist faith (James & Johnson, 1996). Islamic communions represent a growing presence in the United States and must be included in any discussion of faith communities that affect the African American community. African American Muslims represent the largest single ethnic group of American Muslims—about one third of the American Muslim community (McCloud, 1995). Evidence suggests that a substantial percentage of Africans brought to the North American colonies were Muslims who maintained dimensions of their faith. In fact, approximately 30% of the slaves taken from West Africa were Muslims (McCloud, 1995). After centuries of being subjected to Christian indoctrination, which at times was forced on them, some African Americans have chosen Islam as their worldview (Laderman & Leon, 2003).

The historical Black church is one of the earliest organizations to serve as a buffer against the dehumanizing effects of racial segregation, discrimination, and bigotry. It has provided a safe haven for the emotional release of concerns and feelings that could not have been safely expressed in White churches or White society (Birchett, 1992; James & Johnson, 1996; T. Moore, 1991). The first Islamic communities sought to give some identity markers to ex-slaves and first-generation "freed" men and women. Eventually all Islamic communities saw Islam as the "true" religion of Black people and the only way to establish themselves as humans in the world and especially America (McCloud, 1995). Both the Christian and non-Christian Black churches are firmly rooted in the American religious landscape. The African American church emerged as a powerful institution, "second only in importance to the African American family" (S. E. Moore & Collins, 2002, p. 174).

The Black Church Today

Today, the Black church continues to play a vital role in the social, economic, political, and spiritual needs of African Americans. According to Helms and Cook (1999), "the Black Christian church serves as a 'social equalizer' for its members. Regardless of their socio-economic or vocational statuses in the external world, members of a church community can hold very powerful positions within the church" (p. 207). Even with an increase in the integration of churches (mainly Black membership in White churches), the Black church continues to have a strong role and powerful presence in the African American community. Through the use of televised media, the Black church is capable of reaching many people today and is not only a community church but a national and international church as well. Television ministries of many "mega-size" Black churches now expand their services into homes throughout the world and are not limited to community participation. In this respect, the composition of the audience of the Black church has changed to some degree; however, the home base of the church is still in the African American community. According to Rivera, Garrett, and Crutchfield (2004), nothing exemplifies the values of African Americans (e.g., emphasis on being group focused, sensitivity to interpersonal matters, hard work and education, sense of community, cooperation, interdependence, and commitment to religious values, church, and familial bonds) more than the Black church as a source of community for African Americans.

During the late 19th and early 20th centuries, many African Americans found themselves economically frustrated and socially isolated as a result of the undelivered promise of opportunity within urban areas. Many of these African Americans turned to the Black church for assistance only to find churches preoccupied with individual salvation as a requirement of commitment to spiritual growth and mundane betterment. It was not until the civil rights movement that the Black church initiated renewed attention to a fuller range of human needs, including spiritual growth, economic opportunity, social flexibility, and political voice (Pinn, 1998). The Black church once again became an impetus for racial justice, equality, and the promotion of what they regarded as true Christianity (e.g., a spiritually meaningful and empowering version affirming freedom and justice). African American Muslim communities in the latter part of the 20th century represented a broad range of Islamic philosophies, ideologies, and religious understanding that continue to challenge Black Christianity on a variety of beliefs and perceptions. Islamic principles include daily prayer, fasting, and avoidance of pork, alcohol, and drugs. For example, the Nation of Islam asserts that the White man is "the devil" as evidenced in White destruction. In addition, Islam provides an alternative worldview for the African American community, often eradicating drug traffic, prostitution, and other crime in the areas in which they live (McCloud, 1995).

At the beginning of the 21st century, African American Christianity and the Black church face a number of challenges and opportunities that require minimizing negative aspects while augmenting the positive elements of its opportunities (Laderman & Leon, 2003). The Black church faces challenges, such as the faith-based initiative (Segers, 2003), a persistent socioeconomic underclass in the Black community, high divorce and single-parent homes, racial profiling, the growth of nondenominational Christian groups, displacement of people of African descent as the largest racial/ethnic minority group, race-specific aspects of the adversities facing the general U.S. population associated with economic downturns and terrorism, and increased substance abuse problems, violence, and mental health issues (Martin, 1999; S. E. Moore & Collins, 2002). According to McRae, Carey, and Anderson-Scott (1998), the Black church has been called upon to respond to these problems and is in a position to again be the leading force in providing assistance to the African American community. The prominence and size (e.g., membership) of the Black church place it in a position to be a very influential and powerful catalyst for economic, political, and social change and advocacy within the African American community and larger society (S. E. Moore & Collins, 2002). The Black church has both a role and an obligation to respond to these critical issues confronting the African American community.

The response of the Black church to psychosocial and mental health issues includes numerous initiatives such as personal care homes, pastoral private counseling services, reading programs, self-help and support groups, and groups for gang members and parents of gang members. There are also lay health advisory networks that serve as intermediaries between individuals and health and social services, providing many resources not only for its congregation but for surrounding communities as well (McRae et al., 1998). Although too numerous to list and describe within this chapter, there is an extensive array of initiatives presently being undertaken within milieu of the Black church on both macro and micro levels. Many of these initiatives are coordinated by national coalitions including the Congress of National African American Churches, the Interdenominational Theological Center, the Southern Leadership Conference, and the Nation of Islam (McCloud, 1995; S. E. Moore & Collins, 2002).

Religious Beliefs in Support of and Contradiction to Mental Health

Psychology, the discipline with important knowledge in the area of human behavior, is based on very different assumptions than those of the church. The foundation of religious beliefs is faith and spirituality, whereas psychology focuses on the workings of the mind and behaviors (James & Johnson, 1996). Nevertheless, religious involvement of African Americans is inversely related to psychological distress when faced with stressful life events, and having a denominational affiliation is associated with fewer depressive symptoms (Ellison, 1995; Morris & Robinson, 1996). In the Black church, African American ministers balance their role of religious/spiritual leaders providing guidance to members with their role as pastoral counselors. In addition, in the Black church beliefs are reinforced to reduce psychological distress (Crawford, Handal, & Wiener, 1989), worship services are offered that include therapeutic aspects (Griffith, Young, & Smith, 1984), and ministers provide formal and informal pastoral counseling services (Mollica, Streets, Boscarino, & Redlich, 1986; Wiley, 1991; Williams, Frame, & Green, 1999). According to Helms and Cook (1999), both mental health professionals and the clergy have acknowledged the value of forming collaborative relationships in responding to the mental health needs of the community.

For African Americans the belief in faith as the ultimate resolution to many problems serves as a contradiction to seeking mental health services. In addition, many African Americans have an external locus of control in which they believe that many things that happen are beyond their control, and putting their faith in God to alleviate the problem is the best course of action. Other African-derived American religions (e.g., voodoo, hoodoo, conjure) also pose barriers to African American participation in mental health services. The practice of conjure, often used interchangeably with hoodoo, created a space for the power of human agency within an elaborate religious world of spirits, ancestors, charms, divination, and folklore (Laderman & Leon, 2003).

Taylor, Ellison, Chatters, Levin, and Lincoln (2000) indicated that faith-based health initiatives in African American communities are characterized by several factors:

1. The minister or pastor is recognized as a pivotal figure in the church whose leadership and direction are critical for understanding the types of programs organized in the church and the church's relationship with formal service agencies in the broader community.
2. Ministers assume a variety of roles in relation to church-based programs and interventions, particularly as agents of health-related behavioral change and agents of health-related social change.
3. Ministers often function as gatekeepers to formal mental health services.
4. Ministers are sometimes the first and only professional that individuals encounter. As a consequence, pastors' positions as personal counselors and advisers are important ones with respect to the mental and physical health of their congregants. (p. 74)

Understanding the roles of ministers in the Black church is important in gaining access to and support of faith-based mental health initiatives in the church. It is important to note that the quality of mental health services provided by ministers is determined, in part, by their ability to identify serious mental health problems and their willingness to refer people to professional mental health practitioners. Thus, background and training among African American ministers may play a crucial role in their abilities to detect mental illness and emotional distress and in making appropriate client referrals (Taylor et al., 2000).

Using clergy for help with mental health (and other personal problems) has several advantages for African Americans (Taylor et al., 2000). First, the cost of mental health treatment is expensive, and many African Americans do not have the financial means to pay for these services. Ministers do not charge fees for their services or require insurance, copayment, or completion of required forms. A second advantage of using ministers is that they may be readily available and an attractive alternative to the traditional mental health services delivery system. Third, unlike traditional mental health providers who usually are approached after an initial consultation, ministers typically are approached directly by clients, and rarely is contact mediated by referrals. Fourth, ministers make personal visits (e.g., visit the sick in the home or hospital) to those in need, thereby facilitating access to services. Finally, consultations with ministers typically occur within the context of a long-standing personal relationship that may facilitate establishing respect and empathy. (See Table 14.1 for a comparative summary of using clergy versus traditional mental health.)

A Strength-Based Approach in the Black Church

A strength-based approach refers to utilizing the positive attributes of a group of people, community, or society and building on these strengths as a way to implement change and forge progress. The Black church and African American preachers, spiritual healers,

Table 14.1
Comparison of Use of Clergy Versus Traditional Mental Health

Clergy	Traditional
No cost	Fee, copay, insurance
No paperwork	Completion of forms required
No referral required	Consultation, referral required
Personal/home visits	Office visits
Long-standing personal relationship	Formal professional relationship
First source of contact	Mediated contact

prophets, and priestesses have functioned for nearly 400 years as the power brokers and establishment figures within the African American community (Lincoln & Mamiya, 1990), representing a strength-based initiative. "African American communities have a long tradition of human services delivery in the context of religious institutions" (Taylor et al., 2000, p. 77). In fact, the Black church tends to participate in community programs to a greater extent than do White churches (Lincoln & Mamiya, 1990). The African American clergy function as a major mental health response to African American religious congregations and nonchurch members (Cook, 1993). African American clergy provide counseling on a variety of mental health and life issues, including a range of personal emotional problems diagnosed by mental health professionals as some form of mental illness (Mollica et al., 1986). For many clients, particularly African Americans, their religious or spiritual beliefs are strengths that have carried them through life's adversities.

Cook and Wiley (2000) indicated that it is important that the therapists understand their clients' religious beliefs just as they would assess any other defenses (and I would add any supports) used by clients. Cook and Wiley argued that rather than viewing spirituality or religiosity as forces competing against the therapy process, therapists can use these beliefs in relating to their clients. African Americans have created a religious culture of complex depth and range (Sernett, 2000), which consists of interventionlike elements that support psychological health. Alternative strategies are needed for meeting the mental health needs of African Americans, and the Black church is such an alternative that could assist with providing mental health intervention. Some psychologists believe that incorporating spirituality into therapeutic environments could bring new treatment options into the limelight (e.g., Kersting, 2003).

The Black church and Black theology provide a platform on which to dismantle the ideological underpinnings of psychological oppression of African Americans. A church-based mental health model was developed by Dr. Donelda Cook, a psychologist, and Dr. William Shaw, pastor of White Rock Baptist Church in West Philadelphia. Dr. Shaw identified areas in which he perceived that a psychologist would be most helpful to the church. The first area included problems for which individuals sought help from him that were beyond the scope of his training and expertise as a minister. The second area focused on layworkers within the church who needed training in effective communication and basic helping skills so that they could perform assignments of reducing isolation of individual members by being liaisons between the pastor and members of the church congregation. For the final area, the pastor wanted to strengthen the church's impact in the surrounding African American community. It became apparent that traditional mental health practices of counseling psychology were ideally suited for performing mental health intervention within the church setting (Helms & Cook, 1999). Helms and Cook indicated that the church-based mental health model incorporated the primary service modes of counseling psychology: prevention, enhancement of personal development, and remediation to address the problems identified by the pastor.

Individual members of the congregation with professional counseling training and experience were recruited as volunteer service providers. The advantage of using these volunteers is that the congregation trusted the potential volunteer counselors' professional status and cultural and spiritual affiliations with the church (Helms & Cook, 1999). Of course, caution must be taken to ensure confidentiality of clients and to minimize dual relationships in which the counselors have personal relationships with the clients/church members. To facilitate better communication and receptiveness of the congregation to mental health counseling, psychological terminology was changed to be more consistent with the language of spirituality (see Table 14.2). This change in language resulted in the church-based model being named the *Ministry of Spiritual Nurturing*. The Ministry of

Table 14.2
*Comparison of Psychological Terminology
and the Language of Spirituality*

Psychological Terminology	Spiritual Language
Mental health	Spiritual
Counseling/therapy	Nurturing
Services	Ministry
Pathology/dysfunction	Need
Cure	Transcendence
Guidance/facilitate	Assistance/help
Control	Harmony
Health/wellness	Balance
Logic	Faith
Expectations	Beliefs
Counselor/therapist	Adviser/friend/listener
Treatment/intervention	Understanding

Spiritual Nurturing consists of five major areas named to reflect the language of the church community: (a) individual nurturing, (b) group nurturing, (c) reaching out/lending a helping hand, (d) church–community conferences, and (e) networking (Helms & Cook, 1999). Each of these areas is defined below.

Individual Nurturing

Individual nurturing involves brief counseling interventions of a developmental and remedial nature. Individual nurturing intervention includes (a) an initial contact to assess the individual's concern, (b) brief problem-solving-oriented counseling, (c) crisis intervention, (d) brief career counseling, and (e) referrals to an appropriate mental health professional outside of the church setting (Helms & Cook, 1999).

Group Nurturing

The group nurturing component consisting of a variety of group counseling approaches such as single-session workshops and time-limited and open-ended groups may be used to provide preventive, developmental, and remedial interventions. Groups designed to *prevent* the occurrence of various social and psychological problems (e.g., drug abuse, stress management, HIV/AIDS) can be conducted to reach large segments of the community. Groups that address *developmental* issues across the life span prepare individuals for various life transitions. Age-specific groups may be particularly effective in a church setting because the environment can serve to reinforce the value of various age groups. For example, to address youths' sense of isolation as they transition back into the community after incarceration or drug treatment, group leaders could work with the church staff to ensure that the youth members of the congregation are invited to be active participants in ongoing church services and programs. *Remedial* groups (e.g., Alcoholics Anonymous [AA]) frequently hold meetings in churches. The church setting may provide an additional source of hope as people generally connect faith, hope, and acceptance with the spiritual mission of churches (Helms & Cook, 1999). For African Americans this connection may have greater significance because of the sense of connectedness with the community. In addition, when African Americans, who already have been disempowered to a great extent, are required to relinquish self-control to a "higher power" as specified by AA, they see the Black church is a natural conduit.

Reaching Out/Lending a Helping Hand

This component of reaching out/lending a helping hand consists of outreach and con-sultative services that make use of helping auxiliaries within the church to assist in providing services. Mental health professionals can assist these auxiliaries in planning programs and using their resources to reach out to the larger church congregation and the surrounding community. Consulting therapists who utilize reaching-out services will need to familiarize themselves with the overall structure of the church to ascertain how the various auxiliaries and resources might best be used as service components of the church (Helms & Cook, 1999). This step becomes increasingly important in working with the Black church because having an understanding of the structure of the church (e.g., who is in charge of what) will facilitate both church and community participation.

Church–Community Conferences

Conferences are considered to be one of the primary ways in which professionals disseminate research findings and information. The Black church also convenes its own forms of conferences called unions and conventions in which sister churches come together to plan and chart the direction of member churches. Helms and Cook (1999) suggested that mental health professionals can join forces with pastors to hold ongoing conferences with various constituents of the community to (a) respond to the psychological aftermath of community tragedies and disasters, (b) develop strategies for systemic change, and (c) serve as advocates for oppressed groups. Many Black churches are located in the heart of urban decay as well as in rural isolation and in the midst of economic stagnation and racial inequalities, and African American pastors still hold influential positions within the surrounding community.

Networking

Direct service intervention alone will not solve the psychosocial problems of African Americans or their communities. Mental health professionals oriented toward viewing people and their behavior in a sociocultural context (e.g., influenced by culture, sociorace, gender, sexual orientation, age, sociohistorical perspectives) can be instrumental in examining the interaction of these factors in the circumstances of African Americans. Help-givers can use this information to facilitate useful dialogues between African Americans and the social service and public officials as well as other mental health professionals who are making decisions about their lives (Helms & Cook, 1999). In fact, networking is a process that can encourage participation in African American communities.

The Black church as a conduit and a collaborator for mental health intervention for African Americans is a natural support system within the community. Collaborative efforts between the Black church and mental health professionals demonstrate appropriate and culturally sensitive integration of counseling techniques with African Americans. According to Helms and Cook (1999),

> if mental health professionals were to demonstrate cross-cultural competence as much as they preach it, then they would already know how to approach, respect, value, and accept the psychoracial, cultural, and religious perspectives of the indigenous helpers of the people to whom they are rendering services. (p. 272)

It is clear that before collaboration can take place between these two parties, the mental health profession must recognize the utility of the Black church in addressing psychosocial needs of African Americans and respect the leadership role of the church.

The scope and range of outreach programs, including mental health services initiatives, are shaped by congregational, ministerial, and other factors (Taylor et al., 2000). These factors include congregation size (Caldwell, Chatters, Billingsley, & Taylor, 1995), per capita income of church members (Caldwell, Greene, & Billingsley, 1994), and characteristics of the minister (e.g., educational attainment, age, full-time vs. part-time status as a paid minister, theological and political views; Taylor et al., 2000). Lincoln and Mamiya (1990) found that among Black ministers, racial consciousness was related positively to involvement in community outreach programs.

Implications for Professional Practice and Research

The use of the Black church as a strength-based approach to mental health counseling for African Americans calls into question several issues for consideration for mental health professionals. First, mental health professionals must examine their own beliefs about the role of religion and spirituality in counseling. Second, counselors who work with African American clients need to include an appraisal of the clients' religious beliefs and practices or spirituality in initial psychological assessments. Unfortunately, many mental health professionals do not inquire about clients' religious beliefs in the initial phases of counseling despite the possibility that these values are central to clients' views of themselves, the world, and their problems (Zinnbauer & Pargament, 2000). For many African Americans, their religious beliefs may take precedence over scientific methods. Although counselors are becoming more comfortable dealing with religious and spiritual issues, many still misunderstand clients who have religious issues (Judy, 1996). This problem is further complicated when counselors lack an adequate knowledge base of cultural diversity.

Another implication for professional practice concerns competence of counselors to understand the religious and spiritual worlds of their clients. The ethical principles of both the American Counseling Association (1995) and the American Psychological Association (2003) require that counselors and psychologists provide services that are consistent with their competence. Thus, training for mental health professionals in religious and spiritual competence becomes an issue that must be addressed by counselor and psychologist training programs.

Future research is needed to ascertain the perceptions of African Americans regarding religiosity and psychotherapy and the behavioral perspective to psychotherapy and behavior change. Understanding how African Americans view the integration of mental health practice and the church may provide some insight into the role that is played by the Black church and the extent to which the church permits mental health to share its domain. The comparative efficacy of religious and nonreligious treatment in African Americans requires additional research.

Mental health agencies should designate several practitioners to function as full- or part-time liaisons to area Black churches. In addition to being responsible for establishing a point of contact and a channel of communication between churches and the agency, the liaison would serve as a resource linking the church to other human services and programs. Taylor et al. (2000) suggested that the liaisons should include both genders to promote a comfort level for those church members who may be reluctant to approach a minister of the opposite gender than him- or herself.

Some consideration should be given to partnering with existing programs (e.g., cancer screening, blood pressure screening, etc.) as a means of promoting mental health awareness and intervention. Similarly, the partnership model can be used to obtain grants for the church (Taylor et al., 2000), especially with faith-based initiatives.

As with anyone seeking certain credentials and qualifications, training is an area that must be addressed. Mental health agencies might consider conducting in-service training programs to prepare ministers and layworkers to deal with some of the more serious mental health problems confronting church members. For example, agencies across various disciplines (e.g., mental health, psychology, counseling psychology, rehabilitation, social work) may even consider working with universities to establish an interdisciplinary certificate program geared toward individuals seeking certification without seeking a degree.

Finally, African American clergy will need to reexamine their formal training in the area of pastoral counseling to determine if their credentials merit competency as mental health interventionists. Is this to say that because African American pastors have been informally providing counseling services, they are not qualified to do so if they do not possess certain certifications or licensure? Quite to the contrary. African American pastors and the Black church have earned the endorsement of the African American community and continue to be recognized as the stabilizing force in the community. However, the area of preparation in recognizing mental illness and mental health issues among African American ministers (and all ministers) is one in which clergy and mental health agencies might collaborate with one another in addressing the mental health needs and emotional well-being of church members and community residents (Taylor et al., 2000).

Summary

The Black church has had and continues to have a strong presence and influence in the lives of African Americans. The Black church was the first provider of mental health counseling and support for African Americans. Conjoining mental health counseling and the Black church in a culturally appropriate way is an alternative to traditional mental health practices, in which African Americans tend not to participate overwhelmingly. In addition, the terminology used by mental health professionals may circumvent participation of African Americans in traditional services. The use of the Black church–community-based approach to mental health services is an effective way to deliver services to and simultaneously empower African Americans in their own mental wellness.

There is an urgent need for African Americans, including the Black church, to address mental health issues facing their community. Mental health professionals, counselors, and the Black church can help one another in meeting the mental health needs of African Americans. Mobilizing the Black church for intervention, support, and outreach services for African Americans is one way to assist those in need of services to access them without stigma and misunderstanding, as well as increase non-African American service providers' understanding of diversity.

References

American Counseling Association. (1995). *Code of ethics and standards of practice.* Alexandria, VA: Author.

American Psychological Association. (2003). *Ethical principles of psychologists and code of conduct.* Washington, DC: Author.

Birchett, C. (Ed.). (1992). *Biblical strategies for a community in crisis: What African Americans can do.* Chicago: Urban Ministries.

Caldwell, C. H., Chatters, L. M., Billingsley, A., & Taylor, R. J. (1995). Church-based support programs for elderly Black adults: Congregational and clergy characteristics. In M. A. Kimble, S. H. McFadden, J. W. Ellor, & J. Seeber (Eds.), *Handbook on religion, spirituality, and aging* (pp. 306–324). Minneapolis, MN: Augsburg Fortress.

Caldwell, C. H., Greene, A. D., & Billingsley, A. (1994). Family support programs in Black churches: A new look at old functions. In L. S. Kagan & B. Weisbourd (Eds.), *Putting families first* (pp. 137–160). San Francisco: Jossey-Bass.

Cartwright, B., & D'Andrea, M. (2004). Counseling for diversity. In T. F. Riggar & D. R. Maki (Eds.), *Handbook of rehabilitation counseling* (pp. 171–187). New York: Springer.

Cook, D. A. (1993). Research in African-American churches: A mental health counseling imperative. *Journal of Mental Health Counseling, 15,* 320–333.

Cook, D. A., & Wiley, C. Y. (2000). African American churches and Afrocentric spiritual traditions. In P. S. Richards & A. E. Bergin (Eds.), *Psychotherapy and religious diversity: A guide to mental health professionals* (pp. 412–432). Washington, DC: American Psychological Association.

Crawford, M. E., Handal, P. J., & Wiener, R. L. (1989). The relationship between religion and mental health/distress. *Review of Religious Research, 31,* 16–22.

Ellison, C. G. (1995). Race, religious involvement, and depressive symptoms in a southeastern U.S. community. *Social Science and Medicine, 40,* 1561–1572.

Faiver, C. M., O'Brien, M., & Ingersoll, R. E. (2000). Religion, guilt, and mental health. *Journal of Counseling & Development, 78,* 155–161.

Griffith, E. E. H., Young, L. J., & Smith, D. L. (1984). An analysis of the therapeutic elements in a Black church service. *Hospital and Community Psychiatry, 35,* 464–469.

Helms, J. E., & Cook, D. A. (1999). *Using race and culture in counseling and psychotherapy: Theory and process.* Boston: Allyn & Bacon.

James, W. H., & Johnson, S. L. (1996). *Doin' drugs: Patterns of African American addiction.* Austin: University of Texas Press.

Judy, D. (1996). Transpersonal psychotherapy with religious persons. In B. W. Scotton, A. B. Chinen, & J. R. Battista (Eds.), *Textbook of transpersonal psychiatry and psychology* (pp. 293–301). New York: Basic Books.

Kelly, E. W. (1995). *Spirituality and religion in counseling and psychotherapy: Diversity in theory and practice.* Alexandria, VA: American Counseling Association.

Kersting, K. (2003). Religion and spirituality in the treatment room. *Monitor on Psychology, 34,* 40–42.

Laderman, G., & Leon, L. (2003). *Religion and American cultures: An encyclopedia of traditions, diversity, and popular expressions* (Vol. 1). Santa Barbara, CA: ABC-CLIO.

Lincoln, C. E., & Mamiya, L. H. (1990). *The Black church in the African American experience.* Durham, NC: Duke University Press.

Lukoff, D., Lu, E., & Turner, R. (1992). Toward a more culturally sensitive *DSM–IV:* Psychoreligious and psychospiritual problems. *Journal of Nervous and Mental Disease, 180,* 673–682.

Martin, S. (1999). *For God and race: The religious and political leadership of AMEZ Bishop James Walker Hood.* Columbia: University of South Carolina Press.

McCloud, A. B. (1995). *African American Islam.* New York: Routledge.

McRae, M. B., Carey, P. M., & Anderson-Scott, R. (1998). Black churches as therapeutic systems: A group process perspective. *Health Education and Behavior, 25,* 778–789.

Mollica, R. F., Streets, F. J., Boscarino, J., & Redlich, F. C. (1986). A community study of formal pastoral counseling activities of the clergy. *American Journal of Psychiatry, 143,* 323–328.

Moore, S. E., & Collins, W. L. (2002). A model for social work field practicums in African American churches. *Journal of Teaching in Social Work, 22,* 171–188.

Moore, T. (1991). The African American church: A source of empowerment, mutual help, and social change. *Prevention in Human Services, 10,* 147–167.

Morris, J. R., & Robinson, D. T. (1996). Community and Christianity in the Black church. *Counseling & Values, 41,* 59–69.

Peck, M. S. (1997). *The road less traveled and beyond: Spiritual growth in an age of anxiety.* New York: Touchstone.

Pinn, A. B. (1998). *Varieties of African American religious experience*. Minneapolis, MN: Fortress Press.

Poussaint, A. F., & Alexander, A. (2000). *Lay my burden down: Unraveling suicide and the mental health crisis among African-Americans*. Boston: Beacon Press.

Raboteau, A. (1978). *Slave religion*. New York: Oxford University Press.

Richards, P. S., & Bergin, E. (1997). *A spiritual strategy for counseling and psychotherapy*. Washington, DC: American Psychological Association.

Rivera, E. T., Garrett, M. T., & Crutchfield, L. B. (2004). Multicultural interventions in groups: The use of indigenous methods. In J. L. DeLucia-Waack, D. A. Gerrity, C. R. Kalodner, & M. T. Riva (Eds.), *Handbook of group counseling and psychotherapy* (pp. 295–306). Thousand Oaks, CA: Sage.

Segers, M. C. (2003). Introduction: President Bush's faith-based initiative. In J. R. Formicola, M. C. Segers, & P. Weber (Eds.), *Faith-based initiatives and the Bush administration: The good, the bad, and the ugly* (pp. 1–23). New York: Rowman & Littlefield.

Sernett, M. C. (Ed.). (2000). *African American religious history: A documentary witness*. Durham, NC: Duke University Press.

Stuckey, S. (1987). *Slave culture*. New York: Oxford University Press.

Taylor, R. J., Ellison, C. G., Chatters, L. M., Levin, J. S., & Lincoln, K. D. (2000). Mental health services in faith communities: The role of clergy in Black churches. *Social Work, 45*, 73–87.

U.S. Surgeon General. (2001). *Mental health: Culture, race, and ethnicity*. Washington, DC: U.S. Government Printing Office.

Wiley, C. Y. (1991). A ministry of empowerment: A holistic model for pastoral counseling in the African-American community. *Journal of Pastoral Care, 45*, 335–364.

Williams, C. B., Frame, M. W., & Green, E. (1999). Counseling groups for African American women: A focus on spirituality. *Journal for Specialists in Group Work, 24*, 260–273.

Zinnbauer, B. J., & Pargament, K. I. (2000). Working with the sacred: Four approaches to religious and spiritual issues in counseling. *Journal of Counseling & Development, 78*, 162–171.

15

Collaborators: Mental Health and Public Health in the African American Community

Erma Jean Lawson and Ye Jung Kim

The mental health of African Americans is an ignored and neglected public health issue. For example, African American males between the ages of 15 and 24 die more from suicide than homicides and accidents compared with other racial/ethnic groups (Brown & Keith, 2003; U.S. Census Bureau, 2001; U.S. Department of Health and Human Services, 2001). Approximately 90% of people who attempt suicide require mental health services (Healthy People 2000, 1990; Healthy People 2010, 2000; U.S. Census Bureau, 2001). Moreover, African Americans are more likely to experience culture-bound syndromes than non-Hispanic Whites, including sleep paralysis, a brief loss of consciousness, and a sudden collapse preceded by dizziness (*U.S. Surgeon General Report*, 2003).

African Americans also are overrepresented among individuals at risk for mental illnesses, including the homeless, incarcerated, and foster care populations (U.S. Bureau of Labor Statistics, 2001). For instance, although African Americans represent 12% of the population, they constitute 40% of the homeless population (Healthy People 2000, 1990; Healthy People 2010, 2000). Approximately 50% of state and federal prisoners and 40% of juveniles in legal custody are African American (U.S. Census Bureau, 2001). A large number of children in public foster care and more than half of children who wait for adoption are African American (*U.S. Surgeon General Report*, 2003). Such statistics underscore the mental health needs of a large number of African Americans (Landrine & Klonoff, 1996).

Treatment inequities also demonstrate the neglect of public health and mental health services in African American communities. Studies have consistently documented that African Americans have few available mental health services (Brown & Keith, 2003; Healthy People 2010, 2000; U.S. Department of Health and Human Services, 2001). Although they receive treatment, African Americans are more likely to receive poorer quality of mental health care compared with other groups. Specifically, they are incorrectly diagnosed at a greater rate than White Americans (*U.S. Surgeon General Report*, 2003). Compared with other racial/ethnic groups, African Americans are more often diagnosed with a psychotic versus an affective disorder (*U.S. Surgeon General Report*, 2003). As a result, African Americans experience a greater number of days off work compared with other racial/ethnic groups (*U.S. Surgeon General Report*, 2003).

Of importance, African Americans often receive poor quality of psychiatric medication treatment. They are less likely to obtain newer antipsychotic medications with fewer side effects than Whites (*U.S. Surgeon General Report,* 2003). As a result, they often experience severe side effects, which may prompt medication termination at a higher rate compared with Whites (U.S. Department of Health and Human Services, 2001).

African Americans are given more antipsychotic medication injections rather than oral dosages, and they are often prescribed higher doses of psychotropic medications compared with other racial/ethnic groups (U.S. Department of Health and Human Services, 2001). In fact, Whites often participate in individual and group therapies while African Americans continue pharmacological control (*U.S. Surgeon General Report,* 2003).

Public health departments and mental health services collaboration is required to address factors that influence the need for mental health services as well as to explore mental health treatment discrepancies in African American communities. Both disciplines are needed to confront mental health service accessibility disparities and psychiatric treatment inequities among African Americans. Specifically, in 1961, the Joint Commission of Mental Illness and Health recognized the need for collaboration among mental health and public health communities. As early as 1978, the President's Commission on Mental Health encouraged the United States to create mental health systems that embrace community participation and consumer empowerment (Trierweiler et al., 2000; U.S. Department of Health and Human Services, 2001).

This chapter examines the separation between public health and mental health services and its consequence for African Americans. First, it considers the dualism of mental and public health communities to explain the current schism between the two disciplines. Second, it discusses barriers that prohibit public health and mental health research, services, and teaching collaboration. Finally, it presents a model of public health and mental health collaboration.

Dualism in Public Health and Mental Health

Public Health and Mental Health in History

The 19th century stimulated the segregation of public health and mental health (Mazyck, 1970; Scutchfield & Keck, 1997). For instance, public health was based on a population-based model. Such a framework focused on the health of a population and highlighted linkages between positive health and the physical environment. Consequently, public health measures responded to epidemic crises (Institute of Medicine, 1988).

During the 19th and 20th centuries, public health improved the physical health of communities through activities such as the following: assuring food safety and clean water, disposing of sewage, adopting health-promoting habits, and controlling communicable diseases before vaccines and antibiotics. Although public health actions prevented numerous deaths, the federal government provided scarce leadership for the care of the mentally ill (Caplan, 1969; Duffy, 1968). Moreover, the emphasis of mental health focused on the severely mentally ill. For example, in 1865, St. Elizabeth's Hospital was established as the government hospital to provide mental health treatment to the Army, Navy, and the District of Columbia (Caplan, 1969; Deutsch, 1949; Fox, 1978; Rosen, 1950).

In 1854, President Pierce established land grant hospitals for the mentally ill (Cassedy, 1962; Fox, 1978; Scutchfield & Keck, 1997). Consequently, between 1845 and 1945, nearly 300 state mental hospitals were constructed (Deutsch, 1949; Fox, 1978). However, these facilities were racially segregated, and the concerns of African Americans were considered unimportant (Bryd & Clayton, 2000). In fact, until the mid-1960s, state hospitals assigned patients to separate sections on the basis of race. The state mental hospitals that admitted African Americans often provided insufficient, deficient, and meager medical care (Drake, 1970; DuBois, 1977). African Americans, therefore, were not inclined to seek mental health hospital care. They turned to family members, churches, and friends for supportive mental health care. Indeed, the quality of mental health treatment received often provoked African Americans to seek mental health care from other sources (Aptheker, 1945; Bryd & Clayton, 2000; Genovese, 1974; Giddens, 1984).

The National Mental Health Act of 1946 and the federal community mental health centers legislation in the 1960s induced the separation between mental and public health services. For example, the community approach established the belief that mental health problems were also related to factors within communities (Rosen, 1950; Vogel, 1980). Therefore, epidemiological concepts were applied to the identification of population mental health problems (Duffy, 1968; Kiple & King, 1981; Sicherman, 1980). Such health issues as the promotion of mental health and the early diagnosis of mental problems paralleled the traditional public health perspective. Simultaneously, a number of large state mental health hospitals closed (Heller, 1985; Pescosolido & Boyer, 1999). According to studies, the following developments changed the delivery of mental health services, and some events also received federal support (Bennett & DiLorenzo, 2000; Institute of Medicine, 1988; Scutchfield & Keck, 1997):

1. The rapid growth of psychopharmacology.
2. The development of the hospital therapeutic community and inception of the model that therapeutic potential resides in clients and staff. Through the encouragement of a democratic hospital community, the effectiveness of psychological treatment increased.
3. The decentralization of large state mental hospitals.

The mental health community also recognized that such social problems as substance abuse, family violence, and teenage pregnancy are related to mental well-being. Therefore, community mental health centers provided comprehensive and coordinated mental health services (Brown & Keith, 2003; Caplan, 1969; R. L. Jones, 1980; Scutchfield & Keck, 1997; U.S. Department of Health and Human Services, 2001). However, most of the new health and social programs of the 1960s overlooked public health agencies. Although offices were established to mediate between the federal government and local communities, mental health services were often separate from public health departments (Institute of Medicine, 1988; Sicherman, 1980). From the 1960s to the present, the functions of public health were split between numerous agencies. Consequently, public health lost its visibility and clarity as well as an institutional base (Institute of Medicine, 1988; Scutchfield & Keck, 1997).

Public health's lack of focus and vision also solidified the split between mental health services and public health (Bennett & DiLorenzo, 2000; Cassedy, 1962). Therefore, public health practitioners were often limited to routine clinical responsibilities in child health, tuberculosis, venereal disease, immunization, and communicable disease clinics. Additionally, during the 1970s public health departments treated uninsured and Medicaid patients who were often rejected by private practitioners. Importantly, the intense care required for indigent populations eclipsed time for reorganization of the public health infrastructure (Bennett & DiLorenzo, 2000; Fox, 1978).

Although people with no health insurance receive health care from public health departments, U.S. health expenditures for public health decreased when President Reagan cut federal public health funding. Through block grants, he returned power to state health jurisdictions. As a result, state public health agencies devoted little effort to mental health prevention, education, and treatment (Institute of Medicine, 1988). However, the AIDS epidemic and resurgence of tuberculosis refocused attention to public health (Bennett &

DiLorenzo, 2000). Although federal funding was primarily devoted to AIDS research and medical care, consumerism increased attention to public health. Consequently, public health focused on epidemiologic surveillance, AIDS prevention, access to public health, and service evaluation and de-emphasized mental health (Institute of Medicine, 1988; Scutchfield & Keck, 1997).

Core Functions of Public Health Departments

Traditionally, state health departments have focused on six basic public health services: (a) collection of vital records and statistics, (b) control of communicable diseases, (c) environmental sanitation, (d) laboratory services, (e) public health education, and (f) maternal and child health. Concern for the health of the labor force led states to add industrial hygiene services (Bennett & DiLorenzo, 2000; Institute of Medicine, 1988; Scutchfield & Keck, 1997).

Currently, state health departments develop strategies and health programs to address the health of communities. They also furnish technical assistance to local health departments and other governmental and nongovernmental agencies. Health departments also supply direct health services. In most states, local health departments are the primary government entity for direct public health services (Bennett & DiLorenzo, 2000; Institute of Medicine, 1988; Scutchfield & Keck, 1997).

The overlapping and confusing organizational structure between state health and federal agencies increases segregation between the public health community and mental health services. While the federal government considers the public health agenda, state health departments identify goals and strategies to improve community health. However, because of budget cuts, often state health departments manage Medicaid programs and deliver physical health services to uninsured and indigent populations (Bryd & Clayton, 2000; Institute of Medicine, 1988).

The federal government consists of three components: the legislative, judicial, and executive branches. Although the executive branch is usually the focus in public health discussions, often the efforts are uncoordinated, which characterizes a number of government policies and programs. For example, nutritional issues may involve the following federal agencies: the Departments of Agriculture, Defense, Veteran Affairs, and Health and Human Services. Similarly, mental health issues are duplicated by several local, state, and federal organizations (Institute of Medicine, 1988).

Thus, health agencies also increased the dichotomy between public health and mental health. First, according to the Institute of Medicine (1988), the public health system fails to systematically assign mental health services. For example, in only four states are health departments also the state mental health authority. Such an organizational scheme negates client-coordinated mental health planning (Institute of Medicine, 1988; Scutchfield & Keck, 1997).

Second, because health issues are established in various local and state political systems rather than nationally, communities focus on health problems, which reflect diverse social and political priorities. Whereas mental health is a major concern in some states, other states view mental health as inconsequential (Institute of Medicine, 1988; Scutchfield & Keck, 1997). Additionally, variations of mental health agencies exist not only between states but also within states. For example, in some states, physical health is part of a superagency combined with social services but separate from mental health and environmental services. In other states, the local health agency is independent from the social services agency but has mental health and environmental divisions (Institute of Medicine, 1988).

The typical responsibilities of state health departments can be incorporated into four fundamental functions: (a) monitor health of population, (b) promote health, (c) improve health care delivery, and (d) develop health care policy. Major governmental health functions that are assigned to other agencies include mental health, financing of medical care for the indigent, and environmental protection. Indeed, the Institute of Medicine (1988) committee found that regardless of the organization, mental health services are often fragmented along organizational lines. For instance, in one state, substance abuse programs are under the state health agency, but mental health services are responsible to the social services agency (Bennett & DiLorenzo, 2000; Institute of Medicine, 1988). Communication hardly occurs between the two programs. Additionally, public health departments emphasize services for the severely mentally ill. Such segregation negates a public health orientation, including epidemiological surveillance, mental illness prevention, and mental health promotion (Cassedy, 1962; Duffy, 1968; Institute of Medicine, 1988; Scutchfield & Keck, 1997).

Finally, public health agencies often deal with numerous critical issues with few resources, further increasing the dichotomy between public health and mental health services. Public health departments often possess little political authority to rally support. A frequent perception of public health services by citizens is a low and inflexible bureaucracy battling with chaos, waiting to address crises, and consistently reactive (Mazyck, 1970; Scutchfield & Keck, 1997). Public health professionals have failed to effectively present their views and accomplishments to the media, the politicians, and the public. Because public health depends on public understanding and support, such a failure is disastrous (Institute of Medicine, 1988; Mazyck, 1970; Scutchfield & Keck, 1997).

Barriers to Public Health and Mental Health Collaboration

Black Consumer–Practitioner Relations

Following the civil rights movement, interest in the mental health of African Americans increased. The movement had pointed toward the need to examine the mental health problems of African Americans within a sociopolitical context (Azibo, 2003; Dillard, 1983; Dillard & Reilly, 1988; Parham, 2000). Presently, researchers and practitioners in public health and mental health direct attention to the causes and consequences of treatment modalities and to the role of race as it affects treatment outcomes (Brown & Keith, 2003; Kiple & King, 1981; Mays, Coleman, & Jackson, 1996; Neal-Burnett & Crowther, 2000; Pinderhughes, 1989; Siefert & Butter, 1992; Takeuchi, Uehara, & Maramba, 1999).

Although there has been a plethora of critical studies on the mental health service delivery system, a void exists in the literature on the attitudes, beliefs, and behaviors of Whites and various ethnic groups of mental health practitioners. This constitutes a significant knowledge vacuum because the clinicians' behavior influences therapeutic relationships and often prohibits African Americans from seeking mental health care (Brown & Keith, 2003; Green, 1982; Heller, 1985).

Indeed, research has stressed the role of race in the linguistic, behavioral, and attitudinal differences that permeate the White clinician–Black client exchange (Parham, 2000; Pedersen, 2000, 2003). Without knowledge of Black life and history, the clinician will make a futile attempt to evaluate the problem (Harley, Stebnicki, & Rollins, 2000; Lawson & Thompson, 1999; Marsella, 1998). For example, continual subjection to racial stereotypes is undeniably a mental health hazard. A clinician's assumption that most African Americans suffer from low self-esteem because of exposure to racial stereotypes can result in irreparable damage to the clinician–client relationship (Harley, 2000). The lack of diversity training of mental health clinicians may prohibit collaboration with public health, because many mental health programs fail to provide experience in working with diverse populations and many universities fail to hire diverse faculty as well as researchers. As a result, the assessments of mental health symptoms and mental health theories are based on White middle-class models (Johnson, 1934; Pinderhughes, 1989; Vega & Rumbaut, 1991).

The racist theories of mental illness also have prohibited African Americans' mental-health-seeking behavior (R. L. Jones, 1980; Pedersen, 2000; Powdermaker, 1968; Smith, 1995). Theories from the 19th century argued that Blacks' compatibility and adjustment to slavery contributed to their low rates of mental illness. However, following emancipation, Whites increasingly diagnosed African Americans as mentally ill (Drake, 1970; DuBois, 1977). Additionally, historical records have documented Whites' lack of sensitivity to the mental health of Blacks (Aptheker, 1945; Mitchell, 1944; Morton, 1991; Rutledge, Hartmann, Kinman, & Winfield, 1988; Smith, 1995). For instance, public health officials demonstrated little concern for mental or public health services for African American children trapped in the neoslavery of sharecropping (Bryd & Clayton, 2000; Giddens, 1984; Iglehart & Rosina, 1996; Martin, 1990; Rosen, 1950).

Additionally, public and mental health services often ignored the large number of children cleaning and cooking in White households (Johnson, 1934). Segregation in Chicago, for example, led to the exclusion of African American children from White-operated orphanages and restricted Black elderly from White-operated nursing homes (Antler & Antler, 1979; Martin, 1990; Stuart, 1992). Even among services for young delinquents, differential treatment was conducted. In Virginia, although reformatories for White males existed, none were available for African American youths (Drake, 1970; DuBois, 1977; Giddens, 1984; Stuart, 1992). African American youth offenders were confined to jails, penitentiaries, stockades, or chain gangs (Aptheker, 1945; Pinderhughes, 1989).

Given the history of public health and mental health services for African Americans, it is little wonder that they often fail to seek services that have historically reinforced social marginality and racial oppression as well as ignored their social conditions. According to Welsing (1974), the submission and cooperation with one's own oppression are modes of behavior that constitute mental illness. Therefore, resistance to and destruction of the societal oppressive forces constitute mental health for African Americans. In this context, other researchers have also argued that counterracist mental health is the only mental health treatment to alleviate emotional distress for African American people (Dillard, 1983; Nobles, 1991).

Discrimination in Public Health and Mental Health

A history of racism is another significant factor that prohibits collaborative efforts between public health and mental health in the African American communities. For instance, in 1900, the Atlanta Board of Health reported that the Black death rate exceeded the White death rate by 69% (Allen & Britt, 1983; Smith, 1995). Of 431 Black children born in 1900, 45% died before their first birthday, from public health treatable childhood diseases (Duffy, 1968; Giddens, 1984; Johnson, 1934; Litwack, 1979). However, public health often ignored efforts to improve the health status of Blacks and viewed the disproportionate African American mortality rates as confirmation of their biological and moral inferiority (Bryd & Clayton, 2000).

In 1908, the Atlanta Chamber of Commerce expressed concern over the city's high African American death rate. However, the president of the board of health responded that the African American death rate related to their unhygienic and unsanitary lifestyles (Mitchell, 1944; Powdermaker, 1968). A number of Whites argued that African Americans were susceptible to disease because of their inferior intellect, small lungs, and sluggish circulation (Cartwright, 1852; Lawson & Thompson, 1999). Thus, the health crisis of African

Americans justified a racist ideology in which medical journals portrayed African Americans as a disease menace to Whites. Indeed, the public health community used a racist ideology to reinforce ill health and to restrict opportunities while reducing African Americans to functional inferiors (Brown & Keith, 2003; Bryd & Clayton, 2000; Welsing, 1974).

Although the profession's code of ethics endorsed nondiscrimination, public health alienated African American communities. For instance, Blacks were exploited in the Tuskegee Syphilis Experiment (Smith, 1995; see also chap. 8, this volume). From 1932 to 1972 White physicians of the U.S. Public Health Service conducted a study on 400 rural African American men in Macon County, Alabama. Researchers and the public have labeled this study as scientifically unjustifiable and as an unethical experiment that highlighted the racism of American medicine and the federal government (J. H. Jones, 1993).

The U.S. Public Health Service recruited Black men in Macon County, Alabama, to participate in a study of untreated syphilis. Most of the men were sharecroppers with limited education and access to medical care (Kiple & King, 1981; Litwack, 1979; Pinderhughes, 1989). The men were not informed that they had syphilis or that they were research subjects (J. H. Jones, 1993; Kiple & King, 1981). The researchers withheld effective treatment for participants who had syphilis.

Although the study continued for 40 years, it ended because of political protest. The public health community denied that it had performed immoral research (Bryd & Clayton, 2000; J. H. Jones, 1993). A 1973 report commissioned by the U.S. Department of Health, Education, and Welfare found that the study was ethically unjust because subjects failed to provide informed consent and the research participants should have been given penicillin (*U.S. Surgeon General Report*, 2003). In addition, the study convinced many African Americans to distrust public health workers. Such legacy continues still, with many African Americans believing that the federal government created HIV to control the population growth of African Americans (Bryd & Clayton, 2000; J. H. Jones, 1993).

African Americans also have been the target of other public health experiments. For example, the Center for the Study of Psychiatry and Psychology was founded in the early 1970s to organize campaigns to stop the resurgence of lobotomies and other forms of psychosurgery in minority populations. Although public health has often emphasized nonracist treatment philosophically, the public health community has seldom promoted concrete efforts to address such problems (J. Jones, 1985; Kiple & King, 1981). In fact, segregated public health services and facilities were apparent as late as the 1960s.

During the civil rights era, public health officials largely ignored the issues of segregation and health disparities (Bryd & Clayton, 2000; Morton, 1991; Vega & Rumbaut, 1991). Therefore, African American health activism provided mental health programs and services to their communities (Litwack, 1979; Mitchell, 1944; Morton, 1991; Smith, 1995). Finally, 30 years following the civil rights movement, health disparities are a major issue in the public health community. However, some researchers view this emphasis on health inequities as a little too late (Allen & Britt, 1983; Bryd & Clayton, 2000; Heller, 1985; Hine, 1989; Wilkinson & King, 1987).

Removal of Barriers and Public and Mental Health Collaboration

A collaborative model of mental health and public health involves removing various barriers, including (a) organizational and bureaucratic impediments to transdisciplinary collaboration in training and research, (b) the powerful economic interests and political controversies surrounding health reform in the United States, (c) the difficulties entailed in designing sustainable interventions and policies that incorporate the varied views of the African American community, and (d) the methodological complexities inherent in evaluating mental health services and public health in the African American community (Institute of Medicine, 1988; Mazyck, 1970; Scutchfield & Keck, 1997).

Collaborative efforts between public health and mental health are often impeded by bureaucratic and organizational barriers, including the ethnocentrism of university departments and the compartmentalization of health care settings around particular disease categories and professional turfs. These impediments to cross-disciplinary and interagency collaboration must be confronted in future graduate and professional training programs, including graduate psychology and social work programs, as well as in historical Black educational institutions, because often historical Black institutions are compelled to adopt White middle-class norms and European values.

Moreover, a fundamental premise of an inclusive curriculum on historical Black college campuses is that White students and faculty are not prepared to deal adequately with an increasingly multicultural world (Nobles, 1991). Thus, the White ethnocentric character of American education often results in White nationalism on the campuses of a large number of historical Black universities, while African American students are alienated from their history and culture.

In a multiracial society, health education must be interdisciplinary to address issues that produce and sustain ill health. For instance, according to a number of researchers, behavior is labeled mental illness when it contradicts mainstream societal norms (Nobles, 1991; White, Parham, & Parham, 1980). However, some African Americans regard various behaviors as comprehensible and acceptable that may contradict White middle-class norms. An interdisciplinary approach is needed to situate mental illness in the cultural history and in sociopolitical context (Brown & Keith, 2003; Bryd & Clayton, 2000; Nobles, 1991; White et al., 1980). Of importance, American mental and public health often adhere to theories that portray negative perceptions of African Americans in every facet of American life (Harley, 2001; White et al., 1980; Wilkinson & King, 1987).

Collaboration between public health and mental health is complicated by the incorporation of several program components that include multiple organizations and environmental settings (Healthy People 2000, 1990; Healthy People 2010, 2000; Scutchfield & Keck, 1997). Rigorous assessment of multiple programs requires a combination of research methods, such as qualitative and quantitative measures, formative and summative evaluation strategies, interrupted time series, control-series designs, and hierarchical linear modeling (Brown & Keith, 2003; Wilkinson, 1980). When appropriate, comparison communities should be available for inclusion in quasi-experimental models, and simulation models should be considered for program evaluation (Blazer, Landerman, Hays, Simonsick, & Saunders, 1998; Brown & Gary, 1988).

Physical Health and Mental Health Collaboration

Black Community Resources: Public and Mental Health Services

Public health and mental health disciplines often overlook available mental health supportive resources in African American communities. An understanding of such psychological resources as community support, dance, and spirituality allows for collaborative efforts of the two disciplines (Brown & Keith, 2003; Mattis & Jagers, 2001; Morton, 1991). Therefore, a paradigm shift that focuses on psychological resources is needed to understand African American mental health (G. G. Jackson, 1980b; R. L. Jones, 1980).

Community resources and friends often provide mental health support for a large number of African Americans (Pescosolido & Boyer, 1999; Pollard, 1978). For example, research has reported that non-blood-related persons are supportive during a mental health crisis (Giddens, 1984; Morton, 1991; Smith, 1995). For instance, friends are more likely to be a source of emotional support through contributing to personal growth characterized by social companionship and instrumental support (Denton, 1990; Drake, 1970; Grier & Cobbs, 1968).

Community organizations and churches also provide supportive functions in many African American communities. Such societies include historical Black college alumni associations, Black Masons, the Odd Fellows, with sister organizations as well as Black sororities and fraternities. Currently, a number of clubs host social events in the Black community. For instance, the Society of Charlottesvillians provides the names of the sick to local Black newspapers for the provision of community support (Lawson, Rodgers-Rose, & Rajaram, 1999). As early as 1934, the Black Philadelphia newspaper, *The Reflector*, reported that Mr. Roland Poindexter had been sick at his residence (Bryd & Clayton, 2000). Subsequently, neighbors visited the sick and offered emotional support.

Throughout history, dancing also has provided mental health benefits for American Americans (Aptheker, 1945; Blassingame, 1972). Indeed, dancing was an integral component in West Africa. As an agricultural people, the African songs and dances were associated with planting, harvesting, cattle raising, and the preparation of food (Southern, 1971). The slaves were encouraged to dance during the Middle Passage. Additionally, in the West Indies, slaves danced as part of the breaking-in process (Genovese, 1974). For slaves, dancing was a major strategy to escape a life of oppression and torment (Aptheker, 1945; Blassingame, 1972; Genovese, 1974). Realizing the power of music, slaveholders encouraged its use to increase work productivity as well as to prevent depression and suicidal impulses (Blassingame, 1972; Genovese, 1974; Southern, 1971).

The work songs and gospels also contained the remnants of African psychological coping resources (J. Jones, 1985; R. L. Jones, 1980; White et al., 1980). According to Southern (1971), the emergence of gospel singers, whose songs expressed the deep religious feelings of the Black masses, also served as a psychological coping mechanism. For instance, African Americans' improvisation of such songs as "Joshua Fought the Battle of Jericho," "Oh, Mary, Don't You Weep," "I Stood on the Banks of Jordon," and "There Is a Holy City" implied the immanence of God's justice in a race-based society and provided emotional comfort (Southern, 1971). According to DuBois (1977), African American spirituals offered profound psychological strength to an oppressed people who endured prolonged effects of racial stratification and its supportive ideology in the United States.

Moreover, African Americans often use 800 prayer lines, apply prayer oils or cloths, and have ministers lay hands to cast out demons that threaten their mental health (Genovese, 1974). Prayer oils and cloths represent spiritual healing when placed on the affected body. Others may use folk remedies to assist with such mental health problems as depression and anxiety. For instance, one anxious African American female stated,

> I went to a prophet and reader. She interprets dreams. I go to her when I feel stressed. For two weeks, I dreamed of snakes, which meant I was depressed and afraid. The prophet said that she saw my depression ending, and I would receive some money in March. She told me forgo visiting my mother for three days. (Lawson, 2003, p. 12)

The respondent subsequently resumed her daily activities without professional mental health services.

Another respondent stated that a dream she had prepared her for a family death, which assisted in her grief process. She recalled, "I dreamt of children two weeks before my daughter died. I believe children mean death and I need to prepare for a death."

Moreover, beliefs of African origin, prevalent during slavery, have not disappeared in some African American communities. For instance, consistent with African religion, some African Americans believe that dead ancestors return to provide comfort to the living (McGhee, 1984; Pollard, 1978). Additionally, African Americans have connected mental health disorders to superstitions and to intergenerational curses (Snow, 1963). Depression has been associated with exposure to "roots" (voodoo); manic/depressive episodes have been related to the possession of a "veil at birth" (an ominous sign) as well as white doves. Additionally, some African Americans have linked dreaming of children to an accidental, untimely, and unpredicted death, which often results in depression (Lawson, 2003; McGhee, 1984; Snow, 1963). Therefore, often African Americans cook black-eyed peas, collard greens, and chitterlings on New Year's Day to establish mental and physical well-being in the new year (Lawson, 2003).

African Americans also have used numerologists, readers, communicators with spirits, as well as specific herbs, including ginger root, dandelion, and green tea, to combat mental distress (Becerra & Inlehart, 1995; Green, 1982). Such resources should be assessed to understand the mental health of African Americans. However, providing race-specific mental health education, consultation, and services often assumes a low priority in both the public health and mental health. Although funding has been difficult, it is essential to develop outreach preventive mental health services that integrate the African American sociocultural perceptions of mental health resources as well as cultural beliefs about mental illness causation.

A Culturally Appropriate Internet Collaboration

By transcending geographic and temporal constraints, the Internet presents unprecedented opportunities for collaboration between public health and mental health. The recent rapid growth of the Internet suggests some new and exciting directions for future collaboration between public health and mental health. The Internet has included telemedicine and telewellness, whereby mental health services can be delivered rapidly to underserved areas. They provide both public health promotion and mental health resources that are widely disseminated to large segments of the population. The World Health Organization Healthy Cities Program exemplifies the ways in which electronic communication can foster collaboration in the development of effective health policies and community interventions, which can be specifically applied to mental health (Huang & Alessi, 1996; Marsella, 1998).

Although there are distinct advantages to online anonymity, some mental health practitioners question its therapeutic value. First, the lack of access to computers and the World Wide Web among African Americans is racially widening the digital divide. Second, mental health practitioners differ on offering mental health services online. For example, studies have questioned whether it is possible for healthy two-way therapeutic relationships to be communicated through the Internet (King, 1996; King & Moreggi, 1998). Third, there is potential for participants to become engaged in online relationships and exclude other forms of relationships (King, 1996). Finally, the technological breakdown is a major hazard; occasionally computer difficulties occur during a mental health crisis (King & Moreggi, 1998).

Nevertheless, the Internet provides useful mental health services, including an accessible communication tool, especially in rural areas (King, 1996; King & Moreggi, 1998; Kirk, 1997). Moreover, it is less intimidating, and therefore, it may facilitate the client's disclosure of personal information (Holmes, 1998; Huang & Alessi, 1996).

Culturally Appropriate Service Systems

Minimizing Adverse Consequences

A key criterion for measuring the efficacy of public health and mental health collaboration is the extent to which they minimize unintended adverse consequences. Often, well-conceived mental health interventions can lead to problems not anticipated by their creators. These include the stigmatization of the mentally ill caused by programs that overemphasize the individual's responsibility to remain healthy (J. S. Jackson et al., 1996).

Similarly, violence prevention school-based programs can trigger unintended negative, and sometimes dangerous, consequences. For instance, one program emphasized verbal responses to physical threats, although the community norm involved physical aggressive behavior (Lawson & Thompson, 1999). A young man used the program's antiviolence techniques and strategies within an environment that tolerated violence and physical aggressive behavior. Because the program planners ignored varying communication styles, the young man became another victim of violence. Such an example underscores the obligation of researchers and program planners to assess objectively the social ramifications and consequences of mainstream mental health programs within African American communities.

Because traditional American education excludes the African American experience from an integral part of society, culturally competent mental health and public health collaboration is essential and necessary. Textbooks, testing methods, and curricula tend to maximize the values and interests of the dominant White majority (Harley, 2000; Harley et al., 2000; Pedersen, 2003; Takeuchi et al., 1999). As a result, American society often accepts myths of White supremacy while accepting the inferiority of non-Whites. A clinician's lack of understanding of positive mental health strategies of African Americans results in racial stereotypes and damages the mental health encounter. Therefore, the high rate of African Americans' mental health attrition rates can be attributable to therapists' racial ethnocentricity, that is, lack of understanding of their own socialization and beliefs as well as appreciation of a multicultural society (Wilkinson, 1972; Wilkinson & King, 1987).

Components of Culturally Competent Mental Health and Public Health Programs

Key components of culturally competent mental and public health services include access to the best available mental health services that are consumer friendly and provide treatment options. Most importantly, the bureaucracies of mental health care should respond to individual differences and present treatment options (Wilkerson & Mitchel, 1991).

The workforce should include members of ethnic, cultural, and linguistic minorities. Specifically, effective practitioner–client relations can be jeopardized when clinicians ignore the diversity of African Americans. A clinician's failure to shake a client's hand, the neglect to engage in eye contact during an encounter, and the disregard to address as "Mr." or "Mrs." or use a client's professional title can disrupt the mental health visit (Bhui, Christie, & Bhugra, 1995). A culturally appropriate mental health perspective acknowledges that African Americans often value feelings, impulses, and emotions (Azibo, 2003; R. L. Jones, 1980; White et al., 1980). Importantly, culturally competent mental health practitioners should recognize that cultural conditioning to racial beliefs and attitudes has an impact on the client–practitioner encounter (J. S. Jackson et al., 1996).

Because Euro-American mental health practitioners often support an erroneous and negative portrayal of African Americans, applying a cultural component to mental health disputes such negative stereotypes. It recognizes that the African American mental health experience is culturally distinct from the Euro-American experience. Consequently, culturally competent mental health practitioners view their role as change agents in a sociopolitical process (G. G. Jackson, 1980a, 1980b; Mpofu & Harley, 2000; Nobles, 1991; Wesson, 1975).

Mental health practitioners and researchers should understand the existence of mental health disparities among African Americans and the reasons for their existence. For example, it is essential that mental health practitioners realize that social marginality often threatens the mental health of African Americans. They are exposed to stressful events and chronic strains that make them vulnerable to mental distress, including verbal insults, race-based discrimination, and stereotypical mental health interactions. Additionally, culturally appropriate mental health services for African Americans should eliminate disparities in medical care and in housing and economic status and identify communities' expectations of public health agencies.

Culturally effective mental health care involves the removal of treatment obstacles. For example, a number of barriers prohibit African Americans from obtaining optimal mental health care, including cost, fragmentation of services, lack of availability of services, societal stigma toward mental illness, and racial discrimination (Landrine & Klonoff, 1966).

The Institute of Medicine (1988) called for major changes in the training of mental health practitioners to consider various racial/ethnic groups:

1. Include cross-cultural training in the curricula of all health care professionals.
2. Recruit health professionals from diverse racial/ethnic groups.
3. Provide patients with culturally appropriate education programs to learn how to access and to participate in clinical decision making.
4. Require health plans of federal and state government payers to collect and report patient care data for treatment disparities and civil rights violations.
5. Present options for consumers to agree or disagree with the treatment plan.
6. Include mental health care to rural African Americans and to such neglected populations as adolescents in foster care and incarcerated and homeless African Americans.

Culturally competent mental health and public health services are essential because cultural conditioning to Euro-American ideological and value systems pervades mental health systems. Therefore, it is imperative that clinicians are trained to understand African American history and how African Americans develop coping skills to manage social marginality, professional disrespect, and the lack of employment mobility across the life course. Clinicians must understand the underlying premises, ideological translations, and practical applications of mental health services and research (Dillard, 1985; Wilkinson & King, 1987).

Consequently, from a policy standpoint, it is important to recognize the significant differences of mental health issues among various racial/ethnic minorities. Therefore, programs must acknowledge the differences between African Americans and other ethnic groups. With respect to the prevalence of racial myths, it is important to understand the way in which White mental health practitioners operate within the context of 300 years of racial stereotypical theories as a professional exposed to colonialism (Bhui et al., 1995; Pinderhughes, 1989; Wilkinson, 1980). Sensitivity to the perception of the way in which culture influences mental health status is an essential factor in culturally competent mental health and public health services.

Establishing culturally appropriate public health and mental health service systems requires collaboration of organizational and community leaders as well as religious and business leaders. Additionally, both disciplines are obliged to pursue opportunities for continuing education in the fields of Black history, social marketing, media, and communication strategies for African American communities. In fact, a sociology course on race and ethnicity should be required for mental and public health practitioners. Culturally competent mental health services also contribute their expertise in collaborative discussions with community leaders on topics ranging from parenting from an African American perspective, to an evaluation of social and economic progress following the civil rights movement, to relationship trauma including divorce and grief distress.

Future Research

While the discussion has focused primarily on the dualism between public health and mental health, the following specific research areas are needed to affect the dynamics of integrating the two disciplines: (a) the construction of reality-based theoretical paradigms on the experiences and behaviors of African Americans who seek therapy; (b) racial beliefs, attitudes, values, and personalities of White mental health therapists and other ethnic groups who treat African Americans; and (c) the relevance of clinical theories, research, and practice to understanding the life experiences of African Americans.

The following are some future research areas relevant to an understanding of the mental health of African Americans:

1. Child-rearing practices in African American families.
2. A new social psychology of adaptation of African Americans to urban settings, as well as the mental health of African American professionals and the relationship between African Americans and various ethnic immigrants. There is a feeling among some African American urban residents that immigrants have replaced traditional African American neighborhoods and community organizations.
3. An examination of the public educational system on the affective and cognitive development of African American children. Few studies have investigated the way in which African Americans, specifically African American male adolescents, manifest mental disorders and interpret a mental health crisis.

Public health and mental health services can sponsor self-help groups to promote mental health wellness. Such groups provide African Americans with opportunities to meet others who have similar mental health experiences, to provide and receive emotional support, and to work together toward solutions to problems. There is a crucial need for mental health and public health collaboration to understand and to explore all facets of mental health among African Americans.

Eliminating the dualism between the two disciplines is critical to understanding the sociocultural environment of the mental health of African Americans. However, the merger of public and mental health offers both promise and challenges. The challenge is evident in the magnitude of the deterioration of the public health system as well as the opportunity to celebrate a vision of future accomplishments. The success of collaborative efforts must be judged not only by improvements in the mental health treatment, prevention, and promotion of African Americans but also by reductions in the social inequalities between African Americans and other racial/ethnic groups.

Summary

This chapter's discussion of public health and mental health collaboration has focused on the historical dualism between the two disciplines, barriers to collaboration, and a culturally appropriate model for future collaboration with emphasis on African Americans. We have emphasized the history of segregation of public and mental health, focusing on developments that changed the care of the mentally ill. The organizational issues and dualism between public and mental health services centered on the fragmented infrastructure of public health departments. We noted that public health agencies deal with numerous critical issues with few resources and often possess little political authority to rally support. Public health, therefore, is perceived by citizens as a low and inflexible bureaucracy battling with chaos and consistently reactive. Barriers to public health and mental collaboration included Black consumer–practitioner relations, discrimination in public health and mental health, and bureaucratic organizational obstacles.

The integration of public health and mental health services, we have argued, must include the recognition of mental health resources within the African American community and the design of culturally appropriate services. A culturally competent mental health service recognizes that spirituality, as well as the African American community, serves as a valuable psychological resource. As noted throughout, it is important for culturally competent mental health practitioners to understand that in spite of the legacy of slavery, segregation, and ongoing discrimination, African Americans have a tremendous capacity for perseverance and resiliency. We have also emphasized that eliminating the dualism between public health and mental health requires exploring therapeutic outcomes in relation to race. It is also important to consider the sociopolitical context of mental health theories and disorders because, as noted throughout, the mental health of African Americans does not exist in a vacuum.

References

Allen, L., & Britt, D. W. (1983). Black women in American society: A resource development perspective. *Issues in Mental Health Nursing, 5,* 60–79.

Antler, J., & Antler, J. (1979). From child rescue to family protection: The evolution of the child protection movement in the U.S. *Children and Youth Service Review, 1,* 177–204.

Aptheker, H. (1945). *Essays in the history of the American Negro.* New York: International.

Azibo, D. A. (2003). *African-centered psychology.* Durham, NC: Carolina Academic Press.

Becerra, R. M., & Inlehart, A. P. (1995). Folk medicine use: Diverse populations in a metropolitan area. *Social Work in Health Care, 21,* 37–52.

Bennett, J. T., & DiLorenzo, T. J. (2000). *From pathology to politics.* New Brunswick, NJ: Transaction.

Bhui, K., Christie, Y., & Bhugra, D. (1995). The essential elements of culturally sensitive psychiatric services. *International Journal of Social Psychiatry, 41,* 242–256.

Blassingame, J. W. (1972). *The slave community.* New York: Oxford University Press.

Blazer, D. G., Landerman, L. R., Hays, J. C., Simonsick, E. M., & Saunders, W. B. (1998). Symptoms of depression among community-dwelling elderly African American adults. *Psychological Medicine, 28,* 1311–1320.

Brown, D. R., & Gary, L. E. (1988). Unemployment and psychological distress among Black women. *Sociological Focus, 21,* 209–221.

Brown, D. R., & Keith, V. M. (2003). *In and out of our right minds.* New York: Columbia University Press.

Bryd, W. M., & Clayton, L. A. (2000). *An American health dilemma: Race, medicine, and health care in the United States, from 1900 to dawn of the new millennium* (Vol. 2). New York: Routledge.

Caplan, R. B. (1969). *Psychiatry and the community in nineteenth century America: The recurring concern with the environment in the prevention and treatment of mental illness.* New York: Basic Books.

Cartwright, S. A. (1852). Philosophy of the Negro constitution. *New Orleans Medical and Surgical Journal, 9,* 199.

Cassedy, J. H. (1962). *Charles V Chapin and the public health movement.* Cambridge, MA: Harvard University Press.

Denton, T. H. (1990). Bonding and supportive relationships among Black professional women: Rituals of restoration. *Journal of Organizational Behavior, 11,* 447–457.

Deutsch, A. (1949). *The mentally ill in America: A history of their care and treatment from colonial times.* New York: Columbia University Press.

Dillard, J. M. (1983). *Multicultural counseling: Toward ethnic and cultural relevance in human encounters.* Chicago: Nelson-Hall.

Dillard, J. M. (1985). *Lifelong career planning.* Columbus, OH: Merrill.

Dillard, J. M., & Reilly, R. R. (1988). *Systematic interviewing: Communication skills for professional effectiveness.* Columbus, OH: Merrill.

Drake, St. C. (1970). The social and economic status of the Negro in the United States. In T. Parsons & K. Clark (Eds.), *The Negro America* (pp. 3–46). Boston: Beacon Press.

DuBois, W. E. B. (1977). *Black reconstruction in America* (7th ed.). New York: Atheneum.

Duffy, J. (1968). A note on antebellum Southern nationalism and medical practice. *Journal of Southern History, 34,* 256–276.

Fox, R. T. (1978). *So far disordered in mind: Insanity in California, 1870–1930.* Berkeley: University of California Press.

Genovese, E. D. (1974). *Roll Jordon roll: The world the slaves made.* New York: Random House.

Giddens, P. (1984). *When and where I enter: The impact of Black women on race and sex in America.* New York: Morrow.

Green, J. (1982). *Cultural awareness in the human services.* Englewood Cliffs, NJ: Prentice-Hall.

Grier, W. H., & Cobbs, P. M. (1968). *Black rage.* New York: Basic Books.

Harley, D. A. (2000). University partnerships between minority institutions and major research universities: Expanding academic opportunities and strengthening collaborations. *Rehabilitation Education, 14,* 359–368.

Harley, D. A. (2001). In a different voice: An African American woman's experiences in the rehabilitation and higher education realm. *Rehabilitation Education, 15,* 37–45.

Harley, D. A., Stebnicki, M., & Rollins, C. W. (2000). Applying empowerment evaluation as a tool for self-improvement and community development with culturally diverse populations. *Journal of the Community Development Society, 31,* 348–364.

Healthy People 2000. (1990). *National health promotion and disease prevention objectives* (DHHS Publication No. PHS 91-50212). Washington, DC: U.S. Department of Health and Human Services.

Healthy People 2010. (2000). *Understanding and improving health and objectives for improving health* (2nd ed.). Washington, DC: U.S. Government Printing Office. Retrieved from http://www.healthypeople.gov/document/

Heller, D. (1985). *Power in psychotherapeutic practice.* New York: Human Services Press.

Hine, D. (1989). *Black women in white: Racial conflict and cooperation in the nursing profession 1890–1950.* Bloomington: Indiana University Press.

Holmes, L. G. (1998). Delivering mental health services online: Current issues. *Cyber Psychology and Behavior, 1,* 861–869.

Huang, M., & Alessi, N. E. (1996). The Internet and the future of psychiatry. *American Journal of Psychiatry, 7,* 861–869.

Iglehart, P. I., & Rosina, M. B. (1996). Social work and ethnic agency: A history of neglect. *Journal of Multicultural Social Work, 4,* 1–19.

Institute of Medicine, Committee for the Study of the Future of Public Health. (1988). *The future of public health.* Washington, DC: National Academy Press.

Jackson, G. G. (1980a).The African genesis of the Black perspective in helping. In R. L. Jones (Ed.), *Black psychology* (2nd ed., pp. 314–331). New York: Harper & Row.

Jackson, G. G. (1980b). The emergence of a Black perspective in counseling. In R. L. Jones (Ed.), *Black psychology* (2nd ed., pp. 56–66). New York: Harper & Row.

Jackson, J. S., Brown, K. M., Williams, D. R., Torres, M., Sellers, S., & Brown, K. (1996). Racism and the physical and mental health of African Americans: A thirteen year national panel study. *Ethnicity and Disease, 6,* 132–147.

Johnson, C. S. (1934). *Shadow of the plantation.* Chicago: University of Chicago Press.

Jones, J. (1985). *Labor of love, labor of sorrow: Black women, work, and the family from slavery to the present.* New York: Basic Books.

Jones, J. H. (1993). *Bad blood: The Tuskegee Syphilis Experiment.* New York: Free Press.

Jones, R. L. (Ed.). (1980). *Black psychology.* (2nd ed.). New York: Harper & Row.

King, S. (1996). Researching Internet communities: Proposed ethical guidelines for the reporting of the result. *The Information Society, 12,* 119–127.

King, S. A., & Moreggi, D. (1998). Internet therapy and self-help groups: The pros and cons. In J. Gackenbach (Ed.), *Psychology and the Internet: Intrapersonal, interpersonal and transpersonal implications* (pp. 77–109). San Diego, CA: Academic Press.

Kiple, K. F., & King, H. (1981). *Another dimension to the Black diaspora, diet, disease, and racism.* New York: Cambridge University Press.

Kirk, M. A. (1997, February). Current perceptions of counseling and counselor education in cyberspace. *Counseling Today,* 17–18.

Landrine, H., & Klonoff, E. A. (1996). The schedule of racist events: A measure of racial discrimination and a study of its negative physical and mental health consequences. *Journal of Black Psychology, 22,* 144–168.

Lawson, E. J. (2003, March). *Black women's beliefs and health status.* Paper presented at the annual meeting of the Association of Behavioral and Social Sciences, Macon, GA.

Lawson, E. J., Rodgers-Rose, L. F., & Rajaram, S. (1999). The psychosocial context of Black women's health. *Health Care for Women International, 20,* 279–289.

Lawson, E. J., & Thompson, A. (1999). *Black men and divorce.* Thousand Oaks, CA: Sage.

Litwack, L. F. (1979). *Been in the storm so long: The aftermath of slavery.* New York: Knopf.

Marsella, A. J. (1998). Toward a global-community psychology: Meeting the needs of a changing world. *American Psychologist, 53,* 1282–1291.

Martin, G. (1990). *Social policy and the welfare state.* Englewood Cliffs, NJ: Prentice Hall.

Mattis, J. S., & Jagers, R. J. (2001). A relational framework for the study of religiosity and spirituality in the lives of African Americans. *Journal of Community Psychology, 29,* 519–539.

Mays, V. M., Coleman, L. M., & Jackson, J. S. (1996). Perceived race-based discrimination, employment status, and job stress in a national sample of Black women: Implications for health outcomes. *Journal of Occupational Health Psychology, 1,* 319–329.

Mazyck, P. R. (Ed.). (1970). *A half century of public health.* New York: Arno Press.

McGhee, N. (1984). Afterword. In W. H. Watson (Ed.), *Black folk medicine: The therapeutic significance of faith and trust* (pp. 99–100). New Brunswick, NJ: Transaction.

Mitchell, C. M. (1944). Health and the medical profession in the lower South, 1845–1860. *Journal of Southern History, 10,* 442–462.

Morton, P. (1991). *Disfigured images: The historical assault on Afro-American women.* New York: Praeger.

Mpofu, E., & Harley, D. A. (2000). Tokenism and cultural diversity in counselors: Implications for rehabilitation education and practice. *Journal of Applied Rehabilitation Counseling, 31,* 47–54.

Neal-Burnett, A., & Crowther, J. (2000). To be female, middle-class, anxious, and Black. *Psychology of Women Quarterly, 24,* 129–136.

Nobles, W. (1991). African philosophy: Foundations for Black psychology. In R. L. Jones (Ed.), *Black psychology* (pp. 47–63). Berkeley, CA: Cobb & Henry.

Parham, T. A. (2000). *Innovative approaches to counseling African American descent people.* North Amherst, MA: Microtraining Associates.

Pedersen, P. (2000). *Multiculturalism as a fourth force.* Philadelphia: Brunner/Mazel.

Pedersen, P. B. (2003). Culturally biased assumptions in counseling psychology. *The Counseling Psychologist, 31,* 396–403.

Pescosolido, B. A., & Boyer, C. A. (1999). How do people come to use mental health services?: Current knowledge and changing perspectives. In A. V. Horwitz & T. L. Scheid (Eds.), *A handbook for the study of mental health: Social contexts, theories and systems* (pp. 392–411). New York: Cambridge University Press.

Pinderhughes, E. (1989). *Understanding race, ethnicity, and power.* New York: Free Press.

Pollard, W. (1978). *A study of Black self-help.* San Francisco: R & E Associates.

Powdermaker, H. (1968). *After freedom: A cultural study in the deep South.* New York: Atheneum.

Rosen, G. (1950). Public health problems in New York City during the nineteenth century. *New York State Journal of Medicine, 50,* 73–78.

Rutledge, D. N., Hartmann, W. H., Kinman, P. O., & Winfield, A. C. (1988). Exploration of factors affecting mammography behaviors. *Preventive Medicine, 17,* 412.

Scutchfield, F. D., & Keck, W. C. (1997). *Principles of public health practice.* New York: Delmar.

Sicherman, B. (1980). *The quest for mental health in America.* New York: Arno Press.

Siefert, K., & Butter, I. (1992). Incorporating race and gender into the curriculum: An example of a course in social work and public health. *Journal of Teaching in Social Work, 6*(2), 19–32.

Smith, L. S. (1995). *Sick and tired of being sick and tired: Black women's health activism in America, 1890–1950.* Philadelphia: University of Pennsylvania Press.

Snow, L. (1963). Traditional health beliefs and practices among lower class Black Americans. *Western Journal of Medicine, 139,* 829–839.

Southern, E. (1971). *The music of Black Americans: A history.* New York: Norton.

Stuart, P. (1992). The Kingsley House extension program: Racism segregation in a 1940s settlement program. *Social Service Review, 66,* 112–120.

Takeuchi, D., Uehara, E., & Maramba, G. (1999). Cultural diversity and mental health treatment. In A. V. Horwitz & T. L. Scheid (Eds.), *A handbook for the study of mental health: Social contexts, theories and systems* (pp. 550–565). New York: Cambridge University Press.

Trierweiler, S., Neighbors, J., Munday, C., Thompson, E. E., Binion, V. J., & Gomez, J. P. (2000). Clinician attributions associated with the diagnosis of schizophrenia in African American and non-African American patients. *Journal of Consulting and Clinical Psychology, 68,* 171–175.

U.S. Bureau of Labor Statistics. (2001). *Current population survey: Civilian labor force.* Retrieved from http://www.data.bls.gov/servlet/SurveyOutputServlet

U.S. Census Bureau. (2001). *Studies in family violence* (Current Population Reports, Series P-23, No. 162). Washington, DC: U.S. Government Printing Office.

U.S. Department of Health and Human Services. (2001). *Mental health: Culture, race and ethnicity* (A supplement to *Mental Health: A Report of the Surgeon General*). Washington, DC: U.S. Government Printing Office.

U.S. Surgeon General Report on Mental Illness (DHHS Publication No. 8850210). (2003).Washington, DC: U.S. Government Printing Office.

Vega, W., & Rumbaut, R. (1991). Ethnic minorities and mental health. *Annual Review of Sociology, 17,* 351–383.

Vogel, M. J. (1980). *The invention of the modern hospital: Boston, 1870–1930.* Chicago: University of Chicago Press.

Welsing, F. (1974). The Cress theory of color confrontation. *Black Scholar, 5,* 32–40.

Wesson, A. (1975). The Black man's burden: The White clinician. *The Black Scholar, 6,* 13–16.

White, J. L., Parham, W. D., & Parham, T. A. (1980). Black psychology: The Afro-American tradition as a unifying force for traditional psychology. In R. L. Jones (Ed.), *Black psychology* (2nd ed., pp. 56–66). New York: Harper & Row.

Wilkerson, I., & Mitchel, A. (1991, September). Staying alive: The challenge of improving Black Americans' health. *Emerge,* 24–26.

Wilkinson, D. Y. (1972). Racism and American sociology: The myth of scientific objectivity. *Sociological Abstracts, 20,* 1888–1890.

Wilkinson, D. (1980). Minority women: Social and cultural issues. In A. Brodsky & R. Haremustin (Eds.), *Women and psychotherapy* (pp. 284–304). New York: Guilford Press.

Wilkinson, D., & King, G. (1987). Conceptual and methodological issues in the use of race as a variable: Policy implications. *Milbank Quarterly, 65,* 56–71.

Section IV

Application

This section of the book focuses on application of counseling approaches with African Americans. The six chapters explore various topics including community mental health, disabilities, assessment of children and adolescents, spirituality and religion, indigenous counseling, and ethics. In chapter 16, Fabian and Edwards examine community mental health in America historically within the context of racial disparities and currently for African Americans with mental disorders, particularly those with severe disorders who are at risk for developing long-term disability. They discuss key factors such as external barriers to service access and utilization, including differential treatment quality and outcomes, and internal barriers, including stigma, mistrust, and cultural disparities. As part of recommendations for practice, the authors suggest that change needs to occur in several areas: public funding, informal community supports, state and federally funded awareness and educational programs, development of innovative mental health interventions, and culturally responsive practices by counselors and clinicians.

In chapter 17 in his discussion of selective interventions in counseling African Americans with disabilities, Mpofu applies the concepts from prevention science that could help rehabilitation counselors enhance their success with African American clients. He outlines some current prevention intervention concepts and their relevance to counseling disabled populations. In addition, Mpofu discusses the multi-layered identities of African Americans, the sociocultural–historical factors that influence African Americans' participation in counseling services, and counselor and client qualities that influence African American clients' success from a prevention perspective.

Rainey and Nowak, in chapter 18, maintain that if time and effort are not invested at the onset with a young person, more will be required later. Thus, they advocate for a comprehensive, thoughtful, initial assessment for African American children and adolescents. The authors examine general issues in youth assessment, including environmental factors, reliability, validity, norming sample, and test bias. In addition, Rainey and Nowak analyze two areas of mental health in which African American youths continue to be overrepresented: cognition and achievement and social–emotional functioning. Implications for practice are offered across areas of examiner biases; assessment of the individual in context; consideration of multiple traits, settings, and informants; and rule-out and comorbid diagnoses. The authors make effective use of a case study to integrate and illustrate information in this chapter.

In chapter 19, Dillard and Brown Smith explore African Americans' spirituality and religion in counseling and psychotherapy. The authors provide a delineation of spirituality and religion as major dimensions in the lives of most contemporary African Americans and the significance of these dimensions in the therapeutic setting. In addition, they offer suggestions for curriculum modifications for training prospective mental health professionals to work effectively with African Americans' spiritual and religious issues. The authors provide insightful discussion of African custom retention, communal expression of African spirituality, African philosophy as the foundation of African-centered psychology, and spiritual striving and psychological well-being. The authors effectively use case examples to illustrate African American application of spirituality to ward off isolation and achieve a sense of belonging.

Harley further extends the discussion of spirituality and religion in her chapter on indigenous counseling. In chapter 20, she expands on the concepts and values of multicultural counseling. Harley begins with a discussion of the role of traditional healing practice. Next, she compares the advantages and disadvantages of indigenous healing practices, followed by a discussion of integrating indigenous and scientific mental health practices and guidelines for mental health practitioners utilizing indigenous practices, including implications for practice and future research. The author's discussion of ethical implications for the use of indigenous practices is a natural lead into the final chapter in this section.

In chapter 21, Rollins presents the ethical implications in mental health counseling with African Americans. She explores ethical issues inherent in counseling African Americans. In addition, Rollins discusses the reasons for the mental health profession's lack of consensus on multicultural counseling competencies and explores the implications of this discourse for counseling African Americans.

16

Community Mental Health and African Americans

Ellen S. Fabian and Yolanda V. Edwards

Community mental health care has undergone dramatic changes since the advent of the deinstitutionalization movement that began in the 1950s. At that time, the vision of mental health care in America was to replace state mental hospitals with an array of community and neighborhood support systems, a goal that was incorporated in the Community Mental Health Centers Construction Act of 1963 (Pub. L. No. 88-164) during the Kennedy Administration. Unfortunately, the reality proved much different than the vision, and the effort to provide federally funded community-based care for deinstitutionalized individuals with mental health disorders was dismantled in the 1980s. For the decades since deinstitutionalization, several serious consequences of inadequate planning for community mental health care became shockingly apparent in the United States. For example, studies have shown a marked increase in homelessness among individuals with mental illness (Lindbloom, 1991). Other studies have indicated an increased "criminalization" of people with mental health disorders, in that jails and prisons became the only alternative facilities when state hospitals were closed and community services were inadequate (Lamb & Weinberger, 1998). A third consequence of lack of community mental health supports has been the increased burden on families who were forced to take on the added economic and social costs of caring for family members with mental illnesses (Doll, 1976). Ironically, the lack of available community mental health support occurred during an era when advances in clinical and rehabilitative treatments for mental health disorders meant that better and more effective treatments were available to improve the quality of life of the individuals who experienced them (Mueser, Drake, & Bond, 1997).

One response that many states have recently initiated to address systemic public mental health failures is managed behavioral health care, believing that adapting the private health care insurance model to the public sector would reduce expenditures while improving effectiveness because of the focus on performance outcomes and empirically supported treatments (Mowbray, Grazier, & Holter, 2002). However, critics of the system worry that client welfare will be subsumed within the larger goal of cost containment, a scenario that might seriously jeopardize those individuals who tend to rely most heavily on the public mental health care sector, such as African Americans (Dana, 1998). Although the long-term results of managed behavioral health care on communities and clients remain unknown, several studies have already suggested problems with access to and quality of treatment within the states that were the first to enroll clients in the new system (Mowbray et al., 2002).

This brief review of the history of community mental health in the United States presents an important context for considering the racial disparities that have existed within the public mental health sector for several reasons. First, it has been clear through the past 50 years that the public mental health system (from which community mental health is derived) has neglected the needs of many citizens who need assistance, particularly clients from underrepresented groups, such as ethnic minorities, and those with more severe mental health disorders (Torrey, 1992, 1997). These groups include vulnerable populations who, without access to quality treatment, suffer deleterious consequences, such as long-term disability, hospitalization, and even death. Second, as with the rapid and disastrous policy shift that resulted in the deinstitutionalization movement, mental health care policy and programmatic changes that occur without systematic planning and evaluation are apt to fail, owing to the economic demands required by new service systems, the competing constituencies from other equally vulnerable groups, and the lack of a uniform national standard for assessing effectiveness (National Mental Health Association, 1999). Thus, it is important to move forward cautiously in terms of recommending major systemic overhauls that might require shifting public sector dollars so as to avoid some of the systemic failures that occurred after the rapid deinstitutionalization movement. The purpose of this chapter is to consider some of the current issues in community mental health care for African Americans with mental health disorders, particularly those with more severe disorders who are at risk for developing long-term disability. We also describe external and internal barriers to mental health care services and provide recommendations for improved treatment.

African Americans and the Community Mental Health System

Over the past decade or so, there has been increased attention focused on community mental health services for African Americans. Prevalence studies have indicated that about one in five Americans experience a mental health disorder in any given year, with most studies indicating that African Americans and Whites experience similar overall incidence of mental health disorders, even though some categories of disorders may differ between races (Kessler et al., 1996). It is also clear from a variety of data sources that even though rates of mental health disorders of African Americans may be similar to those of Whites, there are several disparities noted between the groups, particularly in the areas of access to and utilization of services (Hu, Snowden, Jerrell, & Nguyen, 1991), quality of treatment (Melfi, Croghan, Hanna, & Robinson, 2000), and treatment outcomes. In addition, there is overwhelming evidence that African Americans rely more on public health and mental health services as compared with Whites and that they are more likely to receive mental health services from primary care physicians, hospitals, and emergency rooms than from community mental health service providers (Snowden, 2003).

These well-known disparities in treatment for African Americans have been noted in the literature. Barriers to equal treatment have been identified and include systemic barriers, such as lack of health care insurance, lack of access to treatment programs, poorer quality of treatment leading to early termination, and racism and discrimination on the part of individuals and institutions (Snowden, 2003). In addition, barriers to treatment that arise from cultural issues have also been noted. These include stigma, mistrust of traditional mental health care treatment, different cultural ideas of health and illness, and differences in help-seeking behaviors, language, and communication patterns (U.S. Department of Health and Human Services [U.S. DHHS], 2001). Combined, external and internal barriers have contributed to a fairly dismal picture for African Americans who do not receive adequate mental health services, such as long-term disability, homelessness, and incarceration.

Finally, inequitable access to mental health treatment for African Americans needs to be considered within the context of need for treatment. As psychosocial stressors increase, individuals who are vulnerable typically experience heightened distress and a subsequent increase in mental health symptoms, such as anxiety or depression. Psychosocial stressors that influence mental health include an array of environmental, social, and physical factors such as poverty, health, and discrimination. As a group, African Americans are relatively poor (U.S. Census Bureau, 2001), experience a much higher incidence of chronic illness and disease (U.S. DHHS, 2001), and continue to be exposed to implicit and explicit racism and discrimination (Clark, Anderson, Clark, & Williams, 1999). However, despite the fact that African Americans experience increased exposure to psychosocial stressors that contribute to mental health disorders, studies indicate that African Americans show the same prevalence of mental health disorders and illnesses as Whites. This suggests, of course, that cultural characteristics of the population, including family and community bonds, informal sources of social support, and individual resilience and coping, may play important roles in mitigating stressors (U.S. DHHS, 2001). However, the consequences of untreated emotional problems for those who experience them underscore the need to explore changes in mental health policy and practices.

The remainder of this chapter describes some of the external (systemic) and internal (social and personal) barriers to mental health treatment for African Americans. We also provide recommendations from the literature for addressing these barriers.

External Barriers

The issue of bias in mental health services and service delivery has been the study of a recent Surgeon General's report titled *Mental Health: Culture, Race and Ethnicity* (U.S. DHHS, 2001). The report cited disparities in treatment of African Americans, Hispanics, and Asian Americans. Snowden (2003) reviewed some of the evidence regarding service and treatment disparities and hypothesized that systemic, cultural, and personal biases might explain them. As mentioned earlier, disparities in mental health services can be loosely clustered into two major categories: barriers due to external or systemic factors and barriers that result from internal or psychosocial factors. In this section, we discuss external barriers, which most frequently include evidence of disparities in utilization of services, in availability and accessibility of services, and in treatment implementation and outcomes.

Utilization of Services

Mental health service utilization is frequently cited as evidence of external (availability) as well as internal (stigma) barriers to mental health services. Studies have generally shown that African Americans, as well as other ethnic minorities in the United States, who need mental health services are less likely to receive them than are Whites (U.S. DHHS, 2001). Data from the National Comorbidity Survey conducted in 1994 found that only 16% of African Americans with mood disorders saw a mental health specialist, and less than one third consulted a health care provider of any kind (Kessler et al., 1996).

African Americans also disproportionately utilize public mental health programs and are more likely to get services from emergency rooms and general health care settings rather than specialized ones (Theriot, Segal, & Cowsert, 2003). These services are generally considered limited and less desirable than more specialized settings (Cooper-Patrick et al., 1999; Hu et al., 1991). Studies have also shown that the percentage of African Americans receiving mental health treatment from any source was only half the rate of Whites, even after eliminating the impact of socioeconomic differences (Swartz et al., 1998), suggesting that attitudinal and other barriers might be influencing utilization rates (Snowden, 2003).

Besides using fewer, if any, mental health services than do White Americans, African Americans appear to choose different health care providers. Snowden and Pingatore (2002) asked U.S. physicians about their patients and found that African Americans with mental health concerns were considerably more likely to seek help from their primary care physician than from a mental health professional, whereas Whites were only slightly more likely to see their primary care physician than a mental health professional. However, studies have also indicated that African Americans are more likely to seek help for mental health disorders than they have in the past (Cooper-Patrick et al., 1999).

One of the most noticeable differences between African Americans and White Americans is their use of inpatient psychiatric care. African Americans are more likely than Whites to be hospitalized in specialized psychiatric hospitals (Snowden & Cheung, 1990). Leginski, Manderscheid, and Henderson (1990) examined the discharge rates from state mental hospitals and found that African Americans were more likely than others to be hospitalized again during the same year.

The disparities also have been noted among African American children and White American children who receive treatment. Cunningham and Freiman (1996) found that African American children were less likely than White children to have made a mental health outpatient visit. Zahner and Daskalakis (1997) examined mental health care by specialists such as physicians and nurses and found that African American children were less likely than Whites to receive treatment and that African American children's underrepresentation varied no matter which source of treatment was used.

Availability and Accessibility of Mental Health Services

According to U.S. DHHS (2001), the availability of mental health services for ethnic minority populations depends on where one lives, the supply of African American clinicians, and the "mental health safety net." Lewin and Altman (2000) characterized the mental health safety net as comprising public hospitals, community mental health centers, and local health departments. Although all of these remain important sources of mental health care for African Americans, recent reports indicate these services are becoming increasingly unavailable in the community as states struggle to fund mental health service programs (Mowbray et al., 2002). Within public mental health programs, there are some that specialize in treatment of African American clients (Blank, Tetrick, Brinkley, Smith, & Doheny, 1994; Cornelius, Simpson, Ting, Wiggins, & Lipford, 2003), a service configuration that has been associated with better treatment outcomes in terms of treatment duration, compliance, and effectiveness (Constantine, 2002).

Although findings indicate that ethnic matching improves mental health treatment outcomes, a significant barrier to the availability of such services is the relative lack of clinically trained African American mental health professionals. A recent national survey of clinicians found that only 2% of psychologists and psychiatrists and 4% of clinical social workers (Holzer, Goldsmith, & Ciarlo, 1998) in practice are African Americans. This is juxtaposed against the finding that African American health care providers are more likely to treat African American patients and that patients report more satisfaction with care under these circumstances (Cooper-Patrick et al., 1999).

The availability of mental health services also depends on where one lives (U.S. DHHS, 2001). Although a relatively high proportion of African Americans live in the rural South, research shows that mental health professionals tend to be concentrated in urban areas (Holzer et al., 1998), thus limiting treatment options and availability. Furthermore, mental health practitioners in urban areas are more likely to be private providers, whereas the majority of African Americans seeking mental health services use publicly funded or Medicaid-reimbursed services (U.S. DHHS, 2001) as nearly one fourth of African Americans have no private insurance at all, a rate that is 1.5 times greater than it is for Whites.

While insurance coverage is one the most important factors for deciding to seek treatment, insurance alone fails to eliminate the disparities in access between African Americans and Whites. Padgett, Struening, Andrews, and Pittman (1995) concluded that provision of insurance benefits with more generous mental health coverage does not increase treatment seeking among African Americans when other barriers, such as mistrust and cultural disparities, still tend to limit access to culturally appropriate treatment.

Differential Treatment Quality and Outcomes

Disparities in treatment quality have been cited as a major barrier to effective mental health service delivery for African Americans. A number of studies have reported, for example, that African Americans are much less likely than Whites to receive "guideline-adherent" treatment protocols for depression and anxiety (Young, Klap, Sherbourne, & Wells, 2001). The evidence of the efficacy of guideline-adherent treatment protocols for African Americans is also lacking, owing to small sample sizes and other methodological problems (U.S. DHHS, 2001).

African Americans with serious mental health disorders are less likely than Whites to receive minimally adequate treatment, including appropriate medication and psychosocial care (Wang, Demler, & Kessler, 2002). Moreover, when African Americans with serious mental health disorders do receive psychotropic medication, they are more likely to receive older, less effective ones (Kuno & Rothbard, 1997).

Treatment quality has also been a concern for older African American clients. Schneider, Zaslavsky, and Epstein (2002) discovered that African Americans enrolled in Medicare were less likely to obtain treatment follow-ups within 30 days as compared with Whites. Also, older African Americans are less likely to receive antidepressant medication (Blazer, Hybels, Simonsick, & Hanlon, 2000). Other studies have shown that African Americans are less likely to receive newer psychotropic medications (Kuno & Rothbard, 1997) and that when medications are prescribed, they have received inappropriately high dosages (Chung, Mahler, & Kakuma, 1995).

Finally, there have been disparities in mental health diagnosis of African Americans. For example, African Americans tend to have higher than expected rates of schizophrenia and lower rates of bipolar disorder, suggesting clinical misperceptions of presenting symptoms (Trierweiler et al., 2000). Lopez (1989) identified what he called two forms of diagnostic bias for African Americans and other ethnic minorities: overpathologizing and minimization. Obviously, problems exist in either domain, with clinicians misinterpreting cultural beliefs as pathology or attributing behaviors and symptoms of mental health disorders to cultural or social practices or stereotypes.

Internal Barriers

In addition to the external barriers identified above, internal or psychosocial barriers also impede access to mental health services. Of course, the conceptual distinctions between internal and external barriers are not that discrete, and there is a reciprocal interaction between them. However, this section highlights three internal barriers: stigma, mistrust, and cultural disparities.

Stigma

In 1999, the U.S. Surgeon General released a report on the status of mental health care in the United States and identified stigma as a key barrier to adequate treatment as well as life opportunities for individuals diagnosed with the most serious mental health disorders (U.S. DHHS, 1999). Stigma also affects reaction to and treatment for other mental health disorders, because it affects the attitudes and beliefs of the individual who is seeking help, family and community members, and the treatment environment. Studies have found that stigma toward mental health disorders disproportionately affects African Americans and subsequently influences help-seeking behaviors (Cooper-Patrick et al., 1997; Sussman, Robins, & Earls, 1987). For example, African Americans have higher rates of civil commitment and are much more likely to be brought to hospital emergency rooms by police (Takeuchi, Sue, & Yeh, 1995). Studies have also found that African Americans living in community group homes are viewed more suspiciously by neighbors and tend to be questioned more frequently by police (Garland, Ellis-MacLeod, Landsverk, Gasnger, & Johnson, 1998). Corrigan et al. (2003) surveyed perceptions of discrimination among adults with serious mental illnesses and found evidence that African Americans perceived more stigmas and experienced heightened discrimination, particularly in employment, housing, and health care.

Stigma also influences individuals' attitudes and behavior regarding seeking mental health services. For example, the fact that African Americans and other minorities are more likely to seek mental health services from general health care practitioners than specialized clinicians may be reflecting individual or cultural beliefs regarding mental health care treatment. Studies have shown that African Americans are more likely to seek help from informal support sources, such as churches (Neighbors, Musick, & Williams, 1998) and self-help groups (Theriot et al., 2003), findings that provide support for offering more diverse community mental health care settings (Cornelius et al., 2003).

Mistrust

Trust is a measure of willingness to seek mental health services, to remain in treatment, and to be able to develop a therapeutic relationship with a counselor or clinician. In each of these areas, there is evidence that lack of trust may influence help-seeking behavior of African Americans.

For example, studies have shown that African Americans are more likely to seek help from informal community sources, such as churches, extended family members, and self-help groups, than formal mental health services (Neighbors et al., 1998; Theriot et al., 2003), which may be a reflection of mistrust or lack of faith in the effectiveness of mental health services. The National Comordibity Study (Kessler et al., 1996) indicated that African Americans had more favorable attitudes toward mental health services before receiving treatment than after. The latter finding suggests that lack of trust in mental health providers and counselors and an inability to establish a therapeutic alliance are major barriers to treatment duration and effectiveness.

Studies of ethnic specificity or ethnic matching between mental health services and clients have suggested that the more similar the two are, the more likely is treatment compliance, including duration and follow-up services (Blank et al., 1994). However, adequate numbers of African American mental health professionals are not available to treat clients who need services, indicating that intensified efforts to overcome cultural disparities and mistrust need to be practiced to encourage service utilization and duration (Cornelius et al., 2003). Moreover, studies have indicated that ethnic-specific mental health services tend to be more effective in overcoming treatment obstacles such as engagement and duration (Blank et al., 1994). These findings again support the need to enlarge traditional mental health services practice to include informal community sources and culturally specific programs.

Cultural Disparities

Issues and concerns that arise from the internal barriers of stigma and trust also influence how African Americans seek and evaluate the mental health services they receive. As several studies have noted, community services, as well as physicians, clergy, and extended families, may be important sources of emotional support for ethnic minorities, including African Americans (Brown, 1984; Neighbors & Jackson, 1984). Studies have also considered that reluctance to using and especially remaining in traditional mental health service systems may be attributable to perceived cultural disparities between professionals and consumers seeking service. And, in fact, mental health programs that are culturally responsive or ethnically matched show more positive patterns of service use and treatment quality than do traditional programs (Akutsu, Snowden, & Organista, 1996; Mathews, Glidden, Murray, Forster, & Hargreaves, 2002). There is also some evidence that African Americans are more frequent users of self-help programs than are Whites (Theriot et al., 2003). This pattern may reflect a preference for using social network supports rather than more traditional mental health services programs, as the former tend to better match the ethnicity of the service user (Goldberg, Rollins, & Lehman, 2003). This preference could also reflect a bias of ethnic minorities to receiving mental health services within their own communities, a preference that has implications for the role that public schools can play in supporting community mental health treatment for children and families.

Finally, as the President's New Freedom Commission on Mental Health (2003) stated, cultural issues affect not only those who seek help but also those who provide services. It follows then that service providers may perceive mental disorders, diagnosis, and interventions in ways that are different for each service provider, as well as different from the cultures of those to whom they are providing these services. Because racial and ethnic minorities are underrepresented in the core mental health disciplines, the ongoing need to train and support the cultural competency of those who deliver community mental health services was underscored in this report, as well as a number of other studies (Constantine, 2002; Ramiriz, Wassef, Paniagua, & Linskey, 1996).

Integration and Recommendations for Practice

It is clear that African Americans experience enormous disparities in mental health services in the United States, the result of systemic and organizational factors as well as psychosocial and cultural ones. As a result of the increased attention to these disparities and the barriers that enable them, there have been many recommendations regarding mental health policy and practice to address barriers. The following are several recommendations that flow from our discussion of barriers to treatment:

1. Publicly funded safety net provisions, particularly those funded through state behavioral managed care plans, need to incorporate the views and recommendations of diverse citizens in organizing and implementing services, particularly African Americans and other ethnic minorities who experience disparities in access and availability. Mowbray et al. (2002) suggested that the most successful state public mental health plans resulted from input and ongoing monitoring by constituents, family members, and consumers of services.

2. Efforts to bolster informal community supports, in which African Americans tend to seek services, can be a cost-effective way to reduce the disparities in service utilization. These efforts can occur on a macro level (e.g., with state mental health authorities reaching out to church and community groups to offer training and support) and a micro level (e.g., within local communities and schools). Schools are a potentially important vehicle for community outreach and dissemination, as school personnel may frequently be in the first line of contact regarding identifying individual and family stress and need for mental health services.

3. State and federal authorities can also heighten awareness on the part of primary and general health care practitioners regarding treatment obstacles and resources for African Americans. This is important as general health care providers may be more frequently sought out for mental health problems. Such educational efforts can include mounting educational programs at health care conferences and in journals, encouraging public health care facilities to incorporate proactive follow-up with patients who report mental health problems, and more intense monitoring of public health care patients within these settings.

4. Federal and state authorities can encourage the development of innovative mental health interventions that are more responsive to the preferences and needs of African Americans. Innovative programs that appear to be effective include 24-hour crisis intervention services within African American communities, self-help and mentor programs, and intensive case management and family services (Cornelius et al., 2003; Snowden & Pingatore, 2002).

5. Counselors and clinicians on an individual basis can incorporate practices that are more culturally responsive to African Americans. These may include using more outreach services (e.g., meeting with clients in community settings rather than mental health offices), using community and church groups as opportunities to educate members about mental health service availability, and constantly improving their multicultural awareness and competence in service delivery.

Summary

The increased national attention to the mental health needs of African Americans and other ethnic minorities presents an opportunity for change at the national, state, and local levels. At this point, more and more is known regarding treatment utilization, accessibility, and efficacy for African Americans in community mental health, but much remains to be understood. Although service innovations in public mental health have been recommended, the need to implement new practices and to evaluate their effectiveness in reducing external and internal barriers to treatment remains a critical area of investigation. During these times of increasing fiscal restraint, the focus of attention can be on finding more responsive and creative means of using existing public mental health dollars to proactively support, and to treat, the mental health needs of African Americans.

References

Akutsu, P. D., Snowden, L. R., & Organista, K. C. (1996). Referral patterns in ethnic-specific and mainstream programs for ethnic minorities and Whites. *Journal of Counseling Psychology, 43,* 56–64.

Blank, M. B., Tetrick, F. L., Brinkley, D. F., Smith, H. O., & Doheny, V. (1994). Racial matching and service utilization among seriously mentally ill consumers in the rural South. *Community Mental Health Journal, 30,* 271–281.

Blazer, D. G., Hybels, C. F., Simonsick, E. M., & Hanlon, J. T. (2000). Marked differences in antidepressant use by race in an elderly community sample: 1986–1996. *American Journal of Psychiatry, 157,* 1089–1094.

Brown, C. L. (1984). Race difference in professional help seeking. *American Journal of Community Psychiatry, 15,* 173–189.

Chung, H., Mahler, J. C., & Kakuma, T. (1995). Racial differences in treatment of psychiatric clients. *Psychiatric Services, 46,* 586–591.

Clark, R., Anderson, N. B., Clark, V. R., & Williams, D. R. (1999). Racism as a stressor for African Americans. *American Psychologist, 54,* 805–816.

Community Mental Health Centers Construction Act of 1963, 42 U.S.C.A. § 2261 *et seq.*

Constantine, M. G. (2002). Predictors of satisfaction with counseling: Racial and ethnic minority clients' attitudes toward counseling and ratings of their counselors' general and multicultural counseling competence. *Journal of Counseling Psychology, 49,* 255–263.

Cooper-Patrick, L., Gallo, J. J., Power, N. R., Steinwachs, D., Eaton, W. W., & Ford, D. E. (1999). Mental health service utilization by African Americans and Whites: The Baltimore Epidemiological Catchment Area follow-up. *Medical Care, 37,* 1037–1045.

Cooper-Patrick, L., Power, N. R., Jenckes, M. W., Gonzales, J., Levine, D. M., & Ford, D. E. (1997). Identification of patient attitudes and preferences regarding treatment for depression. *Journal of General Internal Medicine, 12,* 431–438.

Cornelius, L. J., Simpson, G. M., Ting, L., Wiggins, E., & Lipford, S. (2003). Reach out and I'll be there: Mental health crisis intervention and mobile outreach services to urban African Americans. *Health & Social Work, 28,* 74–78.

Corrigan, P., Thompson, V., Lambert, D., Sangster, Y., Noel, J. G., & Campbell, J. (2003). Perceptions of discrimination among persons with serious mental illness. *Psychiatric Services, 54,* 1105–1110.

Cunningham, P. J., & Freiman, M. P. (1996). Determinants of ambulatory mental health service use for school-age children and adolescents. *Mental Health Services Research, 31,* 409–427.

Dana, R. H. (1998). Problems with managed mental health care for multicultural populations. *Psychological Reports, 82,* 283–294.

Doll, W. (1976). Family coping with the mentally ill: An unanticipated problem of deinstitutionalization. *Hospital & Community Psychiatry, 27,* 183–185.

Garland, A., Ellis-MacLeod, W., Landsverk, J., Gasnger, W., & Johnson, I. (1998). Minority populations in the child welfare system: The visibility hypothesis reexamined. *American Journal of Orthopsychiatry, 68,* 142–146.

Goldberg, R. W., Rollins, A. L., & Lehman, A. F. (2003). Social network correlates among people with psychiatric disabilities. *Journal of Psychiatric Rehabilitation, 26,* 393–402.

Holzer, C. E., Goldsmith, H. F., & Ciarlo, J. A. (1998). Effects of rural–urban county type on the availability of health and mental health care providers. In R. W. Manderscheid & M. J. Henderson (Eds.), *Mental health, United States* (pp. 204–213). Rockville, MD: Center for Mental Health Services.

Hu, T. W., Snowden, L. R., Jerrell, J. M., & Nguyen, T. D. (1991). Ethnic populations in public mental health: Services choice and level of use. *American Journal of Public Health, 81,* 1429–1434.

Kessler, R. C., Berglund, P. A., Zhao, S., Leaf, P. J., Kouzis, A. C., Bruce, M. L., et al. (1996). The 12-month prevalence and correlates of serious mental illness. In R. W. Manderscheid & M. A. Sonnenschein (Eds.), *Mental health, United States* (pp. 59–70). Rockville, MD: Center for Mental Health Services.

Kuno, E., & Rothbard, A. B. (1997). Racial disparities in antipsychotic prescription patterns for patients with schizophrenia. *American Journal of Psychiatry, 159,* 567–572.

Lamb, H. R., & Weinberger, L. E. (1998). Persons with severe mental illness in jails and prisons: A review. *Psychiatric Services, 49,* 482–492.

Leginski, W. A., Manderscheid, R. W., & Henderson, P. R. (1990). Clients served in state mental hospitals: Results from a longitudinal database. In R. W. Manderscheid & M. A. Sonnenhein (Eds.), *Mental health, United States* (pp. 102–114). Rockville, MD: Center for Mental Health Services.

Lewin, M. A., & Altman, S. (Eds.). (2000). *America's health care safety net: Intact but endangered.* Washington, DC: National Academy Press.

Lindbloom, E. N. (1991). *The 1990 annual report of the Interagency Council on the Homeless.* Washington, DC: U.S. Interagency Council on the Homeless.

Lopez, S. (1989). Patient variable biases in clinical judgment: Conceptual overview and methodological considerations. *Psychological Bulletin, 106,* 184–203.

Mathews, C. A., Glidden, D., Murray, S., Forster, P., & Hargreaves, W. A. (2002). The effect on treatment outcomes of assigning patients to ethnically focused inpatient psychiatric units. *Psychiatric Services, 53,* 830–835.

Melfi, C., Croghan, T., Hanna, M., & Robinson, R. (2000). Racial variation in antidepressant treatment in a Medicaid population. *Journal of Clinical Psychiatry, 61,* 16–21.

Mowbray, C. T., Grazier, K. L., & Holter, M. (2002). Managed behavioral health care in the public sector: Will it become the third shame of the states? *Psychiatric Services, 53,* 157–170.

Mueser, K. T., Drake, R. E., & Bond, G. R. (1997). Recent advances in psychiatric rehabilitation for patients with severe mental illness. *Harvard Review of Psychiatry, 5,* 123–137.

National Mental Health Association. (1999, May). *Best (and worst) practices in private sector managed mental healthcare: Part I. Level-of-care criteria.* Alexandria, VA: Author.

Neighbors, H. W., & Jackson, J. S. (1984). The use of informal and formal help: Four patterns of illness behavior in the Black community. *American Journal of Community Psychiatry, 12,* 629–645.

Neighbors, H. W., Musick, M. A., & Williams, D. R. (1998). The African American minister as a source of help for serious personal crises: Bridge or barrier to mental health care. *Health Education and Behavior, 25,* 759–777.

Padgett, D., Struening, E. L., Andrews, H., & Pittman, J. (1995). Predictors of emergency room use by homeless adults in New York City: The predisposing, enabling and need factors. *Social Science & Medicine, 41,* 547–556.

President's New Freedom Commission on Mental Health. (2003). Retrieved September 25, 2003, from http://www.mentalhealthcommission.gov/reports/FinalReport/toc/html

Ramiriz, S. Z., Wassef, A., Paniagua, F. A., & Linskey, A. O. (1996). Mental health providers' perceptions of cultural variables in evaluating ethnically diverse clients. *Professional Psychology: Research and Practice, 27,* 284–288.

Schneider, E. C., Zaslavsky, A. M., & Epstein, A. M. (2002). Racial disparities in quality of care for enrollees in Medicare managed care. *Journal of the American Medical Association, 287,* 1288–1294.

Snowden, L. R. (2003). Bias in mental health assessment and intervention: Theory and evidence. *American Journal of Public Health, 93,* 239–243.

Snowden, L. R., & Cheung, F. K. (1990). Use of inpatient mental health services by members of ethnic minority groups. *American Psychologist, 45,* 347–355.

Snowden, L. R., & Pingatore, D. (2002). Frequency and scope of mental health service delivery to African Americans in primary care. *Mental Health Services Research, 3,* 123–130.

Sussman, L. K., Robins, L. N., & Earls, R. (1987). Treatment-seeking for depression by Black and White Americans. *Social Science and Medicine, 24,* 187–196.

Swartz, M. S., Wagner, H. R., Swanson, J. W., Burns, B. J., George, L. K., & Padgett, D. K. (1998). Comparing use of public and private mental health services: The enduring barriers of race and age. *Community Mental Health Journal, 34,* 133–144.

Takeuchi, D. T., Sue, S., & Yeh, M. (1995). Return rates and outcomes from ethnicity-specific mental health programs in Los Angeles. *American Journal of Public Health, 85,* 638–643.

Theriot, M. T., Segal, S. P., & Cowsert, M. J. (2003). African-Americans and comprehensive service use. *Community Mental Health Journal, 39,* 225–237.

Torrey, E. F. (1992). *Criminalizing the seriously mentally ill: The abuse of jails as mental hospitals—A joint report.* Arlington, VA: National Alliance for the Mentally Ill, and Washington, DC: Public Citizen Health Research Group.

Torrey, E. F. (1997). *Out of the shadows: Confronting America's mental illness crisis.* New York: Wiley.

Trierweiler, S. J., Neighbors, H. W., Minday, C., Thompson, S., Binion, V. J., & Gomez, J. P. (2000). Clinician attribution associated with diagnosis of schizophrenia in African American and non-African American patients. *Journal of Consulting and Clinical Psychology, 68,* 171–175.

U.S. Census Bureau. (2001). *Population by race and Hispanic or Latino origin for the United States: 2000* (PHC-T-6). Retrieved July 2, 2002, from http://www.cnsusn.gov/population.www/cen2000

U.S. Department of Health and Human Services. (1999). *Mental health: A report of the Surgeon General.* Washington, DC: Author.

U.S. Department of Health and Human Services. (2001). *Mental health: Culture, race and ethnicity* (A supplement to *Mental Health: A Report of the Surgeon General*). Rockville, MD: Author.

Wang, P. S., Demler, O., & Kessler, R. C. (2002). Adequacy of treatment for serious mental illness in the United States. *American Journal of Public Health, 92,* 92–98.

Young, A. S., Klap, R., Sherbourne, C. D., & Wells, K. B. (2001). The quality of care for depressive and anxiety disorders in the United States. *Archives of General Psychiatry, 52,* 472–478.

Zahner, G. E. P., & Daskalakis, C. (1997). Factors associated with mental health, general health and school-based service use for child psychopathology. *American Journal of Public Health, 87,* 1440–1448.

17

Selective Interventions in Counseling African Americans With Disabilities

Elias Mpofu

There is evidence to suggest that the helping professions underserve African Americans significantly more than White Americans. Specifically, African Americans utilize the formal helping services less often (Belgrave, 1998; Smith, 2001; Sue & Sue, 2003), have a higher dropout rate from such services (Joseph, 1995), and are less likely to achieve the goals for which they sought consultation (Olney & Kennedy, 2002; Wilson, Turner, Liu, Harley, & Alston, 2002). This is in spite of the fact that the prevalence of chronic illness and disability is higher among African Americans than in the general population (Chumbler, Hartmann, Cody, & Beck, 2001; Smart & Smart, 1997b; U.S. Census Bureau, 2003). The racial disparity against African Americans in the public rehabilitation service system is a case in point. A majority of the studies have documented that African Americans are less well served by the vocational rehabilitation services (Capella, 2002; Moore, 2001, 2002; Rehabilitation Act Amendments, 1992; Wilson, 2002; Wilson, Alston, Harley, & Mitchell, 2002). For example, they are less likely to be successfully rehabilitated (Capella, 2002; Moore, Feist-Price, & Alston, 2002), receive more unwanted services (Wilson, Alston, et al., 2002), and earn lower incomes following vocational rehabilitation services than do White Americans (Moore, 2002; Olney & Kennedy, 2002). Racial disparities in rehabilitation services and potential adverse impact on subgroups of clients can be prevented by a judicious application of counseling interventions that are sensitive to the unique needs of the specific group of clients.

This chapter applies concepts from prevention science that could help rehabilitation counselors to enhance their success with African American clients. Specifically, it briefly outlines some current prevention intervention concepts and their relevance to counseling populations of African American clients with disabilities. The outline on prevention intervention is followed by a discussion on the identities of African Americans and the sociocultural–historical factors that influence their participation in counseling services. Finally, rehabilitation counselor and client service qualities that influence rehabilitation success with African American clients are discussed from a prevention perspective.

Prevention Interventions for Human Health and Service Programs

Prevention, as an intervention, has become an interdisciplinary science (Nation et al., 2003). It has evidence-based efficacy in promoting health in populations at risk for substance abuse, conduct disorder, HIV/AIDS, and other debilitating conditions. Within the health sciences, prevention has historically been associated with interventions for reducing the occurrence of new cases of a health condition in a population (primary prevention), decreasing the prevalence of an existing health condition through early intervention or treatment (secondary prevention), or reducing the severity of the impact of a health condition through rehabilitation (tertiary prevention). This conceptualization of prevention has roots in epidemiology, a specialization on the study of the distribution and correlates of health conditions in populations for the purposes of controlling health problems (Schoenbach, 2003). This chapter argues for the application of prevention science to conceptualize strategies for lowering the incidence, prevalence, and severity of rehabilitation service system failures with African American clients.

Conventional prevention sciences terminology for population-level interventions distinguishes among selective, universal, and indicated interventions (Lochman & van den Steenhoven, 2002; Webster-Stratton & Taylor, 2001). From a prevention perspective, *selective* interventions target groups at risk or subsets of the general population. Selective interventions can be differentiated from universal and indicated interventions. *Universal* interventions are designed for the general population; an example of a universal intervention is the enactment and implementation of legislation for increasing rehabilitation service accessibility to people with disabilities. Selective interventions are presumed to have an impact beyond that which is possible with universal interventions because they achieve their effect by treating the specific vulnerabilities of subgroups within a general population. A community-outreach program for African Americans with disabilities on accessing services that are legislated would qualify for a selective intervention. *Indicated* interventions are designed for people already with evidence of adverse health impact. They are of a remedial nature and seek to reserve or ameliorate existing compromise in health or service status. An example of an indicated intervention is following up unsuccessfully rehabilitated clients with a view to ameliorating or correcting any adverse impact from the failure to rehabilitate.

A target population can be defined at various levels, depending on its complexity or the multiple ways in which a population can be segmented (e.g., African Americans, rural and southern African Americans, etc.; see below). A selective intervention can be universally applied within a population (e.g., with African Americans in general) if the determinants of a health condition within that population are similar. And an intervention that is indicated at the subpopulation level can be selectively applied within a population, depending on the criteria that are used for within-population segmentation.

The application of a prevention intervention for enhancing rehabilitation success with a specified subgroup (e.g., African Americans) presumes a reliable health-condition-specific segmentation (e.g., rural African Americans, African Americans with disabilities). Sensitivity to this within-group segmentation is important to health interventions because the various strata of a complex population have health needs that can be best met by an appropriately targeted intervention.

A number of implications follow from adopting a prevention science approach to counseling members of a specified population (e.g., African Americans). First, designing and articulating counseling interventions to the unique needs of a collective (e.g., race, disability) is good science and not necessarily motivated by group preferences. Second, due to the complexity in the structure of most human populations, considerations about how to counsel members of a selective group (e.g., White Americans, African Americans, Asian Americans) run the risk of distortions from perceiving the group as more homogeneous than it actually is. This is because there are likely to be large within-group differences on clinically significant variables so that the overgeneralizations about a group and its service needs may have the unfortunate effect of perpetuating myths and stereotypes that could narrow the perspectives of practitioners (Cacas, 1995; Mpofu, Beck, & Weinrach, 2004; Weinrach & Thomas, 2002). Third, some interventions are effective across populations (i.e., universal), whereas others could be designed for particular populations or subpopulations (i.e., selective, indicated). Specifically, the level at which a group is defined (e.g., African American) will determine the accuracy with which an intervention can be mapped to a health need within that population. The more general or inclusive the level of the population, the more likely that a universal rather than a selective intervention would be more effective with that population (although a selective intervention could be applied universally within a population). Fourth, although sociohistorical and political factors (e.g., history of segregation or oppression, increase in racial minority population in the United States, migration patterns) preset the context for between- and within-group differences in health-related statuses, they do not in themselves justify differential approaches to health service provision. Ideally, the distribution and determination of health statuses between and within populations should primarily determine the appropriate interventions. However, in societies with a history of racial segregation and oppression, health statuses may covary more highly within rather than between socioracial groups (Belgrave, 1998; Vontress & Epp, 1997) so that consideration of approaches to health services with a designated socioracial group (e.g., African American) is of scientific rather than moral/philosophical interest.

African Americans: Their Identity, Cultural Heritage, and Perceived Context for Counseling

African Americans have multilayered identities from their diverse cultural heritages (Helms & Cook, 1999; Parham, 2002). This rich mix of identities makes for a wide range of both their needs for and responses to counseling services. African Americans are also similar in that they share a long history of being excluded from services available to the general population and of being devalued as individuals or cultural entities (Harley, Jolivette, McCormick, & Tice, 2002; Sue, 2003). These negative experiences precondition their perceptions and experiences of counseling (Smith, 2001; Vontress & Epp, 1997). This section considers the multilayered identities and heritages of African Americans, as well as their perceptions and experiences of counseling, with a view to identifying key issues for selective interventions with African Americans.

Multilayered Identities and Cultural Heritage

African Americans are best regarded as a heterogeneous group of people. They largely comprise descendents of involuntary immigrants to the United States from Africa during the era of slavery and voluntary immigrants from Africa, the Caribbean, Latin America, and Europe who are citizens of the United States by birth or naturalization. There is great variability within the African American community in terms of their identity with original African cultural heritage, whereas that heritage of origin continues to evolve under its own impetus and in interaction with other cultures.

Nonetheless, there seems to be a case for a generic Africa-centric worldview that is different from other cultural heritages and for which behavioral representations are apparent in a majority of African Americans (Cook & Wiley, 2000; Parham, 2002). For example, people of an African cultural heritage have been described as subscribing to an interconnectionist or holistic worldview in which (a) there is a divinely ordained coherence in the workings of humans, the elements, and the universe; (b) events have multilayered causation (physical, metaphysical, and spiritual); (c) the collective and its experiences are treasured lessons for present generations and posterity; (d) humans are essentially spiritual rather than physical; (e) cognition, emotion, conation, and spirit work in synergy in the healthy individual; (f) humans have the capacity to transcend adversity or turn adversity into opportunity; and (g) spirit is the energy that drives human functioning and makes possible insight and intuition.

African Americans also vary widely among themselves in terms of individual statuses in the development of racial identity. Racial identity refers to consciousness of, and affinity with, the cultural heritage of a phenotypic membership (e.g., Black, White). Cross and others (e.g., Cross, 1971, 1990; Helms, 1984) described a series of statuses in individual racial development, with people at the preencounter status at a lower level of racial identity development and those at the internalization–commitment status at the highest level of racial identity development. People at the preencounter status may identify primarily with a dominant cultural heritage of a phenotype different from their own while being unaware of or depreciating their own heritage. Those at the internalization–commitment status have an appreciation of both their own and a dominant cultural heritage. People at the immersion–emersion (or transition status) may overidentify with the cultural heritage of their phenotype while overlooking the enabling characteristics of a dominant culture. Individuals may enact an identity appropriate to their life circumstances or stage of human development (Helms & Cook, 1999). Thus, there is variation in racial identity development within an individual, and some people may not attain the internalization–commitment status of racial identity.

African Americans participate in the broader American culture, which comprises a dominant White cultural heritage and several other cultures. To be better able to function within the White dominant culture, African Americans acculturate as well as contribute to the dominant culture (Sue, 2003). Acculturation is the adoption of cultural elements from the dominant culture. Some African Americans are competent in their own and the dominant culture, a phenomenon called *biculturalism* (LaFromboise, Coleman, & Gerton, 1993). The variability among African Americans with regard to acculturation to the dominant culture and biculturalism adds to the complexity of counseling members of that population.

African Americans with disabilities are an even more heterogeneous group than the general population of African Americans. For example, African Americans with disabilities may identify with the cultural constituency of people with disabilities in addition to having multilayered identities from their specific disability or disabilities, gender, status of racial identity development, acculturation, biculturalism, and other sociocultural participation (socioeconomic status [SES] and education). Regardless of their within-group variability, African Americans with disabilities are at an elevated risk for experiencing discrimination (Adams, 2001; Michilin & Juarez-Marazzo, 2001), and particularly from having a disability and being Black at the same time.

Perceptions and Experiences of Counseling Services

Consultation behavior appears to differ between African Americans and White Americans, and in ways that may explain in part the underutilization of the formal counseling services by African Americans. For instance, a majority of African Americans utilize the nonformal rather than the formal counseling services, such as those offered by the family, church, community leaders, personal experts, and significant others (Cook & Wiley, 2000; Parham, 2002). This service preference pattern is truer of those with lower SES or with lower formal education (Akutsu, Snowden, & Organista, 1996). African Americans from the higher socioeconomic classes tend to use the formal counseling services more than those from the lower socioeconomic classes, although they also use nonformal counseling extensively. The nonformal counseling services may be preferred by African Americans because they are

perceived to be more trustworthy and credible (Belgrave & Jarama, 2000). This perception may be because help-givers in the nonformal counseling services are presumed by
clients to share a basic worldview with them and to have a strong interpersonal orientation.
Worldview refers to beliefs about the self, others, and the world; it also includes values and
the behavioral predispositions that give expression to one's beliefs and values (Sue, 2003).
The preference for nonformal counseling services over formal services by African Americans
is also true for Africans on mainland Africa and could be explained by a respect for the wisdom of the collective (Mpofu, 1994; Mpofu & Harley, 2002). The mistrust of the formal
counseling services by some African Americans could explain the lower rate at which they
access and succeed with counseling services (Helms & Cook, 1999; Vontress & Epp,
1997). If consulting formal counseling services, lower SES African Americans tend to be
referred more by family and other support systems within the nonformal helping sector
(e.g., church, healers, community leaders, personal experts) and welfare services more than
high-SES African Americans (Akutsu et al., 1996).

The major theories of counseling in which counselors are trained are of a Western intellectual heritage and largely inconsistent with the philosophical heritage of people of
African ancestry (Grills, 2002). This difference in cultural–philosophical heritage would
make it likely that counselors working with clients of an African American background
using theories from a Western cultural intellectual heritage could be perceived by their
clients as engaging in oversimplifications (Hays, 2001; Sue & Sue, 2003). For example, a
counselor who sought to explore client cognitions as possible sources of difficulties could
be perceived by the client to be in benign neglect of environmentally or institutionally
generated difficulties the client may be experiencing (e.g., racism). The fact that people of
African ancestry have a history of the experience of slavery and dehumanization solely on
the basis of skin color could lead African Americans to be distrustful of the institution of
formal counseling because of what it may be perceived to "stand for" (i.e., oppression;
Vontress & Epp, 1997). This difference in heritages has been presumed to contribute to
the reluctance by African Americans to access or use the formal rehabilitation services. For
example, while most of the major theories of counseling place a greater emphasis on the
individual's needs (rather than the environment or spirituality) as explaining maladjustment,
African philosophy regards the occurrences in the environment and the spirit world to
play a greater role (Mpofu & Harley, 2002).

Perceptions of African Americans by Counselors

Evidence-based studies on counselor perceptions of African American clients are scarce
(Redmond & Slaney, 2002; Thomas & Weinrach, 2002). However, the few that could be
identified suggest that race is a factor for both African American clients and counselors in
their interactions. For example, there is evidence to suggest that African Americans may receive inequitable treatment from counselors (e.g., Rosenthal & Berven, 1999) and that race
is salient to understanding the needs of African American clients (e.g., Fuertes, Mueller,
Chauhan, Walker, & Ladany, 2002). For instance, Rosenthal and Berven reported the results of a study with White American preservice rehabilitation counselors ($N = 99$) in which
the counselors had lower educational and vocational expectations for a rehabilitation client
who was described as African American than for the same client if White. The counselors
maintained the negative perceptions of the African American clients, even after additional
positive evidence was provided. This study suggested that counselors probably relied on
racially based stereotypes rather than objective evidence when considering vocational potential in rehabilitation clients. The fact that the empirical evidence for racial bias in
counselor expectations for rehabilitation success has come from an analogue study with col-

lege students rather than practicing rehabilitation professionals limits its generalizability to actual rehabilitation settings. Nonetheless, African Americans seeking help from the formal counseling services may be at a disadvantage in that their resources for counseling may be disregarded by counselors who may have predetermined, racially biased, and negative expectations for them.

African Americans experience racial prejudice on a regular basis and at personal, cultural, and institutional levels (Dunbar, 2001; Sue, 2003; Utsey, Ponterotto, Reynolds, & Cancelli, 2000). African Americans experience racial prejudice at a personal level in interactions with White Americans who devalue their personhood or individuality (e.g., when an African American is expected to explain the behavior of all Blacks). African Americans may also experience prejudice at a cultural level when their worldview is devalued (e.g., by a denial of African-centered ways of knowing). At the institutional level, African Americans may experience negative and differential treatment in accessing services for which they qualify (e.g., by lower referrals by health institutions for aggressive diagnostic investigation and treatment). The multilevel and sustained experience of racism by African Americans has been hypothesized to explain the high prevalence of physical and mental health disabilities in that population as compared with White Americans (Belgrave, 1998).

The study by Fuertes et al. (2002) provided empirical evidence that race was an overarching personal and contextual factor in African Americans' perceptions of their interactions in counseling. Fuertes et al. had nine White American counselors report on their recollection of success with rehabilitation clients of an African American background. The counselors were purposively selected for self-reported comfort and success with African American clients. The counselors, who rated themselves average to outstanding in multicultural counseling skills, reported that race was a major factor in establishing the therapeutic relationship and in treatment considerations. The therapists also reported greater success with their African American clients when they openly acknowledged racism as a factor in the clients' experienced difficulties.

The lack of external criteria (e.g., case reports, client satisfaction ratings, supervisor ratings, observational data) to collaborate the counselors' self-reports constrains the confidence with which the results of the study by Fuertes et al. (2002) can be held. However, there is growing consensus that African Americans may experience invalidation by counselors who minimize or deny their claims of racial discrimination and stereotyping (Helms & Cook, 1999; Sue, 2003). For instance, they may be coaxed by counselors to ascribe nonracist explanations for apparent acts of racism against them (Dunbar, 2001; Fuertes et al., 2002; Sue, 2003). This is in spite of the fact that African Americans are less likely than White Americans to ascribe racism to negative personal experiences (Redmond & Slaney, 2002; Ruggiero & Marx, 1999; Sue & Sue, 2003).

It should be apparent from both the diversity of the experiences and cultural heritages that African Americans bring to counseling that they would benefit from selective interventions, some of which could be universally applied across groupings of African Americans. Selective interventions in counseling African American clients that take into account rehabilitation service-related qualities in counselors and African American clients are considered in the next section.

Selective Rehabilitation Interventions With African American Clients

Rehabilitation success with African Americans with disabilities is likely to increase with greater attention by counselors to service-related qualities in both counselors and clients that affect rehabilitation participation (Thomas & Weinrach, 2002). Service-related qualities in African American clients that could hamper rehabilitation may emanate from (a) a lack of awareness of the nature of rehabilitation services, (b) a lower prior preparedness for rehabilitation services, (c) challenges from language use and communication in rehabilitation, and (d) experience of prejudice from service providers. Client service qualities in the counselor that could hinder success with African American clients may include (a) lack of competence in assessing one's own and the clients' worldviews as the basis for selective interventions with African American clients, (b) counselor prejudice, (c) poor communication, and (d) a failure to reach out to the client's level of rehabilitation service participation as previously outlined.

Service-related qualities in African American clients that affect rehabilitation success are discussed first, followed by those in the counselor. The discussion on counselor service-related qualities also considers those from the interface between the characteristics of the client, counselor, and context of service, as appropriate.

African American Clients' Service-Related Qualities

Lack of Awareness of the Nature or Availability of Rehabilitation Services

There is evidence for racial disparities in the sources of referral for African American and White American clients (Akutsu et al., 1996; Belgrave, 1998), with significant implications for selective interventions with African American rehabilitation clients. For instance, African Americans tended to be referred for rehabilitation by extended family, other non-formal support networks, and welfare agencies, whereas White Americans tended to self-refer. White Americans were two times as likely to be referred for rehabilitation services by a physician (Walker, Belgrave, Roberts, & Palmer, 1986). Referral by a physician raised the chances that White Americans would be accepted for services because physicians are better qualified to make disability determinations than are kin and kith. The fact that White American rehabilitation clients were more likely to self-refer or be referred by a physician suggests that they could be more aware of the nature of vocational rehabilitation services and better oriented for rehabilitation services. A selective intervention to counteract this potential source of inequity in service accessibility to African Americans is to use initial contact time with African American clients to educate them about the processes and outcomes of vocational rehabilitation services as well as their entitlements under the relevant laws.

Differences in the qualities of referral sources for African Americans and White Americans could also contribute to the racial disparities in client acceptance for rehabilitation services and success. For instance, the extent to which welfare agencies and nonformal support networks that have a higher referral profile for African Americans are aware of the various rehabilitation eligibility criteria and accurately share them with rehabilitation clients could influence client participation in rehabilitation services. For instance, about 50% of rehabilitation clients had prior documentation to support a disability status at the time of initial visit to vocational rehabilitation services (Whitney-Thomas, Timmons, Gilmore, & Thomas, 1999). This lack of basic documentation on initial consultation suggests inadequate prior client orientation to rehabilitation services at referral. Although in need of empirical verification, it is possible that some welfare agencies are referring a significant number of clients who would benefit from services other than the public rehabilitation system. Thus, racial differences in sources of client referral and their service qualities may introduce bias in the rehabilitation trajectories for clients and necessitate selective interventions for those at risk for negative impact. There is need for studies that audit the service qualities of alternative rehabilitation client referral sources with a view to designing selective interventions to amend any practices that have the potential to cause loss in rehabilitation service qualities with African American clients.

Prior Preparedness for and Accessibility of Rehabilitation Services

Racial disparities in rehabilitation service accessibility and utilization may also emanate from prior racial differences in client preparedness for rehabilitation services. For instance, White Americans have a higher school or college graduation rate than African Americans or other racial minorities (Belgrave, 1998; Sue, 2003). They also have higher access to vocational training than a majority of racial minorities in the United States. The significance of higher levels of formal education to success with rehabilitation service is also attested to by the fact that, regardless of race or severity of disability, people with disabilities with a high school or college graduation had a higher rate of success with rehabilitation than those with less than a high school education (Belgrave, 1998). African American clients are historically significantly underrepresented in the population of people with postsecondary or college education (Cuyjet, 1997; Thomas & Weinrach, 2002). Thus, African Americans with disabilities with a lower level of education and training seeking vocational rehabilitation services are already short-changed by previous exclusions from public services (e.g., education), making it less likely that they would be as successful with the public rehabilitation system as their White counterparts.

Prior racial bias against African Americans in accessing and succeeding in essential public services like education could also make it more likely that African American clients would be subjected to stereotypes associated with lower levels of formal education and training more than would White American clients. For White clients, experience with jobs requiring postsecondary education or college education may add to the chances that they will be perceived by counselors as good prospects for rehabilitation services.

Rehabilitation counselors could minimize negative halo effects on African Americans that are associated with lower levels of formal education by focusing on the unique knowledge, skills, attitudes, and perceptions that individual clients can contribute toward their own rehabilitation. Rehabilitation counselors are gatekeepers to rehabilitation resources and carry a heavy responsibility for helping clients make connections between the resources available to the clients and rehabilitation outcome options. African American clients may require more assistance in that regard, due to the fact that demographic factors that are stereotypically associated with a lack of rehabilitation success (e.g., lower levels of formal education, lower SES, skin color) are historically loaded against them. Community outreach efforts that seek to bring the public rehabilitation services to historically underserved communities would be an appropriate selective intervention to circumvent rehabilitation service disadvantage emanating from the historical past.

Language and Communication Issues

Rehabilitation counselors were particularly resistant to alternative views on disabilities or explanatory models of designing their delivery models, which increased difficulties for their racially diverse clients (Arkansas Research and Training Center in Vocational Rehabilitation, 1992). For instance, counselors may use terms that mystify the rehabilitation process and make it difficult for clients to meaningfully participate in the rehabilitation process (Schaller, Parker, & Garcia, 1998). For example, they may use different terms and meanings from those of the rehabilitation client to discuss a disability, rehabilitation resources, and outcomes (Hays, 2001). Minorities with disabilities were more likely to be uninformed about disability legislation and their role in the rehabilitation process (Smart & Smart, 1997a). Even more significant is the need for rehabilitation counselors to ensure that African American clients have the information that will enable them to make informed decisions.

Counselors may also explain rehabilitation progress in ways that are inconsistent with the African American client's service orientation and preferences (Sue & Sue, 2003). The observation was made previously that a majority of African Americans are relationship-oriented and regard family and community as central to their sense of well-being. Possible selective interventions that would support an interpersonal and collectivistic orientation to health service participation orientation include (a) understanding concerns from the client's perspective and sharing information with the client on resources (personal, family, community) that are likely to be useful in assisting the client to make effective choices and (b) helping the client evaluate the relative merits of each option with regard to the client's values, needs, and preferences. Thus, some African American clients may expect the rehabilitation counselor to assume a leading role in rehabilitation service delivery because their perception of expertness may be that of superiors, not equals (Parham, 2002; Wilson, Henry, Sayles, Senices, & Smith, 2003).

Cultural interpreters may be helpful in bridging communication gaps between counselors and some of their African American clients. They may be particularly helpful in cases in which communication may be hindered by implicit differences in worldviews or culturally restricted use of terms. In this regard, counselors who elect to use cultural brokers may need to take into account enabling practices with cultural interpreters as counselor aides. Some appropriate practices in working with clients with cultural interpreters include (a) facing toward and speaking directly to the client rather than to the translator; (b) keeping the translator fully involved throughout the interview; (c) repeating for confirmation with the client that he or she has been correctly understood; (d) requesting the client to correct any misunderstanding and observing cultural protocols (age, kin, class, gender) about appropriate translators; (e) allowing extra time; and (f) keeping the agenda short and focused (Glasser, 1983; Hays, 2001; Phelan & Parkman, 1995). The question of using family as cultural interpreters needs to be approached judiciously because family members are likely to be involved in the client's presenting situation and may be more helpful as informants and allies in designing, implementing, and evaluating treatment rather than as interpreters (Belgrave, 1998; Putsch, 1985). When possible, cultural interpreters with rehabilitation agencies need to be trained in their role so that they convey the intended messages rather than personal versions (Hays, 2001).

Experiences of Prejudice With Service Providers

In a previous section, the observation was made that rehabilitation failures with African Americans may be exacerbated by the fact that people of color have a history of being socially devalued by the White majority, and hence may enter human service organizations with feelings of distrust. A rehabilitation counselor who prematurely asks a person of color to lead in his or her own rehabilitation may be perceived by the client as engaging in a benign attempt to blame the client for sources of difficulty that are institutionally generated and a part of the oppression of minorities by the majority. The higher unemployment rate among African Americans with disabilities is a case in point. Failure to secure a job placement in rehabilitation service may be perceived by rehabilitation counselors as problems of motivation or lack of skills, when the employment difficulties are better explained by racial prejudice against African Americans in general (Michilin & Juarez-Marazzo, 2001).

There are several selective interventions that counselors could apply to circumvent rehabilitation failure with African American clients due to their long-standing experience of racial prejudice. For example, counselors need to be authentic with clients of an African American background (Hays, 2001; Helms & Cook, 1999; Mpofu et al., 2004). They can be authentic with clients by directly addressing a potential or real difference between the counselors and client perceptions of the goals, resources, and procedures of the rehabilitation service and resolving any differences in a manner that validates the clients' personal worth. Counselors and clients may differ in terms of race, disability status, and gender. Visible differences (e.g., race, disability status, gender) can be addressed in a number of ways: (a) directly asking the client if he or she would work with a counselor who has an apparent difference (racial, disability status, gender, multiple) with the client; (b) openly acknowledging to the client the limitations that one may have in terms of experience in the client's world; (c) encouraging the client to inform the counselor if he or she may be over-looking a significant issue in the client's view; and (d) communicating a genuine willing-ness to learn from the client (Mpofu et al., 2004). There is research evidence in support of the view that openness on the part of the counselor invites the client to share owner-ship of the processes and outcomes of counseling (Ivey, Gluckstern, & Ivey, 1997) and re-sults in lower client dropout from counseling (Fuertes et al., 2002). Directly addressing the cultural differences also minimizes the chances of stereotyping by and of both coun-selor and client (Hays, 2001). It would also assist the counselor–client partnership in de-ciding the extent to which they may draw from minority and majority perspectives in addressing client concerns.

Prejudice against minority clients may also be minimized by appropriately involving family and significant others in all stages of the rehabilitation process (McKenna & Power, 2000). For instance, minority clients could be asked whom they would like involved in their treatment planning. The nominated persons could then be invited to rehabilitation counseling sessions as per the client's need. Involvement of people with a similar worldview to the minority client in rehabilitation service planning and delivery (a) enables the client to draw on the resources of people historically involved in his or her situation, (b) minimizes the negative effects of feeling isolated as a result of seeking rehabilitation services, and (c) enhances the chances that salient issues to the client's adjustment will be addressed. Prejudice against minority clients can also be minimized by locating rehabilitation services at centers that are accessible to minority clients and that include other resources or services relevant to the clients' needs (e.g., community centers; Mpofu, Crystal, & Feist-Price, 2000).

Counselors' Service-Related Qualities

Sensitivity to Own and Clients' Worldviews

Counselors who are not sensitive to possible differences in worldviews with African American clients are likely to be unsuccessful with those clients. Such counselors could en-hance their understanding of the individual client's worldview by using a variety of formal measures of worldviews. A discussion of the potential uses for each of the measures cited in this section is beyond the scope of this chapter. The reader is referred to the original pub-lications for additional information on the prospective use of these measures.

Useful measures of client worldviews include the following: Scale to Assess World View (SAWV; Ibrahim & Kahn, 1987), Value Orientation Scale (VOS; Szapocznik, Scopetta, de los Angeles Arnalde, & Kurtines, 1978), and Cultural Mistrust Inventory (CMI; Terrell & Terrell, 1981). The SAWV is a 45-item Likert-type self-report measure of five value orientations: human nature, social relationships, persons to nature, time, and human ac-tivity. Ibrahim and Kahn (1987) reported internal consistency of .98 and split-half relia-bilities of .95 and .96. An average test–retest reliability of .56 was reported by Mau and Pope-Davis (1993) and .67 by Sodowsky, Maguire, Johnson, Ngumba, and Kohles (1994) over a 3-month period. The VOS is a 22-item scale and requires clients to choose from three responses per item covering perceptions on the nature of human beings, relationship of human beings to the environment, preferred activity level of people, preferred time ori-entations, and relationship of people to others. The internal consistency reliabilities of the VOS in a multiracial sample (Cuban Americans and European Americans; $N = 325$) ranged from .72 to .89. The CMI is a 48-item Likert scale measure of Black people's mistrust of Whites and majority institutions. It assesses cultural mistrust in Blacks in four areas: education and training, politics and legal affairs, business and work, and social and interpersonal relationships. The authors reported a test–retest reliability of .89 (N = 69 students).

Counselors can also use semistructured or qualitative measures developed to assess particular minority status variables of interest to them (Hays, 2001; Mpofu & Houston, 1998). For instance, they may construct a series of open-ended questions to assess disability consciousness, racial identity development, and worldview in clients. The constructs of racial identity development and worldview were discussed previously. Disability consciousness is a multidimensional construct and refers to collective consciousness by people with disabilities of their minority status (Barnartt, 1996), disability-friendly environments, and individual disability identity (Mpofu, 1999). Barnartt (1996) regarded disability consciousness as a collective awareness among people with disabilities of their minority status and the use of that consciousness as the basis for social movements that seek to advance the interests of people with disabilities. It also refers to sensitivity of the environment (e.g., community, workplaces) to disability-related differences. In the case of disability consciousness, the open-ended questions could cover individual, environmental, and collective disability consciousness. Individual disability identity refers to spontaneous self-description as having a disability or not being able-bodied (i.e., people with disabilities). It also refers to consciousness of minority status in people with disabilities and active involvement in disability-related advocacy (i.e., people without disabilities).

People with disabilities who spontaneously self-identify as having a disability or being non-able-bodied are high in individual disability identity or disability consciousness (Mpofu, 1999). Individuals with high disability consciousness may be more sensitive to disability-related prejudice and discrimination (denial of economic opportunities, choice of preferred self-referents, and devaluation of disability-related experiences). They are also more likely to be able to prove discrimination because of a disability-related difference. Individual disability identity or consciousness may be positive or negative. Positive disability consciousness may result in proactive actions to restore the economic, self-identity, and cultural integrity of people with disabilities. For instance, positive disability consciousness may be linked to higher levels of collective disability consciousness in people with disabilities (Barnartt, 1996). Negative disability consciousness is exemplified by lower involvement in activities that would counter minority status effects in people with disabilities or denial of their minority status in communities with high levels of prejudice against people with disabilities. Qualitative measures for disability consciousness that counselors may use would need to be checked for data convergence using multiple-informant methods, observational techniques, and quantitative measures.

Counselors can also measure their own worldviews and multicultural competencies (knowledge, awareness, and skills) using existing quantitative measures such as the SAWV, Cross-Cultural Counseling Inventory–Revised (CCCI-R; Coleman, 1998; LaFromboise, Coleman, & Hernandez, 1991), Multicultural Counseling Inventory (MCI; Sodowsky, Taffe, Gutkins, & Wise, 1994), and Multicultural Counseling Awareness Scale (Ponterotto, Sanchez, & Magids, 1991). The CCCI-R is a 20-item Likert-type scale that assesses counselors' ability to work with racial or ethnic minorities. An evaluator assesses the counselor in three areas that are covered by the scale: cultural awareness and beliefs, cultural knowledge, and specific cross-cultural skills. Internal consistency reliabilities for the CCCI-R range from .88 to .95. The authors reported an interrater reliability of .84. The MCI is a self-report measure and consists of 40 statements on a Likert scale. It measures counselor multicultural competencies in four domains: skills, awareness, relationships, and knowledge. Internal consistency reliabilities of .64 to .78 have been reported for the subscales and .87 for a sample of rehabilitation counselors (Granello & Wheaton, 1998). The reliabilities for the CCCI-R and the MCI are satisfactory for use as identifying counselor multicultural developmental needs.

Use of Culturally Appropriate Approaches to Counseling

There appears to be a growing consensus that rehabilitation success with any identifiable group of clients could not be ascribed to a specific therapy (Luborsky, Singer, & Luborsky, 1975). Change in rehabilitation status appeared to be attributable to relationship with the therapist, intensity of therapy, and client expectations, values, and beliefs about the rehabilitation process and its outcomes (Heinemann & Hamilton, 2000; Robertson & Colborn, 1997). Thus, the value of comparative studies of the effectiveness of various therapies between and within racial and disability groupings is contraindicated by the evidence for generic characteristics of therapy accounting for much of the change in rehabilitation status. Nonetheless, the study by Okonji, Ososkie, and Pulos (1996) documented a preference for directive counseling approaches by lower SES African American males. A limitation of the Okonji et al. study was that it relied largely on preference surveys involving an analogue rather than comparative assessment of rehabilitation effectiveness in field settings.

A majority of African Americans regard spirituality as central to well-being and a primary resource for supporting recovery from a variety of disabling conditions (Cook & Wiley, 2000; Parham, 2002). Most of the major theories of counseling do not take spirituality into account. Rehabilitation success with some people of African descent is enhanced with the incorporation of spirituality into therapy (Cook & Wiley, 2000; Mpofu, 2003; Mpofu & Harley, 2002).

Counselor and Client Racial Matching

There is a growing body of evidence that counseling success does not depend on the racial matching of counselors and clients (Coleman, Wampold, & Casali, 1995; Erdur, Rude, & Baron, 2003; Tomlinson-Clarke & Cheatham, 1993). For example, a meta-analysis of 66 studies on the association of racial, ethnic, or cultural minority status and counseling outcome indicated that clients consistently rated counselor competence higher in their nominations for counselor than racial or ethnic similarity (Coleman et al., 1995). The same meta-analytic study also reported that studies that reported preference for counselors of a similar race/ethnicity were limited by apparent social desirability effects (e.g., choice limited to race/ethnicity/culture only) and sampling bias (ethnic minority students at predominantly White universities). Majority and minority counselors were more alike than different in worldview (Mahalik, Worthington, & Crump, 1999; Redmond & Slaney, 2002); their similarity could be explained by their socialization during professional training or personality characteristics of people in the helping professions. To assume that majority/White counselors are inherently unsuited to counsel African Americans on the basis of color alone smacks of racism and may hurt the needs of African Americans who may prefer the regular, majority counselors (Weinrach & Thomas, 2002). Some African American clients would prioritize compatibility in spiritual values with counselor over race, if given a choice of counselor (Cook & Wiley, 2000). However, Black clients may prefer Black counselors as a result of their desire to be understood culturally and racially.

Summary

African Americans with disabilities have unmet needs for which there are public rehabilitation services and to a greater extent than White Americans. The racial inequity in rehabilitation services utilization against African Americans is, in part, a historical legacy of the U.S. human services system that generally excluded Blacks from full participation. It is also a result of a lack of compatibility between the service needs and preferences of African Americans and existing rehabilitation services. Current rehabilitation service systems could be designed to be more sensitive to the unique experiences and worldviews of African Americans while being respectful of the diversity and individuality among African Americans.

Concepts from prevention science hold considerable promise for the design of appropriate interventions for populations that are at risk for experiencing negative impact from health service systems that lack sensitivity to diversity. Selective interventions with African Americans are likely to result in greater successes with that population. Such interventions could address the service-related qualities in the African American clients, the counselors, and the context of counseling that are associated with unwanted rehabilitation service system failures.

References

Adams, M. (2001, July). *Race, disability: A double minority.* Retrieved October 19, 2003, from www.Sunsport.net/balto.blind

Akutsu, P. D., Snowden, L. R., & Organista, K. C. (1996). Referral patterns in ethnic-specific and mainstream programs for ethnic minorities and Whites. *Journal of Counseling Psychology, 43,* 56–64.

Arkansas Research and Training Center in Vocational Rehabilitation. (1992). *Cultural diversity in rehabilitation: Nineteenth Institute of Rehabilitation Issues.* Fayetteville: University of Arkansas, Arkansas Research and Training Center in Vocational Rehabilitation.

Barnartt, S. (1996). Disability culture or disability consciousness? *Journal of Disability Policy Studies, 7,* 1–19.

Belgrave, F. Z. (1998). *Psychosocial aspects of chronic illness and disability among African Americans.* Westport, CT: Greenwood.

Belgrave, F. Z., & Jarama, S. L. (2000). Culture and the disability and rehabilitation experience: An African American example. In R. G. Frank & T. R. Elliott (Eds.), *Handbook of rehabilitation psychology* (pp. 585–600). Washington, DC: American Psychological Association.

Cacas, J. M. (1995). Counseling and psychotherapy with racial/ethnic minority in theory and practice. In B. Bongar & L. E. Beutler (Eds.), *Comprehensive textbook of psychotherapy: Theory and practice* (pp. 311–335). New York: Oxford University Press.

Capella, M. E. (2002). Inequities in the VR system: Do they still exist? *Rehabilitation Counseling Bulletin, 45,* 143–153.

Chumbler, N. R., Hartmann, D. J., Cody, M., & Beck, C. K. (2001). Differences by race in health status of rural cognitively impaired Arkansans. *Clinical Gerontologist, 24,* 103–122.

Coleman, H. L. K. (1998). General and multicultural counseling competency: Apples and oranges? *Journal of Multicultural Counseling and Development, 26,* 147–156.

Coleman, H. L. K., Wampold, B. E., & Casali, S. L. (1995). Ethnic minorities' ratings of ethnically similar and European American counselors: A meta-analysis. *Journal of Counseling Psychology, 42,* 55–64.

Cook, D. A., & Wiley, C. Y. (2000). Psychotherapy with members of the African American churches and spiritual traditions. In P. S. Richards & A. E. Bergin (Ed.), *Handbook of psychotherapy and religiosity diversity* (pp. 369–396). Washington, DC: American Psychological Association.

Cross, W. E. (1971). The Negro to Black conversion experience: Towards a psychology of Black liberation. *Black World, 20*(9), 13–27.

Cross, W. E. (1990). *Shades of Black.* Philadelphia: Temple University Press.

Cuyjet, M. J. (1997). African American men on college campuses: Their needs and perceptions. *New Directions for Student Services, 80,* 5–6.

Dunbar, E. (2001). Counseling practices to ameliorate the effects of discrimination and hate events: Towards a systemic approach to assessment and intervention. *The Counseling Psychologist, 29,* 279–307.

Erdur, O., Rude, S. S., & Baron, A. (2003). Symptom improvement and length of treatment in ethnically similar and dissimilar client–therapist pairings. *Journal of Counseling Psychology, 50,* 52–58.

Fuertes, J. N., Mueller, L. N., Chauhan, R. V., Walker, J. A., & Ladany, N. (2002). An investigation of European American therapist approaches to counseling African American clients. *The Counseling Psychologist, 30,* 763–788.

Glasser, I. (1983). Guidelines for using an interpreter in social work. *Child Welfare, 57,* 468–470.

Granello, D. H., & Wheaton, J. E. (1998). Self-perceived multicultural competencies of African American and European American vocational rehabilitation counselors. *Rehabilitation Counseling Bulletin, 42,* 2–15.

Grills, C. (2002). African-centered psychology: Basic principles. In T. A. Parham (Ed.), *Counseling persons of African descent: Raising the bar of practitioner competence* (pp. 10–24). Thousand Oaks, CA: Sage.

Harley, D. A., Jolivette, K., McCormick, K., & Tice, K. (2002). Race, class, and gender: A constellation of positionalities with implications for counseling. *Journal of Multicultural Counseling and Development, 30,* 216–238.

Hays, P. A. (2001). *Addressing cultural complexities in practice: A framework for clinicians and counselors.* Washington, DC: American Psychological Association.

Heinemann, A. W., & Hamilton, B. B. (2000). Relation of rehabilitation intervention to functional outcome. *Journal of Rehabilitation Outcome Measures, 4,* 18–21.

Helms, J. E. (1984). Toward a theoretical explanation of the effects of race on counseling: A Black and White model. *The Counseling Psychologist, 12,* 153–165.

Helms, J. E., & Cook, D. A. (1999). *Using race and culture in counseling and psychotherapy: Theory and process.* Boston: Allyn & Bacon.

Ibrahim, F. A., & Kahn, H. (1987). Assessments of world-views. *Psychological Reports, 60,* 163–176.

Ivey, A. E., Gluckstern, N. B., & Ivey, M. B. (1997). *Basic influencing skills.* North Amherst, MA: Microtraining Associates.

Joseph, T. X. (1995). The influence of stages of ethnic identification on evaluations of pre-counseling orientation presentations. *Dissertation Abstracts International Section A: Human and Social Sciences, 55*(12-A), 3749.

LaFromboise, T., Coleman, H. L., & Gerton, J. (1993). Psychological impact of biculturalism: Evidence and theory. *Psychological Bulletin, 114,* 395–412.

LaFromboise, T. D., Coleman, H. L., & Hernandez, A. (1991). Development and factor structure of the Cross-Cultural Counseling Inventory—Revised. *Professional Psychology: Research and Practice, 22,* 380–388.

Lochman, J. E., & van den Steenhoven, A. (2002). Family-based approaches to substance abuse prevention. *Journal of Primary Prevention, 23,* 49–114.

Luborsky, L., Singer, B., & Luborsky, L. (1975). Comparative studies of psychotherapies: Is it true that "everyone has won and all must have prizes?" *Archives of General Psychiatry, 32,* 995–1008.

Mahalik, J. R., Worthington, R., & Crump, S. (1999). Influence of racial/ethnic membership and "therapist culture" on therapists' worldview. *Journal of Multicultural Counseling and Development, 27,* 2–17.

Mau, W., & Pope-Davis, D. B. (1993). Worldview differences between college students and graduate counseling trainees. *Counseling and Values, 38,* 42–50.

McKenna, M., & Power, P. W. (2000). Engaging the African American family in the rehabilitation process: An intervention model for rehabilitation counselors. *Journal of Applied Rehabilitation Counseling, 31*(1), 12–18.

Michilin, P., & Juarez-Marazzo, S. (2001). Ablelism: Social work practice with individuals with disabilities. In G. A. Appleby, E. Colon, & J. Hamilton (Eds.), *Diversity, oppression and social functioning: Person-in-environment assessment and intervention* (pp. 179–194). Boston: Allyn & Bacon.

Moore, C. L. (2001). Disparities in closure success rates for African Americans with mental retardation: An ex-post-facto research design. *Journal of Applied Rehabilitation Counseling, 32*(2), 31–36.

Moore, C. L. (2002). Outcome variables that contribute to group differences between Caucasians, African Americans, and Asian Americans who are deaf. *Journal of Applied Rehabilitation Counseling, 33*(2), 8–12.

Moore, C. L., Feist-Price, S., & Alston, R. J. (2002). VR services for persons with severe/profound mental retardation: Does race matter? *Rehabilitation Counseling Bulletin, 45,* 162–167.

Mpofu, E. (1994). Counsellor role perceptions and preferences of Zimbabwean teachers of a Shona cultural background. *Counselling Psychology Quarterly, 7,* 311–326.

Mpofu, E. (1999). *Social acceptance of Zimbabwean adolescents with physical disabilities.* Unpublished doctoral dissertation, University of Wisconsin—Madison.

Mpofu, E. (2003). Conduct disorder: Presentation, treatment options and cultural efficacy in an African setting. *International Journal of Disability, Community and Rehabilitation, 2,* 1.

Mpofu, E., Beck, R., & Weinrach, S. (2004). Multicultural rehabilitation counseling: Challenges and strategies. In K. R. Thomas, F. Chan, & N. L. Berven (Eds.), *Counseling theories and techniques for rehabilitation professionals* (pp. 386–404). New York: Springer.

Mpofu, E., Crystal, R., & Feist-Price, S. (2000). Tokenism among rehabilitation clients: Implications for rehabilitation education. *Rehabilitation Education, 14,* 243–256.

Mpofu, E., & Harley, D. (2002). Rehabilitation in Zimbabwe: Lessons and implications for rehabilitation practice in the United States. *Journal of Rehabilitation, 68*(4), 26–33.

Mpofu, E., & Houston, E. (1998). Assessment of value change in persons with acquired physical disabilities: Current and prospective applications. *Canadian Journal of Rehabilitation, 12,* 53–61.

Nation, M., Crusto, C., Wandersman, A., Kumpfer, K. L., Seybolt, D., Morrissey-Kane, E., & Davino, K. (2003). What works in prevention: Principles of effective prevention programs. *American Psychologist, 58,* 449–456.

Okonji, J. M. A., Ososkie, J. N., & Pulos, S. (1996). Preferred style and ethnicity of counselors by African American males. *Journal of Black Psychology, 22,* 329–339.

Olney, M. F., & Kennedy, J. (2002). Racial disparities in VR use and job placement rates for adults with disabilities. *Rehabilitation Counseling Bulletin, 45,* 177–185.

Parham, T. A. (2002). Counseling models for African Americans: The what and the how of counseling. In T. A. Parham (Ed.), *Counseling persons of African descent: Raising the bar of practitioner competence* (pp. 100–118). Thousand Oaks, CA: Sage.

Phelan, M., & Parkman, S. (1995). Work with an interpreter. *British Medical Journal, 311,* 555–557.

Ponterotto, J. G., Sanchez, C. M., & Magids, D. M. (1991, August). *Initial development and validation of the Multicultural Awareness Scale* (MCAS–B). Paper presented at the annual convention of the American Psychological Association, San Francisco.

Putsch, R. W., III. (1985). Cross-cultural communication: The special case of interpreters in health care. *Journal of the American Medical Association, 254,* 3344–3348.

Redmond, T., & Slaney, R. B. (2002). The influence of information and race on counselors' attributions. *Journal of College Student Development, 43,* 851–861.

Rehabilitation Act Amendments of 1992, Pub. L. No. 102-569, 106 Stat. 4344-4488 (1992).

Robertson, S. C., & Colborn, A. P. (1997). Outcomes research for rehabilitation: Issues and solutions. *Journal of Rehabilitation Outcomes Measurement, 1*(5), 15–23.

Rosenthal, D. A., & Berven, N. L. (1999). Effects of client race on clinical judgment. *Rehabilitation Counseling Bulletin, 42,* 243–264.

Ruggiero, K. M., & Marx, D. M. (1999). Less pain and more to gain: Why high status group members blame their failure on discrimination. *Journal of Personality and Social Psychology, 77,* 774–784.

Schaller, J., Parker, R., & Garcia, S. B. (1998). Moving toward culturally competent rehabilitation counseling services: Issues and practices. *Journal of Applied Rehabilitation Counseling, 29,* 40–48.

Schoenbach, V. J. (2003, October). *Epidemiology—Definition, functions, and characteristics.* Retrieved October 12, 2003, from www.epidemiolo.net

Smart, J. F., & Smart, D. W. (1997a). Culturally sensitive informed choice in rehabilitation counseling. *Journal of Applied Rehabilitation Counseling, 28,* 32–37.

Smart, J. F., & Smart, D. W. (1997b). The racial/ethnic demography of disability. *Journal of Rehabilitation, 63*(4), 9–15.

Smith, J. M. (2001). The use of q-methodology to assess the possibility that fear is a barrier preventing the use of mental health services by African American men. *Dissertation Abstracts International Section A: Humanities and Social Sciences, 61*(7-A), 2609.

Sodowsky, G. R., Maguire, K., Johnson, P., Ngumba, W., & Kohles, R. (1994). World views of White American, mainland Chinese, Taiwanese, and African students. *Journal of Cross-Cultural Psychology, 25,* 309–324.

Sodowsky, G. R., Taffe, R. C., Gutkins, T. B., & Wise, S. L. (1994). Development of the Multicultural Counseling Inventory: A self-report measure of multicultural competencies. *Journal of Counseling Psychology, 41,* 137–148.

Sue, D. W. (2003). *Overcoming our racism: The journey to liberation.* San Francisco: Jossey-Bass.

Sue, D. W., & Sue, D. (2003). *Counseling the culturally different: Theory and practice* (4th ed.) New York: Wiley.

Szapocznik, J., Scopetta, M. A., de los Angeles Arnalde, M., & Kurtines, W. (1978). Cuban value structure: Treatment implications. *Journal of Consulting and Clinical Psychology, 45,* 961–970.

Terrell, F., & Terrell, S. L. (1981). An inventory to measure cultural mistrust among Blacks. *Western Journal of Black Studies, 5,* 180–184.

Thomas, K. R., & Weinrach, S. G. (1999). Multiculturalism in counseling and applied psychology: A critical perspective. *Educational and Child Psychology, 16,* 70–83.

Thomas, K. R., & Weinrach, S. G. (2002). Racial bias in rehabilitation: Multiple interpretation of the same data. *Rehabilitation Education, 16,* 81–90.

Tomlinson-Clarke, S., & Cheatham, H. E. (1993). Counselor and client ethnicity and counselor intake judgments. *Journal of Counseling Psychology, 40,* 267–270.

U.S. Census Bureau. (2003). *Disability status: 2000.* Washington, DC: Author.

Utsey, S. O., Ponterotto, J. G., Reynolds, A. L., & Cancelli, A. A. (2000). Racial discrimination, coping and life satisfaction, and self-esteem among African Americans. *Journal of Counseling & Development, 78,* 72–78.

Vontress, C. E., & Epp, L. R. (1997). Historical hostility in the African American client: Implications for counseling. *Journal of Multicultural Counseling and Development, 25,* 170–184.

Walker, S., Belgrave, F. Z., Roberts, V., & Palmer, R. (1986). Status of Black disabled in the rehabilitation system. In *Research report of the National Survey of the Howard University Rehabilitation Project.* Washington, DC: Howard University Center for the Study of Handicapped Children and Adults.

Webster-Stratton, C., & Taylor, T. (2001). Nipping early risk factors in the bud: Preventing substance abuse, delinquency, and violence in adolescence through interventions targeted at young children (0 to 8 years). *Prevention Science, 2,* 165–192.

Weinrach, S. G., & Thomas, K. R. (2002). A critical analysis of the multicultural counseling competencies: Implications for the practice of mental health counseling. *Journal of Mental Health Counseling, 24,* 20–35.

Whitney-Thomas, J., Timmons, J. C., Gilmore, D. S., & Thomas, D. M. (1999). Expanding access: Changes in vocational rehabilitation practice since the 1992 Rehabilitation Act Amendments. *Rehabilitation Counseling Bulletin, 43,* 30–40.

Wilson, K. B. (2002). Exploration of VR acceptance and ethnicity: A national investigation. *Rehabilitation Counseling Bulletin, 45,* 168–176.

Wilson, K. B., Alston, R., Harley, D. A., & Mitchell, N. (2002). Predicting vocational rehabilitation acceptance based on race, gender, education, work status at application, and primary source of support at application in the United States. *Rehabilitation Counseling Bulletin, 45,* 132–142.

Wilson, K. B., Henry, M. L., Sayles, C. D., Senices, J., & Smith, D. R. (2003). Multicultural counseling competencies in the 21st century: Are vocational rehabilitation counselors primed for the next millennium? *Journal of the Pennsylvania Counseling Association, 5,* 5–15.

Wilson, K. B., Turner, T., Liu, J., Harley, D. A., & Alston, R. J. (2002). Perceived vocational rehabilitation efficacy by race/ethnicity: Results of a national client survey. *Journal of Applied Rehabilitation Counseling, 33*(3), 26–34.

18

Mental Health Assessment With African American Children and Adolescents

Jo Anne Rainey and Theresa M. Nowak

"LaKesha Wilson" came to the mental health center 4 months ago with her mother, who reported that LaKesha was causing trouble at home and at school. Ms. Wilson was raising three children alone, working two part-time jobs, and seeing a therapist at the center for the past year because of her depression. Now, LaKesha also met with a center therapist every other week, and therapy notes described a compliant girl who answered questions willingly but volunteered little, showed poor insight, and seemed uninterested in the type of intense self-exploration expected by the therapist. LaKesha's mom reported that her daughter consistently did not follow instructions or complete after-school chores that had been explained repeatedly. In addition, 12-year-old LaKesha did not get along with most of the neighborhood youths her age, although she played well with her 9-year-old sister and her sister's best girlfriend and she was kind to her 4-year-old brother. Despite these positive sibling relationships, her compliance was not improving, and now the overwhelmed mother was experiencing such difficulty that she was asking that her daughter be removed from the home, due to incorrigibility. This process required a more comprehensive psychological evaluation than was involved in LaKesha's initial intake.

Mr. Johnson was assigned the evaluation, and he now was preparing to meet LaKesha. He reviewed the mom's and therapist's reports and now was in the process of looking over the youth's school records. He noted that LaKesha was enrolled in a full-time, self-contained, fifth-grade special education class for students with specific learning disabilities (SLD). She had been diagnosed as having learning disabilities in mathematics and reading when she was 8 years old, and she had been receiving special education services since that time. The SLD teacher reported that LaKesha consistently refused to do any schoolwork, showed belligerence toward her, and used profanity routinely. The teacher wrote, "All she wants to do is play with her and the other Black girls' hair. She has a terrible attitude and her mother says she is too busy to come to any more school meetings. She claims she'll lose her waitressing job, but it's obvious that she just doesn't care enough to come." Recently, the teacher had become so frustrated by LaKesha's behaviors that she had called Ms. Wilson to suggest that she ask for a reevaluation. She said she thought LaKesha had emotional/behavioral disorder (EBD). The mom had asked for the school reevaluation, which was in process. Mr. Johnson knew that a diagnosis of EBD would place LaKesha in a different special education class in that particular school, one with a different teacher, and he wondered if that could be part of the teacher's motivation in asking for the reevaluation.

Mr. Johnson went to the waiting room to greet LaKesha. The youth was sitting with her back to her mother, examining her fingernails, which were long, carefully shaped, and painted with tiny stars. Also notable was the young lady's hair, which was intricately styled with braids and weaves. The practitioner complimented LaKesha's nails and hair as the two walked to his office, and the youth beamed. "I do them myself," she attested. "I do my sister's and our girlfriend's, too."

LaKesha cooperated fully during the interview. She smiled appropriately and answered questions willingly, albeit briefly. Mr. Johnson saw none of the negative behaviors described in LaKesha's records, until he broached the topic of school. "It's so stupid!" LaKesha raged. "All those little kids are stupid and the teacher's a _____! We do the same stuff every day and I ain't gonna do that _____!" The practitioner asked LaKesha which subject she liked the most. "None of them," she asserted, at first. Then, when he asked if she ever had fun at school, her affect shifted as she recalled, "Once, when my teacher was out for a long time, we got to go to Home Ec. That was so cool! The teacher was nice and she didn't yell and we got to sew! Want to see? I can draw the apron I made." Mr. Johnson agreed, and the picture, which was immature for a 12-year-old, showed a recognizable apron covered with tiny stars. It reflected more detail than Mr. Johnson would have predicted, based on the youth's vague and general verbal responses. The practitioner followed up with several other questions that required specific memories, such as the previous evening's activities, the day's math lesson, what had been served for lunch in the school cafeteria, and the location of the school gym. LaKesha showed embarrassment when she could not supply the information requested yet did not become hostile or profane.

This case study, which is based on fact, exemplifies the types of biases, misjudgments, and oversights that can lead to a young person not receiving appropriate mental health assessment, diagnosis, and interventions. It also emphasizes the crucial roles of school and community in the total picture of a youth's behaviors. LaKesha was a girl who had "slipped through the cracks" of both the school and community systems, she was in serious trouble, and it was significant that she was an African American youth in two majority Caucasian settings. In this chapter, we explore issues surrounding the mental health assessment of African American youths. At the end of the chapter, we revisit LaKesha and explore how her prognosis improved through collaboration between the professionals in her ecological systems.

Before we proceed, four explanations are necessary. First, we acknowledge that mental health assessments are conducted by a variety of professionals, including social workers, family practitioners, child psychologists, pediatricians, school psychologists, family therapists, psychiatrists, and pastoral counselors. We generally refer to all of these professionals under the general title *mental health practitioners*. Second, we recognize that youth mental health assessments occur in several settings, the most typical of which are mental health centers, health clinics, hospitals, schools, and private offices. No differentiation is made regarding setting-specific assessment techniques; we assert that the keys to good assessment cross setting boundaries. Third, we recognize that service provision for children and youths typically falls within the realms of two major agencies: health and education. Although each of the related disciplines has mental health components, the diagnostic language of the two is different. Health follows the *Diagnostic and Statistical Manual of Mental Disorders* (4th ed., text revision [*DSM–IV–TR*]; American Psychiatric Association, 2000), whereas education has state-approved special education categories that are based on federal law (i.e., Individuals With Disabilities Education Act of 1999). The *DSM–IV–TR* can be purchased at an educational or a medical bookstore. Special education categories can be obtained from state departments of education and typically can be downloaded from their Web sites. Finally, as the authors of this chapter, we have a combined total of over 50 years of experience with children and youths, and we are not naive about the realities, stresses, time limitations, and budgetary constraints that affect youth assessment. We make every effort to keep suggestions reality-based and practical. However, there is no way around the fact that time and effort are required to complete a reliable and valid assessment, which is focused on the current and future mental health needs of a young person. We maintain that, if the time and effort are not invested at the outset, more will be required later, as oversights and errors are remedied. We advocate a comprehensive, thoughtful, initial assessment.

This chapter begins with an examination of general issues in youth assessment, including environmental factors, reliability, validity, norming sample, and test bias. Then, assessment issues in two areas of mental health, in which African American youths continue to be overrepresented, are analyzed, the first being cognition and achievement and the second, being social–emotional functioning. Next, implications for practice are offered, including examples of examiner biases; assessment of the individual in context; consideration of multiple traits, settings, and informants; and rule-out and comorbid diagnoses. To conclude, implications for future research are suggested before LaKesha's case is revisited and analyzed, thus offering a summary of the major points of the chapter.

General Issues in Youth Assessment

When faced with the assessment of children and adolescents, two realities should be noted. The first is that all assessment tools used to describe human behaviors are subjective. Even the most researched, reliable, and valid measures are dependent on human observations and judgments, which are and always will be fallible. That said, when faced with assessing the performances and behaviors of a person, it is better to seek some degree of objectivity than simply rely on impressions, assumptions, hearsay, and brief observations in single settings. The second reality is the importance of taking a developmental approach to assessment. Differences in the ways individuals think, communicate, and behave stem partially from differences in their developmental and life stages. Assessment techniques that are quite appropriate for use with adults generally cannot be scaled down to meet the needs of young people effectively. Ideally, strategies and tools should be designed with developmental levels and needs in mind, from the outset.

Three categories of assessment tools are considered later in this chapter. Standardized tests are discussed in the section on cognitive and achievement assessment, and clinical interviews and behavior checklists are examined in the section on social–emotional assessment. For now, it suffices to offer a few guidelines to provide mental health practitioners with measuring sticks with which to determine whether specific instruments are appropriate for specific clients. Some types of information clearly are delineated in test manuals, whereas other data must be gathered by the practitioner's interactions with the client and the client's significant others.

Environmental Factors

A client's environmental context is the first entity to examine in a well-implemented assessment process involving any individual. Whereas an ideally supportive environment can mask a disability, a difficult environment can make a person's actions appear more internally driven than they are in reality. This assertion may be truer among youths than among typical adults, because youths generally have less control over the environments in which they find themselves. Negative examples of this phenomenon can be seen among clients in mental health settings. For example, if an adult discovers that his or her neighborhood is unsafe, he or she may initiate steps to move. If an adult has inadequate money for food, clothing, or shelter, supports exist that may be accessed directly by the individual. Even an abused adult has legal options that are not offered typically to a youth. No one is implying that it is easy for an adult to change an unhealthy living environment, and, certainly, abused adults can be so stripped of their perceived power that they see no positive, viable options. Nevertheless, adults have rights and privileges not awarded to young people. Thus, it is absolutely fundamental to explore thoroughly the ramifications of the environments of young people who are being assessed. Rather than making a diagnosis and then checking to see if any external factors might be contributing to the youth's behaviors, environments should be investigated *first* and then, if they do not seem to be causing the undesirable behaviors, a more internally driven disorder may be considered.

Reliability

Reliability refers to the consistency of an assessment measure. In the terminology of test experts, "test reliability indicates the extent to which individual differences in test scores are attributable to 'true' differences in the characteristics under consideration and the extent to which they are attributable to chance errors" (Anastasi, 1988, p. 109). A great deal of time, effort, and money are put forth by the publishers of standardized measures to assure that tools are reliable. Reliability is checked through comparing scores of (a) the same people completing the same measure at different times, (b) the same people completing equivalent measures, and (c) measures scored by different scorers. The number and characteristics of the measure completers should be reported. Good reliability does not indicate that an assessment tool does a good job of measuring something; it simply means that it does a dependable job.

Validity

Validity is a reflection of the degree to which an assessment tool actually measures the construct(s) it purports to measure. It is an indicator of whether the assessment fulfills its function. There are several ways to ascertain validity, but naming the types is not crucial to our purposes for this chapter. It is adequate simply to understand that a valid measure does a good job of assessing what it is supposed to assess. Validity is crucial. It does not matter if an assessment tool is reliable if it is not valid. Of what value is it if it consistently measures the wrong thing?

Norming Sample

In the process of developing an assessment measure, the developers choreograph the administration of the measure with people who are supposed to be representative of the people for whom the measure was designed. These people constitute the norming or standardization sample, and their scores lead to the designated norms for the measure. In addition to averages being computed, frequency and range of score variations are examined. This allows practitioners to compare the performances of clients who complete the measure with other similar individuals.

Anyone who administers an assessment measure should check the sample on which the measure was normed. This is especially important when clients are not members of the American mainstream. The question to ask is, "Was an adequate percentage of the people with whom this assessment measure was normed similar to my client?" Several client characteristics should be targeted, including age, ethnicity, socioeconomic status (SES), and geographic location.

Often, it is easiest, when researching an assessment measure for use with a specific youth, to check the test manual for the ages of the norming group first. Recall that adult measurement tools typically are not appropriate for use with young people. In general, it is better to use an instrument for which the client's age is in the middle of the test age range; the scores received at the ages at the ends of the range tend to be less stable. If a measure has not been normed with youths, attention can be shifted to finding a different tool.

If the ages of the norming group are appropriate for the specific client, the next suggested step is to examine its ethnic percentages. The days of major standardized tests being normed exclusively with Caucasian samples are well behind us, but look for more than a symbolic gesture. Look for percentages that closely reflect the U.S. population, according to the most recent U.S. Census Bureau. For example, the 2000 census reported the following percentages for the 35 million youths in the United States who were under the age of 18 years: 61% White, 17% Hispanic, 15% Black or African American, 4% Asian/Pacific Islander, 3% multiracial, and 1% American Indian or Alaskan Native (U.S. Census Bureau, 2000). If a practitioner uses an assessment tool with only one ethnic group, it is fine for the norming sample to contain members of that group only, but results of that measure cannot be compared with those of measures with broader norming samples.

It is worth mentioning, at this point, that as the United States becomes more ethnically diverse, the focus on the needs of African Americans that occurred in mental health and education during the past three decades may be deflected toward young people who come to the United States from other countries. The needs for cultural sensitivity and possible accommodations for young people who, for example, are nonnative speakers of English might be more evident than are the needs of native-born African Americans. It is incumbent upon professionals who promote fair assessment to continue to remind themselves and colleagues that diverse needs occur among both foreign-born and native-born clients.

If the client's ethnic group is represented adequately in the norming sample, then a practitioner can move on to examine the socioeconomic information provided. As with the characteristic of ethnicity, developers of assessment measures designed for national and international use are careful to norm their tools with samples that reflect socioeconomic diversity. However, specific SES information often is not reported in manuals; it is common to list only general categories. Sometimes, demographics related to SES are provided, such as father's income, mother's education, or qualification for free or reduced school meals. If no information is provided, it might be prudent to hypothesize that little or no SES diversity existed in the sample. This is not to assert that the tool cannot be used, but it does diminish the validity of the measure for use with a client whose SES does not fall within the range typical of many convenience samples (i.e., middle to upper SES).

If the tool seems appropriate for the client's SES, a practitioner can progress to checking the geographic locations of the norming sample. Although measures typically are normed across several states, it is wise to check beyond the obvious. If the tool was normed in 15 large cities and a client is from a rural home, the match is not a good one. Again, this does not mean that the assessment measure cannot be used. It does imply that results should be interpreted with caution.

Finally, if a client has a special need or a disability, a practitioner should check to see if people with that disability were included in the norming sample. It is important to ascertain the number of people with disabilities and the types of disabilities represented. If a client has a rarely occurring disability, it is unlikely that his or her specific situation will be reflected in a norming sample, but if no special populations are sampled, assessment results must be interpreted with caution when a practitioner is working with a client with a disability.

Test Bias

Critics of norm-referenced tests have suggested appropriately that testing instruments can be biased against people of color (Barrera, 1996; Townsend, 2002). However, progress in determining norming samples and in test administration has led to better constructed assessment tools that can be applied to wider ranges of the population. In spite of these improvements, mental health professionals need to be aware of biases that can be inherent in norm-referenced testing measures and procedures. The process of determining whether an instrument is appropriate for a specific client rests on the mental health provider asking if the tool is valid for that child or adolescent; the question is whether the test will measure what it purports to measure regarding that specific individual's performances and behaviors.

Content Bias

An instrument is only as good as are its developers. When testing measures are constructed, content can be based on a narrow worldview, thus limiting its functional value across multiple cultures. Laing and Kamhi (2003) suggested that content bias is present when components of an instrument do not reflect the variability in life experiences and opportunities that exist among diverse populations. Such test items and procedures are based on the assumption that all examinees have similar beliefs and values.

Linguistic Bias

Although researchers have concluded, generally, that norm-referenced tests tend not to have content bias (Ortiz, 2002), the ways in which an instrument is administered can bias any measure. This can occur when there is discrepancy in language or dialect between examiner and examinee. For example, when a mental health provider is from the cultural mainstream and speaks standard American English, while an African American youth speaks a vernacular form of English, interpretation of questions and responses may vary more than if both parties speak the same dialect. Outcomes can reflect this discrepancy and result in lower scores, which may be interpreted as based on actual impairment rather than on linguistic differences.

Over- and Underrepresentation

Attempts to correct for biases have led to both over- and underidentification of disabilities among African American youths. This is reflected in data from the Annual Report to Congress on the Implementation of Individuals With Disabilities Education Act, or IDEA (U.S. Department of Education, National Center of Educational Statistics, 2003). This report, prepared by the U.S. Department of Education, Office of Special Education Programs, reflects overrepresentation of African American youths as having mental disabilities and underrepresentation as having gifted abilities. It is notable that norm-referenced instruments typically are used to determine eligibility in these two areas of special education identification. African Americans represent 15% of the American population, whereas 21% of African American youths, ages 6 through 21, are identified as needing special education services. Most educational and mental health professionals, the U.S. Congress, and many members of the American public view this discrepancy as a national concern.

Mental health professionals should be aware of their biases and avoid generalized beliefs when assessing African American youths from various backgrounds (Hanson & Lynch, 2003). Over- and underidentification of minority youths tend to occur when practitioners bring biases, which are based on generalized knowledge of an individual's race, to the evaluation process. The generalized belief that "all African Americans think, speak, and act this way" can lead to one of two interpretive errors. When an atypical result is due to cultural differences and yet is attributed to impairment, overidentification occurs. When a result that is due to true impairment is attributed to cultural differences, underidentification occurs. Only after a practitioner has obtained a thorough knowledge of a child's or an adolescent's background can she or he make a decision as to whether an instrument is appropriate for use with that specific individual.

Issues in Cognitive and Achievement Assessment

Because cognition and achievement typically are assessed within educational or health systems, mental health practitioners generally need to be wise consumers of evaluation reports, rather than administrators of developmental, intelligence, or achievement tests. Toward this goal, this section focuses on the history of intelligence testing, advantages and disadvantages of alternative assessment techniques, and the system through which special education services are accessed for children and adolescents.

History

Although the court system did not become involved in the issue of biased assessment procedures until the 1960s (see *Hobson v. Hansen*, 1967), researchers have had concerns about cross-cultural testing since the early 20th century. Social and political outcry, beginning mid-century, raised society's awareness that assessment results could be reflections of biased measures used with African American children and youths rather than indicators of actual ability. The concern was and continues to be based on the overrepresentation of African American students in special education and underrepresentation in gifted programs.

Legal involvement has not successfully clarified issues surrounding the use of cognitive assessment measures with African American young people (Bersoff, 1982). One can glean the nature of the conflict by comparing legal decisions made in California and Illinois. In 1972, California courts temporarily halted the use of intelligence tests as a method to determine eligibility of African American students for placement in classes for students with educable mental retardation (*Larry P. v. Wilson Riles*, 1972). Years later, after hundreds of hours of testimony, Judge Robert Peckman found a specific IQ test to be racially discriminatory, and he banned the use of any IQ test to determine placement in any special education program other than those for gifted and talented youths. Then, in 1988, a group of Californian parents, who felt that their children were unable to access the special services they needed, filed suit, stating that the ban against IQ tests discriminated against African American students. In 1992, Judge Peckman allowed the administration of intelligence tests with African Americans who had parental consent (*Crawford v. Honig*, 1994). Meanwhile, in a 1980 Illinois court, Judge John Grady listened to the same expert witnesses heard in California (*Parents in Action on Special Education [P.A.S.E.] v. Hannon*, 1980) and asserted that intelligence tests were not discriminatory in determining the need of African American students for special education services. Judge Grady maintained that the Chicago public school system was in compliance, by using a multiprong process in which information was obtained through multiple modes and from multiple sources (Jacob-Timm & Hartshorne, 1998; Sattler, 2001; Turnbull, 1990).

These legal decisions, made in California and Illinois, might appear diametrically opposed. However, the difference in outcomes was based not on whether intelligence tests were biased but on the way in which results from intelligence tests were used. In looking at California's system, Judge Peckman determined that the IQ test was used as the major determinant in the decision-making process for eligibility and placement into special education. Conversely, in Illinois, Judge Grady viewed intelligence tests as one part of a multifaceted evaluation. The issue of using standardized intelligence tests with African American youths still is actively debated.

Different trajectories are taken by researchers to explain variations in intelligence test scores between African American and Caucasian youths. Three prominent positions differ, based on a focus on genetics, environmental characteristics, or testing instruments. The genetic theory, which is the most controversial, posits that African Americans, as an ethnic group, have lower cognitive and achievement abilities, which are reflected accurately by standardized tests. Jensen (1980) and Herrnstein and Murray (1994) made the case that the lower intelligence test scores among African Americans are genetically based. These researchers believe in holding the intelligence testing instrument as the standard for determining individual ability. Conversely, Helms (1992) argued that constructs measured by standardized ability tests culturally favor the mainstream population and that these instruments assess mastery of the mainstream culture.

The environment's vital role with achievement test scores, particularly for young children, is supported by the Early Childhood Longitudinal Study—Kindergarten, sponsored by the U.S. Department of Education's National Center of Educational Statistics (2003). This study has found that kindergarten and first-grade children from minority populations generally score lower in reading achievement. However, when poverty and race/ethnicity are controlled, child and family characteristics (e.g., home literacy environment, early literacy skills, approaches to learning, general health) demonstrate the greatest influence on early achievement. This implies that, for young children, achievement scores reflect environment more than potential ability. This finding is crucial, especially in light of current national and state emphases on academic achievement, at all age and grade levels. In particular, reading is seen as a foundation for school success (Craig, Connor, & Washington, 2003; Ladd, Kochenderfer, & Coleman, 1996). Moreover, early school success influences positive school adjustment and learning, which affect future learning and test scores (Entwisle & Hayduk, 1988; Pianta & Steinberg, 1992).

An association between environment and test results is found with intelligence tests as well. Sattler (2001) suggested that IQ scores reflect both biological and environmental factors and that low scores are indicative of the aptness of educational systems (p. 658). He supported making changes within service provision systems rather than discontinuing the use of individual ability testing instruments. In addition, Helms (1992) warned that to accurately reflect environmental impact on ability functioning, it is imperative that race be distinguished from SES. Specifically, the African American population typically is researched in conjunction with the mono-SES level of poverty. This lack of differentiation assumes homogeneity among African Americans, which inaccurately reflects the breadth of clients seen by mental health professionals.

A third explanation for discrepancies in scores between African American and Caucasian youths focuses on the testing instruments themselves. Bagnato and Neisworth (1991) argued that, especially for young children, standardized tests measure compliance more than developmental ability (p. 39). Experts in this field caution that whenever any school-age child's background is distinctly different from the sample on which a test was normed, using the results for measuring current performance and predicting future accomplishments is inappropriate (Fish, 2002; Salvia & Ysseldyke, 1991). This problem was addressed earlier in this chapter. However, after decades of examining bias in tests, the consensus among many researchers is that the majority of standardized instruments do not contain systematic bias against specific populations (Kamphaus & Reynolds, 1987; Ortiz, 2002; Sandoval, Frisby, Geisinger, Scheuneman, & Grenier, 1998). Once again, however, Helms (1992) asserted that these tests typically are developed by professionals from the mainstream population who have been socialized as such. This results in test items that lack cultural diversity, as exemplified by a dearth of response options that could reflect thinking from various cultures.

Psychoeducational professionals who believe that testing instruments are biased against African American youths have attempted a variety of methods to overcome this problem. One effort in the early 1970s to control for test bias was the development of a culture-specific instrument that purported to reflect the knowledge of African Americans in the inner cities of the United States (Anastasi, 1988, p. 307). The Black Intelligence Test of Cultural Homogeneity (Williams, 1975), known by its acronym as the BITCH test, proved to be ineffective because of the cultural variability of African Americans within and across cities. This example demonstrates the caution that mental health professionals need to use before drawing conclusions and making general statements about African American youths. Another effort was made by Cattell, who attempted to develop a nonverbal instrument that was free of culture, the Culture Fair Intelligence Test (Willard, 1968). This test also did not live up to researchers' expectations, because even nonverbal items are dependent on examinees to perceive, think, and analyze items using a cultural-specific process.

When all is said and done, it appears that most standardized, carefully normed intelligence tests used in America today are not, in and of themselves, biased, although their use and interpretations can reflect subjective partiality (Ortiz, 2002). For example, if an examiner uses the score received on an intelligence test as the sole basis on which to make a diagnosis or to determine eligibility for special services, the end result can be inappropriate labeling or placement. When evaluators do not develop holistic pictures of individuals, inaccurate determinations can be made. Ortiz cautioned that life opportunities provided to young people affect their knowledge base and their ability to do well on these tests; youths whose environments do not offer exposure to tested knowledge will score lower on standardized, norm-referenced tests. Most experts in this field acknowledge that it is impossible to develop a testing instrument that is completely unbiased. For additional information on arguments for and against the use of standardized intelligence tests in assessing culturally and linguistically diverse youths, see Sattler (2001, pp. 658–665).

Alternative Assessments

The process of taking a test may be a biased activity for children and adolescents who have not been exposed to many out-of-context testlike situations within their environments (Battle, 2002). Because test taking is, by its very nature, culturally loaded, it can be hypothesized that other methods of assessment might yield less biased assessment results. Criterion-referenced measures and various alternative assessment measures have been developed to address this goal.

Criterion-referenced measures can be designed by mental health professionals to determine the level at which a child or adolescent is comfortable with independent learning and when she or he has reached a predefined point or goal. These instruments can provide pragmatic information that is useful in assisting professionals to design and implement effective interventions. The advantage of using a criterion-referenced measure when assessing African American youths is that familiar language, materials, contexts, and interaction patterns can be used, thus bypassing a major criticism of norm-referenced instruments (Laing & Kamhi, 2003). Disadvantages of criterion-referenced measures include (a) subjectivity, which can lead to bias, and (b) uncertain or limited reliability and validity. Results, therefore, need to be interpreted and generalized with caution.

Alternative assessment procedures tend to take on a functional approach that gives practitioners insight into how individual children and adolescents learn. These techniques, which do not yield standard scores, sometimes lead directly to appropriate interventions (Campbell, Dollaghan, Needleman, & Janosky, 1997). The common thread through each of the measures can be described by what they are not; they do not emphasize adminis-tration and scores but rather the strengths, interests, and learning styles of young people. Alternative assessments tend to encourage a higher order of thinking than do some stan-dardized, norm-referenced tests. Table 18.1 provides a summary of Laing and Kamhi's (2003) description of several alternative procedures and their advantages.

The best approach to assessing any youth is to use multiple measures to develop a pic-ture of the whole individual. This process may include using a combination of standard-ized and alternative assessments to benefit from the strengths and information of both types. For example, to assure the least discriminatory evaluation possible, a mental health professional may substantiate or refute findings from an evaluation conducted by another agency or provider by performing appropriate alternative assessment procedures. This can be particularly helpful when incongruence exists between test scores and performance.

Access to Special Education Services

The system that provides special services to American students, which includes determi-nation evaluations, has been in place since the passage of the federal special education law, Education for All Handicapped Children Act (Pub. L. No. 94-142) in 1975. Many changes have occurred over the years, and the current system, under the Individuals With Disabilities Education Act (IDEA), is divided into two age groups. If developmental concerns arise when a child is under the age of 3 years, each state has an early intervention system that evaluates the five general developmental areas (i.e., adaptive, cognitive, communication, physical, and social–emotional) and provides services to children who meet state eligibil-ity criteria. Although this system currently falls under Part C of the IDEA Amendments of 1997 (U.S. Department of Education, 1999), evaluators and service providers may not be associated with the educational system. The state lead agency for early intervention may be education, health, social services, or a related agency. Thus, if mental health providers are unfamiliar with this system and they serve children and families who receive early intervention services, they have two options for obtaining evaluation data. They may ask primary caregivers for a copy of children's reports or have caregivers give signed per-mission to have the early intervention lead agency send reports. If developmental con-cerns arise after children pass their 3rd birthdays, school systems are federally mandated through Part B of IDEA (U.S. Department of Education, 1999) to screen or evaluate the

Table 18.1
Alternative Assessment Procedures

Alternative Assessment Procedure	Advantage
Processing dependent measures	Places emphasis on how a youth processes information rather than on prior knowledge and experiences.
Dynamic assessment	Determines a youth's independent performance on a task and suggests supports needed to increase performance.
Test–teach–retest	Assists youths who are weak in language skills. Some young African American children have benefited from this approach.
Task/stimulus variability	Modifies the standardized administration of a test to an action–object orientation presented in a naturalistic environment; African American youths from high-energy homes have been found to respond positively to this approach.
Graduated prompting	Assessment and intervention for a specific behavior occur si-multaneously; has been conducted successfully by modifying norm-referenced tests.

children to determine if special services are needed. Primary caregivers should have a copy of that report, which can be shared, or caregiver-signed permission for the school system to send a report will be required. It is important to note that the initial evaluation may yield the most comprehensive report, describing testing instruments and scores, but it may be out of date. Conversely, reevaluation reports typically provide less formal diagnostic data and more information on the effectiveness of the special services the child or adolescent is receiving (Canter, Hurley, & Reid, 2000). Depending on state regulations and local interpretations, these reports will describe criteria a youth meets to be eligible for special services. Although resulting labels are important in the diagnostic and eligibility process, caution should be used that labels do not bias or restrict the ways in which the youth is seen or the types of goals that are set. Mental health practitioners need to know enough about the evaluation process, as well as familial and cultural mores, to recognize whether interpretations appear valid and reliable and to take corrective steps if they do not.

Issues in Social–Emotional Assessment

Although issues with cognition and achievement often are present, the number one reason for youth referrals for mental health services is demonstration of behavior problems at home, in school, and in the community (Fuery, 1999). The most common diagnoses made for these children and adolescents are attention-deficit hyperactivity disorder (ADHD), oppositional defiant disorder, and conduct disorder (Doll, 1996). These young people are described variously by professionals as exhibiting poor impulse control, externalizing behaviors, conduct problems, acting-out behaviors, noncompliance, antisocial behaviors, behavior disorders, or oppositional behaviors, depending on the philosophy and therapeutic approach of the practitioner. Descriptions commonly heard among nonprofessionals include "He just doesn't care," "She has a real bad attitude," and "He gets mad anytime anything doesn't go his way." In school settings, these youths are labeled as having emotional disorder, behavioral disorder, or both (emotional/behavioral disorder [EBD]).

The bottom line is that some children and adolescents consistently do not do what adults around them want them to do and do not express themselves in the ways many adults prefer, especially adults who adhere to the preferences of the majority, mainstream society. Offering this different perspective on the actions of youths who demonstrate unwanted or unusual behaviors does not make light of the challenges faced by families, school personnel, peers, and community members who deal with these individuals. A young person who consistently does not follow rules, routines, and directions can try the patience of the most understanding individual, prevent individual and group goals from being accomplished, and turn an environment chaotic and even dangerous. A youth who communicates with belligerence and insults—or who refuses to communicate—may be frustrating or unpleasant to be around. Working with these young individuals in a mental health context can be extremely challenging. To formulate a valid assessment and effective intervention, practitioners should first consider risk and protective factors affecting the behaviors of the young person.

Risk Factors

A plethora of environmental stressors can lead to youth social–emotional problems. For example, a student who does not understand a math concept might respond with defiance when asked a question in class rather than admit that he is confused. A child who is neglected or abused might appear uninvolved or distracted because of hunger, exhaustion, illness, injury, self-consciousness, or worries about her personal welfare and safety. A teen who consistently experiences racial discrimination might misinterpret a benign social greeting as an insult and react with anger and aggression. A child who is not accustomed to close adult supervision might react to the rigorous schedules and multiple demands of school with opposition and defiance. An adolescent who is surrounded by chaos and conflict at home might not have access to models to teach him how to react in an effective manner to a police officer who stops him on a sidewalk and demands to know where he is from and where he is going. A child subjected to frequent community violence might appear anxious or resort to violence quickly. A girl who is pregnant might discuss topics deemed inappropriate to some adults.

Several risk factors are supported by research as associated with youth behavior problems. They include poverty, abuse, and neglect; antisocial role models; family history of criminality, substance abuse, or mood disorders; inconsistent parenting; and perception of low social support (Bussings et al., 2003; Hill & Madhere, 1996; L. E. House, 2002; Patterson, 1986; Rainey, 1998; Samaan, 2000). It is important to know that these environmental stressors are found among every ethnic group, every income bracket, and every education level. However, indicators exist that they may disproportionately affect mental health outcomes among African American young people as compared with Caucasians (L. E. House, 2002). Moreover, the truth for African Americans lies not in raw numbers but in percentages. For example, Caucasians are well represented among highly stressed (e.g., impoverished, addicted, incarcerated) American adult populations. However, African Americans are overrepresented in these subgroups; the percentages of African Americans who live with one of these stressors surpass the total percentage of African Americans. Similarly, the percentages of African American young people in high-risk groups (e.g., impoverished, delinquent, violent, pregnant, substance-using) are higher than the percentage of African American youths at large. Some of these percentages are dropping through concerted community efforts (e.g., teen pregnancy), but the percentages are not changing appreciably because rates are dropping across American society as a whole. The reasons for these realities are crucially important and are addressed by other authors (e.g., Canada, 1995; Garbarino, 1999). The point here is that environmental stressors must be acknowledged before the mental health needs of African American youths can be met effectively.

Protective Factors

Although they are much less frequently researched, protective factors are at least as equally important as are risk factors to the mental health of young people. Some of these factors are the commonsense counterpoints to risk factors. For example, just as poor supervision and inconsistent parenting are risk factors for youths, consistent supervision and parenting are protective factors (e.g., Brody, 1999; McDowell, Parke, & Wang, 2003). Similarly, a conflicted family environment is a risk factor, whereas a cohesive family is a protective factor (L. E. House, 2002). A parent with a mood disorder is a risk factor, whereas a parent with good coping strategies is a protective factor. Perception of low social support is a risk factor, whereas high social support is a protective factor (Bussings et al., 2003).

Other factors that buffer African American youths from mental distress are not simply the inverses of risk factors. Most notable among these is involvement with a religion, sometimes termed *religiosity* in the literature. This protective factor, which comes as no surprise to many African Americans, often is overlooked by mental health practitioners conducting assessments and planning interventions. Once again, it is clear that, when working with African American youths, it is important to consider protective factors through a systemic view. Details pertaining to protective factors that are specific to African American culture (e.g., the Black church) are covered elsewhere in this book.

Assessment Tools

Any assessment of human behaviors is destined to be somewhat subjective. This might hold true more for assessment of social–emotional behaviors than of cognition and achievement, which can be evaluated through highly standardized measures. Value judgments vary widely as to what constitute appropriate and inappropriate youth behaviors. This is not to suggest that mental health providers should ignore either their own or their clients' humanity or contexts. It is to recommend that practitioners make concerted efforts to be as professional and objective as possible when conducting or interpreting behavioral assessment. Two tools that can assist these efforts are a skilled clinical interview and behavior checklists.

Clinical Interview

The importance of a skilled, goal-directed clinical interview with a young person and his or her significant others cannot be overemphasized in any discussion of youth mental health assessment. Several commercial interviews are available, such as the Semistructured Clinical Interview (Achenbach, 2002) and the National Institute of Mental Health Diagnostic Interview Schedule for Children (2nd ed.; Shaffer et al., 1993). Many mental health settings specify their own preferred structured or semistructured interview format. Still, a practitioner usually may ask for additional information based on clinical judgment. If the mandated interview is standardized, an interviewer should not violate the standardization. Follow-up questions may be asked after the standardized interview form has been completed.

Ideally, the culturally sensitive practitioner privately interviews the child or teen who is experiencing problems as well as other individuals who are involved in the youth's life. Possible resource persons include the youth's parent(s); sibling(s); peer(s); community member(s) (e.g., neighbor, religious leader, youth program staff); teacher(s); and other school personnel (e.g., teacher aide, special education teacher, school counselor, office staff, principal or assistant principal, bus driver, cafeteria personnel). It is notable that non-professionals almost always are overlooked by assessors, despite their everyday witnessing of young people's behaviors. A person need not know diagnostic criteria or professional jargon to provide important information and insight regarding an individual's behaviors. Certainly, it is unrealistic to assume that all of these people can be accessed for every youth assessment; people are busy, as is the mental health professional. However, extra effort during an assessment can set the stage for more effective and systemic interventions later. To find out the appropriate people to interview, the assessor may simply ask the young person, "Who are the important people in your life?" or "Whom do you care about and who cares about you?" Then, the clinician can inform each prospective interviewee that the youth named her or him as someone who was important or caring. One more word of advice: Youths with behavior problems sometimes make obvious omissions when they list people who know them well; sometimes they do not want the clinician to gain access to important information. A wise assessor will ask other interviewees if all of the appropriate and necessary people are being interviewed.

During each clinical interview, the clinician should ask about environmental factors that tend to be related to the behaviors presented. It is important to avoid professional jargon and judgments so that respondents may understand what is being asked and feel comfortable in speaking honestly. Moreover, the fact that open-ended queries elicit more information than do yes/no questions does not imply that a clinician should be so vague as to encourage nonspecific or elusive responses. Following are specific suggestions for parent/guardian interviews, which are based on one of our own clinical work in family and school settings. They are designed to help respondents not only to understand what is being asked but to focus less on self-interest and more on the needs and experiences of youths. They address important topics and emphasize parental involvement and parental supervision, a dyad proven repeatedly to relate strongly to youth outcome. In this list, a traditional or typical clinical question is posed first and then is followed by one or more alternative suggestions.

- *Typical:* "So, tell me what brings you here today."
  Suggestion: "Tell me about the last time you felt really proud of Monica. What else does she do well?"
- *Typical:* "What kind of structure do you provide for Crystal?"
  Suggestion: "Tell me about the rules you have at home."
- *Typical:* "Does Jonathan follow directions?"
  Suggestions: "What happens at your house when Jonathan doesn't do what you tell him to do? What happens when he disobeys you in public? Tell me about the last time he disobeyed you."
  Follow-up: "What kinds of discipline do you find work best with Jonathan? If that doesn't work, then what do you do?"
  Note: The last question is posed to see if the respondent equates discipline with punishment and to tap into potential abuse.
- *Typical:* "How is Charles's health?"
  Suggestions: "When was the last time Charles was sick? What helped him to feel better?"
- *Typical:* "How is Tabitha's nutrition?"
  Suggestions: "What time did Tabitha eat supper last night and breakfast this morning? What did she eat?"
- *Typical:* "How does Jamal perform in school?"
  Suggestions: "Does Jamal like school? Who's his favorite teacher? What's his favorite subject? What's his least favorite subject? How was his last report card?"
- *Typical:* "Does Belinda complete her school work?"
  Suggestions: "Tell me about Belinda's activities after school. Where does she go when school gets out? When does she do her homework on school nights? Where does she do it? What about on weekends?"
- *Typical:* "Does Carla sleep well?"
  Suggestions: "Tell me what happens at bedtime on school nights. Please describe a typical evening, step by step."
- *Typical:* "Does Michael get along well with his peers?"
  Suggestions: "Who are Michael's friends? Whom have you met? Who has come to your home? Who do you like best? Who do you like least?"
- *Typical:* "Is Ebony involved with any deviant subculture?"
  Suggestions: "What kinds of music does Ebony enjoy? Who is her favorite performer? When and where does she listen to music? What does Ebony like to watch on TV? Does Ebony spend time on a computer? What does she do with the computer? How does Ebony like to dress? How do her friends dress?"
  Note: Meaningful interpretation of responses requires the practitioner to remain informed about current cultural trends among young African Americans.
- *Typical:* "Does Lamar abuse any substances?"
  Suggestions: "To your knowledge, has Lamar ever smoked or chewed tobacco? Has he smoked weed? Has he drunk alcohol? How about oxycotin? Heroin? Has he taken any medicines that were prescribed by a doctor for someone else? What kinds of medicines does he take that you get from the counter at a drug store or

discount store? Has he ever taken any illegal drugs?" If yes to any, "How often does he . . . ?" "Who does he do this with?" If rapport seems good, follow up these inquiries by asking about the parent's or guardian's own substance use.

Note: It is OK to ask a question in more than one way, to get clarification and to check on a respondent's familiarity with a topic. However, be respectful and straightforward. A practitioner who is perceived as trying to set up or trick a respondent will not get honest replies.

- *Typical:* "Is Shamika sexually active?"

  Suggestions: "Does Shamika go out with boys? Is she seeing anyone, in particular? Do her girlfriends have boyfriends? Who does Shamika talk with about sex? Is she on birth control?" If yes to birth control, "Where does she get it? Do you go with her to get it? Do you talk about how to use it?"

- *Typical:* "Does Dominique have access to a dangerous weapon?"

  Suggestions: "Do you ever have a gun in your home, at any time?" If yes, "How many? Exactly where are they, right this minute? Do they have locks? Are they locked, right now? Where are the bullets? When was the last time you saw each gun?"

  Note: Weapon access usually is addressed only during suicide or homicide risk assessments. At some point in the interview, please inform *all* parents of statistics regarding gun-related deaths among African American youths and educate them that youths almost always know the locations of guns and ammunition in their homes, despite their parents' mistaken beliefs.

Behavior Checklists

Mental health services are offered to youths only when they meet certain, specific criteria, and with budgetary problems, those criteria are becoming stringent. In some settings, a child or teen must be deemed harmful to self or others to qualify for services. Often, information from clinical interviews is considered too subjective for such important decisions, and instruments that have shown more reliability and validity are required. To assure some equanimity, to avoid litigation, and to provide services to those most in need, many mental health centers have designated a specific behavior checklist as the assessment tool to be used. Frequently used checklists include the Behavior Assessment System for Children (Reynolds & Kamphaus, 1992), the 2002 Achenbach System of Empirically Based Assessment (Achenbach, 2002), the Personality Inventory for Youth (Lachar & Gruber, 1992), and the Devereux Scales of Mental Disorder (Naglieri, LeBuffe, & Pfeiffer, 1994). Other centers carefully design their own checklists to be used systemwide. As when conducting cognitive assessments, it is important to research the reliability, validity, and norming data for a behavior checklist before adopting it for personal or system use.

Rule-Out Diagnoses

As was mentioned previously, ADHD, oppositional defiant disorder, and conduct disorder are the mental health diagnoses most common among children and adolescents who consistently exhibit problematic behaviors. However, it is important for the skilled clinician to appreciate fully the manner in which other mental health problems can mimic the characteristics of these three diagnoses. It is not the purpose of this section to specify all of the configurations that can apply to forming youth psychiatric diagnoses. Still, the following alternative or comorbid diagnoses are important to consider when assessing a young person who demonstrates antisocial behaviors: abuse/neglect, adjustment disorder, attachment disorder, anxiety disorder, Bipolar I disorder, communication disorder, dysthymic disorder, intermittent explosive disorder, learning disorder, mental retardation, major depression, and substance use disorder. For example, if a disruptive youth's behaviors appear to be in reaction to stressful external events rather than to an internal imbalance, consider the possibility of an adjustment disorder with disturbance of conduct. If a youth misbehaves in school but does fine at home and in the community, consider a possible learning disorder. When a child has trouble with all academic subjects and has been slow to reach most developmental milestones, consider the possibility of a developmental disability such as mental retardation or autism. If the behaviors and peer group of a youth suddenly change, consider a possible new involvement with alcohol or other drugs. If depression seems to lift for no known reason, assess for suicidal intent.

Implications for Practice

Mental health assessment is an avenue to discover a person's pattern of successes and failures and to gain an understanding of her or his view of the world. The process through which this occurs can result in an accurate reflection of a youth or it can begin a long, frustrating journey that involves inappropriate labeling and interventions. It is neither safe to assume that mental health assessments of African American children and adolescents are conducted in a fair, reliable, and valid manner nor that they are inherently unfair and biased. As when assessing any individual, best practices should be followed. The practices targeted here address (a) examiner biases; (b) assessment of the individual in context; (c) consideration of multiple traits, settings, and informants; and (d) rule-out and comorbid diagnoses.

Examiner Biases

Let us be honest. Biases are held by people of both genders and all ethnic groups, levels of education, incomes, sexual orientations, and family structures. The task for mental health professionals is to identify our own preconceptions and then to take control to alter our own biases. It is important to recognize that biases can lead practitioners toward overly harsh or overly permissive attitudes.

First, let us consider biases that can lead to inappropriately harsh attitudes toward African American youths. Of course, these examples are not intended to imply that all professionals within any ethnic group or socioeconomic level have the same thoughts and feelings. They simply are examples of biases that can be witnessed in clinical and educational settings.

- *Fish in water*
  A non-African American practitioner who has had little personal exposure to African American youths or to people who struggle to make ends meet might bring egocentrism, ethnocentrism, or sociocentrism to her work. This bias is reflected in blind assumptions that everyone shares the same values and everyone enjoys the same opportunities. It can help the competent practitioner who deals with this bias in herself and others to keep in mind that the biased person no more understands the privileges he or she has enjoyed than fish understand that they are in water.
- *You're BAD, not EBD.*
  A professional might condemn an African American youth who demonstrates behaviors that he finds inexcusable. This practitioner might interpret behaviors as totally within the youth's control and, thus, as reflecting willful, malicious intent. A corollary of this bias is "You wouldn't be like this if I were raising you."
- *You're making us look bad.*
  An African American practitioner might carry a bias toward African American youths who demonstrate behaviors that are frowned on socially. The professional may feel

that these young people sabotage her personal efforts to move the realities and images of African Americans forward.

- *I did it. What's wrong with you?*
  A practitioner who has worked diligently to improve his educational, financial, and social standing may harbor resentment toward a young person who shows less commitment, tenacity, or success. This professional may be impatient with a struggling youth.
- *My mama raised me like that and I'm OK.*
  A practitioner might rely on memories of counseling, parenting, or teaching techniques from her own youth that, although she disliked and resented at the time, are seen in retrospect as necessary and effective. This professional overgeneralizes about communication styles and disciplinary methods that are appropriate for use with African American youths and maintains that "in your face" techniques are culturally appropriate. The explanation offered usually includes something about "I hate to have to get like that, but sometimes you just have to. And it works."

Each of these biases may lead practitioners to judge troubled African American youths harshly, without demonstrating the objectivity and compassion needed by an effective professional.

Other biases may lead mental health practitioners to take a more permissive approach with African American youths than is therapeutic. Examples follow:

- *Poor thing*
  A practitioner might feel so sorry for a troubled African American youth that he does not give the youth accurate feedback about the youth's behaviors and their consequences. Although this leniency is purported to be supportive of a young person, in reality, it communicates a lack of respect and a belief that the youth cannot gain the self-regulatory skills and insight that may lead to more appropriate behavioral choices.
- *Shouldering the guilt*
  A practitioner who is not African American might feel guilty about the discrimination faced by African Americans, historically and currently. To atone for this mistreatment and to avoid appearing prejudiced or punitive, she might be reticent to supply the limits and structure any youth needs to develop self-control.
- *Please don't hurt me.*
  A practitioner might fear African American youths. This practitioner might ignore behaviors he would confront with a non-African American child or teen because of unrealistic and overgeneralized fears for his own safety.
- *You're just not as smart as we are.*
  A practitioner might believe that African American youths are less capable than are youths of other ethnicities. This practitioner might hold low expectations for African American young people because she assumes that they can do no better. We have been familiar with the consequences of this bias since Rosenthal and Jacobsen (1968) and before.

Being consistently too hard or too easy in dealings with African American youths reflects biases that harm young people. The challenge is to find a balance that communicates genuine empathy, appropriate structure, and reasonable expectations.

Assessment of the Individual in Context

Every person functions within an ecological context that affects her or his behaviors. This might be even truer for young people than it is for adults. Some professionals who specialize in youth assessment assert that the behaviors of children and adolescents are more situation specific, fluid, and evolving than are those of adults, which implies that greater attention should be focused on evaluating environmental characteristics and factors (e.g., A. E. House, 1999, p. 13). A child or adolescent who does not follow common social expectations regarding behaviors does not necessarily have a mental illness; the problem may reflect one or more external factors rather than an internal disability. It is just as inappropriate to assume that a youth's behaviors are *not* reactions to his or her environment as it is to assume that his or her behaviors solely reflect the environment. Both extremes reflect bias. It is crucial, when assessing the behaviors of any youth, to suspend assumptions and view all behaviors through the lens of the person's environments. This is particularly important when psychiatric diagnoses are being contemplated that may have long-term effects on educational and life options.

Multiple Traits, Settings, and Informants

In almost all situations, a child or adolescent should not be diagnosed based only on one act, one person's report, or behaviors demonstrated in one setting. With the possible exception of when a client commits a serious act of violence against self or another person, mental health practitioners should look for patterns of behaviors across settings rather than single acts in one location. This holds true for all clients, and yet it is particularly true for young people who, because of their developmental levels, tend to feel unusual pressure to conform to peer pressure or perceived social norms. Moreover, as has been noted, youths tend to have less control over their environments than do adults. Thus, they sometimes are bound to remain in situations that are dysfunctional for them and then are judged harshly for their reactive behaviors.

For most psychiatric diagnoses, it is mandatory that a youth display disturbed behaviors in more than one setting. This is particularly important when assessing African American youths, whose community or home rules, routines, and expectations might differ markedly from those they encounter in school. For example, if a young person functions well at home, at a local community center, and at church and yet refuses to comply with school expectations, the problem should not be judged automatically as internally based. The problem may be a mismatch between more familiar settings and school expectations. It would be erroneous to diagnose the young person as disabled or disordered without thoroughly exploring ways to bridge the expectation gaps.

In a similar manner, except in unusual circumstances, no youths should be assessed on the basis of behavioral descriptions from only one reporter. Because most children and adolescents function in at least the two very different worlds of home and school, input from members of both environments should be sought to gain an accurate picture of an individual's functioning. It is even better when additional information can be attained from people in the youth's community, such as a neighbor, pastor, or youth leader. The more complete the picture of the youth's functioning in various environments and with various people, the more confidence can be placed in a diagnosis and in interventions.

Rule-Out and Comorbid Diagnoses

When assessing children and adolescents who display unusual or unwanted behaviors, a mental health professional must realize that youths often demonstrate health and mental health problems differently from adults. For example, a child who has trouble paying attention in school might have ADHD. However, she or he might be dealing with abuse, fear, separation, poor nutrition, illness, allergies, low cognitive ability, depression, anxiety, or one of several other internal or environmental factors that could preclude a diagnosis of ADHD. A teen who appears depressed might suffer from a specific learning disability, anxiety, peer rejection, illness, ADHD, poor nutrition, abuse, pregnancy, sleep deprivation, or substance use. It is not sufficient to compare a youth's behaviors with a list of behaviors in the *DSM–IV–TR*, find a diagnosis that matches criterion symptoms, and be done with it. Of course, this would be poor practice when assessing anyone. However, it is especially pertinent when working with African American youths, who may express problems in ways that are different from the social mainstream.

Summary

Implications for Future Research

Areas of study that relate to youth mental health vary markedly in the attention they have received in research literature. Many studies and reviews have focused on delivery of mental health services to African Americans in general. These have yielded qualitative and empirical data regarding African American access to, utilization of, and mistrust of mental health services. Also well researched are risk factors that pertain to youths in general and minority youths in particular. Especially targeted are behaviors connected to social problems for American society, such as youth aggression, drug use, and teen pregnancy. A final common area of study surrounds discrepancies in cognitive/achievement scores between Caucasian youths and youths from minority ethnic groups.

Other areas pertaining to youth mental health assessment are less well researched. This field needs longitudinal studies that deeply explore factors that might be protective for children and adolescents, and for African American youths in particular. Also needed are studies that assess the reliability, validity, and practicality of a variety of assessment techniques that provide alternatives to standardized measures of cognition and achievement. Greatly needed are studies that go beyond simply reporting ethnic differences in scores and behaviors to explore reasons for differences. It can be hypothesized that youth mental health assessment results provide a type of litmus test of access to life options in our society. If so, ethnic and SES clusters, which are found repeatedly through research studies, simply point to unequal access, which continues to exist. This hypothesis can be tested only through truly equal access. If it holds true, then, when every American child and adolescent has equal access to factors correlated with successful choices, such as safe communities, quality education, and mental health support, ethnic and socioeconomic discrepancies should disappear.

Case Study

Let us now revisit the case study of LaKesha Wilson as an application of the suggestions made in this chapter. The reader will recall LaKesha had been referred to the mental health center for an evaluation, as part of the process of her mother seeking her removal from the home. The youth had demonstrated belligerence and noncompliance repeatedly, at home and at school. Mr. Johnson had reviewed the records and interviewed LaKesha.

Mr. Johnson's clinical interview suggested a new possibility for LaKesha Wilson's difficulties at home and at school. The clinician did not automatically dismiss inconsistencies in the youth's responses but rather tried to find patterns in her strengths and weaknesses. LaKesha was skilled in styling her nails and hair, as well as in recalling the visual details of the apron she had made. She showed difficulty in following verbal directions, and she did not complete assigned schoolwork or home chores. Especially notable was LaKesha's evident inability to recall or describe everyday activities and places. Although she was a physically mature 12-year-old, her responses resembled those of a younger child.

Following his interview with LaKesha, Mr. Johnson asked Ms. Wilson to join them in his office. He stopped her immediately when the overwrought mother began to delineate her daughter's misbehaviors and steered her, instead, to talk first about what LaKesha did well at home. He was not surprised to hear that the youth excelled in tasks that required visual acuity and visual memory. Once a more positive atmosphere had been created, Mr. Johnson asked about LaKesha's progress in school, over the years, and about how instructions were provided for LaKesha at home. It became clear that LaKesha had demonstrated difficulty with every academic subject except spelling. He asked LaKesha about her spelling lessons, and she could not explain their format. He asked Ms. Wilson if she would provide written permission for him to talk with LaKesha's teacher and she readily complied. He also suggested that she ask school personnel to evaluate LaKesha's cognitive ability, as they progressed with their reevaluation. Ms. Wilson agreed to talk with the school psychologist, with whom she felt comfortable. She was not certain but thought her daughter had never been given an IQ test.

LaKesha was given a full cognitive assessment by the school assessment team. The youth's full scale score on a traditional, standardized IQ test fell within the range of a mild mental disability, and a nonverbal test reinforced that finding. Her knowledge and skills were evaluated further through a classroom observation and a comprehensive interview with Ms. Wilson that included completion of a measure of adaptive behaviors. In addition, with Ms. Wilson's permission, LaKesha's current teacher, home economics teacher, Girl Scout leader, and Sunday school teacher were interviewed via telephone, and the teacher and mom completed a well-normed behavior checklist. The pattern was clear. Despite LaKesha's phenomenal visual memory, her cognitive ability was low across all other areas. This prevented her from succeeding with most school tasks, contributed to her difficulties with same-age peers, and led to her trouble in following multiple verbal directions. She had made As in spelling because her teacher had an established routine of writing spelling words on the board, as a review, immediately before each spelling test. Because of her excellent visual memory, LaKesha simply remembered the spelling of the words, which she could neither read nor define.

LaKesha's individualized education program was revised to provide her the vocational instruction she needed and enjoyed. Things calmed down at school and at home, and the incorrigibility charge was dropped. LaKesha saw the mental health practitioner four more times before her case was closed. She learned to state her needs more assertively and politely, and she enjoyed the games they played, although she needed assistance, each session, in recalling Mr. Johnson's name and in finding her way to his office from the waiting room.

Analysis

Although LaKesha's need for special education and mental health services had been recognized previously, assessment errors had led to misdiagnosis and, thus, inappropriate interventions. Her lack of success in her home, school, and community environments then was interpreted as reflecting malicious intent rather than LaKesha's difficulties in understanding her various worlds and the accompanying expectations. This was no small problem. LaKesha was very near being removed from her home and identified in school as having an emotional/behavioral disability. Placement in a foster home or residential setting, in addition to placement in classes with peers who did not model acceptable behaviors, could have led LaKesha down an unnecessarily difficult life path.

One may review the major points of this chapter by considering how Mr. Johnson and school personnel collaborated in the assessment of LaKesha's knowledge, skills, and behaviors. First and foremost, they suspended their own biases and preconceptions and considered LaKesha as an individual who was having difficulty dealing with her multiple environments. They spoke, at length, with LaKesha and her mother, as well as with other important people in LaKesha's school and community. They used a variety of assessment measures, some of which were standardized and had been demonstrated as reliable, valid for their purpose, and normed with an appropriate percentage of African American youths, and some of which offered alternatives to traditional instruments. The time and effort put forth by these professionals produced assessment results that more accurately reflected LaKesha's strengths and weaknesses. Once the people in LaKesha's worlds understood her better, the youth's quality of life improved immediately, and her options for successful future choices expanded.

References

Achenbach, T. M. (2002). *System of empirically based assessment.* Burlington, VT: Research Center for Children, Youth, & Families.

American Psychiatric Association. (2000). *Diagnostic and statistical manual of mental disorders* (4th ed., text revision). Washington, DC: Author.

Anastasi, A. (1988). *Psychological testing* (6th ed.). New York: Macmillan.

Bagnato, S. J., & Neisworth, J. T. (1991). *Assessment for early intervention: Best practices for professionals.* New York: Guilford Press.

Barrera, I. (1996). Thoughts on the assessment of young children whose sociocultural background is unfamiliar to the assessor. In S. J. Meisels & E. Fenichel (Eds.), *New visions for the developmental assessment of infants and young children* (pp. 69–84). Washington, DC: National Center for Infants, Toddlers, and Families.

Battle, D. (2002). Language development and disorders in culturally and linguistically diverse children. In D. Berstein & E. Tiegerman-Farber (Eds.), *Language and communication disorders in children* (pp. 354–386). Boston: Allyn & Bacon.

Bersoff, D. N. (1982). Larry P. and PASE: Judicial report cards on the validity of individual intelligence tests. In T. Kratochwill (Ed.), *Advances in school psychology* (Vol. 2, pp. 61–95). Hillsdale, NJ: Erlbaum.

Brody, G. H. (1999). Sibling relationships in rural African American families. *Journal of Marriage and the Family, 61,* 1046–1057.

Bussings, R., Zima, B. T., Gary, F. A., Mason, D. M., Leon, C. E., Sinha, K., et al. (2003). Social networks, caregiver strain, and utilization of mental health services among elementary school students at high risk for ADHD. *Journal of the American Academy of Child & Adolescent Psychiatry, 42,* 842–849.

Campbell, T., Dollaghan, C., Needleman, H., & Janosky, J. (1997). Reducing bias in language assessment: Processing-dependent measures. *Journal of Speech, Language, and Hearing Research, 40,* 519–525.

Canada, G. (1995). *Fist stick knife gun.* Boston: Beacon Press.

Canter, A. S., Hurley, C. M., & Reid, C. L. (2000). A better IDEA for reevaluation. In C. E. Telzrow & M. Tankersley (Eds.), *IDEA Amendments of 1997: Practice guidelines for school-based teams* (pp. 105–150). Bethesda, MD: National Association of School Psychologists.

Craig, H. K., Connor, C. M., & Washington, J. A. (2003). Early positive predictors of later reading comprehension for African American students: A preliminary investigation. *Language, Speech, and Hearing Service in Schools, 34,* 31–43.

Crawford v. Honig, 37 F.3d 485 (9th Cir. 1994).

Doll, B. (1996). Prevalence of psychiatric disorders in children and youth: An agenda for advocacy by school psychology. *School Psychology Quarterly, 11,* 20–47.

Entwisle, D. R., & Hayduk, L. A. (1988). Lasting effects of elementary school. *Sociology of Education, 61,* 147–159.

Fish, J. M. (Ed.). (2002). *Race and intelligence: Separating science from myth.* Mahwah, NJ: Erlbaum.

Fuery, D. C. (1999). Mental health treatment participation patterns of severely emotionally disturbed children and adolescents. *Dissertation Abstracts International, 50*(5-A), 1767.

Garbarino, J. (1999). *Lost boys: Why our sons turn violent and how we can save them.* New York: Free Press.

Hanson, M. J., & Lynch, E. W. (2003). *Understanding families: Approaches to diversity, disability, and risk.* Baltimore: Brookes.

Helms, J. E. (1992). Why is there no study of cultural equivalence in standardized cognitive ability testing? *American Psychologist, 47,* 1083–1101.

Herrnstein, R. J., & Murray, C. (1994). *The bell curve.* New York: Free Press.

Hill, H. M., & Madhere, S. (1996). Exposure to community violence and African American children: A multidimensional model of risks and resources. *Journal of Community Psychology, 24,* 26–43.

Hobson v. Hansen, 269 F. Supp. 401, 514 (D.D.C. 1967).

House, A. E. (1999). DSM–IV *diagnosis in the schools.* New York: Guilford Press.

House, L. E. (2002). And still they rise: An examination of risk and protective factors for depression and antisocial behavior in African American adolescents. *Dissertation Abstracts International, 63*(1-A), 362.

Individuals With Disabilities Education Act. (1999). 34 C.F.R. 300, Regulations Implementing IDEA (1997) (*Federal Register, 1999, 64*(48)).

Jacob-Timm, S., & Hartshorne, T. S. (1998). *Ethics and law for school psychologists* (3rd ed.). New York: Wiley.

Jensen, A. R. (1980). *Bias in mental testing.* New York: Free Press.

Kamphaus, R. W., & Reynolds, C. (1987). *Clinical and research applications of the K-ABC.* Circle Pines, MN: American Guidance Services.

Lachar, D., & Gruber, C. P. (1992). *Personality Inventory for Youth (PIY).* Los Angeles: Western Psychological Services.

Ladd, G. W., Kochenderfer, B. J., & Coleman, C. C. (1996). Friendship quality as a predictor of young children's early school adjustment. *Child Development, 67,* 1103–1118.

Laing, S. P., & Kamhi, A. (2003). Alternative assessment of language and literacy in culturally and linguistically diverse populations. *Language, Speech, and Hearing Services in Schools, 34,* 44–55.

Larry P. v. Wilson Riles, 343 F. Supp. 1306 (D.C. N.D. Cal., 1972).

McDowell, D. J., Parke, R. D., & Wang, S. J. (2003). Differences between mothers' and fathers' advice-giving style and content: Relations with social competence and psychological functioning in middle school. *Merrill-Palmer Quarterly, 49,* 55–76.

Naglieri, J. A., LeBuffe, P. A., & Pfeiffer, A. I. (1994). *Devereux Scales of Mental Disorder.* New York: Psychological Corporation.

Ortiz, S. O. (2002). Best practices in nondiscriminatory assessment. In A. Thomas & J. Grimes (Eds.), *Best practices in school psychology IV* (Vol. 2, pp. 1321–1336). Bethesda, MD: National Association for School Psychologists.

Parents in Action on Special Education (P.A.S.E.) v. Hannon, 506 F. Supp. 831 (N.D. Ill. 1980).

Patterson, G. R. (1986). Performance models for antisocial boys. *American Psychologist, 41,* 432–444.

Pianta, R. C., & Steinberg, M. S. (1992). Teacher–child relationships and the process of adjusting to school. *New Directions for Child Development, 57,* 61–80.

Rainey, J. A. (1998). Early adolescent student aggression: Differentiation of aggression levels in a middle school population. *Dissertation Abstracts International, 59*(6-A), 1908.

Reynolds, C. R., & Kamphaus, R. W. (1992). *Behavior Assessment System for Children (BASC).* Circle Pines, MN: American Guidance Services.

Rosenthal, R., & Jacobsen, L. (1968). *Pygmalion in the classroom: Teacher expectation and pupils' intellectual development.* New York: Holt, Rinehart & Winston.

Salvia, J., & Ysseldyke, J. E. (1991). *Assessment* (5th ed.). New York: Houghton Mifflin.

Samaan, R. A. (2000). The influences of race, ethnicity, and poverty on the mental health of children. *Journal of Health Care for the Poor and Underserved, 11,* 100–110.

Sandoval, J., Frisby, C. L., Geisinger, K. F., Scheuneman, J. D., & Grenier, J. R. (Eds.). (1998). *Test interpretation and diversity: Achieving equity in assessment.* Washington, DC: American Psychological Association.

Sattler, J. M. (2001). *Assessment of children: Cognitive applications* (4th ed.). San Diego, CA: Sattler.

Shaffer, D., Schwab-Stone, M., Fisher, P., Cohen, P., Piacentini, J., Davies, M., et al. (1993). The Diagnostic Interview Schedule for Children—Revised Version (DISC–R): I. Preparation, field testing, interrater reliability, and acceptability. *Journal of the American Academy of Child and Adolescent Psychiatry, 32,* 643–650.

Townsend, B. L. (2002). "Testing while Black": Standards-based school reform and African American learners. *Remedial and Special Education, 23,* 222–230.

Turnbull, H. R., III. (1990). *Free appropriate public education: The law and children with disabilities* (3rd ed.). Denver, CO: Love.

U.S. Census Bureau. (2000). *State and county quick facts.* Retrieved March 31, 2004, from http://quickfacts.census.gov/qdf/states/00000.html

U.S. Department of Education. (1999). *Assistance to states for the education of children with disabilities and the early intervention program for infants and toddlers with disabilities; final regulations, March 12, 1999* (34 CFR Parts 300 and 303). Washington, DC: Author.

U.S. Department of Education, National Center of Educational Statistics. (2003). *The condition of education 2003* (NCES 2003-067). Washington, DC: U.S. Government Printing Office.

Willard, L. S. (1968). A comparison of culture fair test scores with group and individual intelligence test scores of disadvantaged Negro children. *Journal of Learning Disabilities, 1,* 584–589.

Williams, R. L. (1975). The BITCH-100: A culture-specific test. *Journal of Afro-American Issues, 3,* 103–116.

19

African Americans' Spirituality and Religion in Counseling and Psychotherapy

John Milton Dillard and Betty Brown Smith

Spirituality and religion are often significant underlying dimensions of African American clients' concerns brought to the counseling or the psychotherapy milieu. According to Lehman (1993) and Kelly (1994), many prospective clients feel that these dimensions are significantly relevant to counseling and psychotherapy. Moreover, spiritual and religious aspects indeed may be akin to ethnic or cultural experiences clients bring to professional counselors and psychotherapists (Albanese, 1999; Pate & Bondi, 1992; Quackenbos, Privette, & Klentz, 1985). It is well known that African Americans have a rich spiritual and religious heritage that continues to play a significant role in their lives (Albanese, 1999; Potts, 1991).

It is equally important to note that how well practitioners respond to their clients' personal issues may determine the success or failure of their efforts. Prest and Keller (1993) maintained that "because the vast majority of the world's families adopt some identifiable form of expression for their spirituality, it seems only natural that mental health professionals should attend to clients' spiritual belief systems to better understand them and maximize their effectiveness" (p. 137).

This chapter provides a delineation of spirituality and religion as major dimensions in the lives of most contemporary African Americans and the significance of these dimensions in the therapeutic setting. We also suggest curriculum modifications for training prospective mental health professionals to work effectively with African Americans' spiritual and religious issues.

African American Spirituality

Spirituality is defined as a view of an individual's place in the universe (Pate & Bondi, 1992) or a personal inclination or desire for a relationship with the transcendent or God, whereas *religion* is the social or organized means by which people express spirituality (Albanese, 1999; Grimm, 1994). However, spirituality and religion do not necessarily function simultaneously for African Americans. For example, according to Chandler, Holden, and Kolander (1992), "spirituality can occur in or out of the context of organized religion, and not all aspects of religion are assumed to be spiritual" (p. 170).

Spirituality is a widespread, multifaceted presence in the lives of most African Americans. It has the potential to affect their psychological well-being in a preventative manner (Maton & Wells, 1995). From an Afrocultural psychological orientation, Jagers and Mock (1993) stated,

> Spirituality connotes a belief that all elements of reality contain a certain amount of life force. It entails believing and behaving as if nonobservable and nonmaterial life forces have governing powers in one's everyday affairs. Thus a continuous sensitivity to core spiritual qualities takes priority in one's life and indeed is vital to one's personal well-being. Although often expressed in God concepts, this ongoing core spiritual sensitivity is not necessarily tied to formal church doctrine or participation. Indeed, it goes beyond church affiliation. Moreover, it connotes a belief in the transcendence of physical death and a sense of continuity with one's ancestors. (p. 394)

An empirical study by Edwards (1987) revealed that spirituality is the most significant self-determined component of psychological health among African Americans. Much of what African American clients might bring to the therapeutic setting is associated with spiritual material. Meadow and Kahoe (1984), Genia (1990), and Constantine, Lewis, and Conner (2000) contended that spiritual development does not unfold in isolation, separate from other aspects of personal functioning. Rather, it is intertwined with the cognitive, social, emotional, and psychological components of the personality. Hence, deficits in one or more of these areas are likely to be mirrored in the person's spiritual functioning (Genia, 1990; Meadow & Kahoe, 1984). Mental health professionals, however, often fail to attend to the spiritual-related dimensions of clients' concerns. Genia (1990) advocated,

> When clients present dominant [spiritual] themes and concerns in therapy, these issues are often ignored, challenged as inadequate and irrational, or analyzed as symbolic representations of neurotic fears, wishes, impulses, or conflicts. Even when therapists are sympathetic toward religion they seldom work directly with the client's religious material. Instead, such therapists may refer spiritually troubled clients to clergy/persons for spiritual guidance as adjuncts to therapy, without assessing whether such a referral is appropriate or necessary. (p. 39)

African Americans have a long heritage involving spirituality and religious practices that usually are not considered during therapy with professionals who use traditional approaches to mental health (Albanese, 1999).

African Custom Retention

Not that long ago, it was widely promulgated that chattel slavery severed all connections that Blacks in the Americas had with their African homeland and traditions. However, it has been well established that Africanisms—"those elements of culture found in the New World that are traceable to an African origin" (Holloway, 1991)—survived the long voyage across the Atlantic Ocean. Recent research by scholars (Akbar, 1984, 1994; Baldwin, 1991; Nobles, 1973, 1980, 1986) of African descent have successfully demonstrated that Africanisms have been retained by Africans in the Diaspora. Africanisms have been preserved because they are an expression of the deep structure of cultural substance. Cultural substance represents a people's ideological philosophical infrastructure. This deep structure encompasses a group's ontology, axiology, and epistemology and provides a system for organizing, experiencing, construing, and describing their reality (Baldwin, 1991). Simply stated, cultural substance gives meaning to the phenomena, events, and experiences one encounters.

According to Mbiti (1975), African peoples are deeply spiritual. He posited that for African peoples, "to be is to be religious in a religious universe. This notion is the philosophical basis that under-girds African myths, customs, traditions, beliefs, morals, actions and social relationships" (Mbiti, 1975, p. 256). Given this axiom, one would expect a strong spiritual orientation to prevail even under the harsh conditions of chattel slavery. Parenthetically, African American history provides substantial evidence to support this position. The Black church has historically had a central role in African Americans' quest for liberation from injustices. Also, it has unknowingly nourished other African customs and traditions, such as spiritual expression through music, dance, improvisation, orality, call-and-response, the extensive use of metaphors, and symbolic imagery (Albanese, 1999; Constantine et al., 2000; Frame & Williams, 1996).

The structural similarities of Christianity to African cosmology enhanced the Africans' inclination to interpret the new religion in terms of the familiar structure of their native religions. Thus, the conversion of African slaves to Christianity facilitated rather than destroyed the deep structure of the Africans' cultural view of the universe (Paris, 1995). The retention of a strong religious orientation persisted among African Americans long after slavery.

Holloway's (1991) studies of African spirituality in New Orleans, Haiti, and Brazil indicated that spirituality is the most dominant and intact expression of Africanisms. In the 1920s and 1930s, Black Spiritual churches, especially of New Orleans, were uniquely different from other places of worship. The highly participatory nature of services, the use of household objects as sacred, and the sacred and pragmatic approach to healing physical, psychological, or social conditions were all indicators of African custom retention. The Black Spiritual church, often viewed as a corruption of Christianity, characterized the Africans' philosophical understanding of the universe. These churches provided the worshiper with a spiritual world that united the temporal and the eternal (Jacobs, 1990). The African Americans' strong spiritual expression still persists today; the unique forms of song, dance, prayer, and preaching are indicative of the intrinsic inclination to preserve the deep structure of culture (Albanese, 1999; Frame & Williams, 1996; Mulira, 1991). Africanisms, then, are the manifestation of African traditions retained by those in the Diaspora and modified to fit a new environment.

Communal Expression of African Spirituality

From a traditional African frame of reference, spirituality defies the notion of a linear or standard definition. In the dichotomous tradition of the West, spirituality is viewed primarily as a transcendental relationship between an individual and a higher being. Conversely, religion or religiosity is explained as the adherence to the beliefs and practices of an organized church or religious institution (Jackson-Lowman, Rogers, Zhang, Zhao, & Brathwaite-Tull, 1996). From this viewpoint, compartmentalized and expressed in a variety of ways and organized, religion is but one of them. From the traditional African perspective, religion cannot be separated from the daily demands of life; it is understood as pervasive and pragmatic. Religion manifests itself as a way of being in the world. This way of being is spiritual and not only affects how one relates to a higher being but also defines how one relates to all aspects of the universe (both visible and invisible). It is impossible to separate spirituality and religion, because religion is the material manifestation of the spirit (Richards, 1980).

According to Gyekye (1996), religion in the traditional African culture is not an adjunct to daily life, nor is it a means for spiritual uplifting. It is embedded in the culture in practical ways of healing, problem solving, and enhancing physical and material needs. Religion is not designed solely for the salvation of the individual; it is for the use of the people to which the individual belongs. Religion is a celebration of life and the interconnectedness of the universe. By virtue of religious rituals, the traditional African is born into a community that constantly reaffirms a spirit-filled way of being in the world. Therefore, public celebration (drumming, dancing, and singing) of these rites (naming ceremonies, rites of passage, marriage, betrothals, funeral traditions, etc.) is a vital part of the communal lifestyle of the African (Paris, 1995).

In sum, for the traditional African, it is assumed that the essence of material/physical existence is spirit/energy, or what is referred to as *life force*. Therefore, much time is invested in maintaining and strengthening the connection with this life force. According to Leonard Barnett (as quoted in Richards, 1980),

> the supreme value in terms of the African world view is "to live life robustly." That is, we must live life with as much energy and as forcefully as we can. Much of African religious activity, therefore, involves the attempt to strengthen our . . . "life force." (p. 7)

It is clear that what Westerners perceive as a spiritual aspiration, Africans perceive as an inherent way of being in the world that manifests itself in all venues of life. Logically then, it appears more appropriate to discuss African spirituality as a philosophy or worldview versus an entity that can be understood separate from one's cultural view of the world (Montilus, 1989). It is this African philosophy and cultural worldview that provides the foundation of the African-centered psychology that is being used with many Africans in the Diaspora.

African Philosophy: The Foundation of African-Centered Psychology

The philosophical system that prevailed in precolonial Africa assumed the existence of an orderly and harmonious universe. Humans were considered one with God and the whole universe. The concept of a divine connection to the universe stems from the belief that all substances of the universe belong to one vital force. This force is likened to electricity because it is invisible, yet it is the source of all visible energy. People were considered a natural part of the rhythm of nature (Nobles, 1980). Thus, oneness or union with the universe was viewed as an active participatory process; it is in the unfolding of life, the actual living and being, that oneness is internalized (Montilus, 1989).

Internalization of the concept that all life is divinely connected to one source is a complex process. It is through the psyche or mind, which the ancients referred to as the soul, that this divine view of self becomes incorporated. The psyche/soul is multifaceted. It integrates internal emotions and external behavior. It is the seat of intelligence (which is subject to the influence of culture). The human qualities of intent and will are embodied in the psyche and inexplicably intertwined with the development of intellectual maturity. A less evident aspect of the psyche is self-creative power (the power to generate one's own kind). The ability to transmit lineaments of the self to subsequent generations is a spiritual responsibility that is governed by the intellect. It is the intellectual quality of the psyche that acts as the unifying energy force between the spiritual and the material realms of life (Akbar, 1994; Nobles, 1986).

With the emergence of intellectual maturity, diametrically opposed distinctions between phenomena and self apparently melt away. A balance is created between seemingly opposite aspects of the self, that is, rational and emotional, material and spiritual, maleness and femaleness. The synergistic quality of the psyche/soul illuminates the holistic nature of the vital force. This is contrary to the Western view of the self, which is divided into separate and distinctly opposing parts (spiritual vs. material, rational vs. emotional, and male vs. female). For the African these qualities are only aspects of a divine whole that manifests itself in the form of the human self (Akbar, 1994; Nobles, 1986).

The spiritual disposition of African philosophy also dictated the notion of survival of one's people or tribe as paramount. This collective consciousness gave rise to a vital attitude of solidarity (Nobles, 1980). In the African philosophical system, the individual exists in that the group can survive, and his or her individualism is attributed meaning only as the collective prospers (Jackson, 1982; Nobles, 1973). This approach does not deny the uniqueness of an individual; rather, self is defined as a collective phenomenon whereby the person cannot be understood independent of the collective body (Akbar, 1984). Therefore, cooperation and collective responsibility are highly regarded.

Spiritual Striving and Psychological Well-Being

Potts (1991) contended that "in African philosophy, to be human is to be connected with the whole community . . . [by participating] fully in the spiritual practices of the community" (p. 54). Culture, then, appears to order one's behavior, whereas disordered behavior, from the African perspective, would place the individual above the collective and interact with material phenomena as if it were devoid of spiritual content. Disordered behavior (physical, psychological, unnatural) is a threat not only to the individual but to the whole community. Therefore, maintaining cultural order, harmony, and oneness is critical to the survival of a group. Adhering to the intrinsic order of the universe as a living, interactive process for people of African lineage gives rise to a rich heritage (rituals, metaphors, proverbs, offerings, symbols, and ceremonies) that continually reaffirms the philosophical assumption that the universe is divine (Mickel, 1991; Montilus, 1989; Richards, 1980). Substantial deviation from this concept of order would likely result in a disturbance in one's psychological well-being.

Based on the African worldview, research conducted to assess the relationship between spirituality and psychological well-being of Africans in the Diaspora is growing. Rogers (1994) developed a measure of spiritual orientation, the Life Attitude Inventory, which is consistent with an African-centered view of spirituality. Consequently, spirituality is not defined as human potential but as human actuality. One's spiritual orientation, according to Rogers, defines reality and directs all human behavior both ordered and disordered. Rogers contended that this spiritual orientation undergirds all human beings and relationships. It cannot be separated out from any aspect of human existence and manifests itself in everyday activities (Albanese, 1999; Constantine et al., 2000).

Jackson-Lowman et al. (1996) argued that spirituality has the capacity for integrative and disintegrative expression. Integrative expression moves toward ideas like community, harmony, peace, aspiration, transcendence, and balance with nonhuman and superhuman environment, whereas disintegrative expression moves toward discord, disconnection, and desperation. This dynamic nature of spirituality is characteristic of the African worldview. According to Montilus (1989), "harmony is not a given, but an acquired state" (p. 21). Thus, the African's spiritual striving for oneness is a continual process.

Given the dynamic nature of spiritual orientation as defined by Rogers (1994), it is logical to conclude that it would affect one's sense of psychological well-being. As mentioned earlier, Edwards (1987) conducted a study to ascertain what African Americans viewed as the most important component of psychological health. She found that for African Americans, spirituality was the most important component of psychological well-being. Jackson-Lowman et al. (1996) found that high levels of spiritual integration and low levels of spiritual disintegration were associated with marital well-being, whereas the opposite was associated with marital dysfunction.

Potts (1991) defined spirituality as "a way of being and experiencing based upon one's relationship with self, others, nature and whatever one considers the Ultimate or God"

(p. 54). In his study of spirituality and alcoholism, he posited that clinicians pose a serious omission by excluding the spiritual orientation of African Americans when exploring the significant relationships in their lives. According to Potts, this is especially dangerous when working with those who are chemically dependent, homeless, or in severe crisis. He emphasized that the relationship with the Almighty in some instances may be the only relationship that is keeping the client alive. Further, Potts argued for a culturally specific treatment that includes specific questions about spiritual life, beliefs, and practices. He believes that information from these questions could help the clinician and the client understand that the presenting problem is affected by their beliefs (Albanese, 1999).

Other research also shows a connection between spirituality and the psychological well-being of African Americans. Dungee-Anderson and Beckett (1998) conducted a clinical analysis of Alzheimer's disease in African Americans. They found that African Americans, in an effort to reduce stress on the family, preferred the extensive use of informal social support systems in caretaking arrangements of the elderly. God was perceived as a part of this support system, and thus spirituality and faith in God served as a protective coping mechanism to reduce family stress. Additionally, the work of Zimmermann and Maton (1992) demonstrated that African American urban adolescent school dropouts who displayed a spiritual commitment, through their involvement in church, were less likely to use alcohol and other substances.

Another area in which spirituality has been shown to be important to psychological well-being is in the development of community programs. In light of the disproportionate number of young African American males involved in homicides, substance abuse, unemployment, and school disenfranchisement, Watts (1993) investigated several manhood development programs designed to combat these problems from the perspective of community psychology. He found that the participants in his study valued the notion of "giving back" to the community, cultural socialization, and spirituality as vital to manhood development programs. He noted that, while the concept of spirituality was foreign to conventional community psychology, the participants in his study talked about spirituality frequently. Much attention has been given to the psychological well-being of the African American male in general. However, as advocated in the above studies, the role of spirituality and the psychological well-being of the African American male are important areas in need of further investigation.

According to Eugene (1995), "mental health problems are often endemic to the life experiences of Black women, and . . . the ways of womanists within the context of therapeutic Black churches can offer healing responses to . . . [their] problems" (pp. 55–56). The African American woman has a unique role in the well-being of her people. Her unique role affects the manner in which she seeks to reduce stress and maintain her own psychological well-being. The ancients hold the view that the blood of one's lineage is passed on through the mother (Akbar, 1994). Thus, the woman of African origin was traditionally viewed as the spiritual vessel that transmitted ancestral characteristics and wisdom from one generation to another. So, given the traditional spiritual nature of Africans, it is not surprising that Collins and Sussewell (1986) found that Black women view themselves "as a part of the collective whole of the African American community; they could not and do not separate themselves from their children nor their men" (p. 3). This collective view of self makes it easy for African American women to turn to social networks such as the church and clergymen when coping with social, emotional, and psychological difficulties.

McCombs (1986, as quoted in Eugene, 1995)

> argues that effectively aiding African American women with psychotherapy means understanding and appreciating the internal psychological constructions of African American womanhood.

Research that lacks this perspective is less likely to discover and utilize key interventions, including strong community ties, extended family networks, and reliance on other Black women. (p. 57)

According to Jones (in press), when therapeutic goals are being developed for African American women, the variables of religious consciousness and spirituality should be explored as important adaptive coping strategies. Jones suggested that an alternative to the traditional psychotherapeutic process might include outreach and prevention programs that include the church and ministers as partners with mental health providers in the delivery of mental health services. Eugene (1995) delineated four therapeutic interventions provided by the traditions of the Black church that could benefit therapists. Understanding how the Black church contributes to the psychological well-being of Black women can indeed enhance the church's use as a resource in the delivery of therapeutic service. Eugene (1995) posited that the church provides the following: (a) It is a place to articulate personal suffering; spiritual songs and gospel music create an emotional solidarity that is cathartic and healing. (b) It allows for locating the persecutors; prayer meetings are used to talk about troubles and to ask for support and intervention to effect change. (c) It serves as a therapeutic agent and asylum for acting out; here a safe environment, devoid of shame and guilt, is provided for members to experience a much needed break from material reality. In the Black church this is called "getting happy" or "shouting." Eugene (1995) proffered that church members

become therapists for their fellow church members in that they attend to their shouting, encourage them in their feelings, and guard and protect them from possible harm. Every person takes responsibility for the person nearest him or her. . . . It is a collective therapeutic experience. . . . The congregation is actively encouraged to lay its burdens on the altar, and it does. (p. 66)

It is validation of life experiences of the Black women. The Black church provides alternative opportunities, for self-esteem and role continuity, from those available in the dominant society. It is the one safe haven that allows the public accounting of troubles without feelings of self-blame.

It is apparent from Eugene's (1995) statements that the Black church has a positive effect on the psychological well-being of African Americans, especially women. The Black church could serve as a valuable resource for mental health providers. Boyd-Franklin (2003) recommended that mental health professionals partnering with the Black church might help alleviate African Americans' view of psychology as antispiritual. Boyd-Franklin posited that exploring religion in therapy as a way of coping with trauma is key to effective work with African Americans. She challenged mental health professionals to identify methods for bringing the African American families together and utilize their strengths as a means for community empowerment interventions.

Boyd-Franklin (2003) appeared to be arguing for a more traditional African holistic approach to addressing the psychological well-being of African Americans. This approach does not separate religion and spirituality from the person or the person from the community. The literature presents a strong argument for psychology, when addressing the needs of African Americans, to find ways to bridge the gap between the spiritual and the secular in the therapeutic setting. It is evident that Africanisms, such as a strong spiritual orientation, still have a deep and substantive effect on the psychological well-being of African Americans. It is also evident that Mbiti's (1990) description of Africans' religion as "the philosophical understanding behind African myths, customs, traditions, beliefs, morals, actions and social relationships" (p. 256) applies in large measure to Africans in the Diaspora as well. The interconnectedness of spirituality/religion in the daily lives of African Americans makes it imperative for professionals to be more sensitive and open to this cultural aspect in counseling and therapy sessions. The increasing ethical requirements of professional psychological associations add to the demands that psychologists become competent to address the cultural needs of clients. For African Americans, it appears critical that psychologists recognize the impact that spirituality has on their psychological well-being. At the same time, professionals must avoid stereotyping their clients of African origin.

Spirituality in Counseling and Therapy

The theoretical development of African-centered psychology and research in multicultural counseling has contributed much to the concept of self in the context of culture (Constantine et al., 2000; Frame & Williams, 1996; Ivey, Ivey, & Simek-Morgan, 1997). This paradigm shift ushered in recognition of the healing power common to many indigenous people's spiritual systems (Frame & Williams, 1996). *NTU* (pronounced *in-too*) psychotherapy is an application of traditional African spiritual philosophy to the therapeutic setting. NTU is a word from the Batu people of central Africa meaning life force. This approach is rooted in the traditional African value system as it occurs in the African American culture. Humanistic concepts and cognitive techniques from Western psychology are used to augment the applied aspect of NTU (Phillips, 1990).

Phillips (1990) maintained that the therapist–client system is a spiritual and sacred relationship that requires one to trust oneself and the connection to others. The emphasis is on creating an environment in which responding spontaneously and holistically is a priority because it facilitates the natural healing process. In this approach, a lesser emphasis is placed on intervention designed to manipulate behavior. Because the relationship is the focal point in NTU psychotherapy, bonding with the client is paramount. Joining with the client of African descent is approached through affective awareness. The feeling experience is used to concretize cognitive knowledge. NTU is an active participatory process that unites the spiritually intuitive and the rationally scientific epistemology.

Case Illustrations

"Sisters of the Well"

"Sisters of the Well" was a support group organized for African American college women at a predominantly White university in a large metropolitan area. The group was composed of women from their mid-20s to mid-30s, some married and others single, some parents and others not, and some very religious and others not. The common theme for all was a sense of isolation on a predominantly White campus. The objective of the group was to develop a greater sense of belonging while developing relationships. They did this by creating rituals that gave them a shared sense of oneness and identity. Some of these rituals are discussed below.

Tactile Sensation

To promote a collective identity, the members used all of the senses to develop relationships. Hugs were used to promote a concrete sense of belonging and affective comfort. Each member was greeted with a "healing hug" and provided a healing hug whenever needed or requested.

Spiritual Joining

Acid jazz and gospel music were used to relax and share positive energy during breathing and guided imagery exercises. During these exercises, members physically connected by joining hands and breathing in unison. On other occasions, they joined by forming a circle around a member as she expressed herself through dance. Continuity of the present and past was linked through ancestor libation ceremonies, inspirational readings, proverbs, poetry, and songs.

Healing Power of Metaphors

Sisters of the Well was the name chosen by the group because of the spiritual healing power associated with water. Members would spontaneously improvise the metaphor to provide specific support for a fellow member. Versions dealing with the protective powers of water in the womb, the ability to dip in the well for nourishment when needed, the capacity to close the lid on the well so nothing negative could enter, and references to the deep underground source that replenished the well are all examples of how a metaphor can be used spiritually in the healing process.

The use of tactile sensations, spiritual joining, and healing metaphors created rituals the women in the group were able to incorporate into their daily lives. These rituals and techniques are not unique. To help create a change, the African-centered therapeutic approach simply takes full advantage of those things that are woven into what the African American experiences as spiritual. The contextual nature of the traditional Western approach often denies the therapeutic power of spirituality. However, the psychological well-being of African Americans from legal enslavement through postemancipation inequities has been dependent on spiritual survival. Spirituality for the African American is based on African traditions of communalism, religion, music, dance, orality, and social change (Frame & Williams, 1996). If therapeutic settings are going to be effective change agents for people of African descent, it seems logical that additional research and studies should be conducted to investigate the effects of spirituality in therapy.

Black Church: A Therapeutic Asylum and Agent ✳

Mental health problems often permeate the lives of many African American women (Eugene, 1995). According to McCombs (1986), to sufficiently assist African women with these problems, counselors and psychotherapists must begin with ascertaining and appreciating the psychological makeup of African womanists (Eugene, 1995, p. 57). Effective professionals are cognizant that womanhood, in this sense, "includes strong community linkages, extended family networks, and intrasupport among African American women" (Eugene, 1995, p. 57).

Unlike those who can economically afford professional assistance, there are several factors preventing many less fortunate African American women from seeking needed help. Other variables, such as cultural factors, negative experiences, and ineffective communication, also hinder their seeking professional help. This group of less fortunate women must often rely on the therapeutic healing of Black womanists and the Black church. The Black church provides a system that allows its members to release much of their emotional pain or psychological distress.

A sense of community solidarity is usually understood within the Black church congregational services or during special prayer meetings. A spontaneous, collective catharsis (call-and-response or free form, verbal, or physical expressions) in Black churches is a common expression among its members, releasing emotional tension and psychological stress or distress (Eugene, 1995).

Implications for Professional Preparatory Curriculum

We maintain that clients' spiritual and religious issues should be considered in professional preparation programs. Their spiritual and religious beliefs have a legitimate place in the therapeutic encounter between the client and the therapist. Professional literature indicates, however, that many mental health counselors lack adequate training for providing effective assistance to African American clients with spiritual and religious issues (Mickel, 1991). For example, Kelly (1994) surveyed 525 counseling programs to determine to what extent religious and spiritual issues were dealt with in counselor preparation courses, noncourse activities, and intern supervision. Of the 343 responding programs, the results revealed that most of the programs did not have a course (287, or 84%), had no course component (250, or 73%), or had no other learning activities (167, or 49%) dealing with religious or spiritual issues. Also, most of the programs offered little, if any, intern supervision dealing with religious or spiritual issues associated with the client (177, or 52%) or the intern student (171, or 50%). These results were similar to those found among preparation programs for psychiatrists and psychologists (Bergin & Jensen, 1990; Constantine et al., 2000; Kelly, 1994; Kroll & Sheehan, 1989; Pate & Bondi, 1992; Sansone, Khatain, & Rodenhauser, 1990; Shafranske & Malony, 1990a, 1990b).

The need to include spiritual and religious dimensions in the professional preparation programs is further supported with Bergin and Jensen's (1990) research findings. That is, among 425 therapists in a national sample, such as clinical psychologists, psychiatrists, clinical social workers, and marriage and family therapists, only 29% of them affirmed a belief that religious matters were significant to the treatment of all or many of their clients' concerns.

Hence, faculty of professional training or preparation programs might consider modifying their curriculum to enable students to become more sensitive and responsive to their clients' religious and spiritual concerns. Course content should provide opportunities for learning about the African American culture that drives some of the behavior and thought patterns encompassing their spirituality. Pate and Bondi (1992) suggested that the course content would provide such experiences so that "training in intake, client assessment, and diagnosis should include religious beliefs and values as an area for counselor sensitivity and, if appropriate, inquiry" (p. 113). It is equally important to note that both clients and professionals enter into the therapy encounter with their own set of values and belief systems that influence each other's behavior. Preparation curriculum should include experiences encompassing opportunities for prospective professionals to become more cognizant of their own belief systems, values, and spirituality. In providing assistance to African Americans for understanding and working through their spiritual issues, the professional must evaluate his or her own spiritual development (Potts, 1991). Alston and Mngadi (1992) suggested that prospective mental health professionals should engage in a careful self-introspection to assess their own biases, attitudes, and values to attain self-awareness of their own spiritual and religious beliefs. This approach should encourage these professionals to purge their attitudes and behaviors that can impede the overall optimum growth of their clients. Finally, curriculum change should also include courses with integrated spiritual and religious content as well as practicum and intern experiences involving professional supervision with African American clients.

Summary

This chapter presented the meaning of spirituality from an African American perspective in a therapeutic context. The African origin of spirituality formed the basis for delineating the meaning of spirituality for contemporary African Americans. It is clear that both spirituality and religion are major forces in the lives of most African Americans. The Black church continues to play a major role in the spiritual lives of African Americans as it did in the past. We presented case examples of African Americans to illustrate the method used in each case. The beliefs and metaphors of African American traditional spirituality can be successfully integrated with counseling and therapy to attain its therapeutic goals. Including spiritual content in the psychotherapy preparation process can enhance professionals' understanding of their clients. As professionals more accurately understand their clients' spiritual belief systems, they can identify more information pertaining to the clients' concerns. It is also clear that professionals will demonstrate greater effectiveness while working with their African American clients once they have first identified their own spiritual belief systems. It is, therefore, less likely that professionals will deal effectively with African American clients' issues if they themselves are struggling with their own spiritual biases while attempting to provide assistance.

The Black church is recognized as playing a significance role in providing a therapeutic environment that allows for its members to release much of their sorrows. Professional mental health workers might consider partnering with Black churches in the Black community as a method for harnessing the strengths within the community.

Professional literature suggests several barriers to effective therapeutic strategies for working with African Americans' spiritual content. We suggest modifying current training program curricula to prepare prospective mental health professionals to acquire the necessary skills to deal with their clients' spiritual content. Attention should also be given to a wider range of African Americans' mental health needs, including individuals, couples, and families. This might include, for instance, adolescents who are often struggling with identity development, recognized as a spiritual dimension. Also, the developmental period faced by the middle-aged and the elderly requires greater focus on philosophical and spiritual values and is a time when the meaning of life tends to become more of a priority.

References

Akbar, N. (1984). Africentric social science for human liberation. *Journal of Black Studies, 14,* 395–414.

Akbar, N. (1994). *Light from ancient Africa.* Tallahassee, FL: Mind Production & Associates.

Albanese, C. L. (1999). *America: Religions and religion* (3rd ed.). Belmont, CA: Wadsworth.

Alston, R. J., & Mngadi, S. (1992). The interaction between disability status and the African American experience: Implications for rehabilitation counseling. *Journal of Applied Rehabilitation Counseling, 23,* 12–16.

Baldwin, J. A. (1991). African (Black) psychology: Issues and synthesis. In R. L. Jones (Ed.), *Black psychology* (3rd ed., pp. 125–135). Hampton, VA: Cobb & Henry.

Bergin, A. E., & Jensen, J. P. (1990). Religiosity of psychotherapists: A national survey. *Psychotherapy, 27,* 3–7.

Boyd-Franklin, N. (2003). *Black families in therapy: A multisystems approach* (2nd ed.). New York: Guilford Press.

Chandler, C. K., Holden, J. M., & Kolander, C. A. (1992). Counseling for spiritual wellness: Theory and practice. *Journal of Counseling & Development, 71,* 168–175.

Collins, A., & Sussewell, D. (1986). The Afro-American woman's emerging selves. *Journal of Black Psychology, 13,* 1–11.

Constantine, M. G., Lewis, E., & Conner, L. (2000). Addressing spiritual and religious issues in counseling African Americans: Implications for counselor training and practice. *Counseling and Values, 48,* 75–89.

Dungee-Anderson, D., & Beckett, J. (1998). Alzheimer's disease in African American and White families: A clinical analysis. *Smith College Studies in Social Work, 62,* 155–168.

Edwards, K. L. (1987). Exploratory study of Black psychological health. *Journal of Religion and Health, 26,* 78–80.

Eugene, T. M. (1995). There is a balm in Gilead: Black women and the Black church as agents of therapeutic community. *Women and Therapy, 16,* 55–71.

Frame, M. W., & Williams, C. B. (1996). Counseling African Americans: Integrating spirituality in therapy. *Counseling and Values, 41,* 16–26.

Genia, V. (1990). Interreligious encounter group: A psychospiritual experience for faith development. *Counseling and Values, 35,* 39–51.

Grimm, D. W. (1994). Therapist spiritual and religious values in psychotherapy. *Counseling and Values, 38,* 154–164.

Gyekye, K. (1996). *African cultural values.* Philadelphia: Sankofa.

Holloway, J. (1991). The origins of African-American culture. In J. E. Holloway (Ed.), *Africanisms in American culture* (pp. 1–19). Bloomington: Indiana University Press.

Ivey, A., Ivey, M., & Simek-Morgan, L. (1997). *Counseling and psychotherapy: A multicultural perspective* (4th ed.). Boston: Allyn & Bacon.

Jackson, G. (1982). Black psychology: Avenue to the study of Afro-Americans. *Journal of Black Studies, 12,* 241–260.

Jackson-Lowman, H., Rogers, J., Zhang, X., Zhao, Y., & Brathwaite-Tull, M. (1996). Life Attitude Inventory: Preliminary evaluation of a measure of spiritual orientation. In R. L. Jones (Ed.), *Handbook of tests and measurements for Black populations* (Vol. 2, pp. 87–103). Hampton, VA: Cobb & Henry.

Jacobs, C. (1990). Healing and prophecy in the Black spiritual churches: A need for reexamination. *Medical Anthropology, 12,* 349–370.

Jagers, R. J., & Mock, L. O. (1993). Culture and social outcomes among inner-city African American children: An Afrographic exploration. *Journal of Black Psychology, 19,* 391–405.

Jones, P. (in press). *African-American women: The psychotherapeutic process as a coping style.* Washington, DC: American Psychological Association.

Kelly, E. W., Jr. (1994). The role of religion and spirituality in counselor education: A national survey. *Counselor Education and Supervision, 33,* 227–237.

Kroll, J., & Sheehan, W. (1989). Religious beliefs and practices among 52 psychiatric inpatients in Minnesota. *American Journal of Psychiatry, 146,* 67–72.

Lehman, C. (1993, January 30). Faith-based counseling gains favor. *The Washington Post,* pp. B6–B8.

Maton, K. I., & Wells, E. A. (1995). Religion as a community resource for well-being: Prevention, healing, and empowerment pathways. *Journal of Social Issues, 51,* 177–193.

Mbiti, J. (1975). *Introduction to African religion* (2nd ed.). Portsmouth, NH: Heineman.

Mbiti, J. S. (1990). *African religions and philosophies* (2nd ed.). Portsmouth, NH: Heineman.

McCombs, H. G. (1986). The application of an individual/collective model to the psychology of Black women. *Women & Therapy, 5,* 67–80.

Meadow, M., & Kahoe, R. D. (1984). *Psychology of religion in individual lives.* New York: Harper & Row.

Mickel, E. (1991). Integrating the African centered perspective with reality therapy/control theory. *Journal of Reality Therapy, 11,* 66–71.

Montilus, G. (1989). *Dompin: The spirituality of African peoples.* Nashville, TN: Winston-Derek.

Mulira, J. (1991). The case of voodoo in New Orleans. In J. E. Holloway (Ed.), *Africanisms in American culture* (pp. 34–68). Bloomington: Indiana University Press.

Nobles, W. (1973). Psychological research and the Black self-concept: A critical review. *Journal of Social Issues, 29,* 11–31.

Nobles, W. (1980). African philosophy: Foundations for Black psychology. In R. L. Jones (Ed.), *Black psychology* (2nd ed., pp. 23–36). New York: Harper & Row.

Nobles, W. (1986). *African psychology: Toward its reclamation, reascension and revitalization*. Oakland, CA: Institute for the Advanced Study of Black Family Life and Culture.

Paris, P. (1995). *The spirituality of African peoples: The search for a common moral discourse*. Minneapolis, MN: Fortress Press.

Pate, R. H., Jr., & Bondi, A. M. (1992). Religious beliefs and practice: An integral aspect of multicultural awareness. *Counselor Education & Supervision, 32,* 108–115.

Phillips, F. (1990). NTU psychotherapy: An Afrocentric approach. *Journal of Black Psychology, 17,* 55–74.

Potts, R. (1991). Spirits in the bottle: Spirituality and alcoholism treatment in African-American communities. *Journal of Training & Practice in Professional Psychology, 5,* 53–64.

Prest, L. A., & Keller, J. F. (1993). Spirituality and family therapy: Spiritual beliefs, myths, and metaphors. *Journal of Marital and Family Therapy, 19,* 137–148.

Quackenbos, S., Privette, G., & Klentz, B. (1985). Psychotherapy: Sacred or secular? *Journal of Counseling & Development, 63,* 290–293.

Richards, D. (1980). *Let the circle be unbroken*. Trenton, NJ: Red Sea Press.

Rogers, J. A. (1994). Spirituality and liberation (Doctoral dissertation, Duquesne University, Pittsburgh). *Dissertation Abstracts International, 55*(7), 1994-A.

Sansone, R. A., Khatain, K., & Rodenhauser, P. (1990). The role of religion in psychiatric education. *Academic Psychiatry, 14,* 34–38.

Shafranske, E. P., & Malony, H. N. (1990a). California psychologists' religiosity and psychotherapy. *Journal of Religion and Health, 29,* 219–231.

Shafranske, E. P., & Malony, H. N. (1990b). Clinical psychologists' religious and spiritual orientations and their practice of psychotherapy. *Psychotherapy, 27,* 72–78.

Watts, R. (1993). Community action through manhood development: A look at concepts and concerns from the front line. *American Journal of Community Psychology, 21,* 333–359.

Zimmermann, M., & Maton, K. (1992). Life-style and substance use among male African-American urban adolescents: A cluster analytic approach. *American Journal of Community Psychology, 20,* 121–138.

20

African Americans and Indigenous Counseling

Debra A. Harley

Indigenous counseling and psychology refer to a system of psychological thought and practice that is rooted in a particular cultural tradition. The purpose of indigenous psychology is to develop a behavioral science that matches the sociocultural realities of a person's own society (Berry, Poortinga, Segall, & Dasen, 1992). The reason for utilization of traditional culturally based practices of a population is to yield efficacious outcomes. For some African Americans, typically these practices are non-Western in nature and in approach (Heelas, 1981) and are based on cultural nuances of the African culture (Morris, 2000). "Indigenous worldviews and healing approaches are holistic and based on knowledge of self rather than context" (Highlen, 1996, p. 72). Indigenous remedies have appeal to the extent that clinical remedies fail to provide benefit. "Indigenous healers or helpers are designated individuals within a culture from whom people seek various forms of assistance, healing, and/or guidance" (Helms & Cook, 1999, p. 254). According to Jackson (1992), the psychological healer is one who listens to the "sufferer" to learn and understand and, in turn, develops the basis for reassuring, advising, consoling, comforting, interpreting, explaining, or otherwise intervening.

Throughout history, cultures have traditionally found methods for dealing with psychological distress and alternative behavior (Lee & Armstrong, 1995). For African Americans, traditional healing practices have been a hallmark of wellness. In fact, African American clergy, in particular, functions as a major mental health resource to African Americans (Cook, 1993; Rivera, Garrett, & Crutchfield, 2004; see chap. 14 in this book for further discussion on the role of the African American church). An analysis of the practices of people of African descent reveals that indigenous healing practices are part of the strategies used to respond to life challenges (Nicholls, 1993, 1995). People of African descent or African Americans share many cultural attributes with Black Africans. In fact, African Americans have begun to reestablish emotional links and cultural identity with the indigenous peoples of Africa through celebrations (e.g., Kwanza, rights of passage) and pilgrimages back to Africa. Therefore, information in this chapter is presented within the context of African Americans identifying culturally with many of the practices indigenous to Africa. It is not suggested that African Americans and Africans are homogeneous ethnically or racially; nevertheless, parallels can be found in areas of ideology, worldview, and sociocultural mores (Nicholls, 1993). According to Parham (1996), "one can make natural extensions from an African-centered perspective to the understanding of an African American psychology" (p. 182).

Arguably, "Western understanding of indigenous or traditional healing practices in non-Western cultures, including Africa, has been limited" (Levers & Maki, 1995, p. 127). Integration of non-Western and Western healing systems for mental health requires the respect and understanding of indigenous concepts and an analysis within culture-specific ecology. Rogler, Malgady, and Rodriguez (1989) offered an ecological model to increase one's understanding of mental health services for non-European populations. According to Rogler et al., there are five phases within the ecology of mental health services, with culture serving as a major determinant in each phase and one phase serving as a *filter* leading onto the next phase. The first phase, *psychiatric epidemiology*, begins with the emergence of mental health problems in the community (e.g., kinds of mental health problems, how they are manifest, how they are dealt with). This phase acknowledges the notion of indigenous healers and the fact that concepts of mental health and mental illness vary across cultures (Leong, 1996). The second phase is the help-seeking process, *mental health service utilization*, which determines that a person will seek help when he or she experiences a particular threshold of problems. Culture, rather than levels of stress and significant psychological disorder, is assumed to be a central determinant (Leong, 1996). The third phase, *diagnosis and assessment*, begins when an individual makes contact with the mental health system. The fourth phase, *intervention*, involves actual recommendations and implementation of a plan of treatment. In the final phase, *therapeutic outcome*, the individual reintegrates into the community. Because many African Americans do not seek formal counseling and therapy (Helms & Cook, 1999), utilization of an ecological perspective is important to understanding the integration of indigenous healing systems for mental health.

There is some consensus in the consideration of culture as a pathogenic agent, that is, as a factor not only contributing to the occurrence of mental illnesses but also at the same time creating the pathoplasty (graphic and objective appearance) of symptoms or clinical features of these diagnostic categories (Alarcon & Foulks, 1995). Although it is generally accepted that psychiatric disorders exist in all societies, it is not evident that congruence exists between Western categories of psychiatric disorders and those defined by other cultures (Mollica & Lavelle, 1988; Mpofu & Harley, 2002). Mental health methodologies need to further develop an alternative scientific paradigm that provides insight into human action, potential, and creativity. Indigenous psychology's approach, still in its infancy, is an example of this alternative scientific paradigm (Kim, Park, & Park, 2000). The purpose of this chapter is to examine the value of indigenous methods in the mental health of African Americans. The chapter expands on the concepts and values of multicultural counseling. The chapter begins with a discussion of the role of traditional healing practices. Next, a comparison of the advantages and disadvantages of indigenous healing practices is presented. Then, integrating indigenous and scientific mental health practices is discussed. Finally, guidelines for mental health practitioners utilizing indigenous practices, including implications for practice and future research, are provided. The reader is advised to consider the appropriate utilization of information in this chapter to his or her practice in mental health.

The Role of Traditional Healing Practices

For centuries, traditional healers have been major sources for help with psychological distress and behavioral variance throughout the world (Lee, Oh, & Mountcastle, 1992). *NTU* (pronounced *in-too*) psychotherapy is a form of therapy based on Africentric principles of healing, which describes rules for healthy functioning that have been handed down to people of African descent through their classic African ancestors (Helms & Cook, 1999). Africentric frameworks emphasize harmonious connectedness with one's spirituality as a guiding force for optimal functioning. The core principles of NTU are (a) harmony—

being flexibly in charge of one's life without controlling or fighting the unpredictable circumstances of one's life; (b) balance—aspects of life, nature, or oneself that appear to be dichotomous (e.g., masculinity–femininity) are present in all of nature and must be integrated into a unified whole; and (c) interconnectedness—NTU, a cosmic or spiritual universal force, connects all of life (Phillips, 1990). The ultimate outcome of NTU therapy is to help the client "be more keenly aware of self and others, engage life in a more authentic manner, and incorporate effective tools for clear identification, analysis, and resolution of future life difficulties" (Phillips, 1990, p. 72). Fundamentally, African Americans experience reality as a union of the spiritual with the material (Parham, 1996).

Among the Igede (of Nigeria), certain mental illnesses are thought to be caused by supernatural force that is believed to make people "mad" if it enters their head (e.g., *apuruja*; Nicholls, 1993). Someone affected by *apuruja* will sing, talk out loud, and cry for no apparent reason and is even thought to talk in tongues and prophesy. The healing rituals involve signing and dancing while the possessed person is decorated with certain leaves thought to have curative properties. Upon being cured, the individual will become a member of the *apuruja* cult and thereafter will participate in the cure of other *apuruja* patients. Thus, both the cure and subsequent behavior of a person affected by this mental condition have religious overtones and a practical orientation (Nicholls, 1993). This indigenous practice is similar to the practice of using support groups in mental health counseling.

Another example of indigenous practice for mental disturbance is the Ndembu (of Zambia) healing rituals. It is believed that when a person cannot sleep, has recurring nightmares, exhibits depression, has a nervous breakdown, or whose life is otherwise out of balance, he or she is diagnosed as having entered a disunified position within the cosmological order of things. "The cause is attributed to a neglected or forgotten ancestor who requires attention and has chosen that person to become his devotee" (Nicholls, 1993, p. 34). The treatment requires that the patient sit on the ground in an "attitude of humility" while rituals that portray the cosmological order are performed around him or her. Once cured, the individual makes regular devotions to the ancestor. Similar to *apuruja*, the solution for the crisis is conceived to be religious behavior in which the former patient becomes an advocate for the entity that created the disturbance. The focus is on turning a negative into a positive, and the ancestor is seen as awakening the need for filial responsibility and an exploration of the subconscious dimension of life (Nicholls, 1993).

Nicholls (1993) compared the conceptualization of the Ndembu to the ideas of psychologist Carl Jung and Sigmund Freud. Jung's concept of the *collective unconscious* equates in some ways to the ancestral beliefs of Africans. That is, for Jung (1964), the collective unconscious is the "part of the psyche that retains and transmits the psychological inheritance of mankind" (p. 107). At the core of one's personality in the unconscious mind, the collective unconscious (e.g., ancestors) impinges on the individual's consciousness and can affect one's moods, attitudes, and behavior (Nicholls, 1993). Nicholls also described Sigmund Freud's concept of *archaic heritage* (e.g., symbolic archetypes inherited from the human psychic history) as coinciding with these ideas.

African American folk magic (e.g., roots) has long been recognized as an indigenous alternative to scientific medicine. "Though it took western medicine a thousand years to realize the connection between a troubled mind and bodily sickness, the Gullah knew it from the beginning" (Pinckney, 1998, p. 45). The Gullah people are descendants of slaves imported from West Africa who settled in the Sea Islands of South Carolina and the Georgia coast. Thus, from the beginning, Gullah people saw no difference between faith and medicine. An example of mental illness was a Gullah woman who was having "fits" that made her crawl around on the floor, barking and howling like a dog. She was cured by a root doctor who made two conjure bags of ground rattlesnake and had her wear them in her armpits. Pinckey stated that the power of the root works simply because people believe it works.

Indigenous healers sometime intersperse Western medicines and practices with substances and actions that are, at best, bewildering to a Western observer. Hiegel (1994) described four different types of approaches used by indigenous healers to treat people with mental illness: (a) physical treatments (e.g., pain reduction), (b) magic healing methods (e.g., rituals, incantations, sprinkling with magic water), (c) counseling (e.g., advice, information), and (d) medications (e.g., herbs, potions, sometimes Western medicines). Each of these treatments can be used independently of the other or in unison with each other. Ultimately, the purpose is to remove the imbalance between the psyche and the body, restoring the individual to a harmonious existence.

According to Parham (1996), the African-centered worldview begins with *consubstantiation* (recognition that things within the universe are interconnected), and "the sense of interrelationship between all things is essential for understanding the relationship between African American people and the context of their lives" (p. 181). Therefore, any analysis of behavior must include this context. The concept of interrelatedness is also important for understanding congruence among the spiritual, cognitive, affective, and behavioral dimensions of the personality. The African worldview recognizes that there is a spiritual life force that permeates everything, and one's personality is a manifestation of spiritual, mental, emotional, behavioral, and biogenetic factors that interact with the environment in a holistic way (Kambon, 1992; Parham, 1996; Parham & Parham, 1997). In addition, "the African-centered worldview also focuses on the group or tribe, not the individual, as the most salient element of existence" (Parham, 1996, p. 182).

Parham (1996) offered the following definition that provides the essence of an African-centered framework:

> African psychology examines processes, which allow for the illumination and liberation of the spirit (one's spiritual essence). Relying on the principle of harmony within the universe as the natural order of human existence, Africentric psychological perspectives recognize the spiritness that permeates everything that is, the notion that everything in the universe is innerconnected; the value that the collective is the most important dimension of existence; and the idea that self-knowledge is the key to mental health. African psychology then is the dynamic manifestation of the unifying African principles, values, and traditions whereby the application of knowledge is used to resolve personal and social problems and promote optimal human functioning. (as quoted in Parham & Parham, 1997, p. 182)

This definition of an African-centered psychological perspective is a work in progress and is subject to revision as African psychology evolves.

The application of indigenous practices or cultural contextualization is justified in the assessment of mental illnesses and personality and its vicissitudes (Alarcon & Foulks, 1995). Alarcon and Foulks defined *contextualizing* to mean to "put into local and cultural perspective each and every behavior presented by the potential patient, as well as each and every evaluative technique or clinical approach to the assessment of such behavior" (p. 5). It is clear that contextualization serves the critical function of preventing stereotyping and misidentification of behavioral and interpersonal styles (Alarcon & Foulks, 1995; D'Andrea & Daniels, 2001; Helms & Cook, 1999).

Advantages and Disadvantages of Indigenous Healing Practices

Indigenous healing practices in mental health counseling have advantages and disadvantages that are both real and perceived. Questions of trust, genuineness, and practicality must be examined in indigenous practices. On the one hand, the use of herbs, rituals, and meta-physical processes has proved to be beneficial to patients (McCarthy, 1995), while at the same time quacks and charlatans exist among indigenous healers (Hiegel, 1994). On the other hand, spiritual counseling and alternative medicine have proved to be beneficial to patients (Courcey, 1999; Koenig et al., 1992), while at the same time medications with harmful side effects and incompetence among scientific practitioners exist.

Perhaps one of the major advantages of indigenous practices is that many African Americans will not trust psychotherapy or counseling (Cook, 1993; Helms & Cook, 1999). The assumptions of indigenous practices are similar to those of D'Andrea and Daniels (2001) regarding an integrative multidimensional model for counselors. The first as-sumption rests in the belief that the ultimate goal of counseling and psychotherapy is to promote clients' development. "The second assumption involves the importance of un-derstanding the unique and complex multidimensionality of human development and the need to intentionally address the multiple factors affecting clients' development in coun-seling practice" (D'Andrea & Daniels, 2001, p. 418). For Africans and African Americans, mental health is analogous to living in accord with one's natural essence (Parham, 1996).

Inclusion of indigenous practices in diagnostic considerations offers the advantage of examining cultural influences in behavior. In other words, what may be considered dys-functional or abnormal within one context might be considered culturally appropriate or justifiable within another context (Morris, 2000). In fact, opponents of a systematic effort of the *Diagnostic and Statistical Manual of Mental Disorders* (4th ed.; *DSM–IV*; American Psychiatric Association, 1994) to operationally define and provide comprehensive de-scriptions for specific disorders feel that the current diagnostic system is inadequate for cul-turally sensitive evaluators and to culturally diverse clients (Dana, 1998). In a content analysis of the *DSM–IV* focused on diagnostic information, only 15 of the 840 pages ad-dress culture, age, and gender issues (Tseng & Hsu, 1980, as cited in Morris, 2000).

In some ways, indigenous practices are seen as adjunct to clinical therapy rather than as an interference. For example, mental health counseling and psychotherapy promote the concept of a healthy body and healthy mind as beneficial to recovery. Similarly, African American culture emphasizes the importance of the forces of the body, vitality, and spiri-tuality. These forces are in constant relationship with the person's environment and rep-resent the relations of a person with the outside world (Sow, 1977, 1978). Trieschmann (1995) described this model as the *energy model*. In contrast to the clinical method, the en-ergy model integrates the body, mind, emotions, and soul into a philosophy of health and wellness that returns humanity to a linkage with nature. In fact, a cluttered mind, a dis-turbed emotional state, and an unhappy soul are the cause of physical illness, not the re-sult of it. It is this linkage that has been the core of African cosmology and healing for centuries (Levers & Maki, 1995; Phillips, 1990). The relevance of the energy model to men-tal health counseling and psychotherapy rests with an individual's ability to alter one's method of handling stressful life events, conserving and enhancing energy to make one more sensitive to which events trigger the emotional reaction leading to depletion of en-ergy (Trieschmann, 1995).

In the delivery of mental health services using indigenous practices for African Americans, mental health practitioners need to recognize differences in mental health be-havior practices. In an interview in the video *Cultural Diversity in Healthcare: A Different Point of View* (Envision Incorporated, 1994), Dr. Joyce Giger identified three basic health behavior practices: efficacious, neutral, and dysfunctional. *Efficacious* practices may seem odd, but they really are beneficial to the client. For example, a client may chant as a way to cleanse negative thoughts and clear the mind. *Neutral* practices do not have direct med-ical or clinical beneficial effects, but they are psychologically beneficial. For example, a client may put a root or healing bag under the bed for a restful night of sleep. *Dysfunctional* practices are those that are clearly clinically and psychologically harmful. For example, a client may mix medication with certain herbal ingredients that interact negatively with the medication.

Dr. Giger indicated that each of the behaviors identified above is influenced by six cultural phenomena: communication, spatial needs, environmental control, time orientation, social organization, and biological variation (Envision Incorporated, 1994). *Communication* refers not only to style but also to word usage and meaning. African Americans have a "code" for communication in which a word has one meaning in a certain context and another in a different context. Inflection of the voice also provides contextual meaning to words. *Spatial needs* mean the physical proximity to another person. Spatial preference among African Americans varies widely depending on generational differences and acculturation rate. *Environmental control* is the individual's perception of his or her ability to manipulate situations to determine outcome. Environmental control may be either external (e.g., determined by fate, chance, luck) or internal (e.g., behavior affects environment). Many African Americans tend to have an external locus of control (Carter & Helms, 1987). *Time orientation* identifies one's orientation either as past (hold to old values), present (in the here-and-now without linking outcomes to the future or past), or future (use the present to achieve future goals). African Americans are present oriented (Ho, 1987). *Social organization* refers to how culture defines and shapes the person's behaviors and beliefs. African Americans value efforts that contribute to cooperation among people and efforts that facilitate group survival (Parham, 1996). *Biological variation* involves the influence of skin color, race, and so forth in the susceptibility of people to certain conditions and diseases. Although African Americans do not show a propensity for any particular type of mental illness, they do so for certain physical illnesses (e.g., hypertension, diabetes).

Failure to consider clients' behavior practices and cultural phenomena frequently lead to the assumption that everyone will respond to treatment in the same way, thus promoting stereotyping. Counselors, psychotherapists, and medical practitioners are urged to avoid pathologizing behaviors that are considered to be "inappropriate" and "bizarre" among African Americans without first considering the appropriateness of such behaviors from the clients' cultural context (Shimabukuro, Daniels, & D'Andrea, 1999).

Integrating Indigenous and Scientific Mental Health Practices

The Western system of mental health is grounded in the medical and scientific paradigm. Nevertheless, members of the scientific community and numerous other disciplines are recognizing the value of various forms of indigenous and alternative practices as part of treatment for clients and patients. In fact, indigenous psychologies evolved into a worldwide reaction against the unjust claims of universality (Kim & Berry, 1993). For example, a rehabilitation counseling journal published a special issue on spirituality, disability, and rehabilitation (e.g., *Rehabilitation Education*, 1995, Vol. 9, No. 2 & 3) and subsequent articles over the past 9 years. In addition, the fields of counseling psychology, medicine, and social work have devoted increasing attention to the role of indigenous practices, spirituality, and alternative medicine (e.g., Courcey, 1999; also *Journal of Counseling & Development*, 2000, Vol. 78, No. 2; *Monitor on Psychology*, 2003, Vol. 34, No. 11; *The Scientific Review of Alternative Medicine*, 1999, Vol. 3, No. 2).

The *laying on of hands* (therapeutic touch) is an example of a readily acceptable form of indigenous practice (Pinckney, 1998). Another example of indigenous practice is *vibrational medicine* (people comprise a series of interacting multidimensional energy systems that penetrate and surround the body) to rebalance energy templates within the individual (Gerber, 1988). Gerber believes that if these systems become imbalanced, pathological symptoms may occur on the physical, emotional, mental, or spiritual plane. These are only a few examples of the use of indigenous methods in clinical and scientific communities. In addition, the *DSM–IV–TR*'s (text revision edition) inclusion of the "Glossary of Culture-Bound Syndromes" (folk categories) provides further credence to the credibility of culture as a moderating factor shaping or affecting certain psychological disorders (American Psychiatric Association, 2000).

In cross-cultural psychology, three approaches can be identified: universalist, contextualist, and integrationist. The *universalist* approach adopts the methods and goals of traditional, mainstream psychology to discover abstract, nomothetic, and universal laws of human functioning. Within the universalist approach, two types of explanations have been advanced to account for the observed cultural differences. One explanation is that because the goal of psychology is to discover the underlying universal mechanisms, cultural differences, being only superficial manifestations, are ignored or eliminated from the research design. The other explanation is that cultural differences are recognized as being important but are viewed as representing different stages of evolution or development (e.g., from traditional to modern, from primitive to civilized, and from backward to advanced). The *contextualist* approach stresses that every culture has varying priority dimensions of personal diversity and must be considered within its own culture, history, and sociopolitical practices. The *integrationist* approach emphasizes the need to integrate knowledge generated by indigenous psychologies and cross-cultural testing of psychological theories to arrive at verified universal knowledge (Kim et al., 2000).

Integrating these three indigenous approaches along with Western concepts can be accomplished with several alternative models described by Hiegel (1994). In the first model, clients are first examined by scientifically trained clinical practitioners, who then decide on a course of action (traditional or scientific) for the individual. The second model is similar to health maintenance organizations, in which traditional healers examine clients first and then refer those clients who present conditions that healers could not treat to clinical practitioners. In the third model, traditional and clinical systems officially coexist, separately but working in conjunction with one another. The concept of client choice is central to this model. If the clients make a nonbeneficial choice, the practitioner whom they see first refers them to the other. However, this does not exclude, whenever desirable, that the client is evaluated by both the healer and the clinical practitioner.

Sow (1977, 1978) suggested that the traditional African interpretation of illness and mental disorders, and their treatments, can be understood in terms of concentric layers of personality (African personality), which includes three axes that link a person to a state of equilibrium. The first axis links the world of the ancestor to the spiritual principle passing through the other three layers. The second axis connects the psychological vitality principle to the person's extended family (lineage). The third axis connects the wider community to the person, passing through the body envelope to the physiological principle of vitality. According to Sow, a disorder occurs when the equilibrium is disturbed on one or the other of the axes. Therefore, diagnosis consists of discovering which axis has been disturbed, and therapy should focus on reestablishing the equilibrium. It is important to remember "that in African tradition illness always has an external cause; it is not due to intrapsychic phenomena in the person's history, but to aggressive interference from outside" (Sow, 1977, as quoted in Berry et al., 1992, p. 91).

Highlen (1996) stressed that "recent advances in quantum physics and holography, in particular, have made it possible to bridge the chasm between the physical (science) and the metaphysical (spirituality)" (p. 73). This bridge is significant in several ways. First, it helps healers understand and legitimize traditional indigenous and new systems of healing.

Second, it challenges the several key assumptions within traditional counseling and therapy. These assumptions are as follows: (a) Reality consists of distinct and separate objects (e.g., counselor and client, observer and observed); (b) reality consists of what can be observed and measured through the five senses; and (c) space and time are fixed, absolute constructs of reality (Highlen, 1996, p. 73). The application of quantum physics to indigenous practice in mental health counseling demonstrates that matter and energy are dual expressions of the same universal substance, possessing frequency characteristics—the higher the frequency of matter, the less dense it becomes (Gerber, 1988). Highlen explained Gerber's model as one that is recognized by indigenous healers in which one can view subtle energy bodies as matter that vibrates at a higher frequency than the matter of the physical body.

Bohm (1978, as cited in Talbot, 1991) developed the "holographic universe" as the *holomovement*, which describes *enfoldings* and *unfoldings*. That is, "as every part of the holomovement contains the image of the whole, every part of the universe enfolds the whole, which suggests that every cell in the human body enfolds the cosmos" (Talbot, 1991, p. 50). Bohm believes that everything in the universe is part of a continuum and that consciousness is a nonlocal phenomenon that originates in the implicit order (as cited in Talbot, 1991). This suggests that past, present, and future exist simultaneously in the same space; to access the "past" or "future" may simply require a shift in human focus. Therefore, "the holographic principles of the interpretation of whole and part, the unity of manifestation (i.e., distributed information), and spacelessness/timelessness provide an interpretive framework for understanding the indigenous worldview and healing practices" (Highlen, 1996, p. 75). For example, the Afrocentric worldview of the extended self, which includes all ancestors, those yet to be born, all of nature, and the surrounding community, acknowledges the inseparable, interwoven fabric of the cosmos, in which space and time are meaningless (Highlen, 1996).

Guidelines for Use of Indigenous Practices

When deciding to integrate indigenous and clinical or Western healing systems, one must weigh the ethical considerations, especially the ethical principles of beneficence (promoting individuals' well-being), nonmaleficence (avoiding or preventing harm to individuals), and autonomy (respecting individuals' freedom to make choices and decisions). In the case of mental illness, the question of the individual's competence also must be considered. That is, it must be determined whether the individual has the clearness of thought to analyze options and to choose the more prudent course of action. Finding the point of compromise between clinical protocol and indigenous philosophy regarding individual choice with respect to treatment protocol (traditional vs. scientific) may be a major obstacle. From the Western perspective, frequently the principle of nonmaleficence takes precedence over autonomy (Remley & Herlihy, 2001). For many African Americans it is not uncommon for individuals with mental illness to often wander around freely within the community and seemingly find a compromise between the requirements of their internal delusional world and the requirements of their community, unless they behave dangerously. Hiegel (1994) asserted that this supposedly enables individuals with chronic illnesses to behave within acceptable limits for the community and, consequently, to be better tolerated.

Hays (1996) proposed that practitioners use the ADRESSING model (described earlier in this book in chap. 7) for organizing and systematically considering complex cultural influences. The ADRESSING model focuses on nine main cultural influences that need to be considered when working with racial minority groups. These influences include "**A**ge and generational influences, **D**isability, **R**eligion, **E**thnicity (which may include race), **S**ocial status, **S**exual orientation, **I**ndividual heritage, **N**ational origin, and **G**ender" (Hays, 1996, p. 332). The ADRESSING model is intended to incorporate minority groups that have traditionally been marginalized by the mental health and counseling professions in a more integrated way. Hays (2001) recommended the use of the ADRESSING acronym with the *DSM–IV* in making a culturally responsive diagnosis. This approach is essential to increasing the probability that the client will benefit from intervention.

Exactly how can the ADRESSING model help in the multicultural counseling process? On the most basic level, the model can be used in an initial assessment involving consideration of what identities may be relevant for a given client. It provides an easy-to-remember list of minority identities that correspond to each of the ADRESSING influences (Hays, 2001). In some instances the counselor can use the information to establish rapport. In addition, the information can be used to identify what the client identifies or prioritizes as important. For example, if the African American client talks more about his or her ethnic attributes, then ethnicity is important to the client. However, failure of the client to mention certain aspects (e.g., religion, sexual orientation) does not automatically imply nonimportance. The client may not mention it because he or she thought it obvious, private, or defined differently from the dominant culture.

A cultural assessment of the client is important in the use of scientific methods of counseling, indigenous practices, or a combination of the two. In fact, one can surmise that it should be a part of an initial interview or intake. A cultural assessment should include the client's cultural/racial identity, language/communication ability, religious beliefs and practices, illness and wellness behaviors, and healing practices (Envision Incorporated, 1994). Obtaining this information helps to identify the psychological status of the client, expose underlying issues, and prescribe a counseling or treatment plan.

Another important consideration in using indigenous practices is the identification and selection of indigenous healers and helpers. Helms and Cook (1999, p. 271) posed an exercise for this process involving a series of questions in which the practitioner describes a situation in which someone in his or her family was seriously ill and recovered. Next, the practitioner will answer the question, acquiring a sense of the role of indigenous healers in his or her culture, as well as the extent to which mind, body, and spirit are interrelated aspects of healthy functioning.

Cultural sensitivity in mental health practice and psychotherapy is crucial when working with African Americans because the presenting signs and symptoms may be culturally based, not pathological. Parham (1996) stressed that ancient Kemetic and historically African worldview should be considered essential to the application of any theory to African American clients. In addition, the following specific prerequisites should be present:

1. The need to define the African personality, including its spiritual essence, clearly. Clinicians cannot treat what they do not understand.
2. The knowledge of how to support and nurture the spirit of African people. Because spirit is so fundamental to everything that is, clinicians must learn to embrace and nurture the spirit in ways that give it guidance, reassurance, and unconditional love.
3. The need to define appropriate human functioning, including definitions for ordered and disordered behavior. Indeed, what is normal must have a culturally centered frame of reference.
4. The need to promote the liberation of the American mind in helping African Americans move toward a greater sense of self-determination. . . . Black people must be helped to recognize and use a culturally congruent source of validation.
5. The need to express culturally specific treatment strategies and techniques that might help clinicians serve African American people and help African Americans them-

selves achieve a greater sense of harmony and congruence with their own cultural essence. (Parham, 1996, p. 189)

Ultimately, a theory that seeks to help counselors and clinicians work with the human personality must mirror some of its attributes (Parham, 1996).

Implications for Professional Practice and Research

Developing research concepts that link indigenous and scientific (Western) mental health systems requires a more nonjudgmental and objective way of thinking among researchers. One recommendation is the elimination of cultural bias in research trials in which non-Western populations are not included in the sampling process. Kazdin (1999) asserted that the underrepresentation of certain minority groups and people from different cultures as research participants is of concern. Additional support for the correction of scientific bias was augured by Sue (1999), who described this process as "selective enforcement of scientific principles" (p. 1072). Sue offered the following summary of psychological research: (a) Americans are the largest producers of psychological research; (b) the overwhelming subject of the research is Americans; (c) the United States constitutes less than 5% of the world's population; and (d) on the basis of a sample of less than 5% of the world, theories and principles are developed that are assumed to be universal. Sue did not purport that psychological principles and theories cannot be generalized; instead, he advocated that it is in the best interest of science and consistency "to avoid drawing premature and untested assumptions" (p. 1074).

According to Ratner (2002), cultural psychological research requires special knowledge, skills, and procedures and should specifically contain six factors and processes. First, cultural psychology should explore the manner in which activities, artifacts, and concepts penetrate psychological phenomena and constitute their cultural features. That is, cultural psychology investigates the manner in which culture is in psychology, not simply the psychology of people in a culture. The focus is on the internal relationship between activities, artifacts, and concepts and psychological phenomena. Ratner (2002) stressed that this process involves more than "merely ascertaining correlations between activities, artifacts, concepts, and psychology (e.g., depression is more prevalent in the United States than in Zimbabwe)" (p. 106). Moreover, "such correlations overlook the manner in which psychological phenomena *depend on*, *embody*, and *resemble* activities, artifacts, and concepts (e.g., how the specific quality of American depression depends on, embodies, and resembles the features of specific American Activities, artifacts, and concepts)" (p. 106).

Second, cultural psychology should compare cultural origins, formation, characteristics, and functions of psychological phenomena in diverse societies (Ratner, 2002). In addition to comparing characteristics of psychological phenomena in different societies, cultural psychology relates the characteristics of psychological phenomena to cultural activities, artifacts, and concepts. Comparing psychological phenomena in two populations requires recognizing general and specific features. For example, one can decide whether two instances of behavior are similar or different forms of mental illness, or mental illness at all, only if one acknowledges general features of mental illness to serve as a criterion (Ratner, 1997).

Third, cultural psychology should investigate the psychology of individuals to ascertain the presence of various activities, artifacts, and concepts in the formation, function, and character of psychological phenomena (Ratner, 2002). Conclusions about the psychology of groups (in this case African Americans) are derived from investigations on individual members of groups. This process achieves several things: (a) ensures that conclusions about groups are grounded in the reality of the individuals who compose them; (b) helps guard against overgeneralizing about the cultural psychology of group members; (c) enables researchers to identify, from the results, contradictions among groups members; and (d) enables researchers to identify aspects of their cultural psychology that contradict their social position and may be used to change it (Ratner, 2002). It is important to note that "studying individuals to identify cultural aspects of psychology is a methodological strategy that in no way recapitulates the process by which an individual's psychology is culturally formed" (Ratner, 2002, p. 107). It is clear that an individual's psychology is formed first through social process and reflects them, and cultural psychology first investigates the outcome of the individual's psyche and then traces this outcome back to its cultural origins and social distribution.

Fourth, cultural psychology should predict trends in the qualities of psychological phenomena from trends in activities, artifacts, and concepts. Fifth, cultural psychology should identify aspects of psychological phenomena that contradict normative activities and concepts, explaining the origins of these psychological phenomena. Finally, cultural psychology should investigate the cultural formation of psychological phenomena. This includes the social processes of negotiation or domination that adults use when they construct psychological phenomena (Ratner, 1997, 2002).

Multicultural qualitative research in counseling is a research method that attempts to ground research in the lived experiences of those whose lives are being investigated (Marrow, Rakhsha, & Castaneda, 2001). Qualitative research of African Americans and indigenous practices is one way to gain insight into the process of their behavior, explaining why behaviors occur. It is suggested that in qualitative research, "mother wit and wisdom play a huge role" (Marrow et al., 2001, p. 575) and "personal experience is considered very good evidence," and "distant statistics are certainly not as important as the actual experience of a sober person" (Gwaltney, 1980, p. 7). Although traditional (e.g., quantitative) research methods have assembled a wealth of knowledge within the field of counseling, they are based on a Eurocentric paradigm that reflects the perspective of White, middle-class males (Kazdin, 1999; Sue, 1999). Quantitative research methods for multicultural research continue to have inherent challenges to cultural validity (Quintana, Troyano, & Taylor, 2001). Marrow et al. provided an overview of the paradigms guiding qualitative research that guide the formulation of the research questions, the choice of research design, and the analysis and interpretation of data for multicultural counseling. These research paradigms include conventional, interpretivist–constructivist, poststructuralist, ideological–emancipatory, and ethnic and liberatory (see Marrow et al., 2001, pp. 578–580).

The rationale for use of qualitative research for multicultural counseling is that it has several characteristics that make it a "natural" approach to conducting multicultural counseling research, especially with African Americans. Marrow et al. (2001) identified these characteristics in the following way. First, qualitative research includes context as an essential component of the research. Second, it addresses the researcher's processes of self-awareness and self-reflection. Third, qualitative research is uniquely able to capture the meanings made by participants of their experiences. Fourth, it can be used within the paradigms of participants, using the stories, folk wisdom, and common sense of ordinary people. Fifth, scholars in the field of multicultural counseling and psychology have called for expanded methodological possibilities to address questions that cannot be answered using traditional methods. Sixth, its methods provide the opportunity for voices that were previously silenced to be heard and lives that were marginalized to be brought to the center. Finally, qualitative research provides an opportunity to explore previously unexplored or undefined constructs, many of which appear in multicultural counseling. It is clear that research of and counseling with African American clients are to complement each other, and that complement may well rest with inclusion of indigenous practices as part of African Americans' worldview.

Summary

Scientific and indigenous systems of mental health counseling and psychotherapy can co-exist and lend support to one another without compromising and contradicting each other. The selection of one type of mental health system over another (e.g., scientific over indigenous) is becoming more difficult to justify in an extremely dynamic world in which African Americans increasingly move across a diversity of cultures. Similar to self-identity development, the scientific–indigenous challenge is influenced by four levels of history: (a) the general history of humanity, (b) the history of individual societies, (c) the life history of the individual in society, and (d) the history of a particular psychological system (in this instance scientific–indigenous; Dien, 2000).

Professional, intellectual, and academic discourses in the United States regarding scientific–indigenous healing systems must include a perspective on the efficacy of indigenous and alternative intervention systems. The intersection of science and nature is not new, nor is it dichotomous. In fact, mental health counseling and psychotherapy consist of a multiplicity of methods that provide a sense of continuity despite varied approaches.

In summary, a balance between scientific and indigenous systems is a logical and beneficial strategy. Mental health professionals must either move toward change encompassing diversity of influences or become entrenched in static resistance involving monocultural perspectives, risking obsolescence. Similarly, scholars and researchers must also move in a proactive direction. Any movement toward an inclusive approach utilizing indigenous strategies must recognize two issues: Do not romanticize the indigenous perspective, and be aware of African Americans' flexibility to osilate between cultures.

References

Alarcon, R. D., & Foulks, E. F. (1995). Personality disorders and culture: Contemporary clinical views (Part A). *Cultural Diversity and Mental Health, 1,* 3–17.

American Psychiatric Association. (1994). *Diagnostic and statistical manual of mental disorders* (4th ed.). Washington, DC: Author.

American Psychiatric Association. (2000). *Diagnostic and statistical manual of mental disorders* (4th ed., text revision). Washington, DC: Author.

Berry, J. W., Poortinga, Y. H., Segall, M. H., & Dasen, P. R. (1992). *Cross-cultural psychology: Research and applications.* Cambridge, England: Cambridge University Press.

Carter, R. T., & Helms, J. E. (1987). The relationship between Black value-orientations to racial identity attitudes. *Evaluation and Measurement in Counseling and Development, 19,* 185–195.

Cook, D. A. (1993). Research in African-American churches: A mental health imperative. *Journal of Mental Health Counseling, 15,* 320–333.

Courcey, K. (1999). Religiosity and health. *Scientific Review of Alternative Medicine, 3*(2), 70–74, 76.

Dana, R. H. (1998). *Understanding cultural identity in intervention and assessment.* Thousand Oaks, CA: Sage.

D'Andrea, M., & Daniels, J. (2001). Respectful counseling: An integrated multidimensional model for counselors. In D. B. Pope-Davis & H. L. K. Coleman (Eds.), *The intersection of race, class, and gender in multicultural counseling* (pp. 417–466). Thousand Oaks, CA: Sage.

Dien, D. S. (2000). The evolving nature of self-identity across four levels of history. *Human Development, 43,* 1–18.

Envision Incorporated (Producer). (1994). *Cultural diversity in healthcare: A different point of view* [Video]. (Available from Envision Incorporated, 1201 16th Avenue South, Nashville, TN 37212)

Gerber, R. (1988). *Vibrational medicine: New choices for healing ourselves*. Santa Fe, NM: Bear.

Gwaltney, J. L. (1980). *Drylongso: A self-portrait of Black America*. New York: Vintage.

Hays, P. A. (1996). Addressing the complexities of culture and gender in counseling. *Journal of Counseling & Development, 74,* 332–338.

Hays, P. A. (2001). *Addressing cultural complexities in practice: A framework for clinicians and counselors*. Washington, DC: American Psychological Association.

Heelas, P. (1981). Introduction to indigenous psychologies. In P. Heelas & A. Lock (Eds.), *Indigenous psychologies: The anthropology of the self* (pp. 3–18). New York: Academic Press.

Helms, J. E., & Cook, D. A. (1999). *Using race and culture in counseling and psychotherapy: Theory and process*. Boston: Allyn & Bacon.

Hiegel, J. P. (1994). Use of indigenous concepts and healers in the care of refugees: Some experiences from the Thai border camps. In A. J. Marsella, T. Bornemann, S. Ekblad, & J. Orley (Eds.), *Amidst peril and pain: The mental health and well-being of the world's refugees* (pp. 293–309). Washington, DC: American Psychological Association.

Highlen, P. (1996). MCT theory and implications for organizations/systems. In D. W. Sue, A. E. Ivey, & P. B. Pedersen (Eds.), *A theory of multicultural counseling and therapy* (pp. 65–85). Pacific Grove, CA: Brooks/Cole.

Ho, M. K. (1987). *Family therapy with ethnic minorities*. Newbury Park, CA: Sage.

Jackson, S. W. (1992). The listening healer in the history of psychological healing. *American Journal of Psychiatry, 149,* 1623–1632.

Jung, C. G. (1964). *Man and his symbols*. London: Aldous Press.

Kambon, K. (1992). *African personality in America*. Tallahassee, FL: Nubian Productions.

Kazdin, A. E. (1999). Overview of research design issues in clinical psychology. In C. P. Kendall, J. N. Butcher, & G. N. Holmbeck (Eds.), *Handbook of research methods in clinical psychology* (pp. 3–30). New York: Wiley.

Kim, U., & Berry, J. W. (1993). *Indigenous psychologies: Experience and research in cultural context*. Newbury Park, CA: Sage.

Kim, U., Park, Y. S., & Park, D. (2000). The challenge of cross-cultural psychology. *Journal of Cross-Cultural Psychology, 31,* 63–75.

Koenig, H., Cohen, H. J., Blazer, D. G., Pieper, C., Meador, K. G., Shelp, F., et al. (1992). Religious coping and depression among elderly medically ill men. *American Journal of Psychiatry, 149,* 1693–1700.

Lee, C. C., & Armstrong, K. L. (1995). Indigenous models of mental health intervention: Lessons from traditional healers. In J. Ponterotto, J. M. Casas, L. A. Suzuki, & C. M. Alexander (Eds.), *Handbook of multicultural counseling* (pp. 441–456). Beverly Hills, CA: Sage.

Lee, C. C., Oh, M. Y., & Mountcastle, A. R. (1992). Indigenous models of helping in non-Western countries: Implications for multicultural counseling. *Journal of Multicultural Counseling and Development, 20,* 3–11.

Leong, F. T. L. (1996). MCT theory and Asian-American populations. In D. W. Sue, A. E. Ivey, & P. B. Pedersen (Eds.), *A theory of multicultural counseling and therapy* (pp. 204–216). Pacific Grove, CA: Brooks/Cole.

Levers, L. L., & Maki, D. R. (1995). African indigenous healing and cosmology: Toward a philosophy of ethnorehabilitation. *Rehabilitation Education, 9,* 127–145.

Marrow, S. L., Rakhsha, G., & Castaneda, C. L. (2001). Qualitative research methods for multicultural counseling. In J. G. Ponterotto, J. M. Casas, L. A. Suzuki, & C. M. Alexander (Eds.), *Handbook of multicultural counseling* (2nd ed., pp. 575–603). Thousand Oaks, CA: Sage.

McCarthy, H. (1995). Integrating spirituality into rehabilitation in a technocratic society. *Rehabilitation Education, 9,* 87–95.

Mollica, R. F., & Lavelle, J. (1988). Southeast Asian refugees. In L. Comas-Diaz & E. E. H. Griffith (Eds.), *Clinical guidelines in cross-cultural mental health* (pp. 262–304). New York: Wiley.

Morris, E. F. (2000). Assessment practices with African Americans: Combining standard assessment measures within an Africentric orientation. In R. H. Dana (Ed.), *Handbook of cross-cultural and personality assessment* (pp. 573–603). Mahwah, NJ: Erlbaum.

Mpofu, E., & Harley, D. A. (2002). Disability and rehabilitation in Zimbabwe: Lessons and implications for rehabilitation practice in the U.S. *Journal of Rehabilitation, 68,* 26–33.

Nicholls, R. W. (1993). An examination of some traditional African attitudes towards disability. In D. E. Woods (Ed.), *Traditional and changing views of disability in developing societies: Causes, consequences, cautions* (pp. 25–40). Durham: University of New Hampshire Press.

Nicholls, R. W. (1995). Pragmatic spirituality: Enablement on traditional Africa. *Rehabilitation Education, 9,* 147–158.

Parham T. A. (1996). MCT theory and African-American populations. In D. W. Sue, A. E. Ivey, & P. B. Pedersen (Eds.), *A theory of multicultural counseling and therapy* (pp. 177–191). Pacific Grove, CA: Brooks/Cole.

Parham, T. A., & Parham, W. D. (1997). *Therapeutic approaches with African American populations.* Newbury Park, CA: Sage.

Phillips, F. B. (1990). NTU psychotherapy: An Afrocentric perspective. *Journal of Black Psychology, 17,* 55–74.

Pinckney, R. (1998). *Blue roots: African-American folk magic of the Gullah people.* St. Paul, MN: Llewellyn.

Quintana, S. M., Troyano, N., & Taylor, G. (2001). Cultural validity and inherent challenges in quantitative methods for multicultural research. In J. G. Ponterotto, J. M. Casas, L. A. Suzuki, & C. M. Alexander (Eds.), *Handbook of multicultural counseling* (2nd ed., pp. 604–630). Thousand Oaks, CA: Sage.

Ratner, C. (1997). *Cultural psychology and qualitative methodology: Theoretical and empirical considerations.* New York: Plenum.

Ratner, C. (2002). *Cultural psychology: Theory and method.* New York: Kluwer Academic/ Plenum.

Remley, T. P., & Herlihy, B. (2001). *Ethical, legal, and professional issues in counseling.* Upper Saddle River, NJ: Merrill.

Rivera, E. T., Garrett, M. T., & Crutchfield, L. B. (2004). Multicultural interventions in groups: The use of indigenous methods. In J. L. DeLucia-Waack, D. A. Gerrity, C. R. Kalodner, & M. T. Riva (Eds.), *Handbook of group counseling and psychology* (pp. 295–306). Thousand Oaks, CA: Sage.

Rogler, L. H., Malgady, R. G., & Rodriguez, O. (1989). *Hispanics and mental health: A framework for research.* Malabar, FL: Krieger.

Shimabukuro, K. P., Daniels, J., & D'Andrea, M. (1999). Addressing spiritual issues from a cultural perspective: The case of the grieving Filipino boy. *Journal of Multicultural Counseling and Development, 27,* 221–239.

Sow, I. (1977). *Psychiatrie dynamique africaine* [African psychiatric dynamics]. Paris: Poyot.

Sow, I. (1978). *Les structures anthropologies de la folie en Afriaue noire* [The anthropological structures of the madness in Black Africans]. Paris: Poyot.

Sue, S. (1999). Science, ethnicity, and bias: Where have we gone wrong? *American Psychologist, 54,* 1070–1077.

Talbot, M. (1991). *The holographic universe.* New York: HarperCollins.

Trieschmann, R. B. (1995). The energy model: A new approach to rehabilitation. *Rehabilitation Education, 9,* 217–227.

21

Ethical Implications in Mental Health Counseling With African Americans

Carolyn W. Rollins

For almost two decades, the counseling profession has struggled to address issues related to multiculturalism. Two trends have been identified that fuel these issues: (a) increased global interdependence resulting from the expansion of communication networks, marketing, and technology and (b) projected demographic shifts (Lewit & Baker, 1994; U.S. Census Bureau, 1999) that would result in a numerical majority of racially and ethnically diverse individuals (Evans & Larrabee, 2002). The Office of the Surgeon General (2001) noted that while the overall rates of mental illness among African Americans appear to be similar to those of non-Hispanic Whites, differences arise when assessing the prevalence of specific illnesses. It is clear that African Americans are overrepresented in populations at risk for mental illnesses as well as people who are homeless, incarcerated, in foster care and the child welfare system, or exposed to violence. Almost 34 million people identify themselves as African American. Only one third of Americans with mental health problems get care; the numbers for African Americans are fewer (Office of the Surgeon General, 2001).

This chapter explores ethical issues inherent in counseling African Americans. Efforts to define multicultural counseling competencies have heightened awareness of the needs of individuals outside the cultural mainstream, but for African Americans, this awareness has not resulted in increased access to mental health services or improved outcomes. This chapter discusses the reasons for the profession's lack of consensus on multicultural counseling competencies and explores the implications of this discourse on counseling for African Americans. Considerations for providing ethical services to African Americans are identified, and directions for research are suggested.

The Ethical Context of Multicultural Counseling: Competence and Outcomes

There are likely to be several reasons why so few African Americans access mental health services and why those who do do not return. For example, access for some may be limited by a lack of insurance. Consequently, these individuals may use alternative avenues to treatment, such as emergency room services rather than community mental health facilities, alternative health therapies, or no services. Further, skepticism among African Americans concerning counseling services may be a response to the underlying cultural values that guide therapeutic goals and processes. Grounded in Eurocentric, middle-class values, the assumptions of the profession are culturally bound. Further, traditional counseling theories and techniques have operated in ways that are biased against (Ridley, 1995; D. W. Sue, Arredondo, & McDavis, 1992) and harmful to (D. W. Sue et al., 1998) culturally diverse clients. The traditional process and expected outcomes of counseling may be culturally incongruent with the values of some African American clients. For example, the value of autonomy implicitly leads to the expectation that individuals will separate from the family of origin and establish their own nuclear family. Another basic principle in the counseling process involves the client's participation in a talk-cure that involves sharing intimate information with a person who is not a part of the extended family. Neither of these assumptions necessarily applies to African Americans, especially those who hold traditional cultural values.

On the other hand, some reasons for low utilization may be due to counselor, rather than client, characteristics. Some counselors may be unable to provide culturally responsive treatment (S. Sue & Zane, 1987). Ethnocentric monoculturalism (D. W. Sue et al., 1998), a concept embodying both cultural encapsulation (Wrenn, 1962) and cultural racism (Jones, 1972), may help to explain the lack of satisfaction experienced by some African American clients. Ethnocentric monoculturalism describes the set of values, assumptions, beliefs, and practices that establish and enforce a hierarchy of cultural norms and values based on European cultures (D. W. Sue et al., 1998). Counselors contribute to racial oppression by devaluing the outlook and experience of African American clients and expecting that one outcome of the counseling experience ought to be acceptance of the Eurocentric worldview. This perspective is consistent with a deficit model, based in traditional counseling theory, in which the client is viewed as underprivileged, culturally deprived, and unable to cope effectively with the issues of life (R. M. Lee & Ramirez, 2000). Counselors who hold these values are unlikely to recognize their own biases and are unlikely to provide services that empower African American clients to attain their goals. The cultural mismatch between the traditional counseling worldview and African Americans' worldviews epitomizes one reason that cultural competence is needed by counselors who work with African American clients. To promote clarity, it is explicitly understood that ethnocentric monoculturalism, as discussed here, is not racially bound.

Ethics and Standards for Professional Practice

The American Counseling Association's (1995) *Code of Ethics and Standards of Practice* and the American Psychological Association's (2003) *Ethical Principles of Psychologists and Code of Conduct* admonish mental health professionals to

- respect the rights and dignity of clients
- accept their responsibility to be knowledgeable of the cultures of their clients and adapt their methods to meet clients' needs
- neither condone nor engage in discriminatory behavior
- avoid harming clients and promote their welfare
- know and practice within the limits of their expertise.

The public looks to the profession to guide and police individual practitioners. The professional counselors look to their professional associations for leadership, guidance, and training for integrating ethical standards into their practice and addressing issues of professional concern. Documents to inform practice and provide guidance for practitioners in developing multicultural competency have been developed by the Association for Multicultural Counseling and Development and the National Career Development Association and endorsed by the American Counseling Association (ACA; Arredondo et al., 1996; National Career Development Association, 1992; D. W. Sue et al., 1992). The competencies (Arredondo et al., 1996) have also been endorsed by seven divisions in ACA (Weinrach & Thomas, 2004). Divisions 17 and 45 of the American Psychological Association (APA) have adopted the competencies (Arredondo et al., 1996), and the National Association of Multicultural Counseling Concerns, a division of the National Rehabilitation Association, has endorsed professional multicultural rehabilitation counseling competency standards (Middleton et al., 2000) that parallel the competencies (Arredondo et al., 1996) adopted by divisions of ACA and APA. Although preservice training and continuing education opportunities in multicultural counseling have increased, some of the major professional associations do not provide their members with formal guidance for serving culturally diverse clientele. Individuals with no professional affiliation and members of organizations that provide no formal guidance for multicultural counseling competency may have lower levels of multicultural counseling competency than those of counselors who have such guidance (Bellini, 2002).

Multicultural Counseling Competencies

Initially, the multicultural counseling competencies were presented as an aspirational guide (D. W. Sue et al., 1992) and, later, operationalized (Arredondo et al., 1996). Middleton et al. (2000) noted that the operationalized competencies define the minimal, not ideal, level of professional competence for serving historically underrepresented populations. The competencies are intended to be fluid, changing to address the needs of the profession to more effectively serve individuals affected by their diverse cultural attributes or, more explicitly, to promote culturally responsive counseling as the standard of the profession. As operationalized, there are 31 competency statements and 119 explanatory statements. The guidelines for competence in multicultural counseling identify three dimensions for personal and professional development: attitudes and beliefs, knowledge, and skills (Arredondo et al., 1996; Middleton et al., 2000; D. W. Sue et al., 1992).

The first dimension, counselor attitudes and beliefs, refers to counselors' attitudes and beliefs about race, culture, ethnicity, gender, and sexual orientation; recognition of counselors' biases and stereotypes; counselors' orientation toward multiculturalism; and the ways in which counselors' values and biases may affect counseling services (Arredondo et al., 1996; Middleton et al., 2000; D. W. Sue et al., 1992). Second, the dimension of counselor knowledge refers to the counselor's knowledge and understanding of her or his worldview, as well as knowledge about and respect for the heritage and worldviews of the specific cultural groups being served and the sociopolitical factors that influence those groups (D. W. Sue et al., 1992, 1998). The third dimension, skill, refers to the ability of counselors to form counseling relationships and to adapt or develop and implement counseling goals and strategies that are appropriate, relevant, and consistent with the life experiences and cultural values of the client (Middleton et al., 2000; D. W. Sue et al., 1992).

Alternative Views

In the United States, any discussion of concerns related to race is difficult. Consequently, counseling professionals do not yet have consensus on the issue of multicultural counseling competence. As Pistole (2004) noted, even professionals behave in ways that protect and maintain their own cultural beliefs and reject others' cultural perspectives, making discussion of the issues difficult. It is important, therefore, to acknowledge that not all counselors see a need for articulating or adopting multicultural counseling competencies. For example, Patterson (2004) suggested that effective methods and approaches for working with all clients are needed, rather than a compendium of distinct multicultural counseling techniques.

Thomas and Weinrach (2004), Weinrach (2003), and Weinrach and Thomas (1996, 1998, 2002, 2004) have voiced concerns and rationales supporting another perspective. Vontress and Jackson (2004) categorized the objections of Thomas and Weinrach to the competencies into two groups: conceptual–structural and content. The conceptual–structural objections addressed Thomas and Weinrach's perceptions that the competencies

- focused exclusively on African, Asian, Hispanic, and Native Americans
- assumed that mental health problems have an external etiology
- discuss, in the dimensions of personal identity model, dissimilar constructs, such as age, gender, race, and sexual orientation, as if they were parallel constructs
- do not clearly and distinctly distinguish between the terms *multiculturalism* and *diversity.*

The content objections addressed Thomas and Weinrach's perceptions that the competencies

- use race as the basis for individuals' troubles
- suggest that individuals define their own racial or ethnic identity
- suggest that one role of counselors is activism
- may promote extremism. (Vontress & Jackson, 2004)

There are some points in which perspectives may converge. For example, Weinrach and Thomas (2002) suggested that the competencies' emphasis on race is outmoded, as race does not adequately explain the human condition and contributes to America's preoccupation with the color of a person's skin. The fact that, in the 21st century, race still forms a basis for categorizing people means that counselors must understand the meaning of racial group membership and context to provide effective services (Coleman, 2004; Helms & Cook, 1999; Helms & Richardson, 1997). While all might agree that the term *race* is outmoded, in the United States, race still matters. Further, the reality of the experience of race is typically viewed differently by African Americans and other racial minorities and by Whites. Although Vontress and Jackson (2004) asserted that the significance that clients attach to race, not race itself, is most significant, issues of Black and White differences are at the core of the multicultural movement (Malveaux, 1994) and drive the need to sustain the progress gained through the civil rights movement (Arredondo & Toporek, 2004).

Counselors are also likely to agree that all factors affecting a client's situation should be examined. Yet, the suggestion that a self-fulfilling prophecy is created when individuals perceive their race to be an impediment to achievement suggests the belief that the playing field is level, blames the victim, and denies the sociopolitical history of America, including continuing manifestations of racism and its impact on the economic, educational, and psychological status of African Americans. Rather than serving as the basis for excusing any lack of attainment, recognition of inequity and its current and historical impact on experiences and perceptions of African Americans is requisite for effectiveness in assessing the variety of factors that influence life choices and a person's resilience, resources, and capacity for coping with these factors and providing counseling services.

Implications

Outcomes for African Americans who receive treatment are not encouraging, and there is concern about the appropriateness of some diagnostic and treatment procedures (Office of the Surgeon General, 2001). African Americans may be less likely to seek services because they perceive traditional mental health therapies to be grounded in White, middle-class values (O'Connell, 1993) and of little relevance to their concerns. Consequently, the notion that mental health professionals should be able to conceptualize African Americans' mental health issues in a manner that is culturally relevant and develop interventions that are culturally responsive is relevant to ethical practice. Succinctly put, mental health professionals should provide services that are culturally responsive.

The ideal of the culturally responsive counselor evolved as multicultural counseling emerged as the fourth major counseling tradition (C. C. Lee, 1997; Pedersen, 1999) or dimension (D. W. Sue et al., 1998). The culturally responsive counselor recognizes the uniqueness of each individual while considering the client's specific human and culturally based attributes. At the same time, the culturally responsive counselor maintains awareness of the ways in which her or his own personal and cultural experiences can affect perceptions of and responses to the client (C. C. Lee, 1997). Patterson (1995, 2004) suggested that culturally responsive counselors have adopted a universal system or approach to counseling and utilize client-centered strategies. Specifically, Patterson stated that culturally responsive counselors will bring the qualities of respect for the client, genuineness, and empathic understanding; the ability to communicate these qualities to the client; and the willingness to promote understanding through structuring the client's expectations and understanding of the counseling.

Considerations for Planning and Delivering Services for African Americans

Skilled multicultural counselors, understanding that helping styles and intervention strategies may be culture bound, seek to adjust their counseling approaches to the culture, values, and needs of the individual (Bellini, 2002). Adjusting their counseling approaches and implementing appropriate intervention strategies require that counselors be able to accurately assess the cultural characteristics of clients, not simply stereotype individuals based on broadly defined characteristics of their racial or cultural group.

Within-Group Differences

The African American population is diverse. Factors contributing to within-group diversity among African Americans include the immigration of people from African, Caribbean, and Latin American countries; area and region of residence; education; and socioeconomic status. For example, most African Americans (53%) live in the South; in 1997, nearly one fourth earned more than $50,000 a year; in 1999, about 22% of African American families lived in poverty (Office of the Surgeon General, 2001); and many African Americans reside in rural areas (U.S. Census Bureau, 1999). Given such variation among African Americans, effectively understanding the cultural factors that affect clients' presenting issues may be critical in alleviating their concerns (Fischer, Jome, & Atkinson, 1998). One indicator of multicultural competence may be counselors' ability to differentiate and integrate multicultural knowledge pertaining to clients' concerns (Ladany, Inman, Constantine, & Hofheinz, 1997).

Demographic information about African Americans serves as an important indicator of need, risk, and types of interventions and services that might be appropriate (Raajpoot,

2000). To effectively serve African American clients, counselors must recognize and understand the impact of cultural factors on presenting issues and translate this knowledge into appropriate treatment plans (Constantine & Ladany, 2000). Because cultural factors affect individuals in different ways, general cultural knowledge cannot adequately represent the unique ways in which culture influences specific individuals. Each client's culture is a unique composite of factors, including ancestral culture, exposure to and skills for operating within the dominant cultural context, racial/ethnic identity development, and unique personal experiences (Fischer et al., 1998). Counselors who are culturally responsive balance their knowledge about African Americans as a cultural group with their knowledge about the individual client.

Worldview

Worldview generally describes individuals' view of the universe and their place in it (Ihle, Sodowsky, & Kwan, 1996). Worldview, as a reflection of culture, influences individual values and beliefs. Worldview also establishes institutional values and practices, including standards of normality, which influence clinical practice and define therapeutic effectiveness (D. W. Sue et al., 1998). Although the worldviews of individual African Americans may differ, the underlying cultural issues that contribute to their worldview form the basis for the psychosocial development and establish the cultural context for counseling (Ahia, 1997). Acquiring knowledge of African American clients' worldview to facilitate the counseling process requires that counselors are cognizant of specific client characteristics and are self-aware (e.g., aware of their beliefs about those characteristics). Therefore, it is essential that counselors, regardless of race and ethnicity, are aware of their own worldview and the ways in which it may be congruent or in conflict with those of their African American clients. This interplay of worldviews will determine the quality of the counseling relationship, the definition of counseling concerns, and the overall efficacy of and satisfaction with services.

The worldviews of people of African descent have been strongly influenced by African traditions. Significant aspects of African American culture, such as the Black church, extended kinship networks, and expressive communication styles, are thought to have evolved from African cultural heritage (Nobles, 1991, as cited in C. C. Lee, 1997). The concept of African universals has been labeled Afrocentricity (Asante, 1991). Perspectives associated with Afrocentricity have evolved from African traditions, including concepts of time, spirituality, relationships, and holism (Ahia, 1997; C. C. Lee, 1997). For traditional Africans, body, mind, and spirit are interconnected; there is a tendency to respond to external stimuli cognitively, affectively, and behaviorally. Conceptualizations of reality tend to include interactions of the objective and subjective rather than either singularly (C. C. Lee, 1997).

In the African tradition, time is event-driven and fluid rather than fixed. Time exists in two dimensions, past and present. There is no consideration of "future" concerns. Spirituality is an integral part of life in African societies. There is a strong belief in the spiritual world. Life is a spiritual phenomenon, based on the principle of unity. In the natural order of life, humans, plants, animals, and natural phenomena are interrelated. God is the driving force. Human relationships are group centered and characterized by cooperative interdependence. Family identity has obligations and responsibilities. African families are extended; extended family members are often identified as brother or sister. Society is adult oriented rather than youth oriented. Elders are respected and honored. The worldviews underlying the ways in which people of African descent order their universe provide an alternative to the Eurocentric concept of psychosocial development. The degree to which these values and beliefs apply to individual African Americans is not static but an evolving dynamic determined by the life experiences of each person.

Counselors assess mental status through observation, testing, and communication. Miscommunication can occur even when individuals use the same words. The greater the cultural differences, including gender, ethnicity, language, and worldviews, between the counselor and the client, the greater the likelihood of misdiagnosis, inappropriate care, or noncompliance with treatment (Lindsey & Cuéllar, 2000). On the other hand, Lindsey and Cuéllar also noted that communication, empathy, compassion, appreciation, affection, insight, and comprehension increased as knowledge of others increased.

While all African Americans confront issues of racial and social injustice, not all African Americans experience the same type and levels of social stressors. Class differences result in experiences that are qualitatively and quantitatively different. Ford (1997) pointed out that much of what is reported about African Americans characterizes individuals with low socioeconomic status and low levels of achievement. Lifestyles and opportunities differ; some stressors are mediated by higher socioeconomic class status. Despite these differences, however, commonalities also exist, including (a) embracing the predominant culture to some degree, (b) belief in the work ethic, (c) empowerment and strong sense of self, and (d) striving for improved quality of life (Coner-Edwards & Edwards, 1988).

The Next Step

Meeting the ethical responsibility of providing effective services to African Americans can be challenging. Yet, counselors are not without tools for serving African Americans. Patterson (2004) has delineated core qualities that counselors must possess. The multicultural counseling competencies and codes of ethics provide additional guidance. The counseling literature offers a plethora of information about the effectiveness of emerging strategies and approaches for specific cultures in specific settings and situations. Counselors must integrate and utilize this knowledge to achieve successful counseling outcomes and for developing and maintaining counseling relationships with African Americans. For counselors who are uncertain how to do so, two levels of response are needed. First, professional associations and educational programs must respond by providing increased opportunities for training and continuing education. Second, counselors must engage in awareness development and avail themselves to training opportunities.

The counseling profession must be proactive. While there should be no need for such standards (Patterson, 2004), neither the counseling profession nor the global society has evolved to that point. Counselors must continue to engage in the meaningful dialogue that promotes consensus regarding multicultural counseling competence. In addition to dialogue, working toward consensus means that research will focus on defining best practices and providing the knowledge base for multicultural counseling standards. Specifically, Lindsey and Cuéllar (2000) identified three areas necessary for effectively addressing the mental health needs of African Americans:

- comprehensive understanding of the psychological life of African Americans
- comprehensive understanding of the factors related to positive outcomes, growth, and development
- objective understanding of what therapies work best for whom under what conditions and across what settings.

The standards should be understood to be a dynamic document that, like codes of ethics, must respond to emerging knowledge and trends to remain useful and relevant to the profession. Providing the standards makes available tools for counselors that help to promote ethical practice and increase the likelihood of obtaining positive counseling outcomes with African Americans.

Summary

Ethics and ethical competencies among counselors and mental health practitioners working with racial and ethnic minority groups continue to be important issues. The scope of practice in mental health professions is not immune from racism and bias by racially and ethnically insensitive counselors. The determination of competence in the domain of ethics and multicultural counseling competencies is a challenge to research and practice because it requires counselors, faculty, and trainees to think critically about both ethics and multiculturalism (Delgado-Romero, 2003). Therefore, attention must be given to determination of how multicultural ethical competence is different from general ethical competence.

References

Ahia, C. E. (1997). A cultural framework for counseling African Americans. In C. C. Lee (Ed.), *Multicultural issues in counseling: New approaches to diversity* (2nd ed., pp. 73–80). Alexandria, VA: American Counseling Association.

American Counseling Association. (1995). *Code of ethics and standards of practice.* Alexandria, VA: Author.

American Psychological Association. (2003). *Ethical principles of psychologists and code of conduct.* Washington, DC: Author. Retrieved from http://www.apa.org/ethics

Arredondo, P., & Toporek, R. (2004). Multicultural counseling competencies = ethical practice. *Journal of Mental Health Counseling, 26,* 44–55.

Arredondo, P., Toporek, R., Brown, S., Jones, J., Locke, D., Sanchez, J., & Stadler, H. (1996). Operationalization of multicultural counseling competencies. *Journal of Multicultural Counseling and Development, 24,* 42–78.

Asante, M. K. (1991). The Afrocentric idea in education. *Journal of Negro Education, 60,* 170–180.

Bellini, J. (2002). Correlates of multicultural counseling competencies of vocational rehabilitation counselors. *Rehabilitation Counseling Bulletin, 45,* 66–76.

Coleman, H. L. K. (2004). Multicultural counseling competencies in a pluralistic society. *Journal of Mental Health Counseling, 26,* 56–67.

Coner-Edwards, A., & Edwards, J. (1988). The Black middle class: Definitions and demographics. In A. F. Coner-Edwards & J. Spurlock (Eds.), *Black families in crisis: The middle class* (pp. 1–9). New York: Brunner/Mazel.

Constantine, M. G., & Ladany, N. (2000). Self-report multicultural counseling competence scales: Their relation to social desirability attitudes and multicultural case conceptualization ability. *Journal of Counseling Psychology, 47,* 155–164.

Delgado-Romero, E. A. (2003). Ethics and multicultural counseling competence. In D. B. Pope-Davis, H. L. K. Coleman, W. M. Liu, & R. L. Toporek (Eds.), *Handbook of multicultural competencies in counseling and psychology* (pp. 313–329). Thousand Oaks, CA: Sage.

Evans, K. M., & Larrabee, M. J. (2002). Teaching the multicultural counseling competencies and revised career counseling competencies simultaneously. *Journal of Multicultural Counseling and Development, 30,* 131–137.

Fischer, A. R., Jome, L. M., & Atkinson, D. R. (1998). Back to the future of multicultural psychotherapy with a common factors approach. *The Counseling Psychologist, 26,* 602–607.

Ford, D. (1997). Counseling middle class African Americans. In C. C. Lee (Ed.), *Multicultural issues in counseling: New approaches to diversity* (2nd ed., pp. 81–107). Alexandria, VA: American Counseling Association.

Helms, J. E., & Cook, D. A. (1999). *Using race and culture in counseling and psychother-apy: Theory and process.* Needham Heights, MA: Allyn & Bacon.

Helms, J. E., & Richardson, T. Q. (1997). How multiculturalism obscures race and cul-ture as different aspects of counseling competency. In D. Pope-Davis & H. L. K. Coleman (Eds.), *Multicultural counseling competence: Assessment, education, and train-ing and supervision* (pp. 60–79). Thousand Oaks, CA: Sage.

Ihle, G. M., Sodowsky, G. R., & Kwan, K. (1996). Worldviews of women: Comparisons between White American clients, White American counselors and Chinese international students. *Journal of Counseling & Development, 74,* 300–306.

Jones, J. (1972). *Prejudice and racism.* Reading, MA: Addison Wesley.

Ladany, N., Inman, A. G., Constantine, M. G., & Hofheinz, E. W. (1997). Supervisee mul-ticultural case conceptualization ability and self-reported multicultural competence as functions of supervisee racial identity and supervisor focus. *Journal of Counseling Psychology, 44,* 284–293.

Lee, C. C. (1997). (Ed.). *Multicultural issues in counseling: New approaches to diversity* (2nd ed.). Alexandria, VA: American Counseling Association.

Lee, R. M., & Ramirez, M., III. (2000). The history, current status, and future of multi-cultural psychotherapy. In I. Cuéllar & F. Paniagua (Eds.), *Handbook of multicultural mental health: Assessment and treatment of diverse populations* (pp. 279–309). San Diego, CA: Academic Press.

Lewit, E. M., & Baker, L. S. (1994). Children's health and the environment. *Future of Children, 5,* 8–10.

Lindsey, M. L., & Cuéllar, I. (2000). Mental health assessment and treatment of African Americans: A multicultural perspective. In I. Cuéllar & F. Paniagua (Eds.), *Handbook of multicultural mental health: Assessment and treatment of diverse populations* (pp. 195–208). San Diego, CA: Academic Press.

Malveaux, J. (1994). Do African American issues get swallowed in diversity movement? *Black Issues in Higher Education, 11,* 32.

Middleton, R. A., Rollins, C. W., Sanderson, P. L., Leung, P., Harley, D. A., Ebener, D., et al. (2000). Endorsement of professional multicultural rehabilitation competencies and standards: A call to action. *Rehabilitation Counseling Bulletin, 43,* 219–240.

National Career Development Association. (1992). Career counseling competencies: NCDA Professional Standards Committee. *Career Development Quarterly, 40,* 378–386.

O'Connell, L. (1993, August 30). Multicultural training called necessary for counselors and therapists. *Orlando Sentinel,* p. 8.

Office of the Surgeon General. (2001). Mental health: Culture, race, and ethnicity, a sup-plement to mental health: A report of the Surgeon General. Retrieved September 26, 2003, from: http//www.mentalhealth.org/cre/ch2_demographic_trends.asp

Patterson, C. H. (1995). A universal system of psychotherapy. *Person-Centered Journal, 2,* 54–62.

Patterson, C. H. (2004). Do we need multicultural counseling competencies? *Journal of Mental Health Counseling, 26,* 67–74.

Pedersen, P. (1999). *Multiculturalism as a fourth force.* Philadelphia: Brunner/Mazel.

Pistole, M. C. (2004). Editor's note on multicultural competencies. *Journal of Mental Health Counseling, 26,* 39–41.

Raajpoot, U. A. (2000). Multicultural demographic developments: Current and future trends. In I. Cuéllar & F. Paniagua (Eds.), *Handbook of multicultural mental health: Assessment and treatment of diverse populations* (pp. 79–94). San Diego, CA: Academic Press.

Ridley, C. (1995). *Overcoming unintentional racism in counseling and therapy: A practi-tioner's guide to intentional intervention.* Thousand Oaks, CA: Sage.

Sue, D. W., Arredondo, P., & McDavis, R. J. (1992). Multicultural counseling competencies and standards: A call to the profession. *Journal of Counseling & Development*, *70*, 477–486.

Sue, D. W., Carter, R. T., Casas, J. M., Fouad, N. A., Ivey, A. E., Jensen, M., et al. (1998). *Multicultural counseling competencies: Individual and organizational development.* Thousand Oaks, CA: Sage.

Sue, S., & Zane, N. (1987). The role of culture and cultural techniques in psychotherapy. *American Psychologist, 42*, 37–45.

Thomas, K. R., & Weinrach, S. G. (2004). Mental health counseling and the AMCD multicultural counseling competencies: A civil debate. *Journal of Mental Health Counseling, 26*, 41–43.

U.S. Census Bureau. (1999). *Statistical abstract of the United States: The national data book.* Washington, DC: Author.

Vontress, C., & Jackson, M. (2004). Reactions to the multicultural counseling competencies debate. *Journal of Mental Health Counseling, 26*, 74–80.

Weinrach, S. (2003). I am my brother's (and sister's) keeper: Jewish values and the counseling process. *Journal of Counseling & Development, 81*, 441–445.

Weinrach, S. G., & Thomas, K. R. (1996). The counseling profession's commitment to diversity-sensitive counseling: A critical reassessment. *Journal of Counseling & Development, 74*, 472–477.

Weinrach, S. G., & Thomas, K. R. (1998). Diversity-sensitive counseling today: A postmodern clash of values. *Journal of Counseling & Development, 76*, 115–122.

Weinrach, S. G., & Thomas, K. R. (2002). A critical analysis of the multicultural counseling competencies: Implications for the practice of mental health counseling. *Journal of Mental Health Counseling, 24*, 20–35.

Weinrach, S. G., & Thomas, K. R. (2004). The AMCD multicultural counseling competencies: A critically flawed initiative. *Journal of Mental Health Counseling, 26*, 81–94.

Wrenn, C. (1962). The culturally encapsulated counselor. *Harvard Educational Review, 32*, 444–449.

22

Conclusions and Implications for Future Practice and Research

John Milton Dillard

The contributors in this book have presented several challenging issues that can increase the effectiveness in counseling and working with African Americans. The most salient concept among the chapters is empowerment of African Americans in their mental health development. This empowerment must emanate from African American community involvement. In this final chapter, I review and synthesize the important issues raised and suggest considerations for future work in this area.

The central theme of this book is the concept of positive mental health among African Americans. The focus is on exploring factors that contribute to the lives of African Americans. Yet the conventional view of mental health is thought to be universal and applies to Whites and other ethnic/racial groups. However, this view of mental health does not lend itself to African American experiences and conditions such as ethnocentrism and prejudice in the form of discrimination in housing, employment, education, and health. For the most part, African Americans and other populations in general are reported as not having definable mental health disorders. Thus, throughout this book, we have stressed positive mental health for African Americans that is relevant to the life conditions under which adjustment can occur. Despite the many oppressed conditions, African Americans have maintained hope. Factors believed to contribute to positive mental health for African Americans include healthy self-esteem, a successful career, intelligence, a job, access to good health care, well-defined roles of responsibilities, and adequate housing. African Americans never gave up hope for economic changes and improved social conditions, which were significant indicators of resiliency and confidence in self as a people.

Another central theme that was weaved through the book is African Americans' consistent reliance on the Black church. Throughout history, African Americans have used the Black church as a place for psychological strength and solace. Regardless of African Americans' socioeconomic status in the community, they can gain congregational support as they express their emotional pain and feelings about some of their daily encounters with external society. The practice of religion and spirituality within and outside the church is a major function in the lives of most African Americans. When all else seems to fail, their spirituality and religion provide a sense of psychological comfort in spite of negative prevailing conditions. We have seen that other church and personal family members are quite involved outside the church in assisting individuals who experience some forms of mental anguish and heartache.

Because spirituality and religion are major forces in the lives of most African Americans, it is essential that practitioners seriously consider integrating these concepts in their work with African Americans where warranted. It is obvious that this will not be appropriate for all members of this group, because African Americans represent a very diverse group of people who vary in commitment to religious and spiritual beliefs and practices. As suggested in earlier chapter discussions, religion and spirituality are guiding forces in the lives of many African Americans. Much of their worldviews is rooted in religion and spirituality and experiences in the Black church. So to ignore the significance of their religious convictions in counseling or therapy is similar to devaluing their human needs. However, to recognize and respond to their means of achieving comfort is one method of helping to empower African Americans.

As discussed in most of this text, the concept of racism/ethnocentrism is also a major theme that permeates life experiences of many African American men and women and their families. The impact of ethnocentrism happened in the past and continues, however subtly, to affect the psychosocial behavior of African Americans. Earlier illustrations were discussed indicating that many African American men frequently encountered unhealthy situations that were plagued with injustices and unfair treatment, for example, employment practices, unfair wages, and racial profiling. Undoubtedly, such treatment can discourage young men from trying to improve their lives and encourage hopelessness for others to engage in unlawful behavior that often leads to an unproductive life. Some of African American men's frustrations and hostilities with racist treatment are at times negatively vented within their male–female relationships. These relationships are damaged because of such actions.

African American women are also faced with racial stereotypes stemming from history and the media. Further, much of the violence that occurs to African American women is not reported or supported in some communities. These types of conditions call for greater supporting environments containing the needed tools and skills to empower these African American women, as well as men, to learn how to better manage relationships and people in external environments.

One of the most powerful themes discussed in this book is the use of community mental health and how it can be an important vehicle in the mental health arena for African Americans. Communities can, and many do, play instrumental roles in promoting positive mental health among African Americans. Yet a more powerful vehicle is, for instance, the joint operation of public health and community mental health, which when working in collaboration with each other can make significant contributions to both health and mental health concerns of African Americans. The availability of both public health and community mental health services will indeed provide improved quality of life. This joint collaborative effort will likely reduce financial burdens on African American families. Individuals with mental health or health needs, such as HIV/AIDS, alcohol and substance abuse, and the elderly, can receive necessary services for the public within a community. Collaborative public health and mental health service delivery systems would enable people across socioeconomic lines to receive needed assistance. The Surgeon General's report has suggested that psychological and health needs of African Americans are indeed warranted. And equal access must be available to all individuals within the African American service community area.

Self-identity is another important theme that concerns some African Americans. A growing number of people who are biracial or multiracial report being African American in addition to another racial or ethnic group. Counseling and therapy practitioners must be cognizant of the impact that biracial or multiracial identity has on their clients' psychosocial development. In another group, however, among gays, bisexuals, and lesbians, the rationale for self-identity is more than ethnicity as compared with biracial and multiracial individuals. Gays, bisexuals, and lesbians are often more concerned with their gender, sexual, and ethnic identities than just their ethnicity. They must manage these multiple identities simultaneously. Mental health practitioners must be mindful that African American lesbians, gays, or bisexuals are often faced with ethnocentrism, sexism, and heterosexism resulting from various types of oppression. People of both groups (biracials/multiracials and lesbians, gays, and bisexuals) will warrant careful consideration from counselors and therapists in helping to resolve their concerns. What are some of the future implications for the discussions presented in this book?

Positive mental health promotion and mental disorder prevention can improve the psychological health and empower African American communities. Also, collaborative efforts on the part of both public health and community mental health service delivery systems will likely improve mental health for all African Americans. Because many African Americans do not trust community mental health services and are deterred from seeking such services for psychological needs, it is imperative that barriers to such mental health services are removed. These barriers include limited access, negative social factors affecting perception, availability, ethnicity, stigma, and the outcomes of mental health services. Other efforts to promote positive mental heath should include building on African Americans' intrinsic community strengths such as spirituality, positive identity, and traditional values and enhancing educational achievement.

Finally, further research is needed to address issues of counselor and therapist bias and diagnostic accuracy, particularly among providers who are assisting African American clients. Another area of research includes to what extent there are gender and age differences in stress, coping, and resilience as part of the complex of factors that influence positive mental health among African Americans.

Index

A

D

H

I

J

N

S

◈